HOSEA—MICAH

A Commentary in the Wesleyan Tradition

*New Beacon Bible Commentary

HOSEA–MICAH

A Commentary in the Wesleyan Tradition

Timothy M. Green

BEACON HILL PRESS
OF KANSAS CITY

ISBN 978-0-8341-3218-4

Printed in the United States of America

Cover Design: J.R. Caines
Interior Design: Sharon Page

Library of Congress Cataloging-in-Publication Data

Green, Timothy Mark, 1961-
New Beacon Bible commentary, Hosea—Micah / Timothy M. Green.
pages cm
Includes bibliographical references.
ISBN 978-0-8341-3218-4 (pbk.)
1. Bible. Minor Prophets—Commentaries. I. Title.
BS1560.G74 2014
224'.907—dc23

2013046888

10 9 8 7 6 5 4 3 2 1

DEDICATION

To my brothers,
Steve, Dan, and Sam,
who have each been
vivid, living testimonies to the grace of God
and who have defined for me the meaning of "friend"

COMMENTARY EDITORS

CONTENTS

GENERAL EDITORS' PREFACE

The purpose of the New Beacon Bible Commentary is to make available to pastors and students in the twenty-first century a biblical commentary that reflects the best scholarship in the Wesleyan theological tradition. The commentary project aims to make this scholarship accessible to a wider audience to assist them in their understanding and proclamation of Scripture as God's Word.

Writers of the volumes in this series not only are scholars within the Wesleyan theological tradition and experts in their field but also have special interest in the books assigned to them. Their task is to communicate clearly the critical consensus and the full range of other credible voices who have commented on the Scriptures. Though scholarship and scholarly contribution to the understanding of the Scriptures are key concerns of this series, it is not intended as an academic dialogue within the scholarly community. Commentators of this series constantly aim to demonstrate in their work the significance of the Bible as the church's book and the contemporary relevance and application of the biblical message. The project's overall goal is to make available to the church and for her service the fruits of the labors of scholars who are committed to their Christian faith.

The *New International Version* (NIV) is the reference version of the Bible used in this series; however, the focus of exegetical study and comments is the biblical text in its original language. When the commentary uses the NIV, it is printed in bold. The text printed in bold italics is the translation of the author. Commentators also refer to other translations where the text may be difficult or ambiguous.

The structure and organization of the commentaries in this series seeks to facilitate the study of the biblical text in a systematic and methodical way. Study of each biblical book begins with an ***Introduction*** section that gives an overview of authorship, date, provenance, audience, occasion, purpose, sociological/cultural issues, textual history, literary features, hermeneutical issues, and theological themes necessary to understand the book. This section also includes a brief outline of the book and a list of general works and standard commentaries.

The commentary section for each biblical book follows the outline of the book presented in the introduction. In some volumes, readers will find section ***overviews*** of large portions of scripture with general comments on their overall literary structure and other literary features. A consistent feature of the commentary is the paragraph-by-paragraph study of biblical texts. This section has three parts: ***Behind the Text***, ***In the Text***, and ***From the Text***.

The goal of the ***Behind the Text*** section is to provide the reader with all the relevant information necessary to understand the text. This includes specific historical situations reflected in the text, the literary context of the text, sociological and cultural issues, and literary features of the text.

In the Text explores what the text says, following its verse-by-verse structure. This section includes a discussion of grammatical details, word studies, and the connectedness of the text to other biblical books/passages or other parts of the book being studied (the canonical relationship). This section provides transliterations of key words in Hebrew and Greek and their literal meanings. The goal here is to explain what the author would have meant and/or what the audience would have understood as the meaning of the text. This is the largest section of the commentary.

The ***From the Text*** section examines the text in relation to the following areas: theological significance, intertextuality, the history of interpretation, use of the Old Testament scriptures in the New Testament, interpretation in later church history, actualization, and application.

The commentary provides ***sidebars*** on topics of interest that are important but not necessarily part of an explanation of the biblical text. These topics are informational items and may cover archaeological, historical, literary, cultural, and theological matters that have relevance to the biblical text. Occasionally, longer detailed discussions of special topics are included as ***excurses.***

We offer this series with our hope and prayer that readers will find it a valuable resource for their understanding of God's Word and an indispensable tool for their critical engagement with the biblical texts.

Roger Hahn, Centennial Initiative General Editor
Alex Varughese, General Editor (Old Testament)
George Lyons, General Editor (New Testament)

ACKNOWLEDGMENTS

In my early years of undergraduate ministerial preparation, I encountered Abraham Heschel's description of the prophet as one who represents God in the presence of the people and represents the people in the presence of God. From that "aha" moment to this day, the prophetic heartbeat has fueled my own passions and imagination. In light of my deep love for the Old Testament prophets, this project has been a delight and privilege. I extend my sincere gratitude to Beacon Hill Press for the invitation to participate in this series. I particularly appreciate the commitment of Bonnie Perry to the development of this commentary series as well as her personal encouragement and support. Sincere gratitude goes to my friend and colleague, Alex Varughese, who not only has served tirelessly and effectively as general editor of the series but who has provided encouragement, wise counsel, and editorial expertise for me.

The most formative period in my study of the prophets occurred under the instruction of a stellar team of graduate faculty. To these persons, I extend my sincere appreciation for the investment they made in my life and thinking. They opened my eyes to a careful reading of the biblical text. Thank you to Walter Harrelson for teaching the Old Testament prophets in such a way that scholarship and passion were inseparable. Thank you to Douglas A. Knight for introducing me to the profound implications of sociological, political, and economic factors within the prophetic texts. Thank you to James Crenshaw and Mary Ann Tolbert for opening my eyes to a way of reading the text literarily that transformed my reading of Scripture. Sincere appreciation goes to the Vanderbilt Divinity Library staff for allowing me to have full access and privileges to the library's abundant resources for this project.

I am indebted to the community that I have called home for nearly a quarter of a century, Trevecca Nazarene University. The support and encouragement of my colleagues in the staff, faculty, and administration have been a gift across these years. The university's granting of sabbatical leave allowed me the space and time to complete this significant project. Across the years, students who have posed challenging questions and who have compelled me to articulate matters clearly have shaped me immeasurably. My deep appreciation also goes to a community that has been a safe place to have authentic, deep Christian conversation for over a decade, the Covenant Sunday School class.

In particular, I wish to acknowledge the love, support, and encouragement of my family, one of God's richest blessings in my life. During much of the time that I worked on this project, my family has traveled a road filled with uncertainty as one brother battled acute leukemia and as another battled lymphoma. The third floor of the Sarah Cannon Cancer Center often became my "stopover" between a day at work and an evening in the library. However, the hospital rooms were so often places of grace, hope, and healing; from those rooms, I often left more inspired and energized than ever, ready to plunge back into the magnificent prophetic texts. My sincere gratitude goes to my mother for her loving encouragement, wise counsel, and endless support throughout this project. My deep appreciation goes to my three brothers and their families for being instruments of God's grace in ways they could never imagine. Truly, in their weakness, God's power was made perfect.

Finally, I would be remiss if I were not to acknowledge and give thanks for both the prophets of yesterday and the prophets of today. I am deeply grateful for the women and men who boldly proclaim the word of God to their generation. My prayer is that this commentary will provide a small contribution in bridging the message of yesterday's prophets with the proclamation and teaching of prophets in our present setting. May it be so.

—Timothy M. Green

ABBREVIATIONS

With a few exceptions, these abbreviations follow those in *The SBL Handbook of Style* (Alexander 1999).

General

→	see the commentary at
B.C.	before Christ
ch(s)	chapter(s)
ed.	edited by
e.g.	*exempli gratia*, for example
esp.	especially
etc.	*et cetera*, and the rest
fem.	feminine
ff.	and the following ones
HB	Hebrew Bible
Heb.	Hebrew
ibid.	*ibidem*, at the same place
i.e.	*id est*, that is
lit.	literally
LXX	Septuagint (the Greek OT)
MT	Masoretic Text (of the OT)
NT	New Testament
OT	Old Testament
pl.	plural
v(v)	verse(s)
vol.	volume

English Versions

HCSB	Holman Christian Standard Bible
KJV	King James Version
NASB	New American Standard Bible
NIV	New International Version (2011)
NJB	New Jerusalem Bible
NJPS	Jewish Publication Society Tanakh: Jewish Bible (Torah, Nevi'im, Kethuvim)
NKJV	New King James Version
NLT	New Living Translation
NRSV	New Revised Standard Version

Print Conventions for Translations

Bold font	NIV (bold without quotation marks in the text under study; elsewhere in the regular font, with quotation marks and no further identification)
Bold italic font	Author's translation (without quotation marks)

Behind the Text:	Literary or historical background information average readers might not know from reading the biblical text alone
In the Text:	Comments on the biblical text, words, phrases, grammar, and so forth
From the Text:	The use of the text by later interpreters, contemporary relevance, theological and ethical implications of the text, with particular emphasis on Wesleyan concerns

Apocrypha

Bar	Baruch
Sir	Sirach

Secondary Sources

BDB	*A Hebrew and English Lexicon of the Old Testament* (see Brown)

Old Testament

Gen	Genesis
Exod	Exodus
Lev	Leviticus
Num	Numbers
Deut	Deuteronomy
Josh	Joshua
Judg	Judges
Ruth	Ruth
1—2 Sam	1—2 Samuel
1—2 Kgs	1—2 Kings
1—2 Chr	1—2 Chronicles
Ezra	Ezra
Neh	Nehemiah
Esth	Esther
Job	Job
Ps/Pss	Psalm/Psalms
Prov	Proverbs
Eccl	Ecclesiastes
Song	Song of Songs/ Song of Solomon
Isa	Isaiah
Jer	Jeremiah
Lam	Lamentations
Ezek	Ezekiel
Dan	Daniel
Hos	Hosea
Joel	Joel
Amos	Amos
Obad	Obadiah
Jonah	Jonah
Mic	Micah
Nah	Nahum
Hab	Habakkuk
Zeph	Zephaniah
Hag	Haggai
Zech	Zechariah
Mal	Malachi

(Note: Chapter and verse numbering in the MT and LXX often differ compared to those in English Bibles. To avoid confusion, all biblical references follow the chapter and verse numbering in English translations, even when the text in the MT and LXX is under discussion.)

New Testament

Matt	Matthew
Mark	Mark
Luke	Luke
John	John
Acts	Acts
Rom	Romans
1—2 Cor	1—2 Corinthians
Gal	Galatians
Eph	Ephesians
Phil	Philippians
Col	Colossians
1—2 Thess	1—2 Thessalonians
1—2 Tim	1—2 Timothy
Titus	Titus
Phlm	Philemon
Heb	Hebrews
Jas	James
1—2 Pet	1—2 Peter
1—2—3 John	1—2—3 John
Jude	Jude
Rev	Revelation

Greek Transliteration

Greek	*Letter*	*English*
α	*alpha*	*a*
β	*bēta*	*b*
γ	*gamma*	*g*
γ	*gamma nasal*	*n* (before γ, κ, ξ, χ)
δ	*delta*	*d*
ε	*epsilon*	*e*
ζ	*zēta*	*z*
η	*ēta*	*ē*
θ	*thēta*	*th*
ι	*iōta*	*i*
κ	*kappa*	*k*
λ	*lambda*	*l*
μ	*mu*	*m*
ν	*nu*	*n*
ξ	*xi*	*x*
ο	*omicron*	*o*
π	*pi*	*p*
ρ	*rhō*	*r*
ρ	initial *rhō*	*rh*
σ/ς	*sigma*	*s*
τ	*tau*	*t*
υ	*upsilon*	*y*
υ	*upsilon*	*u* (in diphthongs: *au, eu, ēu, ou, ui*)
φ	*phi*	*ph*
χ	*chi*	*ch*
ψ	*psi*	*ps*
ω	*ōmega*	*ō*
ʽ	rough breathing	*h* (before initial vowels or diphthongs)

Hebrew Consonant Transliteration

Hebrew/ Aramaic	*Letter*	*English*
א	*alef*	ʾ
בּ	*bet*	*b*
גּ	*gimel*	*g*
ד	*dalet*	*d*
ה	*he*	*h*
ו	*vav*	*v* or *w*
ז	*zayin*	*z*
ח	*khet*	*ḥ*
ט	*tet*	*ṭ*
י	*yod*	*y*
כּ/ך	*kaf*	*k*
ל	*lamed*	*l*
מ/ם	*mem*	*m*
נ/ן	*nun*	*n*
ס	*samek*	*s*
ע	*ayin*	ʿ
פּ/ף	*pe*	*p; f* (spirant)
צ/ץ	*tsade*	*ṣ*
ק	*qof*	*q*
ר	*resh*	*r*
שׂ	*sin*	*ś*
שׁ	*shin*	*š*
ת	*tav*	*t; th* (spirant)

BIBLIOGRAPHY

Single Author Multi-text Commentaries

Achtemeier, Elizabeth. 1996a. *Minor Prophets I*. New International Biblical Commentary. Peabody, Mass.: Hendrickson Publishers, Inc.

Allen, Leslie C. 1976. *The Books of Joel, Obadiah, Jonah, and Micah*. New International Commentary on the Old Testament. Grand Rapids: Eerdmans.

Barton, John. 2001. *Joel and Obadiah: A Commentary*. Old Testament Library. Louisville, Ky.: Westminster John Knox Press.

Birch, Bruce C. 1997. *Hosea, Joel, and Amos.* Westminster Bible Companion. Louisville, Ky.: Westminster John Knox Press.

Brown, William P. 1996. *Obadiah through Malachi*. Westminster Bible Companion. Louisville, Ky.: Westminster John Knox Press.

Clark, David, and Norm Mundhenk. 1982. *A Translator's Handbook on the Books of Obadiah and Micah*. New York: United Bible Societies.

Coggins, Richard James. 2000. *Joel and Amos.* New Century Bible Commentary. Sheffield: Sheffield Academic Press.

Coggins, Richard James, and S. P. Re'emi. 1985. *Israel Among the Nations: Nahum, Obadiah, Esther.* International Theological Commentary. Grand Rapids: Eerdmans.

Craigie, Peter C. 1984. *The Daily Study Bible: The Twelve Prophets*, vol. 1. Edinburgh: The Saint Andrew Press.

Duhm, Bernhard. 1911. "Anmerkungen zu den Zwolf Prophetien." *Zeitschrift fur die alttestamentliche Wissenschaft* 31:161-204.

Jenson, Philip Peter. 2008. *Obadiah, Jonah, Micah: A Theological Commentary*. New York: T&T Clark.

Kaiser, Walter C., Jr. 1992. *Micah-Malachi*. Communicator's Bible. Dallas: Word.

Limburg, James. 1988. *Hosea-Malachi*. Interpretation: A Bible Commentary for Teaching and Preaching. Atlanta: John Knox Press.

Mason, Rex. 1991. *Micah, Nahum, Obadiah*. Old Testament Guides. Sheffield: JSOT Press.

McComiskey, Thomas Edward. 1992. *The Minor Prophets: An Exegetical and Expository Commentary.* Grand Rapids: Baker.

_________. 1993. *The Minor Prophets: An Exegetical and Expository Commentary*, vol. 2. Grand Rapids: Baker Books.

Nogalski, James D. 2011. *The Book of the Twelve: Hosea-Jonah*. Smyth & Helwys Bible Commentary. Macon, Ga.: Smyth & Helwys.

Simundson, Daniel J. 2005. *Hosea, Joel, Amos, Obadiah, Jonah, Micah*. Abingdon Old Testament Commentaries. Nashville: Abingdon Press.

Stuart, Douglas. 1987. *Hosea-Jonah*. Word Biblical Commentary. Waco, Tex.: Word Press.

Sweeney, Marvin A. 2000. *The Twelve Prophets*, vol. 1. Berit Olam. Collegeville, Minn.: Liturgical Press.

Wolff, Hans Walter. 1977. *Joel and Amos*. Hermeneia. Philadelphia: Fortress Press.

_________. 1986. *Obadiah and Jonah*. Continental Commentaries. Minneapolis: Augsburg.

Hosea

Andersen, Francis I., and David Noel Freedman. 1980. *Hosea*. Anchor Bible. Garden City, N.Y.: Doubleday.

Davies, Graham I. 1992. *Hosea*. New Century Bible Commentary. Grand Rapids: Eerdmans.

_________. 1993. *Hosea*. Old Testament Guides. Sheffield: JSOT Press.

Dearman, J. Andrew. 2010. *The Book of Hosea*. New International Commentary on the Old Testament. Grand Rapids: Eerdmans.

Kelle, Brad E. 2005. *Hosea 2: Metaphor and Rhetoric in Historical Perspective*. Atlanta: Society of Biblical Literature.

Lewis, Theodore J. 1992. Dead, Abode of the. *Anchor Bible Dictionary*, 2:101-5. Edited by David Noel Freedman. New York: Doubleday.

Mafico, Temba L. J. 1992. Just, Justice. *Anchor Bible Dictionary*, 3:1127-29. Edited by David Noel Freedman. New York: Doubleday.

Mays, James Luther. 1969. *Hosea*. Old Testament Library. Philadelphia: Westminster Press.

Mullen, E. Theodore, Jr. 1992. Hosts, Host of Heaven. *Anchor Bible Dictionary*, 3:301-4. Edited by David Noel Freedman. New York: Doubleday.

Noth, Martin. 1966. *The Old Testament World*. Translated by Victor I. Gruhn. London: A & C Black.

Rad, Gerhard von. 1965. *Old Testament Theology*, vol. 2. Translated by D. M. G. Stalker. San Francisco: Harper & Row, Publishers.

Redford, Donald B. 1992. Memphis. *Anchor Bible Dictionary*, 4:689-91. New York: Doubleday.

Walsh, J. P. M. 1987. *The Mighty from Their Thrones*. Philadelphia: Fortress Press.

Ward, James M. 1966. *Hosea: A Theological Commentary*. New York: Harper & Row.

Wolff, Hans Walter. 1974. *Hosea*. Hermenia. Philadelphia: Fortress Press.

Yee, Gale A. 1987. *Composition and Tradition in the Book of Hosea*. Atlanta: Scholars Press.

_________. 1996. The Book of Hosea. *New Interpreter's Bible*, Vol. 7. Nashville: Abingdon Press.

Joel

Achtemeier, Elizabeth. 1996b. The Book of Joel. *New Interpreter's Bible*, Vol. 7. Nashville: Abingdon Press.

Athanasius. 1979. *The Resurrection Letters*. Paraphrased by Jack N. Sparks. Nashville: Thomas Nelson.

Bewer, J. A. 1985. Commentary on Joel. *International Critical Commentary*. Edinburgh: T&T Clark.

Crenshaw, James L. 1995. *Joel: A New Translation with Introduction and Commentary*. Anchor Bible. New York: Doubleday.

Fretheim, Terence. 1988. "The Repentance of God: A Key to Evaluating Old Testament God-Talk." *Horizons in Biblical Theology*, 10:47-70.

Lambert, David A. 2007. Fast, Fasting. *New Interpreter's Dictionary of the Bible*, 2:431-34. Nashville: Abingdon Press.

Levison, John R. 2007. Holy Spirit. *New Interpreter's Dictionary of the Bible*, 2:859-79. Nashville: Abingdon Press.

Prinsloo, Willem S. 1985. *The Theology of the Book of Joel*. Berlin: Walter de Gruyter & Co.

Redditt, Paul L. 1986. The Book of Joel and Peripheral Prophecy. *Catholic Biblical Quarterly*, 48:225-40.

_________. 2008. Locust. *New Interpreter's Dictionary of the Bible*, 3:684-85. Nashville: Abingdon Press.

Segal, Alan F. 2009. Mourning. *New Interpreter's Dictionary of the Bible*, 4:160-61. Edited by Katharine Doob Sakefeld. Nashville: Abingdon Press.

Strazicich, John. 2007. *Joel's Use of Scripture and the Scripture's Use of Joel: Appropriation and Resignification in Second Temple Judaism and Early Christianity*. Leiden: Brill.

Treves, M. 1957. The Date of Joel. *Vetus Testamentum*, 7:149, 156.

Wesley, John. 1975. *Explanatory Notes upon the Old Testament*. Salem, Ohio: Schmul Publishers.

_________. 1984. *The Bicentennial Edition of the Works of John Wesley*, vol. 1. Nashville: Abingdon Press.

Willis, Timothy M. 2007. Elder in the OT. *New Interpreter's Dictionary of the Bible*, 2:233-34. Nashville: Abingdon Press.

Amos

Andersen, Francis I., and David Noel Freedman. 1989. *Amos*. Anchor Bible. New York: Doubleday.

Auld, A. G. 1986. *Amos*. Old Testament Guides. Sheffield: JSOT Press.

Barton, John. 1980. *Amos's Oracles Against the Nations: A Study of Amos 1:3—2:5*. Cambridge: Cambridge University Press.

Crenshaw, James L. 1975. *Hymnic Affirmation of Divine Justice: The Doxologies of Amos and Related Texts in the Old Testament*. Missoula, Mont.: Scholars Press.

Gowan, Donald E. 1996. The Book of Amos. *New Interpreter's Bible*, Vol. 7. Nashville: Abingdon Press.

Hasel, Gerhard F. 1991. *Understanding the Book of Amos: Basic Issues in Current Interpretations*. Grand Rapids: Baker.

Hayes, John H. 1968. The Usage of Oracles against Foreign Nations in Ancient Israel. *Journal of Biblical Literature*, 87:81-92.

_________. 1988. *Amos, the Eighth-Century Prophet: His Times and His Preaching*. Nashville: Abingdon.

Koehler, Ludwig, and Walter Baumgartner. 1995. *The Hebrew and Aramaic Lexicon of the Old Testament*, vol. 2. Translated by M. E. J. Richardson. Leiden: E. J. Brill.
Mays, James L. 1969. *Amos: A Commentary*. Old Testament Library. Philadelphia: Westminster.
Morgenstern, Julian. 1937-38. Amos Studies II: The Sin of Uzziah, the Festival of Jeroboam and the Date of Amos. *Hebrew Union College Annual*, 12/13:1-53.
Paul, Shalom. 1991. *Amos*. Hermeneia. Philadelphia: Fortress.
Robbins, Ellen. 2009. Pleiades. *The New Interpreter's Dictionary of the Bible*, 4:547-48. Nashville: Abingdon Press.
Roth, W. M. W. 1965. *Numerical Sayings in the Old Testament: A Form Critical Study*. Leiden: Brill.
Smith, Gary V. 1989. *Amos: A Commentary*. Grand Rapids: Zondervan Publishing House.
_________. 2005. *Amos: A Commentary*. Grand Rapids: Regency Reference Library.
Terrien, Samuel. 1962. Amos and Wisdom. Pages 108-15 in *Israel's Prophetic Heritage: Essays in Honor of James Muilenburg*. Edited by Bernhard Anderson and Walter Harrelson. New York: Harper & Row.
Watts, John N. D. 1958. *Vision and Prophecy in Amos*. Macon, Ga.: Mercer University Press.
Wolff, Hans Walter. 1973. *Amos, the Prophet: The Man and His Background*. Philadelphia: Fortress Press.

Obadiah

Bartlett, J. R. 1982. Edom and the Fall of Jerusalem, 587 B.C. *Palestine Exploration Quarterly*, 114:13-24.
_________. 1992. Edom. *Anchor Bible Dictionary*, 2:287, 295. New York: Doubleday.
Ben Zvi, Ehud. 1996. *A Historical-Critical Study of the Book of Obadiah*. Berlin: Walter de Gruyter.
Dearman, J. Andrew. 2007. Edom, Edomites. *New Interpreter's Dictionary*, 2:188-91. Nashville: Abingdon Press.
Pagan, Samuel. 1996. The Book of Obadiah. *New Interpreter's Bible*, vol. 7. Nashville: Abingdon Press, 1996.
Raabe, Paul R. 1996. *Obadiah: A New Translation with Introduction and Commentary*. Anchor Bible. New York: Doubleday.
Renkema, Johan. 2003. *Obadiah*. Historical Commentary on the Old Testament. Leuven: Peeters.
Watts, John D. W. 1969. *Obadiah: A Critical Exegetical Commentary*. Grand Rapids: Eerdmans.
Wineland, John D. 2009. Sepharad. *New Interpreter's Bible Dictionary*, 5:169. Nashville: Abingdon Press.

Jonah

Baker, David W. 1992. Tarshish (Place). *Anchor Bible Dictionary*, 6:331-33. New York: Doubleday.
Craig, Kenneth M., Jr. 1999. *A Poetics of Jonah: Art in the Service of Ideology*. Macon, Ga.: Mercer University Press.
Fretheim, Terence E. 1977. *The Message of Jonah: A Theological Commentary*. Minneapolis: Augsburg Publishing House.
Kamp, Albert. 2004. *Inner Worlds: A Cognitive Linguistic Approach to the Book of Jonah*. Boston: Brill Academic Publishers, Inc.
Lacocque, Andre, and Pierre-Emmanuel Lacocque. 1981. *The Jonah Complex*. Atlanta: John Knox Press.
Landes, George M. 1967. The Kerygma of the Book of Jonah. *Interpretation*, 21:3-31.
Lemche, Niels Peter. 1979. Hebrew as a National Name for Israel. *Studia Theologica*, 33:1-23.
Limburg, James. 1993. *Jonah*. Old Testament Library. Louisville, Ky.: Westminster John Knox Press.
Magonet, Jonathan. 1983. *Form and Meaning: Studies in Literary Techniques in the Book of Jonah*. Sheffield: Sheffield Academic Press.
Muldoon, Catherine L. 2010. *In Defense of Divine Justice: An Intertextual Approach to the Book of Jonah*. Washington: Catholic Biblical Association of America.
Perry, T. A. 2006. *The Honeymoon Is Over: Jonah's Argument with God*. Peabody, Mass.: Hendrickson Publishers.
Salters, R. B. 1994. *Jonah and Lamentations*. Old Testament Guides. Sheffield: Sheffield Academic Press.
Sasson, Jack M. 1990. *Jonah*. Anchor Bible. New York: Doubleday.
Simon, Uriel. 1999. *Jonah*. JPS Bible Commentary. Philadelphia: Jewish Publication Society.
Trible, Phyllis. 1994. *Rhetorical Criticism: Context, Method, and the Book of Jonah*. Minneapolis: Fortress Press.

_________. 1996. Jonah. *New Interpreter's Bible*, Vol. 7. Nashville: Abingdon Press.

Micah

Andersen, Francis I., and David Noel Freedman. 2000. *Micah: A New Translation with Introduction and Commentary*. The Anchor Bible. New York: Doubleday.

Ben Zvi, Ehud. 2000. *Micah*. The Forms of the Old Testament Literature. Grand Rapids: Eerdmans.

Hiebert, Theodore. 1992. Theophany in the OT. *Anchor Bible Dictionary*, 6:505-11. New York: Doubleday.

Hillers, Delbert R. 1984. *Micah: A Commentary on the Book of the Prophet Micah*. Hermenia. Minneapolis: Fortress Press.

Luker, Lamontte M. 1992. Moresheth. *Anchor Bible Dictionary*, 4:904-5. New York: Doubleday.

Mays, James Luther. 1976. *Micah: A Commentary*. Old Testament Library. Philadelphia: Westminster Press.

McKane, William. 1998. *The Book of Micah: Introduction and Commentary*. Edinburgh: T&T Clark.

Roncace, Mark. 2009. Moresheth. *New Interpreter's Bible Dictionary*, 4:140. Nashville: Abingdon Press.

Shaw, Charles S. 1993. *The Speeches of Micah: A Rhetorical Historical Analysis*. Sheffield: JSOT Press.

Simundson, Daniel J. 1996. The Book of Micah. *New Interpreter's Bible*, Vol. 7. Nashville: Abingdon Press.

Stade, B. 1881. Bemerkungen uber das Buch Micha. *Zeitschrift fur die Alttestamentliche Wissenschaft*, 1:161-72.

Waltke, Bruce K. 2007. *A Commentary on Micah*. Grand Rapids: Eerdmans.

Wolff, Hans Walter. 1978. Micah the Moreshite—the Prophet and His Background. Pages 77-84 in *Israelite Wisdom*. Edited by John Gammie. Missoula, Mont.: Scholars Press.

_________. 1981. *Micah the Prophet*. Translated by Ralph D. Gehrke. Philadelphia: Fortress Press.

_________. 1990. *Micah: A Commentary*. Continental Commentaries. Minneapolis: Augsburg/Fortress.

General

Ackroyd, Peter R. 1990. Continuity and Discontinuity: Rehabilitation and Authentication. Pages 215-34 in *Tradition and Theology in the Old Testament*. Edited by Douglas A. Knight. Sheffield: JSOT Press.

Anderson, Bernhard W. 1986. *Understanding the Old Testament*. 4th ed. Englewood Cliffs, N.J.: Prentice-Hall.

_________. 2000. *Out of the Depths: The Psalms Speak for Us Today*, 3rd ed. Louisville, Ky.: Westminster John Knox Press.

Bonhoeffer, Dietrich. 1995 (SCM Press, 1959). *The Cost of Discipleship*. New York: Touchstone.

Brueggemann, Walter. 1977. *The Land: Place as Gift, Promise, and Challenge in Biblical Faith*. Minneapolis: Fortress Press.

_________. 1984. *The Message of the Psalms: A Theological Commentary*. Augsburg Old Testament Studies. Minneapolis: Augsburg.

_________. 1986. *Hopeful Imagination*. Philadelphia: Fortress Press.

_________. 2001. *The Prophetic Imagination*, 2nd ed. Minneapolis: Fortress Press.

Buber, Martin. 1970. *I and Thou*. New York: Charles Scribners.

Chaney, Marvin L. 1982. You Shall Not Covet Your Neighbor's House. *Pacific Theological Review*, 15:3-13.

_________. 1989. Bitter Bounty: The Dynamics of Political Economy Critiqued by the Eighth-Century Prophets. Pages 15-30 in *Reformed Faith and Economics*. Edited by Robert L. Stivers. New York: University Press of America.

_________. 1991. Debt Easement in Israelite History and Tradition. Pages 127-39 in *The Bible and the Politics of Exegesis*. Edited by David Jobling, Peggy L. Day, and Gerald T. Sheppard. Cleveland, Ohio: Pilgrim Press.

Cook, S. L. 1995. *Prophecy and Apocalypticism: The Post-Exilic Social Setting*. Minneapolis: Fortress Press.

Davies, E. W. 1991. Land: Its Rights and Privileges. Pages 349-69 in *The World of Ancient Israel: Sociological, Anthropological, and Political Perspectives*. Edited by R. E. Clements. Cambridge: Cambridge University Press.

Donner, Herbert. 1990. The Separate States of Israel and Judah. *Israelite and Judaean History*. Edited by John H. Hayes and J. Maxwell Miller. London: SCM Press.

Doorly, William J. 1994. *Obsession with Justice: The Story of the Deuteronomists*. New York: Paulist Press.

Fretheim, Terence E. 1984. *The Suffering of God*. Philadelphia: Fortress Press.

Green, Timothy Mark. 1997. *Class Differentiation and Power(lessness) in Eighth-Century BCE Israel and Judah*. Ph.D. diss., Vanderbilt University.

Habel, Norman C. 1995. *The Land Is Mine*. Minneapolis: Fortress Press.

Harrelson, Walter. 1990. Life, Faith, and the Emergence of Tradition. Pages 11-30 in *Tradition and Theology in the Old Testament*. Edited by Douglas A. Knight. Sheffield: Sheffield Academic Press.

Heschel, Abraham J. 1962. *The Prophets*. New York: Harper Perennial Modern Classics.

Long, Thomas. 2005. *The Witness of Preaching*. Louisville Ky.: Westminster John Knox Press.

Mendenhall, George E. 1973. *The Tenth Generation: The Origins of the Biblical Tradition*. Baltimore: Johns Hopkins University Press.

Outler, Albert C., and Richard P. Heitzenrater, eds. 1991. *John Wesley's Sermons: An Anthology*. Nashville: Abingdon Press.

Petersen, David L. 1981. *The Roles of Israel's Prophets*. Sheffield: University of Sheffield.

Premnath, Devadasan N. 1984. The Process of Latifundialization Mirrored in the Oracles Pertaining to Eighth Century B.C.E. in the Books of Amos, Hosea, Isaiah, and Micah. Ph.D. diss., The Graduate Theology Union.

_________. 1988. Latifundialization and Isaiah 5.8-10. *Journal for the Study of the Old Testament*, 40:49-60.

_________. 2003. *Eighth Century Prophets: A Social Analysis*. St. Louis: Chalice Press.

Pritchard, James B., ed. 1969. *Ancient Near Eastern Texts Relating to the Old Testament*, 3rd ed. Princeton: Princeton University Press.

_________. 2011. *The Ancient Near East: An Anthology of Texts and Pictures*. Princeton, N.J.: Princeton University Press.

Steck, Odil Hannes. 1990. Theological Streams of Tradition. Pages 183-214 in *Tradition and Theology in the Old Testament*. Edited by Douglas A. Knight. Sheffield: JSOT Press.

Vaux, Roland de. 1961. *Ancient Israel: Its Life and Institutions*. Translated by John McHugh. New York: McGraw-Hill.

Weems, Renita J. 1995. *Battered Love: Marriage, Sex, and Violence in the Hebrew Prophets*. Minneapolis: Fortress Press.

Westermann, Claus. 1967. *Basic Forms of Prophetic Speech*. Philadelphia: Westminster Press.

_________. 1981. *Praise and Lament in the Psalms*. Atlanta: John Knox Press.

Williams, Ronald J. 2007. *Williams' Hebrew Syntax*, 3rd ed. Toronto: University of Toronto Press.

Zimmerli, Walther. 1990. Prophetic Proclamation and Reinterpretation. Pages 69-100 in *Tradition and Theology in the Old Testament*. Edited by Douglas A. Knight. Sheffield: JSOT Press.

HOSEA

INTRODUCTION

A. Hosea the Prophet

Other than the limited material in the book of Hosea itself, we have no additional information concerning the prophet Hosea. Based upon the editorial superscription and the oracles within the book, Hosea's prophetic activity likely began in the middle of the eighth-century B.C. and ended shortly before the Assyrian destruction of Samaria in 722 B.C. The superscription's reference to southern kings may indicate that Hosea made his way to Judah after the fall of Samaria. However, the reference more likely demonstrates that after the material arrived in Judah from the north, it was edited for an audience more familiar with Judah's history (Simundson [2005, 6] suggests that the superscription may "indicate complete disdain for all the kings that came after Jeroboam till the end of the nation"). It is probable that Hosea was informed by and perhaps belonged to the northern Levitical-prophetic school that produced the theological corpus within Deuteronomy and that subsequently engendered the theological convictions in Jeremiah (for a reconstruction of the Levitical migration to the south following 722 B.C., specifically regarding Hosea, see Doorly 1994, 118-21; see also Achtemeier 1996a, 5).

While the text does not specifically mention Hosea's geographical origins, it is not unreasonable to understand Hosea's home as the northern kingdom. The prophet addresses his message primarily to the northern kingdom and focuses upon primary northern traditions and geographical locations (e.g., Jacob, Aram, Gilgal, Bethel, Samaria). Noting the unique "patterns of prophetic speech" and "the many problems of text and vocabulary," Birch describes the book as "the only prophetic book written entirely in the language and idiom of the Northern kingdom" (1997, 12).

Other than the name Beeri (perhaps meaning "my well" or "little spring"), we know nothing else concerning Hosea's father. The only other instance in the OT in which the name occurs is Gen 26:34, in which Beeri is the Hittite father of Esau's wife Judith. While likely coincidental, Esau's intermarriage with a Canaanite provides ironic similarity to Hosea's marriage with an adulterer and with Israel's adultery (i.e., alliances) with other nations. However, as the Hosea text makes no reference to the Genesis text, one is left simply with canonical irony.

While the text makes no specific mention of Hosea's training, various factors within the text seem to demonstrate that he may have experienced some formal instruction. Mays has suggested that the prophet "was a man of ability and culture" who "drew on the resources of Wisdom, was skilled in using a variety of literary devices in the formulation of his speeches, [and] knew the historical traditions of Israel in depth" (1969, 2).

Outside of the text's reference to Hosea's father, the primary biographical material within the text concerning Hosea regards his marriage and children in chs 1 and 3. These narratives have raised a number of questions, including the literal nature of Hosea's family, Gomer's status as a prostitute (both whether she became a prostitute only after the marriage and whether she was a cult prostitute), and the identity of the woman in ch 3 (whether this is Gomer or another woman).

A definitive answer to these questions is impossible. However, as the account of Hosea's marriage to Gomer functions to depict the nature of the relationship between Yahweh and Israel, probable answers emerge. As the text assumes that the people of Israel prostituted themselves only after becoming the people of Yahweh, the narrative likely assumes that Gomer began to prostitute herself after her marriage to Hosea. If this understanding is correct, then the opening statement in 1:2 represents the prophet's perspective "after the fact" (i.e., he was to marry one who would become a prostitute; Achtemeier suggests that Gomer had already engaged in temple prostitution [1996a, 5]). In ch 3 Yahweh receives Israel back from prostitution rather than entering into covenant with a new people. Therefore, it is likely that the woman Hosea redeems in ch 3 is Gomer, his wife who had engaged in prostitution.

Questions concerning the historicity of Hosea's marriage, Gomer, and her children obviously cannot be fully settled. One might state the essence of this question as follows: Is the text allegory with no concrete historical reference, or does a prophet's identity move him to act in such a way as to identify with Yahweh (or similarly, does the experience of a prophet move the prophet into solidarity with Yahweh himself)? Mays has commented that "the very character of prophetic symbolism requires that the divine word be actualized in a representative event." Noting, however, that the text is "kerygmatic" and not primarily interested "in Hosea and the experiences of his life," Mays concludes that "perhaps it was the recognition of this which led to the allegorical approach before prophetic symbolism was properly understood" (1969, 23). In spite of the legitimate intrigue of our modern questions, the primary purpose of Hosea's marriage, whether literal or allegorical, is to provide an image of the relationship between Yahweh and Israel. Like Hosea's marriage, this relationship was intended to be built on trust and fidelity but became tarnished due to mistrust and infidelity.

B. The Historical Context and Audience of Hosea

The superscription places the ministry of Hosea during the reigns of the southern kings from Uzziah (783-742 B.C.) to Hezekiah (715-687 B.C.) and during the reign of Jeroboam II in Israel (786-746 B.C.). Wolff suggests that the approximately thirty years of Hosea's ministry occurred during "the final and most agitated phase of Israel's history," from the final years of Jeroboam II to the siege of Samaria (1974, xxi).

The reign of Jeroboam II was characterized by a lengthy period of prosperity and relative peace in Israel (see historical context of Amos). Following the death of Jeroboam in 746 B.C., however, a rapid succession of six kings, five of whose lives ended violently, occurred until the time of Israel's fall in 722 B.C. Jeroboam's son Zechariah (746-745 B.C.) survived only six months until the time of his assassination by Shallum, who only ruled for one month. At least a portion of the book of Hosea seems to recognize this period of instability and violence that occurred within the kingdom of Israel (see chs 5—8, esp. 7:5-7; 8:4).

Within a year following Jeroboam's death, a new Assyrian ruler, Tiglath-Pileser III, came to power (745-727 B.C.; see 2 Kgs 15). Once on the throne, he aggressively sought to increase the power and expanse of his empire. The coinciding of the death of Israel's long-term king who presided over a period of relative peace and prosperity with the rise of an emperor with grandiose designs created a "perfect storm" for rapid disintegration within Israel. Shallum's successor, Menahem (745-737 B.C.), submitted to Tiglath-Pileser III through the payment of a heavy tribute. However, Israelite landlords rebelled against the large taxes put upon them in order to pay the tribute. Standing behind the assassination of Menahem's son, Pekahiah (737-736 B.C.), Israelite landlords and other local and regional royal functionaries placed Pekah (736-732 B.C.) on the throne.

With the support of Egypt, Pekah formed an alliance with the Syrian king Rezin. Together Pekah and Rezin forcefully attempted to bring Judah into their alliance against Assyria. The eighth-century B.C. prophet Isaiah specifically addressed Judah's King Ahaz concerning this Syro-Israelite alliance, encouraging him not to "lose heart because of these two smoldering stubs of firewood" (Isa 7:4). Interpreting Hos 2 as prophetic rhetoric concerning the alliances of this time, Kelle has convincingly argued that at least some of Hosea's references are less to other gods and more to leaders of nations with whom Israel engaged in alliances (2005, 137-66). When Judah's King Ahaz turned to Assyria for assistance against the Syro-Israelite alliance, Tiglath-Pileser III moved against both Syria and Israel, bringing an end to Syria.

Soon after these events, Hoshea (732-724 B.C.) assassinated the rebel Pekah. Like Pekahiah previously, Hoshea once again submitted tribute to Assyria. During the early years of Hoshea's reign, relative stability returned to Israel (perhaps reflected in Hos 9—11) as the nation pacified Assyria through heavy tribute. However, Hoshea eventually broke from Assyrian submission and looked toward Egypt for assistance (see perhaps 11:5 and 12:1). Upon Tiglath-Pileser III's death, Hoshea refused to pay tribute to the Assyrian successor Shalmaneser V (726-722 B.C.; see perhaps chs 12—14). Shalmaneser V invaded Israel in 724 B.C., putting Samaria under siege and capturing Hoshea. Shalmaneser V's successor, Sargon II (721-705 B.C.), finally brought an end to the northern kingdom with Samaria's fall in 722/721 B.C.

While Hosea witnessed the rapid, tumultuous deterioration of Israel internally, he also witnessed the repeated practice of Israel's kings to turn in every direction (i.e., Syria, Egypt, Assyria) for external assistance. Through political alliances during the latter decades of the eighth century B.C., Israel attempted to survive. For Hosea, Israel's allying itself with other nations was a clear sign of infidelity (i.e., adultery) to Yahweh (see theological vision below). Mays has described Israel's movement between Assyria and Egypt as swinging "back and forth . . . like a pendulum" (1969, 109). The final four decades of chaos in royal succession was only matched by the chaotic uncertainty in international relations. In Israel's vacillating uncertainty, Hosea perceived the nation to be an "easily deceived and senseless" dove "now calling to Egypt, now turning to Assyria" (7:11).

The historical-political situation of the eighth century B.C. provides the context for Hosea's message. His prophetic activity occurred primarily if not entirely in the northern kingdom. The cities of which he specifically speaks are primarily within the tribal boundaries of Ephraim and Benjamin. In contrast to Amos' naming the audience in more general terms, such as Israel or house of Israel (→ The Historical Context and Audience of Amos), Hosea concretely and specifically addresses the power structure of Israel. He speaks of kings seventeen times, princes or rulers eight times, priests four times, and judges twice. His oracles focus upon the political center of Samaria and the religious centers of Bethel and Gilgal. The text contains no reference to Jerusalem.

Like all of the prophetic messages in the OT, the narratives and oracles of Hosea continued to have a living and dynamic function in subsequent generations. Therefore, later audiences that received the text heard Hosea's message in light of their contemporary situation (e.g., the southern kingdom of Judah, a community in exile, a postexilic community, etc.). Therefore, as noted below, apparent subsequent editorial activity within the book of Hosea witnesses to the reality that the prophet's audiences continued far beyond his own lifetime.

C. The Book of Hosea as a Literary Work

1. The Hebrew Text and Versification

Unfortunately, the Hebrew text of Hosea has not been well preserved and is filled with textual corruptions. Andersen and Freedman have described the text of Hosea as competing "with Job for the distinction of containing more unintelligible passages than any other book of the Hebrew Bible" (1980, 66). Perhaps some of the difficulty emerges from subsequent southern attempts to make sense of northern vocabulary and dialect (see Simundson 2005, 2; Mays 1969, 5). In other instances, the text may have undergone damage in transmission as it moved from the northern kingdom to the south during the tumult at the time of the fall of Samaria (see Achtemeier 1996a, 9; Mays 1969, 5).

As noted in the commentary discussion of specific texts, in six instances the Hebrew versification differs from the English versification. These variances occur in the following English sections: 1:10-11; 2:1-2; 11:12; 12:1-14; 13:16; 14:1-9.

2. Literary Devices, Genres, and Metaphors

The book of Hosea is replete with metaphors and images. Certainly the familial images of marriage/marital infidelity (chs 1, 3) and the parent-child relationship (ch 11) dominate the text. However, the text employs numerous other metaphors that include humans (farmer, 10:11; one who traps birds, 7:11-12; physician, 14:4), animals (maggots, 5:12; lions, 5:14; 11:10; doves, 7:11-12; leopards and bears, 13:7-8), and inanimate objects (morning dew, 6:4; hot oven, 7:4-7; bow, 7:16; chaff, 13:3). The image of the divine court provides a context within which the divine accusation and judgment against Israel occur (see discussion of the lawsuit in 4:1; 12:2).

The prose section in the book is limited to the narrative in 1:2-9 and 3:1-5; the remainder of the book is comprised of poetry primarily in the form of prophetic oracles. While a very few of the oracles employ the traditional prophetic conclusion "says Yahweh" (2:13, 16, 21; 11:11), the book contains no use of the typical prophetic messenger formula, "This is what Yahweh says" (contrast the frequent use of the messenger formula in Amos). Although most of Hosea's prophetic oracles are in the first-person singular as Yahweh addresses the people, third-person references to Yahweh also occur (e.g., 4:1-3; 9:1-9; 10:1-8). In contrast to many of the other prophets, the book of Hosea makes no indictments against the surrounding nations (see Amos 1—2, Obadiah, Nahum, Isa 13—23, Jer 46—51, Ezek 25—32).

3. Historical Development of the Text

There are diverse interpretations regarding possible editorial layers within the book of Hosea (for overview of scholarly redaction theories, see Dearman 2010, 5-6). Wolff proposes "three transmission complexes" of redaction (1974, xxix-xxxii; contrast Andersen and Freedman who see "little evidence" of redactionary material and conclude that most of the book "remains archaic, fitting better into an eighth-century setting than anywhere else" [1980, 57]). In addition to the words of the prophet himself, Yee has suggested three primary stages of development within the book of Hosea (1987, 1-25):

- eighth- to seventh-century B.C. collection of oracles
- seventh-century B.C. Deuteronomistic revision during Josiah's reign
- sixth-century B.C. Deuteronomistic/exilic redaction

Doorly also supports the view of the seventh-century redaction of the book; he argues that the Josianic editor of the book has reinterpreted the political sins of eighth-century Israel as cultic and legal sins. The focus of the seventh-century editor was on cultic purity and obedience to the Law that, according to Doorly, is reflected in the final form of the book (1994, 119-20).

4. Structure and Outline of the Text

Generally, the book of Hosea can be divided clearly into two parts: chs 1—3 and chs 4—14 (on the relationship between the two, see Mays 1969, 15-17; Andersen and Freedman 1980, 57-59). Narratives of Hosea's marriage and children in ch 1 and of Hosea's redemption of an unfaithful spouse in ch 3 provide a frame to poetic oracles of divine judgment and restoration of Israel in ch 2.

The opening three chapters of the book function as a narrative and theological introduction not only to Hosea but also to the Book of the Twelve. Ironically, Hos 4—14 never return to the prophet's marriage to an unfaithful spouse. The opening three chapters of Hosea and the general flow within the Book of the Twelve demonstrate a theological movement from infidelity/unfaithfulness to divorce/exile and finally to reconciliation/restoration. Hosea's contemplated divorce (1:2—2:13) that reaches resolution in restoration and reconciliation (2:14-23) parallels the theological conviction of Malachi's divine declarations: "I have loved you" (Mal 1:2) and "I hate divorce" (2:16 NRSV).

Just as the opening three chapters function to introduce the Book of the Twelve, the concluding verse of the book (14:9) serves not only as a reflective epilogue to the book but also as a reflective prelude to the remaining books of the twelve. The language of this verse quite obviously emerges from the wisdom tradition and associates the words of Hosea and the prophets that will follow with the words of the wise. A similar editorial "fingerprint" of the wisdom tradition appears in the Psalter's introductory psalm.

While an obvious progression of thought is not apparent in chs 4—14, one may subdivide this unit of prophetic oracles after ch 11. As a result of this division, three major sections within the book emerge: chs 1—3; 4—11; 12—14). Each section concludes in hope for divine restoration represented in familial images: chs 3 and 14, husband-wife; ch 11, parent-child). In each of the three sections, language of barrenness concludes in language of fertility.

It is possible that the movement of the three sections described above reflects at least a rough chronological movement from Israel's prosperity under Jeroboam, to the chaos following his death (chs 4—11), to Israel's final days (chs 12—14). However, such a chronology within the movement of the book cannot be certain (regarding this loose chronology, see Simundson 2005, 4; Birch 1997, 12; Mays 1969, 15-17; Limburg 1988, 2-4).

Based upon the overall structure of the book of Hosea, the commentary on Hosea will follow the following structural outline:

- I. Superscription (1:1)
- II. Hosea's Marriage (1:2—3:5)
  - A. Hosea, Gomer, and Their Children (1:2-9)
  - B. The Promise of Restoration (1:10—2:1)
  - C. The Lawsuit (2:2-23)
    1. The Charge (2:2-5)
    2. A Blockade (2:6-8)
    3. Stripping Bare (2:9-13)
    4. Alluring into the Wilderness (2:14-15)
    5. Removal of Baals (2:16-17)
    6. The Promise of Peace and a New Marriage (2:18-20)
    7. The Promise of Blessings (2:21-23)
  - D. The Hope of Reconciliation (3:1-5)
- III. Oracles of Judgment and Restoration (4:1—14:8)
  - A. Messages of Judgment and Hope (4:1—11:12)
    1. Yahweh's Lawsuit (4:1-19)
       - *a.* Divine Indictment (4:1-3)

b. Charges against Priestly Leaders (4:4-14)
c. Charges against Worship (4:15-19)
2. Yahweh's Judgment (5:1—6:6)
a. Indictment against Leaders and the People (5:1-7)
b. Sound the Alarm (5:8-15)
c. A Call to Repentance (6:1-3)
d. Yahweh's Exasperation (6:4-6)
3. Rebellion Gone Rampant (6:7—7:16)
a. From the Earliest Days (6:7-11*a*)
b. A Nation of Bandits (6:11*b*—7:3)
c. A Nation as Hot as an Oven (7:4-10)
d. A Nation without Sense (7:11-16)
4. Covenant Broken—the Evidence (8:1-14)
a. Sound the Trumpet (8:1-3)
b. King Makers and Idol Makers (8:4-6)
c. Sowing and Reaping (8:7-14)
5. The Day of Celebration Becomes the Day of Mourning (9:1-9)
6. Ephraim, a Withered Root (9:10-17)
7. A Portrait of Exile (10:1-8)
8. Impending Calamity (10:9-15)
9. The Rebellious Child and the Forbearing Parent: A Glimpse of Hope (11:1-11)
10. A Tale of Two Kingdoms (11:12—12:1)

B. Concluding Messages of Hope (12:2—14:8)
1. Living Up to a Namesake (12:2-9)
2. Divine Faithfulness—Human Rebellion (12:10—13:13)
3. Divine Contemplation—Divine Decision (13:14-16)
4. A Liturgy of Repentance (14:1-8)
5. Wisdom Epilogue: Call for Reflection (14:9)

D. Theological Themes

1. Political Alliances, Infidelity, and Trust in One Deity

The prophet's theology is closely linked to his political stance concerning alliances. Standing in firm opposition to alliances with Assyria and Egypt, the text of Hosea views such reliance as forsaking trust in Yahweh (7:11; 8:9; 12:1; see also the people's turning in trust to their own military strength [10:13-14]). As noted in the historical context above, the text of Hosea ultimately associates these alliances with idolatry and the worship of other deities.

The fertility practices of baalism clearly inform the prophet's articulation of the people's inability to trust in Yahweh. Unable to trust their covenant deity to deliver and to provide, the people of God turn to political, military, and religious systems that promise protection, life, and abundance. Hosea describes this incapacity to trust in Yahweh as the lack of covenant fidelity (*ḥesed*). According to Hosea, the people of Yahweh are not merely an immoral or "bad" community but an unfaithful community.

One might read the text of Hosea as a "call back" to an early form of monotheistic worship of Yahweh. However, in light of the common practices of fertility religion in early Israel, Yee has interpreted Hosea to be more of "a religious innovator, a spokesperson for a developing monotheistic theology" than as a traditionalist who recalls an earlier pure form of religion. According to Yee, Hosea's "new theological ideas would influence the later deuteronomistic writers, for whom belief in the one God Yahweh was normative" (1996, 203).

2. An Inner Disposition

Certainly Hosea points to numerous evidences of infidelity, such as engagement in international alliances, self-sufficiency through military might, and the worship of other deities. However, the prophet is insistent that the issue at stake in the life of covenant community goes beyond unfaithfulness and lack of trust. He perceives that something deeper is at stake. Something within the very mind-set of the people compels and motivates their actions of infidelity. He refers to this mind-set as a "spirit of prostitution" (4:12; 5:4). Recognizing that the community has been "joined to idols," the prophet declares, "Leave him alone" (4:17).

Hosea understands that the people's "disposition" seduces them and controls their actions. He shares a similar conviction concerning the people's nature with Jeremiah. The prophet Jeremiah compares the people of God to animals in heat (Jer 2:23-25), to Ethiopians who cannot change their skin, and to leopards that cannot remove their spots (Jer 13:23). Jeremiah portrays sin as etched on the people's hearts with an iron pen (Jer 17:1). Describing this disposition as an "inner flaw," Anderson likens Israel's struggle with the predicament of "persons who are so completely enslaved by habitual ways of thinking and living that they lack both the imagination and the willpower to change themselves" (1986, 311). Hosea's insightful and reflective perceptions undoubtedly contribute to subsequent theological understandings concerning the utter helplessness of the human dilemma in relationship to sin.

3. Knowledge of God

While Hosea is keenly aware of the deeper, inner dilemma of human infidelity, he is also convinced that fidelity to Yahweh is not possible apart from the community's knowledge of God (6:6). For Hosea, faithfulness to this covenant deity is possible only when the people are fully aware of this God—of his mighty acts of deliverance and provision and of his loyal and merciful character. The prophet is further convinced that instruction (Torah) of the community is the responsibility of the religious leaders, particularly the priests. Therefore, if the priests fail at their task, it becomes impossible for the community to *know* Yahweh (see 4:1, 6-9). Hosea is adamant that the sacrificial system cannot serve as a substitute for or an alternative to the knowledge of God and the faithfulness that accompanies such knowledge (6:6; 8:13).

4. The Reality of Divine Judgment and the Victory of Divine Grace

The book of Hosea communicates a perspective of judgment consistent with the Deuteronomic conviction of retribution. The life lived by a community will ultimately come back upon that community (2:9; 4:3; 7:11-16; see Obad 15). Hosea employs the fitting metaphor of planting; the seed one sows will produce a specific and definite fruit (Hos 8:7; 10:12-13). For the prophet, divine judgment is neither arbitrary nor capricious. Rather it is the "logical" result of the people's actions; it is the fruit of sown seed.

At the same time that Hosea portrays divine judgment in direct correlation to the transgressions of the people, the text depicts the redemptive nature of divine judgment. Particularly in ch 2, as Yahweh allures Israel into the wilderness, the suffering of exile becomes the "door of hope." The people of God discover grace not apart from death and destruction but in the midst of the very calamity brought on by their own rebellion (2:14-15). Within that context, Yahweh will speak tenderly to the heart of his people and will rejoin them in marriage so that they will indeed *know* the Lord (2:16-20).

While Hosea unquestionably announces a verdict of guilt upon Israel, the book presents a clear theology of grace and restoration, described aptly by Anderson as "an 'optimism of grace'" (1986, 305). Each major section concludes with a definitive statement concerning the final victory of divine grace. Birch observes that in the book of Hosea "the character of God was not exhausted in divine anger and punishment. God's judgment was transcended by God's love" (1997, 8). In the end divine grace triumphs. Thus Hosea ultimately imagines a future in which "God promises to do what human beings ought to do but cannot" (Achtemeier 1996a, 3).

COMMENTARY

I. SUPERSCRIPTION: HOSEA 1:1

BEHIND THE TEXT

The superscription locates Hosea within a particular period in the larger story of the people of God. Similar superscriptions with historical references are found in Isaiah, Jeremiah, Ezekiel, Amos, Micah, Zephaniah, Haggai, and Zechariah. Superscriptions in the Latter Prophets, perhaps provided by a final editor, function to authenticate and legitimate the message that is to follow as coming from Yahweh himself. Hosea, like other books that have superscriptions with historical references, identifies the prophet and makes reference to his ancestry, and locates the period of his ministry in relationship to the kings of Judah and Israel.

IN THE TEXT

■ 1 Verse 1 introduces the content of the book as **the word of *Yahweh* that came to Hosea son of Beeri**. The superscription functions to authenticate and legitimate the material that is to follow; it also communicates the conviction that the prophet is a person who is entrusted with **the word** [*dābār*] **of *Yahweh***. The word that **came** (lit. ***happened***) conveys the notion that this "word is not the product of human speculation or wisdom" but rather this word "happened as an event of revelation to a particular man, and his proclamation is reflex and expression of that event" (Mays 1969, 20).

The prophet's name **Hosea** (*hôšēaʿ*) means "salvation"; it is derived from the verb *yāšaʿ*, which means "to save." According to Num 13:8, 16, this was the original name of Joshua. It is also the name of the northern kingdom's last king (2 Kgs 15:30). The significance of the name of the prophet, however, is never noted in the text, nor does the text ever appear to use the name as a pun. However, the prophet makes the declaration in ch 1 that Yahweh will *save* (*yāšaʿ*) Judah not by bow, sword, war, horses, or horsemen but ***by Yahweh their God*** (1:7). Similarly, toward the end of the book (13:4 NRSV, see also 13:10), Yahweh declares, "I have been ***Yahweh*** your God ever since the land of Egypt; you know no God but me, and besides me there is no savior" (*môšîaʿ* derived from *yāšaʿ*). The prophet's name seems to symbolize salvation for Israel as Yahweh's ultimate plan for the nation, though it is now faced with the reality of his judgment. As to the name of Hosea's father, **Beeri**, nothing is known.

Verse 1 places the ministry of Hosea during the reign of **Uzziah, Jotham, Ahaz and Hezekiah**, southern kingdom kings from 783 B.C. to 681 B.C. and during the reign of **Jeroboam** II, who ruled the northern kingdom from 786 B.C. to 746 B.C. Since Hosea carried out his ministry in northern Israel and since the text lacks reference to other northern kings, it is reasonable to assume that Hosea was active in the north sometime during the reign of Jeroboam II, a contemporary of the Judean king Uzziah (783-742 B.C.). Particularly, the oracles of the prophet reflect a concern over the house of Jehu; Jeroboam II was a great-grandson of Jehu. It is possible that the prophet fled to the south and continued his ministry in Judah soon after the death of Jeroboam II and prior to or during the revolt against the house of Jehu and the assassination of Zechariah, Jeroboam's son. The reference to Jotham, Ahaz, and Hezekiah seems to suggest a Judean ministry, but it is difficult to establish a precise date for the ministry of the prophet.

FROM THE TEXT

The presence of the superscription should not be quickly dismissed as a mere formal factor of the prophetic book. It serves to locate not only the prophet and the text but also the reader. The superscription locates the reader in a particular theological world, a sociohistorical world, as well as a creative-dynamic world of the prophetic word.

The book of Hosea in its final canonical form is located within the broader historical and theological tradition of Deuteronomy and Joshua—2 Kings (Deuteronomic theology and Deuteronomistic History). The Deuteronomic theological tradition is ultimately traced to Moses, the prophet par excellence (see Deut 34:10-12). This broader tradition of the Prophets (*Nevi'im*) provides a significant context for intertextual reading of the book of Hosea as well as a valuable theological backdrop for the reading of the text.

The prophetic message does not speak into an empty world but into the concrete realities of human existence and into the situations in which God's people find themselves at any given moment in history. The superscription of Hosea invites readers of subsequent generations to be keenly aware of the fact that the prophet's message cannot be completely dislodged from the concrete world of the people of God in the eighth century B.C. The reference to Jeroboam, Uzziah, Jotham, Ahaz, and Hezekiah is a reminder of volatile and crumbling political, social, and religious realities for Israel and Judah. Verse 1 presents the coming of God's word as a historical reality in the midst of Israel's crisis-filled existence. The content of the book of Hosea shows that God speaks directly into the context of the crisis of his people—words not only of severe judgment but also of intense hope.

The superscription also serves to authenticate the message of the prophet as the word from Yahweh. The message of the prophet is directly linked to the creative and life-giving word of Yahweh. The reader or hearer of the text must keep in mind the ongoing creative-dynamic effect of this prophetic word from God as it is taught and proclaimed in contemporary settings. From a Christian perspective, as this word speaks into diverse contemporary settings, the Living Word, Jesus Christ, is made present among us; through him, and by the help of the Holy Spirit, the people of God experience the ongoing dynamic of divine creativity and newness conveyed by the word.

II. HOSEA'S MARRIAGE: HOSEA 1:2—3:5

A. Hosea, Gomer, and Their Children (1:2-9)

1:2-9

BEHIND THE TEXT

The book of Hosea begins with a personal narrative of the prophet's life, a narrative that clearly images the life that God experienced subsequent to the covenant he made with Israel. The narrative is in the third person (see ch 3 for a first-person narrative of Hosea); it deals with the marriage of Hosea and the birth of three children. The narrative has four parts: part one (vv 2-3) describes the marriage of Hosea as commanded by Yahweh and the birth of the first child; part two (vv 4-5) contains Yahweh's command to Hosea to give a symbolic name to the first child; parts three (vv 6-7) and four (vv 8-9) deal with the birth and the naming of the second and the third child. Parts two, three, and four also include a brief explanation of the meaning of the symbolic names of the three children.

In the MT, v 9 concludes ch 1; 2:1 in the MT is 1:10 in the English versions. The theme of judgment dominates the marriage narrative of Hosea; however, 1:10-11 (English; MT 2:1-2) formally concludes the marriage narrative with an oracle of salvation to the people of Israel and Judah.

The narrative (1:2-9) reflects two worlds that are interrelated to each other: prostitution and infidelity in the marriage relationship (i.e., adultery). Yahweh commands the prophet to take a wife of prostitution.

The prophet Hosea and subsequent prophets (especially Jeremiah and Ezekiel) utilize the language of prostitution primarily to emphasize Israel's unfaithfulness toward Yahweh with a secondary emphasis upon the people hiring themselves out for wages provided by their "lovers" (see particularly Jer 3 and Ezek 16). Hosea, Jeremiah, and Ezekiel also utilize the metaphor of prostitution for Israel's political alliances with powerful nations such as Egypt and Assyria. This unfaithfulness demonstrated through alliances appears to be subsequently broadened to include unfaithfulness in the worship of Yahweh through the worship of other deities and particularly through participation in the rituals of the fertility cult. Hosea frequently refers to the activity of the people of God as prostitution (various forms derived from the verb *zānâ*) and twice speaks of a *rûaḥ zĕnûnîm* ("spirit of prostitution") that has taken over the minds and conduct of the people (4:12; 5:4).

Prostitution in the OT

In the OT, the verb *zānâ* (and its derived noun) is often used simply to refer to the act of prostitution whether or not it is related to the fertility cult. In certain instances, the OT portrays prostitution as the presumed last resort for the woman to bear a child or even to provide for herself if she is unmarried or her husband is deceased (e.g., see the story of Tamar in Gen 38; perhaps also see the woman in Prov 7). In other instances—such as the narratives of Rahab (Josh 2:1), Jephthah (Judg 11:1), or Samson (Judg 16:1)—the specific context of the prostitute is not provided. However, in these various instances, the term likely refers to a woman's act of hiring herself out for acts of sex. In certain instances, the term may simply be used more generally of a woman who has engaged in sexual activity outside of (prior to) her marriage (see Deut 22:13-21).

Prophets and Symbolic Acts

The marriage of Hosea to Gomer is clearly a symbolic act. Such symbolic acts were certainly not uncommon by the prophets of the OT. We see various symbolic acts by the prophets Isaiah, Jeremiah, and most certainly numerous symbolic acts by the prophet Ezekiel. However, for the prophet Hosea, this symbolic act is not merely an object lesson to the people but is clearly experienced by the prophet himself. He himself intimately knows the suffering and hurt of unfaithfulness by his wife. The prophet is truly one who suffers along with the heart of God.

Heschel on Hosea's Personal Suffering

A mere knowledge of what has come to pass between God and Israel would have enabled him to have genuine sympathy for the present emotion, the disillusionment, but not for the whole gamut of experience. . . . One must share the experiences, or similar experiences, in order to share the emotional reactions to them. . . . For this purpose, the full story was re-enacted in the personal life of the prophet, and the variety of divine pathos experienced and shared in the privacy of his own destiny: love, frustration, reconciliation. (Heschel 1962, 63-64)

IN THE TEXT

■ **2** Verse 2 describes ***the beginning of the word of Yahweh to Hosea*** or the instance in which the prophetic word of Yahweh began to come to Hosea. This word comes in the form of the command to ***take a wife of prostitution*** (*zĕnûnîm* from the verb *zānâ,* which means "to commit fornication"). The noun *zĕnûnîm* (plural) is indicative of a state of being or personal quality rather than simply the activity itself, so that prostitution characterizes who this woman is. The verbal root *zānâ* does not necessarily link prostitution with the marital status of the prostitutes. Thus it may be engagement in sexual intercourse outside of marriage or fornication by unmarried women or prostitution as a profession. Later the prophet uses the vocabulary of *zānâ* to describe the actions of the daughters of the Israelites (4:13*b,* 14*a*), and in this case the term does appear to refer to and is used in parallelism with temple prostitutes. The prophet also uses this vocabulary to describe the broader activity of the people as a whole (4:15*a*; 5:3*b*) as well as the mind-set that has overtaken the people (4:12*b*; 5:4*b*).

The text does not make clear whether Yahweh's command to Hosea is to marry a woman who is already a prostitute or a woman who in all likelihood would follow that path of life after Hosea marries her. A casual reading of the text suggests the former. However, based on the narrative's primary concern (i.e., the unfaithfulness that occurs once the marriage has taken place), the latter view is to be preferred here. Birch suggests that the phrase "wife of prostitution" does not characterize Gomer as a professional prostitute but merely as one whose promiscuity mirrors the behavior of a prostitute (1997, 20). Yee, from a feminist perspective, argues that Gomer is a wife of prostitution "not because she is a prostitute; she is never labeled a *zona,* the technical term for a prostitute. Rather, she is a 'wife of whoredom' because she is habitually promiscuous. Her sexual acts are evaluated pejoratively as being '*like* a whore,' although she is not a prostitute by profession" (1996, 216; for a summary of interpretation of the nature of Gomer and when her promiscuity began vis-à-vis the marriage to Hosea, see Yee 1996, 215-16).

Finally we should note here that since Hosea's marriage ultimately serves metaphorically for the covenant between Yahweh and Israel, the concern is not what Israel was *prior to* the deliverance from Egypt and covenant at Sinai. In fact, the only prophetic speculation concerning Israel's nature *prior* to deliverance and covenant is Ezekiel's description of Israel as an unwanted baby flailing about in its blood (Ezek 16:3-7) that was made beautiful by Yahweh only subsequently to prostitute itself with anyone who would pass by (Ezek 16:8-22).

Was Gomer a Cult Prostitute?

The prostitution envisaged in Hos 1 reflects the practice of cult prostitution familiar in ancient fertility rites. However, the prophet does not specifically point to Gomer as being a cult prostitute (see von Rad 1965, 138-39, for the view of Gomer as a cult prostitute). Wolff interprets the reference to be to a "young Israelite woman, ready for marriage, who had demonstrably taken part in the Canaanite bridal rite of initiation that had become customary" (1974, 15). Mays is likely correct in observing that much of the language used to describe Gomer, particularly in ch 2, emerges out of the fertility cult; however, he notes that the emphasis in the text concerning Gomer is upon sexual promiscuity. In the end, however, Mays believes that "the foil for Hosea's use of marriage as a model of Yahweh's relation to Israel and of sexual promiscuity as the *leit-motif* of his portrayal of Israel's sin is to be found in the fertility cult of Canaanite religion." As a result, he does conclude that Gomer was neither a "woman of unknown promiscuous tendencies" nor a "common prostitute" but "one whose sexual promiscuity was a matter of the very harlotry of Israel in the cult of Baal" (i.e., a cult prostitute, Mays 1969, 25-26). These various perspectives suggest that Gomer may have been a cult prostitute.

The Hebrew text clearly does not state in v 2 that the prophet is "to have" children of prostitution; rather, the verb "to take" appears to include the children. The MT reading, which is reflected in the NIV, is as follows: ***take for yourself a wife of prostitution and children of prostitution***. Some English versions supply the verb "have" after the conjunction "and" (see NRSV). The phrase ***children of prostitution*** (genitive construct in Hebrew) most likely refers to children born to their mother as she was practicing prostitution or infidelity. However, the report of the first child's birth (v 3) specifically states that the woman Hosea took as his wife "conceived and bore *for him* a son." Verse 3 does not appear to think of this child as belonging to anyone other than Hosea. Hosea does appear to take on the parental role of naming the children, though he himself does not choose the names, but they are given by Yahweh. The statements in vv 6 and 8 do not link Hosea with the conception or birth of the second and the third child; neither do these verses indicate that the children were conceived by another man. Overall, the narrative indicates that the birth of the children took place while Hosea was married to Gomer and that during this time of their marriage, the wife/mother has been unfaithful and played the part of one who receives payment for her sexual services.

Mays observes that the reference to the children as being children of prostitution does not convey a message about the children's character but rather that they came from the womb of a mother that was a participant in the fertility cult and thus were "religiously the offspring of harlotry" (Mays 1969, 26). Following the line of reasoning that Gomer had participated in common Canaanite bridal rituals of her day, Wolff argues that the children "were not necessarily born before the marriage and by no means were they born outside of marriage. They are so named because the mother had acquired her ability to bear children in marriage by her participation in a pagan rite which in Yahweh's judgment was 'whoredom'" (1974, 15).

Verse 2 also gives the specific reason for Yahweh's rather strange and difficult command to Hosea. ***The land commits great prostitution*** by turning itself away from Yahweh. Throughout the book of Hosea, the prophet places great concern upon ***the land***, particularly the manner in which the land has been affected by the harlotry-like actions of the people. The phrase ***children of prostitution*** is also linked to the last part of v 2. The emphasis of v 2 is on Yahweh's assessment of a present reality in Israel. Covenant infidelity is the characteristic way of life of the present generation of Israel. Every individual Israelite is born into the context of Israel's turning away from its relationship to Yahweh.

■ **3** Verse 3 reports the prophet's obedience to Yahweh's command (***so he went and took*** . . .). The command came without further instructions on the identity or the family of the woman. Verse 3 identifies **Gomer daughter of Diblaim** as the woman Hosea took as his wife. The identity of Diblaim is not given. Some commentators see in this name a linguistic connection to *dĕbēlim* ("cakes of figs"; see 1 Sam 25:18; 1 Chr 12:40), which may be linked to the Canaanite fertility cult. Hosea 1:3 indicates that Gomer conceived and gave birth to a son, and the child actually belongs to the prophet. In fact, the text describes the action as bearing a son ***for him***.

■ **4** The naming of the first child by Hosea is also an act of obedience to Yahweh's command. In other words, Yahweh decides on the name of Hosea's son (**Jezreel**, meaning "God sows"), and Hosea simply gives the name chosen by Yahweh. In the birth narrative of Hosea's children, all the names function in a symbolic way, similar to "prostitution" in v 2. Verse 4 vividly depicts the direct effect of the harlotry of the people (***the land*** in v 2) upon the land itself. The name **Jezreel** is a clear and visible symbol of the "fruit" that has been conceived and born in the midst of the union between Yahweh and his adulterous people. In v 4 Yahweh also gives the reason for the name **Jezreel** and its significance to the past, present, and future history of Israel.

Jezreel

Jezreel is first remembered for the great victory of Gideon over the Midianites (Judg 6—7). The name is subsequently tarnished by the violent and bloody massacre of the Omri dynasty by Jehu in the ninth century B.C. (see 2 Kgs 9—10). First Kings 19 narrates how King Ahab took possession of the vineyard owned by Naboth the Jezreelite in Jezreel after a successful plot by Jezebel to kill Naboth for refusing to sell his property to the king. First Kings 21 and 2 Kgs 9 contain prophetic judgment on the house of Ahab made by Elijah and Elisha. Elijah announced that dogs would lick up the blood of Ahab and eat Jezebel's flesh in the boundary of Jezreel, in the same place where dogs licked up the blood of Naboth (1 Kgs 21:17-24). Elisha commissioned one of his disciples to anoint Jehu as king over Israel and to strike down the house of Ahab (see 2 Kgs 9:1-10). Jehu carried out his commission, which resulted in the violent death of both King Joram, Ahab's son (9:17-26), and Jezebel in the territory of Jezreel (9:30-37), the murder of Ahab's descendants (10:1-17), and the prophets, priests, and worshippers of Baal in northern Israel (10:18-27). Jezreel's notoriety as a place of violence and bloodshed suggests that Hosea's naming of the first child was akin to one's naming a child after the location of massive violence in more recent history, such as naming a child Hiroshima or Columbine.

The name of the first son, Jezreel, is ironic in many ways. Its meaning—
"God sows"—has many shades of meaning. First, it is linked to the fertility cult
of Baal religion, which believed in the idea of sowing seeds with subsequent 1:4
bountiful harvest made possible by the god Baal. It is ironic that the house of Ahab, which fervently supported the Baal fertility religion, was overthrown in a territory named "God sows." In that sense, Jezreel stands here for God sowing his seeds of judgment on northern Israel for its long history of covenantal unfaithfulness and Baal worship.

Another irony in this name is that, long after the commissioning of Jehu by Elisha and Jehu's violent extermination of the Omri dynasty, Hosea suggests that Jehu's violence had polluted the land itself. During the revolution of Jehu, blood had been "planted" in the land; now the effects of the violence are coming back upon Israel. Again, the name Jezreel implies it is now time for God to sow seeds of judgment on Israel for Jehu's shedding of blood in the land or sowing violence in the land. The spilled blood in the land of Jezreel must now be reckoned.

Verse 4 also states that Yahweh will ***visit*** or ***attend to the blood of*** [*dĕmê*] ***Jezreel*** concerning the house of Jehu. The reference to the blood here indicates a natural product out of its natural state; thus, the description is of spilled or shed blood. This violently shed blood will be attended to or visited by Yahweh. The verb *pāqad* (meaning "to visit," "to attend," "to punish," etc.) does not first convey punishment but divine visitation. It is the act in which Yahweh will give attention to a particular individual or group. Oftentimes this verb can be understood as a gracious visitation (e.g., Gen 21:1; Exod 13:19; Isa 23:17). However, when the sins of a people are attended to by Yahweh, then the idea is that of divine visitation to bring punishment (see the NIV: **I will soon punish the house of Jehu**; see also Amos 3:2, 14; Exod 20:5; 34:7; Deut 5:9).

Yahweh's visitation upon the spilled blood of Jezreel is intended to bring an end to the kingdom of the house of Israel. This house or dynasty that re-emerged as a legitimate people of Yahweh under the reform of Jehu (see 2 Kgs 10:15-28) had lost its legitimacy to exist as it prostituted itself against the very God who had authorized it to come into existence (see 2 Kgs 10:29-31).

■ **5** Verse 5 indicates that on the day of Yahweh's visitation (***on that day***) Yahweh will shatter the symbol of northern Israel's mighty military power—the bow (e.g., see Gen 9:13-16; 49:24; 1 Sam 2:4)—in Jezreel, the very place where the spilled blood cries out. Ironically, the might and power of the kingdom of Israel that had reemerged under Jehu in the Valley of Jezreel will be brought to an end in the Valley of Jezreel.

■ **6** Without any explanation of the role played by Hosea, v 6 reports the conception and birth of the second child, this time a daughter. Yahweh commands the prophet to name the child **Lo-Ruhamah**, meaning "Not pitied" or "No compassion." Yahweh also explains the name by saying that he will no longer extend his compassion to the people of Israel: ***I will not continue to have compassion upon the house of Israel that I would indeed (truly) lift them up***. The name of the second child ("Not pitied" or "No compassion"—from *rāḥam*, which means "to have compassion") would likely have conjured up in the minds of the people the oft-repeated affirmations that Yahweh has compassion toward his people particularly after their rebellion against him and even after their exile (see Exod 33:19; Deut 13:17; 30:3; 2 Kgs 13:23; Jer 12:15; Ezek 39:25; for the lack of divine compassion upon Yahweh's people, see Isa 9:17 [9:16 HB]).

Israel's theological tradition affirmed that Yahweh's ***compassion*** (*rāḥam*) is an important demonstration of his covenant faithfulness to his people, and indeed an essential characteristic of Yahweh (see Exod 34:6-7; Num 14:18; Neh 9:17, 31; Ps 103:8; Jonah 4:2). In Hos 1:6 Yahweh declares he will no longer have such covenant-grounded mercy toward his people. Verse 6 ends with the negative outcome of the end of Yahweh's compassion—Israel will not be "lifted up." The verb "lift up" (*nāśā'*) often means "forgive"; the use of the infinitive absolute here adds a sense of emphasis to Yahweh's declaration. The translation of this verb in the Septuagint indicates that God will resist or oppose the house of Israel. This reading reflects *sane'* (meaning "to hate") rather than *nāśā'* as the Hebrew word underlying the Greek translation. It is possible that the Greek translators would have simply reversed the first two Hebrew consonants. There is no Hebrew manuscript evidence for the LXX reading. The prophet's statement emphatically claims that Yahweh's mercy and compassion in times of their rebellion that has led Yahweh to forgive iniquity, transgression, and sin (see Exod 34:6-7; Num 14:18) has come to an end. The result of **Lo-Ruhamah** (***no compassion***) is no forgiveness. Nevertheless, later in the book the prophet announces divine compassion as warm and tender again; this suggests the end of Yahweh's compassion that has grown cold (see Hos 11:8-9).

■ **7** In spite of the effect of Yahweh's lack of compassion upon the northern kingdom of Israel, Yahweh continues to extend his faithfulness to Judah, the southern kingdom. Some commentators see this verse as a later addition because of its focus on Judah in the middle of a narrative that deals with the northern kingdom. Verse 7 makes explicit mention concerning the divine ***compassion*** (*rāḥam*) toward Judah that would move Yahweh to ***rescue*** (*yāšaʿ*, meaning "to save") the southern kingdom. This statement is likely a reference to the sparing of the south when the Assyrians invaded and destroyed both Syria and the northern kingdom of Israel in 722/721 B.C. Yahweh announces that he himself would directly bring salvation and deliverance to Judah, though Judah has placed its trust in nations that have superior military resources and war equipment (**sword, horses, horsemen**). Judah's dependence on Assyria for its survival in the context of a military threat from the Syrian-Israelite coalition may have been the context of this salvation word announced to Judah.

■ **8** Verse 8 reports the birth of the third child, a boy, who was conceived by Hosea's wife after she had weaned Lo-Ruhama. Again, there is no reference to the involvement of Hosea in the conception of this child.

■ **9** Yahweh is again the one who determines the name of this child. The name **Lo-Ammi** (***Not My People***) is followed by a reason for the name. By naming the child Lo-Ammi, Yahweh declares that Israel is not his people (**my people**) and that he is not their God (**I am not your God**; lit. "I myself will not be for you" [plural pronoun]). Certainly, the child's name ***Not my people*** (derived from *ʿammî*, "my people") and the reason for the name given by Yahweh (**You are not my people, and I am not your God**), would clearly evoke in the communal memory Yahweh's covenant with Israel at Sinai. The most critical aspect of this covenant was the relationship between Yahweh and Israel. The naming of the child reverses the covenant promise, "I will be your God and you will be my people" (Jer 7:23; see Exod 6:6-7; Deut 26:17-19; Jer 31:33; and Ezek 36:28). This means that Israel is deprived of the divine compassion and no longer exists in a covenant or marriage relationship with Yahweh. The marriage between Yahweh and Israel is annulled.

FROM THE TEXT

The narrative of Hosea's marriage to Gomer and the three symbolic names of his children reflect the intimate relationship between the message proclaimed and the messenger who proclaims. Hosea's marriage to Gomer vividly demonstrates his call to associate his life directly with his message and thus to associate it directly with the life of God's people. The life of the prophet Jeremiah reveals this prophetic agony much more explicitly than that of Hosea. The narrative suggests that the message cannot be separated from the messenger, nor can the messenger stand aloof from the message proclaimed. Limburg rightly observes that "for Hosea there was no separation between office and home, vocation and family life. No doubt that is why he spoke with such passion. The pain in the heart of the prophet became a parable of the anguish in the heart of God" (1988, 10). Certainly, for the prophet Hosea, to speak the word of God is to participate in the very message that is spoken.

Through the prophet's firsthand knowledge of living in a relationship of infidelity, Hosea has contributed immensely to the understanding of the nature of the relationship between Yahweh and his people and ultimately between Christ and his church. Of all of the images that might have been chosen to portray the covenant relationship, the image of marriage particularly evokes in the consciousness of the hearer a relationship of anticipated loyalty and mutual fidelity.

The awakened husband's declaration in the opening narratives of scripture—***This time, bone of my bone and flesh of my flesh*** (Gen 2:23)—and the subsequent announcement that the two will cling to one another and become one flesh (2:24), clearly anticipate marriage between a man and a woman to be a relationship of oneness and mutual love. Likewise, the relationship shared between God and his covenant people is also a relationship of mutual faithfulness. The people of Yahweh are not simply called to an abstract religious idea or practice; they are called to a relationship of loyalty to the God who redeemed them. They are called to faithfulness and fidelity.

Over time, subsequent generations have further reinterpreted the image of marriage. Both Jeremiah and Ezekiel utilize this image in vivid ways. The Song of Songs, while originally a wedding song demonstrating the love between husband and wife, is later interpreted by the people of God as the relationship shared between Yahweh and Israel and subsequently the relationship shared between Jesus Christ, the groom, and the church, his bride. The NT community likewise draws upon this image of the relationship between Christ and his followers (Mark 2:19-20; Eph 5:21-33; Rev 19:7-9).

The narrative makes clear that the marriage relationship is between God and his people, and not simply a privatized relationship between God and the individual. In the midst of heavily individualistic and consumer-oriented cultures, one might easily apply the covenant relationship to the individual rather than to the community. The prophetic understanding of Israel as the wife of Yahweh cautions against such quickly reached individualistic and privatized conclusions. The issues at stake within covenant fidelity are much broader than simplistic individual behaviors. These issues especially challenge the faithfulness of a community called the *people* of God.

For the Christian, the loyalty and fidelity of the church vis-à-vis Christ is at stake. The narrative, through its image of marital fidelity, invites the people of God *as a community* to reflect on the means by which communal commitments and loyalties compete for the attention of the people of God. The narrative also challenges the people of God to be aware of those instances in which even well-intentioned religious systems or programs call for allegiance that distracts from undivided commitment to and complete trust in Yahweh. Likewise, the text calls upon the people of God *communally* to examine their behavior and activities to be conscious of those ways in which communal preoccupations demonstrate either fidelity or infidelity to the God with whom they share covenant and to whom they owe their very reason for existence.

The opening narrative of the book of Hosea calls for the reader to perceive the direct effects of a relationship of infidelity with Yahweh. The image of the broken marriage between Hosea and Gomer vividly portrays the dire consequences of the people's infidelity to the covenant with Yahweh. Chapter 2 will particularly flesh out the ramifications of these consequences; however, in a general sense, the covenant cannot and will not continue to stand if one member of the marriage is resolutely committed to infidelity. The tragic outcome of covenant infidelity is that a people who were once *my* people will no longer be *my* people. A community that was founded in and by the compassion of God will no longer be the recipient of God's compassion.

This text makes quite clear that the effect of the broken covenant is not simply upon the people of Yahweh but also upon Yahweh himself. Yahweh is not the stoic Greek god who stands aloof and cannot be touched by this people; he is affected by his people's life and commitments. Israel is not the only member of this marriage; Yahweh is the other member, and he has been hurt by the unfaithfulness of his covenant partner. Birch quite accurately notes that "the marriage and family metaphors force us to face the woundedness to God and ourselves that results from idolatrous unfaithfulness to our covenant commitment" (1997, 23).

The narrative also indicates that the effects of covenant infidelity are ultimately upon creation itself. Yahweh is God not merely of a called-out people or even simply of the human race but is ultimately the God of all creation. This theological understanding of God that underlies the text is linked to its proclamation that "the land" is also directly affected by the people's covenant infidelity. The *missio Dei* (mission of God and likewise of God's people who partner with him) does not stop with a mission to members of the covenant community or to the human race. Ultimately, the divine mission is one *to* and *with* all of creation. When the people of Yahweh have broken covenant fidelity with their God, the ramifications extend into creation itself.

B. The Promise of Restoration (1:10—2:1)

BEHIND THE TEXT

Hosea 1:10—2:1 is 2:1-3 in the MT. This unit is an oracle of salvation to both Israel and Judah. This oracle of salvation provides the necessary balance to Hosea's opening message of judgment (1:2-9). The messenger formula is lacking; Hosea is the speaker and he conveys Yahweh's future activities on behalf of the people who live under his judgment. Jezreel, Lo-Ammi, and Lo-Ruhamah all hear Yahweh's words of the reversal of their judgment. The reversal of the judgment on Jezreel, Lo-Ammi, and Lo-Ruhamah is also the theme in 2:21-23.

Some commentators view these verses as later editorial additions to Hosea, subsequent to the Babylonian exile of Judah. However, the restoration theme reflected in these verses is highly consistent with the overall message of Hosea. Hosea links the theme of the restoration and God's renewed covenant relationship with Israel to Israel's collective memory of God's promises to the patriarchs concerning his descendants (see Gen 22:17; 32:12), and to David concerning the Davidic kingdom (2 Sam 7:16). Hosea's message of the remaking of the covenant and the reemergence of a united monarchy under Davidic kings receives further development in later prophetic traditions, particularly in Jeremiah and Ezekiel (see Jer 30:9, 22; 31:1, 31-34; 32:38, 40; 33:14-26; Ezek 37:15-25, 26-27).

IN THE TEXT

■ **10** In v 10 the prophet holds out hope for the people of Israel, and this hope has its basis in God's promise to the ancestors. This verse anticipates a time when the people of Israel shall be **like the sand on the seashore, which cannot be measured or counted**. The language of this promise reflects the promises to the patriarchs concerning the multiplication of their descendants in Genesis (see 22:17; 32:12; also 15:5). Even in the midst of covenant breaking and unfaithfulness on the part of Israel, Yahweh remains committed to his unconditional promises to the patriarchs. The nation of Israel will not be reduced to nothing, but its number will continue to increase; even in judgment, the promise of increase in population is at work.

The second part of Hos 1:10 introduces another promise to Israel. The word of judgment in v 9 is reversed in v 10. Israel's relationship with Yahweh has been annulled ("Not my people") because of its covenant breaking (v 9). That means the end of any hope for Israel's continued existence in the world as a people who belong to Yahweh. The surprising element of v 10 is the promise of a new identity to Israel. Yahweh's faithfulness to his covenant promises to the ancestors will make it possible for Israel to be known as **children of the living God** (*bĕnê ʾel-ḥāy*). One would have expected the title "my people," the old covenant formula, in this reversal of Israel's judgment. **Children of the living God** conveys a more intimate and familial relationship. Israel will be brought to life from death by the life-giving power of the Creator God who lives and who is the source of all that exists. This God, who from the beginning of creation has been about *giving* life, will not allow death and annulment to be the final word.

■ **11** Not only will restoration between God and his people take place, but restoration between a divided people will occur as well. The text envisions the northern and southern kingdoms once again becoming a united people; reconciliation will come between the divorced nations. Restoration of fidelity with Yahweh engenders restoration with one's human comrades as well. Israel will experience covenant in its fullest sense—relationship between God and community as well as relationship within the community itself. These two divided nations will join together to come under one ***chief*** (*rōʾš*; lit. "head"). The language used in the text is actually reminiscent of the chieftains during the period of the judges or tribal leaders (e.g., Exod 18:25; Num 1:16; Deut 1:15; Judg 10:18). Later in the text, Hosea specifically names David (Hos 3:5), or a descendant of David, as the one who will lead these people. However, in this instance he uses the monarchical term "king" (*melek*) in contrast to the tribal leader or chieftain. Perhaps the prophet does not use the customary title "king" in 1:11 because of its negative image during the days of Hosea (see 7:3-7; 8:4; 10:4, 7). Hosea seems to envision here Israel's restoration as a united kingdom as it was during the days of King David or as a unified people in the days of Moses and Joshua.

Verse 11 ends with a promise that is directly linked to the land. The nation united under one leader **will come up out of the land** (see "they shall take possession of the land" in the NRSV). This land is specifically referred to as **Jezreel**, the territory where the shed blood of the polluted land served as a vivid illustration of the broken relationship. The prophet makes clear in v 11 that the renewal of covenant between Yahweh and his people—the change of name from "Not my people" to **Children of the living God**—will occur in the very location where the brokenness had first taken place. The place of brokenness and bloodshed will become the very sign of a mighty day of deliverance and restoration (**the day of Jezreel**).

■ **2:1** While one could interpret 2:1 as an introduction to vv 2 ff., it is more likely that it concludes the hope and restoration described in 1:10-11. The restoration and renaming of Lo-Ammi and Lo-Ruhamah is the theme of 2:1. Yahweh will restore and rename Lo-Ammi and Lo-Ruhamah to Ammi and Ruhamah.

Verse 1 reads literally as follows: **Say *to* your brothers, "My people [*Ammi*]," and *to* your sisters, "*Pitied* [*Ruhamah*]."** While one might first read Ammi as being in apposition to brother and Ruhamah as being in apposition to sister (so that certain translations keep brother and sister in the singular), the translation of the plural **brothers** and **sisters** in the NIV is consistent with the Hebrew text. The imperative verb **say** is likewise in the plural. Yahweh is speaking to Lo-Ammi and Lo-Ruhamah, who represent the covenant people as they have broken covenant with Yahweh. Yahweh gives them new names and thus reverses the judgment implicit in the names Lo-Ammi and Lo-Ruhamah. After the days of judgment, Yahweh will once again take his wife and children back into his home, and they will be restored to their rightful identity. Yahweh commands them to speak to each other and address themselves as the restored and renamed people of Yahweh—Ammi and Ruhamah. The prophet clearly envisions here a remarkable reversal of Yahweh's divorce from Israel, his wife, and of the disavowal of children, and the impact that this reversal will have upon subsequent generations of God's people.

FROM THE TEXT

A vibrant message of hope is obvious in this brief oracle. One of the clearest declarations of hope is found in the statement that the very place of brokenness, the territory that had become polluted, will become the place of restoration and optimism. The same irony is expressed in 2:15 where the prophet speaks of the transformation of the Valley of Achor (trouble) into a *door of hope*. That which was deemed as catastrophic and final becomes the threshold to new life and a road into the future.

This short passage especially demonstrates well the overall purpose of the book of Hosea. Whatever devastation is to occur as Yahweh visits his people is not intended by God to be the end purpose of the divine visitation. Rather, the purpose of judgment is found in the broader context of God's ultimate intent for the salvation, restoration, and hope of his people. Limburg has observed that for the prophet Hosea and thus for Yahweh, "he wants his wife to quit her prostitution and adultery so that there can be a reconciliation. The husband still hopes that his marriage can be saved and looks forward to a time when their relationship will be like it was in the courting days" (1988, 10-11). Rather than a declaration that Yahweh desires to divorce his people, Hosea's parabolic marriage is a message of the effect of infidelity upon the covenant relationship between Yahweh and his people.

In the end, the divine spouse seeks the restoration and healing of his wayward partner. Tremendous irony is provided in the final arrangement of the collection of the twelve, with Hosea at the outset declaring a divine divorce and yet Malachi at the end declaring that Yahweh is a ***hater of divorce*** (Mal 2:16). However, even before the book of Hosea has come to an end, the message is clear that Yahweh in the end will not settle for divorce; he seeks restoration.

When the child's name is changed to Lo-Ammi, the name change seeks to come full circle so that the people who are "Not My People" will once again become "My People." When Yahweh declares the withdrawal of divine compassion from a people who have repeatedly been the recipients of divine compassion, such a declaration ultimately seeks to restore compassion to its fullest extent. The ultimate and tragic effect of judgment is death and destruction of the population, the loss of freedom and the exile of the people from the land of promise. But as we will see in Hos 2, these tragedies do not mean the end of Israel. They are simply the path toward a restored future, the threshold to hope.

C. The Lawsuit (2:2-23)

BEHIND THE TEXT

This poetic text takes the common form of the legal controversy (i.e., lawsuit; Heb. *rîb*). In ancient Israel, the juridical procedure that determined an innocent or guilty verdict was conducted in the city gate (see Exod 23:2; Ruth 4). Occasionally the OT prophets have utilized this procedure to present the case Yahweh (plaintiff) has against his people (defendant) in their oracles (see Isa 1:2-9; Jer 2:4-13; Mic 6:1-16 for examples of this genre). The lawsuit consists of three primary movements: a summons to come to trial; the trial itself, which may include presentations by both the defendant and the plaintiff; and the verdict (see Mic 6:1-16, where these three movements are clearly present).

Hosea 2:2-23 lacks the summons and the trial but preserves other features of the lawsuit genre. The text begins with the charge against the mother/wife (vv 2-5). Here the plaintiff uses the very words of the defendant to establish the guilt of the defendant (v 5). The charge is followed by three "therefore" pronouncements of Yahweh (vv 6-8, 9-13, 14-15). Verses 6-8 and 9-13 convey punishment; vv 14-15 announce the restoration of the unfaithful wife. The text ends with three eschatological (***on that day***) oracles (vv 16-17, 18-20, 21-23). These oracles develop the theme of restoration conveyed in vv 14-15. The final segments thus clearly indicate that restoration, and not divorce, is the ultimate goal of Yahweh, who brings the case against his unfaithful wife.

Yahweh is the speaker throughout this text (see the frequently found "I" in this text). However, the text permits the reader to interchange between Yahweh and the prophet as speakers in this text, since they both share the same experience of marital unfaithfulness. Both are present in the text as scorned and rejected spouses. Though the children are asked to speak to the mother, they do not speak, because the identity of the children is wrapped in the identity of the mother. Nowhere in the text does the spouse/mother reply, perhaps a result of the patriarchal background of this hearing.

In addition to being filled with language of a promiscuous spouse in her desperate search for lovers, ch 2 is replete with language and thought that emerges from the ancient Near Eastern fertility cult and particularly Baal worship. The language of dry and barren land (2:3, 6, 12) as well as fertile agricultural produce (2:5, 8-9, 12, 21-22) points to a subsistence society's great concern over the growth of crops for the sake of sheer survival of the family.

Fertility Cult

The promise of abundance of rain and fertile crops was an important aspect of ancient Near Eastern fertility cult. An underlying religious notion of the fertility cult is that the male and female deity in the heavens mimicked the sexual activity of their worshippers on earth. As the god of fertility and his consort would engage in sexual activity, fertility on earth would result. The rains would come and the crops would grow. Fertility and growth were the "wages" from the fertility god(s) as the worshipper engaged in appropriate worship of the deity who was the owner or master (lit. "the *baʿal*") of the land. Hosea 2 clearly assumes the practices of the fertility religions of the ancient Near East and its impact upon the thought and practices of the ancient Israelites.

IN THE TEXT

I. The Charge (2:2-5)

■ **2** The speaker is not identified, but it is clear that Yahweh is the speaker throughout this unit. Verse 2 begins with the imperative (in plural) **rebuke** (*rîbû* means "bring a charge/case against") followed by a reason clause (*kî* clause in Hebrew). The children are the addressees; Yahweh commands them to make a legal charge against their mother. The reason for the charge is that there exists no husband and wife relationship between Yahweh and his wife. What is essential to the marriage relationship is the commitment between **wife** (*ʾiššâ*) and **husband** (*ʾîš*) (see Gen 2:22-25). Yahweh charges that his marital partner, Israel, no longer regards herself as his wife (*ʾištî*, **my wife**); neither does she acknowledge Yahweh as **her husband** (*ʾîšāh*). At the outset, this charge seems to suggest the first step in a divorce proceeding. However, the second part of Hos 2:2 implies that divorce is not the goal of the lawsuit. Yahweh simply wants his unfaithful wife to put an end to her life as a prostitute. He says: **Let her remove *her prostitution* from her face**. Likewise, she should remove ***her adultery*** [*na'ăpûp*] **from between her breasts**. Wolff sees in these lines a reference to "certain marks or emblems, e.g., headbands, belts, rings, necklaces, or similar jewelry, placed on a woman who had participated in the Canaanite sex cult" (Wolff 1974, 33-34; see also Mays 1969, 38). Yee argues that these terms do not suggest "some sort of signs" that display the profession of a prostitute, but the woman's "cosmetics and jewelry" that she puts on "to make herself attractive" (1996, 224). These two lines perhaps convey the image of a woman who is unfaithful to her marriage covenant. The text calls the unfaithful partner to turn aside from all unfaithfulness and to turn back toward her husband by removing any indications of such infidelity. Wolff thinks that the call here is for the removal of "the sanctuaries of Baal," the marks of Israel's prostitution, "from the face of the land" (1974, 34).

■**3** In v 3 Yahweh announces his actions that he would undertake should his spouse, Israel, refuse to respond to his urgent appeal. The threat here is filled with language of barrenness and infertility. While the threat begins with the language of being stripped of one's garments, the language proceeds with vivid imagery of forcibly placing (*yāṣag*) the wife into the circumstances of a newborn child, helpless and naked. The imagery conveys the idea of conditions that threaten life as well as shame and humiliation. While ancient Israelite laws go as far as to prescribe capital punishment for the adulterous wife (Lev 20:10; Deut 22:24), the prophet does not speak of capital punishment but of the removal of basic needs provided by a husband to a wife (e.g., see Exod 21:10).

The second part of Hos 2:3 links the removal of clothing to three terms that express the barrenness of the land: ***wilderness***, **parched land**, and **thirst**. The language of barrenness fits very well with the context of the popular fertility cult, which the prophet is convinced in the end cannot produce what it promises. Yahweh is the true provider of life and fertility for his people Israel; their trust in other sources of fertility would result in the loss of fertility and the barrenness of the land.

■**4** The mother's refusal to remove her marks of harlotry does not merely affect her, but her refusal has a direct impact upon **her children**, upon all that has been conceived by her and born from her. The children born into this broken marriage will not have the ***compassion*** (*rāḥam*) of their father. The declaration of no paternal compassion upon the sons ironically recalls the name given to the second child, a daughter (Lo-Ruhamah). Yee has suggested that because of their mother's sexual promiscuity, even the paternity of the children is held suspect in v 4 (1996, 224).

■**5** Verse 5 describes two reasons for the threat announced in v 4. This verse describes the mother's shameful activity in specific and concrete terms. The first reason (*for*; Heb. *kî*) is that **their mother has *committed adultery*** and that she has **conceived them in *shame*** (or, ***she who conceived them has acted in shame***). The reference to shame here is of tremendous significance. In an ancient Near Eastern culture such as Israel, in which honor and shame were paramount, the activity of the adulterous spouse (and ultimately of the people of Yahweh) is an affront to the honor of the husband, the family, and ultimately the community in which this family finds itself.

The second reason (***for***; Heb. *kî*) is that she is determined to **go after** her **lovers**, whom she claims as the source of her basic provisions (***bread*** and **water**) as well as luxuries of life (**wool** and **linen**, **olive oil**, and **drink**). The *piel* participle *mĕʾahăbay*, translated as **lovers**, could be translated either as "the ones who love me" or "the ones that I love." Israel is portrayed not simply as the adulterer waiting for lovers to come to her; the intensive stem of the verb (*piel*) indicates that she wantonly and actively seeks her lovers (see "lovers" as political allies in 8:9; see also Jer 22:20, 22; 30:14; and Ezek 16:33, 36, 37; 23:5, 9, 22). In Hos 2:5, **lovers** may refer to other deities. Verse 5 indicates that Israel has abandoned its confession of faith during harvesttimes, which acknowledged the fruit of the ground as a gift from Yahweh (Deut 26:1 ff.; see 26:10). The people attribute fertility and other blessings to other sources—other deities or political allies.

2. A Blockade (2:6-8)

2:5-7 **■ 6** The verses that follow v 5 provide three sequential divine responses that will be given to the wayward covenant partner. Yahweh will block the path of his unfaithful wife (vv 6-8); he will strip her naked (vv 9-13); he will allure her into the wilderness (vv 14-15). Each of these responses is introduced by the particle **therefore** (*lākēn*).

The first divine action in response to the shameful activity of the unfaithful spouse is to **block her path** to her lovers (v 6). The goal of this divine action is to make it impossible for the unfaithful spouse to reach her lovers.

Two different images convey the blockade. The fence of ***thorns*** and the stone **wall** both indicate the obstacles that Yahweh plans to place on Israel's path that would make it difficult for her to find her way to her lovers. Mays has noted that in light of the customary penalty for adultery in ancient Israel (i.e., stoning of the guilty partner), this response by the faithful spouse is actually one of grace in spite of its tremendous severity (Mays 1969, 39).

■ 7 Verse 7 describes the unfaithful wife's determination to disregard the blockade and to **chase** [*rādap*] **after her lovers**. **She will look** [*bāqaš* also means "to seek"] **for them** conveys the same idea. The intensive stem (*piel*) of the Hebrew verbs here expresses the idea of fervent and frenzied pursuit and desperate yearning of the spouse to find her lovers. Seeking other gods at cultic sites is perhaps the idea being conveyed in v 7. Hosea elsewhere utilizes the verb *bāqaš* ("to seek") to describe the act of seeking Yahweh in worship (see Hos 5:6, 15; 7:10). Verse 7 also shows the futility of the spouse's fervent seeking of her lovers. She will not ***reach them*** or **find them** also conveys the effectiveness of the blockade of her path by Yahweh.

The second part of v 7 introduces a change in the mind-set of the unfaithful spouse. Her failure to find her lovers prompts her to make a decision to ***return*** (*šûb*) to her ***first*** **husband** (*ʾîš* means "man" or "husband"), whom she has abandoned for other lovers. This decision is also prompted by her recognition of the truth that life was indeed better for her when she was with him than at the present moment. In ch 3, the prophet Hosea anticipates the return of the people to Yahweh (3:5) and their subsequent restoration.

■ **8** In v 8 Yahweh speaks about his unfaithful wife's lack of knowledge (**She has not acknowledged**) of the true source of her provisions. Knowledge of Yahweh is a key concern in the book of Hosea. The Hebrew verb (*yādaʿ*) conveys the idea of knowing someone in intimate, personal, and covenantal relationship. Verse 8 implies that the unfaithful wife exists without a covenantal relationship with her husband, the clear evidence of which is her lack of recognition of Yahweh as the true source of the provisions she enjoys in her life. **Grain**, **new wine**, and **oil** are the three staple agricultural products of ancient Israel. The prophetic-Deuteronomic tradition views these three products as the blessing of Yahweh to those who live in an obedient and faithful relationship to him (see Deut 7:12-14; 11:13-15).

In addition to the three primary agricultural products, Yahweh had also **lavished on** (*rābâ* means "to increase," "multiply," etc.) the people **silver and gold**. However, the people have used the precious metals in the service of Baal, presumably in the making of images. The Hebrew phrase here (*ʿāśû labāʿal*) could be translated as **they used for Baal** or ***they made into Baal***. The former translation suggests the use of these metals as possible ornaments of decorative jewelry (perhaps a reference back to the marks of adultery in Hos 2:4); the latter leads to the suggestion that the people used these metals for the construction of idols (see also 8:4; 13:2; Isa 44:9-17). Whichever translation is adopted, Hos 2:8 makes clear that the people have replaced their devotion to Yahweh with their devotion to Baal.

3. Stripping Bare (2:9-13)

■ **9** The particle *lākēn* (**therefore**) introduces the second divine response (vv 9-13). Yahweh the husband will remove the blessings and gifts (**grain, new wine, wool, linen**) that he gave to his wife. The grain and wine will be taken back ***in its time*** and ***in its season***; both phrases likely refer to harvesttime. Since Yahweh is the giver of these provisions for life, and since these provisions belong to him (**my grain, my new wine, my wool, my linen**) he also has the right to take them back or withhold them from his unfaithful wife. These are

Yahweh's provisions for life (grain and wine) and for clothing (wool and linen) to **cover her naked body**.

■ **10** In v 10, Yahweh threatens to **expose** the **lewdness** of his wife. Some commentators see here the idea of stripping naked and the public exposure of genitals (Wolff 1974, 37; Yee 1996, 225). The husband's intent is to bring disgrace and public humiliation to his wife, who shamelessly exposed herself before **her lovers**, her other gods and political allies. The verb **expose** or uncover (*gālah*) in v 10 is also the root verb used for "to go into exile." Exile ultimately is the revealing or uncovering of the shameless and lewd character of God's people. Verse 10 ends with the note that these powers can do nothing to save her from the ***hand*** of Yahweh; they will be powerless and helpless before the mighty power of Yahweh at work in judgment against his unfaithful people.

■ **11** Yahweh's judgment also includes an end to Israel's cultic festivals, the context of great ***rejoicing*** (*māśôś*) for the nation. The lack of agricultural produce has a direct impact on the ability of the people to bring offerings and eat and drink and enjoy life during festival times. Hosea begins with the announcement of the cessation of the feasts that were celebrated annually, monthly, and weekly. **Festivals** (*ḥag*) refer to the three annual festivals—Passover, Weeks, and Tabernacles (Exod 23:14-17; 34:18-23). These three major festivals recalled the three primary events in the salvation story of the Israelites (deliverance from Egypt, covenant at Sinai, and provision in the wilderness). These festivals perhaps had their origin in and were celebrated alongside the three primary harvest periods (barley harvest, wheat harvest, and harvest of olives and grapes).

The **New Moons** (*ḥādaš*) describes the monthly celebrations while the **Sabbath** (*šabāt*) obviously refers to the weekly celebration. Hosea states that Yahweh will cause all of these festivals to cease (*šābat*, i.e., he will bring a "sabbath" to them). The ***appointed times*** (*môʿēd*) may refer to the annual, monthly, and weekly festivals in their totality but may also indicate all other communal gatherings of the people that occur throughout the year, such as fast days, gatherings prior to war, and so forth. The prophet describes these festivals as **her** feasts. They appear to have become festivals for Israel's own self-serving purposes rather than for the worship of Yahweh.

■ **12** Not only will Yahweh bring an end to the self-serving cultic celebrations, but he will also destroy all signs of fertility—**her vines** and **her fig trees**. The unfaithful spouse has claimed her vines and her fig trees as **her pay from her lovers**. The noun **pay** (*ʾetnâ*) is most likely a reference to a prostitute's wage. Verse 12 ends with the verdict that what was at one time sumptuous and lush will become no more than forest herbage for the **animals** of the field to **devour**.

■ **13** In v 13, Yahweh announces his plan to **punish** (*pāqad* means "to visit," "to punish," etc.) his people for their allegiance to **the Baals** (in plural). The verb *pāqad* conveys the idea that Yahweh will visit his people and that visitation will set things straight; in this case, he will bring his punishment upon his unfaithful people. The plural **Baals** (see also 2:17 and 11:2) may be an indication of the numerous Baal shrines scattered throughout Canaan (Mays 1969, 43). Verse 13 indicates Israel's Baal worship included the offering of **incense** (*qāṭar*) to the Baals and the wearing of **rings and jewelry**. The unfaithful spouse adorned herself as she **went after her lovers** (see 2:2). Wolff thinks that the phrase **went after** refers to a ceremonial procession in the sanctuaries of Baals (1974, 40), though it may simply refer to Israel's pursuit of other gods. Israel's pursuit of the Baals meant that she **forgot** Yahweh. The language of forgetting recalls the Deuteronomic call not to forget Yahweh (see Deut 6:10-14 in which forgetting Yahweh is directly linked to following after other gods; see also Deut 8:11-20).

4. Alluring into the Wilderness (2:14-15)

■ **14** The final response of the betrayed spouse (vv 14-23), introduced by the third **therefore**, begins in v 14. The divine activity in these verses reflects courtship before marriage and thus something completely different from the threat announced in the two previous "therefore" passages. The husband here announces that he will **allure** [*pātâ*] **her . . . into the wilderness and speak tenderly to her**. The verb *pātâ* conveys the activity of enticing or seducing young and simpleminded individuals (see Prov 7:7 ff.). It is used in other texts to describe the seduction of a virgin (Exod 22:16 [22:15 HB]) or a husband (Judg 14:15; 16:5).

Yahweh's plan to bring his unfaithful spouse into the wilderness recalls the days subsequent to the deliverance from Egypt. The text here anticipates a new beginning in this broken relationship. The intent of the divine visitation is not to bring further punishment but to **speak tenderly** (lit. ***speak upon the heart***), to offer salvation and hope to an unfaithful people. The goal of his speech is not only to demonstrate Yahweh's tender and compassionate attitude to a people under judgment but also to alter the communal mind-set of the people. The heart (*lēb*), the seat of human emotion and will and decision making, is the recipient of Yahweh's speech. Hosea anticipates that through the catharsis of this wilderness experience, a change will occur in the heart/mind (*lēb*) of the people as Yahweh speaks to their *lēb*.

■ **15** The imagery of courtship continues in v 15. Yahweh, who allures and speaks tenderly to his unfaithful spouse, plans to lavish upon her gifts and thus to display his love for her. She will receive **her vineyards** as gifts from her suitor. The reference may be to the restoration of the vineyards that have been laid waste (v 12) or possibly to the gift of the land that points to an entirely new beginning in the Yahweh-Israel relationship. In either case, the text makes clear that the land and its productivity are gifts not from the Baals but from Yahweh. Moreover, Yahweh promises to make the **Valley of Achor** (lit. ***Valley of Trouble***) into an entryway to **hope**. The Valley of Achor is a reminder of the military defeat and trouble that Israel experienced because of the sin of Achan (Josh 7). Yahweh's promise is to erase from the collective memory of Israel its past troubles; he promises to give his people hope for their new beginning in the land of promise. The wilderness itself is a reminder of Israel's troubles in the past. However, the text here places the wilderness as the setting of the words of hope. The judgment announced in vv 6-13 is not the end of the people; it is actually the threshold to a new beginning.

Verse 15 also anticipates the response of the unfaithful wife, who hears the words of hope. **She will respond** to her husband **as in the days of her youth**. Wolff finds here an anticipation of Israel's willful following of Yahweh and her acceptance of his hand in commitment to "begin her marriage relationship anew" (1974, 43). The text as a whole (vv 14-15) suggests an entirely new beginning in the Yahweh-Israel relationship.

5. Removal of Baals (2:16-17)

■ **16-17** Verse 16 indicates that on the **day** of this new relationship (**in that day** usually denotes an eschatological day), Israel will address Yahweh as **my husband** (*ʾîš*) and not **my master** (*baʿal*). Yahweh also promises to **remove the names of the Baals** from the lips of his people (v 17). Yahweh's direct work on behalf of his people is what enables them to put an end to the worship of other gods. Verses 16-17 thus speak of the changes that will take place in Israel's worship of Yahweh. They will worship him not as a deity who can be manipulated for wages but as their intimate marriage partner with whom they enjoy a covenantal relationship. They have lacked this knowledge of Yahweh (2:8; 4:1, 6). But their way of thinking will be transformed when they enter into this new relationship with Yahweh; then they indeed will know him as their covenant partner (see 2:20).

6. The Promise of Peace and a New Marriage (2:18-20)

■ **18** In the eschatological day of Israel's restoration and renewed relationship with Yahweh (**in that day**), Yahweh will make for Israel a covenant (*bĕrît*) that will bring security and rest for the nation (e.g., see Deut 28:1-14). In the next century, the prophet Jeremiah will build upon and elaborate the language of this new covenant in which the people will truly know Yahweh (see Jer 31:31 ff.). All that which threatens the people's existence, from destructive animals to human instruments of war, will be brought to an end.

This covenant, though it is on behalf of Israel, will be with all the creatures—**the beasts of the field, the birds in the sky and the creatures that move along the ground** (v 18). The list of the creatures here reflects the list of creatures in the creation account (Gen 1). The covenant with the animal kingdom means that these animals will not destroy or do harm to Israel's population or agricultural fields and crops (Wolff 1974, 51).

Yahweh also promises to destroy the weapons of warfare and to bring an end to war itself in the land. This promise echoes the language of Isaiah and Micah (Isa 2:4; Mic 4:3; see also the language of the peaceable kingdom in Isa 11:6-9 and Ezek 34:25-31). The outcome of this covenant is peace and security to Israel. **Safety** in v 18 is derived from the verb *bāṭāḥ*, which means "to trust." The security or safety of Israel here reflects the trust or quiet confidence that the people will have in Yahweh as their deliverer and provider (see Isa 30:15).

■ **19** In v 19 Yahweh promises to enter into a marriage relationship with Israel. Israel's unfaithfulness to Yahweh has resulted in the legal abrogation of the marriage between Yahweh and Israel (the Sinai covenant) (see 1:9; 2:2). The offer here, **I will betroth you to me**, is for a completely new and legally binding act of marriage (Wolff 1974, 52). This offer is found three times in 2:19-20.

Hosea describes this new marriage as a permanent (*ʿôlām*, **forever**) relationship, unlike the old marriage that was revoked by Yahweh. In ancient Israel, betrothal is "the final step in concluding a marriage"; what remains is the actual cohabitation (Mays 1969, 50). The bridal gifts that Yahweh offers to Israel are not material goods, but his essential attitudes and actions toward his bride that guarantee a healthy and lasting relationship—**righteousness** (*ṣedeq*), **justice** (*mišpāṭ*), ***covenant loyalty*** (*ḥesed*), and **compassion** (*raḥămîm*). Each of these terms is deeply rooted in the covenant theology of ancient Israel. **Righteousness** conveys the idea of rightness or right-relatedness; **justice** involves the maintenance of the rights and claims of others in a relationship; ***covenant loyalty*** calls for faithfulness in relationship; **compassion** conveys intensified feeling and is often understood as a maternal emotion.

■ **20** Yahweh announces a fifth and final bridal gift in v 20. He will betroth his bride with the gift of **faithfulness** or ***steadfastness*** (*ʾĕmûnâ*). Yahweh promises to Israel to be a reliable and trustworthy covenant partner. Hosea anticipates that Yahweh's lavish gifts he graciously bestows upon his bride will lead her to ***know*** (*yādaʿ*) her husband (i.e., enter into an intimate and personal relationship with him). While such knowledge clearly begins with the teaching (*torah*) of the priests and the proclamation of the prophets (see 4:4-6), this knowledge appears to go further. Bernhard Anderson has rightly observed that "Hosea was talking about the knowledge of the heart—that is, the response of the *whole person* to God's love" (1986, 310).

7. The Promise of Blessings (2:21-23)

■ **21-23** The concluding statement of the passage expresses Yahweh's direct control over the fertility of the land. The announcement here is linked to the two previous **in that day** announcements (v 21; see vv 16, 18).

There is a downward movement of actions in these verses. Yahweh will **respond** to the sky; the sky will respond to the earth; **the earth will respond to the grain**, the **wine**, and the **oil**; these primary agricultural products will respond to the cry of **Jezreel**, which initiates this chain of actions. Jezreel (meaning "God sows") has come to represent both the unfaithful people and the land polluted with spilled blood (see 1:4-5). If one traces the logic, unfaithful people and the polluted land cry out to the produce of the land, which in turn cries to the land, which in turn cries to the heavens (from which rain comes), which then ultimately cries out to the source of fertility, Yahweh himself.

However, Yahweh will ultimately deal directly with **Jezreel**; he himself will ***sow*** (*zāraʿ* means "to sow," the root form of the noun **Jezreel**) Jezreel. Though in v 23 the reference to Jezreel is in the feminine (**her**, meaning "the land"), it is possible that the promise here includes not only the productivity of the land but also the growth of the population of Israel.

Yahweh's promise to sow Jezreel for himself indicates that the identity of the people and the land will be changed. Verse 23 ends with the name change of Lo-Ruhamah and Lo-Ammi, the other children of Gomer. Yahweh extends ***compassion*** (*rāḥam*) to the one from whom he withheld compassion (Lo-Ruhamah). In the same way, Yahweh says to those whom he declared as Lo-Ammi (**Not my people**) that he will call them his people (**You are my people**). Without the names of the Baals on their lips, they will then be able to respond, **You are my God**. Verse 23 anticipates the full restoration of Israel. The text also anticipates the full participation of the people in the covenant with Yahweh. The words **You are my people** by Yahweh and the people's response **You are my God** reiterates the Sinai covenant relationship expressed by the formula, "You will be my people, and I will be your God" (Jer 30:22; see Exod 19:5; Deut 26:17-18; Jer 31:1).

FROM THE TEXT

This image-filled passage reveals a number of convictions central to the book of Hosea and evokes thoughtful reflection upon various critical issues in Israel's covenant relationship with God. This text invites the reader to think about issues such as covenant fidelity, popular religion, divine punishment, and restoration.

The people's claim, "my food and my water, my wool and my linen, my olive oil and my drink" (v 5), and God's declaration, "my grain . . . my new wine . . . my wool and my linen" (v 9) powerfully illustrate a central issue of conflict in this text. The ultimate question for a people in covenant has always been, "Who owns the wine and bread?" Are these *gifts* from Yahweh to be *received* by the people of God, or are they *payments* to be *earned* by the people of God? Are they gifts of grace, or are they the results of human works—personal, even privatized, possession derived from human performance through religious, political, and/or economic systems?

The struggle of God's people over covenant fidelity and undivided allegiance is particularly clear in the confusion over the source of blessing, life, and growth (i.e., fertility). The sin of the people was not their materialism or their desire for "stuff." Rather they were guilty of their misunderstanding of who actually provided the "stuff" of their lives (i.e., the baals) (Mays 1969, 39). Mays appropriately describes this dilemma that the people of God face both *then* and *now*: "What Yahweh gave as his blessing under covenant, expecting only thanksgiving and confession in return, Israel thought it necessary to purchase through a ritual of sympathetic magic" (1969, 43).

In the name of fertility or *growth*, the people of God often prostitute themselves to other systems, believing that as homage is given to these systems, they will receive abundant blessings. Oftentimes, these systems are "sanctified" by the people of God. At times, the institutions may be specific political forms of government that promise freedom, economic structures that assure prosperity and independent wealth, or ecclesial polities and programs that ensure numerical, financial, and even spiritual growth.

The people of God must remain vigilant regarding the subtle manner in which even means of God's grace can become means of divine manipulation. When any political system, economic structure, or religious practice, regardless of how ancient and highly regarded it may be, becomes a means to manipulate and control the deity, it is no longer a means through which the deity might work but a means of manipulation. It becomes "magic" in the hands of the citizen, the investor, or the worshipper. It becomes a contemporized "baal." Birch provides important caution to the church today concerning the "lure on every side by products, programs, settings, and schemes that promise us control in achieving the good life. . . . The church, like the ancient Israelite prophets, claims that the good life comes as the gift of God to be received and not to be manipulated by our own societal rituals for our own benefit" (Birch 1997, 34). The text is also a timely warning to the church not to engage in syncretistic worship in which the "baals" of the contemporary society and popular religion are blended with Yahweh, who delivers and provides without the manipulative work of his people.

The heart of the issue for the people of God is clearly reflected in Hosea's concern that the people do not know Yahweh as the source of their lives (v 8). They live a life of forgetfulness, without any regard for the Deuteronomic challenge not to forget Yahweh their God who brought them into the land. Deuteronomy clearly cautions the people of God not to assume that they were saved by their own righteousness or prowess (see Deut 6:10-15; 7:7-11; 8:11-20).

The text also speaks clearly to the matter of divine judgment. This passage does not view the actions taken by God as a divine temper tantrum in which Yahweh seeks to "get even" with his people. Consistent with the Deuteronomic-prophetic theology, Hosea describes what comes upon the people of Yahweh as a divine *visitation*, a visitation that is ultimately portrayed as the life lived by the people coming back upon them. Hence, as they have trusted in sources outside of Yahweh for their protection and provision, so they will have only those sources to protect and provide for them. When the people are unable to make their way to these sources, the sources are revealed as powerless in their ability to make their way to the people.

In light of this understanding of the divine visitation, Jezreel plays a prominent role in the text. The land that God had sown became infertile and barren as it was polluted with covenant infidelity and spilled blood. The text challenges contemporary readers to imagine further the ways in which covenant fidelity or infidelity of God's people has a direct impact upon "the land" and its productivity, and ultimately upon all of creation. Texts such as Hos 2 reflect the divinely assigned vocation of human beings to protect and serve the ground (Gen 2:15). They further challenge the people of God to explore the relationship between faithfully discharging all covenant responsibilities and the direct effect that these responsibilities have upon creation.

As to the role and purpose of God in this divine visitation, Wolff has appropriately emphasized that this passage is underscored with one basic reality: "God suffers under Israel's deceitful love affair. He refuses to accept as final the divorce his wife both desired and initiated." He continues by noting that "Yahweh passionately strives, in various ways, to achieve *one* aim: that Israel turn to him anew" (1974, 44). The final purpose of this passage and for that matter the book of Hosea is not to frighten the original audience or a contemporary audience into divine damnation and destruction. It is to hold out hope—even to a people lost in the wilderness—that Yahweh who makes covenant with his people is a faithful and compassionate God who will transform the greatest valley of trouble into a door of hope. Subsequent generations looking back upon the text of Hos 2 would affirm that in the midst of the catharsis of exile and death, new life emerged.

There is a striking parallel between the response of the wayward spouse left alone behind the hedge as well as the readiness of the husband to woo her back, and that of the wayward son and his father in the gospel story of the faithful father (Luke 15:11 ff.). In the NT story, the wayward son squanders away what has been given to him as gift. In the midst of his emptiness and isolation, he comes to recognize that it would be better to return even as a hired hand to his father's house. In both narratives, the emphasis finally rests upon the faithfulness of Yahweh to receive back rebellious family members and restore them not simply with "enough" but with superabundance. The image of the parent-child in Hos 11 will likewise mirror this NT parable of the extravagant love and mercy of God.

D. The Hope of Reconciliation (3:1-5)

BEHIND THE TEXT

The brief narrative of ch 3 picks up where the narrative of ch 1 left off; however, the first chapter is reported in the third person while the third chapter is reported in an autobiographical first person. However, chs 1, 2, and 3 have important literary and theological connections. Chapter 1 serves as the prose introduction to the poetic oracles in 2:2-13. Chapter 3 is also linked to ch 2 in that the former emphasizes the manner in which the prophet is to take in the adulterous woman as his wife. This is parallel to Yahweh's love for his unfaithful wife and his marriage to her in 2:14-20. In its final canonical shape, ch 2 with its first part describing the marital-covenantal brokenness and its second part describing the marital-covenantal restoration is bordered by the narratives of chs 1 and 3. Noting numerous parallels between the second and third chapters, Wolff interprets ch 3 as an immediate continuation and original conclusion to 2:2-20 and thus functioning as "the prophet's personal seal upon the foregoing series of threats and promises" (1974, 59). Thematically and theologically, while ch 1 portrays the faithlessness of God's people, ch 3 in contrast portrays the faithfulness of God.

The passage is not specific as to whether the woman described in ch 3 is Gomer or another individual. This lack of clarity has raised some debate concerning her identity. The discussion centers on two critical issues: (1) ch 1 makes no reference to her leaving Hosea; (2) Yahweh's command to Hosea in ch 3 is to marry "a" woman. However, as the narrative genre reemerges in ch 3, the final canonical shape appears to present ch 3 as the narrative continuation of the story that was left suspended at the end of ch 1. The narrative of the unfaithfulness of Gomer and the birth of the three children is suspended or interrupted by the poetry of ch 2. The poetry of ch 2 provides an interlude in which the character of Yahweh is identified with Hosea, and Israel is identified with Gomer. With that identification made, in ch 3 Hosea is now instructed to imitate the nature and character of Yahweh in Hosea's relationship with his unfaithful wife.

The narrative begins with Yahweh's command to Hosea (v 1), followed by a report of the prophet's obedience (v 2). Verse 3 contains Hosea's instruction to the woman that she is not to have sexual relationship with anyone. Verse 4 relates the meaning and application of v 3 to the Israelites. The narrative ends with a statement about Israel's restoration (v 5).

IN THE TEXT

■ **1** The narrative begins with an introductory phrase, ***Yahweh said to me again***, followed by the divine command to Hosea. The particle ***again*** (*ʿôd*) indicates that this encounter between Yahweh and Hosea occurred at a time different from the one reported in 1:2. The divine speech begins with the command **go** (also in 1:2). In contrast to the command in 1:2 for Hosea to take for himself an adulterous wife (or wife of prostitution), the command in 3:1 is for the prophet to **love** a **wife** (*ʾiššâ* also means a "woman") who is **loved by** a ***friend*** (or simply another person). The wife/woman here is most likely Hosea's wife Gomer. **Love** (*ʾahab*) is a word that finds itself at home in the covenantal language of ancient Israel. While the word is completely absent in the relationship described in ch 1, it appears in 3:1 four different times. ***Friend*** or another person (*rēaʿ*) can mean a sexual companion (e.g., see Jer 3:1 and Song 5:16).

The woman whom Hosea is to love is further described as an **adulteress** (*mĕnāʾāpet*, from *nāʾap*, which means "to commit adultery," conveys the idea of unfaithfulness in a marriage relationship; see Exod 20:14). In ancient Israel, a married man was guilty of adultery only when his sexual relationship was with a married woman. However, a married woman was guilty of adultery when her sexual partner was anyone (married or unmarried) other than her husband. In both cases, the marital status of the woman determined the sin of adultery.

The command to Hosea to love a wife/woman is followed by a rationale (see also 1:2). Hosea is commanded to love just **as *Yahweh* loves the *people of Israel***. The love for the adulterous wife is to be patterned after the love (*ʾahab*) Yahweh has for Israel. Hosea elsewhere describes the divine love as it is embodied in specific actions, such as deliverance from captivity (11:1) and healing of infidelity (14:4). This love is what is at work in Yahweh's promise concerning his unfaithful wife in 2:14. Hosea's demonstration of love to his unfaithful wife should be the same.

Verse 1 also indicates that the object of the divine love is a people who have engaged in corporate infidelity by turning to **other gods**. The verb used here (*pānâ* means "to turn") conveys the sense of turning for the purpose of looking upon or toward another. In other words, Israel has turned her face toward other gods and has looked to them for protection and provisions. Moreover, though Israel is the object of Yahweh's love, her love (*ʾahab*) is directed toward **raisin cakes**. The significance of raisin cakes, made by pressing dried grapes, is not clear in this context. As an imperishable food product, it would have been used as a military provision for soldiers or as food for long-distance journey. Isaiah describes these cakes in light of the Moabites' great self-pride (16:6-7), while the prophet Jeremiah speaks of producing such cakes for "the

Queen of Heaven" as a family affair in Judah (Jer 7:18; 44:19). It appears that these cakes represent plentiful grape harvest and would likely have been linked to the fertility cult (the NIV adds **sacred** to convey its link to the fertility worship). The people's love of the raisin cakes is an indication of their devotion to the gods whom they worship with such cakes.

■ **2** In v 2, the prophet proceeds to describe the manner in which he **bought** this wife. The seldom-used verb *karâ* (meaning "to get by trade") indicates that the transaction was made through bargaining. While the text does not specify the situation from which Hosea purchases his wife, it is clear that she now finds herself in a situation in which she has become a commodity available for bargaining and purchase by others. The Hebrew text also conveys the idea of Hosea purchasing the woman for himself and thus legally making her his personal possession (*lî* means "to/for me"). The bargain includes the exchange of **fifteen shekels of silver and a about a homer and a lethek of barley** (the LXX adds, "and a jar of wine"). The shekel weighs approximately four-tenths of an ounce; thus the amount of silver exchanged would have been around six ounces. Both the homer and the lethek (half a homer) are capacity measurements for dry products. The equivalency of a homer has been estimated to be anywhere from 3.8 to 6.6 bushels; the exchange thus includes approximately six to ten bushels of barley. Some commentators estimate the value of barley to be around fifteen shekels, which would make the total price Hosea paid to be around thirty shekels (Wolff 1974, 61).

The payment Hosea made could be viewed as a prostitute's fee, perhaps a fee to purchase the prostitute permanently. The payment could also be interpreted as the price for the purchase of a slave. The Covenant Code establishes the price of thirty shekels for the purchase of a mature female slave (Exod 21:32; Lev 27:4; see also the purchase of Joseph for twenty shekels, Gen 37:28). In any case, it is possible to assume that Hosea emptied out both his monetary and material resources (thus bankrupted himself!) to purchase this adulterous woman.

The text does not make specific mention of the one with whom Hosea carries out the transaction. The woman appears to be a passive figure in the narrative, exchanged between two dealers. Hosea's payment of the price here is parallel to the bride price Yahweh promises to pay when he would take Israel to be his wife again (see 2:19-20).

■ **3** In v 3 Hosea speaks to the woman and gives her instruction that she must remain under his sole proprietorship. She must **live with** her husband alone **many days**. The phrase ***you shall live with me*** (*tešbî lî* literally means "you shall dwell to me or dwell as mine") conveys the idea of her forced confinement to Hosea's house (parallel to Yahweh hedging up Israel's path in 2:6). **Many days** indicate an extended period of time; however, in the end it is temporary and not permanent. Moreover, she must not return to her life as a **prostitute** (*zānâ*; the same verbal root is used in the description of Gomer in 1:2) or seek another man. The final part of v 3 may be literally translated as follows: "you shall not become to a man, and even I to you." Sexual relationship of the woman seems to be the issue here. It is likely that Hosea's instruction to his wife is to remain celibate and have no sexual contact with anyone; he further says to her that he will also refuse to engage in sexual relationship with her during this period. He will not seek her to satisfy his own passions or desires. The prophet (and Yahweh) seeks an authentic response of love from his partner and not a forced relationship (see 2:6-7). Mays states, "The pathos and power of God's love is embodied in . . . strange tactics . . . a love that imprisons to set free, destroys false love for the sake of true, punishes in order to redeem" (1969, 58).

■ **4** Verse 4 explains the significance of Hosea's actions to the people of Israel. They, too, will remain for **many days** under severe restrictions—**without king or prince, without sacrifice or sacred stones, without ephod or *teraphim***. Just as the situation described in 2:9-14 will not last forever but restoration will occur (2:15-23), so, too, will this time period come to an end (see "afterward" in v 5). Nevertheless, during this period (directly related to the period in the wilderness described in ch 2), the institution of the monarchy will cease to exist. The people will be without both king (*melek*) and prince (*śār*). The term *śār* likely refers to the various royal officers, including military leaders, who rule on behalf of the king. Throughout his oracles, Hosea expresses concern over the irresponsible conduct of the kings and the political leaders who governed Israel (see 5:10; 7:3, 16; 8:4; 13:10).

Yahweh also announces an end to Israel's meaningless cultic activities during this period. The list begins with sacrifices that have become meaningless rituals (see Amos 5:21-22; Isa 1:10-11). The people will also remain without the **sacred stones** or monuments (*maṣṣēbâ*), representations of the Canaanite male deity (e.g., see Exod 23:24; Deut 7:5; 12:3; 2 Kgs 3:2). The cultic objects that the people illicitly used as means of divination—**ephod** and ***teraphim***—likewise will not be available to the people. The ephod, though listed among priestly vestments (Exod 28:4), here refers to an idol (see Judg 8:22-28). ***Teraphim*** likewise refer to **household gods** (see Gen 31:19). The removal of political leaders and false worship and illicit cultic devices means that the people will exist without the sources they depended upon for their political and religious survival and all that were hindrances to their true relation to Yahweh.

■ **5** The phrase **afterward** indicates the end of Israel's "many days" of living in isolation. Yahweh promises that Israel will **return** (*šûb*) and will **seek** (*bāqaš*) Yahweh their God. The language of *šûb* ("turn," "return," or "repent") is frequently found in Hosea (see 2:7; 5:4; 6:1; 7:10; 11:5; 12:6; 14:1, 7). The verb conveys the idea of one's acknowledgment of sin and commitment to go back to faithful relationship. Mays describes the verb as a reference to the people's "going back to the original relation to Yahweh . . . to take up the religious situation of the Exodus time" (1969, 59). The verb **seek** (*bāqaš*), in the setting of worship, indicates the act of a worshipper approaching the presence of a deity. The description of Yahweh as **their God** conveys the idea of the desire of the people to restore their covenant relationship with Yahweh. The desire to seek Yahweh will be accompanied by the desire to seek **David their king**, Yahweh's Anointed One. Israel will seek that which Yahweh had removed because of Israel's failure to keep the covenant.

Verse 5 also describes the manner in which Israel would come to Yahweh. **They will come trembling** (*pāḥad*) conveys the sense of dread or awe as they respectfully submit to Yahweh as their God. As they come to seek Yahweh, they will also be in dreadful awe of his ***goodness*** (*ṭôb*, **blessings**). Yahweh's ***goodness*** here is his mercy and compassion that ultimately allows a rebellious, stubborn, and idol-worshipping people to once again experience the reality of his presence as they enter into genuine worship.

FROM THE TEXT

This brief passage represents covenant love in multiple layers: divine love for the covenant people, Hosea's love for his wife that mirrors God's love for his unfaithful people, love of covenant people for false gods, and love that always moves to reconciliation and restoration. Mays articulates this divine love paralleled by the action of Hosea as "both exclusively jealous and passionately generous" and a love that closes the door on sin and opens the door for restoration (1969, 58).

In these few verses, the unfailing love of God is contrasted in an almost embarrassing manner with the people's fickle and weak love of other gods and their worship practices. While the emphasis in ch 1 is upon the unfaithfulness of the wayward spouse, the emphasis in ch 3 is upon the unending love of the betrayed spouse. The divine love compels both the prophet and his God to love the adulterous partner.

This divine love embodied in the prophet's action toward his wife is not a cheap love. It is more than an affection or feeling. Neither does it seek a love in return that is simply an affection or feeling. It seeks authentic trust, fidelity, and covenant faithfulness. It desires the removal of all that has prevented the rebellious partner from trusting and loving fully and faithfully. It requires abiding (dwelling) in the presence of the faithful spouse. Demanding the practices of infidelity to stop, it seeks to remove the obstacles that entice the wayward partner to a lack of complete trust and love no matter how sentimental and sacred those obstacles have become.

Perhaps one of the most significant portraits of Yahweh that arises from the book of Hosea is the nature of the divine love that *precedes* the people's response to him. This divine love is demonstrated through a prevenient grace, a grace that hopes for and even anticipates a faithful loving response from the covenant partner. While this love will allure the people into the wilderness, such a divine love remains noncoercive, refusing to manipulate and overpower the other partner of the covenant. In the same manner that God will not permit his people to manipulate him, so, too, he will not coerce and manipulate the love of his people. Rather, he waits for them to love him in response to his love. Birch accurately describes the love portrayed in Hosea: "Love is not the reward for having returned to right relationship, but love makes return possible . . . Relationships are made possible by love risked even in the face of brokenness" (Birch 1997, 45).

In the end, this divine love dreams and envisions of an "afterward" (v 5). It holds out hope; it believes; it endures; and it trusts to the very end. It dares to imagine a restored relationship of fidelity, loyalty, and mutual love. It refuses to let rebellion, political alliances, or an adulterous spouse be the final word. Rather, it boldly dares to imagine that divine compassion, mercy, and goodness will once again pass by and that the people will be restored. This love works to bring healing to the heart of the rebellious people so that they indeed will be able to love Yahweh their God with all their heart, with all their soul, and with all their strength.

One cannot miss in this brief account, however, that the self-giving love of God is not an abstract idea to be pondered. In the end, it is to be fleshed out through the prophet. To know this divine love is to live this divine love. To know the God of reconciliation is to become a person and even more a community of reconciliation. This message of love speaks powerfully both to individuals who know the love of God and to the church whose very being was birthed by the love of God. To have known this love is to make this love known; to be loved in this way is to love in this same way. One cannot help but hear the admonition of John, "Dear friends, since God so loved us, we also ought to love one another" (1 John 4:11). The prophetic task of the church ultimately goes beyond speaking a message of judgment or salvation. It in the end is to participate so authentically in the life of God that the love of God is realized and embodied through the people of God.

III. ORACLES OF JUDGMENT AND RESTORATION: HOSEA 4:1—14:8

A. Messages of Judgment and Hope (4:1—11:12)

1. Yahweh's Lawsuit (4:1-19)

In this passage, Yahweh presents a lawsuit (*rîb*) against his people. The lawsuit consists of three major sections: the indictment (vv 1-3), specific charges against the priests and the people (vv 4-14), and specific charges against the worship of the people as a whole (vv 15-19).

a. Divine Indictment (4:1-3)

BEHIND THE TEXT

As in ch 2, the legal procedure provides the context for the opening verses. The prophet employs the traditional language of the covenant between Yahweh and Israel, i.e., faithfulness (*ʾemet*), covenant loyalty (*ḥesed*), and the knowledge of God (*daʿat ʾĕlōhîm*). The language Hosea uses to describe the bride price in 2:19-20 reemerges in Yahweh's charge against his people. The theme of the unproductive nature of the land, a key issue in ch 2, reemerges as well.

IN THE TEXT

■ **1** In the opening verse, the prophet summons the people to **hear the word of *Yahweh***. The call to **hear** (*šāmaʿ*) includes the call "to obey" (see Deut 6:4). The **word** (*dābār*) that the prophet calls the people to hear/obey is the word that comes from Yahweh (see Hos 1:1). ***The people of Israel*** as a community are the recipients of the prophetic word.

The second part of v 1 states the reason for the divine word; Yahweh speaks to Israel because he has a ***lawsuit*** (*rîb* also means **charge**, case, dispute, etc.) ***with the inhabitants of* the land**. The third part of v 1 states the charge itself. The charge includes a list of three negatives that indicate what is totally lacking in the land (v 1*c*): ***trustworthiness*** (*ʾemet*), ***covenant faithfulness*** (*ḥesed*), and ***the knowledge of* God** (*daʿat ʾĕlōhîm*). ***Trustworthiness*** (*ʾemet*) is one's reliability and dependability in a relationship. ***Covenant faithfulness*** (*ḥesed*) is one's firm commitment to the covenant relation with another person, expressed through love, devotion, kindness, mercy, and other actions required by the covenant. In the context of Israel's covenant with Yahweh, the ***knowledge of God*** includes the cognitive understanding or remembrance of what Yahweh has done as well as the people's recognition of Yahweh as their *only* God (see 13:4). These qualities function as the standard by which the prophet measures covenant fidelity throughout the remainder of the book.

4:1-3 ■ **2** Verse 2 lists what Yahweh finds in the land: ***swearing***, **lying**, **murder**, **stealing**, **adultery**, and violent **bloodshed**. Swearing or using the divine name for unworthy purposes is a violation of the third commandment, which upholds the sanctity and the power of God's name. Lying is a violation of the ninth commandment, which affirms the integrity of the legal system. The last three activities relate directly to the sixth, seventh, and eighth commandments (murder, adultery, and stealing). The prophet vividly depicts the manner in which Israel breaks the commandments, the stipulations of the Sinai covenant; they **break all bounds** (***burst forth***) in much the same way that water breaches through a dam. Social chaos has ruptured the fabric of the community. The prophet's list of broken relationships in v 2 reaches its climax with the phrase ***spilled blood touches spilled blood.*** Violent bloodshed permeates the land; shed blood is everywhere.

■ **3** Verse 3 describes the tragic effect of the disintegration of communal relations on the land. The land, polluted by shed blood, is personified in v 3; it ***mourns*** (*ʾābal*) because it is deeply affected by the violent bloodshed (see Gen 4:10). The land is lamenting because the violence of its inhabitants has resulted in its loss of fertility (see Gen 4:12).

The land's loss of fertility has caused the languishing (*ʾāmal*) of **all who live in it**, both animal and plant life (Hos 4:3). Verse 3 indicates that Israel's sins have caused the withering of plant life and the barrenness of humans and animals. Even **the beasts of the field, the birds in the sky and the fish in the sea** have not escaped the destructive effects of human sin. Barrenness and deathliness permeate every corner of creation.

FROM THE TEXT

The text invites the reader to explore the hallmarks of the covenant relationship between Yahweh and his people: fidelity, trustworthiness, and the knowledge of God. How do the people of God express these characteristics of the covenant community in the contemporary setting? In what specific ways do the people of God fall short?

Hosea's central concern of "knowing" God also challenges the reader to discover the relational intimacy between God and his people within the context of the covenant. Throughout the OT, the term *to know* even expresses the sexual intimacy between a husband and wife (e.g., see Gen 4:1; 24:16; 1 Sam 1:19; 1 Kgs 1:4). The verb conveys the sense of oneness shared between two members of a relationship. In his expressed concern for the people to "know" Yahweh, Hosea suggests that the core identity of the people lies in something other than the rituals of worship, the structures of politics, and the practices of economics. The identity of Israel rests in a corporately-shared trust in their God.

For Hosea, the people do not embody this intimacy/trust in God through emotional feelings or intellectual impressions. Rather, they embody it through the same undivided loyalty and wholehearted commitment that necessarily characterizes the intimate relationship between a husband and wife within the covenant of marriage. All other trappings of marriage, from family rituals to family structures and responsibilities, are meaningless apart from the intimacy of authentic participation in the marriage relationship.

Certainly the Christian reader hears a very similar echo in Paul's description of the emptiness of rituals, structures, and responsibilities apart from this authentic participation in the life, death, and resurrection of Christ. He states:

> I consider everything a loss because of the surpassing worth of *knowing* Christ Jesus my Lord, for whose sake I have lost all things. I consider them garbage, that I may gain Christ and be found in him, not having a righteousness of my own that comes from the law, but that which is through faith in Christ. (Phil 3:8-9, emphasis added)

While the prophet Hosea calls the hearers of the text to the knowledge of God, he demonstrates no understanding whatsoever of a privatized, individualized covenant separated from its social realities. For Israel, a covenant with Yahweh is one and the same as a covenant within and between members of the covenant community. Both the Decalogue (Exod 20:1-17) and the Covenant Code (Exod 21:1—23:19), found within the literary-theological context of the covenant ceremony of Exod 19 and 23, make clear the intricate relationship of Israel's covenant with God and relationship with neighbor. As the deliverance from Egypt demonstrated to Israel the character of their covenant God, the people cannot escape the social implications that such a character would have upon subsequent communal relationships. True to this understanding, this text shapes for the reading community a clear worldview that appreciates the intricate relationship between the lack of the knowledge of God and acts of human violence. For Hosea, as for Jesus, there is no separation of loyalty to and love for God from loyalty to and love for one's neighbor (see Mark 12:28-34; Matt 22:34-40; see also 1 John 4:20-21). One does not exist without the other.

This text also makes quite obvious that the implications of covenant infidelity are not limited to brokenness with God and with one's neighbor and/or to the personal and social arenas. Perhaps the area in which the text challenges contemporary readers as much as any is the relationship between covenant infidelity and ecological devastation. Limburg has insightfully observed that the roots of "ecological crisis are to be found in the same attitudes of arrogance, irreverence, selfishness, and greed which expressed themselves in the failure to acknowledge God or to care for the neighbor" (Limburg 1988, 18). The prophet poignantly describes the broader effect of the people's unfaithfulness upon all of creation. The text challenges the reader to recognize that there is no bifurcation between personal or communal sin and the rest of creation. When humanity breaks its covenant with God, all of creation suffers.

b. Charges against Priestly Leaders (4:4-14)

BEHIND THE TEXT

Hosea deals with two critical issues in this passage. In vv 4-10, the prophet condemns the priests as mindless, self-serving worship leaders who have led the people astray, thereby making them mindless as well. The prophet expands his indictment in vv 11-14 to include the people who have incorporated elements of the Baal cult into their worship. Together the priests and the people participate in practices of worship that are antithetical to their identity as people in covenant with Yahweh. The passage as a whole has continuity with vv 1-3. The primary charge here, as in vv 1-3, is the people's lack of knowledge of God. In vv 1-3, the case (*rîb*) is against the inhabitants of the land; here the case is specifically against the priests (v 4).

The charge against the priests assumes the prominent role of the priests in providing instruction (*torah*) and the consequence of their failure to carry out their responsibility in ancient Israel. When the priests failed to carry out this task, the outcome was the people's lack of the knowledge of God and his instructions concerning the way they were to live their lives as the people of God (vv 4-6).

This passage also includes several direct references to Israel's involvement with the common practices of the Canaanite fertility cult. The practice of divination to receive communication from the deity involved the use of a piece of wood and a stick or a staff (v 12). The Canaanite rituals of worship regularly occurred at the highest place ("mountaintops" or high places; v 13) in a village. The Canaanites also conducted their worship under large green and luscious trees, which represented the capacity of the deity to provide fertility to the land (see v 13). Most often the worship site included a pile of stones (*maṣṣēbāh*) and a sacred pole (*asherah*), symbols of the male and female deities. The worship sites or the so-called temples were places where worshippers engaged in sexual relationship with "prostitutes" employed by the temple (v 14). This text thus addresses both the sins of the priests and the people and the breakdown of Israel's covenant relationship with Yahweh.

IN THE TEXT

■ **4** The prophet's indictment begins with the use of a unique particle (*ʾak*) that can function as a restrictive particle, such as **but** or "yet" (NRSV), or as a particle of emphasis ("Surely" or "No doubt"), which is most likely its usage here. Hosea declares that ***surely*** no one could now bring a ***lawsuit*** (*yārēb* from *rîb*, **charge**) or could make a legitimate ***argument*** (*yôkaḥ* from *yākaḥ*, **accuse**) against Yahweh's indictment in vv 1-3. Whether or not a priest made an actual attempt to argue against Hosea, the prophet declares that all counterarguments must cease.

The closing line of v 4 is difficult to translate. The NIV attempts to provide a possible rendering of the Hebrew text: **Your people are like those who bring charges against a priest**. However, Yahweh's accusation against the priest(s) in the following verses has prompted commentators to see here Yahweh directing his lawsuit against the priest(s). The alternative reading, ***My lawsuit*** ["contention" (NRSV)] ***is with you, O Priest***, requires only minor textual emendation. This alternative reading conveys the most likely intent of the text here. The text refers to the **priest** in the singular. Perhaps the prophet is speaking to a representative priest who has stepped forward to rebuke the prophet, or perhaps he is addressing the priesthood as a whole. However, in v 7 Hosea's address makes an obvious shift from the singular to the plural; there he addresses the various individuals within the totality of Israel's cultic leadership. The divine charge is directed toward the priests and the priests alone (see Wolff 1974, 77; Yee 1996, 237).

■ **5** In v 5, Hosea proceeds to portray the priestly leaders as tottering or stumbling like drunkards. He also includes the prophets in his accusation in this verse. Except for this verse, Hosea's denunciations in the book are directed primarily toward the priestly and political leadership. Here the prophet portrays the totality of the religious leadership as having no sense of direction. Verse 5 ends with a word of judgment; Yahweh will cut off, or more literally "cause to cease" (*dāmâ*), the priest's mother. The judgment word gives no hope for the survival of the priestly family. The death of mothers indicates the end of the line of priestly descendants.

■ **6** Verse 6 begins with the consequence of the dereliction of duty by the priests. The people are those who pay the price. Because the priests have been unfaithful in providing the *torah*, the very essence of life and welfare to the people (see Deut 30:11-20; 32:46-47), the people are being cut off or **destroyed** (*dāmâ*). The prophet uses the same verb to describe the fate of the mother of the priests and that of the people. Hosea sees no future for the people. The reference to the people as **my people** indicates Yahweh's intimate covenant relationship with them. Their **lack of knowledge** is the cause of their destruction. In 4:1, this same lack of knowledge in the land serves as the basis of the divine indictment.

The people are destroyed for lack of knowledge because the priests have ***refused*** [*māʾas*, **rejected**] **knowledge**. This indicates not only the priests' dereliction of duty to provide instruction to the people but also their refusal to live in a covenant relationship with God. As a direct consequence of their disobedient action, the priests who have refused knowledge hear the word of Yahweh's rejection (*māʾas*) of them from being his priests (v 6). Similarly, in direct relation to the priests' forgetting (*šākaḥ*) the *torah* of God, Yahweh announces that he will ***forget*** (*šākaḥ*) the descendants of the priestly leaders. The emphatic use of the first-person pronoun (***I, I myself, will forget your children***) indicates Yahweh's direct involvement and determination to carry out his judgment on the priests.

■ **7** In vv 7-8, the prophet depicts the manner in which the priests used their office for self-serving purposes. As the priesthood ***increased*** and multiplied in number, so did its rebellion. Yahweh's charge that **they sinned** [*ḥāṭāʾ*] **against me** probably refers to their role in promoting the setting of worship as a place for sinful conduct of the people rather than a context for remedying the effects of sin. It is also possible that the reference may be to their violent and greedy behavior (see 1 Sam 2:12-17, 22-23, 29). Hosea 4:7 implies that the priests used the authority of their religious office to exploit and manipulate the people, who already had no knowledge of God, to their own advantage and for their own profit. This verse echoes Amos' charge against the priests at Bethel and Gilgal that they have made these places of worship as places for the people to multiply their sins (Amos 4:4). Both prophets understood the illegitimate places of worship in northern Israel as places of rebellion against Yahweh.

Verse 7 ends with Yahweh's announcement that he will exchange the honor accorded to the priests with humiliating shame. Based on some ancient versions, the NIV translates this line as follows: **they exchanged their glorious God for something disgraceful**. The MT reads: ***I will exchange their glory into shame***. Thus, the subject of this exchange of honor in the MT is Yahweh and not the priests. Though ***their glory*** could legitimately refer to the glory of Yahweh (*kābôd*), in this context the phrase indicates the highest honor and esteem that Yahweh bestowed upon the priesthood. Based on v 6 where Yahweh is the one who refuses and forgets the priests, it is possible to conclude that he is also one who brings ***shame*** (*qālôn*) to the priests in v 7.

■ **8** Verse 8 indicates that the priests exploited the sacrificial system to satisfy their own appetites. Hosea describes the priests as eating the ***sin*** (*ḥaṭṭa't*) of the people or making a living off the sins committed by the people. The next line literally reads as follows: "to their iniquity they lift up their soul." The Hebrew phrase conveys the idea of greed or yearning; the priests have a gluttonous appetite or a deep yearning (they **relish**) for the ***iniquity*** (*'āwōn*) of the people. The priests who have been set apart to give life and to teach the ways of Yahweh actually find their own strength in the people's sin. They have made the sacrificial system, God's provision for the atonement of sins, a substitute for the true knowledge of God and a means to become prosperous and satisfied.

■ **9** The meaning of the opening phrase (***and it shall be like people like priest***) is not clear. Hosea may be saying here that the fate of the priests will be the same as that of the people (see the judgment word against the people in ch 2). Alternatively, it is possible to see here the announcement of the same fate for both the people and the priests. Yahweh announces that he will ***visit*** the ways of the priests and the people upon them and will ***return*** (**repay**) their deeds to them. It is clear in this context that Yahweh's visitation is for the purpose of punishing a rebellious and sinful people. Yahweh is not so much "paying back" the people as he is returning what they have done upon them. In other words, what they sow is what they will reap.

■ **10** Verse 10 describes how the deeds of the priests and the people will come back to them. Although they **eat**, they will never be satisfied. Although **they . . . engage in prostitution**, both literally and metaphorically, they will not multiply. In other words, their search for provision (eating) and fertility (prostitution) will be futile.

The prophet concludes v 10 by giving an explanation for barrenness and hunger. Both the priests and the people have forsaken Yahweh, their sole source of nourishment and life (13:4). Their abandonment of Yahweh means that they do not trust him as their provider and protector. The Hebrew text of v 10 simply ends with the infinitive "to guard" or "to keep" (*šāmar*) without a direct object.

The reader likely infers from the context that they abandon Yahweh in order to keep their involvement in the fertility rituals of the Canaanite religion.

■ **11** Because of the lack of a direct object at the end of v 10, many translations, including the Greek Septuagint, regard the opening word **prostitution** (v 11) as the object of the verb "to keep or guard" (v 10). These versions thus consider **wine and new wine** as the subject of v 11 (NRSV). The NIV links prostitution, wine, and new wine as part of the object of the verb in v 10. In the Hebrew text, prostitution is one of three subjects in v 11; thus prostitution along with wine and new wine takes away the minds of the people. It is certainly possible that the word for prostitution originally occurred twice, once at the end of v 10 and once at the beginning of v 11. In the transmission of the text, the second appearance might have eventually dropped out (see Mays 1969, 72). **Wine and new wine** depict symbols of fertility and abundance.

Regardless of where one places the word **prostitution**, Hosea's concern is clear. The prophet declares that the practices of the fertility cult have taken away the ***heart*** (*lēb*) of the people (see "my people" at the beginning of v 12). The word *lēb*, often translated as ***heart***, refers to the human will and thought processes. The popular worship practices of the day have not simply impaired but have removed the ability of the people of God to discern and think clearly. Mays suggests that a proverb expressing the notion that "harlots and wine take away a man's mind" could certainly have existed in ancient Israel (1969, 73). It is possible that in v 11 the prophet applies this wisdom observation to the fertility rites associated with both cultic prostitution and the extravagant consumption of wine.

■ **12** In vv 12-13 the prophet portrays a corporate insanity that has swept over the community. Verse 12 begins with a description of a method of divination in which the people asked questions of a piece of wood, and a staff or wand gave oracles. This reference may be to the Asherah pole common at Canaanite worship sites. He describes an almost mindless state of being, in which a mind-set of adultery (*rûaḥ zĕnûnîm*, **spirit of prostitution**) actively moves the people to wander about aimlessly. Hosea concludes v 12 with the observation that the people ***played the harlot*** instead of following God in faithful covenant relationship (v 12). The spirit of prostitution has completely taken over the community.

■ **13** The prophet vividly portrays the hyperactivity of the people's worship in v 13. The people of God sacrificed on **mountaintops** and high **hills**. In the ancient times people saw these places in proximity to the heavens where gods lived. The sacrificial worship incorporated various symbols of fertility, including **oak**, **poplar**, and **terebinth** trees that provide shade. Hosea specifically names the trees here, but other biblical texts simply refer to "every spreading tree" (see Deut 12:2; 1 Kgs 14:23; Jer 2:20).

Hosea 4:13 ends with a statement of the outcome (**therefore**) of Israel's involvement with the fertility cult of the Canaanites. What the people practice on the mountaintops and high hills has become a way of life for the **daughters** and **daughters-in-law**. They practice prostitution and adultery; the reference may be to these women's involvement in sacred prostitution at the local shrines. More likely, the text refers to the breakdown of morality in the towns in which the people lived. The text perhaps links the spread of immorality and sexual disorder in the society to "the disease of harlotry contracted at worship" (Mays 1969, 74).

■ **14** Although everyone in the community is culpable for the sin of prostitution and adultery, Yahweh exempts the **daughters** and **daughters-in-law** from punishment (v 14). He places the guilt squarely upon the men who participate in the worship orgies. The men are guilty because they **consort with harlots** and they **sacrifice with *the temple* prostitutes** (*haqqĕdēšôt* in fem. pl. from *qādēš*, meaning "the holy women"). They are the ones who spread the sin of harlotry through their full participation in the worship rituals of the fertility cult. Verse 14 ends with the description of the community as a mindless and senseless people without discernment. These people who are without understanding will be ***thrust out*** (*lābaṭ*). The Hebrew verb conveys the idea of utter and devastating ruin.

FROM THE TEXT

The text addresses the issue of faithful religious leadership and the accountability and responsibility of religious leaders. Limburg rightly observes in this text "a call to theologians, to all who speak about God, to carry out their task with faithfulness and effectiveness" (1988, 21).

Faithful leadership means faithful teaching of the ways of God and the promotion of the knowledge of God even in an environment where popular religious ideas and practices dominate the society. The rejection of this responsibility on the part of religious leaders is a clear sign of their rejection of the knowledge of God, which is vital to the survival and spiritual growth of the community. When there is lack of knowledge of God, the people of God will engage in senseless behavior that will ultimately lead them on the path of their destruction. The future of the people of God depends on the commitment of religious leaders to faithfully preach, teach, and lead the people in the ways of God. Paul echoes the concern of Hosea when he states: "How can they believe in the one of whom they have not heard? And how can they hear without someone preaching to them?" (Rom 10:14).

The text suggests two ways in which contemporary church leaders may be tempted to carry out their task for self-serving purposes: by feeding upon the sins of the people and by engaging in modern forms of baalism. The first is to appeal to the fears, the frustrations, the failures, and even the sins of a community and manufacture ways for people to overcome their brokenness. The second is to view the fellow believers as consumers who have an insatiable appetite for creatively packaged religious commodities. This text challenges religious leadership and the people of God as a whole to a renewed commitment to the knowledge of God through forms of proclamation and teaching that refuse to serve selfish ends for both the individual and the institution. Birch observes that

> many clergy of ordinary congregations find themselves lured by the rewards of a professionalism purchased at the expense of people's genuine needs. They find themselves locked into institutional systems that reward institutional needs over attention to instruction in the knowledge of God. Time spent in membership expansion brings salary and prestige, but hours of teaching and instruction rarely do so. (Birch 1997, 53)

This text also challenges the community as a whole to see and confess its fascination with popular religious forms that attempt to manipulate and control divine power. Popular religions of our modern world have their own forms of the fertility rites of baalism. They simply carry new names and offer quick fixes, rapid remedies, and do-it-yourself self-help modes of salvation. The text reminds us that these systems, though they guarantee successful outcome, cannot deliver or provide for God's people. Most importantly, the text warns us that contemporary forms of baalism can accomplish only one thing: lead the people of God to trust in their own power to produce.

The "spirit of prostitution" is a real danger that the people of God face today. It is a way of life or a mind-set that controls one's life. The central issue here is one's refusal to trust God with an undivided heart—to love him with one's whole heart, soul, and strength. This spirit cannot be overcome with one's own effort. Only through the work of God's grace can one overcome this mind-set and be transformed to love God with an undivided heart and be completely loyal to him (see Deut 30:6; Jer 31:33-34; Ezek 36:23-28). Paul expresses the futility of self-effort to liberate oneself from this mind-set that dominates the sinful life when he says: "What a wretched man I am! Who will rescue me from this body of death?" But he also answers with hope: "Thanks be to God, who delivers me through Jesus Christ our Lord!" (Rom 7:24-25).

c. Charges against Worship (4:15-19)

BEHIND THE TEXT

This passage continues the prophetic indictment begun with the charges brought against the priests in 4:4-14. Here, the prophet broadens those charges by pointing to the worship of the people as a whole. Specific names and places held in high esteem by the northern kingdom appear in this passage.

The people of the northern kingdom regarded both Gilgal (see its significance in Josh 4:19—5:12; 1 Sam 11:14-15) and Bethel (see Gen 28) as significant sacred sites. In 922 B.C., Jeroboam I, the first king of the north, established Bethel and Dan as the two primary worship sites for northern Israel. He set up at these places the bull as representation of Yahweh the God of Israel, and thus introduced idolatry in the northern kingdom. By the eighth century B.C., Bethel had become the more prominent of the two worship sites.

Over thirty times in the book, Hosea refers to Israel as Ephraim, the most significant tribe in northern Israel, as a substitute name for the whole nation (4:17). It is possible that Hosea's affinity with the northern kingdom might have led him to use nomenclature that was common in the north. However, it is more likely that the prophet employs this term for literary-theological reasons, to convey his concern over Israel's involvement with the fertility cult. The ancient tradition associated the name Ephraim to fruitfulness (Gen 41:52). A common motif throughout Hosea is the fruitfulness of the land. Hosea's preference for this name seems to convey his criticism that the people whose very name is "fruitfulness" seek their "fruitfulness" outside of Yahweh, thereby failing to live up to their namesake.

IN THE TEXT

■ 15 The passage begins with Hosea's plea to northern Israel not to contaminate the people of Judah. Hosea attempts to save Judah from any association with Israel and her guilt. Some commentators see here the reflection of a later southern editor who seeks to use the devastation of Israel as a warning to Judah that survived the ordeal of the Assyrian onslaught in 722 B.C.

Verse 15 does not make clear if the imperatives, **Do not go to Gilgal; do not go up to Beth Aven** (in plural), are addressed to both Israel and Judah or only to one of these two kingdoms. It is possible that the directive here is a warning to Judah to disassociate with the cultic sites of northern Israel. Bethel ("the house of God") has become **Beth Aven** ("the house of wickedness"). What takes place in the name of worship at these places is nothing more than sinful acts (see Amos' indictment of Bethel and Gilgal in Amos 4:4; 5:4-5).

A third imperative in Hos 4:15 forbids the people from using the traditional oath formula, **As surely as *Yahweh* lives**. In its proper use, this statement recognizes God as the witness of the solemn oath taken by an individual (Deut 6:13). The prohibition here is against such oath taking by a people who worship Baal as the fertility deity while claiming to be the people of Yahweh (see Exod 20:7).

■ 16 In v 16, Hosea compares the hard-hearted nature of the people of Israel to the stubbornness of a **heifer**. The people are set in their ways and refuse to allow Yahweh to provide nourishment. Therefore, the situation is hopeless. The NIV and the NRSV have the second part in the form of a question. These translations seem to say that though Yahweh wishes to lead Israel like a shepherd would lead his lamb in a meadow, the stubbornness of the people makes it impossible for him to lead and guide them. However, the interrogative particle is lacking in v 16, and therefore, the second part of v 16 is not necessarily a question. The text literally reads as follows: "now, Yahweh will graze them like lamb in an open place." The Hebrew text thus indicates that even though the people of Israel are like a stubborn heifer, Yahweh will bring them in submission to his authority as their shepherd and they will continue to be fed by him (see NJPS translation; also Yee 1996, 242).

■ **17** Verses 17-19 depict the people of God as hopelessly committed to the fertility cult. Ephraim is in league with **idols**; their relationship is like a knot that cannot be loosened. The Hebrew text also conveys the idea that Ephraim is under the spell of idols. The last line of v 17 (**leave him alone**) employs a verb in the causative stem (*hannaḥ* from *nûaḥ*, meaning "to give rest"); it conveys the idea of giving rest or causing one to be quiet. The NIV and the NRSV convey this simply as an exclamation of divine exasperation and hopelessness. Yee, however, observes here Yahweh's commitment to provide rest to his people like a shepherd provides rest to a flock (1996, 242; see Yee's interpretation of v 16*b* cited above).

■ **18** In v 18, the prophet portrays the interconnectedness of wine drinking and prostitution within the fertility cult. The people of Israel turn to prostitution when their wine is gone. Israel's drunkenness and involvement with prostitutes show how deeply the nation was immersed in the fertility cult. Mays exclaims: "Wine and women in the holy place! Worship has become an orgy!" (1969, 78). The meaning of v 18*b* is not clear. The following is a possible reading of the Hebrew text: "her shields truly love shame." Shields may be veiled reference to the rulers. The Hebrew word for ***shame*** (*qālôn*) also appears in v 7. There the prophet speaks of Yahweh's changing the honor of the priests into shame or disgrace. Israel's leaders not only participate in the fertility cultic rituals but also dearly love them.

■ **19** In v 19, the prophet reemphasizes the hopeless nature of the people's situation. This verse literally depicts a *rûaḥ* ("spirit" or "wind") that has restrictively bound (*ṣārar*, meaning "bind") the people in its wings. This spirit or wind both captures the people in such a way that they cannot return to Yahweh and carries them away from Yahweh (see the "spirit of prostitution" in 4:12; 5:4). The closing line of 4:19 indicates that the **sacrifices** of the people will only bring shameful humiliation. The cultic rituals have no power to protect or provide for the people.

FROM THE TEXT

The text constructs a vivid portrait of Israel's worship practices that have become self-serving and addictive. The people can find no way out. They are like a stubborn heifer set in its ways, and they only move from bad to worse.

The most holy sites of Israel's sacred history have become places of idolatry rather than places that reminded them of God's saving actions. The people frequented these places to engage in the endless rituals of the fertility cult. They have become one with the very idols they worshipped. A mind-set has trapped them, and it took them in the path of humiliating shame.

The prophet's depiction of this addicted religious community functions as a mirror for contemporary readers of Hosea. The text challenges the people of God to examine their own religious practices that might also have emerged from the popular culture of the day. It invites them to recognize that sacred traditions are not immune to the influences of religious perversion. Bethel, the house of God, can become Beth Aven, the house of wickedness.

The text further challenges God's people to come face-to-face with the reality of religious addiction and to explore ways in which certain styles of worship, preaching, or programs of evangelism and church growth can become addictions of the worshipping community. For example, religious addiction occurs when the people of God flock to one particular style of worship and come to think of it as the only true form of worship, and consider all other styles of worship as less spiritual or less desirable for one's spiritual growth. The text reminds us that the people of Israel were stubborn and set in their particular way of worship, which was attractive and alluring even though this form of worship was self-serving and idolatrous. Worship, when it becomes a means to fulfilling one's personal agenda and needs, loses its holy character and purpose. The text reminds us that key to true worship is not one's obsession with the style or format of worship but earnest desire to encounter the holy God, the object of our praise and worship.

2. Yahweh's Judgment (5:1—6:6)

a. Indictment against Leaders and the People (5:1-7)

BEHIND THE TEXT

The indictments against the Israelite priesthood and the people in ch 4 continue in ch 5. In this oracle (5:1-7), however, the indictment expands to include the royal house.

Thus it is a judgment oracle against the whole nation. Two geographical locations play a significant role in this passage. These place names also emerge from Israel's shared traditions, as in the case of Bethel and Gilgal in 4:15. Hosea mentions these places to remind his audience their long history of turning away from God.

Samuel chose Saul, a member of the Benjamite tribe, as king through the casting of lots at Mizpah, located in the Benjamite territory (1 Sam 10:17-27). Commentators think that Tabor was one of the sites of Baal worship in ancient Israel. Mount Tabor, at the southern edge of the Jezreel valley, was also the place where some of the Israelite tribes gathered under the leadership of Deborah and Barak for battle against Sisera, the general of Hazor (Judg 4).

IN THE TEXT

■ **1** In v 1, the prophet makes use of three imperatives: **hear**, **pay attention**, and **listen**. Taken together, these imperatives demand the audience to listen intently to the prophetic message. The prophet also specifically identifies the targeted audience. **Priests** are the first among the addressees, though they were already addressed in ch 4. The ***house of Israel*** is mentioned next. This phrase often refers to the whole nation. Mays thinks that the phrase here in the context of v 1 refers to the representatives of the people or elders of the clans, or those who are in positions of authority in the land (see Mays 1969, 80; Yee interprets it as a reference to the nation itself [1996, 244]). The third group in the list of addressees is ***the house of the king***. This group would include the king and all those who rule along with the king in the palace. Taken together, the three addressees represent all-inclusively the power base of the Israelite political, economic, and religious system.

Yahweh's judgment against the power structure of Israel contains language familiar to the judicial setting at the city gate (v 1). The text literally means, "For the judgment concerns you." The word translated as **judgment** (*mišpāṭ*) frequently appears in translations as "justice." However, the term refers to a decision rendered in a case. Yahweh has already presented his case (ch 4); now he is about to render a verdict along with its penalty.

The divine verdict in v 1 utilizes two metaphors taken from the hunting scene. At Mizpah, Israel's leaders became like a trap of two spring nets that come together to catch birds (**snare**). At Tabor, they spread out a **net** used to entangle its prey. Both metaphors portray the leaders as vicious hunters and the people as their unsuspecting prey.

■ **2** The first part of v 2 literally reads as follows: "Rebels make deep slaughter." The meaning of this phrase is unclear. Mays and others emend the Hebrew words *wĕšaḥăṭâ śēṭîm heʿĕmîqû* ("rebels made deep slaughter") to *wĕšaḥăt hašiṭṭîm heʿĕmîqû* ("they made deep the pit in Shittim"). This emendation makes this line parallel to v 1*b* where we find reference to two place names and the metaphors of snare and net (Mays 1969, 79; Wolff 1974, 94). The hunting metaphor thus most likely continues in v 2 with the image of a deeply carved-out pit that catches unsuspecting victims. The charge here is that both religious and political leaders used their offices to ensnare the people and brought destruction upon them.

Verse 2 ends with Yahweh's announcement that he will **discipline** (*mûsār,* from *yāsar,* "to discipline," "chasten," "instruct") the religious and political leadership of Israel. In Proverbs the dominant idea is instruction and correction (see Prov 1:8; 4:1; 13:1). One may assume that the goal of Yahweh's disciplinary action is the rectification of wrong deeds committed by the leaders and the establishment of proper leadership and appropriate exercise of power in the land.

■ **3** With the emphatic use of the first-person pronoun, Yahweh declares that he knows **Ephraim** (thus, the NIV adds **all about**). This divine knowledge (*yāda'*) of Israel has its basis in Yahweh's covenant with his people. Though Israel lacks the knowledge of God (2:8; 4:1, 6), Yahweh knows the ways of his people, and they are not **hidden** from him. The passive form of the verb *kāhar* ("conceal," "cut off") likely portrays Israel as hiding itself. Yahweh knows them and their ways, and Yahweh will indeed find them.

The second part of v 3 describes Israel as a people who have become **corrupt** (passive of *ṭāmē'*, meaning "become unclean") by turning into **prostitution** or idolatrous religious practices. Ezekiel, a prophet with a priestly background, also links the practice of idolatry with the uncleanness of the people (see Ezek 36:17-18, 25). As a result of their ritual uncleanness, the nation as a whole is removed from the presence of Yahweh.

■ **4** In v 4, Hosea announces that the adulterous deeds of the people prohibit them from returning (*šûb*; see 2:7; 6:1; 14:1, 4) to **their God**. The people are so accustomed to their adulterous practices that they remain in a paralyzed state from which they are unable to return to Yahweh on their own initiative. In the second part of v 4, Hosea returns to the theme of a **spirit of prostitution** (see 4:12); this time he relates this as a spirit that is ***in their midst*** or a spirit that dwells within the community. This spirit is "at home" with them, and they are "at home" with it. The tragic outcome of this communal spirit is that the people do not ***know Yahweh***. The community has lost its identity as a people who know God; they are instead known as a people led by a spirit of prostitution.

■ **5** Yahweh does not need any verbal response to his charges from Israel. Israel's self-exaltation provides all the testimony needed (v 5). The text literally read that "the pride of Israel answers in his mouth." The ***pride of Israel*** is Israel's self-proclaimed majesty and claim of splendor. This perhaps includes their claim of wealth, power, buildings, and the fertile land.

The second part of v 5 announces that Israel as a whole and the dominant tribe of ***Ephraim shall stumble in their iniquity***. The reference here is most likely to the calamity that is coming upon the nation because of its sinful way of life. The imagery here is that of a drunken person unable to stand up because of the influence of alcohol. Verse 5 ends with the note that the people of Judah also will stumble with Israel. In 4:5, Hosea attempts to save Judah from any guilty association with Ephraim. The text here indicates Judah's involvement in idolatry and its drunkenness with the spirit of prostitution. Commentators think that reference to Judah may be the work of a later editor.

■ **6** Verse 6 gives evidence to the syncretistic nature of Israel's worship. The people of Israel, though they follow other gods, continue to offer sacrifices to Yahweh and seek him in worship. **Flocks and herds** imply superabundance of offerings and lavish worship. They lack covenant faithfulness but are loyal to the established religious practices. Hosea warns that worship of Yahweh by his unfaithful people, who have not given up their loyalty to other gods, will not produce its intended result. Yahweh has **withdrawn himself** (or removed himself) from his people (see also 5:15); therefore, **they will not find him** when they seek him. The covenant people may not be able to hide from Yahweh (v 3), but Yahweh is able to hide himself from them.

■ **7** The focus of v 7 is on Israel's betrayal of God. Hosea states that the people have ***acted treacherously*** (**are unfaithful**) against Yahweh. The people have been disloyal to Yahweh, and they related to him in devious and fraudulent ways. Such disloyalty resulted in the birth of generations of children whom Hosea describes as ***strange children***. Even their children are strangers to Yahweh and his covenant with them.

Verse 7 ends with the pronouncement of judgment. The judgment will come in the most unexpected way. The people who **are unfaithful** to Yahweh participate in religious activities such as the **New Moon feasts**, thinking that these cultic rituals would bring them blessing from Yahweh. Hosea announces that instead of blessings, these festivals would ***swallow up*** both the people and **their fields**. The people who seek protection, prosperity, and enjoyment of life will find instead death and destruction. Their frantic search to save their lives has ironically become for them the sentence of their death.

FROM THE TEXT

The struggle with the communal mind-set or "spirit" of prostitution described in this text continues to be a part of the story of God's people even to the present day. Christians who live within certain cultural, social, and historical contexts may find the narratives, values, and ethics of the dominant culture attractive, and they may be tempted to adapt them to their faith and living. The outcome is that such ways of thinking or "spirits" may become entrenched and even reified in the minds of the community. The dominant cultural, sociopolitical, and economic narrative would begin to define and give shape to both the identity and the practices of God's people. Eventually the community would become blind and deaf to alternative realities, and it would find it practically impossible to turn back to the God who has defined for them their existence.

This text calls the covenant people in any given generation to honestly reflect on the dominant narrative that defines them. While no community stands aloof and separate from the dominant cultural narrative in which the people of God live, this text challenges the faithful community to rediscover its core identity in the story of the God who graciously frees and provides for his people. The text confronts the reading community with the practices of the popular religion of the dominant culture and calls for an examination of the convictions, values, and narratives that inform them.

Hosea makes clear in this text that God hides himself from those who seek him through manipulative worship practices. The prophet also makes clear that true worship is the context for God's people to experience his presence. Hosea invites the people of God to become an alternative community of people that worships God the Father "in the Spirit and truth," a community of worshippers that God "the Father seeks" (John 4:23).

b. Sound the Alarm (5:8-15)

BEHIND THE TEXT

This passage appears to reflect a memorable incident in the political life 5:8-15
of both Israel and Judah. Historically, it likely emerges out of the geopolitical developments in the ancient Near East during 735-732 B.C. The Assyrian imperial expansion program under Tiglath-Pileser prompted the Syrian king Rezin and Israel's king Pekah to form an army coalition to defend their nations against Assyria (see 2 Kgs 16; Isa 7). Judah refused to join this coalition, which led to an attack of Judah by the coalition army. This attack prompted Ahaz, king of Judah, to appeal to Tiglath-Pileser, the Assyrian king, for help. Assyria responded by invading Syria and Israel, and incorporated their major cities into the Assyrian Empire. As for Israel, the kingdom lost not only much of its territory but also most of its population to Assyria's deportation program. A total takeover of Israel by Assyria was prevented by Hoshea, who murdered Pekah and became a tribute-paying vassal of the Assyrian king in 732 B.C. (2 Kgs 15:29-30). As for Judah, it also became a tribute-paying vassal of Assyria (2 Kgs 16:7-9).

As in other oracles, the prophet makes direct reference to three locations that played significant roles in the early history of the northern kingdom. Gibeah, Ramah, and Beth Aven (Bethel) are all cities located in the southern border of northern Israel. Although the name Gibeah is linked to a city in the hill country of Judah (Josh 15:57) and to a town in the hill country of Ephraim

(Josh 24:33), here it most likely refers to the Gibeah in the Benjamite territory, also known as Gibeah of Benjamin (Judg 19:14; 20:10; 2 Sam 23:29). It was the home of Saul (1 Sam 10:26; 15:34) and the provincial capital during his reign as Israel's first king (see 1 Sam 22:6; 23:19). Ramah was also a city in the Benjamite territory (Josh 18:25). Gibeah and Ramah were en route from Jerusalem to the worship shrine at Bethel. As previously noted, the name Beth Aven ("house of wickedness") is a derogatory pun on the name Bethel ("house of God"; see Hos 4:15).

The history of war between Israel and Judah over the border towns of Gibeah and Ramah goes back to the earliest days of the divided kingdom (see 1 Kgs 15:6-22). It is likely that during the Syrian-Israelite invasion of Judah, these cities were taken over by the Israelite army (2 Kgs 16:5). Some scholars speculate that Hos 5:10 refers to a Judean attempt to reclaim these cities during the Assyrian invasion of Israel. The precise event that underlies v 10 is not clear. Ephraim's turning to Assyria may be a reference to Israel's submission to Assyria during the days of Menahem (745-736 B.C.) or to Hoshea's submission to Assyria in 732 B.C. (see Mays 1969, 86-88; also Wolff 1974, 110-12, and Yee 1996, 246, for various scenarios of historical events).

IN THE TEXT

■ **8** Using two imperatives in v 8 (**sound the trumpet**, **raise the battle cry**), Hosea functions as a military watchman and sounds the warning of an invasion to the cities of **Gibeah**, **Ramah**, and **Beth Aven** (Bethel). He urges the tribe of **Benjamin**, located just north of Judah, to be alert to the enemy's imminent invasion. The command to sound the trumpet and the horn and to raise the battle cry suggests an imminent attack against the people (see similar terminology in the march around Jericho in Josh 6:16). The order of the list of the towns, from Gibeah in the south to Bethel in the north, suggests the movement of the invading army from the south to the north. The invader could thus likely be Judah that is attempting to reclaim its territory in Benjamin (Mays 1969, 88). On a much grander scale, however, the text may refer to the Assyrian invasion of northern Israel in 733-732 B.C. (see Wolff 1974, 111; Yee 1996, 248).

■ **9** The reference to Ephraim's destruction and the **day of reckoning** in v 9 suggests the possibility of the Assyrian invasion rather than a Judean attack (see v 8). The invasion of Ephraim means that its day of reckoning has come. The invading army will make Ephraim/Israel into a desolate wasteland. The **day of reckoning** (*yôm tôkēḥâ*, from *yākah*, means "rebuke," "correct," "reprove"; "day of punishment" [NRSV]) conveys a sense of corrective reprimand. The text views the invasion of Ephraim by the enemy as divine judgment with the intent to rebuke or correct the nation for its failure to keep the covenant with Yahweh.

In the second half of v 9, the prophet declares that his warning to the various tribes of Israel is **certain** or trustworthy. The people can depend on this word spoken by the prophet. The prophet is not merely proclaiming this reliable word, but he makes it known (*yāda'*). The people may not *know* Yahweh (4:1, 6), but Yahweh will make certain that they know through the prophetic proclamation the devastating effects of their infidelity.

■ **10** The reference to Judah in v 10 disrupts the continuity of the judgment words on Ephraim. However, the word against Judah here shows that Judah is not exempt from God's judgment. The **leaders** (*śārîm* could mean "rulers," "princes," "captains," etc.) of Judah could refer to local or tribal authorities, but here the term likely refers to military leaders. Judah is also involved in treacherous and deceitful acts. The text clearly reflects the legal prohibition against the displacement of boundary markers from a neighbor's field (e.g., Deut 19:14; Prov 22:28; 23:10). Judah has violated the covenant stipulations and so Judah receives the divine verdict. Judah will experience the overflow of divine rage poured out upon it **like a flood of water.**

■ **11** Hosea returns to the judgment words on Ephraim in v 11. Ephraim is under military invasion and oppression by the Assyrians. Though the nation is crushed by the judgment, it continues to have a determined, stubborn will to follow after **idols**. The meaning of the Hebrew word *ṣāw* (**idols**) is not clear. Mays and Wolff follow the emendation of *ṣāw* to *ṣār* (meaning "enemy") and see here Israel's determination to be in league with Syria, its longtime enemy, to resist Assyria and to wage war against Judah (Mays 1969, 85, 90; Wolff 1974, 114). The Septuagint translation here presupposes the Hebrew word *šāwĕ'* meaning "vanity" (NRSV) or "emptiness" (**idols** conveys this idea).

■ **12** Hosea announces Yahweh's verdict against Ephraim and Judah with vivid, even crude images in v 12. The prophet likens Yahweh's devastation of the northern kingdom to ***maggots*** within open sores (see NRSV; Wolff suggests "pus" [1974, 115]). The NIV **moth** describes the eating away little by little at a garment from the outside until the garment completely wastes away. Judah is not exempt from judgment; Hosea compares Judah's destruction to the decay and rottenness that a worm brings to a piece of wood from the inside out.

■ **13** In v 13, the prophet describes the incurable and terminal disease of both Israel and Judah. The **sickness** of Ephraim and the **sores** of Judah perhaps refer to the massive military destruction of Israel and Judah by the Assyrian army. Verse 13*b* reports Ephraim's attempt to find a cure for its sickness. Ephraim turns to the very same nation that is bringing devastation upon it. The leaders of the nation sent its delegation to **Assyria** and to **the great king for help**. The text most likely refers to seeking political help or submission to a great king.

The great king here is most likely Tiglath-Pileser, the Assyrian emperor who began the program of Assyrian expansion in the mid-eighth century B.C. The text most likely refers to Hoshea's submission to Assyria in 732 B.C., following the assassination of Pekah, to save Israel from a total takeover by the Assyrian army (2 Kgs 17:3 ff.). Judah was already a vassal of Assyria during this period.

Hosea 5:13 ends with Hosea's announcement that the Assyrian king will not be able to **cure** the sickness of Israel or **heal** the sores. Hosea is well aware of the tradition that Yahweh is the healer of his people (6:1; 7:1; 11:3; 14:4; see Exod 15:26; Pss 103:3; 147:3). The closing line of Hos 5:13 simply states that the very wound that is filled with infection will not depart from the people. Even though the covenant community will seek assistance from the mighty power of Assyria, they will remain with their incurable sickness and pus-filled wound.

■ **14** In v 14 Hosea uses the imagery of a predatory animal attacking and destroying its victim to portray Yahweh's judgment on Israel and Judah. Like a lion that tears its victim into pieces, Yahweh will tear these two nations. No one can rescue these nations from the powerful grip of Yahweh. The image of a lion (see also 11:10; 13:7-8) depicts the ferocity of Yahweh in this verse.

In the second half of 5:14, double repetition of the first-person pronoun along with the verb communicates the absolute certainty that the people's collapse is Yahweh's doing. The verb **tear . . . to pieces** (*ṭārap*) conveys the violent ripping of a prey into pieces by wild animals, such as a lion or wolf. The prophet does not provide a direct object to the sentence. The text assumes the object of the divine "tearing" to be Ephraim and Judah, or the whole nation of Israel.

Verse 14 concludes with one swift action after the other: ***I will go, carry off, and there will not be a rescue***. Just as a lion mangles its prey and then walks away with the prey as food in its mouth, so Yahweh will come with destruction and depart. Neither cultic rituals at the Baal sites nor alliances with the nations will be able to deliver the ruptured prey from the mouth of this divine lion.

■ **15** In the first line of v 15 Yahweh declares what he will do after destroying Israel: ***I will go, I will return to my place***. Just as the lion returns to its den after devouring the prey, so Yahweh will return to his hiding and wait. In the midst of the people's terror, they will experience the absence of God. The particle **until** (*ʿad*) indicates that Yahweh's departure from his people is not forever.

The absence of Yahweh from among his people will end once the people have experienced the suffering that accompanies their guilt. The NIV **until they have borne their guilt** is a possible reading of the Hebrew text. The Hebrew verb *ʾāšam* means "to incur guilt" or "to suffer the consequences of guilt"

(Mays 1969, 93). The verb often indicates one's bearing the results or sufferings of one's guilt. The phrase **in their misery** ("in their distress" [NRSV]) in the last line is parallel to **their guilt**.

Hosea anticipates that the experience of the suffering that accompanies their guilt will prompt the people to **seek** (*bāqaš*; see 3:5; 5:6; and 10:12) Yahweh's **face**. The notion of the face of Yahweh often refers to the divine presence. Hosea describes the people's dire situation in the closing line. The noun translated as **misery** depicts the utter depths of human destitution and desperation. In the midst of the people's great agony, they will ***diligently look*** (*sāḥar*) for Yahweh. The verb *sāḥar* often means one's looking for an object or person at the earliest part of the day when the sun first rises.

FROM THE TEXT

Hosea portrays in this text the emptiness of God's people who have sought blessing and protection from the imperial power. The covenant people come to the end of their own resources and become fully aware of the inability of the empire and its political, economic, and military might to provide a cure for their deep and deadly wound. In that moment, even the God of covenant fidelity appears as the enemy, as destruction and destitution eat away at the people's existence from the inside out. Eventually, the God who had delivered, provided, and healed withdraws himself from the people and becomes silent. However, the text anticipates an end to the divine absence just as it also anticipates the seeking of God's face by the people in their misery. Their prayer of return to God follows in 6:1-3.

This text certainly does not lead us to conclude that the catastrophes that occur in one's life or in the life of a community are the result of the sufferer's sin. Nor can one conclude from this text that the devastating calamities of life are the works of a God who is manipulating people through their suffering. The God who refuses to let his covenant people manipulate him also refuses to manipulate his covenant people. Within the larger context of the Bible, the sufferings of Job, the calamities of the Apostle Paul, and certainly the suffering and death of Jesus Christ serve as a corrective to an ideology that views suffering in such a way. This text does not seek to provide an answer to the enduring question of "why" suffering and devastation occur in our world.

However, as we read this text in the setting and theology of the book of Hosea, it becomes clear that catastrophic life experiences create the occasion for both individual and communal reexamination of the object of their trust. The catharsis of such events opens the individual and the community to realities to which they easily become numb and blind. This text, in the midst of incurable wounds and fatal injuries—socially, politically, economically, religiously, and even physically—invites the suffering individual and community to recognize the source of life and blessing. The text reminds us the real source of life and help is "the LORD, the Maker of heaven and earth" (Ps 121:2). The text also reminds us that our alliance with the world powers, whether human or divine, cannot produce the security and welfare that we seek from them. Ultimately they will all fail because none of them have the power to prosper or heal or save.

c. A Call to Repentance (6:1-3)

BEHIND THE TEXT

Though 6:1-3 is a distinct literary unit, these verses are a natural extension of 5:14-15. Chapter 5 concludes with Yahweh's anticipation that his people will earnestly seek his face. This unit seems to provide the response of the people.

These verses seem to function as a call to and prayer of confession and repentance. Commentators offer various explanations on the authenticity and the genuineness of the words found in these verses. Some scholars see in these verses a prayer that Hosea offers on behalf of the people or the genuine confession and prayer of the people themselves. Others have argued that this prayer is the insincere expression of either a desperate people who approach Yahweh as if he were a Baal or of priests who attempt to satisfy Yahweh through their ordinary practices of national lament (e.g., see Mays 1969, 94-95; Wolff 1974, 116-17). However, Yee argues that one should read "the Hosean text like a musical score whose notes are read both horizontally in a linear progression and vertically to create chords" (1996, 249). Therefore, although the prophet expresses exasperation at the short-lived fidelity of the people in v 4, the prayer of vv 1-3 could certainly reflect an authentic prayer of repentance.

The prayer avoids all language of a fast or any particular rituals involved in the communal observance. This lack of reference to rituals may also be used as an argument against the view that the prophet is quoting here an insincere and shallow prayer of the people. The call to the people focuses upon the familiar themes of the people's return to Yahweh (*šûb*). It also associates this return with the people's desire to know (*yāda*ʿ) Yahweh. The prayer also expresses hope that Yahweh will bind and heal his people and will cause them to rise again. This idea is consistent with the traditional theology of the power of communal repentance to persuade Yahweh to replace divine curse with divine blessing (see Joel 2:21-27).

IN THE TEXT

■ **1** The prayer begins with an invitation. The plural imperative **come** introduces a command to the people as a whole. However, the phrase **let us return** places the command in the mouths of the people themselves. Thus the desire to return to Yahweh is a corporate wish expressed by the community (see the theme of return in Hos 3:5; 12:6; 14:1-2; also Jer 3:12, 14, 22; 4:1; 31:21, etc.).

After the initial call and desire to return, the prayer changes into a confession or acknowledgment by the people that Yahweh has **torn** them **to pieces** and that he has **injured** them (Hos 6:1). The Hebrew verb *nākâ* (**injure**) means "to strike violently" or "to smite," and thus it conveys the idea of Yahweh's destructive attack upon the people. These verbs echo the language of the divine attack in 5:14. The people are in full agreement with Yahweh that they are bearing the consequences of their guilt. However, the people also express their hope that Yahweh will **heal** them and **bind up** their **wounds**. Binding depicts the wrapping of bandages around the wounds caused by the divine attack. The people thus indirectly admit the futility of their trust in the king of Assyria to heal them (5:13).

■ **2** The hope of the community continues in 6:2. The focus shifts from Yahweh's healing and binding to his power to **revive** (*ḥāyâ* means "to make alive" or "revive") and ***raise*** (*qûm*) his people. **After two days** Yahweh will revive the destitute, and **on the third day he will *raise*** them up. Wolff argues that the idea here is not the giving of life but the preservation of life because of the lack of specific reference to death (1974, 117). Hosea, however, describes here the condition of a nation that is torn to pieces—the nation is as good as dead. The hope of the mortally injured people is that they will be brought back to life so that they will rise as living and healthy beings. The precise meaning of **two days** and **on the third day** is not clear; it is likely that these phrases indicate a short period of time (Mays 1969, 95). The people express their confidence that they will not have to wait a long period of time for their revival and restoration to become a reality. Some commentators connect the language of dying and rising to the familiar Canaanite belief in the rising of the fertility god from death in the underworld to bring fertility upon the land. However, this verse cannot be linked to the Baal myth because the subject of rising here is human beings and not deities.

Verse 2 ends with the hope of the people that their restoration by Yahweh will make it possible for them to live in the presence of Yahweh. The healing and the reviving is a means to a greater end. The ultimate desire of Yahweh for his people is not simply that they experience wholeness from their wounds but that they experience life in his presence.

■ **3** Verse 3 expresses the corporate desire of the people to know Yahweh (***let us know***). This is parallel to the desire, "let us return to the LORD," in v 1. The verb "to know" (*yāda'*) appears twice in v 3; its first occurrence (***let us know***) does not have a specific direct object (the NIV adds **the LORD**). As if in midthought, the prophet, however, continues: **Let us press on *to know Yahweh***.

For Hosea, this knowing is not an abstract knowledge for the people to attain. In the end, this knowing embodies itself in the pursuit of knowing Yahweh. The verb *rādap* (meaning "to pursue"; **press on**) provides a vivid image of the people's diligent effort to pursue Yahweh in order to enter into a personal and covenantal relationship with him (knowledge of God).

Verse 3 concludes with the affirmation that Yahweh will come to the people as the giver of blessing, fertility, and life. Yahweh's appearance to his people is as certain as the rising of **the sun** at dawn. Yahweh's coming also means the bestowal of his blessings to his people. **Like the *showers*** and **spring rains** provide water to the land, Yahweh's coming will bring fruitfulness to the land that has suffered so greatly because of the people's sins and lack of knowledge of God (1:2; 4:1-3). Hosea is careful not to portray Yahweh's appearing to the people as the means of fertility; instead he portrays Yahweh as the provider of fertility. Yahweh comes to his people in their wounded condition and he himself heals and binds. He comes to his people in their dryness and barrenness, and he himself provides rain and nourishment.

FROM THE TEXT

This text reveals a God who does not heal his people from wounds and festering sores simply for the sake of healing or to make his people "feel better." God heals his people, binds their wounds, and breathes new life so that they might live in his presence. The prophet is not concerned with a once-and-for-all healing that leaves the people "healed." He is concerned with a once-and-for-all healing that prepares them to live as a healed people in God's presence.

It is important to note that all statements of the passage are in the first-person plural. The return to God is corporate. The healing and the binding are corporate. The resurrection and life subsequent to resurrection are corporate. The pressing on to know God is corporate. The participation in the gift of life and blessings of fertility is corporate. Such an emphasis on the corporate nature of God's work might strike the modern reader of the text as odd. However, Hosea makes clear that salvation is not a mere individualized, privatized experience. This divine act of salvation and renewal is for the reviving of a community, specifically the people of God. This text particularly confronts the privatized, consumer-oriented notions of the modern reader of the text and challenges the reader to explore the corporate and communal nature of God's life-giving activity.

Christian readers of this text will find in Phil 3:8-14 an echo of Hosea's call to ***press on to know*** God (Hos 6:3). The Apostle Paul declares his deep desire "to know Christ . . . to know the power of his resurrection" (Phil 3:10). For Paul, like Hosea, to know this God is to participate in the very life and presence of this God. The knowledge of God is not merely the cognition of the story of God. Rather, it is participation in the divine story, and ultimately that story is Jesus Christ himself. The knowledge of God is participation—"becoming like him"—in the suffering and crucifixion of Jesus Christ (Phil 3:10-11). The knowledge of God is life in the presence of the resurrected Christ.

The text constructs a theological world of hope in the revival of the people "on the third day" that ultimately reaches its pinnacle in the resurrection of Jesus Christ. Hosea paints a portrait of reviving or making someone alive as well as raising someone up. It is not surprising that Hos 6:2 has been viewed by Christian interpreters as a veiled reference to the resurrection of Jesus Christ. In the immediate context of the eighth century B.C., the prophet expresses the exuberant hope for a people that they will indeed return to God and experience healing from their catastrophic wounds. As a statement of hope, this text declares without reservation that defeat is not the final word for God's people. The aroma of life will overcome the stench of death that has filled the air. Where defeat has occurred, the victory of God will prevail. The hope of Hosea continues to echo in the resurrection faith of the Christian community, which grounds its hope in the resurrection of Jesus Christ.

d. Yahweh's Exasperation (6:4-6)

BEHIND THE TEXT

The divine frustration in vv 4-6 clearly emerges out of the prayer in vv 1-3. This unit focuses on the ephemeral nature of Israel's covenant faithfulness. Verse 6 implies a religious condition that placed more importance to rituals than the covenant way of life. Whether or not the prayer of vv 1-3 was sincere, v 4 clearly demonstrates that the people consistently failed to serve their covenant God faithfully. These verses show that the people's struggle with infidelity played itself out in the ritual practices of the sacrificial system. 6:4-6

IN THE TEXT

■ **4** In an almost "hand-wringing" exasperation, Yahweh cries out separately to both **Ephraim** and **Judah**, **What can I do with you?** The second part of v 4 indicates that the quickly dissipating covenant loyalty of the people is the reason for Yahweh's frustration expressed in this question.

In the second part of v 4, Yahweh compares the covenant people's **love** (*ḥesed*) for him to the early **morning mist** (lit. "morning cloud"), to the **dew that disappears** early in the day. In the Hebrew vocabulary, *ḥesed* belongs to the context of a covenant relationship; it refers first and foremost to covenant faithfulness or one's loyalty within a commitment made to another. The prophet's accusation in v 4 is not the absence of loyalty but rather fickleness of loyalty. This erratic and inconsistent nature of the people's allegiance to Yahweh lies at the heart of the prophet's concern.

■ **5** Verse 5 shows what Yahweh has done to deal with the fleeting loyalty of his people. Yahweh reminds the people that he **cut** with his **prophets** and **killed *them* with the words of** his **mouth**. The language here echoes the violent language of 5:14. It is likely that the third-person plural refers to previous generations as well as the present generation. The **prophets** in the first line is parallel to the phrase **the words of my mouth** in the second line. The text does not identify the prophets; Hosea may have been thinking of powerful personalities in the past (such as Elijah) and contemporary figures (such as Amos, Isaiah, and Micah). Although the prophetic utterances were capable of speaking life and blessing into the community, Yahweh has used them to bring destruction to the people who were fickle in their covenant loyalty.

Verse 5 ends with the statement that Yahweh's **judgments** (*mišpāṭ* in plural; "your judgments" [MT] imply God's judgments upon the people) ***come out*** as light. While this flash could depict the light of the **sun** or a flash of "lightning" (HCSB), however, the reference may be simply to the phenomenon of "light" itself (NRSV). Mays thinks that the reference to light here may be an indication of the clarity of the words of judgment (1969, 97). Yee links the text to Gen 1:3 and argues that the focus of the text is on judgments going out of God's mouth and simultaneously the people experiencing the effect of Yahweh's judgments pronounced upon them (1996, 252). The people compared the certainty of their hope in Yahweh's coming to heal them to the rising of the sun (Hos 6:3). Yahweh now responds to this hope by saying that the people can be certain of his judgment just as they are certain of light appearing at dawn.

■ **6** In v 6, Yahweh declares that his deepest **desire** for his people is their ***covenant loyalty*** (*ḥesed,* **mercy**) and their ***knowledge of God*** (*daʿat ʾĕlōhîm*). These core covenantal concepts are the basis for Yahweh's case against Israel in 4:1. Yahweh expresses his **desire** (*ḥāpēṣ* means "to take delight in," "be pleased with," "desire") to a people who have preoccupied themselves with **sacrifice** (*zābaḥ*) and **burnt offerings** (*ʿôlâ*). In the whole burnt offering, the worshipper holds back nothing; the fire consumes the animal on the altar completely. In the sacrificial system of worship in the OT, this offering is the clearest demonstration of one's total devotion to God. Verse 6 implies that though the worshipping community demonstrates through rituals its total commitment to Yahweh, it lacks two fundamental qualities that are essential to the ordering and well-being of the community and its relationship to Yahweh. These qualities—***covenant loyalty*** and ***knowledge of God***—determine the efficacy of sacrifices and offerings. God delights in these qualities and desires to find these qualities among his people. Obviously the prophet neither demonizes nor rejects the notion and practice of sacrifices. Rather, he renders them meaningless and empty if they are not accompanied by that which they are to represent in the first place, that is, the loyalty of God's people and their intimate covenant knowledge of God.

FROM THE TEXT

Hosea's use of the image of a quickly disappearing morning dew to portray Israel's covenant loyalty engages the imagination of readers. This image vividly makes clear the great dilemma of God's people, then and now. The text presents a people who are attached to their God; however, their fidelity to God is sporadic and easily distracted.

The text also makes clear to its readers that God is not interested in occasional expressions of praise, gratitude, affection, or obedience from his people. What he seeks from his people is consistency of relationship and wholehearted devotion. Such consistency and commitment embodies itself first and foremost in the knowledge of God and in uninterrupted covenant fidelity. This does not mean, however, that Hosea discounts acts of sacrifice. The prophet places rituals within the context of covenant loyalty so that they become expressions of faithfulness and knowledge of God rather than substitutes for these qualities. When these qualities are absent, then rituals become meaningless and empty.

A plethora of voices across the pages of Scripture share Hosea's conviction concerning acts of worship and service. Samuel warned Saul, Israel's first king, that obedience "is better than sacrifice" (1 Sam 15:22). Amos spoke about God's hatred of elaborate worship offerings of the people who are not committed to doing justice and righteousness in the society (Amos 5:21-24). Micah announced that burnt offerings, rivers of oil, and even the sacrifice of one's firstborn child do not suffice. Rather, God desires justice, covenant faithfulness, and humble walk with him (Mic 6:6-8). Isaiah challenged the worshipping community that was preoccupied with offerings and sacrifices to seek justice and protect the poor and the helpless in the community (Isa 1:10-17). Jeremiah extended a similar call to the worshippers in the temple in Jerusalem who were confident in God's presence with them, though they were engaged in wholescale covenant-breaking activities (Jer 7:1-15). The Apostle Paul reminds his readers that ecstatic worship experiences and demonstrations of self-sacrifice empty of love are nothing more than meaningless activities (1 Cor 13:1-3).

Jesus' use of Hos 6:6 illustrates the significance he has placed on the relationship between covenant faithfulness to God and relationship to one's neighbor. He responds to the criticism of the Pharisees that he eats with sinners: "It is not the healthy who need a doctor, but the sick. But go and learn what this means: 'I desire mercy, not sacrifice.' For I have not come to call the righteous, but sinners" (Matt 9:12-13). Jesus thus makes clear that covenant fidelity to God does not exist apart from covenant fidelity to one's neighbor. The gospel text portrays a merciful Savior who was more concerned with reaching out to sinners with his acts of mercy than religious pretensions and legalistic observance of the religious laws of his day.

3. Rebellion Gone Rampant (6:7—7:16)

BEHIND THE TEXT

Various oracles in this passage enumerate the hopeless and seemingly helpless situation of the people and their leadership as their rebellion against Yahweh has gone out of control. As in previous passages, the prophet cites various place names in order to describe the rebellious history of the people. Although the text does not link a specific incident to the locations, all three place names (Adam, Gilead, Shechem) represent the earliest period of Israel's settlement in the land.

a. From the Earliest Days (6:7-11a)

IN THE TEXT

■ **7** The beginning phrases of v 7 create some ambiguity. The text literally reads as "and they like Adam transgressed the covenant; there they acted treacherously with me." Most translations take Adam as a place name and translate *kĕʾādām* as **at Adam** (lit. "like Adam"). The literal phrase could point to the story in Gen 3 and the "original covenant rupture" in Eden (Mays 1969, 100). The term *ʾādām* could even refer simply to human frailty in general. Reading **Adam** as a place name is more logical here because of the second line, ***there they acted treacherously with me,*** and also because of other place names in this passage. Adam is the place where the waters stood in a heap as the Israelites crossed over (*ʿăbar* means "to cross over" or "to transgress") the Jordan (Josh 3:16). There seems to be a play on the word *ʿăbar* at work in this text. Soon after Israel "crossed over" into the land of promise, they ***transgressed*** the covenant (*ʿăbar*) and dealt faithlessly (*bāgad*) with Yahweh. Hosea uses the verb *bāgad,* which means "to deal faithlessly," "deal treacherously," and so forth, in Hos 5:7 where he links the people's interaction with Yahweh to the foreign children born into the covenant family. However, no preserved tradition indicates a rebellion of the people at this site. Wolff links the reference to "some recent action by the cultic community which demonstrated its unfaithfulness to the covenant" (1974, 121). It is also likely that the intent of the text is to depict the people as rebellious from the very moment they entered the land, that is, even at the location where the waters stood in a heap.

■ **8** From Adam, the prophet proceeds in v 8 to **Gilead** on the eastern side of the Jordan. Gilead is the mountainous region where the Transjordan tribes of Reuben, Gad, and half-tribe of Manasseh settled. Here they built a large altar soon after the tribes had been dismissed to their various territories (see Josh 22:1-10). Other tribes viewed this as an act of treachery and rebellion against Yahweh (Josh 22:10-34). The reference to violence in Gilead in Hos 6:8 may refer to an event that occurred more around the time of the prophet.

The prophet describes Gilead in its present state as a ***gathering place*** (*qiryâ*). It is a gathering place of ***those who do*** or ***work*** iniquity (*ʾāwen*). Verse 8 indicates that doing iniquity was a communal activity in Gilead. The next phrase, **footprints of blood**, describes the violent nature of the iniquity shaped by the people of Gilead.

■ **9** In v 9 Hosea compares the **priests** to thieves who lie in wait together in order to make a unified attack. Once again, Hosea portrays the priests as a whole united and banded together and engaged in criminal activity against the people (see 4:7-8). The text portrays the priests carrying out their **wicked schemes** on the way to **Shechem**, the place where Israel gathered together to renew the covenant with God in their early history in the promised land (see Josh 24).

■ **10** The prophet concludes his portrayal of the rampant rebellion by saying that he has witnessed **a horrible thing in Israel** (v 10). Hosea is most likely referring to the abuse and perversion of priestly power. The reference to **Israel**, however, leads us to think that the nation as a whole is the subject of v 10. The next line specifically describes **Ephraim**'s **prostitution**; as a result, **Israel** [Ephraim] **is defiled**. Prostitution here and elsewhere in Hosea is Israel's engagement in the Canaanite fertility rituals; the result of prostitution is ritual uncleanness. Thus, the horrible thing witnessed by the prophet may be the participation of both the priests and the people in the fertility rituals at the Canaanite cultic sites, resulting in the defilement of the whole nation.

■ **11*a*** So as not to leave the southern kingdom innocent in their covenant relationship with Yahweh, in v 11*a* the prophet announces that **Judah** will reap **a harvest**. This harvesttime is appointed by Yahweh—it will be the time to harvest what the nation has planted (see 8:7). The specific sin of Judah is not mentioned here. Yahweh's judgment is coming upon both Israel and Judah.

b. A Nation of Bandits (6:11b—7:3)

■ **11*b*** The concluding line of v 11 functions as poetic parallelism with the opening line of 7:1; therefore, one should consider v 11*b* along with the subsequent verses. Verse 11*b* anticipates a time when Yahweh would **restore** [*šûb*] **the fortunes of** his **people**. **Fortunes** conveys the idea of the material wealth in a general sense. The text refers to the return from exile and the subsequent restoration of the people in the land (see Deut 30:1-5). The text also assumes the removal of the land's blessings when the people were taken into exile. The word *šěbût* thus most likely refers to both the exiled people and wealth of the nation that was removed from the land by the enemy.

■ **7:1 Whenever I would heal Israel** (7:1*a*) functions as a parallel statement to "whenever I would restore the fortunes of my people" (6:11*b*). The focus of these two lines is thus on Yahweh's activity of restoration and healing of his people (see also 5:13; 6:1). Since the verbs in both 6:11*b* and 7:1*a* are infinitive constructs, the remainder of 7:1 is necessary for the expression of a complete thought. The rest of v 1 indicates that when the people approach Yahweh for healing and when Yahweh turns away from his wrath to initiate healing and restoration, it results only in the further disclosure of Ephraim's ***corruption*** (*ʿāwōn*) and Samaria's ***evil deeds*** (*rāʿôt,* from *rāʿâ*). The verb *gālâ* ("to uncover," "to expose") is linked to both Ephraim's corruption and Samaria's evil deeds. The NIV repeats the verb (**exposed, revealed**) though in the MT the verb occurs only once. This verb is used in 2:10 to describe the uncovering of the shame of the wife. The verb conveys the idea of revealing and exposing that which has been hidden, which in the text here is the corruption and evil deeds of Israel. ***Corruption*** (*ʿāwōn*) refers to the polluted residual effect that accompanies transgressions and sins committed by an individual or a community. The word in the singular here (NIV has **sins**) indicates the overall effect of the people's sin in its totality in contrast to the individual and specific sins of the people. As the consequence of sins, the term is often translated as guilt or punishment. In the next line, Hosea parallels Samaria's ***evil deeds*** (lit. "the evils of Samaria") to Ephraim's corruption of the previous line. Samaria, the capital of the northern kingdom, represents the center of Israel's power structure and thus the whole nation. The parallel lines indicate that corruption and evil have become the characteristic traits of northern Israel. In the closing lines of v 1, the prophet identifies **deceit** and thievery as the evil deeds of Israel that have been brought to light by Yahweh's attempt to heal the nation. With the reference to Samaria, the work of deceit or falsehood may depict the direct involvement of the political leaders in creating and enacting fraudulent and dishonest practices within the Israelite political and economic system.

■ **2** Not only does this treacherous activity occur in the open, but according to the prophet, the perpetrators **do not realize** that Yahweh remembers **all their evil** (v 2). The image created in this line is that the people do not even remind themselves of Yahweh's awareness of their activity. Ironically, the people who have forgotten Yahweh (2:13; 4:6; 8:14; 13:6) have also forgotten that Yahweh remembers. Verse 2 of ch 7 ends with the note that the community has come face-to-face with its deeds as those deeds completely surround (**engulf**) them. These same deeds are also before Yahweh; they are out in the open to both the people themselves and to God.

■**3** From the highest office of the king to those at peripheral power centers (*śārîm*, **princes**), the leadership finds merriment in the evil and deceptive practices of the people (v 3). The theme of **wickedness** (*rāʿâ*) in vv 1-2 is continued in v 3. Throughout the book of Hosea, the prophet demonstrates a particular fondness for the word *kāḥaš*, translated in v 3 as **lies** (4:2; 9:2; 10:13; 12:1), the deceptive and evil practices of the people.

c. A Nation as Hot as an Oven (7:4-10)

■**4** Hosea utilizes the guiding metaphorical motif of the book when he describes the people and probably the priesthood in particular as **adulterers** (*nāʾap*; see 3:1 and 4:2) in 7:4. **They are all adulterers** indicates that the engagement in infidelity was a community activity; apparently no one refrained from it.

Beginning with v 4*b* and continuing through v 8, the language of the text imaginatively evolves from vocabulary of adultery into diverse images of heat produced by an oven. Verse 4 compares the people and particularly the priests to a portable stove or firepot used for baking, which keeps its fire continually burning.

■**5** In v 5, Hosea deals with the burning heat of Israel's political leaders brought on by wine. It is not clear what **the day of the festival of our king** means in this context. The language of vv 5-7 seems to suggest the intoxication of the king and his royal entourage, which would have provided the perfect setting for an assassination attempt. Mays interprets the phrase "the day of the king" as a reference to "the coronation day of the candidate in whose behalf the conspirators acted" (1969, 106). Though the meaning of the concluding line of v 5 in the Hebrew text is not certain, it appears to depict the king as stretching out his hand to persons who only bring mockery and scorn. The portrayal is perhaps of the capacity of wine to bring scorn and mockery to those in the palace by making them drunk and more open to overthrow. On the other hand, the reference may be directly to a conspirator's partnership with scornful persons (i.e., rebels and assassins) in his attempt to gain the throne through a coup d'etat.

■**6** The text continues to develop the portrayal of the palace intrigue in v 6 by comparing the **hearts** of the conspirators to a burning **oven**. Like the heat within a stove, a fire burns within the minds (*lēb*, **hearts**) of the conspirators. Hosea's depiction of the heat within the people demonstrates that the actions of the people emerge from a fire that first burns within them. They first think about what they are planning to do. Then **all night** long their anger **smolders** as they continue to make their final preparations (see also Mic 2:1 for a similar depiction of nighttime planning and daytime action). The portrait is one of hot coals just waiting to burst into flames. Finally when **morning** arrives on the day of their attempted coup, the inner-burning fire and the nighttime's smoldering embers explode into a full-fledged **flaming fire** that brings destruction. The fire that had existed only in the stove finally erupts and spills over into acts of violence.

■ **7** This burning heat, like the adultery in v 4, is all-pervasive. Out of their heat and passion, they finally consume their **rulers**. The text appears to depict palace overthrows in Israel. In v 7, **rulers** actually refer to those persons who carry out judgment or justice (*mišpāṭ*) in the community. Out of their passionate heat, the people consume the ones whose responsibility was to announce upright and just verdicts in order to protect the social, economic, and political order of the community. Moreover, the kings refuse to call upon Yahweh for help though they are falling from their place of leadership. The kings' refusal to call out to Yahweh had become the consistent pattern of kingship.

■ **8** In vv 8-9, Hosea leaves the domestic intrigue of palace overthrow and enters the international intrigue experienced by Israel throughout its history as it shifted from one alliance to another. The text continues to employ diverse metaphors. The metaphorical images include confusion, burnt bread, weakness, and old age. In v 8, the text describes **Ephraim** as mixing itself (*bālal*) with the peoples and thus bringing confusion upon itself. The term *bālal* (meaning "mix," "mingle," "confuse"), also found in the story of Babel, reflects here the activity of mixing ingredients such as oil and dough together in preparation of making bread (see Lev 2:4-5; Num 28:5, 9). The use of the reflexive stem of the verb implies that the people had brought confusion upon themselves. Such confusion or mixing portrays well the entire history of Israel as it sought security through alliances with one nation and then another.

The prophet provides a second comparative depiction of Ephraim by describing a cake of bread that remains unturned. Such a loaf of bread would be burnt on one side and dough on the other side. Although the meaning of this metaphor is not quite clear, in light of the context of mixing with the nations, Hosea may be portraying the international policy of Israel as not clearly thought out. In the end, it is certain that such bread that is "half-baked," neither all dough nor all cooked, is good for nothing. Like lukewarm drink, half-baked bread must finally be discarded.

■ **9** Verse 9 describes Israel as a nation being devoured by **foreigners** (*zārîm*). The prophet utilizes the same term (*zārîm*) in 5:7 to describe the children born out of the people's adultery. In 7:9, Hosea may be thinking of the self-serving interests of the nations with whom Israel allied itself throughout its history. Israel expects these allies to help and deliver Israel, but these allies have their own agenda. They have come not to save but to ***devour*** (*ʾākal* means "eat," "consume," "devour," etc.) Israel, the half-baked cake, and to destroy its **strength**. Tragically, the people of God do not even realize that foreigners are eating away their strength. In the second part of v 9, Hosea utilizes the image of gray hairs sprinkled upon the head and compares Israel to one who is unaware that aging is rapidly occurring and that the end is soon approaching. Again, the people are oblivious to the aging and dying process that is taking place within them as a people.

■ **10** Hosea observes in v 10 that the ***pride*** or self-exultation of Israel serves as the witness against the people of God (see 5:5). In spite of an unquestionable evidence against them, the people neither ***turn back*** (*šûb*, **return** or "repent") to Yahweh, nor do they seek (*bāqaš*) him. Pride prevents Israel from turning to Yahweh in repentance. The people of God have set their mind on seeking alliances with other nations, and they refuse to seek Yahweh their God.

d. A Nation without Sense (7:11-16)

■ **11** In v 11, Hosea describes the mindless nature of Ephraim's foreign policy actions through the image of an **easily deceived** dove. The text indicates Israel's vacillating alliances with **Assyria** and **Egypt**. Menahem submitted to Assyria and paid tribute to Tiglath-Pileser (2 Kgs 15:19), but Pekah joined a coalition to resist the Assyrian power (2 Kgs 15:29, 37). Hoshea submitted to Assyria but revolted and appealed to Egypt for help (2 Kgs 17:4). The phrase **easily deceived** literally means "simple" or "open-minded." In Israel's wisdom tradition, such simplicity or open-mindedness reflected an immature simple-mindedness that others can easily deceive and entice (e.g., see Prov 1:4, 22, 32). Hosea also describes Israel's activity as **senseless** (lit. "there is no heart" or "without mind"), which indicates that Israel was not engaged in proper decision-making processes. This is clearly evident in the nation's going back and forth between Assyria and Egypt. Hosea's reference to these two powers points back to his comments in vv 8-9 concerning Israel's mixing with the nations and the devouring of Israel's strength by foreigners.

■ **12** The bird imagery continues in v 12. Yahweh declares that he will throw his net on the mindless dove Ephraim who flies back and forth (***as they go***) between the nations for help (v 12). The purpose of this divine action is to ***bring them down*** and to ***discipline them***. The Hebrew text of the final words in the last line in v 12 is difficult to understand. The text literally reads, "I will discipline them [*'aysirēm*, from *yāsar*, which means "discipline," "chastise," "instruct"] *according to the report of their appointed time (or appointed place or gathering)*." The NIV reading (**When I hear them flocking together, I will catch them**) seems to be determined by the emendation of the verb *yāsar* to *'āsar* (meaning "bind" or "imprison"). The report given at an appointed time or place could refer to Yahweh's announcement of the verdict concerning his people. Regardless of the difficulty of this text, it makes clear Yahweh's intent to discipline his people.

■ **13** Hosea begins v 13 with an announcement of **woe** upon Israel. The term often implies a denunciation or even a curse upon the recipient. In the next line, Hosea describes the wandering of the people (lit. "fluttering away") from Yahweh as the reason for the pronouncement of the woe upon them. In the announcement of **destruction** that follows, Hosea states the rebellion (*pāšaʿ*) of the people against Yahweh as the reason (**they have rebelled against me**) for the judgment on the people. Violent devastation is announced upon the people because of their deliberate crossing over the boundaries that Yahweh had established for them. In the midst of divine woe and destruction, Yahweh interrupts his own speech by declaring his desire to rescue his people. With the emphatic use of the first-person subject pronoun, Yahweh declares, ***I will redeem them***. The Hebrew word *pādâ* conveys a transaction in which one ransoms or purchases an individual or property from another (see the more common word *gāʾal* (meaning "redeem" in 13:14). The purchasing transaction of this text recalls the action of Hosea toward his adulterous wife in 3:2. Verse 13 of ch 7, however, ends with a disappointing note. The divine desire to ransom the people cannot come to fruition because the people respond to Yahweh by speaking **falsely** (*kāzab*) about him. The falsehoods are most likely their false worship and idolatry, and mixing of Yahweh worship with the Baal cult (Mays 1969, 111). The people live in a world of idol worship and alliance making and stubbornly refuse to be redeemed by Yahweh, who deeply desires to save them.

■ **14** In vv 14-16, the prophet portrays the people as a substandard, defective bow. They do not fulfill that for which their maker designed them. Verse 14 describes the manner in which the people demonstrate their defective character; on the one hand, they refuse to cry out to Yahweh with sincerity **from their hearts**. Yet, on the other hand, they are engaged in drastic acts in order to receive grain and new wine from the fertility deity. Instead of crying out to Yahweh, they go through extreme contortions and rituals of the fertility cult and howl in agony or **wail on their beds**. **They slash themselves, appealing to their gods** implies the worshippers' self-mutilation in order to manipulate the deity into action (see 1 Kgs 18:28-29; also the prohibition against self-mutilation in Deut 14:1). This reading is based on the LXX and some Hebrew manuscripts; the MT reading *yitgôrārû* (*grr* means "to drag oneself away") suggests the idea of the worshippers dragging themselves to the pagan places of worship. The goal of the worshippers who either drag themselves to the pagan shrines or cut themselves is the provisions of **grain and new wine**. **They turn away from me** indicates that the people do not come to Yahweh for these provisions for their life.

■ **15** In utter disbelief, Yahweh remarks in v 15 that although he was the one who trained his people, they have "double-crossed" him. The text once again employs the verb *yāsar* (see 5:2; 7:12; **trained**) to refer to the discipline or corrective measures that Yahweh carries out in the life of his people. In the

MT, there is no direct object (the NIV supplies **them** as the direct object). The next line, **I . . . strengthened their arms**, describes the manner in which Yahweh disciplined or trained his people. Yahweh is the one who made the nation strong. In spite of Yahweh's personal care and concern for his people to become strong, they have ironically turned around to **plot evil** against him. Their actions against Yahweh are calculated and carefully planned. Yahweh regards Israel as his people; they regard Yahweh as their enemy.

■ **16** The first line of v 16 states that the people do not turn to God. Commentators think that *'al* here is a shortened form of *elyon* (**Most High**). They also link this verse to Ps 78:56-57, which also makes reference to a **faulty bow** and *elohim elyon* ("God Most High"). If this is the case, the text describes the people as having not turned to **the Most High** (thus NIV). The image of the **faulty bow** vividly portrays the people as not fulfilling their purpose. The people of God have failed to be what Yahweh made them to be.

The destruction of the ***rulers*** of Israel is the theme of the rest of v 16. Hosea attributes the destruction of the rulers to the offensive ***indignation*** (*zā'am*) that is on ***their tongue*** (**insolent words**). Mays describes the rulers as "the architects of the royal assassinations in the search for an alignment of security" (1969, 113). The text indicates that because of their insolent words that have likely brought on the violent revolutions in Israel's history, they themselves will **fall by the sword**. Their own violence will now meet violence.

Verse 16 ends with the announcement that Israel will become a laughingstock in Egypt. Hosea anticipates here Israel's return to Egypt for help (see 8:13; 11:5). The very nation with which Israel allies for help will end up disparaging it. Once in its history, Yahweh delivered Israel from Egypt; now Israel plans to return to Egypt only to be ridiculed and mocked by the Egyptians.

FROM THE TEXT

The oracles in Hos 6:7—7:16 present us with a plethora of diverse and vivid images that reflect the hopeless unfaithfulness of God's people. These images paint vibrant portraits of the contrast between the divine desire for covenantal faithfulness and the knowledge of God (v 6) and the quickly evaporating fidelity of God's people (v 4). Metaphors of bandits in wait, hot ovens and half-baked bread, the aging process, senseless birds caught in a trap, and defective bows combine to paint an image of community completely oblivious to their addiction to infidelity. No wonder Hosea compares their faithfulness to a morning mist. Yet even when God attempts to restore and heal his people, the result is simply further revelation of their unfaithfulness (6:11*b*—7:1). These images, though they portray infidelity, also present an alternative reality—the vision of God for his people to be a faithful people in their relationship with him and with others in the community. The imagined world of the text is thus a world of covenantal faithfulness, trust, and dependence on God not only for physical needs but also for security and protection from enemies.

Contemporary readers of this text cannot help but see themselves reflected in the various images of this text. These images further reveal to the contemporary worshipping community its close association with the mindset and practices of the ancient covenant community. The text in that sense functions not only as a reminder to its modern readers of their own covenant infidelity to God but also as an invitation to acknowledge and confess sin and seek restoration of relationship with God.

4. Covenant Broken—the Evidence (8:1-14)

BEHIND THE TEXT

This passage continues the prophetic accusation that Israel has broken the covenant with Yahweh (8:1). The text begins with a summons to sound the trumpet to announce the approaching enemy. The enemy is most likely the Assyrian army. Wolff assigns 733 B.C. as the date for this unit (1974, 137). Mays suggests a date immediately after 733 B.C. (1969, 114). The text mentions setting up kings, idol worship, and foreign alliances as specific illustrations of Israel's covenant breaking.

The biblical tradition maintains two perspectives on kingship in Israel. Both perspectives have as their theological basis the idea of God's kingship, which is fundamental to Israel's existence as a covenant people (see Exod 15:18; see also Judg 8:23). One perspective indicates Yahweh's involvement in the making and removal of kings in Israel (see 1 Sam 9—10; 15:26; 1 Sam 16:1-13 and 2 Sam 7:1-17; 1 Kgs 19:16; 2 Kgs 10:28-31). The other perspective maintains kingship as an office established by God, with the stipulation of the king's strict adherence to his law (Deut 17:14-20). For this reason, while some prophets (such as Hosea) appear to view kingship as rebellion against Yahweh, others (such as Isaiah) understand kingship as the basis for an anticipated Messiah.

The history of Israel's idolatry goes back to the Sinai incident of the making of the golden calf under the leadership of Aaron (see Exod 32). When the northern kingdom was established, Jeroboam, its first king, constructed temples at Bethel and at Dan and set up the calf as the symbol of the deity for his nation (1 Kgs 12:25-33; for an overview of the iconology of the golden calf, see Davies 1992, 201). Hosea in this text clearly connects kingship and idolatry as two sides of the single issue of infidelity and broken covenant. For Hosea, both kingship and idolatry indicate the rejection of Yahweh's sovereignty over his people (see 1 Sam 8:7-8).

Hosea adds the issue of political alliances as another clear sign of Israel's broken covenant with Yahweh. The reference to Israel going to Assyria in v 9 most likely belongs to a particular historical context. After Hoshea's murder of Pekah, Hoshea quickly resumed payment of tribute to the Assyrians in 733 B.C. just as Menahem had done previously. Earlier in 7:8-12, Hosea alludes to this turning toward Assyria for aid. The annals of Tiglath-Pileser III make specific reference to the tribute given by Hoshea to Assyria. The Assyrian king reports that

> Israel . . . all its inhabitants (and) their possessions I led to Assyria. They overthrew their king Pekah . . . and I placed Hoshea . . . as king over them. I received from them 10 talents of gold, 1,000 (?) talents of silver as their [tri]bute and brought them to Assyria. (Pritchard 1969, 284)

Hosea 8:1-14 is made up of three subsections. In vv 1-3, the prophet warns about an impending enemy invasion. Israel's rejection of Yahweh through kingship and idolatry is the theme of vv 4-6. The prophet describes Yahweh's judgment in vv 7-14. Judgment is described here in terms of reaping what one sows. This section also deals with Israel's foreign alliances and idolatry, through which the nation has forgotten its maker.

IN THE TEXT

a. Sound the Trumpet (8:1-3)

■ 1 Verse 1 begins with Yahweh's command to the prophet to sound the trumpet. The text depicts the enemy as a bird of prey (*nešer*, perhaps a ***vulture***); it has already begun to circle over its victim. While one cannot be certain of the specific historical milieu, the urgency of impending doom reflects a time period shortly after the Syro-Ephraimite war and the coming Assyrian invasion (see 5:8 ff.; see Mays 1969, 114-15). According to the prophet, this predator is already **over the house of *Yahweh***. The house of Yahweh does not most likely mean a particular worship site, such as Bethel or Jerusalem. The next line, ***they* have broken my covenant**, indicates that the house of Yahweh is Israel. This is a departure from the usual expression "house of Israel" or "house of Ephraim" for Israel.

The bird of prey circles over the house of Israel because the people of God have overstepped or **broken** (*ʿăbar*; see 6:7) or crossed over Yahweh's covenant (**my covenant**). The covenant the people have broken belongs to Yahweh. It is his possession. The last line makes clear that overstepping what rightfully belongs to Yahweh is an act of purposeful rebellion (*pāšaʿ*) against Yahweh's ***instruction*** (*tôrâ*). The Hebrew word *tôrâ* includes not only God's law but also the narratives that shape Israel's present and future.

■ 2 The people who refused to cry out to Yahweh (see 7:14) now cry out, **O *my God, we, Israel, know you!*** This cry is most likely prompted by the urgency of the situation. The people identify themselves as **Israel** to God to remind Yahweh of their unique covenant identity and thus make a claim of their relationship to him. Such a self-identification and call for help is a familiar practice in the outcries found in the laments (e.g., see Pss 22:1; 63:1, etc.).

The cry of the people also includes the claim that they actually ***know*** (*yādaʿ*) Yahweh. The people speak directly to Yahweh (***we, Israel, know you***). Their declaration is particularly ironic in light of the numerous accusations made by Hosea concerning Israel's lack of the knowledge of God (see 4:1, 6; 6:3). It is possible that the prayer of the people here is a sincere acknowledgment of Yahweh as Israel's national deity. However, it is clear in Hosea's oracles that the people consistently failed to show covenant fidelity to Yahweh in their religious and national life.

■ **3** In spite of their various attempts to make covenant claims upon Yahweh, in v 3 Yahweh declares that they have rejected that which is **good** (*ṭôb*), or that which is appropriate and fitting for the people. Rejection of good also means the embracing of evil. Verse 3 ends with the consequence of rejecting the blessing of covenant life (i.e., "the good"); **an enemy will pursue** and bring Israel to its destruction. The people who have rejected the good and the call to pursue the knowledge of God (see 6:3), and have pursued alliances with other nations (12:1), will be pursued by an enemy. The evil of destruction is what is awaiting those who have rejected Yahweh.

b. King Makers and Idol Makers (8:4-6)

■ **4** Yahweh announces in v 4 his evaluation of Israel as king makers (***they made kings but not through me***) and idol makers. This verse also portrays Israel's kings and idols as "Israel-made" objects. Israel's kings were either self-appointed rulers or rulers chosen by the will of the people. Their authority to rule the nation did not come from Yahweh. While the prophet's reference in some ways goes to the beginning of the monarchy with Saul, it particularly reflects the palace intrigue and overthrows of Hosea's day (see esp. 7:5-7). They put military officers or **princes** (*śar*; see 7:5) into places of national leadership, but Yahweh had no knowledge of them (*yādāʿtî*, **without my approval**). Yahweh's knowledge here most likely refers to his covenantal relationship with them. Yahweh does not acknowledge leaders who do not participate in the covenant with him.

The second part of v 4 focuses on the theme of idol making, the other primary embodiment of the people's disloyalty to Yahweh (see 4:17; 13:2; 14:8). The people **make** for themselves **idols** with the precious metals of **silver** and **gold** with the expectation that they will bring blessing and fertility to them. But what they really get instead is their **destruction** (*kārat* means "cut off"). The passive form of the verb *kārat* in the text here actually conveys the idea of the people being cut off from any source of life and fertility. The verb is often used to describe the making of a covenant ("to cut" a covenant). The covenant-making ritual includes the cutting of an animal into two pieces (see

Gen 15:7-11). The underlying idea is that the covenant partner who breaks the covenant terms stands under the threat of being cut off, just like the animal that was cut into two pieces. The strange irony is the people do not even realize the fact that they are engaged in an action that in the end will turn out to be the cause of their own destruction.

■ **5** The first line of v 5 reads as follows: ***he rejected your calf, Samaria***. Because of the change to first person in the next line (**my anger burns**), the NIV changes the verb in the perfect tense in the MT to an imperative (**throw out your calf-idol**). Yahweh declares that he has rejected the calf. In the same way that the people have spurned or rejected (*zānaḥ*) the good (Hos 8:3), Yahweh has spurned or rejected (*zānaḥ*) their calf. The meaning of the reference to the calf of Samaria is not clear. Israel's history began with the setting up of calves as idols in the shrines at Dan and Bethel by King Jeroboam (1 Kgs 12:25-33). Since Samaria was the capital of the kingdom, and since Bethel was the king's sanctuary and the temple of the kingdom (see Amos 7:13), it is also likely that the reference here is to the calf idol of the nation as a whole. Yahweh announces in the next line that his **anger** is burning **against them**—kings and idols, and the people who have made them. Yahweh's burning anger echoes his reaction to Aaron's calf at the base of Sinai (Exod 32:10).

Hosea 8:5 ends with a rhetorical question: **how long will they be incapable of *innocence*?** According to Hosea, the people have lived and continue to live a life of sin; they are not capable of freedom from their sinful way of life. Mays describes this question as "a cry of anguish and sorrow over Israel's inability to live in innocence, free of the deeds that disqualify for relation to God" (1969, 119). As long as Israel is committed to idolatry, they cannot find freedom from their sin and guilt.

■ **6** In a direct polemic against the **calf** of Samaria, the prophet exposes the emptiness and vanity of idolatry (v 6). He declares that this idol has no divine powers whatsoever. The minds and hands of the people of Israel birthed it. An ***engraver*** (**metalworker**) in Israel produced it (see Isa 40:18-20). Hosea emphatically claims that this idol is ***not divine*** (*ʾĕlōhîm*). Both the NIV and NRSV translate *ʾĕlōhîm* as **God,** thereby inferring that the calf is not Yahweh. Perhaps the intent here is to declare that the calf is not a god or a deity. Hosea 8:6 ends with the description of the destiny of the calf. As a nondivine, humanly shaped vessel, this calf—along with all other humanly devised and humanly shaped idols—will ultimately become ***splinters*** (**broken in pieces**).

c. Sowing and Reaping (8:7-14)

■ **7** Hosea employs in v 7 the image of sowing and harvesting to convey the integral relationship between the behavior of the people and their imminent devastation. They have sown **wind** (*rûaḥ* means "breath," "wind," or "spirit"); now it is time to harvest what they have planted. Israel has planted the seed that has no potential for growth or yield. The obvious reference here is to Israel's investment in the fertility cult in the hope of an abundance of harvest. Hosea warns that what Israel will reap is not merely wind but the **whirlwind**, a mighty storm. What this whirlwind means for Israel is the focus of the remainder of v 7. In agricultural terms, the whirlwind does not mean an abundance of harvest, but rather a harvest that yields little or nothing. Hosea portrays here the image of standing stalks without grain, which in turn means no **flour** for the farmer. Hosea concludes v 7 with the observation that even if the people reap a token of grain, **foreigners would swallow it up**. They have trusted in their alliance with other gods and other nations; in the end these allies would swallow up even the meager resources that are left in the land (see 7:9).

Sowing and Reaping in the OT

In the matter of sowing and reaping, Hosea's thought is quite consistent with the Deuteronomic-prophetic conviction in which the community's conduct ultimately comes back upon the community. This conviction informs the promises of both blessing and curse in Deut 28. This conviction also shapes the prophets' understanding of judgment and salvation in terms of divine visitation. Perhaps this conviction best expresses itself in the prophetic understanding of the Day of Yahweh in such prophets as Joel (1:15; 2:1, 11, 31; 3:14), Amos (5:18-20), and Zephaniah (1:7, 14-18; 2:2). The prophet Obadiah most clearly and succinctly summarizes this conviction in his statement toward Edom: "The day of the LORD is near for all nations. As you have done, it will be done to you; your deeds will return upon your own head" (Obad 15).

■ **8** Israel's alliance with the nations is the subject of vv 8-10. The concluding line of v 7 introduces the transition to Israel's foreign alliances. Verse 8 describes Israel as a nation **swallowed up** by the great empire. Not only is Israel a tribute paying nation, but it has lost much of its land to the Assyrian Empire as well. After the invasion of 733 B.C. Assyria annexed a significant portion of Israel, including Galilee and Gilead, into the Assyrian Empire as its provinces and deported the inhabitants of these areas (see 2 Kgs 15:29). As a result, Israel is now scattered **among the nations**. The people of the covenant have lost their unique identity; they are just like any other nation that Assyria has swallowed up. The people who have lost their identity now exist as a ***worthless vessel***, a vessel in which no one takes pleasure or a vessel that is of no use even to the nation that subjugated it.

■ **9** Hosea compares Israel's going up to **Assyria** to **a wild donkey wandering alone** (v 9). The reference here is most likely to Hoshea's decision to submit to Assyria after his assassination of Pekah in 732 B.C. to save the nation from a complete takeover by Assyria. Earlier in Israel's history, Menahem (745-738 B.C.) paid tribute to Assyria to secure his kingship. The analogy of the wandering wild donkey indicates Israel's wandering away from Yahweh (see 7:8-11). Instead of going up to Yahweh for help, the covenant people have **gone up** to a mighty political power. The text emphasizes that the people themselves made the initiative in turning to Assyria (***They, they themselves, went up to Assyria***). The last line, **Ephraim has sold herself to lovers**, reiterates the theme of tribute payment to Assyria. Hosea compares **Ephraim** (*ʾeprayim*) to a **wild donkey** (*pereʾ*); there seems to be a play on the words here since these words share the same consonants. The unusual use of the plural form of the noun "love" perhaps suggests the various demonstrations of love. At the time of Hosea, Israel's demonstrations of love would be the regular tribute paid to Assyria along with the political loyalty required in international alliances. It is ironic that the prostitute Israel is the one who is actually paying out wages instead of receiving it from her lovers.

■ **10** Although Israel is paying out wages for love, Yahweh plans to gather the people together (v 10); this divine gathering of Israel is for judgment (Mays 1969, 121). They will not receive the protection they hope to receive from Assyria. The judgment will come in the form of oppression and suffering; the people of Israel will soon writhe in severe pain and anguish (**waste away**) on account of the ***burdensome load*** (*maśśāʾ*, **oppression**) imposed upon them by the Assyrian king (*melek śārîm*, **mighty king**; lit. "king of princes"). Again the irony here is that the Assyrian king to whom the people turned to for help will turn out to be the agent of Yahweh's judgment.

■ **11** In vv 11-13, Hosea returns to the popular cultic rituals of the day. In the same way that Israel will harvest what she has planted through alliances, the acts of the fertility cult will also return upon the people in terrorizing ways. Verse 11 is an indictment against the numerous sacrificial altars that Israel has built ***for sin offering*** (*lāḥăṭōʾ*, from *ḥăṭṭāʾâ*; *ḥăṭṭāʾâ*, could mean "sin" or "sin offering"). However, these altars have become in Israel **altars for sinning** (*lāḥăṭōʾ*). The Hebrew text thus plays on the double meaning of the word *ḥăṭṭāʾâ* ("sin" or "sin offering"). The people built altars to expiate sin through sin offering. Without any regard for the "many things" in Yahweh's law (see v 12), the people have taken the matter of atoning for their sins into their own hands. They presumed that ***multiplying*** (*rābâ*) altars will expedite the process of atonement. However, in reality they were involved in multiplying their sin through their sin offerings at these illegitimate places of worship. The sin offerings themselves thus became sinful acts instead of rituals to expiate sin. In Israel, sin has become an institution with the proliferation of cultic centers (Mays 1969, 121). Other eighth-century B.C. prophets also reiterate Hosea's view of worship as an opportunity to sin (see Isa 2:10-17; Amos 4:4-5; 5:4-5, 18-24; Mic 6:6-8; also Hos 4:7; 5:6).

■ **12** The prophet contrasts the conduct of the people with the conduct of Yahweh in v 12. The people multiplied their altars (v 11) in spite of Yahweh's multiplied or **many** [adjective *ribbô*, from *rābab*, means "many," "much," etc.] ***instructions*** (*tôrâ*; see 4:6; 8:1) that he had written for the people. However, the people have totally disregarded Yahweh's *tôrâ* and they have treated it as something very ***strange*** (see 5:7; 7:9*a*; 8:7*b*). Ironically, the covenant people are more at home with "foreigners" (8:7) who devour their strength and who swallow them up than they are with Yahweh's instruction, which though it is integral to their story has become foreign to them.

■ **13** Yahweh's displeasure with Israel's sacrificial system in v 13 once again shows that Yahweh and his covenant partner are moving in the opposite direction. The people **offer sacrifices as gifts** given to Yahweh (**me**). The meaning of the plural form of *habhab*, translated as "gifts," is somewhat uncertain since this word occurs only here in the Hebrew Bible. The text as it stands in the MT seems to depict the people as making sacrifices to other deities either from gifts that Yahweh has given to them or from gifts that they should give to Yahweh. However, the next line, ***they eat flesh***, suggests that the text may be dealing with the people's activity of consuming the sacrifice that should be offered to the deity. Whether these sacrifices were intended to be for deities other than Yahweh or for Yahweh himself, by eating the sacrifice the worshippers participate in the life of the deity worshipped in the cult. Mays suggests that Hosea is dealing with the people's attempt to "establish solidarity with God" (1969, 123). The worshipper's attempt is to become one with the god to whom the worshipper makes sacrifice and with whom the worshipper shares the meal.

In the next line of v 13, Hosea announces that Yahweh is **not pleased with** any of these rituals the people do to participate in his life. Instead he will **remember** [*zākar*] **their *iniquity*** (*ʿāwōn*) and ***visit*** [*pāqad*] **their sins** (*ḥăṭṭāʾâ*). The people have forgotten Yahweh (2:13; 4:6; 8:14; 13:6), but he will remember his people's wayward ways (7:2; 9:9). Yahweh's visitation of the sins of his people here is for punishment and not for salvation from their oppressors. This divine visitation will result in the return of the people to **Egypt**, where their story began as captives and where they first experienced Yahweh's deliverance. It is ironic that Yahweh's judgment will take the people right back to Egypt, the original place of their bondage and suffering (v 13).

■ **14** Verse 14 depicts the people's forgetfulness of Yahweh, the **Maker** of Israel. The verbal participle (*ʿōśēh*, ***maker***) conveys ongoing and continuous activity. Yahweh is not merely the one who "made" the people; he is the one who is "making" the people (see Yahweh as the "Maker" in Pss 95:5; 134:3; 149:2; Prov 22:2; Isa 44:2; 45:11; 51:13).

Israel's forgetfulness of their maker is evident in their effort to make for themselves ***temples*** (*hêkāl*, **palaces**) and **fortified . . . towns**. Wolff suggests that *hêkāl* here may be applied to both temples and palaces (1974, 146). Self-sufficiency and self-reliance are the root cause of the peoples' amnesia (see 2:13; 4:6; 13:6).

Hosea ends his oracle with an announcement of destruction by fire of all the structures that Israel as a nation trusted in for blessing and security. Yahweh's judgment will completely destroy these structures. Nothing will survive—not even the safest and the strongest structure in the land.

FROM THE TEXT

Hosea presents in this text king making, idol making, and foreign alliances as strong evidences of Israel's broken covenant with God. These religious and political realities of the eighth century B.C. continue to exist even in our present day as powerful threats to covenant faithfulness. Although the content of these political and religious systems has evolved over time, the form of these realities endures. This form embodies itself through human constructs easily manipulated by God's people in order to secure their own existence and to bring blessing upon themselves.

In Hos 8, these human constructs include altars of sacrifice. Hosea notes that altars that are intended to overcome sin actually promote sin in Israel (v 11). Israel built altars and increased their offerings as an expression of their religiosity, but without any true commitment to live an obedient life in faithfulness to the covenant with God and his instructions to them. Mays observes that these "altars come between Yahweh and his people instead of bringing them to encounter. Sacrifice has become an end in itself . . . and has displaced attention to the will of their Lord" (1969, 122). The contemporary readers find in this text a clear warning against any attempt to manipulate God through self-serving acts of busy worship and many offerings. Hosea reminds the contemporary readers that our busy worship is not a substitute for faithful worship and that indeed it may become a context of sin.

The text also paints a vivid picture of the subtlety of alliances with the empire. Making alliance with the nations meant abandoning God with whom the people have made a covenant. The text challenges the people of God to explore how the various political, economic, and religious systems depicted in Hosea embody themselves in the contemporary setting. The message of Hosea in ch 8 raises a whole series of questions for the reading community to ponder. What are the alliances that the people of God believe necessary in order to survive? How do such alliances compromise the people's undivided allegiance to God? The text clearly warns that alliances the people of God make with the world are a sure sign of their forgetfulness of God, their maker. Hans Walter Wolff has quite effectively articulated the service rendered by this text to the contemporary reading community. He states:

> Especially this chapter discloses the wrong path taken by God's New Testament people whenever they place a false authority over themselves; whenever they succumb to the idolatry of their accomplishments; whenever they seek help in their own works; whenever they give in to unbelief; whenever they take delight in their "worship services" instead of hearing and obeying the will of God; whenever they delude themselves with self-glorification and a false self-confidence, instead of placing their future in the hands of their Creator. (1974, 148)

This passage also assists in constructing a significant worldview in which sowing and reaping share an integral relationship. The text is clear in its description of the closer association between the life that is lived (planting) and what eventually grows from that life in the end (harvesting). This Deuteronomic conviction is not limited to the OT, but it continues into the early Christian proclamation and teaching as well. In Luke 6:37-38, Jesus reflects a very similar understanding in his admonition, "Do not judge, and you will not be judged; do not condemn, and you will not be condemned. Forgive, and you will be forgiven; give, and it will be given to you" (NRSV).

However, Hosea and the larger canon caution us against two extreme perspectives of the concept of sowing and reaping. On the one hand, the concept does not promote the idea of sowing and reaping as a form of sympathetic magic. God cannot be manipulated by our religious performances of any kind. God calls for a life of trust in his daily provisions and not trust in our religious activities or "sowing" with the expectation of an abundant "reaping." Blessings from God are his gifts to us, not a measured return for what we do for him.

On the other hand, the testimony of the whole scripture cautions us against viewing any event in life as the "harvest" of what one has "sown." Such a view links tragedies in one's life as the consequence of one's sin. The book of Job, as well as Jesus' response to disciples concerning the blind man, show that sickness and other tragedies in life are not always the result of sin by the individual(s) affected by such experiences in life (John 9:1-3). What Hosea and the Scriptures as a whole make clear is that what one has planted will eventually grow in one's life and will produce its fruit one way or the other.

5. The Day of Celebration Becomes the Day of Mourning (9:1-9)

BEHIND THE TEXT

Hosea articulates in this unit the devastation that will come upon the people who have built many altars, made alliances with nations, and have forgotten Yahweh their Maker. Hosea pronounces this message of destruction in the setting of the Feast of Tabernacles or Booths (Sukkot), one of the three great annual pilgrimage festivals of the people, the other two being Passover/Unleavened Bread and the Feast of Weeks. Roland de Vaux describes this festival, which lasted for a full week, as "the most important and the most crowded" of the three annual festivals (1965, 495). The autumn festival of Sukkot likely originated in the annual harvest of grapes and olives, two of the principal agricultural products of the Israelite people. The people erected small "huts" (*sûkkôt*) made of tree branches in the vineyards and orchards during the harvest season (de Vaux 1965, 501; see the postexilic custom in Neh 8:15-16). The practice of dwelling in huts reminded the people of the tent dwelling days of their ancestors in the wilderness (Lev 23:43). The festival was one of merriment and joy (regarding the practices and the anticipated merriment of the "Festival of Yahweh," see Lev 23:39-43; Deut 16:13-15; Judg 21:19-21). According to 1 Kings, Jeroboam I, northern kingdom's first king, instituted for his people their own version of the Festival of the Tabernacles at Bethel (1 Kgs 12:32). Bethel or one of the other sanctuaries in Israel may have been the location of this prophetic speech. Mays assigns this oracle to a date after 733 B.C. when the people would have returned to normal life activities, after Hoshea's submission to Assyria (1969, 125).

This unit has three sections. In Hos 9:1-3, the prophet calls the people to put an end to their rejoicing and celebration. The prophet proceeds to declare the end of offerings and sacrifices and festivities in the land and the exile of the people from the land (vv 4-6). The unit ends with the announcement of Yahweh's visitation of his people to carry out his judgment (vv 7-9). Hosea addresses the people directly in vv 1, 5, and 7 and in the third person in the rest of this unit.

IN THE TEXT

■ **1** The prophet seems to interrupt the people of Israel who are in the midst of their jubilation. He commands them not to rejoice and be exultant like the nations around them. The MT reads literally as follows: "Do not rejoice, O Israel, to rejoicing like the peoples." Most modern translations follow the LXX reading and read the preposition *ʾel* (meaning "to") as *ʾal* (negative particle meaning "no," "not"). The reading then would be, ***Do not rejoice, O Israel; do not rejoice like the peoples***. The first part of v 1 thus is a strong reminder to the people that the time for rejoicing is not now. The context of this prophetic call is most likely the Feast of Tabernacles (Mays 1969, 125; Wolff 1974, 153). The second line also suggests that Israel's jubilation was patterned after similar customs among ***the peoples*** (*ʿammîm*). Though the prophet does not use the usual term *gôyim* for the non-Israelite nations in v 1, it is clear that here the reference is to the surrounding nations as well as the inhabitants of the land who participate in the fertility rites and who attribute the harvest to the gods worshipped in the fertility cult.

The second part of v 1 states the reason for this call to cease rejoicing and celebration. The people of Yahweh, like other nations, regard their bountiful harvest as the reward for their involvement in the fertility cult. They have been thus **unfaithful** (lit. "you have played the harlot") and have wandered away from their covenant God (**your God**). Moreover, the harlot Israel loves **the wages of a prostitute** (*ʾetnān*; see 2:12); apparently the people have come to regard the **threshing floor** as the place where they received their wages/blessing from the fertility deities.

■ **2** Though the people trusted in the ***threshing floor and wine vat*** for their food and drink, Hosea states that these will fail to provide for the people (v 2). The people expected the threshing floor and wine vat to **feed** (lit. "pasture" or "tend") the people in return for their loyal service to the fertility gods. The wine vat is perhaps a reference to the winepress or even the deep trough into which the juice from the grapes flowed once the grapes were trampled. Verse 2 ends with the announcement that **the new wine will fail** or be lean (or "deceive" or "lie"). Deception has been the way of life for the people; they will be deceived by the very same source in which they placed their trust for their sustenance.

■ **3** A further effect of Yahweh's judgment is that the people will not be permitted to ***dwell in the land of Yahweh*** (v 3). The land is the land of Yahweh. The people are merely aliens and sojourners in Yahweh's land (see Lev 25:23). Yahweh's decision is to send them away from his land. The people who are not permitted to ***dwell*** (*yāšab*) in the land **will return** [*šûb*] **to Egypt**, the place where their ancestors were in bondage. Moreover, Israel will also have a new home—**Assyria**. As they make their new home in Assyria, they will become unclean by means of their daily diet, which will include **unclean food**. Thus the two powers to which the people of Israel have sworn allegiance will become their homes (see Hos 5:13; 7:11; 11:5, 11; 12:1). The Assyrians invaded northern Israel and annexed a large part of the kingdom and deported the people to Assyria in 733-32 B.C. (see 2 Kgs 15:29). It is possible that some of the Israelites would have escaped to Egypt during this time (see Mays 1969, 127).

■ **4** The exile of the people to foreign lands will bring an end to the worship of Yahweh through the established forms of ***drink offerings of wine*** and **sacrifices** (Hos 9:4). The Law specifically mentions the offering of wine as a drink offering during Israel's individual and communal worship (see Exod 29:40; Lev 23:13; Num 15:1-5). This practice will cease when the people are removed from the land of Yahweh. Life in exile and eating unclean food in unclean lands also mean that the sacrifices of the people will be unclean and thus not sweet or pleasing (*ʿārab*) to Yahweh. Instead, the sacrifices of the people will be like the **bread of mourners** (*leḥem ʾônîm*; *ʾônîm*, from *ʾawen*, means "trouble" or "sorrow" here). The reference is most likely to the food in a house where people mourn the death of someone in that house. The Law associated the dead with uncleanness; contact with the dead rendered individuals and objects unclean in ancient Israel (Num 19:11-22). The bread of mourning will only make the people unclean. Unclean offerings, moreover, serve only to satisfy the hunger of the people; they are unacceptable to Yahweh and will not have any place in the proper worship of Yahweh in ***Yahweh's temple*** (*bêt yhwh*). The text suggests that worship in the lands of exile will be unclean since it is done outside the legitimate place of worship in the Jerusalem temple.

■ **5** The prophet proceeds to address the people concerning their response on the day of the ***appointed gathering*** (*mô'ēd*) and on ***the day of the festival*** [*ḥag*] ***of Yahweh***? The answer is clear; the impending exile of the nation will bring an end to Israel's festival days. The question implies that the judgment words in vv 2-4 are about to be fulfilled; the jubilant nation will soon spend its days in sorrow and lamentation.

■ **6** Verse 6 announces destruction as an inescapable reality. Even if some may ***walk away*** [i.e., **escape**] **from destruction, Egypt will gather** [*qābaṣ*] **them, and Memphis will bury** [*qābar*] **them**. Egypt will become the burial ground for those who escape death and destruction by the hand of the Assyrians. Memphis served as the capital and primary place of residence for the Egyptian rulers throughout most of ancient Egypt's history. Hosea may have been thinking of the impressive necropolis located in Memphis when he describes the burial of the Israelites by Memphis (see Redford 1992, 690; Wolff 1974, 156).

The precious possession of silver (**treasures of silver**) in the last line of v 6 may be a reference to the idols made of silver, which Israel had used in the fertility cult. When the judgment of death and destruction comes, ***thistles*** will overtake these prized idolatrous vessels. Rather than vats of oil and wine along with storehouses of grain, **briers** will fill the **tents** of the people. The booths constructed in the vineyards during the annual harvest festival will be taken over by weeds and thorns.

■ **7** Verse 7 announces that the day of Yahweh's visitation (*pāqad*) has arrived. As in other texts, Yahweh's visitation conveys the idea of **punishment**. The second line reiterates the theme of punishment; **the days *of Yahweh's visitation*** are indeed the days **of reckoning** (*šillum*, from *šālēm*, means "to complete") or making things complete. Judgment of Israel began with the events of 733 B.C.; Yahweh will soon complete his judgment of Israel. The first part of v 7 thus anticipates a further attack on Israel by Assyria and Israel's total destruction in the near future (Mays 1969, 129). The remainder of vv 7-9 focuses upon the Israelite prophets and Hosea in particular. These verses seem to indicate that the people gathered to celebrate the festival of Sukkot totally rejected the prophetic message and mocked the prophet and his message. These verses contain the response of the prophet to his opponents.

The third line of v 7 reads as follows in the MT: "Israel shall know" (**Let Israel know this**). The MT reading suggests that Israel will know or recognize Yahweh's judgment when it arrives. Some commentators emend the MT *yēdʿû* to *yārîaʿ* and translate this line as "Israel cries" (NRSV). This reading assumes that the following line ("the prophet is a fool; the man of the spirit is mad" [NRSV]) contains a quotation of the people concerning the message of Hosea (see Wolff 1974, 156; Mays 1969, 129; Limburg 1988, 32). Wolff suggests that even without the textual emendation, the text here introduces a quotation of the words of the people.

The rebellion of the people is further demonstrated through their estimation of the spokesperson of Yahweh; the people perceive him simply as a **fool** and **maniac**. The word **fool** (*ʾĕwîl*) is used frequently in the wisdom tradition as a foil to wisdom (thirteen times in Prov 1—27). Hosea's opponents perceive themselves as wise, and they judge the prophet to be a fool and a madman. The phrase **the inspired person** (*ʾîš hārûaḥ*; lit. "the man of the spirit") is an eponym for the prophet; the Spirit of God was at times associated with the activity of the prophet (e.g., 1 Kgs 18:12; Isa 61:1; Ezek 2:2; Joel 2:28-29; Mic 3:8, etc.). Such possession by the Spirit of God could result in ecstatic or mantic forms of prophecy (e.g., see Num 11:17, 25, 26; 1 Sam 10:6, 10; 16:15-16), thus perhaps at times leading to a negative view of the prophet. The term translated as **maniac** or madman (*mĕšuggaʿ*) refers to one who is not sane (see 1 Sam 21:12-15); it is used in a disparaging way for a prophet who is not considered rational by his opponents (see 2 Kgs 9:11; Jer 29:26).

The people's assessment of Hosea comes out of their own sinfulness and **hostility** toward the prophet. The prophet is well aware of this popular sentiment, and he seems to agree with what the people say about him in a mocking tone: "(Yes, I have gone mad) ***because of your great iniquity and great animosity"*** (*maśṭēmâ*). In the next verse, however, he makes clear his true role as Yahweh's prophet in Israel.

■ **8** The prophet makes it quite obvious in v 8 what the true prophet of Yahweh is to be and thus how the people of God are to regard Yahweh's authentic prophet. The true prophet of Yahweh is a sentinel or a **watchman** who keeps watch over the people of God and alerts the people concerning what is imminent (see Ezek 3:17; 33:1-7). The MT is difficult to make sense of since it reads Ephraim as a "sentinel with my God" (regarding the rearrangement of the accent marker so that the prophet is viewed as the sentinel and not Ephraim, see Yee 1996, 266). This task has been given to the prophet by his God (**my God**). The prophet understands himself as carrying out his task in the presence of God and within the arena of God's activity. The word he speaks is the word of God.

According to Hosea, although the prophet functions as Yahweh's faithful sentinel over Ephraim, what he finds is the ***fowler's trap in*** **all his paths**. In 5:1, Hosea describes the religious and political leaders as involved in laying traps against others. However, in this case the trap is specifically laid against the prophet. As a result, all that he encounters is hostile ***animosity*** (*maśṭēmâ*; see v 7) and it has crept even into **the house of his God**. The text makes clear that the prophet is doing the bidding of *his* God in the house of God; however, that setting has become the place of intense hostility. The house of God perhaps is a reference to the land in general (see Mays 1969, 131).

■ **9** In v 9, the prophet vividly announces how deeply corruption has cut into the very identity of the people of God (**sunk deep into corruption**) and its disastrous effect on the nation. The language of deep cutting in v 9 (*ʿāmōq*) is reminiscent of a deeply cut valley. The corruption is likened to the events that took place at Gibeah, the home of Saul the first king of Israel. The phrase **days of Gibeah** is perhaps a reminder that the establishment of monarchy was a rebellious act against Yahweh. It is also possible that Hosea may be thinking of the rape of a Levite's concubine by the citizens of Gibeah and the subsequent war against Benjamin by the rest of the tribes that almost wiped out the tribe of Benjamin (see Judg 19—21). Yahweh will not forget Israel's hostility toward the prophet; he will remember the iniquity and punish the sins of the people. The prophet invokes the memory of the days of Gibeah perhaps to remind the nation that the days of Israel's extermination are on the way. The text does not seem to give any hope for Israel's future as a nation.

FROM THE TEXT

The setting of the Feast of Tabernacles provides a significant context within which the reading community interacts with this text. This festival particularly called upon the people to remember what Yahweh has done in their collective story. Such a setting of remembrance provides a contrast to the forgetfulness suffered by the people of God (see Hos 2:13; 8:14; 13:6). Yee has noted that "through ritual acts of remembering, the people 'relived' the days when God protected and sustained their forebears in the desert" (Yee 1996, 273).

Such remembrance continues to this day in the life of the people of God as they participate in the remembrance of the life, death, and resurrection of Christ as well as the birth of the church through the festal days of Christian time. Such remembrance and participation in the life of Christ himself is experienced each time the bread and wine are received in the Eucharist.

In light of the message of Hosea, the festivals celebrated and the meal eaten by God's people today should not only be observed, but the narratives that give rise to them should be recounted and ultimately reenacted through the daily lives of the people of God. The festivals of Christ and his church should not only be enjoined but should be embodied, fleshed out, in the lives of the followers of Christ. The meal of the broken body and shed blood should not only be received as a remembrance but enacted as a way of life so that the body of Christ indeed does become the broken body and shed blood of Christ in the world. Yee notes that

> saying grace is not so important as "doing grace," actually living a grace-filled life and being thankful for it. Putting Christ back into Christmas entails more than displaying a crèche or sending greeting cards illustrating the birth of the Christ child. It means reflecting deeply upon the mysterious source of our salvation and how God became a vulnerable human being in order to achieve that salvation. (1996, 273)

Perhaps a contributing factor to the "forgetfulness" of God's people is their deep love of and their fascination with the harvest itself. Focus given to the bountiful harvest celebrated at the Feast of Tabernacles led the people of Israel to forget the one who has provided the harvest and the blessing. As a result, they have failed to remember the unique narrative that informed the great Feast of Tabernacles to begin with. Mays observes that the festival of Sukkot became an "expression of Israel's apostasy" as the very character of the people's worship "sunk to the level of the nations around them" (1969, 125).

The prophet does not speak in generalities and outside of the life of the people. Rather, the prophet goes directly into the worship festivals with which the people are intimately familiar. Speaking from within the context of the festival that has been perverted and even confronting that which has become most sacred in the life of the people, the prophet lives in "real time" and addresses "real time." Yee has very aptly observed that

> it is often said that prophets are well ahead of their time, but it seems more accurate to say that prophets have a special insight into their time. They see the present more clearly and keenly. . . . The prophets fearlessly called their contemporaries to task to deal with the contemporary situation. (1996, 268)

The portrayal of the prophetic office as that of a sentinel or watchman is particularly noteworthy to the reading audience. Although such an image becomes more common in later prophets (e.g., Jer 6:17; Ezek 33:1-7), Hosea is the first of the prophets to describe himself in this manner. The primary task of such a watchman was to remain alert to all that was occurring and particularly to warn of oncoming dangers. He is to report what he has witnessed and for him not to do so would be to fail at his primary responsibility to protect the people under his watch. Similarly, the primary task of the contemporary prophet, the preacher, is to give witness to that which he or she has seen in the world and in the presence of God. Suggesting that perhaps *witness* is the most appropriate image for the preacher, Long observes that

> the preacher is listening for a voice, looking for a presence, hoping for the claim of God to be encountered through the text. Until this happens, there is nothing for the preacher to say. When it happens, the preacher becomes a witness to what has been seen and heard through the Scripture, and the preacher's authority grows out of this seeing and hearing. (2005, 47)

Limburg finds in this text the following questions that confront those who are called to preach the word of God in contemporary society: "Would anyone call me 'meshugga' [i.e., *maniac* or *madman*] because of a sermon preached or a position taken? Or have my words become only smooth and soothing words, designed to avoid conflict at any cost and to evoke kind reactions at the doorway?" He continues, "Hosea could preach of God's grace like no other, but he also knew that this was not the only task of the one who speaks for God. That person is also a watchman and, when the time is right, a watchman must sound the alarm" (1988, 34).

Modern readers of Hosea should not be surprised by the hostility of his audience toward him, who was determined to speak on behalf of God. Israel's true prophets were often viewed as troublemakers (1 Kgs 18:17; 22:1 ff.) or were told to speak no more (Amos 7:12-13) or were shut out by family and friends (Jer 12:6) or were rejected, opposed, even persecuted by the political and religious establishment (Jer 20:1-2; 26:7-9; 28:1 ff.; 36:20-26; see Matt 23:34). The NT also provides ample stories of opposition and hostility toward God's faithful messengers, beginning with Jesus and the apostles and the Christian community as a whole. Hosea and these biblical witnesses show that facing opposition because of preaching God's word is certainly not a sign of weakness or foolishness. Paul was convinced that "the message of the cross is foolishness to those who are perishing, but to [those] who are being saved it is the power of God. . . . For since in the wisdom of God the world through its wisdom did not know him, God was pleased through the foolishness of what was preached to save those who believe" (1 Cor 1:18, 21; see also 2 Cor 11:1, 16, 21).

6. Ephraim, a Withered Root (9:10-17)

BEHIND THE TEXT

As in the previous verses of ch 9, the context of the Feast of Tabernacles continues to inform this text. The oracle for the most part is a divine saying in the first person that is interrupted by two prophetic sayings (see vv 14, 17). The prophet utilizes once again historical events to compare and contrast

Yahweh's past relationship with his present attitude to Israel. The wilderness tradition reflected in v 10 echoes a period of intimacy and Yahweh's affection for the nation. The reference to Baal Peor (v 10*b*) recalls the beginning of Israel's long history of involvement in the fertility cult of the Canaanites. Yahweh's punishment of Israel for the idolatry of Baal Peor is the focus of vv 11-13. Verse 15*a* introduces the wickedness of Israel in Gilgal, followed by the sentence of judgment in vv 15*b*-16. The prophetic sayings in vv 14 and 17 show the prophet's agreement with the divine verdict.

IN THE TEXT

■ **10** Verse 10 begins with Yahweh's nostalgic recollection of the earliest days of Yahweh's relationship with Israel. Yahweh compares his meeting with Israel's ancestors to someone finding **grapes in the desert** and **early fruit on the fig tree**. The language of Yahweh's finding (*māṣa'*) Israel in the wilderness reflects Hosea's view of the early years in the wilderness as a positive experience in the covenant relationship between Yahweh and his people (see also Jer 2:2 ff.). When Israel was found by Yahweh, they were a cause for jubilation and celebration. Obviously, grapes would ordinarily not be found in the barren wilderness; the text simply seeks to convey the sense of an unanticipated discovery that brings joy to someone who least expects such a finding. The early spring figs are characteristically more tender than those that ripen later in the summer. In other words, they were innocent and appropriate; they were Yahweh's joy and delight. Nothing yet had the opportunity to taint or corrupt them.

The second part of Hos 9:10 describes how quickly Israel became a corrupt and idolatrous people and Yahweh's disappointment with Israel. Toward the end of Israel's wilderness journey, at **Baal Peor**, located in the land of Moab, the Israelite men participated in the worship of Baal by engaging in sexual relationships with the Moabite women (see Num 25). Yahweh recalls here that at Baal Peor, the people ***devoted themselves*** (*nāzar*) or separated themselves to an idol that he describes as a ***shameful thing*** (*bōšet*; see Jer 3:24; 11:13). The verb *nāzar* is the root of the word "Nazirite," a person who is consecrated or set apart for Yahweh either for a lifetime or for a short period (see Num 6).

Hosea 9:10 further describes the change in the identity of the people who were once found as grapes in the wilderness and early fig fruit. They have become exactly like the thing they have worshipped and **loved**—**a vile** or detestable **thing** (*šiqquṣ*). The word *šiqquṣ* is often used in the OT to describe idols themselves or the practices of idolatry (see Deut 29:17 [29:16 HB]; Jer 4:1; 7:30).

■ **11** In v 11, Yahweh describes the consequence of Israel's participation in the fertility cult; the **glory** (*kābôd*) of Israel/Ephraim, the esteemed place it once had in its relation to Yahweh, will **fly away like a bird**. Wolff comments that "whatever made the grape and early fig Israel esteemed, glorious, and delightful in Yahweh's sight, whatever accounted for her honorable election by Yahweh, it shall disappear" (1974, 166). There will be **no birth, no pregnancy**, and **no conception** in the land. The people who anticipated productivity through the fertility cult will end up with total barrenness. The text describes barrenness using the language of the maturation of the embryo in the reverse order—from childbearing to pregnancy to conception. Yee notices here the application of a negative logic; no conception, but even if there is conception, no pregnancy; even if there is pregnancy, no childbirth (1996, 270).

■ **12** Verse 12 states what will happen should there be childbirth and rearing of children in the land, though that likelihood is negated in v 11. Yahweh announces that he will make the people childless or **bereave** (*šākal*) them of ***humanity*** (*ʾādām*). No sign of human life will remain. Such a declaration is a fascinating irony for a people whose earliest memories were grounded in a divine promise of descendants who would be as numerous as the sand on the seashore and the stars in the sky (Hos 1:10; see also Gen 15:4-5; 22:17; 26:4; 32:12).

The second part of v 12 is a **woe** announcement; total destruction and death is what awaits the people when Yahweh turns away from them. Yahweh's turning away implies the departure of his glory from among the people (see v 11 for the disappearance of "Ephraim's glory"). Where the glory of Yahweh is not found, bereavement and infertility is a certainty. Where the divine giver of life and blessing is not present, only death and curse remain.

■ **13** The meaning of v 13 is somewhat obscure in the Hebrew text. The second half of the verse is actually much clearer than the first half. The NIV presents a translation that reflects the MT. In the Hebrew text, a more positive statement (in contrast to the second half of the verse) concerning Ephraim is presented; the NIV reading, **I have seen Ephraim, like Tyre, planted in a pleasant place**, assumes the meaning of *ṣôr* in the MT as Tyre (the NRSV translates *ṣôr* as a "young palm"). The LXX reading is parallel in meaning to the second half of the verse (***Ephraim shall bring forth his children to slaughter***). If Tyre is intended here, it may be an allusion to Tyre's revolt against Assyria and the resulting five-year siege of Tyre by the Assyrian army (see Yee's reference to Josephus' account of this incident; 1996, 270). Likewise, Hoshea's revolt against Assyria resulted in a three-year siege of Samaria by the Assyrians. Yee, who sees a possible linkage of the two incidents, suggests that Hosea anticipates here Ephraim/Israel leading its children to slaughter in its attempt to defend Samaria against the Assyrian siege (see Yee 1996, 270). Mays finds here a reference to Pekah's war against Assyria only to be utterly destroyed by the mighty armies of Tiglath-Pileser (1969, 134).

■ **14** In v 14, the prophet speaks directly to Yahweh and declares his verdict on the people. What do the people deserve from Yahweh? The prophet utilizes the verb **give** (*nātan*) three times in this verse as he cries out to Yahweh. Hosea first speaks in the imperative (**give them**), then asks a reflective question (**what will you give them?**), and concludes with another imperative (**give them**). The people participated in cultic rituals and sought fertility and blessing from idols that have no power to give life. Therefore, what the people deserve from Yahweh, the true source of life, is not the blessing of life but the curse of ***miscarrying womb*** and ***dry breasts***. The womb is where life takes its shape, and breasts are organs that provide nourishment to the developing child. This curse calls for an end to all possibilities of life in the land. There is an intriguing literary-theological irony here; the word "compassion" and the word "womb" belong to the same root (*rāḥam*). Hosea calls for this judgment of an infertile womb on the covenant community that Yahweh has already called *lo-ruhamah* (no compassion or pity; see 1:6). A people without the compassion of Yahweh are given here no hope for fertility and life.

■ **15** Yahweh's speech continues in v 15 with a reminder of another place of apostasy in the early history of Israel. The first line of v 15 in the MT reads as follows: ***all of their evil was in Gilgal***. The mere reference to Gilgal conveys all that is wrong in Israel—its alliances with other nations, its corrupt monarchy, and its idolatrous worship (→ 4:15 for notes on Gilgal).

The second line of v 15 traces Yahweh's hatred of Israel to Gilgal. The phrase ***There I hated them*** conveys the idea of the beginning of the disrupted relationship between Yahweh and Israel. At Gilgal, the future of the covenant between Yahweh and Israel was threatened. It has now come to the point of breakup or divorce. Yahweh declares that he will, because of the long and continued history of Israel's **sinful deeds**, **drive** the people **out of** his **house**. The text reflects the ancient practice of divorce, the sending away of an unfaithful wife by a man from his house (see Deut 24:1-3). The verb *gāraš* in the intensive form conveys the idea of forced expulsion from the location in which one resided (see Gen 3:24; 4:14; 21:10; Exod 6:1; 11:1; Josh 24:12). The reference to **my house** here and elsewhere in the book conveys the idea of the land as Yahweh's residence (see also 8:1; 9:8). Verse 15 ends with another statement of Yahweh's present attitude toward Israel; he no longer loves his people. Israel's covenant tradition is deeply rooted in the theology of Yahweh's love for Israel (11:1; see Deut 7:8; Mal 1:2-3). For Yahweh to love his people means to be in covenant with his people; for him to hate his people means they have stepped out of covenant with him and thus they are no longer the object of his love for them. Hosea 9:15 ends with an alliteration that attempts to emphasize the stubborn rebelliousness (*sōrĕrîm*) of the political **leaders** (*śārêhem*) of Israel. The leaders and the people alike are rebellious, and therefore Yahweh can no longer permit them to live in his land (see 4:16 where the people are compared to a "stubborn heifer").

■ 16 Verse 16 contains another set of images that describes once again the barren, infertile nature of Ephraim. The first half of the verse compares Ephraim to a **blighted** plant with ***dried up*** root. A plant that has no prospect of life cannot yield fruit. Such is the condition of Ephraim. The second half of the verse uses more direct language to describe the end of life in the land. Should this nation that is cursed with the curse of barrenness give birth, Yahweh will **slay *the most precious offspring of their womb***. Death of children means the nation has no prospect of a future. The covenant people who hoped to have children through their worship of Baal would receive instead barrenness and death from Yahweh.

■ 17 Chapter 9 ends with another prophetic speech. In the concluding verse, Hosea again supports the divine decision to bring death and destruction to Ephraim (see v 14). The prophet acknowledges his covenant faith by addressing Yahweh as **my God**. Hosea is certain that his God will **reject** (*māʾas*) Ephraim, the nation that has rejected its covenant God. The reason for Yahweh's rejection of his people is that **they have not *listened*** [*šāmaʿ*] ***to* him**. The wordplay (*māʾas, šāmaʿ*) conveys the nature of the covenant relationship and the consequence of covenant-breaking. The people rejected by their God will become nomads or **wanderers** [*nōdĕdîm* from *nādad*] **among the nations**. The word *nādad* refers to those who wander abroad without a home of their own (see Gen 4:12-14 where Cain becomes a wanderer [*nād*] on earth). The reference here is likely to the scattered community subsequent to their dispersion after 722/721 B.C.

FROM THE TEXT

The imagery of "grapes in the desert" and "early fruit on the fig tree" (v 10) makes clear that God's plan and purpose for his people is that they become a vineyard that would produce fruit that reflects their faithful relationship with God and their mission to the world. The destiny of the people of God is to be a source of joy and delight to God and a source of blessing to the world in which they live (see Gen 12:2-3). They are called by God to be God's special possession, "a kingdom of priests" and a holy people (see Exod 19:5-6). They are to embody the life of God in the world. God's people can fulfill this destiny only if they remain faithful to God through their obedience—constant listening/paying attention to the voice of the one who has called them to be his people. The text describes the tragic consequences of disobedience. Instead of blessing, the disobedient people of God hear words of curse; instead of the promise of life, they hear words of death; instead of life with God in his "house," they hear the sentence of expulsion and wandering among the nations.

The special relationship between God and his people is a significant theme in the NT also. Paul describes the church as the "handiwork" of God "created in Christ Jesus to do good works" (Eph 2:10). First Peter reiterates the language of Exod 19:5-6 and Hos 1:9-10 in the description of the identity of the Christian community (1 Pet 2:9-10). The epistle writer also makes clear that the duty of those who have been called "out of darkness into . . . light" is to proclaim the wonderful deeds of the one who called them to be his people (1 Pet 2:9).

New Testament writers also challenge the Christian community to be involved in producing fruit worthy of their calling. Jesus himself teaches the key to fruit-bearing when he states: "I am the vine; you are the branches. If you remain in me and I in you, you will bear much fruit; apart from me you can do nothing" (John 15:5). However, Jesus also warns the Christian community that trees that do not bear fruit are ultimately cut down (Luke 13:6-9) and burned (John 15:6; see also Matt 3:10).

The text also presents the great irony that the people received in return what they desperately tried to avoid through their participation in the fertility rituals. They attempted to overcome their fear of barrenness and death; what they received instead was the judgment of barrenness and death. The religious rituals and cultural customs that promised fertility yielded nothing but the prospect of no life in the land. The goal of the people's worship was to gain life rather than to celebrate the giver of life. When worship becomes the means to an end, it becomes idolatrous and in the end results in death and lifelessness. Yee observes, "By going off to the god of fertility, Ephraim causes the true God of fertility to 'depart from them' and to bring woe upon the nation" (1996, 270). Those who sought life ended up losing life. However, the gospel promises life to those who give up life for the sake of the one who is the true source of life (see Mark 8:35).

A final comment should be made about the strong language of hatred and love in this text. Buber states that whoever hates is actually "closer to a relation than those who are without love and hate" (1970, 68). In this passage, the reader very clearly enters into a vivid narrative-poetic world in which God has just as much at stake as his people do. The deity described by Hosea is not the aloof, stoic god of the Greeks. This God is a relational, covenantal God who is directly affected by his people. He feels: he loves, and he hates. He shares covenant relationship; he is moved to end covenant relationship. He is not the passive unmoved mover, but he is moved to action in response to his people. Certainly, in the broader context of Hosea, he is not the "baal" that is manipulated, but he is the "husband" and the "parent" who is moved by divine passion toward his people (see Hos 2:16; 11:8-9). Hosea also presents this relational God as a God who changes his mind in order to keep his relationship with his people and traces it to the character of God as a holy God (11:9). Buber reminds us that relationship between God and humanity is reciprocal. He states,

> That you need God more than anything, you know at all times in your heart. But don't you know also that God needs you—in the fullness of eternity, you? How would man exist if God did not need him, and how would you exist? You need God in order to be, and God needs you—for that which is the meaning of your life. (1970, 130)

7. A Portrait of Exile (10:1-8)

BEHIND THE TEXT

The prophet once again pronounces judgment on Israel's religious and political centers and attacks the practices of the fertility cult and the institution of monarchy and its alliances with other nations. The calf of Bethel (Beth Aven), the religious center of Israel, and Samaria the seat of Israel's political power receive particular attention in this text as the focus of Yahweh's judgment. This judgment speech begins with accusations directed against Israel's cultic practices, monarchy, and political alliances (vv 1-4). Verses 5-8 focus on the fate of the people, their idol, the king, and cultic places.

IN THE TEXT

■ **1** Verse 1 begins with the description of Israel as **a spreading** [*bāqaq*] **vine**, a fertile, healthy, and growing people. The nation has taken root and has **brought forth fruit**. It is likely that the prophet has in mind not only the population growth but also the economic and political strength of the nation. The second part of v 1 is an accusation; though the nation prospered, along with its prosperity also came a growth or increase of altars in the land. Alongside the land's prosperity (*ṭôb*, meaning "good"), the people **adorned** (causative form of *yāṭab*, the root of the adjective *ṭôb*, **he adorned**) **sacred *pillars*** (*maṣṣēbâ*). According to Mays, Israel saw a "functional relation" between "welfare and cult." He states that Israel's "altars and pillars were the holy machinery which produced the prosperity—a typically Canaanite understanding of the cult" (1969, 139).

■ **2** The accusation moves to an indictment in v 2. In spite of the increased and beautified worship sites, the hearts of the people remained **deceitful** (*ḥālaq*). The verb *ḥālaq* conveys the idea of a divided heart. The prophet declares that the people are guilty and that **they must bear their guilt** because of their divided loyalties. Verse 2 ends with the divine sentence of judgment. Yahweh will **demolish** the **altars** and **destroy** the **sacred *pillars*** in which the people trusted for their increased fruitfulness. The destruction of the cultic objects announced here was carried out in the next century by King Josiah during the religious reformation he carried out in the land (see 2 Kgs 23:14-15).

■ **3** Verse 3 introduces in the form of a quotation of what the people will say. The verse opens with the expression ***for now***, which suggests that the quotation is the response of the people to the accusation and indictment in vv 1-2. The meaning of the statement of the people (**We have no king because we *do not fear Yahweh***; ***and the king, what would he do for us?***) is ambiguous. Mays finds in this verse the acknowledgment of the people "when Yahweh's judgment drives them to self-knowledge and penitence." Thus, according to Mays, the people will confess that that they are a people without a king and that they did not allow Yahweh to rule them as king (1969, 140). The last part of the quotation, ***The king, what would he do for us?*** seems to convey the nonchalant, calloused, and cold attitude of the people toward their human king, most likely Hoshea (see Wolff 1974, 174). In their exile, they will recognize that their human king can do nothing for them.

■ **4** Verse 4 seems to convey a present reality in the land. Those who would spurn their human king in the days of their exile, nonetheless, are at the present time engaged in and support the activities of their king. The first part of v 4 lists three activities: they ***speak words***, they ***swear falsely***, and they ***make covenant***. The community is characterized here by its propensity to speak empty and meaningless words, words that have no value. Moreover, the people enter into treaty relationship by taking false oaths. Empty promises and worthless covenants permeate the character of the community. Wolff suggests that words, oaths, and covenants in v 4 refer to political agreements, palace revolts, and treaties between king and people that were empty, all characteristic of the final decades of Israel's history (1974, 175).

Verse 4 ends with a statement on the consequence of empty words and falsehood in relationship in the community. What the prophet observes in the land where promises are made lightly and covenants are not kept is a tragic perversion of justice. Hosea states that the judgments (*mišpāṭ*, **lawsuits**) that are given sprout a venomous herb in the furrows of the field (i.e., plowed field). The focus here is not so much on lawsuits, but rather on judgments pronounced in the courts, which are anything but just. Justice in the land is poisonous and life-taking rather than life-giving. This saying is parallel to Amos' statements concerning those who have turned justice into bitter wormwood (Amos 5:7; 6:12).

■ **5** In Hos 8:5, the prophet continues his portrayal of the utter ruin of the people as he describes their tremendous grief and shame over the loss of the calf of Beth Aven (see vv 5-6 for Yahweh's rejection of the calf of Samaria). As in other texts, Hosea refers to Bethel, the primary northern worship site, as **Beth Aven** (see 4:15; 5:8). The meaning of the MT "calves" (in plural) is not clear; it may refer to multiple religious sites in and around Bethel or the prophet may simply be addressing the deity of the people in a sarcastic tone (see Yee 1996, 272).

The inhabitants of Samaria are the elite and the powerful in the land. They are in dread because they now realize that the calf deity they worshipped is unable to save them from the hands of the Assyrians. Not only that but they are in dread because they do not know how to protect the calf deity from the impending danger. The people of Samaria do not have a covenant with Yahweh; they belong to the calf deity (**its people**). The text anticipates that soon the calf will be taken away into exile and that there will be mourning over the loss of it in the land. Both the people and the priests will mourn for the deity.

Hosea here describes the priests as **idolatrous priests** (*kōmer*; see 2 Kgs 23:5; Zeph 1:4) or priests in service of idols. The text poses some difficulty here. The MT reading, "and its idolatrous priests, over it shall rejoice, over its glory, because it has departed from it," conveys the idea of the priests rejoicing over the glory of the calf as it is taken away; that is, even on the way to its exile, the people would continue to give honor and worship to the calf. The NIV reading suggests the rejoicing of the priests more as a previous rather than a present action. The glory or the **splendor** (*kābôd*) of the calf refers to the brilliant metal and costly decoration of the idol. Whether it is in grief or exultation, the people see themselves as the people of the calf rather than as the covenant people of Yahweh.

■ **6** The destiny of the calf and its worshippers is the focus of v 6. The highly honored calf of Bethel will be taken away to **Assyria** as a tribute or an offering to **the great king**. The MT seems to convey the idea of the calf being taken to Assyria as payment to the Assyrian king for military assistance. Both the NIV and the NRSV follow the emendation of the text to read here *rab* (meaning "great") and thus translate the phrase as the **great king**. The closing line of v 6 states that Ephraim/Israel will in the end suffer shame and disgrace because of ***his counsel*** (*ʿēṣâ*), perhaps the counsel or even assistance given by the Assyrian king. The NIV reading, **foreign alliances**, reflects political counsel sought by Israel from the Assyrian king. In Hosea's view, Israel's calf deity is destined to suffer shame; likewise, Israel's political alliances and trust in the counsel of others will also yield nothing but shame.

■ **7** Verses 7 and 8 announce the death of Israel's politics and religion. The king of Samaria will cease or ***perish*** (v 7). In light of the overall context of the passage, Mays interprets the king to refer to the calf deity rather than to the ruler at Samaria (1969, 142). The second line of v 7 uses vivid imagery to describe the end of Israel's king; he will be like a small piece of wood that floats away **on the surface of the waters**. The Hebrew text here is vague as to whether the reference is only to the king of Samaria or to both the king *and*

Samaria. There is no conjunction and the words **Samaria** and its **king** are simply placed side by side.

■ **8** Destruction of the religious centers is the focus of v 8. The phrase **the high places of wickedness** (*bāmôt ʾāwen*) most likely refers to fertility worship sites at Bethel, which the prophet often portrays as Beth Aven in his oracles. Hosea identifies these places of idolatry as **the sin of Israel**. Yahweh's judgment will also result in the shame and disgrace of the nation. They hoped for productivity and growth through their engagement in idolatry, but what the land will produce is **thorns and thistles**, which will overtake even the worship sites that were thought to bring fertility and life. This will result in a terrifying cry of despair that will be heard in the land. The people will cry to the **mountains** and **hills**—places where they worshipped the fertility gods for life and security—to fall upon them so that they might come to a swift and complete end. Those who have rejected Yahweh choose for themselves death rather than life (see Deut 28; 30:15-19).

FROM THE TEXT

Like much of the book of Hosea, this text ultimately creates a literary-theological world in which the people of God are called not merely to trust God but to trust him wholly and without rival. Covenant faithfulness to God is wholehearted faithfulness and undivided loyalty. In spite of all of the religious trappings and rituals of worship, the people of God can fall short of full trust in God. When their focus is more upon what they need to do in the name of worship in order to increase their prosperity, then they perceive God as a Baal who returns the favor and insist on more manipulative forms of worship.

Hosea's God has nothing to do with that sort of worship; he is a gracious God who freely delivers and provides for his people, and a covenant partner who shares intimate life with his people. Hosea portrays here a people who have totally misunderstood blessing, which contributed to their misunderstood worship. Mays observes that

> the heart of Israel was neither whole nor faithful toward Yahweh; they worshipped him, but what they really had in mind was the produce of grain, wine, and oil which they thought their worship would secure. Instead of an encounter with their God, the cult had become an evasion of him. (1969, 139)

The text also imagines and hopes for the reader a world in which the people of God would live in covenant loyalty and faithfulness to each other in the community. Hosea lives in a world where people make covenants only to break them, a world not unlike the world of the reader today. Individuals come to share life with one another in such a way that they speak mere words that mean nothing and make promises that are empty. The disintegration of society that the text portrays is something that we witness in our day in our homes, marriages, workplace, churches, neighborhood, and friendships. The text makes clear that where words do not mean much, justice will be absent. The people who suffer the most in such a world are the poor, the disadvantaged, the powerless, the voiceless, and the defenseless. The poisonous effect of injustice is death and not life for the most helpless members of a community. The text invites its readers to participate in community life not only as promise makers but also as promise keepers, bringing hope and life to the world in which they live.

The depiction in v 8 of the utter helplessness and the ultimate ruin of those who reject God would likely have influenced the reflection and imagination of subsequent generations who read the text. The text clearly warns the future generations to remain loyal to God in their political and religious life or face the tragic consequences of apostasy. The images of Hosea would certainly have influenced readers of the Deuteronomic text that God indeed had set before the people "life and prosperity, death and destruction" so that each subsequent generation would hang in the balance of decision as they are called to "choose life, so that you and your children may live" (Deut 30:15, 19).

The Revelator echoes the language of Hosea when he portrays the scene of God's judgment of all humanity:

> Then the kings of the earth, the princes, the generals, the rich, the mighty, and everyone else, both slave and free, hid in caves and among the rocks of the mountains. They called to the mountains and the rocks, "Fall on us and hide us from the face of him who sits on the throne and from the wrath of the Lamb! For the great day of their wrath has come, and who can withstand it?" (Rev 6:15-16)

These are the very ones who had slain those who remained faithful to God. Both Hosea and the Revelator warn the wicked in the world of their day of judgment from which there will be no escape.

8. Impending Calamity (10:9-15)

BEHIND THE TEXT

The theme of judgment dominates this unit; sandwiched between judgment speeches (vv 9-11; vv 13-15) is a prophetic call to the audience to practice righteousness and to seek Yahweh so that they may enjoy the blessings of his righteousness. The judgment speeches in vv 9-11 and 13-15 allude to war scenes (Gibeah in vv 9-10; destruction of Beth Arbel in v 14; see Gibeah in 9:9).

The exact historical context of the war scene in 10:14 is not clear; also, the identities of Shalman and Beth Arbel are not definite. Commentators propose several possibilities for Shalman, including Shalmaneser V who destroyed Samaria in 722 B.C., and a Moabite king by the name Salamanu. Commentators also identify Beth Arbel with modern Irbid in the Gilead region of Transjordan (see Mays 1969, 149; Wolff 1974, 188). To whichever incident in Israel's history the prophet makes an allusion, it is apparently filled with such horrific memories that it can be used as a metaphor for later violent atrocities. According to Hosea, in this gruesome event even mothers and their children were dashed into pieces. Such sadistic activity was particularly practiced by armies in order to obliterate an entire populace from a region (see 2 Kgs 8:12; Ps 137:9; Isa 13:16; Nah 3:10).

IN THE TEXT

■ **9** The message of this oracle is addressed to **Israel**. The unit ends with a word about the destruction of "the king of Israel" (v 15). The goal of v 9 is to show that Israel has not made any progress at all in its way of life **since the days of Gibeah**, the dark days of Israel's early history. The phrase **you have sinned** (*ḥāṭāʾ*) implies Israel's covenant-breaking. Though a specific incident is not mentioned here, **the days of Gibeah** evoke memories of barbaric acts of violence and treachery narrated in Judg 19—21 and of rebellious actions on the part of King Saul, who was from Gibeah.

Hosea states that at Gibeah Israel ***stood*** or took a stand to show their persistence or refusal to change their rebellious ways. The phrase ***there Israel stood*** could also mean that the people gathered at Gibeah in a determined voice and took a position together against Yahweh and against the norms of the community. The prophet then proceeds to ask, **Will not war again overtake the evildoers in Gibeah?** Gibeah will again be the site of another war, this time the war that Yahweh will wage against Israel. It is ironic that the prophet refers to Israel as *bĕnê ʿalwâ* (***children of injustice;*** **evildoers**) instead of the traditional *bĕnê yiśrāʾēl* ("children of Israel").

■ **10** Hosea proceeds in v 10 to announce Yahweh's direct judgment upon his people. The opening phrase of the Hebrew text (*bĕʾawwātî* from *ʾāwâ*) literally reads, ***In my desire*** (**when I please**). This phrase would indicate that Yahweh will act according to his desire. The LXX reads here "I will come" (reading the opening word as the verb *bôʾ*, meaning "to come"; see NRSV). The LXX reading makes more sense here. The purpose of Yahweh's coming is to discipline the people or to chastise them (**punish**; the verb *yāsar* means "to discipline," "to chastise," etc.; see 7:12, 15).

The rest of 10:10 describes how Yahweh intends to carry out his disciplinary action against Israel. He will gather the nations against Israel, and the nations will **put them in bonds**. Yahweh will bring the nations together to punish the nation Israel for its **double *iniquity*** (*ʿāwōn*). Yee has suggested that the **double *iniquity*** may refer to the two great atrocities that had occurred at Gibeah, that is, the civil war and the establishment of monarchy in Israel. However, as

Yee also suggests, **double *iniquity*** may not refer to any specific historical incidents but simply to Israel's past and present covenant violations (1996, 275).

■ **11** The first part of v 11 describes what Ephraim's relation to Yahweh was like in the past (**Ephraim *was* a trained heifer**). The prophet compares Israel in v 11 to a well-trained heifer that loves to thresh the grain willingly and without being muzzled by a yoke. The image of the **heifer** (*ʿeglâ*) here contrasts with the image of Ephraim as a "stubborn heifer" (*pārâ*) in 4:16 (Yee 1996, 275).

The next line, **so I will put a yoke on her fair neck**, is based on a textual emendation of the MT that literally reads, "I passed by her fair neck" (*ʿābartî ʿal-ṭûb ṣawwāʾrâ*). The MT suggests that Yahweh spared the neck of the animal ("I spared her fair neck" [NRSV]) from the yoke and let the animal enjoy its freedom. The NIV reading implies Yahweh's decision to put a yoke on the neck of the nation, the trained heifer, so that he can now use the nation to do more difficult work.

The textual difficulty here cannot be easily resolved. Whether or not the animal was once free, the metaphor in the final part of the verse is that of an animal that is being made to do a more difficult task. Yahweh's statement, **I will drive Ephraim**, conveys the idea of a farmer behind the plow making the cow to do the hard work of plowing the field. The reference to Judah in the next line is difficult to explain. Commentators see here the work of a Judean redactor who included Judah to this verse. Both Ephraim and Judah must do the hard work of plowing and breaking the ground.

Commentators are divided on the nature of the task assigned to Ephraim and Judah (the nation as a whole). If v 11 is a continuation of v 10, then the yoke and the hard work imply the hard life of the nation under the Assyrian bondage. However, if v 11 is understood as an introduction to v 12, then the task assigned to Israel in v 11 is to break the ground and prepare the soil and get ready to sow the seed of righteousness. Though both readings are possible, this commentary favors the latter and views v 11 as a preamble to v 12.

■ **12** The agricultural metaphors in v 11 are directly related to the imperatives, given also in agricultural terms in v 12. The imperatives define Israel's mission in the world as the people of God. Yahweh's charge to the people who are under his yoke is to prepare the soil and plant the seed of righteousness, which in turn will lead them to reap **the fruit of unfailing love** in the land. **Righteousness** (*ṣĕdaqâ*) is right-relatedness; this relational concept is directly related to covenant faithfulness (see 2:19). This concept reflects actions that are consistent with the expectations within a previously established relationship.

Yahweh also admonishes the people to harvest the fruit of righteousness, which is *ḥesed* or covenant fidelity (see also 2:19). **Unfailing love** is one of the many meanings of the Hebrew word *ḥesed*. As the people sow right-relatedness, they will reap covenant faithfulness, which Hosea describes as lacking among the people (see 4:1; 6:4). For this to happen, the people must prepare the soil by breaking up the **unplowed ground**. Hosea then makes clear what the agricultural imagery of the cultivation of the ground means in the next line.

The prophet explains that the present time is the appropriate season to **seek** (see 5:6; see also Amos 5:4-6, 14) Yahweh. The people's preparatory action is first neither to plant seed nor to reap a harvest; instead, they are to seek Yahweh, for it is Yahweh and Yahweh alone who is ultimately the God of fertility who can make the seed grow and bring a bountiful harvest. Moreover, they must seek him **until he comes** and ***rains*** [*yārâ* literally means "to throw" or "to shoot"] **righteousness** upon the people. The preposition **until** indicates an epoch or a future turning point (see BDB 725). As Mays suggests, Hosea may be anticipating here Yahweh's work of sending salvation to his people who cultivate their ground by seeking him through their faithful adherence to his words (1969, 146).

■ **13*a*** What Israel has done is directly the opposite of what Yahweh admonished the nation to do. Instead of sowing seeds of righteousness, the people ***plowed*** **wickedness**, and as a result of that they have **reaped** violent deeds of ***injustice*** (*ʿāwĕlâ*). The harvest of the people is the result of what they have plowed. **You have eaten the fruit of deception** reiterates the idea of reaping what one sows. The people who practice deception eat **the fruit of** their **deception** (*kāḥaš*; see 4:2 and 9:2 where the prophet uses this term to describe the activity of the people). Hosea seems to imply that the current political crisis is the direct consequence of Israel's long history of deceptive and wicked dealings not only in relationship to God but also in its communal life.

■ **13*b*-14** Verse 13 ends with a specific reference to Israel's wickedness and deception in the area of its political existence. The dependent clause, **because you have depended on your own strength and on your many warriors**, introduces a judgment speech that is continued in v 14. The covenant nation does not depend on Yahweh for protection from enemies. It has put its trust in its **own strength** (lit. "in your way") and in the size of its army. Israel's self-sufficiency and self-reliance reveals its pride and arrogance and independence from its covenant partner.

Verse 14 indicates that war, destruction, and terrible human casualty will be the fate of the nation that practices wickedness and deception. Moreover, the people have put their trust in their military power; therefore, another military power will now overtake them. The people will hear the uproar of an invading army coming for battle. The enemy forces will destroy Israel's mighty fortifications, which the people have trusted for their protection.

Hosea then compares the destruction the enemy will inflict upon the nation to the devastation of **Beth Arbel** by **Shalman**. Hosea recalls for his audience a terrifying incident that the enemies carried out against the people of Beth Arbel. The enemies, as part of their war strategy, committed the vicious crime of murdering mothers with their children. Such acts indicate extreme cruelty on the part of an invading army; they were also meant to induce great fear among the victims of war. Hosea seems to suggest that such horrifying fate awaits the people of Israel who have pursued a wicked, deceptive, and arrogant way of life.

■ **15** Whatever the place name of Beth Arbel may refer to, Bethel will suffer the same fate (v 15). The cause of Bethel's massive destruction is its ***great evil*** (*ra'at rā'atkem*). Verse 15 indicates that the day of Bethel's destruction will also be the day of the destruction of **the king of Israel**. Yahweh's judgment is upon both the religious and the political institutions of Israel. Both were instrumental in promoting idolatry, wickedness, deception, and self-sufficiency in the land. The oracle ends with an announcement of the end of the kingdom, kingship, and the illegitimate worship center of Israel.

FROM THE TEXT

The people who are rebellious and unfaithful hear in this text words of hope; the prophet invites them to "sow," "reap," "break up," and "seek" and thus to become the people that God had called them to be in the world. They are to become a people who cultivate righteousness in the land and harvest faithfulness or devotion (*ḥesed*) in their relationship with God and others (v 12).

In the reading of this text, the community truly encounters gospel, the good news of hope that in the midst of a rebellious and apparently hopeless people, God does not give up on his covenant people but engages with them to produce that which they have been called to be and to do from the beginning. The invitation of this text does not presume that the people of God can accomplish the challenge of the text by themselves or in their own strength. God is the partner in this work, and planting the seed and harvesting the fruit are done in partnership between God and his people. God's people partner with him, but only God himself can bring the growth. Paul recognizes this reality when he states: "I planted the seed, Apollos watered it, but God has been making it grow. So neither the one who plants nor the one who waters is anything, but only God, who makes things grow" (1 Cor 3:6-7).

9. The Rebellious Child and the Forbearing Parent: A Glimpse of Hope (11:1-11)

BEHIND THE TEXT

In ch 11 the prophet introduces the metaphor of a loving and caring father and his rebellious child. Though there is a shift here from the marriage metaphor of chs 1—3, the parent-child metaphor continues the theme of Israel's covenant-breaking way of life. This chapter seems to provide a historical overview of Israel's past and present relationship with Yahweh. Hosea recalls the core traditions of deliverance from Egypt (v 1) and guidance in the wilderness (v 3). The themes of Israel's attachment to the fertility gods and Yahweh's love for Israel (see ch 2) also recur in ch 11. The prophet also utilizes the epic story of Sodom and Gomorrah in his reference to Admah and Zeboyim. These two cities allied themselves with and subsequently experienced destruction alongside Sodom and Gomorrah (Gen 14:2; 19:24-25; see also Deut 29:23). As typical of other parts of the book, Ephraim is the preferred name in Hos 11 for northern Israel (vv 3, 8, 9).

The text seems to reflect the chaotic and devastating political events that happened during the final years of King Hoshea (v 6). Hoshea had withheld tribute payment to Assyria and turned to Egypt for assistance, which prompted Shalmaneser V (727-722 B.C.) to invade the northern kingdom (2 Kgs 17:4-5). The reference in Hos 11:5 to Israel's return to Egypt may reflect Hoshea's pro-Egyptian stance. On the other hand, the reference may refer to the flight of some Israelites to Egypt during Tiglath-Pileser III's attack in 733 B.C. At this time, Assyria acquired most of the territory of Israel and had deported at least some Israelites to Assyria (see Wolff 1974, 197; Mays 1969, 155; Limburg 1988, 38-39). The divine distress over the fate of the covenant people in v 8 seems to presuppose destruction well underway in Israel. The reference to the return of the people from Egypt and Assyria in v 11 implies voluntary exile of some of the Israelites to Egypt and forced migration of others to various parts of the Assyrian Empire.

Most commentators take the whole chapter as a single literary unit. Wolff designates this chapter as a *historic-theological accusation*, structured in the form of a lawsuit made by a father against his rebellious child (1974, 193). Yahweh speaks in first person throughout this text except in v 10. The divine sayings address Israel in the third person in vv 1-7 but shift to direct address in vv 8-9. Wolff suggests that vv 1-7 constitute the complaint brought before the court by the plaintiff, whereas vv 8 ff. contain a "proposal to reach a settlement" "addressed directly to the defendant" by the plaintiff (1974, 194). The text begins with Yahweh's recalling of his redemptive act of Israel ("out of Egypt"; v 1) and ends with the promise that Israel will return from their exile in Egypt and Assyria and that Yahweh will settle them "in their homes" (v 11). The text thus anticipates a second exodus, this time not only from Egypt but also from Israel's exile in the Assyrian lands.

In the Hebrew text, ch 11 ends with v 11; v 12 in English translations is 12:1 in the MT. In this arrangement, the series of accusations and judgments in chs 4—10 ends with a portrayal of the divine love. This pattern is similar to the depiction of divine love at the conclusion of chs 1—3. Chapters 12—14 also end with statements about divine grace and mercy (see 14:4-9).

IN THE TEXT

■ **1** The unit begins with Yahweh's reminiscence of his deliverance of Israel from Egypt when the nation was at a tender age. The Hebrew term *naʿar* may mean an infant, a weaned child, an adolescent, or a household servant or personal attendant. Mays suggests that the term here conveys the idea of "helpless dependence on an adult" (1969, 153).

Verse 1 makes clear that divine love was the motivation for Yahweh's deliverance of Israel from Egypt. The link between Yahweh's love and his redemption of Israel is central to the theology of the book of Deuteronomy (see Deut 7:8, 13; 10:15; 23:5). Hosea is the first prophet to describe love as the basis of Yahweh's relationship with Israel.

In v 1, **I loved him** is parallel to **I called my son**. Divine love prompts and motivates the divine call of Israel or the election of Israel to a unique relationship between Yahweh and Israel that would culminate in the covenant at Sinai. The preposition *min* ("from") can certainly mean **out of;** thus **out of Egypt** may refer specifically to Israel's exodus or going out from Egypt. However, v 1 also seems to suggest that Yahweh's call of Israel is broader than the saving event. The call came even when Israel was in bondage and slavery in Egypt. The prophet clearly understands the interrelationship of Egypt and Yahweh's covenant with his people (2:15; 12:9; 13:4).

The phrase **my son** describes the relationship of covenantal love shared between Yahweh and his people. This metaphor demonstrates the manner in which "Israel is to be closely and inseparably united with Yahweh" as his "personal property" and as his "holy people" (Wolff 1974, 198; see also Deut 14:1).

■ **2** Verse 2 sums up Israel's rebellious response to Yahweh's continued and consistent calling of his people. The MT literally reads, "They called them; they walked from them." Most English translations reflect the LXX reading ("I called them; they walked from me"). The third-person reference in the MT could refer to the call extended to Israel by the prophets to live by the covenantal instructions and Israel's stubborn refusal to pay attention to the prophets. Both the MT and the LXX convey the reality of Yahweh's ongoing care and protection of his people. Mays observes that each subsequent act of Yahweh "is a validation and renewal of election that makes the Exodus a constantly contemporary reality for Israel" (1969, 154). The people's movement away from Yahweh was not simply a departure from God. It was also a turning toward the Baals and the idols to whom the people made sacrifice and offered incense (see 2:13; 4:12-14, 17).

■ **3** In v 3 Hosea depicts Yahweh as a parent who taught Israel how to walk. The prophet employs an unusual verb related to the foot (*rāgal*) to convey the divine training. The divine activity is not simply a teaching to walk but a training of the feet themselves. In a moment filled with pathos, Yahweh recalls taking his child by the child's arms, presumably to give the child ongoing support and guidance as the child learned to walk. In spite of the vigilant parental care, the people of God ***did not know*** (*yādaʿ*) that Yahweh was the one **who healed them**. For Hosea, the healing activity of Yahweh demonstrates the divine rescue from that which endangers the people of Yahweh, particularly political threats (see 5:13; 6:1; 7:1). The people of Yahweh have failed to know him as the provider of grain, wine, oil, silver, and gold (2:8), and as their healer. This lack of knowledge of Yahweh (see 4:1) is what led them to turn away from him and to put their trust in other religious and political powers.

■ **4** In v 4, Hosea returns to the image of the faithful divine parent who led his people out of Egypt and guided them through the wilderness. Both the NIV and NRSV translate the opening Hebrew phrase (lit. "cords of human") as **cords of human kindness**. While such cords often mean captivity and subjection (see 1 Kgs 20:31, 32) or a trap (see Job 18:10; Ps 140:5 [140:6 HB]), Yahweh used them to bring freedom and life to his people. **I led them** (*māšak*) here conveys the idea of gently drawing, though the verb can also mean hostility that results in captivity (e.g., see Judg 4:7; Pss 10:9; 28:3; Ezek 32:20) or dragging an undomesticated animal (see Deut 21:3-4). **Ties of love** (lit. "twisted cords of love") serve as parallel to **cords of human kindness**. God's love for his people is the basis of his humane treatment of his people. In the next line, Yahweh states that he was to Israel like one who lifts the yoke off of the ***jaws*** of an animal in order to feed the animal with gentleness. Some translations prefer an alternative reading *ʿul* (infant) instead of the MT *ʿōl* (**yoke**). This reading conveys the image of a parent lifting up a nursing child to one's cheeks (see NRSV).

The textual evidence appears to support the image of taking off the yoke from an animal's jaws in order to feed it. Nevertheless, one might also argue for the image of the child over against the animal in order to maintain consistency with the opening verses (see Yee 1996, 277; Mays 1969, 154-55; Wolff 1974, 191, 199-200). Certainly the images of both son and animal seem to merge together in Hos 11:1-4, similar to their merging in Jer 31:18-20.

The last line of Hos 11:4, ***I bent down to him and fed,*** continues the image of Yahweh as a caring and self-giving divine parent. He nourished his people who were weak and powerless with care and love by reaching down to them at their level of weakness and helplessness. Wolff finds here an "expressive picture of divine condescension" (1974, 200).

■ **5** The transition from v 4 to v 5 is quite abrupt. Verse 5 begins with the negative particle *lōʾ* ("not"), which seems to negate the verb **return** (thus, literally, "he will not return to the land of Egypt"). One might also translate this statement as a rhetorical question, as the NIV does (the NIV changes the subject to third-person plural). Based on the LXX, some translations assume here a scribal error (confusion caused by similar sounding words) and emend the MT *lōʾ* to *lô* ("to him") and attach this prepositional phrase to v 4 ("I bent down to him and I fed him"; see NRSV). A third possibility is to keep the negative particle in place and to see here Yahweh's announcement that the people will actually not return to Egypt, but rather they will experience a new captivity in Assyria (see Limburg 1988, 39). The difficulty with this interpretation, however, lies in Hosea's other statements concerning both the people's return to Egyptian captivity (see 8:13; 9:3, 6) and their eventual return from Egyptian captivity (see 11:11).

The rest of v 5 and v 6 reflect a wartime situation, most likely the invasion of Israel by Shalmaneser V as a punitive action during the early part of his reign. The reference to the return to ***the land of*** **Egypt** suggests Hoshea's pro-Egyptian politics. Though Assyria is clearly the ruling power with which Hoshea has made a treaty, the nation seeks political alliance with Egypt in the hopes of gaining freedom from the Assyrian rule. Seeking Egyptian help is futile, because Egypt cannot save Israel from the Assyrian rule. Yahweh has given Israel over to the Assyrian king for him to exercise his kingship (the verb *mālak* means "to be king") over Israel. Israel is in this predicament because it refuses to **repent** (*šûb*) or return to Yahweh, the true king of Israel, who alone can save the nation from its enemies.

■ **6** In v 6, the prophet simply describes the warfare that will overtake the people. ***The sword will whirl about*** in the cities of Israel. The plural form of *bad* can refer to "empty or idle talkers" (see Job 11:3; Isa 16:6). As both Isa 44:25 and Jer 50:36 use the word to describe the empty-talking false prophets, so too Hosea may employ the term to depict the **false prophets** of his day. Some commentators think that the second line of Hos 11:6 refers to the destruction of the empty-talkers or the oracle-giving priests and the false prophets in the city gates (see the NRSV). This meaning fits well with the last line that deals with **an end to their plans**; that is, plans of the empty-talkers. The reference may be to the pro-Egyptian and anti-Assyrian political counsel that the priests and the false prophets were giving to King Hoshea and his officials.

■ **7** Destruction of war and an end to their political counsel do not prompt the people to turn to Yahweh for help. They remain stubborn in spite of their precarious situation. In v 7, Yahweh sums up Israel's long history of turning away from him. Though the nation is determined to turn away from him, Yahweh still describes them as **my people**. Yahweh loves his people, but they do not reciprocate with their love but rather with their stubborn turning away from him. Instead of calling on Yahweh for help, they call to *ʿal* who does not ***raise*** them up. While the reference to **Most High** (*ʿal*) often denotes the God of Israel, some understand the use of the term here as a reference to Baal (perhaps a textual error or misspelling of *baʿal*). It is not clear if the subject of the verb ***raise*** is Yahweh or Baal. If Yahweh is intended, the message is that he will not help the stubborn and rebellious people. If Baal is the subject, then the message is that Baal cannot help Israel because Baal is an idol with no power.

■**8** Verse 8 introduces a transition in the divine speech, which turns from judgment to a ray of hope for the people who are faced with warfare, captivity, and total destruction. The plaintiff experiences deep inner struggle because of the prospect of death that faces the defendants and moves to act with compassion. Verse 8 begins with rhetorical questions (introduced by the particle *ʾêk* twice) that convey Yahweh's anguish over his rebellious child as well as his determination to spare the child from the sentence of death. Addressing the nation as Ephraim and Israel, Yahweh announces that he cannot **give** them **up** or **hand** them **over** to their enemies who would destroy them completely. The people of Israel do not belong to Egypt or Assyria or to Baal; they belong to Yahweh. Therefore, he cannot treat them like **Admah** and **Zeboyim**, the cities that were destroyed along with Sodom and Gomorrah (see Deut 29:23).

The concluding lines of Hos 11:8 explain why Yahweh's attitude to his people has changed. Yahweh declares that his **heart** has been turned or overturned (*hāpak*) upon himself. In the Hebrew thinking, the **heart** (*lēb*) represents the seat of the intellect and will. The statement, **My heart is changed within me,** conveys the idea that the divine will or thought process has overturned the intended divine plans. Yahweh states that he has changed his mind.

The concluding line of v 8 describes the impetus behind the divine change of mind. In the NIV, Yahweh declares that his **compassion** (lit. "my compassions"; *niḥûmāy*, from the verb *nāḥam*) has been **aroused**. The verb *nāḥam* often conveys a sorrow or grief that leads one to repent or to change one's mind. When Yahweh is the subject, the verb conveys the divine change of mind concerning previous intentions (e.g., see Exod 32:12, 14; Joel 2:14; Jonah 3:9). The plural form of the noun ("my compassions") likely refers to "a quality, a characteristic, a state, or the concept of an action" (see Williams 2007, 2). The prophet uses a unique verb (*kāmar*) to describe what has occurred to the "compassions" of God. A warming to the point of making tender has taken place. That which was firm and established has become soft and pliable. The suffering, grieving nature of God has been affected and warmed so that the divine plans for the people have changed.

■**9** Verse 9 indicates the result of Yahweh's change of mind; he **will not carry out** his **fierce anger**. Yahweh now refuses to express his anger through destructive activities. He will not turn against Ephraim and destroy it. In the second half of v 9, Yahweh provides a theological rationale for his change of mind and new attitude toward Israel. He is **God** (*ʾēl*) and not **man** (*ʾîš*). He is divine; he is not mortal (see also the contrast between divine and human in Num 23:19; Isa 31:3; Ezek 28:2). Human beings are stubborn and hard-hearted, and they refuse to turn back to Yahweh. However, Yahweh is amenable and tender-hearted; he does not desire the destruction of his people but desires their salvation. He does not come in wrath but comes in mercy and compassion.

Yahweh further explains that he is **the Holy One** (*qādôš*) in the midst of the people. This One who is unique and distinct from the commonplace and mundane nature of humanity and creation itself does not take life but gives life. The reference to Yahweh as the one in the midst of the people frequently conveys Yahweh's protection over his people (see Num 14:14; Josh 3:10; Isa 12:6).

Yahweh's announcement that he is divine and not human has an inherent irony in light of the human emotion and pathos found in the preceding verses. In spite of all human depictions of God as spouse and parent, the intensity and depth of the divine love ultimately distinguishes him from all that is human. Divine love—holy love—goes beyond the limits of human love, even the human love between husband and wife, child and parent. Mays has noted that "Hosea's many anthropomorphisms are meant as interpretative analogies, not as essential definitions. The metaphors are incarnations in language. . . . But he transcends the metaphor, is different from that to which he is compared, and free of all its limitations" (1969, 157).

The closing line of Hos 11:9 presents some difficulty. The literal rendering, "I will not come in [upon, against] a city" could be taken to mean that Yahweh has changed his mind concerning the destruction of the cities (**I will not come against their cities**). Because the word for city (*ʿîr*) can mean wrath or rage (see Jer 15:8), some translations render the last line as "I will not come in wrath" (see NRSV). Both renderings clearly denote Yahweh's change of mind. Such a change of mind vis-à-vis the rebellious son stands in direct contrast to the legal stipulations provided in Deut 21:18-21, in which the rebellion of a child results in stoning.

■ **10** The closing verses (Hos 11:10-11) depict the people's return to Yahweh and their settlement in the land. The opening line of v 10 portrays Yahweh as a roaring lion and the people as those who follow the commanding voice of Yahweh with **trembling**. Though the word "trembling" might be taken to mean dread or even fear, it conveys here the idea of trembling or shaking experienced by a startled person. The prophet describes the people as coming from **the west**. "West" (*yām*) also means "sea." If "sea" is the intended meaning here, then it refers to the Mediterranean coastal regions (see Wolff 1974, 203).

■ 11 Verse 11 continues the theme of the return of the people to their homeland. The exiled people will come trembling like birds from Egypt and Assyria. Throughout the book of Hosea, the prophet has spoken against the people's reliance upon these nations (5:13; 7:11; 8:9; 12:1; 14:3) and warned against captivity to these nations (8:13; 9:3, 6; 10:6). The immediate text appears to focus upon the people's physical return from Egypt and Assyria. However, within the broader context of the book, the return from Egypt and Assyria may also indicate Israel's return from its dependency upon these powers to dependency upon Yahweh who alone can rescue and provide for them (see 2:7).

The return of the people will ultimately result in their resettlement in the land of promise. Yahweh himself will cause his people to inhabit or to dwell in their houses once again. He will not merely bring them back, but he will settle them down.

FROM THE TEXT

Hosea 11 is undoubtedly a literary and theological masterpiece within Scripture. The passage stands as a pinnacle to the testimony of the nature of God's grace, wrath, and redeeming love. The text not only allows the otherness of God and the mercy of God to stand side by side, but in the end it depicts divine holiness and divine love as one and the same.

The world portrayed in the text is a world where divine grace is at work

even before Israel has become the covenant community at Sinai. Divine love expressed through divine call precedes any response from the people. In his sermon "On Working Out Our Own Salvation," John Wesley observes that there is no human being "that is wholly void of the grace of God" (Outler and Heitzenrater 1991, 491).

Chapter 11 demonstrates that the same divine grace that went before the people and brought them into initial covenant with God continued to call them back to God in the midst of their infidelity. Paul echoes Hosea's understanding of God's grace at work when he states, "Where sin increased, grace increased all the more" (Rom 5:20).

This grace is ultimately the people's only hope for salvation and restoration. Divine grace finds its expression in a remarkable display of divine love in this text. Wolff finds in this text the tenacious nature of God's love expressed in a number of ways. Israel rejects God's love, but God continues to train and nourish his people. God's "suffering love" "struggles against the divine wrath" and "bears the anguish of neglect within itself" (1974, 203).

The text also portrays the wrath of God particularly in Hos 11:5-7. Limburg notes that "God's love is a 'tough love' which knows that there is a time in the parent/child relationship for punishment" (1988, 41). However, in light of the fuller context of Hosea, the reader must ask just what this "tough love" or wrath described in vv 5-7 really is. Rather than interpreting vv 5-7 as divine judgment against the people, Wolff interprets these verses to be a description of "the consequences of Israel's reactions and Yahweh's new actions" (1974, 194). Mays describes God's wrath as "his active refusal to let Israel go her own way"; God's purpose of punishment is to bring the people back into their status as a covenant people and therefore wrath is not the "final decree" of God (1969, 157). Thus for Hosea, divine wrath is clearly set within the context of covenant. In the midst of his expression of wrath, his will to save and restore the covenant with his people remains firm. In Hosea, as well as in the rest of Scripture, hope is the last word for those who are under the wrath of God (see Eph 2:1-10).

The text reaches its crowning achievement in displaying the holy character of God. Hosea's ultimate concern in ch 11 is not the people's rebellion or God's wrath. It is the gracious love of God that in the end would triumph over both human rebellion and divine wrath. Wolff has argued that the prophet "is much less a witness and plaintiff against Israel's history than he is a witness to the divine love which struggles with Israel as within itself" (1974, 203).

Regarding the holy character of God depicted in ch 11, the reader legitimately might question whether the text portrays God in internal conflict between wrath and love. Fretheim argues that "it is going too far to speak of conflict in God here, for judgment is never the will of God for the people; yet it is God's will to save that makes for an internal tension, and hence suffering, in God when confronted with the concomitant need for justice to be done" (1984, 144).

The reader of the text might then more appropriately speak of the suffering of God in the text rather than conflict within God. The suffering God depicted by Hosea is indeed a vulnerable, relational being. As a relational being, the divine suffering is directly linked to God's being affected by the "other" (i.e., the covenant partner) within the relationship. Hosea's two primary images that both emerge from the domestic setting (i.e., the unfaithful spouse and the rebellious child) particularly lend themselves to a portrayal of God as a vulnerable covenant partner who can be affected by the other. In this text, God grieves over his rebellious child and longs to restore the broken relationship. The vulnerability of the divine parent and his authentic relationship with his child bring about divine suffering, which is clearly evident in this text.

Hosea's God in this text is a God who is capable of and willing to change his mind (will). God's heart turns upon God himself. An outside source has not changed the mind of God. What prompts God to change his mind is his commitment to keep his relationship with his rebellious child who causes suffering and agony to God's heart. He refuses to carry out his own requirement to destroy his defiant child.

Ultimately, mercy is what is at work in God's change of mind. God's mercy—his grace—refuses to leave the people where they are; therefore sinners have hope. The optimism of grace declares that where human rebellion abounds, the grace of God ultimately prevails. Bernhard Anderson rightly points us to the source of the people's optimism when he states, "Israel's hope was grounded solely in the constancy of Yahweh's love for the people" (1986, 305).

So what is the reader to make of such a God as depicted by Hosea? Does Hosea's portrait of God diminish the sovereignty of God? Does such a depiction go too far in bringing the deity down to a human level and thus overlook or even nullify the holiness of God?

Hosea would respond to such an honest question with a resounding "No!" For Hosea this vulnerable, suffering, relational character of God is not an exception to the sovereignty of God. It *is* the sovereignty of God. It is not a contrast to the holiness of God. It *is* the holiness of God. The holy God of Hosea is the God of holy love. Hosea defines holiness in this text as love, which is central to our understanding of God's sovereignty. God expresses his sovereignty in the best way possible—by loving the unlovable, the defiant and rebellious, and by making every effort to restore the broken relationship.

For the reader of the text, that which is ultimately at stake in the text is the very nature of God. For the Christian interpreter, God is not merely a God who seeks relationship; his very being *is* relationship. The One whose name is "Father, Son, and Holy Spirit" does not merely love; he *is* love. He is the holy God in the midst of his people. He calls his people to "participate in the divine nature" by becoming a holy community (2 Pet 1:3-4).

Hosea's portrait of the holy God also defines for God's people what it means to live in the world as those who are transformed by his grace. The text invites its readers to be firmly committed in their faithful relationship to God and others in the world. Participation in the divine nature also means living lives in this sinful and broken world as authentic images of the holy God. Birch states that "the perseverance of God's love and compassion encourages the church to turn toward a broken and rebellious world with the hope of a promise and not the finality of a judgment" (1997, 102).

As the Christian reading audience engages with Hos 11, it has seen and continues to see in Jesus Christ the faithful Son who was called out of Egypt and who remained obedient to the Father's will (Matt 2:15; see Mays 1969, 153, who describes sonship in Hosea as a metaphor for the covenant relationship). It sees in Christ the embodiment of the one who looked upon his war-torn and harassed people and had compassion upon them (see Matt 9:36; 14:14; 15:32; 20:34). Undoubtedly it hears in Christ's parable of the father who received back his wayward son an echo of the divine Father who refused to give up on his rebellious child (Luke 15:11-32).

10. A Tale of Two Kingdoms (11:12—12:1)

BEHIND THE TEXT

The text most likely belongs to the days when King Hoshea broke the treaty with Assyria that he made in 733 B.C. and turned to Egypt for help during a regime change in Assyria in 727 B.C. (12:1). Olive oil was probably the payment Israel made to Egypt for its military help. When Israel turned toward Egypt, Assyria took punitive actions against Israel. The Assyrian invasion of Israel led to the siege and destruction of Samaria in 722/721 B.C.

IN THE TEXT

■ **12** Israel's deceitful relationship with Yahweh seems to be the main theme of v 12. Yahweh states that the people have **surrounded** him much like one surrounds an enemy prior to attack. In whatever direction Yahweh looks, all he sees is falsehood and fraudulent activity that has become characteristic of and prevalent throughout God's people.

The second line of v 12 (**And Judah is unruly against God, even against the faithful Holy One**) is enigmatic. Translations show the difficulty of the Hebrew text (compare the NIV with the NRSV). The Hebrew verb *rûd* (**unruly** in the NIV) conveys the idea of wandering or roaming (thus "roaming with God"), but the next phrase describes Judah as being ***faithful*** to ***the holy ones***. If the reference to God (*ʾēl*) and ***the holy ones*** mean Israel's God and his divine council, or the faithful people in the land, then it is possible to see here the portrayal of Judah in a positive light (see the NRSV). However, if the noun *ʾēl* refers to the Canaanite deity (Baal), then ***the holy ones*** may mean the temple prostitutes of the Canaanite religion. In that case, the people of Judah are also portrayed in a negative light; they roam with Baal and participate in the fertility cult (see Yee 1996, 282; Mays 1969, 160; and Wolff 1974, 210, for various interpretations of v 12).

■ **12:1** In 12:1, Hosea returns once again to Ephraim's deceitful actions. **Ephraim** chases after or hastily pursues **the east wind all day**. The east wind is a destructive wind that brings intense and unbearable heat that "oppresses and drains every form of life" (Noth 1966, 32). The east wind here is most likely a reference to the mighty and destructive power of Assyria. The text may thus allude to Israel's alliance with Assyria in 733 B.C. The text indicates that the nation chases after a power that will ultimately destroy it. Israel entered into a ***covenant*** (*bĕrît*) with Assyria, but it now sends **olive oil** to Egypt. Even in political life, Israel acts without loyalty to the nation to which it pledged fidelity. This kind of treachery already characterizes Israel's covenant relation with God.

FROM THE TEXT

Hosea portrays here a world where the people are busily involved in tending and pursuing that which profits them nothing but will lead only to their destruction. He also portrays here a way of life that can be best described as treacherous, without any commitment to fidelity in relationships. The text of Hosea portrays a worldview that is not different from the worldview subscribed by many in our own world today. The text invites its readers to explore and examine their preoccupations that consume their time, energy, resources, and allegiances to whatever the world may have to offer as sources of security and prosperity. The text also invites its readers to move out of their world of self-sufficiency and treacherous ways of life and move into the world of covenant faithfulness and fidelity in relationships. The text clearly shows that destruction is what awaits a life that is lived by deception and manipulation. The text is also powerfully suggestive. It invites its readers to imagine the blessings that await those who follow the path of fidelity to God and others in their relationship.

B. Concluding Messages of Hope (12:2—14:8)

1. Living Up to a Namesake (12:2-9)

BEHIND THE TEXT

As in ch 2, the prophet draws upon the familiar genre of the lawsuit, but instead of a guilty verdict the defendants hear from the judge a call to repentance and transformation. The text also utilizes the familiar traditions of Jacob, the ancestor of the twelve tribes of Israel. Hosea often draws upon the traditions of the exodus and wilderness period. His use of the preexodus period is unique to this text. The reference to the deception of Jacob links the passage with the previous unit (11:12—12:1).

The prophet makes direct reference to the tradition of Jacob's struggle with his brother in their mother's womb (Gen 25:21-26), Jacob's wrestling with God (Gen 32:22-32), and Jacob's encounter with God at Bethel (Gen 28, 35). However, the text does not seem to provide a strict chronology of the events narrated in Genesis. God met with Jacob at Bethel when he was fleeing from his brother (Gen 28). Jacob's struggle with God took place when he was on his way back to Canaan (Gen 32). According to Gen 35, Jacob returned to Bethel and there God renewed the covenant promises. Hosea seems to have collapsed the two Bethel stories into one; he focuses on Jacob finding God at Bethel and talking with him there.

IN THE TEXT

■ **2** Verse 2 begins with the announcement of Yahweh's litigation or **charge** (*rîb*) against Judah. As we have seen before, similar charges are made against Yahweh's spouse (2:2) and against Israel in 4:1. These charges are located at strategic places in the book. Thus each major section of the book (chs 1—3; 4—11; 12—14) consists of a charge, the development of the accusation, and finally an announcement of restoration.

The prophet's mention of Judah rather than Israel is odd because the remainder of the passage concerns northern Israel (see 11:12 above). Mays is likely correct in observing that "the Judean editor whose work may be seen in 11:12*b* and 12:5 changed the text as a way of applying the message to the other descendants of Jacob in the south" (1969, 162; see also Wolff 1974, 210-11). Hosea does not specify Yahweh's charge, but proceeds to announce Yahweh's plan to **punish Jacob**. The defendant here is most likely Israel, the northern kingdom. The reason for Yahweh's punishment of Jacob is his **ways/deeds**, or the path he had followed. Yahweh will cause to return (**repay**) to the people what they have done.

■ **3** In v 3, the prophet outlines the biography of Jacob, the ancestor of the nation. Hosea begins with the infamous incident that is linked to the name Jacob. Jacob ***took by the heel*** or supplanted (*ʿāqab*, the root verb of the name *yaʿăqōb* or Jacob) his brother (see Gen 25:26) in his mother's womb. The text in Genesis tells that Jacob grabbed the heel of his brother as he came out of the womb. Hosea goes a step further than the Genesis narrative and claims that Jacob was a heel-grabber even within his mother's womb. Hosea thus shows that Jacob was born with the nature of deception, which characterized his life. Hosea also describes Jacob as a full-grown man who **struggled** [*śārâ*, the root verb of the noun "Israel"] **with God**. Hosea uses here a rare term (*ʾôn*) for Jacob, which emphasizes the vigor of full manhood or even "wealth" (in v 8 Hosea uses this term where Ephraim boasts of its wealth).

■ **4** In v 4, the prophet repeats the verb *śārâ* when he describes Jacob's struggle **with the angel**. Hosea is not reporting another incident but the struggle with God mentioned in v 3. Not only did Jacob prevail in this struggle (however, the text is ambiguous here regarding who prevailed over whom), but he also **wept and begged for** God's **favor**. Hosea here makes a shift from a negative portrayal of Jacob toward a positive one.

The second half of v 4 brings the narrative of Jacob to a concluding crescendo. The prophet returns to an earlier event in the life of Jacob that occurred at Bethel. The identity of the subject and the direct object is not clear in the text. Who met whom at Bethel? Did Jacob meet Yahweh, or did Yahweh meet Jacob? The last line in the Hebrew text actually reads, ***he spoke***

with us; this reading presupposes Yahweh as the subject. It is likely that Hosea attempts to bring his audience here into the story of their ancestor to show that they themselves *are* Jacob. The patriarch is one and the same with the people; the people are one and the same with the patriarch. Hence as Jacob (both ancestor and descendants) contritely seeks the divine favor, Yahweh meets Jacob (both ancestor and descendants) at Bethel, Israel's worship center. Hosea seems to give his audience a true understanding of what should take place at Bethel. It should be a genuine place of worship where people seek Yahweh's favor with contrition, a place where the penitent people will hear Yahweh speaking to them. Bethel, the house of God, which has become Beth Aven (see 4:15; 5:8; 10:5), the house of iniquity, can indeed become Bethel once again, the place where Yahweh himself will speak with his people Israel.

■ **5** The liturgical declaration in v 5 clearly identifies the one who spoke with Jacob at Bethel (see similar liturgical declarations in Exod 15:3; Amos 4:13; 5:27). This declaration, ***Yahweh God of hosts; Yahweh is his name***, was likely a significant element of the legitimate Yahweh cult at Bethel. Hosea does not use the usual word for **name** here but employs the word *zēker*, which means "remembrance" or "memorial." Yahweh's name brings to remembrance that he is the God who commands all the cosmic and earthly armies to do his battles (***God of hosts***). It is this mighty and awesome God who meets and speaks with his people at Bethel (see the association of the divine name with the warrior God particularly in Exod 15:3).

God of Hosts

The prophet's epithet of Yahweh as "God of hosts" occurs only at this place in Hosea although the phrase is very common in other prophetic texts. Of the 285 occurrences of the term as a part of the divine epithet in the OT, 251 of those occurrences are in prophetic texts, primarily Jeremiah, Isaiah, Zechariah, Malachi, Haggai, and Amos. The epithet seems to have a strong affiliation with the biblical tradition of the divine warrior. Early in the tradition, the "hosts" likely refers either to the divine army led by Yahweh or to the divine council that carries out the bidding of Yahweh. According to the prophetic view as commander of both divine and human armies, Yahweh directed earthly and cosmic affairs "through the proclamation of his divine decree, delivered by either heavenly or prophetic messages" (Mullen 1992, 303).

■ **6** The prophet makes a direct appeal to the people in v 6. Hosea's words are emphatic: **you must return**. Hosea's call to **return** (*šûb*) here is the typical prophetic call to repentance. The verb is an imperfect that denotes ongoing action. The God to whom the people are called to return is **your God**, the God with whom the people have made a covenant. The closing lines of v 6 express the posture of the people as they return to God. Hosea urges his audience to return to Yahweh in ***covenant faithfulness*** (*ḥesed*) and **justice** (*mišpāṭ*) and to eagerly **wait for** their **God** (see Mic 6:6-8). Covenant faithfulness and justice are not new themes for the prophet (see 2:19; 5:1, 11; 6:6; 10:4, 12). Hosea's words here have an unusual resemblance to Micah's words about Yahweh's requirement from his people. They are to do justice (*mišpāṭ*), to love covenant faithfulness (*ḥesed*), and to walk humbly with God (6:8). The verb *qāwâ* suggests the notion of eagerly waiting or fervently anticipating. Thus, the people's keeping of justice and covenant faithfulness as well as their waiting for Yahweh to act in their lives is not passive; they remain active and attentive.

Justice (*Mišpāṭ*) in the OT

The term *mišpāṭ* finds its home within the law court and generally refers to the rendering of a judgment in a legal case (see Hosea's use in this regard in 5:1, 11; 10:4). Such renderings ultimately sought "the restoration of a situation or environment which promoted equity and harmony (*shalom*) in a community" (Mafico 1992, 1128). Walsh describes justice understood within the Yahweh-worshipping community of Israel in this way:

> The kind of particular *mishpat* Israel understood to be Yahweh's will had to do with the way people dealt with one another, especially in the economic and political sphere. His *mishpat* mandated compassionate regard for defenseless people . . . who would be easy prey for acquisitive and violent men. This interest in the dispossessed or "marginated" was backed up by Yahweh's passionate involvement. Compassion for the widow and the orphan was not just one option among many possible ways of arranging social relationships: it was what the acceptance of Yahweh's *mishpat* operatively meant. (1987, 31)

■ **7** Hosea proceeds to move from the depiction of the ancestor Jacob to specific examples of the fraudulent and haughty character of the people. In v 7, Hosea describes the deceptive practices of the **merchant** (*kĕnaʿan*) who holds dishonest scales in his hand. The term *kĕnaʿan* also refers to "Canaan"/"Canaanite." Hosea's reference in v 7 likely refers to merchants in general. Mays says that Hosea uses this term to convey the message that "Israel has taken on the character of the dwellers in the land and lost his identity as Israel. When God looks at him he sees only a Canaanite trader standing in the market place with crooked scales" (1969, 167; see also Birch 1997, 108). Hosea goes on to say that merchants love to **defraud**. Deceitfulness is not an occasional activity for them, but a passion they pursue in their everyday life.

■ **8** With the impudent face of a deceitful merchant, Ephraim brags about its wealth (**I am . . . rich**) and claims that it ***found*** [*māṣāʾ*] ***wealth*** or vigor (*ʾôn*). However, it also claims that **iniquity or sin** will not be found (*māṣāʾ*) in all of its wealth. The people are not only engaged in deception but also deceive themselves. Through self-deception they remain blind to the relationship between their wealth (*ʾôn*) and their guilt (*ʿāwōn*).

■ **9** Verse 9 begins with Yahweh's self-identification: ***I am Yahweh your God from the land of Egypt*** (or, ***I am Yahweh your God since the land of Egypt***); this statement echoes the preamble statement of the Decalogue (Exod 20:2). This announcement serves the purpose of confronting the people with the reality of God's power both to save them and to bring his judgment upon them for their sins against him. He saved them by his power when they were in captivity in Egypt. Now he announces that he will make them **live in tents again**. They already have a taste of living in tents; during the Festival of Tabernacles or Booths they lived in tents to commemorate the tent dwelling days of their ancestors (see Lev 23:33-43; Deut 16:13-17). The threat here is most likely to the impending exile of the nation and the loss of their homes.

FROM THE TEXT

The text provides significant insight into the function of ancient sacred traditions and even provides a significant example of both a biblical hermeneutic and homiletic. Hosea neither allegorizes the story of Jacob nor explains the story of Jacob. The prophet simply invites the people of the eighth century B.C. to see themselves in and through their ancestor Jacob. By collapsing the world of the "then" and the "now," Hosea's audience became one with the biblical narrative. The movement from "him" to "us" (v 4) was not only natural but also legitimate. Through this mode of interpretation (i.e., hermeneutic), the sacred tradition becomes the narrative that not only defined the character Jacob but also defined Hosea's listeners. Becoming characters in the story, they stand within the text as participants rather than outside of the text as observers.

The text also provides a legitimate structure by which to deliver a message (i.e., a homiletic), moving very naturally from "bad news" to "good news." In the first movement, the prophet depicts the deceitful and game-playing Jacob. In the second move, he portrays the contrition and seeking of divine favor. In the third move, he announces the divine presence accompanied by divine word. With the arrival of Yahweh, the prophet breaks into a liturgical affirmation concerning the very nature and being of God as revealed through his name. In a final move that emerges directly out of the affirmation of Yahweh's being, the prophet charges the people to embody their divine encounter through faithfulness, justice, and hope.

This very natural movement we find within the text also conveys to us two theological affirmations central to Hosea. In the first place, before the prophet ever calls the people to return or makes promise of their return, he declares the name of Yahweh. The gracious and merciful God known in his name and embodied through his acts always precedes the divine call to repentance or the divine promise of hope. Without this divine initiative, repentance is nothing but the human attempt of "trying harder," and hope is nothing but the human endeavor of "positive thinking."

Second, the text insists on the possibility of human transformation. Jacob the heel-grabber becomes Israel the God-wrestler. According to Hosea, the God-wrestler becomes a contrite seeker of divine favor. This human transformation through the divine encounter also points to the possibility of the transformation of the "house of iniquity" (Beth Aven) to the "house of God" (Beth El). Divine-human encounter changes people and the way they worship God. Yee notes the manner in which Jacob "becomes, through his world-changing struggle with God, the nation's paradigm for repentance. He urges his descendants to undergo a similar transformative confrontation with God" (1996, 284). The optimism of divine grace in this narrative as presented by Hosea clearly holds out hope for a covenant people whose faithfulness has been like the morning mist. The God who calls his people to wholehearted fidelity continues to meet his people. Regardless of the wickedness that resides in the "house" (Beth Aven), hope remains that God will move in and once again reside in the "house" (Beth El).

The text also communicates a word of warning to its readers. It clearly shows the possibility of wealth becoming the source and a hideout of pride and iniquity. The final outcome of wealth through deception is self-deception. The people of Israel boast in their wealth, which is the fruit of their injustice and oppression, and fail to see any iniquity in their life. Birch provides an important warning to the people of God today: "Unfortunately, the boastful, self-centered trader is not really an unknown figure to us in our nation and churches. Many believe that success vindicates their methods of reaching it. Many confuse the traits and values of contemporary culture for God's values" (1997, 109). The warning of the text to its readers also serves as an invitation—a call to create a faithful community in which transparent introspection and honest confession are practiced by all of its members.

2. Divine Faithfulness—Human Rebellion (12:10—13:13)

BEHIND THE TEXT

This text, which is comprised of a series of oracles, contains a mixture of Yahweh's recollection of his numerous attempts to bring the people back to himself and incidents of the rebellion and unfaithfulness of Israel. The text concludes with the announcement of Yahweh's judgment of Israel (13:9-13). This collection of oracles provides a summary of the prophet's message. The text revisits various themes and images already found in the book. Places such as Gilgal (4:15; 9:15) and Gilead (6:8), concern over idol-making and the worship of the calf (8:4-6), the people's pride (5:5; 7:10), their forgetfulness

(2:13; 8:14), deliverance from Egypt (11:1; 12:9), the image of the morning dew (6:4), and the destructive lion (5:14) all reappear in the text.

Hosea also introduces an episode in the life of Jacob for the first time in the book—the story of Jacob going to the land of Aram and working there to get a wife (Gen 27:42-46; 29:1-30). Hosea seems to introduce this story to emphasize the significance of Aram in the history of the northern kingdom. The term "Aram"/"Arameans" refers to the territory of Syria/Syrians. Aram-Damascus on Israel's northeastern border was one of the most powerful city-states in the ninth and eighth centuries B.C. Throughout the history of the northern kingdom, it had frequent military conflicts with Aram-Damascus. In the last quarter of the eighth century, however, Israel joined with Aram to resist the Assyrian imperial power, which eventually led to the annexation of both nations into the Assyrian Empire. Wolff suggests that the passage with the reference to Aram might have originated within a decade after the Syrian-Israelite alliance against Assyria (1974, 209).

In addition to the Jacob/Aram tradition, Hosea also draws upon the tradition associated with Moses as the premier Israelite prophet. Without specifically naming Moses, Hosea also draws upon the Deuteronomic tradition of Moses as the father of the great line of Israelite prophets. The text in Hosea is likely one of the first to describe Moses as a prophet, a tradition later developed in Deuteronomy.

12:10 The text begins with Yahweh's recollection of his consistent attempt to speak to Israel though his prophets (12:10-13). However, Ephraim/Israel's response was a contemptuous disregard for Yahweh's prophets and his words; moreover, the nation only multiplied its sins (12:14—13:2). Yahweh pronounces his judgment on the nation in 13:3 and calls for their undivided loyalty to him in 13:4-5. The text concludes with another oracle that focuses on Israel's sins and Yahweh's judgment on his people (13:6-13).

IN THE TEXT

■ **10** Yahweh is the speaker in v 10; he begins by describing his method of communication to the prophets. In 6:5 Hosea speaks about Yahweh using his prophets to destroy the unfaithful people with the words of his mouth. Here the focus is on the prophets (*nābî'*) as the recipients of divine revelation, which they then communicated to the people. Not only did he speak (*dābār*) his word, but he also increased the number of prophetic **visions** (*ḥāzôn*). Prophets both heard and saw the word of Yahweh. The people cannot blame their situation on lack of divine revelation. Yahweh has been faithful.

The concluding line of 12:10 is difficult. The translation, **and told parables through them**, is based on reading the verb as *dāmâ* ("speak a parable"). The NRSV reading, "through the prophets I will bring destruction," assumes the verb *dāmam* ("bring destruction"). The NIV reading suggests parables as a third means of communication. However, it is also possible that Hosea may be reiterating what he says in 6:5. Prophets were messengers of words of salvation as well as words of destruction (Jer 1:10).

■ **11** Gilead's wickedness and the impending destruction of its inhabitants and altars is the theme of Hos 12:11. The first half of the verse (***If Gilead is iniquity, they will become nothingness***) implies the destruction of the people of Gilead, most likely by the Assyrians. The prophet also depicts Gilgal as a place of corrupt worship practices and announces that the altars where the people sacrifice will become **piles of stones on a plowed field**. Total destruction of the cultic centers in Gilgal is announced here.

■ **12** In v 12, Hosea returns to the story of Jacob, his flight from Esau, and his service to Laban to gain Rachel as his wife (Gen 29). However, again as in Hos 12:2-4, the prophet retells the story according to his theological and didactic purposes. The emphasis of this verse is on Jacob's activity to **get a wife**. Literally, the text reads, ***Israel served in exchange for a wife, and in exchange for a wife he kept*** (NIV adds **sheep**). Hosea portrays Jacob as a person who is engaged in hard labor in order to gain what he desired. Mays has suggested that "the reference to Jacob's service for the sake of a wife could be an allusion to Israel's proclivity for the sexual cult of Canaan" (1969, 169-70; see also Wolff 1974, 216). Even more broadly, the character of Jacob reflects the character of the nation Israel, which toils with and enters into relationship with both nations and gods to achieve blessing and security. Jacob's fleeing to Aram and serving there can function in the text as a veiled reference to Israel's submission and servitude to the various nations.

■ **13** The theme of Israel's servitude continues in v 13. Hosea shifts his attention to Israel's bondage in Egypt and portrays Jacob/Israel in bondage as the recipient of Yahweh's salvation. He brought Israel out of Egypt through the agency of a prophet. Not only did Yahweh deliver Israel by means of a prophet, but he ***watched over*** Israel by means of a prophet. Certainly Hosea has in mind the agency of Moses the prophet par excellence through whom Yahweh led Israel out of Egypt.

■ **14** Rather than listening to the voice of Yahweh via the prophets, Ephraim **aroused** Yahweh's **bitter anger** (see Judg 2:12; 1 Kgs 14:9, 15; 16:33; Jer 7:18-19; 11:17; 32:29, 32, etc.). Although the NIV speaks of anger, the text states that Ephraim has provoked "bitterness." The actions of the people have brought about deep, bitter grief in the heart of God. The text does not explicitly state what the people have done to affect Yahweh. In light of the preceding verses, the people appear to have rejected Yahweh's prophetic activity among them.

In the second half of the verse, the prophet presents the verdict. Interestingly, Hosea refers to Yahweh as **Lord** (*ʾādôn*), a divine title that conveys his authority over his people. Mays observes that "the one who rules Israel will turn the reproach back on the guilty as a revelation of his lordship" (1969, 171). Ephraim's **Lord** will not cover up the crime of the people, but he will ultimately return upon the people their own contempt. Yahweh will leave the spilled blood upon the people. This indicates the guilt of shedding innocent blood by the people. Death is the penalty for bloodshed (see Lev 17:4; 20:9-16, 27). Hosea 12:14 ends with the note that Yahweh will **repay** the guilty for their total disregard for Yahweh.

■ **13:1** In 13:1-3 Hosea proceeds to describe the rebellion and infidelity of the people. He begins v 1 with a reminder of the early glory of **Ephraim**. While Hosea oftentimes uses the term "Ephraim" in its broader sense to refer to all of the northern kingdom, the immediate context in v 1 seems to refer specifically to the tribe of Ephraim. As the center of the northern kingdom's political, economic, and religious life, Ephraim had been ***raised above*** the other tribes of Israel; others **trembled** (*rĕtēt*) when they heard the words of Ephraim (see Isa 7:2).

In spite of Ephraim's exalted position, the people are guilty on account of Baal. Though **Baal worship** certainly conveys the sense of the text, the text more broadly states that the guilt is simply on account of Baal. Yee suggests that the expression "in" or "at" Baal likely refers to a place, perhaps Baal-Peor (1996, 288) (Num 25:1-18). At Baal-Peor, the people did not experience the fertility that baalism had promised but instead suffered death, the result of their guilt. In Hosea's time, death continued to be at work, this time through the agency of the Assyrian army, which began its devastation of the northern kingdom in 733 B.C.

■ **2** With the opening particle in v 2 (**now**), the prophet moves from the past rebellion of the people. Though death has come upon the people, they continue or even increase their sin by making for themselves **idols** (*massēkâ*) of molten metal (see Exod 32:4, 8). The text does seem clearly to have in mind the golden calf set up by Jeroboam I at Bethel (see 1 Kgs 12:28-30). Although the prophet speaks of this image in the singular, the subsequent reference to ***idols*** and ***calves*** indicates that the practice extended far beyond the one calf at Bethel. These idols are made by the people according to their own discernment or the knowledge and understanding that they possess (**cleverly fashioned images**).

The closing line of Hos 13:2 presents a difficulty in translation. Literally the Hebrew text reads as follows: ***They say, "Ones who sacrifice humanity*** [*ʾādām*] ***are kissing calves."*** The grammatical construction indicates that the prophet clearly has in mind the atrocity of human sacrifice. This statement suggests that the people were involved in human sacrifice as a way of showing their allegiance to **calf-idols**. The cultic ritual of kissing the images of the deity indicated the worshippers' loyalty to them (1 Kgs 19:18).

3 In 13:3, Hosea describes the effect of the people's rebellion by introducing the images of four objects that disappear rapidly. These images are stacked together to display the intensity of Yahweh's judgment. The people will become like **the morning mist**, that is, just as their covenant faithfulness has all too frequently been (6:4). They will become **like the early dew that disappears**. They will become like **chaff *storm-driven* from a threshing floor**. Here the prophet uses a verb that indicates more than an object blowing in the wind but rather an object caught up in the ferocity of a howling wind. Finally, they will become like **smoke escaping through a window**. The mighty and exalted Ephraim will soon vanish completely from the stage of human history. The nation known as Ephraim ("to be fruitful") will evaporate into nothingness.

4 The theme of Yahweh's faithfulness, Israel's forgetfulness, and Yahweh's judgment is continued in 13:4-8. Verse 4 echoes the preamble statement in the Decalogue (Exod 20:2-3; see also Hos 12:9). Yahweh has been to his people their covenant God (**your God**); his self-identification is linked to his redemption of his people from their bondage in Egypt. The NIV does not fully convey the sense of the second half of 13:4. Rather than a command to acknowledge no God but Yahweh, the text actually declares that the people ***do not know*** (*yāda*ʿ) any other God but Yahweh. The call here is for complete exclusivity in relationship to Yahweh. Yahweh is the only God with whom Israel shares covenant (see the similar language of Yahweh's covenant knowledge of Israel in Amos 3:2). The statement sets Yahweh apart from all other deities as Israel's *only* God. In the last line of v 4, Yahweh claims that Israel has known no other **Savior** except Yahweh. To know Yahweh as God is to know him as Savior. Hosea's name (*hôšēa*ʿ means "salvation") most clearly resounds the conviction of the prophet that salvation is found in Yahweh alone.

5 In v 5, he proceeds to address Yahweh's continual provision in the wilderness (***I knew you*** **in the wilderness**). The NIV (**cared for you**) does not adequately convey the idea of the Hebrew verb *yāda*ʿ in this verse. The verb here depicts "the recognition extended by a suzerain through treaty to a vassal" (Mays 1969, 175). Thus this covenant-making God who ***knew*** his people acted upon that knowledge by actively demonstrating covenant faithfulness to his people. The description of the wilderness as ***a land of drought*** extends the meaning of the knowledge of Yahweh to his involvement in the life of his people in the wilderness. The recipients of Yahweh's covenant knowledge were also the recipients of his loving care and protection.

6 In the first half of v 6, Hosea describes Yahweh's provision in the wilderness and the ungrateful response of the people. Yahweh's provision included his feeding of his people; the imagery thus shifts from the infertile barrenness of the desert to the fertile and green pasturage into which a shepherd guides his flock. In this lush pasture, the sheep of Yahweh were satisfied even to the point of saturation. Midway in v 6, the story abruptly changes. When the people became saturated with the blessings of God, their heart became proud and exalted. Their pride led them to their forgetfulness of the source of their provisions (see the warning in Deut 6:10-13; 8:11-20). To have forgotten Yahweh is in effect not to know Yahweh (Hos 2:8; 4:1, 6; 5:4; 6:6).

■ **7-8** In 13:7-8, the divine shepherd who has protected his flock from wild beasts becomes the predator who attacks and destroys his flock. The images of predatory beasts (**lion**, **leopard**, **bear**) emerge out of the context of ancient Near Eastern curses against the party who might break the treaty (Mays 1969, 175-76). Hosea joins these wild animals to dramatic verbs in order to portray the horrific action that Yahweh will take against his people (a leopard's watching slyly, a bear's encountering and ripping open, a lion's devouring, and a wild animal's breaking wide open). The people who became proud and ungrateful will experience painful death and suffer total destruction.

■ **9** Hosea makes clear the reason for the destruction of Israel in v 9. The Hebrew text also makes clear that Yahweh is the subject of the destructive activity (the text literally reads as follows: ***He will destroy you, O Israel***). In the second line, Yahweh speaks in first person. Translations attempt to remove this ambiguity either by the use of passive construction as in the NIV (**You are destroyed, Israel**) or by emending the first line to a first-person speech (see NRSV: "I will destroy you, O Israel"). The second line of v 9 is not completely clear in the Hebrew text. Literally, it reads, ***Because in me*** [is] ***in your helper***. The twice occurring preposition ("in") can function in an adversative manner. Thus the text could be read as follows: **Because [you are] against me**, **against your helper** (see NIV). The Hebrew text thus suggests that the people are being destroyed because they have acted against their divine helper. The LXX reads this line as a question ("Who is your helper?" See NRSV, "Who can help you?"). Israel's tradition affirmed its faith in God as the **helper** (*ʿēzer*) (see 1 Sam 7:12; Pss 115:9-11; 121). Israel at this point in its history is without a helper, either divine or human.

■ **10** The first line of Hos 13:10 is also problematic. In the Hebrew text, Yahweh simply declares, ***I am*** [will be] ***your king***. However, with the simple reversal of the last two consonants (from *ʾhy* to *ʾyh*) the phrase changes to an interrogative particle ("where"). The text would then read, "Where is your king?" rather than "I am your king." Both the NIV and NRSV translate the statement as a question (**Where is your king . . . ?**). In light of the content and structure of the remainder of this line (**that he may save you**), it is reasonable to assume that the MT may have suffered textual corruption here. This question perhaps reflects the takeover of Israel by the Assyrians, particularly the arrest of King Hoshea by Shalmaneser V (2 Kgs 17:4). In the remainder of the verse, Hosea broadens the political arena to include the royal entourage, likely those persons who rendered judgment on behalf of the king in the various regions of the kingdom. The people rejected Yahweh's kingship and demanded a human king, so that they would be like other nations (1 Sam 8:4-5). The king and the rulers the people have chosen for themselves are of no help to the people; they cannot save themselves or the people from Yahweh's judgment.

■ **11** In v 11, Hosea continues his reminder to the people that Yahweh did not contrive the idea of a king (see Hos 8:4). This idea emerged from the people. Yet out of his **anger**, he **gave** them a king; however, out of his overflowing rage, he now **took** the king **away** from the people. The verbs "to give" and "to take" indicate that Yahweh remains as king in spite of the failed monarchy and maintains his sovereign rule over both his people and their king.

■ **12** In v 12, the prophet reminds Israel that their **guilt** (*ʿāwōn*) and ***sin*** (*ḥaṭṭāʾâ*) have been **stored up** and **kept on record**. Mays relates the language here to "the practice of tying together papyrus and parchment documents and putting them in a depository for safe-keeping (cf. Isa 8:16)" (1969, 180). Yahweh has enough evidence of his own to carry out his judgment against those who have violated his covenant stipulations.

■ **13** The metaphor in Hos 13:13 compares Israel to an infant in its mother's womb; though the time of its birth has come, it refuses to be born. The text depicts Ephraim as **a child without wisdom**. When the time of delivery comes, he is not able to position himself at the opening of **the womb**. The people choose the destiny of an infant that would rather die in the womb than welcome the opportunity for life by coming out of its mother's womb. They welcome death and reject the offer of life.

FROM THE TEXT

The text reflects the realities of the world that God has called his people to enter into, and the actual world in which the people live and shape their destiny. God called the people from their bondage in Egypt and declared himself as Israel's only God. The people were to know no other God but the God who saved them from the land of Egypt. They were to have no other savior but the God who delivered them from their bondage. This salvation was not a once-and-for-all moment in the life of the people. Rather it ushered in a continuous covenant relationship in which God would be Israel's God and Israel would be his people.

The text, however, makes clear that God's people have habitually rejected Yahweh (12:10, 13). In rejecting the prophetic word, the people have rejected God himself. The divine messenger and his God are inexorably linked. To reject one is to reject the other. Jesus reiterates this theme when he speaks to the seventy: "Whoever listens to you listens to me; whoever rejects you rejects me; but whoever rejects me rejects him who sent me" (Luke 10:16; see also 2 Thess 2:14). For the Christian reader of the text, the prophetic message uniquely lays "bare the offenses committed by those who misjudge or who reproach the witnesses to Jesus Christ" (Wolff 1974, 218).

The prophetic statement concerning the fall of the once mighty Ephraim serves as an enduring warning to both individuals and institutions. One cannot engage in this text without being reminded of the fleeting and temporary nature of prestige, power, and wealth. Within the larger context of the canon, one also hears in this text the echoes of Jesus' warning about gaining the whole world but forfeiting one's soul (Mark 8:35-36).

The text also confronts its reading community with the call to exclusivity in its relation to God and to acknowledge God as its sole deliverer and provider (Hos 13:4). The text suggests that the key to maintaining exclusivity in relation is the community's commitment to return to the narrative that defines and shapes its identity as the people of God. Their narrative is first and foremost a narrative of redemption. They know no other God; they have no other savior (Deut 6:4-5; Mark 12:28-30).

The text is also a powerful warning to God's people against pride that leads to destruction (Hos 13:6). Israel's pride led to their forgetfulness of God and his past and present provisions for life. Their forgetfulness of Yahweh led them to their frenzied attempts—from human sacrifice to kissing a calf—to get what they wanted in their life. Mays observes that "they seek salvation by means of what is actually sin, and so hope to find life in what works death" (1969, 172). The text invites its readers to reflect on worship that evokes memory of God's redemptive work, instill faithfulness in the worshipping community, and nurture gratitude for God's gracious provisions in life. The outcome of faithful worship—worship in the Spirit and truth—is abundant life, life lived in true fellowship with God through Jesus Christ (John 4:24; 10:10).

3. Divine Contemplation—Divine Decision (13:14-16)

BEHIND THE TEXT

The closing verses of ch 13 emerge directly out of the preceding passage, which conveys the image of Ephraim as an unborn child in the womb. In v 14, Yahweh engages in a direct speech addressed to the power of death. The term *Sheol* ("the grave") twice appears in parallelism with "death" (*mawet*) in this verse.

Sheol

Sheol is a familiar concept throughout the OT. It functions poetically as a legitimate synonym for death as the ancient Hebrews understood Sheol as the abode of the dead. It was neither a place of reward nor a place of punishment. Texts often describe one as "going down" into Sheol, and typically writers depict Sheol as dark, dusty, and silent. Oftentimes, images of watery chaos appear

alongside Sheol. These depictions simply represent poetic images of the grave itself. It is likely that the common ancient Near Eastern understanding of the place in which the dead reside may have informed the ancient Hebrews' understanding of Sheol (regarding the ancient Near Eastern view of death and the depiction of Sheol in the OT, see Lewis 1992, 101-5).

The closing lines of v 16 appear to depict the terror brought on during the collapse of Samaria by Shalmaneser V's destructive forces. The Assyrian troops are on the verge of bringing down the city that had served as the northern kingdom's political and economic nerve center since the time of King Omri (see 1 Kgs 16:24). The statement likely depicts the final years of Hoshea's reign, perhaps as he was making his last attempts to overcome the Assyrian power or as the city lay under the three-year siege by the Assyrians (2 Kgs 17:5).

IN THE TEXT

■ **14** Yahweh is the speaker in Hos 13:14. The womb of the mother in v 13 is depicted here as the dark and watery chaos of Sheol. What the text itself conveys, however, is quite ambiguous, and the text can ultimately convey two extreme opposite thoughts (see Yee 1996, 291).

On the one hand, the text may be read as Yahweh's decision to intervene and deliver the infant that refuses to come out of its mother's womb (see
v 13): **I will deliver . . . I will redeem**. On the other hand, the text could be 13:14
read as questions that convey Yahweh's determination to let the infant die in its mother's womb: ***Shall I ransom. . . . Shall I redeem*** (see NASB, NLT, NJB, NRSV). In either case, the text personifies the power of death as having grasped the people. They are already in the clasp of death. Therefore, the only possibility of life for the people remains in Yahweh's power to **ransom** (*pādâ*) and **redeem** (*gāʾal*) his people. The verb **ransom** conveys the sense of making a payment to free an object or a person. Mays describes the verb as conveying the activity by which one is freed "from legal or cultic obligation through the payment of a price" (1969, 182). Biblical texts often use this verb to describe Yahweh's activity both in his bringing the people out of Egypt (e.g., Deut 7:8) and in his bringing the people out of exile (e.g., Isa 35:10; Jer 31:11).

The verb **redeem** similarly conveys the sense of purchasing an individual or object. Biblical texts use words derived from this verb to convey the next of kin who takes in the wife and children of a deceased man (e.g., Boaz in the story of Naomi and Ruth). This verb also often conveys the salvific activity of Yahweh in delivering his people from Egypt (Exod 6:6) as well as from exile (Isa 43:1; Jer 31:11).

In the next two lines of Hos 13:14 the word *ʾĕhî* (***I will***) appears twice. The LXX translates the verb as the particle *ʿayyeh* ("where") and translates the lines as Yahweh's questions to death and Sheol: "Where are your plagues . . . ? . . . where is your destruction?" (NRSV; see NIV). Paul apparently quotes from the Greek translation of Hosea in 1 Cor 15:55. The LXX reading (and the NIV) conveys the idea that the mother's womb will not be the child's grave. Death will not have final victory over God's people.

Nevertheless, the MT *ʾĕhî* (***I will***), changes the meaning of the verse completely. Rather than a rhetorical question of optimism and victory, the prophet makes a declarative statement in which Yahweh himself will become the very means of death and destruction for his people. He declares, "I will be your plagues, O Death; I will be your destruction, O Sheol" (see KJV, NKJV). In this scenario, the very God who takes his people from the grips of the death and destruction of Egyptian captivity and wilderness barrenness now becomes the one who brings pestilence and destruction upon his people (see Ps 91:6, where these two words also occur alongside each other to convey destruction through plague). Further description of devastation and barrenness in Hos 13:15-16 justifies the interpretation of v 14 as dealing with destruction and not salvation. Why has this life-giving savior become a life-taking deity? In the closing line of v 14, Yahweh simply declares that comfort or **compassion** (*nōḥam* also conveys the idea of "change of mind" or "repent"), which grew warm and tender in 11:8, is hidden from the divine vision. Yahweh cannot even see or imagine a possibility in which he could change his mind (or, repent).

13:14-16 ■ **15** In 13:15, the prophet continues the theme of the destruction of Ephraim. The verb used in the first line (*pāraʾ* means "to be fruitful"; the name Ephraim means "fruitfulness") implies the idea of Ephraim's fruitfulness. Though Ephraim flourished or thrived among his brothers, in the end, he will suffer destruction by **an east wind** that Yahweh will send from the desert. **East wind** most likely is a reference to the Assyrian power in this context. The nation Assyria, in which Ephraim trusted, will become the very power that will destroy the people. For Hosea, this eastern wind of Assyrian power making its way across the great desert is not simply a coincidence of history, however. This wind is the very *rûaḥ* (wind, breath, or even spirit) of Yahweh himself. It will so dry up the people's wells that they will become like an arid wasteland. The fury of Yahweh's *rûaḥ* will further plunder the **storehouse** of **all its treasures**. The text clearly alludes to the impending Assyrian invasion and the plundering of the palace, the royal treasury, and the temples of the nation and the removal of its wealth as war spoil by the enemy.

■ **16** The unit concludes with the prophet's announcement that the great political-economic center of Samaria will ultimately carry the weight of its guilt (v 16). In the MT, this verse is the opening verse in ch 14. The city is guilty of rebelling against her God. The NIV translates the verbs and the singular pronoun in the first line as plural forms (thus, instead of "Samaria must bear her guilt because she has rebelled against her God," the NIV reads: **The people of Samaria must bear their guilt, because they have rebelled against their God**).

Hosea then proceeds to graphically describe the punishment the city must bear for its sin against God. Yahweh will carry out his punishment of the city through the agency of Assyria. The Assyrian invasion will result in the death of the citizens of Samaria by the sword. The atrocities of warfare will include the dashing of children to the ground and the ripping open of pregnant women. The horrific language of this verse is quite familiar in the biblical text (see 2 Kgs 8:12; Ps 137:9; Isa 13:16; Amos 1:13; Nah 3:10). Not only will warriors be destroyed, but the very signs of fertility (children and fertility) and any hope for life will be removed from the land.

FROM THE TEXT

The difficult text of 13:14 raises a question about the nature and character of God. Is this God bent on destruction or on salvation? Is he the plague and the famine that destroy life, or is he the healer and the fresh rain that renew life? What does the reader make of a text in which God might say, "I will be your plagues, O Death; I will be your destruction, O Sheol"?

If the text is meant to be questions that God asks, then, based on the reading of the entire book of Hosea, one might conclude that these questions come from the God who is in deep agony because of the stubborn refusal of his people to acknowledge him as their covenant God. God who asks these questions suffers loss, grieves over broken relationship, and agonizes over rejection. The God of Hosea is a God whom the readers can identify with because he identifies with them. Therefore, whatever grace characterizes the God of Hosea, it is not by any means a "cheap grace." It is costly, because God's grace comes to a rebellious people out of the deep hurt of God. The entire book of Hosea is a powerful testimony to the overwhelming display of God's suffering love, which Hosea defines as holy love. The holy love ultimately sets God apart from humans. In the end, he does not, and will not act as humans and leave sinners to their death/grave. That is good news for all who read Hosea today, who will again find this God who comes to deliver, to give hope to the dead, in the concluding chapter of this book.

For the Easter community, Hosea's words in v 14 have become tremendous words of hope. Paul expresses this hope, "'Death has been swallowed up in victory.' 'Where, O death, is your victory? Where, O death, is your sting?'" (1 Cor 15:54-55). Wolff observes, "Paul takes the command which summons death for Israel and makes it a mockery of death because God 'gives us the victory through our Lord Jesus Christ'" (1974, 229). The love of the Father for the Son that has brought him to life through the Spirit breathes that resurrection life into the people of God who are dead in their trespasses and sins.

Therefore, Paul could also declare, "I am convinced that neither death nor life . . . will be able to separate us from the love of God in Christ Jesus our Lord" (Rom 8:38-39).

4. A Liturgy of Repentance (14:1-8)

BEHIND THE TEXT

In the concluding verses of the book of Hosea, the prophet calls for the people to return to Yahweh. In an orderly, liturgical manner, ch 14 moves from a call to return (v 1) to words of repentance (vv 2-3) to the divine response (vv 4-7) and finally to a benediction that opens wide the people's future in reliance upon Yahweh (v 8).

IN THE TEXT

■ **1** Hosea addresses Israel directly in v 1 (MT v 2) and urges the nation to **return** [*šûb*] . . . **to *Yahweh* your God** (see similar language in 6:1). In spite of the rebellion of the people, Yahweh remains to be the covenant God of Israel. The people have broken the covenant with Yahweh, but there is a way to restore the relationship with him. The call to **return** in Hosea and other prophets is a call to repentance, which involves recognition of sin, confession of guilt, and commitment to turn around and walk in the path that God has laid out for his people.

The second line of v 1 in the NIV does not fully express the meaning of the Hebrew text, which literally reads, ***Because you have staggered on account of your iniquity***. The verb here implies the unsteady movement of a drunkard (see the use of same verb for the behavior of priests and prophets in 4:5). The prophet then identifies the source of Israel's staggering. They have stumbled along the way because of their ***iniquity*** or guilt. The word ***iniquity*** (*ʿāwōn*) describes the residue or aftereffect of sin. That which the people's transgressions have left behind has caused them to stagger like drunkards. Therefore, the prophet calls upon Israel now to come back to Yahweh.

■ **2** In 14:2-3, Yahweh graciously *gives* the words to the people that would make it possible for them to return to him. The words of the prayer are directly associated with the people's return to Yahweh. The people are not merely to utter empty words, but their words must be accompanied by action. The prayer of repentance commences with a request that Yahweh ***lift up*** [*nāśāʾ* in this context means "to remove" or **forgive**] **all *iniquity*** (*ʿāwōn*). The people seek Yahweh's forgiveness of all their iniquity.

The prayer proceeds with the request that Yahweh now ***take*** that which is appropriate or ***good*** (*ṭôb*) from the people. Thus the people are being asked to give an offering to Yahweh or to give something back to him, in return for the words they take from him. The NIV translation (**receive us graciously**) does not adequately convey the sense of the Hebrew text.

What the people are to offer is made clear in the next line. The text reads literally as follows: ***Let us make complete*** **the fruit of our lips**. The NIV, **we may offer the fruit of our lips**, conveys the general idea of the passage, but the prayer is quite specific in its request to Yahweh. The verb *šālēm* (means "be complete"; root of *shalom*, "wholeness or completeness") conveys the idea of the people completing or fulfilling the vows that they have made to Yahweh, which often involves a peace offering (*shelem*). The text is not completely clear as to the nature of the sacrifice. The Hebrew text refers to *pārîm*, which means "bulls." The translation would then read, "We will offer the bulls of our lips." The LXX reading assumes the Hebrew word *peri* ("fruit"). English translations follow the LXX reading here (**We *will* offer the fruit of our lips**). **The fruit of our lips** in this context could mean the vows taken by the people (i.e., some specific sacrifice) or more likely the confession of complete dependence upon Yahweh expressed in v 3.

■ **3** The confession of the people in v 3 affirms the central conviction of the prophetic book: political alliances (**Assyria**), military might (**warhorses**), and religious systems (***the work of our hands***) will neither deliver nor provide. The people acknowledge that they will never say idols are ***our God***. Verse 3 thus affirms the truth that Yahweh alone is the savior of his people. Only in the true God of their life (**in you**) do the hopeless find hope, the helpless find help, and the weak find strength. The God to whom the people make their confession is the God of **compassion** (*rāḥam*), the God who shows mercy to the defenseless and "defends the cause of the fatherless and the widow" (Deut 10:18; see also Pss 10:14; 146:9).

■ **4** In Hos 14:4-7, Yahweh responds to his people who confess their trust and dependence on him. He will come with his healing and love for his people. Verse 4 indicates that Yahweh will do more than **heal** and bind up the people's wounds. He will heal them of their ***turnings*** (*mĕšûbâ*; see also Jer 3:22). The hope expressed in Hosea's conclusion goes beyond a divine restoration of the people of God; his message begins to imagine some form of divine transformation of the people. What had appeared to be a hopeless cycle of rebellion and infidelity will experience divine healing. The God who had called the people to covenant faithfulness will act in their lives in such a way that he will enable them to live a life of covenant faithfulness.

Verse 4 also announces that Yahweh will **love** his people **freely**. The people cannot coerce God into loving them. Unlike Baal, Yahweh loves his people voluntarily or freely.

Yahweh also announces that his **anger has turned away** (*šûb*) from the people. The language of the anger that turns recalls the image of the divine compassion in 11:8-9, which portrays Yahweh's change of mind so that he will not turn (*šûb*) to destroy Ephraim. As the people turn *toward* Yahweh (14:1), his anger turns *away* from them.

■ **5-7** In vv 5-7, Hosea describes the benevolent effects of Yahweh's mercy in vivid depictions of fertility. Verse 5 begins with Yahweh's first-person description of his involvement in the fertility and growth of Israel. This God who had become like a ravenous lion (13:7) and plagues and destruction of death itself (see 13:14) will now become to Israel life-giving nourishment of **the dew**. Yahweh will provide nourishment to Israel in the same way that the dew provides moisture to the ground. As a result of Yahweh's nourishment, Israel will experience the fertility for which it had turned to gods and nations to receive.

The images employed in the rest of v 5 and the first line of v 6 (**blossom like a lily**, **cedar of Lebanon** sending down **roots**, and **shoots** going out) all reflect significant movements toward growth and fertility. Above ground, flowers blossom and leaves sprout; below ground, roots go deep. The prophet compares the bounty of Israel's fertility to Lebanon three times in vv 5-7. Although the NIV refers twice to the **cedar of Lebanon**, the Hebrew text simply refers to Lebanon itself. In v 6, Hosea draws upon the image of the **olive tree** to compare the splendor of Israel in its abundance of fertility and growth. In v 7, the prophet brings to a conclusion his vivid portrayal of Israel's coming fertility. In the opening line of the verse, the pronoun **his** before **shade** results in some ambiguity. Since the reference to Yahweh as dew in v 4 and the luscious tree in v 8 convey nourishment and fertility, **his shade** could mean the shade of Yahweh. The image of Yahweh as "shade" is familiar to the OT (see Pss 17:8; 36:7; 91:1). However, this reading interrupts a series of descriptions of Israel's restoration (e.g., lily, Lebanon, olive tree, grain, vine, and wine). It is also possible that **his shade** here is the shade that comes from Yahweh's restored people. If this is the intent of the text, then Hosea describes Israel as once again capable of providing nourishment and safety to its inhabitants and perhaps even to surrounding nations. Israel will not only be fertile but its fertility will provide life to others.

Hosea 14:7 also refers to grain and grapes, two other primary agricultural products of Israel that are symbols of fertility and growth. Like the grain, the people will live; like the vine, they will blossom. As a result, Israel's **fame** will be spread throughout the earth like that of **the wine of Lebanon**. Its fertile, abundant reputation will abound. The depiction of the fertility of a repentant and restored Israel recalls the images in 2:21-22. Jezreel ("God sows") regains her rightful place in history as the place of fertility in which God has sown. At the conclusion of the book, God not only sows but also waters. Through his watering, the fertile abundance occurs. Without question, Hosea demonstrates Yahweh God of Israel as the source of life.

■ **8** Yahweh's response concludes with a pronouncement of life and blessing upon the people as they move into the future (v 8). Addressing Ephraim directly one final time, Yahweh inquires concerning idols. Hosea has earlier described Ephraim as "joined" to these humanly devised and humanly fashioned vessels that they make from their own silver and gold (4:17; 8:4; 13:2).

The Hebrew text of the first line of 14:8 literally reads, **O *Ephraim! What*** [are] ***idols yet to me?*** The adverb *ʿôd* (**more**) conveys the sense of continuance or persistence in an action. Hence the question conveys some type of an ongoing relationship to idols. As both the NIV and NRSV suggest, the text can be read as follows: **What more have I to do with idols?** In this sense, Yahweh is rhetorically stating that in any type of ongoing relationship he has nothing to do with idols. Therefore, if the people are to be his people, they, too, must have nothing to do with idols.

In light of this declaration concerning idols, the prophet proceeds to affirm that Yahweh and Yahweh alone is the deity who answered and who will watch carefully for Ephraim. With the emphatic use of the first-person pronoun, Yahweh declares, **I will answer him**. This promise echoes 2:21; Yahweh is responsive to his people and will bless his people with fertility. Yahweh's answer in the immediate context likely refers to the divine answer to the people's prayer of repentance in 14:2-3. Yahweh also promises to **care for** (*šûr*, "watch over"; contrast to "lurk" in 13:7) his people, to protect them from their enemies.

Verse 8 goes on to describe Yahweh as the very sign of the fertility of his people. Yahweh will be like a noble ***fir tree*** that is **flourishing** and luxuriant. Frequently in the Deuteronomic-prophetic story of Israel, the symbol of the flourishing tree depicts the site that worshippers sought as a place of fertility (Deut 12:2; 1 Kgs 14:23; 2 Kgs 16:4; Jer 2:20; 3:6, 13). Yahweh announces to his people that he himself will be that leafy, flourishing tree to them. He becomes the very emblem of life and blessing to which they had gathered in the past.

The concluding line of v 8 magnificently summarizes the entire message of the prophet Hosea. Yahweh's statement, ***Your fruit is found in me*** (**your fruitfulness comes from me**), is his indisputable claim as the source of Israel's life and fertility. No other god or political power can make this claim. Yahweh's claim comes from the fact that he is the Creator God.

FROM THE TEXT

For the reader of the full text of Hosea, these eight verses function as the ideal conclusion. In reading the book, the reading community has looked into the mirror and has seen its own idolatry, infidelity, brokenness, and devastation. How then is the community to respond? The liturgical movement of this text offers the reading community a model of repentance and confession necessary for divine restoration to become a reality. Moreover, the text functions as a liturgy for all generations of the people of God.

The texture of the response attempts to maintain the delicate balance between the role of God and the role of his people in the covenant relationship. On the one hand, this God will not permit his people to manipulate or coerce him. He makes the call to his people to return before they ever pray. He provides them with words to pray. The action of his people does not control or manipulate the divine love for his people. His love is voluntary and freely bestowed. He is not Baal or an idol that the people can manipulate for their self-serving purposes.

At the same time, the prayer balances this portrait of the voluntarily loving God with a people whom this God does not manipulate or coerce. He does not overpower them and make a decision for them. He invites them to return. He provides a prayer for them, but he does not say the prayer for them. His prayer must become their prayer. Their words are accompanied by their return. Like their God, they are an authentic member of this covenant relationship. They are not a game piece in the hands of their God.

Therefore, as throughout the book of Hosea, the closing liturgy refuses to portray the covenant as unilateral. It is authentically a bilateral agreement. It is initiated by grace that goes before (i.e., prevenient grace) through both a divine call to return and a prayer that God provides. However, the people of God must be responsible to that grace. They cooperate with the grace extended. This text particularly shapes a liturgy in which the reading community can continue to experience the significant balance between divine grace and human responsibility.

The reader experiences a means of grace embedded within this text. The words given by God as a prayer for his people to pray (vv 2-3) clearly function as a vessel whereby the divine grace can bring healing and restorative love to the people. As the community both then and now participates in this means of grace provided by God, the divine restoration and transformation of the people is at work.

At the heart of this prayer is a turning away from the powers that promise life and blessing and a turning toward the God who alone can bestow life and blessing (v 3). In this "turning away" and "turning toward," the people practice authentic repentance. They recognize the delusion of the powers both outside of their own strength (Assyria) and within their own strength (horses). Recognizing the delusion, they confess that none of these powers are divine. Moreover, the community names itself—orphans—a helpless, defenseless, and hopeless people. Hope emerges out of this confession. The hope of the community is God and not the powers of the world. As the reading community engages in this prayer, the delusions of self-sovereignty and the false promises of the powers of politics, economics, and popularly practiced religion are stripped of divine power. The text prompts the readers to imagine in their own life and in their community existence who Assyria is and what the horses are. It then moves them to confess the utter emptiness of both Assyria and horses.

As the reader continues through the liturgy of this passage, God's pronouncement gives even further hope (v 4). God the healer of Israel announces that he not only will mend their wounds but also will heal their *turnings*. The persistent struggle of the people that always ends in failure is not a cycle that must continue. This gracious God will act in such a way that he will enable his people to be faithful and loyal. Hosea's optimism reaches a high point here. He is confident that the grace of God not only can restore his unfaithful people but can actually transform his people in such a way that they will love God undividedly with all of their heart and soul and strength (see also Deut 30:6; Jer 31:33-34; Ezek 36:25-29).

Finally, as the reading community comes to the conclusion of this liturgy, it celebrates the fertility and life of God in its midst. The text challenges all subsequent generations to affirm God as the source of their blessing and productivity. Apart from him, the people of God, the church, can do nothing.

The image of the luxuriant tree and its fruit brings to the reader's mind the teaching of Jesus in John 15:4-6. Jesus' words, "Those who abide in me and I in them bear much fruit, because apart from me you can do nothing" (NRSV), could be understood as appropriate commentary on Hosea's words, "Your fruitfulness comes from me" (Hos 14:8).

5. Wisdom Epilogue: Call for Reflection (14:9)

BEHIND THE TEXT

The final verse not only functions as the epilogue to the book of Hosea but also serves as a prologue to the remainder of the Book of the Twelve as the subsequent prophetic messages will build upon many of the themes of Hosea. Within its context of the flourishing tree described in v 8 as well as in its address to the wise, v 9 is reminiscent of the prologue to the Psalter that compares the wise/righteous person to a tree "planted by streams of water, which yields its fruit in season and whose leaf does not wither—whatever they do prospers" (Ps 1:3). The emphasis upon the "ways" of Yahweh as "right" and the portrayal of both the righteous and transgressors traveling this way are also reminiscent of the first psalm.

Just as Ps 1 emerges out of and reflects the ancient Israelite wisdom tradition, so, too, does the language in the closing verse of Hosea. In addition to the various motifs and guiding theology, the verse clearly draws upon three central words to the wisdom tradition: *ḥākām* ("wise"), *bîn* ("understand"),

and *yāda* ("know"). In the opening statement of the prologue to the book of Proverbs, all three words are represented in the purpose statement of the book (1:2). These terms recur regularly throughout the book of Proverbs and in the broader wisdom tradition.

IN THE TEXT

■ **9** The concluding admonition to the book of Hosea begins with a single question: **Who is wise** [*ḥākām*]**?** The response is, ***He will understand*** [*bîn*] ***these*** [***things***]; ***the one who understands*** [*bîn*] ***will know*** [*yāda*] ***them***. The NIV composes two questions and translates the double occurrence of a form of *bîn* with two entirely different words (**realize** and **discerning**).

The book's concluding question and its answer affirm that the wise person is the one who ***will understand these*** (things). What are these (things)? The prophet may have in mind the entirety of his message, which includes Yahweh's case against Israel, his judgment, and the hope he gives for the future of Israel. The wise would know that Yahweh is the source of life and Israel's only Savior. They have wisdom to discern the futility of idols, alliances, kings, and military might.

In the closing half of v 9, the prophet reiterates the wisdom tradition's emphasis on **the ways of the LORD.** The metaphor of the way or the path is a central motif in the wisdom tradition (see Ps 1:1, 6; Prov 1:15; 2:18, 20; 4:11, 14; 8:13, 20, etc.). The phrase "walk in the ways of Yahweh" is a common Deuteronomic reference to obedience (Deut 8:6; 11:22; 19:9). The path that Yahweh sets for his people to walk is **right** or straight (*yāšar*). It is not twisted, crooked, or perverse. Those who are in right relationship with God and with their neighbors (**righteous**) **walk** in the ways of Yahweh. However, the scenario is quite different for those who rebel against God; they **stumble** (*kāšal*) upon these paths in the same manner that a drunkard would totter.

But how is one to *know* and *understand* this straight path? What are these "ways" in which they are to walk? How do they walk the way of wisdom? The text of Hosea has clearly set out for the reader what this path looks like. So, too, the short messages of the subsequent prophets in the twelve (Joel—Malachi) will elaborate upon many of the themes begun in Hosea. The closing line of Hosea thus functions as a wise introductory admonition for all who will read the remainder of the Book of the Twelve. The call of Hosea also echoes into the next century as Jeremiah declares, "Stand at the crossroads and look; ask for the ancient paths, ask where the good way is, and walk in it, and you will find rest for your souls" (Jer 6:16).

FROM THE TEXT

The book of Hosea ends with an invitation to its readers to walk in the ways of God. The lesson of the book is clear; there is in reality only one path that God sets before humanity. This path is the path of righteousness. The righteous walk along this path by keeping the rules of the road; they will enjoy God's guidance as they journey along this path. However, those who follow their own rules as they travel on this path will find their journey hazardous and unsafe; they will totter, stumble, and ultimately fail to reach their destination.

Hosea reminds his modern readers that life in the kingdom of God requires total allegiance to God. There is only one way to walk in the path of God; that is the path of right living, because the path of God is right. The final verse of Hosea also serves as a warning to those who claim to be members of God's kingdom and at the same remain loyal to the kingdoms of this world. They will find life unsteady, unsafe, and leading to nowhere. They have no real identity; they do not know to which kingdom they really belong.

The book of Hosea also ends with a challenge to its readers to continue to seek discernment and wisdom. The final verse of Hosea anticipates that its readers would seek wisdom through their continued reading and reflection of the prophetic word. This closing statement is perhaps strategically placed here as the concluding verse of Hosea by the compilers of the twelve. They
have perhaps intended this verse to be an invitation to the readers to read and 14:9
reflect not only the "word of the LORD" communicated by Hosea but also the "word of the LORD" in the remaining prophets (Joel—Malachi) to discover "the ways of the LORD."

JOEL

INTRODUCTION

A. Joel the Prophet

The book of Joel provides very little information concerning the prophet himself. The name Joel occurs once in 1 Sam 8:2 (the oldest son of Samuel) and seventeen times in the postexilic books of Chronicles, Ezra, and Nehemiah (regarding the various references, see Crenshaw 1995, 21). However, none of these instances are in reference to the prophet. In contrast to many of the superscriptions of prophetic books (e.g., Isa 1:1; Jer 1:1-3; Hos 1:1; Amos 1:1), the superscription in Joel provides no names of reigning Israelite or Judaean kings. The lack of reference to kings provides the book with a more ahistorical setting.

The text of Joel demonstrates significant familiarity with the Jerusalem cult, particularly in relationship to communal fasts and temple offerings. This awareness may indicate that the prophet was a part of the temple staff. In his extensive study of Joel's "very astute knowledge" and use of ancient Israelite traditions and sacred texts, Strazicich concludes that Joel's activity and influence is "in close proximity to the temple" (2007, 51; see Strazicich's exhaustive examination of the text's use and function of prior scripture, 59-252; see also Cook 1995, 171). The text's familiarity with the creed-like confession of Exod 34:6-7 in Joel 2:13 is apparent. Other references to prophetic traditions—such as Isa 2:2-4; 13; Ezek 47:1-12; Amos 1:2; Mic 4:1-4; Zech 14:8—clearly demonstrate the text's familiarity with the prophetic tradition. In spite of the extensive use of earlier traditions and texts in the book of Joel, it is not possible to determine precisely if these texts are in the mind of the prophet Joel or rather if they reflect the hand of the editors of the prophetic collection (i.e., the *Nevi'im* or the Book of the Twelve).

B. The Historical Context and Audience of Joel

As previously noted, the editorial superscription provides no historical context regarding kings of Israel or Judah. One cannot decisively conclude from the absence of royal names that there were no kings at the time of Joel. If the prophet was active during either the exilic or postexilic period, however, it is obvious why the superscription lacks a reference to reigning kings. The oracles of the prophet never address a king nor comment on the behavior of a king or his royal entourage. In contrast to a monarchic setting, the text assumes a temple-centered community presided over by the priesthood.

Various indicators in the text point to a much later postexilic context. The text understands a reunited north and south. References to Edomite involvement at the time of Jerusalem's fall and to the exile of Jerusalem's leaders indicate a date after the events of 587 B.C. While the text describes no king reigning in Jerusalem, neither does it depict Assyrian, Babylonian, or Persian domination. However, the text does clearly depict a standing temple, an operating cult with daily offerings, a well-developed Zion theology, and a priestly staff in Jerusalem (1:9, 13-16; 2:14, 17). The wall that surrounds the city (2:7, 9) is likely the one constructed under Nehemiah's leadership in the middle of the fifth century B.C. Specific reference to slave trafficking with Greeks and Sabeans (3:6, 8 [4:6, 8 HB]) particularly points to the fifth century B.C. (for detailed description of sociohistorical and linguistic evidences within the text, see Crenshaw 1995, 23-28; Strazicich 2007, 51-55).

Based upon the presence of a reconstructed temple in Jerusalem, Birch proposes a very open-ended period for the book of Joel—sometime after the temple's construction in 515 B.C. (1997, 126). Suggesting a broad period during which the prophet might have been active (500-350 B.C.), Achtemeier establishes a terminal date as 343 B.C., the date of the Greek destruction of Tyre and Sidon, which are still standing in 3:4-8 (1996a, 115-16; see extensive argument by Wolff 1977, 4-6, in which he suggests the first half of the fourth century B.C.).

The dominating "historical event" that informs the book of Joel is a "foreign invasion" of locusts. Metaphors of devastating armies of locusts allow the "ahistorical text" to depict subsequent military invasions as well (regarding whether the text is referring to locusts, armies, or both, and the literary motif of locusts for armies in the ancient Near East, see Crenshaw 1995, 96, 117). Unfortunately the threat of both locusts and armies was frequent in preexilic and postexilic periods. In the present form of the text, the common invasions of locusts and armies take on apocalyptic proportions as they anticipate a final divine battle against evil. Crenshaw has suggested three primary ways in which one might interpret the relationship between the locusts, military armies, and the apocalyptic nature of the book:

- A locust invasion functions as a "precursor" to the Day of the Lord.
- A locust invasion provided the images for a "semi-apocalyptic description" of the Day of the Lord.
- The book of Joel, including the locust invasion, is comprised of "symbolic descriptions of military attacks" (1995, 116-17).

Whether or not a specific locust plague was an originating event for the subsequent descriptions of the Day of the Lord in the book of Joel, the ultimate concern of the book is "the threatening army as the fulfillment of the enemy nation proclaimed by prophecy and commanded by Yahweh" (Wolff 1977, 46). In turn, the book is concerned to articulate the proper response of the people of God at the time of such a catastrophic calamity. The call of the priestly-prophetic book is for the community to turn to Yahweh in trust and worship.

The audience to whom Joel speaks within the literary text is the general populace of Judah and Jerusalem as it experiences the devastating effects of a locust invasion. More specifically, he addresses the temple priests and staff who are responsible for leading the communal fast and who will ultimately officiate over the temple offerings of wine and grain. However, the ahistorical nature of the book suggests an "audience" beyond the general populace and the temple personnel. In its present form, the book speaks more into a "future history" than it speaks into a past event. Informing the book of Joel is a conviction concerning the faithfulness of Yahweh to deliver his people from a tragic calamity in the past. As the prophet called upon the people and the priestly community to turn to Yahweh then, the book of Joel calls upon the people once again to turn to Yahweh at an unspecified time when the great and fearful Day of the Lord is upon them. The "historical context" of the past thus functions in the book of Joel as a paradigm for the present and even more as a paradigm for the future. The ongoing retraditioning of this text that is apparent in Peter's sermon on the day of Pentecost in Acts 2:15-21 is true to the spirit, conviction, and function of the book of Joel. Undoubtedly Peter and the writer of Luke-Acts understood themselves to be Joel's "audience." In many respects, the nature of the book of Joel allows for the prophet's "audience" to remain "open" throughout time.

C. The Book of Joel as a Literary Work

1. Literary Devices and Genre

As a report of the great catastrophic event of a locust plague, metaphorical images with hyperbolic proportions appear throughout Joel 1:2—2:11. These vivid metaphors ultimately engender proto-apocalyptic language and ideas in ch 3 (ch 4 HB). Because of the priestly background to Joel, the classical prophetic language of judgment and warning merges with the priestly concerns for a cultic response of lamentation and communal fast. With unique interest in cultic matters, the prophetic text often employs imperative verbs in order to express the priestly call to cultic observance (e.g., wail in 1:5 and lament in 1:8; put on sackcloth in 1:13; call a fast in 1:14; call an assembly in 2:15; blow a trumpet in 2:1, 15; fast and weep in 2:12-15).

While Joel demonstrates a unique concern for priestly-cultic matters, however, the text equally demonstrates a unique understanding and use of previous prophetic texts and traditions (see discussion of the person of the prophet above). Joel or perhaps a redactor of the text uniquely incorporates various prophetic passages and references into the text. Although certainly not as elaborate as other prophetic oracles against the surrounding nations (Isa 13—23; Jer 46—51; Ezek 25—32; Amos 1—2), Joel pronounces judgment against the nations for their crimes against humanity (3:4-8, 19 [4:4-8, 19 HB]).

2. Historical Development of the Text

As early as 1911, Bernhard Duhm suggested that Joel's original text dealt solely with the locust plague and that the eschatological references in the final chapter were additions as late as the Maccabean period (Wolff 1977, 6-8; for extensive discussion of scholarly work on the formation of the text of Joel, see Crenshaw 1995, 29-34). While such a proposal has merit, Achtemeier has more recently and rightly commented that "the eschatological passages of the book are integral" to the message of Joel and "the book as a whole has a remarkable symmetry" (1996a, 117). In the present state of the book of Joel, it is not possible to determine precisely the nature and degree of editorial work that might have occurred subsequent to the prophet himself.

3. Reliance upon Prophetic Tradition

As noted above, Joel is unique in its incorporation of other prophetic texts. In some instances, the text borrows complete statements from earlier writings, such as Isa 13:6 in Joel 1:15 and Amos 1:2 in Joel 3:16 [4:16 HB]). In other instances, the text employs phrases from prophetic passages such as Amos 9:13 and Obad 17. Familiar prophetic traditions such as the Day of Yahweh, divine judgment on surrounding nations, and the enemy from the north are present in the book of Joel (for detailed discussion of Joel's use of prophetic material, see Wolff 1977, 10-11). Wolff has observed that in its integration of diverse prophetic traditions and texts, the book of Joel functions as "a literary critique of prevailing ideologies and institutions" as it is "sustained by an enormous passion for understanding . . . in relation to earlier prophecy which had already become Scripture" (1977, 10).

4. Hebrew Versification

Similar to the change in versification between the Hebrew text and the English translation of Hosea, the book of Joel also changes in versification. Whereas the English translation of the depiction of transformation in v 28 continues ch 2, Hebrew versification quite appropriately acknowledges the change in perspective and content and begins a new chapter (ch 3). Thus the English passage 2:28-32 is 3:1-5 in Hebrew versification. Chapter 3 in the English translation is then ch 4 in the Hebrew text, so that 3:1-21 in the English translation is 4:1-21 in the Hebrew text.

5. Flow of Text and Structure

The text of Joel may be examined in two primary divisions. The first section of the book focuses upon the dilemma of the locust plague and its resolution (1:2—2:27). The second section focuses upon the Day of Yahweh (2:28—3:21) and the eschatological ramifications of this day of divine visitation. As the language of a catastrophic locust plague merges with the language of a destructive military invasion, the text reaches its climax in proto-apocalyptic images in which cosmic catastrophe and transformation occur.

The book articulates both the locust plague in the present and the eschatological vision of the future in terms of the Day of the Lord; this day of divine visitation connects the two sections. In agreement with early Israelite tradition, Joel understands the Day of Yahweh to be a day of divine visitation upon the nations. However, in agreement with prophets such as Amos, Joel also understands the Day of Yahweh to be the time of Israel's accountability to Yahweh and thus the day of divine visitation upon the covenant community as well.

The shift in 2:19-27 from the locust plague to the future judgment and salvation precedes the prophet's reflections upon the cosmic, eschatological Day of Yahweh beginning in 2:28 (3:1 HB). This movement from catastrophe to salvation is similar to the structural movement within the genre of the lament as it moves from outcry of grief to assurance of and praise for divine restoration.

The hinge between the catastrophe of the locust plague in 1:2—2:11 and the shift toward hope in 2:19-27 is the people's outcry in 2:12-17. In response to the community's outcry, the Lord responds with jealousy and pity in 2:18. The community's calling upon the Lord in 2:12-17 provides the basis for and even foreshadows the declaration in 2:32 that "everyone who calls on the name of the LORD will be saved."

Based upon the general structure of the book of Joel, the commentary will follow the structural outline below:

I. Superscription (1:1)
II. Locust Plague and Resolution (1:2—2:27)
    A. A Portrait of Calamity (1:2-7)
    B. Call to Mourning (1:8-20)
    C. Enemy on the Horizon (2:1-11)
    D. Call to Repentance (2:12-17)
    E. A Jealous God Acts (2:18-27)
III. The Cosmic Day of Yahweh and the Establishment of the Reign of God (2:28—3:21)
    A. After Deliverance . . . (2:28-32 [3:1-5 HB])
    B. Judgment against the Nations (3:1-16*a* [4:1-16*a* HB])
    C. Final Restoration (3:16*b*-21 [4:16*b*-21 HB])

D. Theological Themes

1. Disaster and the Call to Prayer/Call to Return

The significant hinge in 2:12-17 (see discussion of structure above) concerning the outcry of the people in the midst of their calamity provides insight into a dominant theological concern of the book of Joel. In response to this communal outcry, the Lord becomes jealous of his people and has pity upon them (2:18). While Joel relies upon traditional priestly responses to disaster, i.e., lamentation and fasting, he ultimately calls upon the people in a prophetic manner to turn or to return to the Lord (*šûb*, repent; see 2:12-13). Wolff (1977, 13) describes this unique call to return as being "based not on the Torah . . . but on prophetic proclamation." As the people turn back to their covenant God, he is faithful and chooses not only to remove the calamity from their midst but to transform their barrenness to fertility, their death to life.

2. Who Knows? The Qualification of Prophetic Theology

In the prophet's call for the people to turn back to the Lord, Joel is careful to make certain that the people's repentance is not simply a matter of human action and divine consequence. He reflects the prophetic caution toward any cultic action that might appear as manipulative or idolatrous. His restrained qualification of "Who knows?" (2:14) assures that the people do not view their repentance as a means employed in order to coerce divine action. The free grace and sovereignty of God remain at work even within the context of human repentance.

3. The Day of the Lord as Both Judgment and Salvation

As noted previously, the familiar concept of the Day of the Lord clearly informs both Joel's interpretation of the locust plague and his anticipation of a final universal judgment (for extensive overview of the concept of the Day of the Lord in Joel, see Crenshaw 1995, 47-50). Wolff has commented that "no other Old Testament witness gives it [*the Day of the* LORD] as detailed and systematic a treatment as he does" (1977, 12). Similar to the prophets Ezekiel, Amos, and Zephaniah, Joel does not limit the Day of the Lord to the surrounding nations alone. He clearly understands that Yahweh will hold his covenant people accountable (1:15; 2:1, 11; see also Ezek 7:1-20; Amos 3:1-2, 14; 5:18, 20; Zeph 1:7-18; 2:2-3; 3:8). Perhaps informed by his priestly theological background, Joel understands an integral relationship between divine judgment and the land of promise itself (see priestly understandings of this relationship in Lev 18:24-28 and Ezek 36:16-21). As divine judgment occurs, the Lord's gift of land along with its crops and animals are all adversely affected.

While Joel understands the Day of Yahweh to be a day of accountability for and judgment upon the covenant community, he likewise understands it to be Yahweh's judgment upon the nations of the world and the restoration of the covenant community to their rightful place (2:31; 3:14). In this understanding, Joel shares similarity with the early popular notion of the Day of the Lord, which viewed it as the divine visitation upon surrounding enemy nations. Joel's well-developed Zion theology clearly influences the manner in which he understands Yahweh's final establishment of Jerusalem and its temple as the center of the universe to which all people will flow (see also other exilic and postexilic prophetic texts, such as Isa 63:1-4; Obadiah; Zech 14:1-9). Thus Joel uniquely balances the perceptions of the Day of the Lord as Israel's judgment and as Israel's deliverance/the enemies' defeat. Wolff has observed that "by developing the theme in both directions, Joel stands at the threshold between prophetic and apocalyptic eschatology" (1977, 12).

4. The Past as Paradigm for a Hope-filled Future

The structure of the book of Joel reveals a significant theological conviction of the prophet concerning the relationship between the past and the future. The manner in which God has formerly acted (i.e., judgment through and subsequent deliverance from the locust plague) provides the interpretative lens by which one might see the future. Birch has articulated Joel's mode of operation as follows: "This experience of salvation in a present crisis leads to the prophet's vision of God's future salvation, when the day of the Lord does come" (1997, 129).

5. The Spirit of God

Similar to other exilic and postexilic prophetic texts, Joel envisions the pivotal role of the Spirit of God in enlivening and re-creating the covenant community (see also Isa 48:16; 59:21; 61:1; Ezek 36:26-27; 37:14; 39:29; Hag 1:14; 2:5; Zech 4:6; 7:12; however, see Mic 3:8). For Joel, the divine restoration of the devastated city and its citizens occurs only as God "pours out" his Spirit (→ 2:28-29 [3:1-2 HB]). Joel does not envision the Spirit of God in a parochial manner. As the segregating lines of gender, age, and status evaporates, the Lord will empower "all flesh" to carry out the prophetic activity of receiving and giving a word from God. Neither does Joel envision the "pouring out" of the Spirit as merely a privatized, individualized experience with God. While Joel understands individuals to be directly affected by the pouring out of the divine Spirit, this gift of God is first and foremost at work in the salvation and empowering of the covenant community as a whole.

6. Zion Theology

A well-developed Zion theology provides a significant theological thread throughout the book of Joel (see 2:1, 15, 23, 32; 3:16, 17, 21). While earlier references to Zion speak of blowing trumpets in preparation for the invasion and for the communal fast (2:1, 15), later references depict Zion as a place of rejoicing over fertility (2:23) and as a place of escape (2:32). The obvious movement in the text from invasion, devastation, and communal fast to escape, deliverance, and communal joy is the result of Yahweh's habitation in Zion (3:16, 17, 21). As the elevated hill upon which Yahweh's temple/palace stood, not only was Zion the visible manifestation of Yahweh's reign over his people, but it ultimately demonstrated to all that Yahweh was with his people or as Ezekiel concluded: "*The* Lord *is there!*"

7. Proto-Apocalyptic Thought

The book of Joel transforms the familiar and common occurrences of insect infestations and foreign intrusions into images of divine reign, imminent judgment, and cosmic transformation. Presenting the Day of Yahweh as the divine visitation upon the nations as well as the people of God (→ 3. The Day of the Lord as Both Judgment and Salvation under D. Theological Themes), the text proceeds to develop the concept to the final and utter cosmic transformation from death to life. Contrary to the popular ancient Israelite notion (perhaps including Amos' understanding of the Day of the Lord for Israel), Joel's ultimate concern for the Day of the Lord was not final destruction. For Joel, this day of divine visitation moves toward salvation in the end. Wolff insightfully comments, "I hear the 'learned prophet' Joel say in a world changed since Jesus of Nazareth: Let the catastrophic threats to the present and the future move you to a total reorientation towards the attested and coming compassion of God!" (1977, 15). For Joel, hope survives catastrophe; life survives death.

COMMENTARY

I. SUPERSCRIPTION: JOEL 1:1

IN THE TEXT

■ **1** The superscription introduces the content of Joel as ***the word of the Lord which was*** or ***happened*** (*hāyâ* means "to be," "to become," "to happen," etc.; **came to**) to Joel. ***The word of the Lord which was*** or ***happened*** (usually translated as **came**) is a familiar phrase found in many other prophetic superscriptions (→ Hos 1:1; see Mic 1:1 and Zeph 1:1). The use of the verb *to be* or *to become* depicts the commissioning of the divine word to the prophet (see Crenshaw 1995, 79).

The very brief superscription simply provides the prophet's name and that of his father. The name Joel, which means "Yahweh is God," is rare in the OT. It actually is the reversal of the two primary components of the name Elijah ("My God is Yahweh"). The only other occurrences of the name are Samuel's son (1 Sam 8:2) and various genealogical references in the Chronicler's history, none of which provide further detail. However, the frequency of the name in the Chronicler's history seems to suggest that it was a common name in the postexilic period.

The name of Joel's father, Pethuel, appears only here, and the meaning is uncertain. Unlike many prophetic superscriptions, the text provides no historical context of kings, empires, or specific situations (compare Isa 1:1; Jer 1:1; Ezek 1:1-2; Hos 1:1; Amos 1:1). While the text depicts a locust plague, such incidents recurred throughout Israel's history. The lack of historical references suggests that perhaps the intent of the text was to purposefully speak beyond a specific setting in order to address more broadly subsequent natural and/or political crises that arise in the life of the community.

II. LOCUST PLAGUE AND RESOLUTION: JOEL 1:2—2:27

A. A Portrait of Calamity (1:2-7)

BEHIND THE TEXT

Locust invasions, a common occurrence in the ancient Near East, had devastating effects upon both the physical, economic, and political life of the community. These six-legged insects easily leaped significant distances with the strength of their two larger back legs. In large swarms, they would consume all vegetation in their path.

The significant impact of these insects upon agrarian people is demonstrated in the plethora of terms (eleven in all) in the OT for types of locusts. Three of these terms likely describe the locust stages (see 1:4; 2:25). These stages include: the larva or wingless stage in which the insect is able to hop ("young locusts" [NIV]; "hopping locust" [NRSV]), the cocoon stage ("other locusts" [NIV]; "destroying locust" [NRSV]), and the young flying stage ("locust swarm" [NIV]; "cutting locust" [NRSV]). Four additional terms depict the collective or swarming nature of the insect (see Redditt 2008, 684-85).

IN THE TEXT

Looking both to the past and the future, vv 2-3 place the devastating effects of the locust invasion within the narrative framework of God's people. Former generations had never seen such an event; future generations would remember it forever.

■ **2** In v 2, Joel balances two imperatives (**hear** and **listen**) with two vocatives (**elders** and **all who live in the land**). A similar construction of imperatives and vocatives occurs in Hos 5:1. A rhetorical question follows the summons to **hear** and **listen**. Joel's first addressees, the **elders**, frequently in the OT are those who exercise tribal authority at the city gates (see Willis 2007, 234). However, Joel's appeal to memory suggests that the reference here perhaps encompasses those persons advanced in years. Crenshaw observes that "Joel's interest lies in accumulated years, not in special rank and privilege" (1995, 86). "He appeals to those individuals in society who had the longest memory" (ibid.; see also Achtemeier 1996a, 306; however, compare Wolff 1977, 25, who interprets this reference to be to "the real leadership group" that gained prominence in the postexilic period). Joel's subsequent references in 2:16 and 28 certainly seem to indicate age.

The second group of addressees, **all who live in the land** or ***the inhabitants of the land***, occurs twice more in Joel (1:14; 2:1). The prophet addresses the land dwellers whose lives have been severely impacted by the locust invasion.

The rhetorical question, **Has anything like this ever happened in your days or in the days of your ancestors?** indicates the uniqueness of the catastrophe. The ambiguous demonstrative pronoun (**this**) refers to some unspecified catastrophe; a full disclosure of the event is made in v 4. Joel claims that the magnitude of the catastrophe in his day is incomparable with anything in the past.

■ **3** The prophet moves from memory of the past to the future in v 3 and commands the people to ***recount*** or ***rehearse*** (**tell**) this event to their children. In turn their children are to recount the event to their children into perpetuity. The narrative chain is all-inclusive: ancestors, present generation, the next generation, and all future generations. This catastrophe has and will continue to have unfolding implications for subsequent generations. In light of the broader context of the book, this devastating invasion provides the backdrop for the subsequent invasion portrayed later in the text. As the subsequent generations remember Yahweh's deliverance from the locust plague, they will anticipate Yahweh's deliverance from the enemy nations.

■ **4** In v 4, the prophet proceeds to flesh out the ambiguous **this** of v 2 by graphically describing the utter devastation brought about by four types of locusts. Joel uses four terms to identify the locusts. The precise meaning of these terms is not clear. The terms may depict four stages of the locust or four different types of locusts.

The first term, **locust swarm** (*gāzām*), reappears in 2:25. The noun likely indicates the biting or devouring activity of these insects ("cutting locust" [NRSV]). The second term, **great locusts** (*ʾarbeh*), likely derives from the verb meaning "to be many" and perhaps indicates the swarming nature of locusts.

The third term, **young locusts** (*yeleq*), may depict the quick hopping activity of the insects (see Nah 3:16, where the term denotes the quick manner in which a party scatters and disappears ("hopping locust" [NRSV]). The final term, **other locusts** (*hasî*), consistently describes the destructive nature of the insect (see Deut 28:38; 1 Kgs 8:37; 2 Chr 6:28; and Ps 78:46). In Joel's sequencing of the terms, this final one does appear to indicate the nature in which these locusts finally destroy or "finish off" whatever had remained behind ("destroying locust" [NRSV]).

■ **5** In Joel 1:5-7, the prophet calls upon the slumbering people to grieve over the utter ruination. Joel begins with a call to the people to **wake up** (v 5). The command is given to the people who are sluggish and have become lethargic because of their drunkenness. The prophet's call is intended to awaken them from their stupor. The command to **weep** is given to those who are unable to weep because of their drunken condition. Only when they wake up and see their loss, including the loss of wine, would they be able to join the prophet and weep over the destruction that is taking place in the land.

The **drinkers of wine** addressed in v 5 here are probably not a different group from the drunkards in the first line of this verse. The intoxicated people are commanded to **wail** or to howl (*yālal*) in distress over an extremely painful condition. They are to howl in distress over the loss of the ***sweet*** **[new] wine** (*yāsîs*). Wolff describes this wine as "the juice of the new vintage" (1977, 28-29). In 3:18, the text once again specifically refers to this sweet wine as the mountains drip sweet wine with restored fertility.

The prophet depicts this sweet wine as being ***cut off*** **(snatched)** from the people's mouths. The image of cutting off is particularly appropriate in light of the cutting activity of the locusts. As the wine is "cut off," the gladness and merriment brought about by wine is replaced by grief-filled wailing.

■ **6** With vivid images of a hostile invading army, v 6 portrays the massive swarm of locusts as a mighty nation's conquest. The national and military images foreshadow the appearance of the invading nations that appear in subsequent chapters. The land against which these invaders have come belongs to Yahweh himself; it is **my land**. Yahweh has something personal at stake in the matter.

Powerful and uncountable (**without number**), the invaders are of tremendous magnitude both in the capacity to utterly destroy and in sheer mass.

The prophet depicts their ruination of the crops through metaphors of lions' teeth and lionesses' jaw teeth (**fangs**). Their strength and their number render their victims powerless.

■ **7** Verse 7 depicts the devastation brought about by the powerful jaws of the locusts. Fertile vegetation of the vineyards lies ***desolate***; the bark of the fig tree has ***splintered***. The vines (**my vines**) and the fig trees (**my fig trees**) that have grown on the land belong to the Lord (see "my land" in v 6).

In ancient Israelite tradition, the grape vine and the fig tree represent a life of safety and abundance; the devastation of these fruits indicates the end of all security and blessing.

FROM THE TEXT

In the opening verses, the prophet calls upon the generation experiencing this devastation to make the event memorable for future generations so that they will be shaped by its narrative. The structure of the book itself reflects the significance of such memory. Greater calamities may occur in the life of God's people, but their memory of past experiences may serve as the anchor that will hold them steady when they will engage in the horror, pain, and loss brought upon by future "locust plagues." This text reminds the people of God that the memory of the past is the proper context within which one might engage the difficult challenges of the present and the future.

Unfortunately, subsequent generations hearing this text might too easily conclude that all natural and social disasters such as this one come directly from the hand of God for punitive or didactic purposes. The reading community must give special care not to hear this text as a statement of God's direct hand in such natural or humanly caused disasters. As Joel is not concerned here to present a theodicy, the text does not function to locate the source of such disasters. Although the prophet will later call for a fast, the opening lines do not depict the devastation as divine punishment for past sin. Rather, the text utilizes this event as a backdrop for the approaching Day of Yahweh. Beyond this immediate catastrophe, the people are to prepare for the rapidly approaching visitation of God (1:15). However, these opening verses do not themselves depict this day but rather depict the communal helplessness and despair brought about by the horrific disaster.

Through its vivid portrait of devastation, fear, and loss, the text shapes a world of communal terror similar to what we find in individual and communal laments in the OT. In doing so, it invites the reader to engage in the terrorizing emotion of such loss. While not seeking to frighten the reader into a response of repentance, the text brings the reading community into a world of images that allow the audience to see, identify with, and confess its own "locust plague." It compels the reader to remain in the text in order to seek an appropriate communal response to such a crisis. Ultimately it prepares the reading audience to hear the invitation to come before the Lord in utter trust and dependency through communal prayer and fasting.

B. Call to Mourning (1:8-20)

BEHIND THE TEXT

In vv 8-13 the prophet calls for public mourning over the loss of fertility. Three times the prophet mentions sackcloth, the traditional garb of mourning. In each case, it is directly related to the priestly temple service of wine and grain offerings. Regular temple service, which included such offerings, ensured future fertility. Infertility in the field and vineyard will now begin a cycle of infertility as temple offerings come to an end. In vv 13-20, the general call to mourning becomes specified as a communal fast.

IN THE TEXT

■ **8** This section begins with another imperative, a command from the prophet to the people to **mourn like a virgin** (v 8). Mourning for the dead in the ancient world was a public expression of grief (also seen in the Middle Eastern setting even today). Segal has noted that "not to do so was considered insulting to the dead and to the grieving relations, as it implied lack of affection and respect for the dead, the family, the clan, and the nation" (2009, 160).

The term translated **virgin** (*bětûlâ*) refers either to a woman at the age of marriage and thus already married or an engaged woman who, while still a virgin, is considered a wife (see Deut 22:24). The phrase **the betrothed** [*baʿal*] **of her youth** makes it difficult to understand the actual status of the woman. Crenshaw observes that the phrase "recalls the early years of marriage" (1995, 98). In contrast, Wolff sees here the image of a woman who has "lost the beloved of her youth shortly before marriage" (1977, 31). With either interpretation, the image of the grieving young woman depicts the hope of life and fertility overcome by the despair of death and barrenness.

In accord with accepted rituals of mourning, the grief-stricken woman girds her waist with the coarse material made from goat or camel hair (**sackcloth**). This material along with ashes represents the traditional manner of expressing grief. While the text employs the image of the virgin, the addressees particularly seem to be the temple priests (see vv 9, 13).

■ **9** In v 9, the prophet describes the **mourning** (*ʾābal*) of the temple leaders over the loss of the crop. What Joel generally described in v 5 as "cut off" (*kārat*) from the people's mouths, he now specifically describes as **cut off** from the house of the Lord. Mourning before God was part of the intercessory ministry of the priests, particularly during national calamities and plagues (see also 1:13). The loss of crops in the land means the cessation of **grain offerings** and ***wine offerings*** in the temple. The priests lived on their share of these offerings for their nourishments. Their mourning reflects their sorrow over the loss of nourishment for themselves. However, beyond personal loss, the mourning of the priests also indicates sorrow over the cessation of proper communion with God that was accomplished through the offerings of the people.

■ **10** According to v 10, the grief is not confined to the human community. The **fields** [*śādeh*] **are ruined** or devastated (*šādad*) by the violent, life-taking attack of locusts. As a result, the ***soil*** (*ʾădāma*, **ground**) also ***mourns*** (*ʾābal*, **dried up;** see also the same verb in v 9 above and in Hos 4:3).

The second part of Joel 1:10 describes the impact of the ruin of the field on the three primary agricultural products (**grain**, **new wine**, and **oil**). The prophet here uses the same verb (*šādad*) to describe the ruin of both the fields and the grain; the grain has become just like the fields that produce them. Both lie in their **ruined** condition (NIV translates *šādad* as **ruined** for the fields and **destroyed** for the grain). The prophet describes **the new** or fresh **wine** as **dried up** (*yābēš*), or completely evaporated. This same verb appears three times later in v 12 and once again in v 20. Joel concludes with the observation that the fresh olive **oil** has ***grown weak*** or languished (*ʾāmal*, **fails**). The three verbs together graphically portray the complete loss of agricultural produce through ruin, dryness, and frailty. These images of dryness prepare for a textual transition from locust plague to draught that culminates in v 20.

■ **11** In v 11 the prophet directs those persons most directly invested in the fertility of the soil to grieve: ***ploughmen*** (**farmers**) who grow the grain and ***vinedressers*** who tend grapes, olives, and fruit trees. Verse 11 begins with a command to the ploughmen to ***be ashamed*** (*bōš*, **despair**). The verb *bōš* here sounds similar to *yābēš* ("dried up" in v 10), which suggests that perhaps a play on words (pun) is intended here. As new wine has dried up (*yābēš*), shame (*bōš*) comes upon tenders of the soil. Lack of agricultural produce meant the withdrawal of divine blessings in the ancient Mediterranean world, which in turn brought disgrace upon the farmer (see Wolff 1977, 32). The prophet also calls upon the vinedressers to ***howl*** or **wail** (see the same imperative in 1:5). The second part of v 11 specifically mentions **wheat** and **barley** among **the harvest of the field** . . . **destroyed** (*ʾābad*) by the locust plague.

■ **12** The prophet continues the use of picturesque verbs to describe the prevalence of hopeless infertility in v 12. The vine has **dried up** (*yābēš*) just as the fresh wine in v 10. The fig tree, stripped of its bark in v 7, has become ***feeble*** just as the olive oil in v 10. **Pomegranate**, **palm**, and **apple**—the fruit **trees of the field** that most represent fertility—have also **dried up** (*yābēš*). **All the trees of the field** indicate the farmers' loss of everything they had hoped to harvest. Verse 12 ends with a depiction of how the devastation has penetrated deeply into the communal psyche. Rejoicing associated with the harvest season has been completely **dried up** (*yābēš*) in the same manner that the crops have **dried up**. This devastation has affected the entire human community (*bĕnê ʾādām*, **the people**), not just the wine drinkers, priests, and farmers. Joy has been taken away from all who live in the land; no one is exempt.

■ **13** Joel returns to address the priests in vv 13-14. Joel begins with a command to ***gird*** themselves (*ḥāgar*), most likely with **sackcloth** (see v 8). The priests are those **who minister before the altar**, those who officiate in the temple rituals. They are also described as those **who minister before my God**. The service at the altar is essentially their service before God. Their ministry before the altar was directly tied to the **grain offerings** and **drink offerings** that they supervised at the altar of God (see v 9). These offerings were occasions of great rejoicing in the temple. The command to **mourn** and **wail** indicates the disappearance of joy from the temple because these offerings have been ***held back*** from the temple. The withholding of these offerings meant the disruption of priestly ministry as well as severe shortage of food supply to the priestly families that served in the temple.

The reference to the temple as **the house of your God** directly links the priests to the God before whom they minister in the temple. In the preceding line, the text refers to the priests as those who minister before **my God**. The God on whose behalf the prophet speaks is the same deity before whom the priests minister.

■ **14** The prophet commands the priests in v 14 to ***set apart*** or ***sanctify*** a communal **fast**, another ritual Israel observed when the nation experienced calamities of war or natural disasters. **Fast** usually consisted of day-long deprivation of food and perhaps water. Joel also commands the priests to **summon** both **the elders** and **all who live in the land** to participate in the public grief (v 14). **Elders** here most likely denote the tribal and clan leaders who would be most directly involved in the communal fast. The phrase **all who live in the land** perhaps includes both human and nonhuman creatures.

The assembly is to be a solemn and holy event in **the house of the Lord your God** where offerings have become extinct (1:9, 13, 16), but where fertility will one day flow abundantly (3:18). The prophet's summons to the nation to **cry out** to God is rooted in the memory of God's faithful, covenantal response to his people's cry in the past (see Exod 2:23; Judg 3:9, 15; 4:3; 6:7-8).

■ **15** The prophetic summons in v 14 also anticipates an even greater and imminent threat—**the day of the Lord** (v 15). While this day is not presently upon the people, it is **near**. The devastating agricultural crisis prepares the way for the greatest of calamities, which is rapidly approaching the nation.

The Day of Yahweh: Salvation or Judgment?

The Day of Yahweh was popularly understood in Israel as God's visitation in order to vindicate his people. In this visitation, he would bring judgment upon the nations and exalt Israel in the eyes of the nations. From a nationalistic perspective, the notion easily led to self-security on the part of God's people. Amos reversed the popular notion of the Day of Yahweh and described it as Yahweh's visitation to hold his people accountable for their sins; hence in Amos, this is a day of desolation and darkness rather than jubilation and light (Amos 5:18, 20). Amos' perspective is maintained by subsequent prophets (e.g., Isa 2:6—3:15; Ezek 7:19; Zeph 1:14-18). However, in postexilic prophets, the concept of the Day of Yahweh once again points to the salvation of God's faithful people (Zech 14:1-21; Mal 3:16—4:6). The prophet Joel particularly portrays the day first as one of judgment against the covenant people but ultimately as a day of judgment against the nations.

The opening interjection **alas** (*ʾăhâ*) introduces the terror of this imminent day (Joel 1:15). The Day of Yahweh will arrive with violent ***havoc*** or ***ruin*** (*šōd*, **destruction**). Through paronomasia, Joel describes the day as *šōd*, from *šadday*, or ***havoc*** **from the Almighty**. Neither in this instance nor in the other occurrences of the Day of Yahweh in Joel (2:1, 2, 11, 31; 3:14) does the book link this day specifically to the sin of God's people. Rather, the popular phrase depicts the horror and devastation brought about on this day of divine visitation and serves as the motivation to turn to Yahweh (and the house of God, i.e., the temple) for security.

■ **16** In v 16, Joel returns to the description of the destruction resulting from the locust plague. The people have witnessed their food supply disappear (**cut off**; see 1:5, 9) from their sight (**before our very eyes**). They have also witnessed the disappearance of **joy and gladness** from God's house. Verse 16 places **food** in direct parallelism with **joy and gladness**. Not only were offerings carried out in the context of jubilant mirth, but they likewise brought jubilation back upon the worshipper. As festival becomes fast, grief and painful outcry replace the familiar merriment.

■ **17** The precise meaning of the first line of v 17 is unclear. The verb *ʿābaš* (**shriveled**), the noun *pĕrudâ* (**seed**), and the noun *megrāpâ* (**clods**) occur only here in the Hebrew Bible. The verb *ʿābaš* likely conveys a sense of shriveling or shrinking. The noun *pĕrudāh* may derive from the verb that means "to divide" or "separate." Hence, the word could refer to the grain of seed that separates from the plant. The noun *megrāpāh* likely derives from the verb that means "to shovel," "scoop up," or "sweep away." In light of these possible word meanings, the line would describe the manner in which the seeds of grain shrivel under the shoveled clods; this would thus depict the lack of a seed harvest. The second half of v 17 vividly describes the emptiness of the harvest. The

storehouses are ***desolate*** (*šāmēm*) and the **granaries** are **broken down** (*hāras*). The emptiness of the storehouses results from the drying up of the grain; there is nothing to harvest and thus nothing to be stored up in the granaries.

■ **18** In v 18, Joel indicates that even the animals are affected by the calamity. They, too, **moan** to show their grief. Because of the lack of sufficient pasturage, entire **herds** of oxen aimlessly ***wander about*** in confusion. The last line of v 18 reports the suffering of the **flocks of sheep** caused by the catastrophic locust attack. The Hebrew text is difficult to understand. The Greek translation, followed by both the NIV and NRSV, interprets the verb to be derived from *šāmēm* ("be desolated," "devastated," "ravaged"). In the broader context of v 17, the NIV reading, **even the flocks of sheep are suffering**, makes sense.

■ **19-20** Verses 19-20 are in the form of a prayer. This is a prayer of utter dependency on Yahweh. The prayer opens with a direct address to Yahweh: **to you, Lord, I call**. Rather than a "crying out" (*zāʿaq*; see 1:14), the prayer is a **call** (*qārāʾ*) to God. The first-person subject most likely stands for the prophet, but the "I" also includes the suffering community as a corporate unity.

The remainder of vv 19-20 returns to the primary themes of vv 17-18. The experienced realities become expressions of prayer. They confess the devastation; they bring the situation as it is to their God. ***Fire eats up*** the pasturage of **the wilderness** (*midbār*). **Flames** set ablaze **all the trees of the field**. No sign of life remains; the destruction is comprehensive. ***The cattle of the field long*** (*ʿārag*) for Yahweh (v 20). The verb here points to a sense of deep longing or desire rather than to an action of outcry (see similar expression in Ps 42:1). With ravines dried up and pastures eaten by fire, the animals thirst and starve. As there is neither grain to eat nor wine to drink for the human community, there is neither pasturage (food) nor water ravines (drink) for the animal kingdom. All living beings are devastated by the effects of the agricultural crisis.

FROM THE TEXT

These oracles make a clear call for the reading community to participate in honest grief and transparent lament. In the vivid description of comprehensive devastation, there is no attempt to conceal or ignore the realities as they are. There is no move to rationalize or to explain the devastation away. Through the porous language of the text, the reader sees and experiences the reality of devastation as it is. As a result, the reading community can also honestly confess devastation and lifelessness. However, the text does not stop short in naming the despair. It proceeds to confess the source of life, fertility, and blessing. All of creation—both human and nonhuman—declares its utter dependency upon Yahweh, the giver and sustainer of life.

The text through its emphasis upon the joint lament of all of creation, human and nonhuman, land and vegetation, reminds the reading community of the scriptural understanding of the interconnectedness of creation. Humanity is not separate from creation but integral to and interconnected with all of creation. Human suffering and creational suffering occur side by side. When creation suffers, humans suffer; when humans suffer, creation suffers. The two are not and cannot be divorced. Indeed, the Apostle Paul affirms that creation itself groans along with humanity as it, too, eagerly awaits its redemption (Rom 8:22-23).

C. Enemy on the Horizon (2:1-11)

BEHIND THE TEXT

The context of ancient warfare provides the backdrop for this passage. The text depicts the common practice of warning the community of enemy invasion through the blast of the ram's horn (*šôpār*). Stationed at towers along the city wall, sentinels alerted citizens of imminent danger (see Ezek 33:2-6) so that they might gather within the city walls.

Traditional images of theophany (a physical manifestation of a deity) comprise the opening verses. Similar depictions of blasting horns, fire, smoke, cloud, darkness, and quaking also occur in the divine appearance at Sinai (Exod 19:16-19; 20:18; Deut 4:11-12; 5:22-23) as well as the ancient theophany hymn of Hab 3:3-11.

Although the language in Joel 2:1-11 emerges from the locust invasion of ch 1, the locusts recede in the background; the locust invasion provides the backdrop for the even more destructive Day of Yahweh that looms on the horizon in chs 2—3. Achtemeier has noted that beginning in ch 2 there "is no mere locust swarm." Rather, "this is God's army, come to destroy God's enemies, before which no one can escape" (1996b, 316; see also Crenshaw 1995, 116-17; Wolff [1977, 47] compares Joel 2:1-11 with Isa 13).

IN THE TEXT

■ **1** In vv 1-2, the prophet warns of the rapidly approaching Day of Yahweh. Terrible darkness accompanies the day of divine visitation. Through poetic parallelism in the first two lines, the prophet gives the command to sound the alarming war cry (**Blow the trumpet . . . sound the alarm**). The blast of the **trumpet** (*šôpār*) emerges from Jerusalem, the economic, political, and religious center of life. The house of God is located here (1:9, 13, 14; 3:18); indeed, the Lord himself "dwells in Zion" (3:21). Hence, both life and judgment proceed from here.

According to 2:1, all land dwellers, both human and nonhuman, quiver in fearful dread over the imminent divinely led attack. In v 10, Joel describes even the land as trembling in the presence of this destructive army. Joel's description of this day as ***imminent*** adds intensity to dreadfulness of this day.

■ **2** In v 2, the text proceeds to describe the nature of this day through stunning images. Using language of **darkness** and ***gloomy darkness*** (*ḥōšek, ʾăpēlâ*) and ***cloudiness*** and ***thick cloud*** (*ʿānān, ʿărāpel*), the prophet depicts the deathly and desperate nature of the divine visitation (see Zeph 1:14-15; also Amos 5:18; 8:9). The language of darkness portrays the catastrophic nature of the divine visitation. Joel may be thinking here of the experience of the Egyptians when their land was turned to black by the massive number of locusts that covered the surface of the land (Exod 10:14-15). Joel proceeds to compare the advancing army of Yahweh to the morning dawn that spreads itself like a garment over the mountains. Just as the early dull light of dawn rapidly blankets the countryside, so does this numerous and strong army permeate every corner of the land.

Joel 2:2 concludes with a report on the uniqueness of the day of Yahweh's visitation. Both in past memory and for the anticipated future, the event stands alone. The catastrophic effect of this day supersedes everything else, including the locust plague suffered by Egypt (Exod 10:6, 14), and the locust invasion that Israel has experienced in its present history (Joel 1:2-3).

■ **3** With vivid imagery, 2:3-5 describes the appearance, activity, and destructive effects of the invading army. In v 3, the text depicts the army's utter devastation of the land through images of devouring **fire** and blazing **flame**. The destruction is all-encompassing. Fire precedes the army and follows them (see 1:19).

The prophet compares the land to the **garden of Eden** before the invasion of the Lord's army on the Day of the Lord. The scenario of "before and after" depicts the utter desolation of the land that was once fertile and life-giving, like the garden of Eden (see Gen 2:8, 18). The land will become a ***desolate wilderness*** in the aftermath of the invading army. The army, as it marches forward, destroys everything in its path; nothing escapes its destructive power.

■ **4-5** The prophet describes the army using the particle of simile (*kĕ, **like***) five times in vv 4-5. The appearance of the invaders is ***like*** the appearance of **horses; like *war steeds* (cavalry)** they charge forward. They make noise **like** the rumbling of **chariots** and **like crackling fire**; they are **like** a powerful **army** preparing for war. Taken as a unit, the images vividly depict the army's swift, powerful, and destructive character. The depiction of intense rumbling and loud crackling brilliantly moves the audience beyond a mere visionary experience to an auditory one. They see the devastation taking place before their eyes; they also hear the sound of devastation.

Unlike an army of simple chariots that rides upon the mountaintops, this army moves so swiftly that it ***leaps*** or ***skips about*** from one location to the other (see also Nah 3:2). This destructive army devours even the chaff before them. In the end, this strong army is prepared for the ensuing battle as they are orderly arranged (**drawn up**). Not only is it capable by means of its might, swiftness, and destructive nature, but it is likewise logistically prepared as it is ready to invade in a systematic fashion.

■ **6** This invading army is a force with which to be reckoned and from which there is no escape. With such a powerful and prepared army's advance imminent, the people groups (lit. ***peoples***) are in writhing **anguish** (see the use of this language to convey the anguish of the people brought about by invading armies in Deut 2:25; Jer 4:19; Ezek 30:16). The phrase **at the sight of them** conveys the idea that the very presence of this powerful army evokes tremendous angst. However, the Hebrew text reads the pronoun in singular ("it"/"him"), which could refer to the army in its totality or to Yahweh himself (see Wolff 1977, 46).

The second half of Joel 2:6 further describes the physical manifestation of the people's angst. In the *face* of the enemy, their *faces* become panic-stricken (see Isa 13:8). The meaning of the word *pā'rûr* (**pale**) is not clear; it occurs only here and in Nah 2:10 [2:11 HB]. The text obviously depicts the distressed look of the persons under imminent attack who are faced with the threat of their impending doom.

■ **7-9** Various action-filled verbs in Joel 2:7-9 depict the army's orderly invasion. The army first charges toward the city and proceeds to **scale** its defensive **walls** (v 7*a*). It continues its organized **march** into the city (vv 7*b*-8*a*) and overpowers the weaponry within the city (v 8*b*). Finally, it climbs the house walls and, like a thief, enters **through the windows** (v 9).

Charging and scaling the city walls, each warrior reflects an orderly, prearranged attack. Each stays on his set path without interfering with his companion. The theme of an established, well-defined path (*derek*) repeats itself throughout vv 7-8. Familiar in the wisdom tradition, the notion of the straight path represents the wise and prudent life.

The concluding phrase of v 7 in the Hebrew text infers that the warriors neither take nor give a pledge (*'ābaṭ* means "to take a pledge"). However, most translations read here *'ābat* ("to swerve," "twist," "weave"; **not swerving from their course**). The preceding and subsequent lines of the text support this reading.

Continuing the theme of the orderly march, v 8 depicts each warrior keeping in line without interfering (**jostle**) with the other. Each warrior **marches straight ahead** (*měsillâ* conveys the idea of a public road or open highway) and remains clearly focused in order to carry out his task.

The army successfully enters the city and proceeds to **plunge through** the weapons. Joel seems to describe the manner in which the invaders successfully thrust themselves through the ***weaponry*** (*šelaḥ*) hurled at them. The NIV **defenses** conveys the general idea intended by the text (see Crenshaw's interpretation of this text as the army entering the city through Siloam tunnel [1995, 124]). Verses 8-9 quite graphically depict the inability to stop the army's advance once they have entered the city. Without a direct object, the concluding line of v 8 simply states that "they do not cut off." The NIV reading, **without breaking ranks** (by adding the word "ranks"), maintains consistency with the orderly procession of the army indicated in the text.

In the concluding description of the warriors in v 9, a plethora of action words describe systematic yet hurried activity. They **rush** (*šāqaq*) in a roaming manner. The verb here depicts the quick occurrence of a threatening activity, by military chariots (Nah 2:4), wild animals (Prov 28:15), or locusts (Isa 33:4). As they **run along** the walls, they proceed to climb through windows into houses. Their quick, unexpected entrance recalls the action of a thief.

■ **10-11** In vv 10-11, the prophet leaves no doubt concerning the true nature of the imminent invasion. The mighty invaders are Yahweh's army. This event is ultimately the divine visitation upon the nations and upon the covenant people; Joel makes it clear that it is indeed the Day of Yahweh through signs traditionally related to this dreadful day.

Both land and sky experience the effect of the divine visitation. The ***land*** itself ***quakes*** (*rāgaz*; see 1 Sam 14:15; Ps 77:18 [77:19 HB]; Amos 8:8), and the **sky** ***shakes*** (*rā'aš*) (see also Joel 3:16). The orderly separation between land below and sky above (Gen 1:6-10) becomes threatened. The luminaries (Gen 1:14-19)—**sun, moon,** and **stars**—become dark (see Joel 2:2, where Joel describes this day as a day of gloomy darkness and thick clouds; see also Isa 13:10-13 and Ezek 32:7-8). These cosmic signs are triggered ***before him*** (both NIV and NRSV read **before them**). The singular pronoun (***him*** or ***it***) may refer to Yahweh who **thunders at the head of his army** (see Joel 2:11) or to the army in its totality, in contrast to the individual warriors (i.e., **them**).

In v 11 the prophet describes Yahweh's immediate and direct relationship to this dreadful event. Yahweh ***gives*** (**thunders**) his voice **at the head of his** [the mighty] **army** (see Crenshaw 1995, 128, concerning the thundering voice of the storm gods of the ancient Near East). The army is **his** and he is the commander in chief of this army (see 2:25).

The second half of v 11 begins with the announcement that **the day of the Lord is great**; indeed, **it is** a **dreadful** day. Previous verses have graphically described the terrifying effect of this day. Verse 11 ends with the rhetorical question, **Who can endure it?** (see a similar statement in Mal 3:2). No one is able to contain this overwhelming invasion. One cannot begin to capture the

Day of Yahweh; one can only be captured by it. The reference to the Day of Yahweh in Joel 2:11 provides a significant literary inclusio with v 1. At the same time, within the larger literary context, the rhetorical question prepares the way for the call to repentance that will follow in v 12.

FROM THE TEXT

These eleven verses make indubitably clear the horrific terror of the invading army. The use of graphic images engages the audience in such a way that it can participate in the horrific nature of the onslaught. Such texts filled with creative and graphic images remind subsequent audiences of the significant role played by language in both ancient and contemporary prophetic proclamation.

As with the laments, the honest naming of terror and destruction permeates this text. Such articulation of the horrific reality faced by God's people allows the community of faith to see, experience, and articulate their own contemporary situation with honesty. As terror is put to words, the text refuses to shape a community in which faith conceals harsh realities of life. Those who hear this prophetic text can acknowledge and engage in the catastrophe and subsequent catastrophes that occur in the human family.

The portrait of God commandeering his army needs to be viewed through the lens of the full Christian canon. In light of the overall tenor of Scripture, the reading community should be cautious in seeing in this text a link between horrific and terrorizing events and the direct activity of God. The purpose of this text is not to provide a final and definitive answer as to why all devastating events occur (i.e., the judgment of God). Rather, it seeks to describe the final and consummating activity of God against evil and the ultimate establishment of his reign over his people, the nations, and all creation.

The cosmic disruptions of quaking and darkness reflect familiar language of the theophany. The Christian reader recalls similar cosmic disruptions at the time of Christ's death and resurrection (see Matt 27:45, 51-52; 28:2). These depictions of the death and resurrection of Christ reflect the establishment of the reign of God. As Christ has died and has risen to life, the Day of the Lord has indeed begun to occur.

The text of Joel does not give definitive details concerning a final divine judgment on the Day of the Lord. However, the text demonstrates a resolute conviction that divine judgment will occur. Ultimately, the reader cannot separate these depictions of disaster in 2:1-11 from what follows in vv 12-17 (i.e., the turning to God in time of disaster). In that sense, this text serves both as a warning and as an invitation to those under judgment to turn to God for salvation.

D. Call to Repentance (2:12-17)

BEHIND THE TEXT

The call to repentance is a familiar theme throughout the story of ancient Israel. This call is deeply rooted in the theological conviction of God's favor toward the covenant people (see Exod 34:6-7). Israel's traditional confession of God's faithfulness to and forgiveness of his people serves as the backdrop for Joel's words in 2:12-17. The community's turning to God is possible only because of divine grace preceding human response. In this text, the call to repentance is found in the context of the urgency and desperation of the people because of the impending Day of Yahweh.

IN THE TEXT

■ **12** The call to repentance comes from Yahweh. The opening phrase, **Even now**, indicates the urgency of the situation and the need for immediate action. The people's **return** to Yahweh (**to me**) is the immediate action that is being called for. The oracle formula *nĕʾum-ʾădōnay* (***an oracle of Yahweh***) makes the urgency of the declaration even more apparent. Although this formula is familiar in other prophets, it occurs only here in Joel.

The imperative, **return to me with all your heart**, brings to mind the Deuteronomic call to love the Lord with "all your heart" (Deut 6:5; 30:2, 6) (regarding the **heart** in Hebrew anthropology as the organ of the will and rational thought, → Hos 2:14).

Verse 12 concludes with a list of three activities—**fasting**, **weeping**, and ***contrite wailing***—that were linked to grief and repentance in ancient Israel during calamities such as war, disease, plague, or drought. The prophet urges the people to carry out these activities as expressions of their repentance. Communal abstinence from food reflects the corporate nature of grief. The entire community participates in the fast. Fasting is to be accompanied by **weeping** and ***contrite wailing***, signs not only of grief but also of repentance.

■ **13** In v 13, Joel admonishes the people not simply to follow the ordinary mourning custom of ripping (**rend**) their **garments** (e.g., Gen 37:29; Ezra 9:3; Job 2:12). Instead, he calls upon them to tear their **heart** (*lēb*). This action calls for the decision of the communal will to be genuine in its expression of grief. Internal grief is brokenness of the heart, grief that occurs within the human heart, which finds expressions in the rituals of fasting and weeping.

Verse 13 reiterates the call to **return** (*šûb*) to Yahweh. Achtemeier concludes that this text clearly calls upon God's people "to turn away from apostasy and return to God in a deliberate act of will" (1996b, 319). Joel identifies **the Lord your God** as the object of the people's turning. The divine name ***Yahweh*** and his covenant relationship (**your God**) (see Jer 31:33; 32:38; Hos

7:10; 12:5-6) set the context for the prophet's description of the character of Israel's God, which also serves as the theological reason for the call to return.

Joel finds hope for the nation in the unchanging character of Yahweh as **gracious** (*ḥannûn*), **compassionate** (*raḥûm*), **slow to anger** (*ʾerek ʾappayim*), and **abounding in love** (*rab-ḥesed*). The God of Israel also **relents from sending calamity** (*niḥām ʿal-hārāʿāh*). This faith is rooted in Yahweh's revelation at Sinai as a gracious and compassionate God who showed mercy and grace to his people who broke their covenant with him and participated in idolatry (Exod 34:6-7). This confession is one of the most oft-repeated confessions of God's character in the OT (see Num 14:18; Neh 9:17, 31; Ps 103:8; Jonah 4:2).

God's graciousness is his undeserved mercy that he extends to his people; this divine attribute depicts the benevolence a superior shows to an inferior person (see its various uses in Exod 22:27; 2 Chr 30:9; Ps 86:15 [86:16 HB]). The second divine attribute, **compassionate** (*raḥûm*), reflects the merciful divine love toward the people. This adjective conveys the gentle, affectionate, parental nature of Yahweh's love (see Hosea's use of the root in 1:6; 2:1, 23; 14:3). Yahweh is also **slow to anger**; he is not quick to act upon his anger with wrathful acts. The description of Yahweh as **abounding in love** (*ḥesed*) conveys the idea of the greatness of his covenant faithfulness. It extends to the thousandth generation (see Exod 34:7). The final line, **he relents from sending calamity**, indicates that God's grace and covenant loyalty move him to relent (*niḥam*) or change his mind about what he planned to do to his people. However, this change of mind is not arbitrary; it is directly associated with his sorrow, mercy, and forgiveness (regarding the OT portrayal of God's changing of mind, see Fretheim 1988, 47-70).

■ **14** In v 14, Joel turns his attention to God's sovereign freedom. While Yahweh is gracious and forgiving, he is also sovereign and free to respond as he chooses. The very name of God, ***Yahweh***, conveys that this deity will be whoever he will be. The question, **Who knows?** indicates that the covenant community can neither coerce nor manipulate this God. According to Crenshaw, this rhetorical question "contains an implicit negative response: 'nobody knows'" (1995, 138). Even in their repentance, the people cannot presume upon God; he remains sovereign. The statement, **he may turn** (*šûb*) and change his mind (*niḥam*, **relent**), reiterates the theme of divine freedom (see Jonah's similar statement in Jonah 3:9). The prophet has previously called upon the people to turn (*šûb*) to Yahweh; now he declares that Yahweh may turn (*šûb*) to them.

Joel is optimistic that Yahweh might bring **blessing** (*bĕrākâ*) rather than "calamity" or evil (*rāʿâ*; v 13). This vivid contrast between life-death, blessing-curse, good (*ṭôb*)-evil (*rāʿâ*) occurs in the classic call to choose life in Deut 30:15, 19.

Joel 2:14 concludes by observing the effect of divine blessing. Fertility replaces infertility; life replaces death. This blessing will make it possible for the people to bring **grain offerings** and **drink offerings** to the temple for Yahweh, the God of Israel (**your God**). Verse 14 makes clear that there is an integral relationship between divine grace, the community's return, divine blessing, and the community's worship.

■ **15** In vv 15-17, in a staccato-like series of seven plural imperatives, each followed by a brief indefinite direct object, the prophet directs the religious leaders to make preparations for the fast. While the text does not specify the intended recipients of the commands, the command to set apart a communal lament and to sanctify a congregation points to the priests. He calls for the blowing of the *šôpār* to announce the fast (see 2:1, where it alerts the people to an invading army). The religious leaders are then commanded to set apart or ***sanctify*** (*qādaš*) a fast (**declare a holy fast**) and to call for **a sacred assembly** to take place (see 1:14).

■ **16** Joel then instructs the religious leaders to **gather the people** (*ʿam*) and to set them apart or ***sanctify*** (*qādaš*, **consecrate**) this organized body or **the assembly** (*qāhāl*). From the oldest to the youngest members of the community, including the nursing infants, are to be a part of this gathering; no one is excluded. Even the celebration of marriage is placed on hold for this communal fast. The bridegroom is to come out from his private chamber room and the bride from her bridal chamber. The urgency of the threat requires everyone in the land to participate in the fast.

■ **17** In v 17, Joel extends the call to the priests, those **who minister before the Lord**, to take the lead in the communal fast through weeping. Their expressions of grief should take place just outside the temple between ***the outer porch*** (*ʾûlām*) and **the altar** (*mizbēaḥ*; see Solomon's sacrifice in 2 Chr 8:12). As temple service has all but ceased, the text emphasizes the mourning that occurs within the precincts of the temple itself.

The prophet also calls the priests to pray on behalf of the people, and thus to perform their intercessory function. Joel provides the language of prayer, which has three parts. The first part of the prayer is an urgent appeal to Yahweh to **spare** or to have pity on his people. This intercessory prayer originates in Israel's understanding of Yahweh as its covenant partner who is bound to Israel by his covenant faithfulness (*ḥesed*). This appeal acknowledges Israel as Yahweh's people (**your people**), his covenant partner.

The second part of this prayer is an appeal to Yahweh to not let Israel, his **inheritance,** become **an object of scorn** or **a byword among the nations**. Old Testament texts frequently describe Israel as Yahweh's inheritance or personal *property* (*naḥălâ*; see Deut 4:20; 9:26, 29; 1 Sam 10:1; 1 Kgs 8:53; Isa 19:25; Joel 3:2; Mic 7:14). While all of the earth belongs to Yahweh, through the covenant at Sinai Israel is uniquely his possession (Exod 19:5-6; see also Amos 3:2). This appeal is rooted in the belief that the shameful state of the people of Israel has a negative impact on the honor and reputation of Yahweh **among the nations** in the world (see Ezek 36:16 ff.). Other prophets spoke of God making Israel an object of shameful reproach and a byword among the nations through his judgment (see Jer 24:9; 29:18; Ezek 5:14-15). The prayer here is an urgent plea to God to spare Israel from judgment so that God's honor in the world would not suffer shame. Nations in the world would ask among themselves the question, **Where is their God?** This is a concern often found in the laments (see Pss 42:3, 10; 79:10; 115:2). Not only would Israel's reputation come to ruin among the nations, but even more Yahweh's reputation would be tarnished. The nations would perceive Israel's covenant God to be either a deity who does not care to rescue his people or who is not capable of such rescue.

FROM THE TEXT

The prophetic call to repentance provided by this passage has served across generations as the call to observe the Lenten season through honest confession and contrition. This text invites the readers to acknowledge their shortcomings and their utter dependence upon God. Through this text, the reader understands confession as the appropriate and right response to a merciful and forgiving God. The practice of the fast in faith functions as a means whereby divine grace is at work in the life of God's people, bringing transformation. John Wesley emphasized that "godly sorrow for sin" should be associated with fasting. He also taught that fasting ultimately should

> work in us the same inward and outward repentance; the same entire change of heart, renewed after the image of God, in righteousness and true holiness; and the same change of life, till we are holy as He is holy in all manner of conversation. (1984, 610)

The text makes clear that there should be a significant balance between ritual (e.g., fasting, imposition of ashes, weeping) and the inner disposition. As the text calls for both, it refuses to negate either. Like his prophetic predecessors, Joel recognizes the lure and even the danger of ritual observance that is void of the inner disposition. Yet the text calls upon the audience to carry out the ritual of the fast as the ritual emerges from the depth of the inner being—the mind, or in the Hebrew thinking, the heart. In his *Festal Letters,* Athanasius emphasized the call to sanctify (i.e., make holy) a fast. He observed the holy manner in which the fast must be carried out, noting that many people, though they go through the motions of a fast, are still polluted in their hearts because they do evil against their brothers and sisters or because they dare to cheat. And many, if nothing else, think more highly of themselves than of their neighbors, thereby committing a great offense (1979, 51).

We find in the text the portrait of God who permits for a divine change of action, the God who stands in authentic relationship with the community. Clearly the God of this passage is not the stoic, immovable God whose "mind is made up." On the contrary, he will lovingly move into the morrow with his people and will act for their good and for their salvation. Consistent, never-changing covenant faithfulness engenders graciousness, mercy, and forgiveness. These in turn provide the context for the Lord to change his course of action vis-à-vis the covenant community. Such change is the sign of fidelity, grace, and covenant relationship. It is the embodiment of a God who is in genuine covenant relationship with his people in such a way not only that he affects them but that they in turn affect him.

The text also tenaciously maintains a firm understanding of divine sovereignty. Therefore, in the midst of the call to repentance, Joel exclaims, "Who knows . . . perhaps . . ." While the prayer of confession expresses the relational nature of the divine character, it refuses to allow divine grace, mercy, and forgiveness to become an idol that can be manipulated and controlled. Wesley warned God's people about the danger of thinking that they merit God's mercy in return for their fasting. He observed that "fasting is only a way which God hath ordained wherein we wait for his *unmerited* mercy; and wherein, without any desert of ours, he hath promised *freely* to give us his blessing" (1984, 609).

While the text focuses upon the relational character of God, it also imagines a faithful community that defines itself as a relational people who embody the character of their covenant God in their communal life. To be a community formed by a God of this character is to be a community transformed into the character of this God. The text challenges the reading community to envision itself as gracious, compassionate, slow to anger, abounding in love, and relenting from sending calamity . . . and to live toward that vision.

E. A Jealous God Acts (2:18-27)

BEHIND THE TEXT

From 2:18 to the end of the book, the text depicts a reversal of the devastation described earlier in the text. In vv 18-27, the prophet depicts the plenteous harvest that Yahweh will bring about through the fertility of grain, wine, and oil. Joel calls upon all creation, including soil and animals, not to fear and provides the divine promise that the people will never again experience such shame. These verses prepare the way for the annihilation of the enemies and the establishment of the covenant community depicted in ch 3.

IN THE TEXT

■ **18** In v 18, Joel gives the assurance of God's action to the lamenting community. **The Lord *will be* jealous** (*qānāʾ*) may be best understood as God's zeal, his commitment to that which belongs to him. The object of divine jealousy (or, his zealousness) is **his land**; the object of divine **pity** is **his people**. The verb *ḥāmal* (***take pity***) means more than an emotional sense of empathy or compassion; it also depicts pathos put to action by means of sparing or rescuing one from calamity. According to Israel's faith, both the people and the land belong to God, and both are objects of his saving work.

■ **19** Verses 19-20 contain Yahweh's direct response to the people. Through a series of first-person verb forms, Yahweh outlines the actions he will undertake to reverse the misfortunes of his land and his people. The first line of v 19 is a continuation of the prophetic assurance in v 18. Joel assures the lamenting community that Yahweh ***will reply to his people***; the Hebrew text infers the covenant relationship between Yahweh and ***his people*** Israel.

The divine response is one of immediacy, conveyed by the particle *hinnēh* (often translated as ***lo*** or ***behold***). The text clearly indicates the divine presence presently acting on behalf of the community. Yahweh's reply is addressed directly to his people (see the second person **you** [plural] in vv 19-20).

Yahweh's reply begins with the announcement that he is **sending** to his people (you) **grain, new wine and *oil***. Yahweh's activity begins with the reversal of the curse of dryness and destruction, the withdrawal of the fertility of the land. Empty storehouses and granaries (1:17) and parched fields (1:10) will be no more; the people will now have excess. The phrase **satisfy you fully** conveys the idea of satiation or superabundance.

Yahweh also promised to bring an end to the disdain of the people in the eyes of the nations in the world. No longer will Yahweh make his people an **object of scorn** or disgrace. The return of fertility to the land will be a sure testimony to the zealousness of Yahweh for his people.

■ **20** Yahweh promises to drive out and destroy the ***northerner*** in v 20. Destructive invasions often occurred from the north (e.g., Assyrians, Babylonians, and Persians); Joel follows here the prophetic tradition of describing the invading army as the ***northerner*** (see Jer 1:13-15; 4:6; 6:1, 22; see also Ezek 38:6, 15; Zech 2:6). The precise identity of this army is not given. Some commentators interpret the word ***northerner*** as a reference to the locust swarms that attacked the land (Allen 1976, 88). However, it is likely that the reference here is to an evil force that had served the purpose of God's judgment of his people. Again the locust invasion provides the backdrop for this verse. Rather than simply destroying the ruthless army, Yahweh will banish it to a **parched and barren land** (see also Isa 41:18; Jer 26:6; Hos 2:3 [2:5 HB]).

Barren land in other texts is a devastated wasteland, burned and ravaged (Isa 1:7), and without human inhabitant (Exod 23:29). This army once devastated Yahweh's land; Yahweh will now banish it to a devastated land. The verb ***banishing*** or **pushing** (*nādaḥ*) conveys the idea of the exile of this nation (see Deut 30:1; Jer 46:28; Ezek 4:13 for the use of this verb for the Judean exile).

Joel 2:20 also identifies the arid wasteland as two bodies of water: ***the eastern sea*** (**Dead Sea**) and ***the western sea*** (**Mediterranean Sea**). ***The front columns*** (**the eastern ranks**) of the army will go into the site of utter lifelessness, the salty Dead Sea. ***The rear columns*** (**western ranks**) will go into the salt water of the Mediterranean. The army, from beginning to end, will drown in arid lifelessness. As a result, the deathly stench of this once-mighty army will ascend in a manner similar to the stench of dead fish and frogs in Egypt (Exod 7:18, 21; 8:14).

Joel 2:20 ends with a praise, **Surely he [*the* LORD] has done great things!** (see also the last line of v 21), in response to Yahweh's promise of the destruction of the enemy and the return of fertility and blessing to the land and the people (see Ps 126:2-3). In Joel, it is a confession that comes from the mouth of the prophet on behalf of God's people for his promised salvation.

■ **21-22** Verses 21-27 contain an oracle of salvation; it begins with the customary admonition, ***Do not fear*** (vv 21, 22). This admonition is addressed to the ***ground/soil*** and the ***animals of the field***; it originates in the prophet's confidence that God has done great things.

Animals of the field may be **wild animals** (v 22) or larger cattle that graze in the pastures that had been devastated in the catastrophe. As a result of the new life that has come upon the ground/soil, the ***open*** **pastures** will sprout grass and become green, and thus once again become a feeding ground.

Joel includes the fruitfulness of trees in his description of the abundant fertility of the land in v 22. **Fig** trees that once lay waste (see 1:7) now yield a plentiful crop. **The vine** produces at its highest level of efficiency.

■ **23** In v 23, Joel invites the people of Zion to **be glad** and **rejoice** in ***Yahweh*** **your God**. Those who worship Yahweh upon Mount Zion now have a reason to rejoice in their God (see Ps 149:2-3). ***Yahweh***, the covenant God of Israel (**your God**), has brought fertility back to the ground by sending the much-needed rain for the ground to produce its yield.

Yahweh has given the ground both the **autumn** and **spring** rains. The emphasis is on abundant showers. Joel describes the autumn rains as given ***in righteousness*** (*ṣĕdāqâ* means "right-relatedness" or "proper order"; **because he is faithful**). Wolff concludes that God's provision of fertility to his people is "appropriate to Yahweh's covenant relationship with Israel" (1977, 63). God shows himself as righteous God by bringing order to the communal existence of his people. However, the phrase ***in righteousness*** could reflect the broader understanding of the order of creation itself. The autumn rains arrive at the appropriate time within God's created order (see Crenshaw 1995, 155).

■ **24** Verse 24 depicts the result of the autumn and spring rains. The primary agricultural produce of Israel—grain, grapes, olive oil—that was once absent from Judah (1:10) will become plentiful once again. The locust plague made the storehouses desolate (1:17), but the rain from God will yield a plentiful harvest that will fill ***the harvest*** **floors** with grain. Likewise, **the vats** that had become dry when the fruit trees were destroyed (1:12) will overflow with **new wine** from pressed grapes and **oil** from crushed olives (see 3:13 where Joel uses the language of 2:24 to describe the reversal of the fortunes of Israel's enemies).

■ **25** Yahweh's promise to reverse the misfortunes of Israel continues in vv 25-27. In v 25, Yahweh announces that he will ***make whole*** or complete (*šālēm*, from which the noun *šālôm* is derived; **repay**) that which his people have lost. He will restore wholeness to the people by restoring all that has been destroyed by the locust swarm, his **great army** that he sent among them.

■ **26** The same satiation depicted in v 19 characterizes the people's future in v 26. The Hebrew verb form (infinitive absolute) conveys the idea of the abundance of food for the people's continual eating (**plenty to eat**). A satisfied satiation will result from this uninterrupted nourishment. The reading, **You will have plenty to eat, until you are full**, does not adequately convey the ongoing sense of both the eating and the consequent satisfaction.

The people's satiation will engender their praise of God. The reference to **the name of the Lord** points to the divine reputation. God's character is reflected in the divine name, Yahweh. For Israel, Yahweh is indeed not merely God or a God but **your God**. In the same way, Israel is not just another people in the world, but they are **my people**, God's covenant partner, a people belonging to God through the covenant relationship. The people's praise is directly related to the ***awe-inspiring deeds*** carried out by Yahweh (**worked wonders for you**) in behalf of his people. The reference to these deeds emerges out of the paradigmatic events of the deliverance from Egypt and the provision in the wilderness. Yahweh was known and praised throughout Israel's history for these mighty acts. Verse 26 ends with God's promise that his people will never again be put to shame.

■ **27** The final line of v 26 is repeated again at the end of v 27. Moreover, both verses reiterate the language of covenant relationship between Yahweh and Israel (**your God, my people**). Central to this covenant relationship is the acknowledgment of the covenant community that Yahweh is **in Israel**. This affirmation of God's presence in the midst of his people serves as the crescendo to the book of Joel (3:21). Echoing the language of the Decalogue in Exod 20:2-3, Joel 2:27 links Yahweh's presence to the people's unrivaled loyalty (**I**

am the Lord your God, and . . . there is no other). **There is no other** is God's claim of his unrivaled place in the God-Israel relationship; however, it also elicits the faithful response of the people that they have no other God but Yahweh. The twice-repeated covenant language (**your God**, **my people**) and the twice-repeated promise that Israel shall never be put to shame in vv 26 and 27 show the inexorable link between the covenant relationship and Yahweh's fidelity to the covenant. The promise that Israel shall never again be put to shame is found in these verses as a unilateral promise from Yahweh. This promise, however, anticipates the faithful response of the people that Yahweh is their only God and that there is no other.

FROM THE TEXT

In the depiction of divine action, the text paints a vivid portrayal of a covenant-oriented God, a relational deity that challenges common notions and popular assumptions about the character of God. Divine jealousy for what is his prompts a divine response. He is not detached from the cry of his people but rather is affected by their outcry (Exod 2:23-25; 3:9-10; 22:21-24; see also Gen 21:15-19). Consistent with the testimony of Scripture, Joel portrays God as changing the course of his actions and acting out of his compassion on behalf of the people to whom he is committed through his covenant, though they have deserted him. Becoming flesh and dwelling among mortals, this God, moved by compassion, opened blind eyes (Matt 20:34) and restored withered bodies (Mark 3:6). That is good news for the readers of Joel today.

The text also challenges the reading community to faithfully respond to God, who does great and wonderful things (Joel 2:20, 26). The text of Joel anticipates the people of God engaging in praise and worship and living in true covenant relationship with him. The invitation of the text to its readers today is to be true witnesses of God's faithful and compassionate work in the world. God's faithfulness to his people and the witness of his people to his gracious divine character thus characterize the nature of the relationship between God his people, both then and now.

III. THE COSMIC DAY OF YAHWEH AND THE ESTABLISHMENT OF THE REIGN OF GOD: JOEL 2:28—3:21

2:28-32

A. After Deliverance . . . (2:28-32 [3:1-5 HB])

BEHIND THE TEXT

Joel 2:28 in the English text is the beginning of a third chapter (consisting of five verses) in the Hebrew text. Likewise, 3:1 in the English text begins a fourth chapter in the Hebrew text, which continues to the conclusion of the book.

Beginning in 2:28, the oracles shift to divine judgment upon the nations and the exaltation of God's people, particularly Zion. The devastating events in 1:1—2:17 and the divine deliverance in 2:18-27 serve as a backdrop for this ultimate divine visitation upon all peoples. The transition to universal judgment emerges quite naturally from the concern for the nations' mocking of God's people in 2:17, 19, 26-27. The Lord will set things right, that is, give justice/judgment vis-à-vis the nations. From 2:28 on, the destructive armies of the preceding verses evolve into a military showdown between God and the nations that have devastated both God's land and people (3:2-3).

The oracles that follow 2:28 seem to depict a more remote and distant future; it is likely that they emerge from a period later than that of 1:1—2:27. The portrait of God's sovereignty over the nations and God's ultimate commitment to Jerusalem clearly conveys an eschatological tone that is lacking in the preceding verses. The opening phrase "and afterward" introduces a more distant time in which salvation surpasses even that described in 2:18-27.

IN THE TEXT

■ **28-29** The temporal statements **and afterward** (v 28) and **in those days** (v 29) clearly mark vv 28-29 as a literary unit. Yahweh is the speaker in vv 28-29, and his word comes as an eschatological promise to the covenant community. The opening phrase **and afterward** (*wĕhāyâ ʾaḥărê-kēn*) links the depiction of disaster and deliverance in the preceding verses to the divine promise in vv 28-32 and the oracles in ch 3. According to Wolff, this phrase presupposes the fulfillment of the preceding oracles and confirms "the expectation of the much greater future response" (Wolff 1977, 65; see also Achtemeier 1996b, 326, who interprets the phrase **and afterward** as indicating a future "indefinite time").

Yahweh's speech begins with his promise that he **will pour out** his **Spirit on all people** (v 28). The language of Yahweh pouring out (*šāpak*) his Spirit is unique to Joel and Ezekiel (see Ezek 39:29; Zech 12:10 speaks of "a spirit" rather than "my Spirit"). The verb **pour out** indicates that Yahweh does not hold back or limit the availability of his Spirit, but rather he offers his Spirit in a superabundant manner. Barton describes the Spirit (*rûaḥ*) as "the principle of YHWH's own life, the breath in YHWH's own nostrils" (Barton 2001, 94). Thus, what is being promised here is a gift of the life-giving vitality of God to his people; this promise is parallel to God's promise of the satiating showers of fertility in 2:21-27. The activity of the Spirit is frequently found in the stories of Judges and 1 Samuel (Judg 6:34; 14:6, 19; 15:14; 1 Sam 10:6, 10; 11:6; 16:13). Israel's early traditions portray the Spirit as an empowering Spirit, "a gift given in order that the recipient might do a particular job for God" (Achtemeier 1996b, 326).

The reference to **all people** (*bāśār* literally means "flesh," which indicates the frail and weak condition of humanity) means all members of the community. Although the immediate context obviously points to Israel or more specifically Judah, Barton is correct in noting that the phrase here means "all humankind without exception" (2001, 96; Crenshaw interprets the phrase as referring to "all Judahites" [1995, 165]; also Wolff 1977, 67).

Joel also indicates that the Spirit's outpouring will not be limited to certain privileged members of the community. The community as a whole—**sons, daughters, old men, young men, servants**—will experience the life-giving, animating Spirit of God. The outcome of God's outpouring of his Spirit upon all people is the ability to **prophesy**, to **dream dreams** and **see visions** (see the spirit and the activity of prophesying in Num 11:25-29; 1 Sam 10:6, 9-13; see also Isa 48:16; 61:1; Hos 9:7; Mic 3:8). The outpouring of God's Spirit will enable its recipients to speak a prophetic word (**prophesy**) and receive a prophetic word (**dream dreams** and **see visions**). Like all true prophets, everyone in the community will be spokespersons for God and will have direct communication from God. This same emphasis is found in Acts 2, where Peter quotes this text in his famous sermon on the day of Pentecost.

■ **30-31** Verses 30-31 focus on another entirely different way God will show himself to all humankind "afterward" or "in those days" (vv 28-29). The portrait of God changes from one who pours out his Spirit to one who comes to judge all humanity. Signs (**wonders**) of this day of his **coming** will be visible both in **the heavens and on the earth**. The signs of **blood and fire and billows of smoke** echo the ancient traditions of Yahweh's intervention and deliverance of Israel from Egypt and the destruction of the enemy (see Exod 4:9; 7:20; 13:21-22; Num 14:14). In Joel 2:31, the text continues to depict the signs of the divine visitation. **The sun** and **the moon**, the heavenly bodies of light, will be turned into **darkness** and **blood** respectively. Crenshaw describes these occurrences as possible effects of solar eclipses that "aroused consternation among ancient peoples" and "sandstorms that give the moon a reddish appearance" (1995, 168). While the images may emerge from such natural events, the text likely envisions a reversal of the created order itself. These wondrous signs will occur **before the coming of the great and dreadful day of the LORD.** The wondrous divine signs that have pointed to Yahweh's delivering power in the past now prepare the way for the divine visitation upon both his people and the surrounding nations.

■ **32** Joel announces in v 32 that this dreadful day of divine visitation will also be the day of salvation to ***all who call upon the name of Yahweh***. Those who call on God's name invoke God's assistance in a specific situation. Psalmists often call on God in the midst of their distress to show their total dependence on God for their deliverance (see Ps 141, for example).

The promise of Joel 2:32 is that those who seek God **will be saved** on that day from the imminent catastrophe. Joel uses here the verb *mālaṭ*, which signifies an escape from a grim disaster (see Job 1:14-19; Ps 124:7; Amos 2:14-15) instead of the more common verb (*yāṣaʿ*), which conveys the idea of salvation.

Joel identifies **Mount Zion** and **Jerusalem** as the specific locations where the people will experience escape or deliverance in the midst of catastrophes in the heavens and on the earth (see Obad 17). The verb used in the second part of v 32 (*pālaṭ* means "escape," "deliver") resembles the verb *mālaṭ* in the first part of the verse in form and meaning. Those who call upon Yahweh's name will discover safety in the holy abode of Mount Zion. The phrase **as**

***Yahweh* has said** reveals that this escape of those who call on his name is the fulfillment of Yahweh's promise.

The concluding statement in v 32 is difficult to interpret. The promise of salvation is already extended to all who call on Yahweh's name; now, the prophet speaks of those whom Yahweh calls as being among the survivors. Yahweh is now the subject of the calling rather than the object. The participial verbal form indicates God's calling as a continual, ongoing action rather than a one-time event. The NIV reading (**even among the survivors whom the LORD calls**) suggests that Yahweh's deliverance will be experienced even by those who live beyond the borders of Zion/Jerusalem. In Joel's context, the **survivors** most likely refer to those who have been deported to other parts of the world by the Assyrian and Babylonian invasions. Salvation is a gift that God offers to all who call upon his name.

FROM THE TEXT

The Apostle Peter interpreted the events on the day of Pentecost as the fulfillment of Joel 2:28-32 (see Acts 2:17-21). The words of Joel thus hold a prominent place in the life of the Christian community.

The hope of Joel reminds subsequent generations of both human frailty and the necessity for divine vitality for the life of God's people in the world. Conscious of their frailty, the early church testified to the reality that only the life-giving power of God's Spirit would enable them to continue the work of Jesus Christ and thereby to give witness to him in the world (Acts 1:8; 2:4). When we hear this text today, and understand it in light of the words of Peter on the day of Pentecost, it will become clear to us that every generation of God's people since the days of Joel lived and continue to live within the context of Joel's anticipation.

Both the Gospel of Luke and the book of Acts demonstrate that in Jesus Christ and subsequently in the life of the church, the kingdom is enacted through the power of the Holy Spirit (Luke 1:35; 3:21-22; 4:1, 18-21; 23:46; Acts 1:2, 8, 16; 2:4, 17-21, 38). Acts further shows the manner in which the church participates in—even *fleshes out*—the life, death, and resurrection of Jesus Christ. For the Christian reader, the hope of Joel has become reality.

This text makes clear to its modern readers the implications of *being* a prophetic community. Although the text addresses individual categories such as gender, status, and age, the primary focus of the prophet's declaration is communal. In Acts, a prophetic community has emerged in the name of Jesus of Nazareth. What Moses anticipated for Israel (see Num 11:29) and what Joel prophesied as an eschatological event are now part of the experience of the people of God today.

The nonexclusive nature of the prophetic community that we find in this text is remarkable. The NT community clearly understood itself to be inheritors of this extraordinary vision. It saw no distinction between Jew and Greek (Rom 10:12) and affirmed the dissolution of barriers created by ethnicity, gender, and social status (Gal 3:28-29). Indeed, the promise of repentance, baptism, and the gift of the Holy Spirit was for even those who were *far off* (Acts 2:38-39). Indeed, all who call on the name of the Lord will be saved (see also Ps 91:14-15; John 6:37).

B. Judgment against the Nations (3:1-16*a* [4:1-16*a* HB])

BEHIND THE TEXT

Joel 2:28-32 provides the backdrop for the arrival of the Day of Yahweh to bring his judgment against the nations (3:1-16*a*). Though OT prophets primarily spoke as the mouthpiece of Yahweh to the covenant people, calling them either to judgment or restoration, they also understood and declared Yahweh's sovereignty over the nations. They frequently pronounced judgment against the nations that have carried out war atrocities or exercised power in a haughty, self-serving manner (e.g., see Isa 13—23, Jer 46—51, Ezek 25—32, Amos 1—2, Obadiah, Nahum). These judgment speeches convey Yahweh's visitation upon the nations as the Divine Warrior on the Day of Yahweh. These passages also portray the Divine Warrior as the judge of the nations that have failed to recognize his sovereign authority over them.

The prophetic announcement of judgment against the nations consists of a prose declaration (Joel 3:1-3) followed by a brief digression to judgment against the Philistine and Phoenician coastal region (vv 4-8). The depiction of cosmic judgment resurfaces in v 9 in the form of poetry. In vv 9-16*a* the text continues the divine act of setting things right (i.e., *mišpāṭ* or "justice") by means of a call for the nations to prepare for battle. These nations have mocked the covenant people (2:17) and treated both people and land with contempt (3:2-3).

IN THE TEXT

■ **1** The opening statement of 3:1 (4:1 HB) begins with the particle of immediacy (*hinnēh*), followed by the phrases **in those days** and **at that time**. Similar to "afterward" in 2:28, these phrases describe a specific yet undefined future time. Joel depicts the divine visitation as the time in which Yahweh will ***return*** or turn back (*šûb*, **restore**) **the fortunes of Judah and Jerusalem** that had been captured by the enemies of Israel. The term **fortunes** (*šĕbut*) is linked to the verb *šābâ*, which means "to take captive." Verse 1 depicts the divine intention to bring total restoration by returning the people along with all that was captured to their homeland.

■ 2 In v 2 the text proceeds to depict a judicial scene in which Yahweh enters into ***judgment*** (*mišpāṭ*) with the nations. The judicial proceeding will begin with Yahweh's gathering of all the nations and bringing them to **the Valley of Jehoshaphat**. Though the name **Jehoshaphat** is familiar in the OT (see particularly the Davidic king in 1 Kgs 22; 2 Chr 17—20), no specific valley is associated with this name except here in the OT.

The Jewish, Christian, and Muslim traditions have identified this site as the Kidron Valley, located between Jerusalem and the Mount of Olives. Rather than having a specific geographical location in mind, Joel likely employs the term based on its etymology: Yahweh (*Jeho*) judges (*šāpaṭ*; provides *mišpāṭ*). The Chronicler reports the judicial reform that Jehoshaphat carried out by appointing judges to provide impartial judgment that would reflect the impartiality of Yahweh's judgment (see 2 Chr 19:6-7). This tradition of the reform may have influenced Joel.

The second half of Joel 3:2 indicates the reason for Yahweh's gathering of all nations. Yahweh's plan is to put them on **trial** because of what the nations have done to his (**my**) **inheritance**. Yahweh's land and people are the divine property (*naḥălâ*). The nations have scattered his (**my**) **people** and divided up his (**my**) **land**. To assault either is to assault Yahweh's peculiar possession (see 2:17-18).

■ 3 In 3:3 the text vividly depicts the horrifying atrocities that the nations have committed against the covenant people. Not only did the nations divide Yahweh's land as if it belonged to them, but they also traded Yahweh's **people**, including **boys** and **girls,** by casting lots for them. The nations treated Yahweh's covenant people (**my people**) as a commodity exchanged in the marketplace. Casting lots for invaded lands and people seems to have been a usual practice in the ancient world (see Josh 18—19; Obad 11; Nah 3:10). Joel 3:3 further describes the nations' heinous practice of exchanging the captured boys for prostitutes and young girls for wine. The nations have treated Yahweh's people with contempt by using them as economic goods for self-indulging activities, such as sexual satisfaction and getting drunk with wine.

■ 4 Verses 4-8 convey Yahweh's response to the nations, specifically the people of Tyre, Sidon, and all the regions of Philistia. The question, **What have you against me?** is most likely about the way the nations have treated Yahweh's people and Yahweh himself. Yahweh asks these nations if they are trying to pay him back for his judgment he carried out against them (**Are you repaying me *this recompense*?**). Before God deals with the nations according to the nations' dealings with his people, he asks if the nations' dealings toward Judah were simply matching the way Yahweh had previously dealt with the nations.

Verse 4 ends with God's warning that if the nations were ***repaying*** him (**paying me back**), then he would **return** (*šûb*) their ***repaying*** (**what you have done**) upon their heads. Yahweh will not exonerate the nations for their treatment of his people and land even if that treatment was somehow their way of "getting even" with Yahweh. What they have sown, they will now reap. God will not delay the penalty of this verdict but will promptly carry it out.

■ **5** In v 5 Yahweh sums up the nations' violation of God's possessions (**my silver, my gold, my finest treasures**). The reference to **my finest treasures** (*maḥămadday*) likely indicates the ruined temple treasures of **gold** and **silver** and the other valuables that the nations treated with contempt (see Isa 64:11; Lam 1:10-11). They took them and brought them to the temples of their national gods (**your temples**).

■ **6** Joel returns to the accusation of human trafficking in v 6, and indicts the nations for selling God's people to **Greeks** (*yĕvānîm*; see Ezek 27:13). Joel's question to Tyre, Sidon, and the Philistines in 3:4 now becomes a direct accusation against these coastal city-states. They captured both humans and temple treasures to trade with these merchants who sailed the Mediterranean from Greece.

■ **7** Yahweh announces his judgment on the coastal cities in vv 7-8. As a prelude to his judgment, he will restore his people (**rouse them**) back to their homeland from the places to which they were sold (v 7). Yahweh will also **return** the nations' repayment (**what you have done**) upon their heads. The text employs the same language as in v 4.

■ **8** Verse 8 indicates how God will repay the nations. In the same way the nations have sold God's people, God will **sell** the Phoenician and Philistine children into the hands of the Judeans. In turn the Judeans will **sell** the children over to the **Sabeans**. Like the ancient Greeks, the Sabeans represent a distant nation (see v 6).

The concluding statement of v 8, ***For Yahweh*** **has spoken**, conveys the effectiveness of the prophetic word. What the prophet has announced is certain and sure; there is no revoking of the prophetic word.

■ **9** Beginning with v 9 and continuing through v 12, the prophet calls upon those persons who muster the armies to gather the people for battle. The text's employment of a series of succinct imperatives and declarations ("sanctify," "awaken," **draw near**, "go up") reflects the rapid movement of battle preparation. The nations are to **prepare** themselves **for war**. The warriors are to be awakened or stirred up (**roused**) and quickly to **draw near** and go up to battle (**attack**) (v 9).

■ **10** Verse 10 begins with a command to the nations to take their agricultural tools, such as **plowshares** and **pruning hooks**, and crush or **beat** them into weapons of war (**swords** and **spears**). The call here is to convert tools of harvest that serve as agents of life and nourishment to be instruments of death and destruction. Here we have a reversal of the words of Isaiah and Micah (see Isa 2:4; Mic 4:3). These eighth-century B.C. prophets anticipated the end of warfare and violence and the nations converting their instruments of warfare (swords and spears) into agricultural tools (plowshares and pruning hooks).

The second half of v 10 suggests that the nations should build their armies by enlisting even the most fragile members of the community for battle against God. These weak and unfit people are to assume the role of soldiers; they are being told to say that they are **strong** (*gibbôr*), as the "warriors" (*gibbôrîm*) who are aroused in v 9.

■ **11** Finally the prophet calls upon **all** the surrounding (**from every side**) nations to come and be gathered (**assemble**) for battle (v 11). The meaning of the word translated as **quickly** (*ʿûšû*) is uncertain in the Hebrew text. The NIV reading, **come quickly** (see also NRSV), presents it as a call to come hurriedly.

Verse 11 ends with the prophet's call to Yahweh to cause his mighty **warriors** (*gibbôrîm*) to descend upon the nations' "warriors" (*gibbôrîm*) (see vv 9-10). The battle scene is set. Citing Ps 103:20 and Zech 14:5, Achtemeier describes these warriors as "angelic hosts" (1996b, 332).

Yahweh as Divine Warrior

The idea of Yahweh as divine warrior is articulated in some of the most ancient poetry of the OT (e.g., Exod 15:21; Judg 5; Hab 3). The familiar title Yahweh Sabaoth (Lord of Hosts) reflects the image of the divine warrior whose military hosts (astral, angelic, and human) carry out warfare on God's behalf. The ark of the covenant likely functioned as the embodiment of Yahweh's military leadership of his warriors in battle (see Num 10:35-36; Josh 6; 1 Sam 4—7).

■ **12** Joel 3:12 provides a balanced conclusion to the initial call to arms in v 9. With repetitions from the opening call in vv 1-3 (e.g., Jehoshaphat, judge, and a designated *place*), v 12 also brings the call of vv 1-3 to its expected conclusion. Yahweh (*Jeho*) will take his seat as a judge in order to render his decision of justice (*shaphat*; i.e., "to judge") concerning **all the nations on every side** (i.e., surrounding nations; see phrase also in v 11). The warrior God victorious in battle now sits (*yāšab*) to mete out judgment upon the people.

■ **13** The passage reaches its climax in the depiction of the Day of Yahweh through three succinct, vivid movements in vv 13-16. Following the divine verdict in v 13, v 14 depicts a courtroom filled with defendants. Finally, vv 15-16 portray the Day of Yahweh in images of darkness and a roaring voice.

The time of Yahweh's harvest is at hand. Verse 13 describes the **ripe** nature of the harvest as boiling or cooking (*bāšal*), perhaps a reference to fully ripened grapes (see Wolff 1977, 80). While the term *maggāl* (**sickle**) may refer to the tool employed for harvesting grain, it may also denote the pruning knife used to cut grapes from the vine. In this case the text may describe the full process of the grape harvest from cutting grapes off the vine to overflowing vats (see Achtemeier 1996b, 333).

The imperatives (**come, trample**) convey urgency of the situation; the **winepress** is full of harvested grapes to be pressed (see 2:24). Likewise, the troughs (**vats**) that receive the juice are overflowing. The last line, **so great is their wickedness**, reveals the reason why Yahweh is issuing the urgent call to harvest. The harvest day is the day of God's judgment on the nations; God's judgment is coming upon them because wickedness is widespread among them.

■ **14** Verse 14 begins with a report of the confusion and the uproar of the crowd that Yahweh has gathered in the valley where he will soon make his decision or judgment (***Tumultuous roaring! Tumultuous roaring*** **in the valley of decision!**). The term *hămônîm* conveys the sense of a large crowd (thus **multitudes**) or the chaotic roar raised by such a crowd.

In v 14 the text moves beyond the proper name Jehoshaphat (3:2, 12) and describes the location as **the valley of decision**. The term *ḥārûṣ* indicates a strict, diligent decision. In contrast to more popular interpretation, the valley of decision is not the location where the nations decide, but rather, the place Yahweh will decide how to deal with those who have opposed him and his covenant people. As the name Jehoshaphat indicates, *Yahweh will judge*.

■ **15-16*a*** The text employs traditional language of the Day of Yahweh in vv 15-16*a* (see very similar language in Jer 25:30-31). The darkening in Joel 3:15 appears word-for-word in 2:10. However, in v 16*a* Joel heightens the voice of Yahweh (**roar, thunder**). **Zion/Jerusalem**, the location of Yahweh's residence, is the place from where the roaring/thundering voice of Yahweh will be heard. The roaring depicts a lion seeking prey (see Judg 14:5; Ps 104:21; Amos 3:4, 8). Canonically Amos begins where Joel concludes: "The LORD roars from Zion and thunders from Jerusalem" (Amos 1:2). For both the text of Amos and Joel, the Day of Yahweh is a central theme. However, for Amos the divine lion roars not only against the nations but also against the covenant people (see Amos 3:2-4).

After all of the momentum toward a divine verdict, the text gives no specific decision. In Joel 3:16*b*, the focus of the text turns to Yahweh's deliverance of his people (→ Joel 3:16*b* below). Only after the text portrays divine deliverance will it briefly return to the divine decision upon Egypt and Edom in 3:19.

FROM THE TEXT

The text presents to its readers the reality of divine judgment against persons who regard life and land as mere property. As commodities to be traded for greater goods, land becomes simply a means to another end while humans become means of exchange for something of greater value. The text challenges the reading community to examine and to confess contemporary practices that treat human life and the gift of creation itself as mere commodities to be bought and sold.

The text depicts divine judgment not simply against bad people or bad actions but rather against evil and its embodiment in social, economic, and political structures. This evil and its various incarnations stand in direct opposition to the reign of God. The theme of God's victorious battle against evil is found in both Testaments (e.g., Ezek 38—39; Isa 24—27; Dan 10—12; Matt 24—25; Rev 4 ff.). The early Christian community understood that this battle was a struggle not simply against flesh and blood but against *cosmic powers* (Eph 6:10-17).

The graphic violence employed in this text can be distasteful to modern ways of thinking. In the talk of a gracious and loving God, this destructive God seems foreign. Achtemeier, however, quite perceptively comments that "evil and sin are very real, and their forces are very strong, encompassing the ability to torture and degrade, to warp and destroy every form of life. . . . A God who is merely friendly is no match for such evil" (1996b, 334b; see also Achtemeier's quote from Tertullian's *Against Marcion* 1, 26-27).

The Christian reader understands the battle portrayed in texts such as this from the perspective of the cross. God does not conquer the enemy by violence but by his self-giving love fleshed out on a cross. The one who overcomes the enemy is indeed a lamb that has been slain (Rev 5:6). Ultimately people from all nations become part of the priestly kingdom of God—not through the blood of the enemy but by the blood of this slaughtered lamb (Rev 5:9-10). This Christian understanding of God's redemptive work on behalf of the whole world must guide our reading of Joel's text in 3:9-16*a*.

C. Final Restoration (3:16*b*-21 [4:16*b*-21 HB])

BEHIND THE TEXT

In the concluding lines of the book, the text returns to various concepts and images from the opening chapter. However, it reverses those images. A famine of wine ends with an overabundance of wine. Deprivation of cattle concludes with freely flowing milk. Drought becomes water that pours profusely from the temple mount. While v 16*b* brings the preceding passage to an appropriate conclusion, its emphasis upon the salvation of God's people introduces the closing verses. Therefore v 16*b* will be considered alongside the concluding verses, which emphasize the implications of Yahweh's protection of his people.

IN THE TEXT

■ **16*b*** Verse 16*b* states that when Yahweh roars and thunders his voice against the nations, his people will experience him as the source of their security (**refuge, stronghold**). The **people of Israel** are **his people**; Yahweh is their God. The language of Yahweh as "refuge" and "stronghold" is frequently found in the psalms (see, for example, Pss 27:1; 46:1; 61:3-4).

■ **17** When Yahweh brings his judgment on the nations and offers security and protection to Israel, then his people will **know** (*yāda'*) that Yahweh dwells **in Zion** (see 2:27). Statements similar to Joel's **Then you will know that I *am Yahweh*** are found throughout the book of Ezekiel (see 12:20; 13:9, 14, 21, 23; 23:49; 24:24; etc.). Joel reiterates here the OT tradition of **Zion** as Yahweh's dwelling place. The text returns to this same language in the book's final affirmation in 3:21: "The LORD dwells in Zion!" The book's ultimate hope for the people's deliverance and ongoing life rests in the reality that God dwells with his people in Zion (see the name "THE LORD [***Yahweh***] IS THERE" for the restored Jerusalem in Ezek 48:35).

Zion, the dwelling place of Yahweh, is his **holy hill**, the place set apart for Yahweh (see Obad 17). As the city that hosts this mountain, **Jerusalem** is also **holy** or set apart for Yahweh's purpose. Although the nations previously

pillaged Jerusalem and its temple, the restored holy city and holy temple precinct will never again see strangers (**foreigners**) ***cross over*** (**invade**) its borders. Verse 17 thus ends with Yahweh's promise of protection to Jerusalem from future enemy invasions.

■ **18** Verse 18 introduces the final four verses as an eschatological promise. The opening phrase, **in that day**, points to the time of Israel's restoration. The language in v 18 is similar to other prophetic declarations of the restored community's future fertility (see Ezek 36:8-12; 47:1-12; Hos 2:21-23).

Various images in Joel 3:18 portray the future as a period of productivity and fruitfulness of the land. The hyperbolic language of this verse cannot be interpreted literally. Images of dripping **wine**, flowing **milk**, and rushing **water** depict the land and life in the land as God intended for his people. Reference to water flowing in the **ravines of Judah** conveys the idea of life and fertility even in the areas susceptible to drought and lack of growth.

The **fountain** flowing **out of the LORD's house** echoes the language of Ezek 47:1-12. The **valley of acacias** most likely is not a specific location but a general reference to dry and arid areas of the desert of Judah. Even the driest part of the land will experience fertility and growth because of the life-giving presence of Yahweh in the temple in Zion.

The Temple and Fertility

In ancient Near Eastern thought, the divine palace/temple functioned as the centerpiece of divine blessing and fertility. The depiction of the four rivers flowing from Eden in Gen 2:10-14 reflect a similar understanding (see also Ps 46:4-7; Zech 14:8). The narrative of David's securing a site for the temple links fertility and temple (2 Sam 6:11-12; 24:18-25). The iconography of the temple included symbols of fertility, including pomegranates, palm trees, and lilies. Ezekiel's vision of the river flowing from the temple draws heavily upon the idea of the temple/the dwelling place of God as the source of life and productivity. The vision of Rev 22:1-2 returns to these primordial life-giving waters. These texts suggest that biblical writers may have understood the temple as a representation of the primordial garden with life-giving streams.

■ **19** Verse 19 contrasts the blessings of God's people with the desolation of **Egypt** and **Edom**, two ancient enemies of Israel. Both nations attempted to destroy Israel in the earliest days of its history—Egypt through bondage and oppression, and Edom through violent treatment and border attacks. Joel does not refer to a particular historical incident as the reason for this judgment word. The general indictment is that these nations carried out **violence** (see Obad 10) toward the people of Judah, pouring **innocent blood** upon the land. For Joel, these crimes demand some form of reprisal. They will both become a devastated wasteland (see 2:3; 3:18-19).

■ **20-21** In the concluding two verses, the text returns to the perpetual life and vitality that becomes the norm for the future of the covenant community. At one time no sign of life (plant, animal, or human) was evident; however, habitation will reappear and will remain from one generation to the next.

While most of the Hebrew text of Joel is fairly straightforward, the next to the last line of v 21 is quite obscure. The NIV reading, **Shall I leave their innocent blood unavenged? No, I will not**, conveys Yahweh's determination to avenge the violence against his people and will not acquit the guilty nations of their violent deeds (see **innocent blood** in vv 19 and 21). The NIV follows the Septuagint reading of this verse. This translation makes perfect sense within the context of Egypt and Edom in v 19 (for extensive discussion of the textual issue, see Barton 2001, 110).

The book's concluding line, ***Yahweh* dwells in Zion**, affirms the hope expressed previously in 2:27 and 3:17. This hope was grounded in the conviction that "everyone who calls on the name of the LORD will be saved; for on Mount Zion and in Jerusalem there will be deliverance" (2:32). As long as Yahweh dwells with his people, they are secure. This prophetic affirmation of Yahweh's presence in Zion engenders the certainty of divine safety and fertility for the people (→ 3:17 above).

FROM THE TEXT

The movement of Joel's message from natural and political catastrophe to God's salvation of his people and his faithful presence with them functions to engender hope in the readers of their own deliverance and salvation. God's faithfulness in the past is the historical basis for hope in his faithfulness in the future. This hope is anchored in the conviction that the God who acted to save his people in the past is a God who dwells with his people. Joel, in the typical Israelite tradition, reminds of this truth about God by declaring to them that Yahweh dwells in Zion.

Christian readers of Joel may ask, "Where is Zion?" "What is God's temple?" The Gospel writer John makes clear that the tabernacling presence of God is with his people in and through the presence of the Word made flesh (John 1). John reports Jesus' own words about himself:

> Jesus answered them, "Destroy this temple, and I will raise it again in three days." They replied, "It has taken forty-six years to build this temple, and you are going to raise it in three days?" But the temple he had spoken of was his body. (John 2:19-21)

Wolff reminds us that to gather in Zion is to gather "around the fate of Jesus which was sealed in Jerusalem; around his death as guarantee of God's compassion; and around his resurrection as pledge of new, eternal life. The fulfillment exceeds the promise by far" (1977, 86).

The Christian community, through its participation in the broken body and shed blood of Jesus Christ, also understands itself to have risen to new life into the body of Jesus Christ himself. This community called the church *is* the body of Christ; it *is* the temple of God (1 Cor 3:16-17; 2 Cor 6:16).

The hope-filled message of Joel continues to be a source of hope to the Christian readers of Joel who participate in the life of the resurrected Christ. They, too, hopefully anticipate and hope for abundant life, the defeat of evil, and the abiding presence of a living God. These very realities reappear in the hope of the Revelator. While the hope-filled future is breaking in upon God's people, the reading community continues to anticipate God's promise in which the life-giving waters will flow abundantly to all of creation (Rev 22:1-5).

AMOS

INTRODUCTION

A. Amos the Prophet

The editorial superscription describes Amos as "one of the shepherds of Tekoa" (1:1). Amos describes himself as "a shepherd" and as one who cares for "sycamore-fig trees" (7:14).

Amos was from the village of Tekoa (1:1), located approximately ten miles south of Jerusalem in the southern kingdom of Judah. Amos directs almost all of his oracles toward the northern kingdom of Israel (see Judah in 2:4-5; 6:1). It is likely that Amos carried out his prophetic activity near or at Bethel (3:14; 4:4-6; 7:10, 13).

The superscription (1:1) places Amos' ministry during the days of Uzziah, king of Judah, and Jeroboam, king of Israel, and more precisely, "two years before the earthquake." It is likely that the reference here is to the earthquake also noted in Zech 14:5. There are indications that an earthquake occurred at Hazor around 760 B.C. (see Mays 1969, 20).

Amos' prophetic activity was likely brief, perhaps as short as a year or even a few months or weeks (see Mays 1969, 20). Wolff rejects Morgenstern's view that Amos "made but one speech lasting only twenty to thirty minutes, during a single appearance at Bethel"; he suggests a short period of "a few weeks or months" for Amos' ministry (1977, 90). Achtemeier thinks that once Amos completed his task, he returned to Judah "to resume his normal life" (1996a, 166). Gowan cautions against speculations and efforts to recover the "historical Amos" and encourages the interpreter of Scripture to focus "on the book of Amos, or what may also be called the Amos tradition" (1996, 341).

B. The Historical Context and Audience of Amos

The superscription places Amos' ministry during the reigns of Uzziah (783-742 B.C.) king of Judah and Jeroboam II (786-746 B.C.) king of Israel. During the reigns of these kings, both the northern and southern kingdoms experienced relative peace and prosperity.

Deuteronomic historians report that Judah and Israel enjoyed territory expansions and building activities under both Uzziah and Jeroboam respectively (2 Kgs 14:21-29). Direct and indirect references from the eighth-century B.C. prophets (Amos, Hosea, Isaiah, and Micah) provide further insight into the political and social situation at the time of these kings. The northern kingdom of Israel pushed back threats from Syria to the north and experienced relative peace without any foreign interference during this period. This period also witnessed tremendous economic prosperity for the state and for its powerful elite. The wealthy and powerful leaders of Israel included not only those who resided in the royal precincts of Samaria but also those families who ruled in outlying cities and villages on behalf of the king. The political and economic power of the few wealthy people in the land engendered socioeconomic and judicial oppression against the overwhelming majority of the population. The wealthy exacted taxes, fines, interest, and other forms of imposed debt from the tenants, which resulted in the tenants' debt slavery and the loss of their inheritance. Birch is likely correct in attributing the socioeconomic situation of Israel in the mid-eighth century B.C. to "the growing commercial life of the kingdom with its aggressive business practices" (1997, 244) (for extensive discussions of the eighth-century B.C. historical situation and its socioeconomic ramifications, see Chaney 1989 and 1991; Green 1997; Premnath 1984). Therefore, the biblical interpreter must hear the socioeconomic critiques of prophets such as Amos and Micah within the broader political structure of eighth-century B.C. Israel and Judah. To view an economic stratum separate from political power in the eighth century B.C. is likely an anachronistic read of the text.

Based on Amos' exchange with Amaziah the priest of Bethel, we may safely assume that Amos' ministry took place prior to Jeroboam's death in 746 B.C. (see 7:10-13), and before Tiglath-Pileser III's accession to the Assyrian throne the year following. It is likely that Amos carried out his ministry somewhere between 760 and 750 B.C. (see Mays [1969, 2] and Achtemeier [1996a, 169-70], who both argue for a date closer to 760 B.C.). Tiglath-Pileser III expanded the Assyrian Empire westward in 740 B.C. and annexed Syria and placed heavy tribute upon Israel by 738 B.C. Eventually in 721 B.C. Assyria destroyed Samaria and exiled the population into various parts of the Assyrian Empire. Although these events occurred subsequent to Amos' prophetic ministry, they confirmed the validity of his message concerning Israel's downfall and thus contributed to the preservation and continuation of Amos' message.

As noted before, Amos' addressees are most often Israel, the people of the northern kingdom. According to Gowan, Amos addresses anyone in Israel "who turns justice to wormwood, takes bribes, cheats in buying and selling" (1996, 417). Gowan also notes that "this is more realistic than any analysis based on class struggle, for not all suffering is the fault of the rich and those in power. The poor also prey on the poor" (ibid.). While Gowan's observation for subsequent generations of readers is valid, the society into which Amos spoke was not one in which "the oppressed" made judicial decisions by taking bribes, nor was it one in which "the poor" were capable of buying and selling in the manners depicted by Amos. In the various socioeconomic indictments of Amos, the prophet is clearly speaking to persons who have political-judicial power that has resulted in their economic advantage. As a result of their positions within the community, they are able to carry out concrete forms of social injustice, political oppression, and economic fraud. Within the context of ancient Israel's political-economic structure, Amos primarily, if not entirely, addresses political functionaries who oversee the land and who are responsible for making judicial decisions regarding those entrusted to their supervision. Smith is likely correct in his conclusion that Amos' condemnation is not against "an economic system or a class of people," but rather against "the abuse of workable economic arrangements by persons having significant economic control to manipulate things to their advantage" (1989, 252).

The preceding observations call for a final comment concerning the audience(s) of Amos. The narratives and oracles of Amos functioned and continue to function dynamically far beyond the eighth century B.C. One must take into account subsequent contexts and audiences that received Amos' message and heard it in light of their own situation. These situations included the southern kingdom of Judah (which continued to survive a century and a half beyond the fall of Samaria), the Jewish community in Babylonian exile, and the postexilic community both in Palestine and throughout the Jewish diaspora. As described below, subsequent editorial activity of the book of Amos undoubtedly demonstrates that the prophet's audiences continued to exist far beyond Amos' lifetime. These audiences did not merely "hear" the words of a text. They took the living and dynamic words into their own situation and made them their own.

C. The Book of Amos as a Literary Work

Most of the book of Amos is comprised of brief oracular sayings of only a few verses. The classic messenger formula, "This is what the LORD says," and the concluding messenger saying, "Says the LORD," appear quite frequently in Amos. Amos' oracles of judgment adhere to the familiar pattern of an accusation with depiction of specific crimes followed by an announcement of punishment. Attempting to engage in dialogue with his audience, the oracles of Amos frequently present an argument by first quoting the words of the addressees (2:12; 4:1; 6:13; 8:5-6; 9:10).

In addition to the brief oracles, longer sections include a collection of brief judgments or curses against the nations (1:3—2:8). Oracles against surrounding nations are a common feature in prophetic books (e.g., Isa 13—23; Jer 46—51; Ezek 25—32). Amos' oracles incorporate the graded numerical saying from the wisdom tradition (1:3, 6, 9, 11, 13; 2:1, 4, 6) to introduce the crime of each nation. Though poetic oracles comprise most of the book of Amos, prose sayings are found in the vision accounts in chs 7—8 and in Amos' exchange with Amaziah in 7:10-17. At least on one occasion Amos employs the language of a funeral dirge with its 3+2 meter (*qinah*) (5:1-2).

The opening oracle of Amos in 1:2 is a brief theophany or depiction of a divine appearance. Closely related to this opening theophany and functioning as an intermittent thread throughout the book of Amos are three doxological fragments likely taken from a single hymn (4:13; 5:8-9; 9:5-6). Each hymn fragment ends with the declaration, "***Yahweh*** is his name!" The reader of the text gains a better appreciation for the unity of the hymn by reading it in its entirety. It is possible the editors of Amos understood the hymn as a hymnic response to the theophany of Yahweh in 1:2. However, in the present structure and organization of the book, Amos' accusations against the worshippers "interrupt" the hymn, thus creating the appearance of "hymn fragments" (regarding the placement and function of the hymn fragments, see Mays 1969, 83-84, 145; Auld 1986, 74-77). The hymn affirms that the God who creates and gives life can and will destroy and take life. Ironically, the hymn itself declares Amos' essential conviction concerning the Day of Yahweh: it can bring life to Israel, and it can destroy the life of Israel.

D. Historical Development of the Text

The present canonical shape of the book of Amos reflects later editorial activity. The introductory and concluding formula given to the oracles, the insertion of a third-person narrative (7:10-15) into the series of vision reports (chs 7—8), the vision reports themselves, and the arrangement of the oracles against the nations in 1:3—2:3 are also likely the result of subsequent editorial activity. The manner in which the doxological fragments are interwoven through the text may likewise demonstrate the work of literary editing.

The present redacted book of Amos likely does not emerge before exile, and the concluding statement of hope in 9:11-15 may certainly be as late as the postexilic period. Wolff discusses as many as six stages in the historical development of the text: three eighth-century stages from either Amos or his followers and three subsequent additions for the purpose of "updating" (1977, 106-13). Mays suggests that "the larger part of the material can be attributed with confidence to Amos"; however, he concedes that some subsequent editing is likely to have occurred (see Mays 1969, 12-14). Regarding the historical development of the text, Gowan's conclusion is especially significant for interpretation of any biblical text:

> The book of Amos may all have come from him, may be mostly his with a few later additions, or may have been heavily redacted. Each of these opinions may be found in the work of very able scholars, but we cannot demonstrate that any one of them is true or false. (1996, 341)

In light of such a reality, Achtemeier appropriately encourages the biblical interpreter to seek "the theological meaning of this message, as it has been handed down and now lies *in its entirety* before us" (1996a, 172).

E. Flow and Structure of the Text

In addition to the editorial superscription and the opening statement in 1:2, the book of Amos is comprised of four major sections: the curses against the nations climaxing in the curse against Israel (1:3—2:8); the specific oracles of judgment against Israel (2:9—6:14); the series of five visions and the prophetic encounter with the priest Amaziah (7:1—8:3); additional oracles of judgment (8:4—9:10); a late, brief editorial conclusion of hope (9:11-15).

Based upon the overall flow and content of the book of Amos, the commentary will follow the structural outline below. As the outline reveals, the commentary will examine the five visions as a single unit.

I. The Roaring Voice of Yahweh (1:1-2)
II. Indictment against the Nations and Israel (1:3—2:5)
   A. Aram (1:3-5)
   B. Philistia (1:6-8)
   C. Tyre (1:9-10)

D. Edom (1:11-12)
E. Ammon (1:13-15)
F. Moab (2:1-3)
G. Judah (2:4-5)

III. Oracles against Israel (2:6—6:14)
A. Israel's Crime and Punishment (2:6-16)
B. Covenant Responsibility (3:1-2)
C. Cause and Effect (3:3-8)
D. Indictment against Samaria and Bethel (3:9-15)
E. Indictment against "Secondhand" Oppressors (4:1-3)
F. Call to Worship (4:4-5)
G. A Rehearsal of Divine Attempts to Save (4:6-12)
H. Doxology One (4:13)
I. A Song of Death (5:1-3)
J. A Second Call to Worship (5:4-7)
K. Doxology Two (5:8-9)
L. Social Justice and a Call to Proper Worship (5:10-15)
M. An Unexpected Day of Mourning (5:16-20)
N. Reflecting on True Worship (5:21-27)
O. Indictment against Indulgence and Pride (6:1-14)

IV. The Visions of Amos and the Confrontation with Amaziah (7:1—8:3; 9:1-4)
A. The Visions of Amos (7:1-9; 8:1-3; 9:1-4)
1. Vision of Locusts (7:1-3)
2. Vision of Fire (7:4-6)
3. Vision of a Plumb Line (7:7-9)
4. Vision of a Basket of Summer Fruit (8:1-3)
5. Vision of the Temple Destruction (9:1-4)
B. Interlude: Amos-Amaziah Confrontation (7:10-17)

V. Oracle against Israel (8:4-14; 9:5-10)
A. Social Condemnation (8:4-14)
B. The Final Doxology (9:5-6)
C. A Leveling of Identity (9:7-10)

VI. Editorial Conclusion: Hope Beyond Judgment (9:11-15)

F. Theological Themes

1. The Day of Yahweh

Amos' book as a whole speaks to a nation that upheld a popular view of the Day of Lord as a day of its salvation and the day of the judgment of its enemies (see 5:18, 20). The covenant community expects and desires the day to come but fails to perceive that God would hold his own covenant people accountable for their sins (3:2). Mays refers to Israel's crime as "a sin of belief, the sin of excepting oneself from Yahweh's judgment and therefore from his sovereignty. Israel's dogmatic security is a real declaration of independence from Yahweh which lies behind all their other transgressions" (1969, 163). For Amos, Yahweh's judgment of both the nations and the covenant community pointed to the Lord's reign over all the earth. According to Achtemeier, Amos declares "that the God of the covenant is on the move, toward the goal of the day of the Lord, when God will set up his kingdom on earth" (1996a, 166).

2. Deuteronomic-Prophetic Retribution

Underlying Amos' notion of the Day of Yahweh is the common Deuteronomic-prophetic conviction of divine judgment. For Amos, divine judgment is no arbitrary punishment. It is always directly related to the crime committed. Cities that march out strong are left with no survivors (5:3). Persons who construct stone mansions will in the end not dwell in them (5:11). Individuals who feast on the finest will ultimately neither feast nor recline (5:4-7). While this understanding of judgment demonstrates a consistent Deuteronomic-prophetic perspective, it is likewise grounded in a creation-oriented conviction of divine order that is at home within the wisdom tradition. Nogalski articulates this prophetic-wisdom concept in this way: "God has structured the world so that actions have consequences, and when human beings work at cross purposes to God's intentions, God will allow, or cause, those consequences to come to fruition" (2011, 354).

3. Justice, Covenant, and Worship

The political-economic situation in Amos' day provides a concrete context in which Amos expresses the divine plea for justice and righteousness. For Amos, justice and righteousness were not merely abstract concepts to ponder. They were actions to be embodied within the practices of authoritative power, economic exchange, and judicial decision making. For Amos, Israel's God demanded social justice and not simply criminal justice. Yahweh demanded right relatedness in day-to-day affairs and human relationships. He demanded that right decisions occur in the social, economic, political, and judicial arrangements. He particularly demanded persons invested with economic, political, and ideological/religious power to carry out their responsibilities with a protective eye on those under their supervision and care: the weak, the oppressed, the afflicted, and the poor.

The prophet's understanding of appropriate decisions and interactions within communal relationships assumed that covenant existed not only between Yahweh and the community but also between members of the community. The covenant with Yahweh assumed covenant with one's neighbor. Just as Yahweh had committed himself to his people, so those in power had committed themselves to the powerless. If one aspect of covenant broke down (i.e., neighbor), the entire covenant broke down (i.e., with God). For Amos, a single thread loosened from the fabric of the community/covenant endangers the entire community/covenant. It is not clear if a fully developed "theology of covenant" (particularly as traditionally understood in terms of a vassal treaty) had emerged by the time of Amos. Perhaps prophets such as Amos actually contributed to that development. However, the notion of relationships of mutual reciprocity between Yahweh and Israel and between members of the community clearly informs the message of Amos (see Achtemeier 1996a, 167-69).

For Amos, any form of public worship that separates itself from covenant responsibility within the community is absurd. Even more than absurd, worship apart from justice is horrific and detestable in the eyes of the covenant God (4:4-5; 5:21-23). To gather in worship of this covenant deity at locales such as Bethel and Gilgal is mockery (4:4; 5:4-5) when the powerful elite have consistently and repeatedly broken covenant with their sisters and brothers in daily affairs. For Amos, the worship of God and fidelity toward one's neighbor are so intertwined that for a single thread to become loose, the entire cord is broken. Amos would be apt to state with John, "Whoever does not love their brother or sister, whom they have seen, cannot love God, whom they have not seen" (1 John 4:20).

4. Lord of the Nations

Although Amos clearly assumes a unique relationship between Yahweh and Israel, he also assumes that Yahweh is God of the universe and God of the nations. The doxological fragments vividly depict the Lord as Creator who brings to life and who destroys. The curses against the nations in chs 1—2 likewise assume that Yahweh has the prerogative to accuse and to judge the nations for their war crimes against humanity. Amos' unique statement in 9:7 appears to assume that Yahweh has provided deliverance and life to Israel's greatest foes, the Philistines and the Syrians.

5. The Divine Change of Plans

The overall message of Amos does not emphasize Yahweh's change of plans regarding the destruction of Israel in the same manner that Hosea (11:9), Joel (2:13-14), and Jonah (3:9—4:2) do. However, the narratives of Amos' first two visions reveal Amos' understanding of Yahweh as a God who responds to sincere appeal for mercy and compassion (7:1-6). Though Yahweh shows him visions of destruction, when Amos cries out, Yahweh relents. Amos shows in this text his deep-rooted conviction that, though the nation stands under the threat of destruction, its future rests on Yahweh's willingness to relent in response to his people's cry for mercy. For all the judgment announced by Amos, the book assumes that the Lord is merciful, gracious, and compassionate, a theme consistently found in the biblical narrative (see this issue also explored in the commentaries on Hosea, Joel, Jonah, and Micah in this volume).

COMMENTARY

I. THE ROARING VOICE OF YAHWEH: AMOS 1:1-2

BEHIND THE TEXT

The superscription to the book of Amos follows the basic form of other superscriptions. This superscription most likely comes from the editor of the Latter Prophets; it functions to provide the historical context of the prophet.

The first half of v 2 shares similarities with Joel 3:16. One cannot know for certain if one book influenced the other or if both authors simply employed familiar expressions. Nevertheless, in the present canonical ordering of the books of the twelve, the metaphor of Zion's roaring lion links the two texts. Amos mentions Zion only one other time in the book (see 6:1). He depicts Yahweh's voice as the roaring of a lion again in 3:8.

IN THE TEXT

■ 1 The superscription identifies the content of the book as **the words of Amos** (similar to Jer 1:1); it lacks the phrase "the word of the LORD that came" found in the superscriptions of other prophetic books (e.g., see Hos 1:1; Joel 1:1; Mic 1:1; Zeph 1:1). Among the prophetic superscriptions, Amos stands alone in referring to **words** (*dibrê*) that the prophet **saw** (*ḥāzâ*; compare with Isa 1:1). Visions are an important medium of revelation in the book (see Amos 7:1, 4, 7; 8:1; 9:1). Thus the text may also intend the reader to understand the double meaning of *dābār*: "word" and "thing." Amos communicates through his words (*dĕbarîm*) the things (*dĕbarîm*) he saw in his visions.

The superscription depicts Amos as being among the shepherds (*nōqdîm*) from Tekoa. In contrast to the common term for shepherd (*rōʿeh*), *nōqēd* may indicate that Amos bred or even traded sheep (see 2 Kgs 3:4). In Amos 7:14, the prophet refers to himself as a cattleman (*bôqēr*; perhaps a misread or miscopy of *nōqēd* due to confusion between the consonants *bet/b* and *nun/n*, and *resh/r* and *dalet/d* in Hebrew).

Tekoa is associated with the wisdom tradition (2 Sam 14:2). In light of the use of the term *nōqēd* and Tekoa's proximity to Jerusalem, Amos may have been involved in raising sheep for temple service. However, specific details of his occupation are unknown (see Mays 1969, 19; Gowan 1996, 351).

The superscription also specifies that his words were about the northern kingdom of **Israel** even though Amos was from Judah (see 7:12). Although the superscription mentions both **Uzziah** (783-742 B.C.) and **Jeroboam** (786-746 B.C.), the book only refers later to Jeroboam (7:10-11). **Jehoash** is a variant of Joash (see NRSV). The lengthy reigns of both Jeroboam and Jehoash reflect the prosperity and security experienced by Israel and Judah during this period.

The details of the **earthquake** to which the superscription refers remain unknown. The earthquake may be the quaking depicted in Amos' fifth vision (9:1). Certainly the occurrence of an earthquake two years after Amos' ministry would have provided validation to his entire message. The reference to the earthquake provides affirmation to the subsequent visions and words in the text (see Zechariah's reference to an earthquake more than two centuries after Amos [Zech 14:5]) (→ Introduction).

■ 2 The opening oracle in Amos 1:2 establishes the context for the book's oracles and visions. Yahweh has spoken; therefore, the prophet must speak. Joel employs similar language (Joel 3:16). While one prophet may have followed the lead of the other, it is likely that both prophets employed widespread images of Yahweh's roaring and thundering voice. Canaanite texts also depict Baal with a thundering voice. The image of a roaring lion appears twice more in Amos (3:4, 8). However, in these passages in which the prophet addresses the northern kingdom alone, the prophet makes no reference to Jerusalem or Zion (contrast 6:1).

The language of 1:2*b* suddenly shifts. While one might expect the lion's roar to result in panic or in the devouring of prey, the imagery shifts to drought. Again the language recalls Joel who describes the watercourses as ***mourning*** and the pastures as ***consumed*** (Joel 1:20). The reference to the pastures' ***mourning*** (**dry up**) depicts the suffering grief of the ground itself (see Joel 1:10). Amos later expands the ground's mourning to include human mourning (5:16; 8:8; 9:5). The text's reference to **the shepherds** (from the broader term *rōʿeh* rather than *nōqēd* as in v 1) confirms that these pastures provide nourishment needed for herds to survive.

The last line of v 2 conveys the drying up of the source of water for **the pastures of the shepherds**. Reaching over seventeen hundred feet above sea level, Mount Carmel extends approximately twenty miles southeasterly from Haifa and supplies abundant fresh water to the streams below. Not only does the term **Carmel** mean a fertile vineyard or beautiful garden, but the mountain itself symbolized such fertility (see 2 Kgs 19:23; Song 7:5; Isa 35:2). This fertile site provided the setting for Elijah's challenge to the prophets of the fertility deities (1 Kgs 18).

Amos depicts in 1:2 the disappearance of all signs of life and fertility. Both pasture and stream have disappeared. Subsequent verses proceed even more concretely to describe the devastating consequences of the divine word upon the nations, including Judah and Israel.

FROM THE TEXT

The superscription reminds the reader that prophets and their messages are located within and speak into concrete and specific situations. While the words they speak are not limited to the prophet's generation, they cannot be divorced from their historical context. In the same way, contemporary readers of the prophets also hear the prophetic words in the concrete realities of their own life and times.

Special reference to Amos' vocational background shows that the prophet brings his background, personality, and convictions into the message. Amos and his message cannot be separated from his own life experiences of being among "the shepherds of Tekoa." What he witnessed and experienced as a shepherd and a dresser of sycamore trees in Tekoa gave authenticity to his words and particularly to his indictment of the wealthy and oppressive citizens of the northern kingdom. Personal experiences of God's spokespersons play a role in the shaping and delivery of God's word.

From the outset, the text reminds its reading audience of the source and power of the prophetic "words of Amos." The prophet does not merely give voice to his own opinion and agenda. He first "saw" words/things as the Lord initiated them; he subsequently articulates this sight into words. Verse 2 indicates the destructive power of the divine roaring. Though this verse indicates the judgment tone of the book of Amos, the prophet also speaks words of life: "seek the LORD and live" (5:6); "seek good, not evil, that you may live" (5:14). The prophetic words, both then and now, have life-giving and life-taking power (Heb 4:12).

II. INDICTMENT AGAINST THE NATIONS AND ISRAEL: AMOS 1:3—2:5

BEHIND THE TEXT

Beginning with 1:3, the prophet pronounces a series of curses against the surrounding nations and Israel. Each curse has the introduction, "this is what the LORD says" (***thus Yahweh said***), and the conclusion, "says the LORD" (***Yahweh said***). This framework of the messenger formula authenticates both the prophet and the prophetic message as originating with Yahweh. The oracle proper, comprised of indictment and punishment, articulates the divine message as a curse (regarding the oracle structure of indictment and punishment, see Westermann 1967, 142-76).

Curses against nations are familiar features of the prophetic books (e.g., Isa 13—23; Jer 46—51; Ezek 25—32). The books of Obadiah and Nahum are entirely devoted to curses against Edom and Assyria respectively. Curse oracles against the nations may have their origin in the holy war tradition of Israel. War oracles provided divine affirmation of war plans, Israel's success, and defeat of the enemies (e.g., see 1 Kgs 20:28; Gowan 1996, 354-58; Hayes 1968). Amos, however, concludes his oracles with a series of curses against Judah and Israel.

Structurally the curses follow the pattern of the graded numerical saying: **for three . . . even for four**. The graded sayings found in the wisdom tradition often open with a title line that introduces a list (e.g., see Job 5:19-26; 33:14-18; Prov 6:16-19; 30:15-31). However, Amos simply uses the title line without providing a list. Each oracle presents a single crime for a specific nation (see Mays 1969, 23-24). The text does not imply that God has forgiven three crimes but cannot or will not forgive four. The graded saying emphasizes the multiple crimes committed by the nations. Each oracle focuses more upon divine judgment against a nation than a list of specific crimes of that nation.

Before climaxing with divine judgment against Israel (2:6-16), the text makes evident that Yahweh is sovereign over the nations that encircle Israel (Syria to the north; Philistia and Phoenicia to the west; Edom, Ammon, and Moab east of the Jordan; and Judah immediately to the south). The divine visitation follows the depiction of each war crime.

The series of curses against neighboring nations is directly related to the concluding curse against Yahweh's own people. In the present form of the book, the oracles against the nations invite the audience into a sympathetic hearing of the prophetic curses. However, as the hearers participate in the various curses against their neighbors, they cannot run away from the final curse against them. While Yahweh holds the nations responsible for war crimes, he particularly holds the covenant people responsible for their crimes (see 3:1-2).

IN THE TEXT

A. Aram (1:3-5)

■**3** In vv 3-5, the prophet addresses Aram and its capital, **Damascus**, which lies northeast of Israel. The numerical saying refers to the ***transgressions*** (*peša*ʿ, **sins**; see also 1:6, 9, 13; 2:1, 4, 6) of Damascus. Amos describes the crimes of Aram and the nations in terms of purposeful rebellion. They have knowingly and willfully transgressed acceptable law and custom (for the political nature of the term *peša*ʿ, see Mays 1969, 28). The atrocities carried out by the nations are ultimately crimes against humanity.

Throughout the curses against the nations, the prophet repeatedly declares that Yahweh ***will not turn it back*** (**I will not relent**; *šûb* means to "turn" or "return"). The ambiguous third-person pronoun suffix at the end of the verb (***it***) perhaps refers to Yahweh's wrath ("punishment" [NRSV]). However, the pronoun could also refer back to Yahweh's roaring in v 2 (see Gowan 1996, 354).

The second part of v 3 states the specific indictment against Damascus. The Aramaeans **threshed Gilead** with iron **sledges**. The prophet uses vivid language to describe the violent attack on Gilead. The image of a sharp instrument (**iron teeth**) dragged over grain at harvest depicts the intensively destructive nature of Damascus' actions. This same image appears in Assyrian texts to portray complete victory in battle (see Paul 1991, 47).

Throughout the ninth and early-eighth centuries B.C., the Aramaeans engaged in border skirmishes with Israel (see 1 Kgs 22; 2 Kgs 6—7; 13). While the incident with Gilead noted by Amos cannot be determined precisely, 2 Kgs 13:3-7 depicts a real possibility. Second Kings 13:7 observes that the Aramaeans had made Israel "like the dust at threshing [*dûš*] time." Amos uses the same term in 1:3 to describe the Aramaeans' threshing (*dûš*) of Gilead. Although the event in 2 Kings would have preceded Amos by nearly half a century, such great violence against Gilead would have served as a graphic example of war atrocities.

■ **4** The oracle against Aram sets a pattern for the subsequent oracles with the exception of the oracle against Israel itself (2:6-8). Divinely sent **fire** will come upon **the house of Hazael** and **consume the fortresses of Ben-Hadad**. Hazael is mentioned in 1 Kgs 19:15-17 as the individual whom Elijah was to anoint as king over Aram. Hazael murdered Ben-Hadad (2 Kgs 8:7-15) and established a dynasty (**house of Hazael**). His son, also named Ben-Hadad, succeeded him. Amos is perhaps referring to the dynasty of Hazael and Hazael's son. Hadad was the storm deity worshipped in Damascus; it is also possible that the name **Ben-Hadad** (i.e., son of Hadad) was a throne name of Aramean kings.

Yahweh's judgment will destroy both the ruling family and its military strongholds (*ʾarmĕnôt*); **fortresses** represent all that was virtually impenetrable by the enemy. Although this term appears in all of the oracles against the nations, it particularly resembles the first nation cited, Aram (*ʾarām*), in both sight and sound.

■ **5** Verse 5 describes the divine visitation upon the capital city Damascus and all of Aram. The sites mentioned here cannot be clearly identified today: **Valley of Aven** ("valley of evil"; perhaps Baalbek, north of Damascus) and **Beth Eden** ("house of Eden"; perhaps Bit-adini in Akkadian texts). Yahweh will **destroy *the one who inhabits* (the king who is in) the Valley of Aven**. The NIV reading is appropriate in the context of the next line, which mentions a ruler **who holds the scepter in Beth Eden**.

Destruction will come, and in the end **the people of Aram will go into exile** (*gālâ* means "to uncover" or "to remove"; see 1:6, 15; 5:5, 27; 6:7; 7:11, 17). Yahweh will remove the Aramaeans back to the land from which they originated (see Kir also in Amos 9:7). The Assyrian king Tiglath-Pileser III deported the Aramean people to Kir (2 Kgs 16:9). It is not possible to identify this precise location today.

B. Philistia (1:6-8)

■**6-8** In vv 6-8, Amos moves from Aram in the northeast to Philistia in the southwest. He begins with an accusation against **Gaza**, one of five city-states comprising the Philistine Pentapolis (also Ashdod, Ashkelon, Ekron, and Gath). Just as Damascus represented Aram, Gaza represents Philistia. The Philistines initially arrived off the Mediterranean Sea from the west about the same time the Israelites entered the hill country from the east. They were a constant threat to Israel in the early part of Israel's history in Palestine. Gaza, located two and a half miles from the sea, controlled a primary trade route connecting Egypt with Mesopotamia.

Gaza's specific crime was that ***they carried into captivity*** **whole communities** and **sold them** to the Edomites. Gaza, with its strategic location on trade routes with both Edom and Arabia, likely engaged in various forms of human trafficking (see v 9, where Tyre is charged with the same crime).

In vv 7-8, Amos announces destruction; the language here is similar to vv 4-5. Yahweh will **send fire** that will **consume** the strongholds (**walls** and **fortresses**) of the city-state. Just as the oracle in v 5 broadened beyond Damascus, so v 8 broadens beyond Gaza to include three other Philistine city-states and ultimately all of Philistia (regarding Gath's omission, see Mays 1969, 33).

The word of punishment against the ***inhabitant*** (**king**) **of Ashdod** is the same as in v 5. The second line (**one who holds the scepter**) makes clear that the judgment word is against the political rulers of the Philistine cities of Ashdod and Ashkelon. Divine power, often portrayed through the metaphor of the **hand**, will come upon the city-state of Ekron as well. In the oracle's closing statement, the prophet incorporates the entirety of Philistia. Whoever among the Philistines remains (**the last**) will die. Just as the Philistines had carried out wholesale exile without respect of persons, Yahweh will carry out wholesale destruction against the Philistines.

C. Tyre (1:9-10)

■**9-10** In vv 9-10, the prophet moves northward along the Mediterranean coast and condemns Tyre for human trafficking, the same crime committed by Gaza. Like the Philistine cities, Tyre capitalized on its coastal location through maritime trade. Though an island city, Tyre had become the leading Phoenician city in the eighth century. Therefore the oracle mentions Tyre alone without referring to Phoenicia more broadly.

The biblical text generally portrays Tyre's relationship with Israel in a relatively positive light. During the reigns of David and Solomon, Tyre played a significant role especially in the construction of the temple (see 2 Sam 5:11-12; 1 Kgs 5—9). Nevertheless, subsequent prophetic texts speak judgment against Tyre (see Isa 23; Ezek 26—28; Joel 3:4).

Amos 1:9 differs from the preceding oracle only slightly, with its additional charge that Tyre disregarded (*lōʾ zākrû*, "did not remember") **a treaty** [*bĕrît*] **of brotherhood**. The sibling language depicts the reciprocity of allied nations. The text does not specify the identity of the "other brother" with whom Tyre shared and broke a treaty. Amos may have in mind Israel since close relationship existed between Tyre and Israel during the days of David and Solomon (1 Kgs 5:1-12). It is also possible that the text may be referring to the Edom/Israel (Esau/Jacob) relationship of brotherhood (see Deut 2:4-8; 23:7-8; Wolff 1977, 159). Tyre's action of delivering up Israelites into the hands of the Edomites would demonstrate a blatant disregard for the unique relationship between Israel and Edom. "Coming between" brothers in such a way would have made Tyre a third party to the crime of covenant breaking. The text specifically addresses the brother-nation Edom in the next oracle. Interestingly, despite Edom's involvement in human trafficking in Amos 1:6 and 9, the text makes no reference to human trafficking in the specific accusation against Edom in v 10.

D. Edom (1:11-12)

■ **11-12** Amos, after dealing with nations to the north and to the west of Israel, addresses the Transjordan nations of Edom, Ammon, and Moab in 1:11—2:3. The charge against Edom, located south-southeast of Jordan, is Edom's intense anger and violent pursuit of his brother.

The Jacob-Esau narrative (Gen 25:19—35:29) depicts the sociopolitical relationship between Israel and Edom. Although the narrative portrays mutual enmity and deceit, it concludes with reconciliation (Gen 33:4-17) and their coming together to bury their father, Isaac (Gen 35:29). Despite Israel's acknowledgment of and respect for this brotherhood (see Deut 2:4-8; 23:7-8), skirmishes regularly occurred between the two nations (e.g., 1 Sam 14:47; 2 Sam 8:13). Vitriolic enmity and hostility toward Edom especially emerged following the destruction of Jerusalem in 587 B.C. (see Ps 137:7; Joel 3:19 [4:19 HB]; Obadiah; Mal 1:3-4).

Amos describes Edom as ***violently chasing after*** (*rādap*; **pursued . . . with a sword**) his brother in order to end his life. The text recalls Isaac's words to Esau and Esau's hatred for his brother Jacob (Gen 27:39-41). In a series of three phrases, Amos depicts Edom's violent action as it is motivated by unchecked wrath.

In Amos 1:11, the prophet charges Edom with the crime of destroying his brother's ***wombs*** (lit. "his wombs"; *reḥem* means "womb" and also conveys the idea of compassion, hence "cast off all pity" in NRSV). The NIV interprets the plural of *reḥem* here as **women** and adds the phrase **of the land**; see Paul 1991, 64-65).

Amos adds to his charge against Edom his perpetual anger toward his brother. The phrase **his anger** [*ʾap*; see also Gen 27:45] ***tore*** **(raged) continually** conveys the idea of Edom's anger as ripping apart (*ṭārap*) (see this verb alongside "anger" [*ʾap*], in Job 16:9). The final line of Amos 1:11 is parallel to the preceding line (**his fury flamed unchecked**). The reference to **fury** suggests excessive or overflowing wrath vis-à-vis Israel. The verb *šāmar* ("to guard," "to keep") depicts Edom keeping its anger into perpetuity (see Gen 27:44-45 where Rebekah expresses her hope that Esau's fury would subside and that he would forget what Jacob did to him).

The divine verdict against Edom in Amos 1:12 recalls the preceding oracles (vv 4, 7, 10). Primary cities of southern Edom and northern Edom represent the entire nation. **Teman** was the largest city in the south. It was situated on the King's Highway, the primary route in Transjordan that stretched from Elath on the Gulf of Aqaba in the south to Damascus in the north. **Bozrah** was located in the northern part of Edom. Like Teman, it also can function to represent the state as a whole (see Isa 34:6; 63:1; Jer 49:13, 22).

E. Ammon (1:13-15)

■ **13-15** In Amos 1:13-15, the prophet moves from Edom in the southern Transjordan to **Ammon** in the north. The biblical narrative depicts Ammon, along with his half-brother Moab (see 2:1-3) as a son born to Lot's incestuous relationship with his daughter (Gen 19:30-38). Amos' indictment of Ammon concerns the horrific war crime of violence carried out against pregnant women and their unborn children. The prophet graphically depicts the Ammonites as breaking through or cutting to pieces (**ripped open**) **the pregnant women of Gilead** (see similar violence in 2 Kgs 8:12; 15:16; Ps 137:9; Hos 10:14; 13:16). Mays observes that such practices occurred in border disputes in order to bring terror upon a nation as well as to annihilate a population (1969, 37).

With abundant pasturage, **Gilead** lay just north of Ammon. Both its location and its fertile land made it susceptible to border invasions by the Ammonites (e.g., Judg 10:8; 11:4-5; 1 Sam 11:1-4). According to the text, Ammon carried out such war crimes **in order to extend his borders** (Amos 1:13).

The divine judgment in response to Ammon's crime is directed against **Rabbah** (v 14). This ancient citadel is present-day Amman, Jordan (see 2 Sam 12:26-31). As in preceding oracles, this primary city serves to represent all of Ammon. However, unlike previous oracles, the text provides a much more elaborate description of the actual destruction. A war cry and a tempestuous storm accompany the text's repeated image of devastating fire. While the shout indicates a battle scene, the storm conveys the onslaught of a violent wind. Divine battle and tempestuous windstorm are typical images in theophany narratives. For Amos, the Day of Yahweh is looming on the horizon for the

Ammonites. Yahweh will send the **king** of Ammon and his **officials** into **exile** (*gôlâ*) (v 15). The power structures of Ammon that committed atrocities will be driven out of their homeland.

F. Moab (2:1-3)

■ **1-3** The text completes the Transjordan series in 2:1-3 with charges against the central territory of **Moab**, located between Ammon and Edom. Like Ammon, the biblical tradition traces Moab to Lot's incestuous relationship with his daughter (Gen 19:30-38). The biblical narrative depicts diverse relationships between Israel and Moab throughout Israel's history (see Judg 3:12-30; Ruth; 1 Sam 14:47; 2 Sam 8:2; 1 Kgs 11:1, 3; 2 Kgs 3:1-27).

Unlike the charges against the other neighboring nations for their crimes against Israel, the crime of Moab is against **Edom**. By means of this unusual twist, the prophet subtly conveys that Yahweh is more than a mere national deity who defends his own people. He is God of the nations. Yahweh not only brings charges against the other nations but also provides justice on behalf of the nations that suffer maltreatment. In spite of Edom's perennial struggle with Israel (see Amos 1:11-12), Yahweh holds Moab responsible for its crime against Israel's notorious enemy brother.

The oracle charges Moab with the war crime of burning the Edomite king's bones **to ashes** or ***as if to lime*** (2:1). Amos suggests the crime of either burning alive an Edomite king who was captured in battle or desecrating the tomb of a dead king and burning his bones to ashes. As in previous oracles, the divine response includes **fire** that will devour (**consume**) Moab's strongholds. **Kerioth** was likely a principal Moabite city (see Jer 48:24, 41). It may be associated with the city of Ar (see Mays 1969, 39). According to the Moabite Stone, King Mesha (ca. 840-820 B.C.) of Moab had dragged the chieftain of an Israelite city to Kerioth.

Similar to the preceding oracle against the Ammonites, Amos 2:2*b*-3 provides a more detailed depiction of the destruction of Moab. The oracle announces that Moab will ***die*** (*mût*, **go down**). Its death will occur within the context of a crashing uproar (*šāʾôn*, **great tumult**; see the military context of this term in Isa 13:4; Jer 25:31; 48:45; Hos 10:14). War cries and trumpet sound, signaling a call to battle, will be heard throughout Moab. Amos 2:3 depicts Yahweh's judgment on the ruling class of Moab. He will ***cut off*** (*kārat*, **destroy**) Moab's **ruler** and **kill all** the **officials** in the land who rule on his behalf. Judgment on the ruling class implies the end of the nation's ability to continue the path of violence against other nations.

G. Judah (2:4-5)

■ **4-5** In vv 4-5 Amos addresses Judah, located directly south of Israel, and thus completes his judgment speeches against all the nations around Israel.

Although Amos comes from Judah, he seldom directs an oracle solely to his homeland. In contrast to the preceding six oracles, the text does not focus upon the war crimes of Judah. Neither does Amos focus upon the social injustices that he will cite against Israel (2:6-8). Judah's crime is twofold: first, it **rejected the law of the Lord** (*tôrâ*) and did not keep Yahweh's **decrees**. Rejection of Yahweh's *tôrâ* is tantamount to the rejection of Yahweh himself. Amos makes it very clear that the crime of Judah is covenantal in nature; the covenant community failed to live by the covenant stipulations and its agreement with God. Second, **false gods,** or ***lies, led the people astray*** (**they have been led astray**). The plural form of the noun *kāzāb* means ***lies*** or ***deceptive things***. Amos is most likely thinking of false gods as well as Judah's political alliances with other nations. The ***lies*** caused the people to wander away from their covenant commitment to Yahweh. Amos also indicates that this is not something new that just happened in Judah's history; the present generation is simply following the ***lies*** that its **ancestors followed**.

The concluding statement in v 5 employs the same language of **fire** and consumption as in the preceding oracles. Likewise v 5 singles out Jerusalem, the dominant city of the nation. Later Deuteronomic thought may have influenced the prophetic indictment against Judah (see Mays 1969, 41-42; Wolff 1977, 163-64; however, contrast Paul 1991, 20-24).

FROM THE TEXT

Amos' oracles against the nations challenge the reader of the text to recognize that the Lord is not a parochial, sectarian deity. Rather, he is the sovereign Lord and judge of all nations, all peoples, all ethnicities, and all cultures. He holds all nations accountable for their actions. Though he has a special covenant with Judah, he does not exempt them from judgment for their violation of his covenant with them. Amos makes clear that the crimes committed by the nations will be returned back to them in the form of divine judgment.

Amos' judgment word against Moab portrays God as a God who does not merely defend his own people. As God of the universe, he acts on behalf of all who are defenseless, abused, and without hope. Amos will later say that this God even provided emancipation for the Philistines from Caphtor and the Arameans from Kir (9:7) in spite of the divine accusations against them in the opening oracles. This theme is consistent with Amos' portrait of Israel's God as the God of all nations.

This text shapes a narrative universe in which humane treatment of one's fellow human beings is a divine expectation of all people groups. Shalom Paul has aptly observed that the Lord's "moral laws operate and are binding within the international community of nations" (1991, 72). Therefore, the text graphically confronts inhumane treatment of *the other* regardless of *the other's* temporal, geographical, or ideological location. The text boldly challenges the reading community both in war and in peace to examine the manner in which one's society, nation, and culture objectifies, vandalizes, vilifies, demonizes, and treats with contempt one's fellow human beings. The text invites the reader to explore and confront contemporary incarnations of inhumane treatment that occur through human trafficking, unbridled outrage, rape and murder of the living and the yet to be born, unchecked greed for empire building, war crimes and abuse of prisoners of war, undignified handling of the dead bodies of enemies—both soldiers and civilians—and destructive violence.

The text moves the reading audience to examine not only how it might actively engage in these atrocities but also how it might live within a society or an empire that engages in such acts of violence. Through the text, the reading community must face its own passive participation in cruel and violent crimes against humanity. The text confronts the reader to ask how, where, and why human beings have become mere commodities for exchange and objects for destruction. It challenges the reading audience to recognize that in all human interaction, including warfare, there is a divinely defined line that one must keep. When human beings become mere objects for economic exchange, violent mutilation, and self-serving destruction for the sake of an economic, political, or religious cause, the perpetrator has crossed that line. When human dignity is stripped from the other, crime against humanity becomes crime against God the Creator. This is the central message of Amos' introductory oracles.

It is important to note that Amos also holds transgression of the instructions of the Lord by his covenant people in the same scale as war crimes and other inhuman activities committed by the surrounding nations. There is a clear invitation in this text to the people of God to live in faithfulness to God's instructions as well as to be God's voice in the world for just and humane treatment of all human beings, even one's enemies. In the world in which we live, where nations trust in their military power and their capability to destroy other nations, Amos reminds God's people that they have a responsibility to be mediators of peace and reconciliation rather than supporters of hostility, violence, and destruction of human lives. The Gospel writer Matthew makes clear Jesus' instruction (*tôrâ*) to his disciples: "Blessed are the peacemakers, for they will be called children of God" (Matt 5:9).

III. ORACLES AGAINST ISRAEL: AMOS 2:6—6:14

A. Israel's Crime and Punishment (2:6-16)

BEHIND THE TEXT

The oracles against the surrounding nations begun in 1:3 provide the context for this passage. The basic pattern and language established in 1:3—2:5 continues on into 2:6-8.

With the accusation against Israel in 2:6-8, the series of oracles against the nations comes to an end. However, the unit in vv 9-16 develops the thought established in vv 6-8. In vv 9-11, the prophet rehearses Yahweh's mighty acts in the life of his people. These acts include three primary traditions that informed ancient Israel's early faith: the exodus from Egypt, provision in the wilderness, and the possession of the land. Verse 12 depicts the people's rebellious response to Yahweh's mighty acts. The unit ends with the pronouncement of divine judgment (vv 13-16).

IN THE TEXT

■ 6-8 Unlike the crimes of the nations and Judah in 1:3—2:5, Amos depicts in 2:6-8 Israel's "neighborly war crimes," which destroyed the fabric of the covenant community life.

In the opening accusation against Israel (v 6*b*), the prophet depicts economic transaction in which the vulnerable of society have become commodities that are purchased and sold. These persons move from relationships of reciprocity into relationships of debt-slavery (see 2 Kgs 4:1-7). The prophet describes the manner in which members of the landholding ruling stratum **sell** [*mākar*] **the *righteous*** (*ṣaddîq*, **innocent**) with **silver** and the **needy** [*'ebyôn*] **for a pair of sandals**. Within the well-established political-economic structure of eighth-century Israel, the ***righteous*** were those who were *in the right* (i.e., **innocent**) or at the receiving end of their dependency relationship to their overlord. The term **needy** also conveys the dependency relationship of tenants who were vulnerable and depended on their overlords for land, basic provisions, protection, and well-being. Instead of protecting and providing for those who depended on them for their survival, the wealthy were exploiting them for profit. The reference to selling for silver may also indicate the practice of a tenant selling himself to his overlord in lieu of the silver that he owed. The **pair of sandals** is likely an idiom depicting the transfer of land or other valuable property (e.g., Deut 25:9-10; Ruth 4:7-8). Amos portrays here the transfer of ownership of the vulnerable members of the covenant community by the wealthy in the same way they exchanged ownership of land and other property.

In Amos 2:7*a*, Amos' accusation focuses on the perversion of justice by the ruling class who were responsible for rendering appropriate judgments (i.e., justice) to dependent persons. Rather than providing justice, these powerful persons pulverize (*šā'ap*, **trample**) the heads of the ***helpless*** (*dal*) into the dust of the earth. The participial form of the verb *šā'ap* depicts this crushing as an ongoing activity. The ruling is also being charged with the denial of the ***way*** (*derek*, **justice**) of the ***weak*** (*'ānî*, **oppressed**). The term *derek*, which usually means "way," "path," and so forth, can also mean **justice** (see Mays 1969, 46).

Amos cites a specific example of perversion of justice in v 7*b*: ***a man and his father go to the young maiden***. The term ***young maiden*** (*na'ărâ*) commonly depicts a young woman of marital age; here the sexual exploitation of a young woman by a father and son indicates that the exploited person was a debt-servant to a wealthy family (thus a maidservant) (see Lev 18:8, 15; Deut 27:20 for laws against improper sexual conduct of family members). The laws in Exod 21:7-11 address the just treatment of young female slaves. Throughout Amos 2:6-7, the prophet has portrayed the ruling stratum as viewing and treating fellow human beings as objects to be used and commodities to be exchanged (see Wolff 1977, 167; Gowan 1996, 365). This type of conduct for the sake of self-gratification not only dehumanized the powerless in the community but also resulted in the disintegration of primary social relationships (husband-wife, parent-child, patron-client).

Using the priestly language, Amos states that Yahweh's **holy name** was profaned by this perversity and total lack of concern for a vulnerable and helpless human being. Preservation of the sanctity of the **holy name** of Yahweh is a key aspect of the covenant relationship between Yahweh and his people. This concern emerges from the priestly conviction that the life of the community should be a reflection of the divine nature itself (Lev 11:44). Amos charges that instead of preserving the sanctity of Yahweh's holy name, the ruling class in Israel is engaged in activities that **profane** his holy name. They have made the one who is holy something/someone ordinary and unclean in Israel and among the nations (see this dominant concern in Ezekiel).

In Amos 2:8, Amos charges Israel's ruling class with the crime of utilizing that which they have gained through exploitation and perversion of justice in their worship of Yahweh. Amos' reference to **garments taken in pledge** suggests the practice of handing over one's outer garment as a guarantee for a financial obligation (see Paul 1991, 83-85, regarding the seizure of property for unpaid debt). Exodus 22:25-27 stipulated that one's cloak be given back by evening even if the debt were not paid (see the unique case for widows in Deut 24:17*b*). According to Amos, the wealthy kept the garments and used them as a cushion to recline upon (**lie down**) beside every altar. The reference to **every altar** may indicate that the practice had become widespread in Israel. Amos shows here how perverted political-economic practices have made their way into the place of worship and have thus corrupted the worship of Yahweh in Israel.

Amos concludes his accusations with the charge that the wealthy are drinking **wine taken as fines** (Amos 2:8). Presumably, these fines were exacted from the vulnerable dependents by the ruling class as a *payment in kind* (see Mays 1969, 47). Similar to pledged garments, levied fines were also legitimate (e.g., Exod 21:22; Deut 22:19). Amos accuses the wealthy of their self-indulgent drinking of the levied wine **in the house of their god**. Though the text does not make it clear, the phrase **their god** likely refers not to other deities but to Yahweh, the God whom the wealthy claim to worship in the shrine at Bethel ("house of God") (see Amos 3:14; 4:4). Again, corrupt political-economic practices have made their way into the setting of worship, and the wealthy were oblivious to the incompatibility between the deity they worship and their hedonistic way of life.

■ **9-11** Before announcing the divine response to Israel's crimes, the text describes Yahweh's gracious activity toward his covenant people (vv 9-11). The multiple examples of divine graciousness contrast sharply with the rebellious actions of vv 6-8.

Amos reminds the wealthy who control the corrupt political-economic structure and claim ownership of the land that they are exploiting the poor in Yahweh's land that he gave to Israel by destroying its previous inhabitants (v 9). The reference to the **Amorites** denotes either the entire population that lived in Canaan or a particular segment that lived there. The image of trees of height and strength (**tall as the cedars** and **strong as the oaks**) reminds the Israelites of their inability to enter the land in their own might (see Num 13:22-33; Deut 2:10, 20-21; 7:7-9; 8:12-18). Yahweh not only destroyed the formidable Amorites but also utterly annihilated their produce (**fruit**) and all that might nourish future produce (**roots**).

In Amos 2:10 the prophet reminds his audience of the three mighty acts of Yahweh: exodus from Egypt, guidance in the wilderness, and giving Israel the land of the Amorites. Yahweh delivered Israel from their bondage in Egypt and **brought** them **out of Egypt**. He **led** Israel **in the wilderness** for **forty years**, a place where it was impossible for anyone to survive. The text makes clear that the purpose of this divine rescue and leading of Israel was to give Israel **the land of the Amorites**. God did not merely deliver the people *from* the land of Egypt but delivered them *for the purpose* of life in a new **land** (*'ereṣ*). The phrase **to give you the land** literally reads ***to inherit the land*** (*yāraš* means "to take possession"). Amos reminds his audience that they took possession of the land that did not belong to them; it was given to them as a gift, as the fulfillment of God's promises to the patriarchs.

Amos includes in his list of God's saving acts on behalf of Israel the rise of **prophets** and **Nazirites** from among their young men (v 11). From their own **children**, Yahweh brought forth **prophets** or spokespersons (*nābî'*) who delivered his words to the people. From among their **youths**, he brought forth Nazirites. In the life of the Israelite community, the Nazirite reminded the people of their collective consecration and devotion to Yahweh (see Num 6 for legislation regarding the Nazirite vow). With God's raising up both prophets and Nazirites from among the people's own children, he continued to act in the life of his people, reminding them of their unique place among the nations of the world.

Yahweh concludes the overview of his faithfulness with a rhetorical question, **Is this not true, people of Israel?** (v 11). The story of Israel, which includes both Yahweh's faithfulness and the people's rebellion, speaks for itself. The historical sketch of God's covenant loyalty toward Israel prepares the way for the divine verdict.

■ **12** Verse 12 depicts how Israel *shut down* the gifts of God. They **made the Nazirites drink wine** and thus caused them to break their vow of separation from intoxicating drinks. They commanded **the prophets not to prophesy**, and thus they gave a direct mandate to the prophets to break their loyalty and commitment to God, who called them to a special vocation. Both of these activities show how the people showed no regard for fidelity or loyalty to their covenant with God. They have perverted themselves and forced those persons who have set themselves apart for God to follow their perverted way of life.

■ **13-16** In vv 13-16, Yahweh responds to Israel's crimes. In v 13, God announces the specific divine action: ***Behold, I am pressing you under***. The participial form of the verb depicts ongoing application of divine pressure. The remainder of the verse compares God's activity to the pressure of a loaded cart. The weight of the cart **crushes** whatever lies underneath it.

The divine pressure will *press out* the strength of the strongest members of the community so that even the most powerful will not endure. In vv 14-16, the text employs and repeats various terms that describe the weakness of the mighty. The **swift**, the **strong**, and the **warrior** all represent the fastest and the strongest persons in the land. These are the people who are capable of escaping any type of calamity, either by running to places of escape or fighting against enemies. When God's judgment comes, even the strongest in the land will find themselves weak and defenseless. The same thought continues in v 15 by listing three groups of warriors: archers, foot soldiers, and infantry. Again, these groups represent the highly skilled in the land who are trained in military strategies. Depicting God's judgment by using the language of warfare, Amos gives no hope to even the strongest in the nation of Israel. In v 16, the text reaches a crescendo as the prophet announces what will become of the mighty warrior who is ordinarily strong in his heart (i.e., **bravest**). He will lose all courage and run away **naked**. Those who trusted in their own strength will suffer shame and disgrace **on that day** (i.e., the day of Yahweh's visitation, see 3:14; 5:18, 20; 8:9).

FROM THE TEXT

Amos' oracles against the neighboring nations reach their final target in this text. The placement of Israel at the end of the series of oracles that begins in 1:3 clearly reveals Amos' strategy to expose Israel as the worst criminal, worse than any other nations in the world because it committed "war crimes" against its own people. This text compels Israel to point the finger of accusation that Israel pointed at others back upon itself. The Day of the Lord is not merely divine judgment against the outsiders (i.e., the nations); it ultimately is the season of accountability for the insiders (i.e., the people of God). In this announcement, the text boldly speaks to subsequent generations of God's people that wag the finger of accusation against "the world" but fail to see their own injustices and crimes. It challenges the people of God to reexamine its perception of final judgment solely as "sinners in the hands of an angry God." The Lord's judgment holds the people of God accountable for the unique covenant relationship they share with God.

The text invites subsequent generations to explore the manner in which they live out their covenant identity and the divine investment given them. In Matthew's eschatological discourse (Matt 24—25), Jesus likewise challenges his followers to understand their calling as more than privilege. The call to follow Jesus as Lord entails responsibility. As vividly demonstrated in Jesus' parables of the faithful and unfaithful servants (Matt 24:45-51) and the investment of talents (Matt 25:14-30), the people of God are in no way exempt from the judgment of the nations. The ones who inherit the kingdom are those persons who clothe the naked, care for the sick, and visit the imprisoned (Matt 25:31-46).

The text of Amos constructs a graphic portrait of a community engaged in "warfare" within itself. The covenantal relationships of reciprocity have disintegrated in such a way that human beings are mere commodities for exchange. Particularly the vulnerable, dependent members of the community have become mere objects for self-serving leaders. This text challenges the reader to explore where such relationships exist in contemporary society and how these relationships deteriorate to serve only persons in power. It moves the reading community to identify its own weak, dependent, and vulnerable members.

Amos' depiction of the political-economic situation of eighth-century B.C. Israel especially challenges subsequent generations to examine the use and the abuse of political, economic, and religious power. Do authorities employ power *for the sake of* or *to the harm of* weaker members of the community, the society, and the world? While the text does not specifically object to the reality of power itself, it unabashedly opposes the use of power for self-indulgence and self-aggrandizement. The text blatantly objects to the use of power that seeks to take life from "the other" rather than to give life to "the other." It challenges every level of political, economic, and religious leadership that uses established relationships for self-serving purposes.

The text not only challenges the abuse of power but also constructs an alternative to human infidelity in its depiction of enduring divine faithfulness. Human infidelity through self-serving power serves as the foil for divine fidelity through self-giving power. The abusive misuse of neighbor contrasts with God's deliverance of and provision for his people. Broken communal covenants contrast sharply with the unbroken divine covenant. What the people have received, they have not given. The Lord delivers only now for them to enslave; the Lord provides only now for them to hoard. The text shapes a narrative world into which it now draws the reader. It prepares the reader to respond just as the Lord himself will respond in the subsequent chapter.

B. Covenant Responsibility (3:1-2)

BEHIND THE TEXT

Amos 3:1-2 serves as an introduction to the subsequent oracles of judgment in the book. These opening verses express the ironic and paradoxical conviction underlying Amos' message to Israel. On the one hand, all of v 1 and the first half of v 2 reflect the historic tradition of the people of Israel that Yahweh delivered them from Egypt and entered into a unique covenant relationship with them at Sinai. This conviction undergirded the priestly (e.g., Exod 19:3-6) and the Deuteronomic-prophetic (Deut 6:4-15, 20-25) testimonies concerning Israel's unique identity.

Although the NIV translates the twice-used particle *ʿal* in v 1 as "against," one should not limit this particle to an adversative meaning. It can also function to specify the object to which a verb (i.e., "has spoken") applies. Therefore one may translate the particle as ***concerning*** or ***with regard to***. The entire house of Israel is the recipient of Yahweh's word. In the context of eighth-century B.C. thinking about the Day of Yahweh, Amos' audience would have hoped to hear a word about their salvation. However, vv 1-2 show that Yahweh's word *concerning* Israel is paradoxically a word *against* them.

IN THE TEXT

3:1-2 ■ **1** Amos begins with a familiar call for the **people of Israel** to **hear** (*šāmaʿ* means "hear," "obey"; see Deut 6:4) a specific **word** (*dābār*) that Yahweh has **spoken** (*diber*). The term ***clan*** (*mišpāḥah*, **family**) is a reminder to the people that even as a nation they are the ***clan*** or the **family**. The word is addressed to **the whole family**. Some scholars speculate that this phrase presupposes both Israel and Judah, and thus the phrase belongs to a later period. However, it is also likely that the reference is simply to the northern kingdom people. **I brought up out of Egypt** indicates Yahweh's direct and personal involvement in the deliverance of Israel from their bondage in Egypt (see Amos 2:10). This divine act of salvation sets the context for Yahweh's speech in 3:2.

■ **2** Verse 2, a direct address (**you, your**), begins with Yahweh's declaration that out of all the clans/**families** [*mišpāḥôt*; see v 1] **of the earth**, he has ***known*** (*yādaʿ*; **chosen**) only this clan/family whom he brought up from Egypt. The particle **only** emphasizes the exclusive nature of the Yahweh-Israel relationship. In the context of the ancient suzerain-vassal treaties, "to know" means covenantal commitment to each other by both parties (see Paul 1991, 101-2). The text asserts that though Yahweh is the Lord of all nations (chs 1—2), and though he has worked on behalf of other nations (9:7), only with Israel has Yahweh entered into a covenantal relationship. The phrase **all *the clans*/families of the earth** echoes the language of God's promises to the patriarchs (Gen

12:3; 28:14). The linkage of this verse with Gen 12:3 and 28:14 also suggests that God established this covenant relationship with this particular family so that it may be the mediators of God's blessings to all the families of the earth (its priestly responsibility among the nations; see Exod 19:4-6).

Amos 3:2*b* indicates that the covenant relationship between Yahweh and Israel is the basis (**therefore**) for Yahweh's impending visitation of Israel. The preceding oracle (2:6-12) firmly established the failure of Israel to fulfill their responsibility to Yahweh. They have broken the covenant by their failure to do justice to the poor and the oppressed among them. **Therefore**, Yahweh says, he will ***visit*** (*pāqad*, **punish**) Israel for **all** their **sins** (*ʿāwōn* means "iniquity"). The literal translation of *pāqad* (***visit*** or ***attend to***) conveys Yahweh's visitation of Israel or the nations either in salvation or judgment. His visitation may be his gracious overture toward those who are in need of his help. It can also be for the purpose of punishing those who violate his moral and ethical demands. In such case, **punish** is an appropriate translation, as in the NIV. The Hebrew term *ʿāwōn* indicates the residue, aftereffect, or even guilt of sins committed. The word contrasts with purposeful rebellion or transgression (*pešaʿ*) and sin as the intentional or unintentional "missing of a mark" (*ḥaṭṭāʾt*).

FROM THE TEXT

This text challenges the reading audience and the church in particular to examine the issue of election and "chosenness." The language of the text reflects the election of a people rather than the election of an individual. God initiated this election as an act of grace in relationship to *both* the community itself *and* the world. The election is not to eternal salvation or eternal damnation; it is election to a specific role in and to the broader world. As divine election is not the end in itself, the chosen community functions as the means of divine grace in relationship to the nations and all of creation. The privilege of election entails responsibility. To be the "chosen people" is not grounds for superiority over the world; it is grounds for ministry in and service to the world. The book of Amos vividly portrays the subtle temptation faced by God's people to understand itself in a privileged, even superior, position. These verses remind the covenant community that the Lord will hold his chosen people accountable for their unique calling. Indeed, those to whom much is given, of them will much be required (Luke 12:48). This text invites "a kingdom of priests and a holy nation" (see Exod 19:4-6 and 1 Pet 2:9-10) to explore and understand its privileges as well as its covenant responsibilities to each other and to the world.

C. Cause and Effect (3:3-8)

BEHIND THE TEXT

While vv 3-8 are distinct in content and genre, this unit emerges directly from the announcement in vv 1-2. These verses seem to be Amos' response to Amaziah the priest who commanded Amos not to prophesy at Bethel (see 7:10-17). These verses convey how and why the prophet has no option but to speak (see 1:1). The prophetic word spoken is simply the divine word given. Amos establishes himself as a legitimate and authorized spokesperson of Yahweh.

Amos utilizes here a logically argued disputation style of speech in order to persuade the hearers/readers to acknowledge the authenticity of the prophet and his message. Mays describes these verses as "an authentic apologetic" (1969, 60). The disputation speech, which finds its home in the wisdom tradition, may contain a series of rhetorical questions emerging from commonplace life experiences (see 3:3-6). The image of the roaring lion (vv 4, 8) frames the disputation as well as links the disputation to the book's opening oracle in 1:2. From the outset of the book, the divine roar has dramatic effects.

In the rhetorical questions in 3:3-6, seven examples of cause and effect appear. In vv 7-8, Amos applies these examples to the prophetic message itself. The argument of the disputation is in effect as follows: before Yahweh acts (effect), he speaks to the prophet (cause); therefore, when the prophet speaks (effect), Yahweh has spoken (cause).

IN THE TEXT

■ **3-6** The opening three verses of this unit (vv 3-5) provide five rhetorical questions that depict the cause and effect (beginning with the effect). Each question, which utilizes the interrogative particle, posits a specific situation (an effect), and each situation then concludes with its cause. While v 3 depicts the cause-effect relationship between two persons who agree to meet and proceed to journey together, vv 4-5 depict two examples of a lion and its prey and two examples of trapped animals.

The two rhetorical questions in v 6 employ two *if* statements followed by a negative interrogative statement. Both statements refer to disastrous calamities within a city. The statement in v 6*a* reverses the order from effect-cause to cause-effect as the prophet portrays the invasion against a city. When the **trumpet** sound is heard in the city (cause), the people are terrified (effect). The statement in v 6*b* returns to the order of effect-cause as seen in vv 3-5 and concludes with the first direct mention of Yahweh himself. If a great **disaster** comes upon a city (effect), Yahweh himself has **caused it**. This unique arrangement of v 6 provides a chiasmus of *cause-effect—effect-cause* with the text concluding with Yahweh as the cause of the city's calamity.

■ **7-8** The disputation reaches its climactic application in vv 7-8. God **does nothing** unless he reveals his counsel to his servants the prophets. (Mays 1969, 61-62, interprets this verse to be a subsequent editorial comment.) The reference to God as ***Lord Yahweh*** (**Sovereign** L**ORD**) appears twice in these two verses. The term LORD (*ʾădōnāy*) reflects Yahweh's lordship or sovereignty over all that takes place. This divine sovereign speaks (v 8) and acts (v 7).

In v 7, Yahweh reveals **his plan** (*sôd*) before acting. The term *sôd* implies the counsel that is carried out and received within a circle of friends or within a council of colleagues (1 Kgs 22:13-40; Jer 23:18, 21-22). The phrase **his servants the prophets** is characteristic of Deuteronomic-prophetic thought (see, e.g., Deut 3:24; 34:5). It conveys the authenticity and credibility of the word given by the prophets (see Deut 18:15-22).

The disputation reaches its climactic conclusion in Amos 3:8 as the prophet declares that **the lion has roared . . . the Sovereign** L**ORD has spoken**. Amos' oracles are indeed the words received from the roaring deity (1:2). If creation itself responds to the roaring lion, how much more must the covenant community respond.

Once again reversing the pattern followed in 3:3-6 (effect-cause), the text depicts the cause (the lion's roar) first. The effects of the divine roar are the reverent **fear** (*yāraʾ*) of the people and the proclamation by the prophet. If the prophet fears Yahweh, he must speak the prophetic word; if the people fear Yahweh, they must *hear* the prophetic word.

The prophet concludes v 8 by returning to one more question in his disputation speech: ***Who will not prophesy?*** Amos makes the bold claim that the words he prophesies are the words spoken by Yahweh. The source of his prophetic authority is Yahweh, who has spoken and commanded him to "go, prophesy" to the people of Israel (7:15). Those who hear the words of Yahweh can do nothing but speak Yahweh's words on behalf of him.

FROM THE TEXT

Contemporary readers of 3:3-8 recognize in these verses a central theological issue: the authoritative nature of the prophetic word. The word spoken by the prophet carries with it divine authority; therefore, the people of God must *hear* and subsequently *obey* the word of God. They simply cannot and must not ignore the word. This word is not the fanciful creation or self-serving agenda of the prophet. It is God's word to his people, and thus God will hold his people accountable.

At the same time, the prophetic person must take seriously the reality that the word spoken is the word from God. "Thus says the LORD" conveys the source of the word delivered. Only as the prophetic message comes from God does it carry authority over the people. Thus the prophet must also stand under the authority of the God who gives the word delivered. Words that originate with God have no room for self-serving agendas or programs. Prophet stands as the messenger of God, and not a spokesperson for particular political ideologies or economic and social programs.

Amos demonstrates the role of the prophetic person in communicating the divine word. Those who hear God speaking are invited by this text to enter into a partnership with God and become his spokespersons in their world. Such a partnering with God is not a light task. Nevertheless, the prophetic messenger is indispensable to the people's hearing the divine message. To the Romans, Paul raised the questions, "How can they believe in the one of whom they have not heard? And how can they hear without someone preaching to them? And how can anyone preach unless they are sent?" (Rom 10:14-15).

Finally a caution: the cause-and-effect language of the text does not establish a theological principle that traces all that happens in the world to God. The prophet utilizes the cause-and-effect language to establish the relationship between God's word and the prophetic word, and God's call and his response. Reading this text out of context may result in the perspective that God is the source and direct cause of all that occurs (see esp. 3:6*b*). The full canon, both the OT and the NT, will not support that conclusion.

D. Indictment against Samaria and Bethel (3:9-15)

BEHIND THE TEXT

Three distinct units comprise vv 9-15. In vv 9-11, the prophet calls upon Ashdod and Egypt to serve as witnesses against Israel. This oracle follows the basic form of the prophetic lawsuit: call to witnesses (v 9), indictment/verdict (v 10), and announcement of punishment (v 11).

The indictment is against Samaria, the political center of Israel. Omri established Samaria, located about thirty-five miles north of Jerusalem, as the capital of the northern kingdom in the early ninth century B.C. (see 1 Kgs 16:23-24). Amos frequently mentions Samaria in his criticism of the national, political, and social life of the citizens of the northern kingdom (see 3:12; 4:1; 5:7-12; 6:1; 8:4-6). It represents for the prophet the *pacesetter* for the other towns and villages of the northern kingdom. Mays observes that "Samaria was a special case, because the tune was called there and sung throughout the land" (1969, 64).

The brief oracle in 3:12 announces the devastating effect of the divine visitation upon Israel. However, the verse obviously continues the images of destruction found in v 11.

Calling upon the witnesses (see v 9) to hear and testify against the covenant people, vv 13-15 focus upon the imminent destruction that will occur both to the primary worship shrine of Bethel and to the luxurious dwellings of the elite. Bethel, located ten miles north of Jerusalem, is the subject of Amos' indictment. Bethel also receives Amos' repeated criticism (see 4:4; 5:5-6; 7:10-13). Bethel, where Jacob built an altar (Gen 28:10-22), was one of the two cultic centers (the other being Dan) established by Jeroboam I shortly after the division of the kingdom in 922 B.C. (1 Kgs 12:25-33). According to 1 Kgs 13:1-5 "a man of God came from Judah to Bethel" and announced its destruction under a king named Josiah (see 2 Kgs 23:15-17). The depiction of Amos' denunciation of Bethel during the time of Jeroboam II (see Amos 7:9-17) is strangely reminiscent of this earlier prophetic voice at the time of Jeroboam I. Amos also announces the destruction of the opulent houses of the wealthy citizens of Israel (3:15).

IN THE TEXT

■ **9-10** The oracle begins with a summons to the mighty powers of Ashdod and Egypt to witness Samaria's crimes from **the mountains** that encircle the royal city. Amos makes reference to **fortresses** four times in this text, twice in reference to other nations and twice to Israel. **Ashdod** was one of five cities of the Philistine Pentapolis (see 1:6-8). What an irony that surrounding nations who have committed horrendous crimes are being called here to testify against Israel, God's covenant people. These nations will see **great unrest** and **oppression** taking place in the midst of Samaria (**within her** and **among her people**). The plural form of **unrest** (*mĕhûmâ*) conveys the idea of tumultuous disturbances that cause panic within the community. These disturbances occur more frequently and in large scale (**great**; *rabbôt* perhaps means ***many*** here). The concluding line of v 9 relates the unrest in the city to acts of ***oppressions*** (*ʿăšûqîm*). In v 10 Amos describes the fortresses of Samaria as storehouses of ***violence*** (*ḥāmās*) or that which has been gained by violence (hence **plundered**). The parallel term ***loot*** (*šōd*) also conveys the idea of ***violence***. The inhabitants of Samaria commit violence and oppression because they do not **know how to do right**. Violence is all that they know; lack of knowledge of how to do right is the direct outcome of lack of commitment to the covenant with God.

■ **11** Amos announces the destruction of Samaria's **fortresses** in v 11 (see similar announcements in 1:3—2:5). These sites of military defense indicate the pride, self-security, and misplaced trust of the people (see 6:8). Although the strongholds are now filled with "treasures of violence," the **Sovereign Lord** announces that an adversary (**enemy**) will bring down these places in which they seek refuge (**strongholds**). The adversary will violently take that which was violently gained. With no safe place for the people to run, the Day of Yahweh will be for them as it will be for all nations. That which they sowed, they will harvest (see Obad 15); that which they plundered will be plundered. The adversary is not identified, though based on our knowledge of the geopolitical developments on the horizon we may identify this enemy as Assyria.

■ **12** With graphic images, v 12 depicts the complete destruction of Israel's fortresses. The image of a lion appears once again (see 1:2; 3:4, 8) here as a violent predator that destroys a sheep. Amos compares the rescue of Samaria to a shepherd's attempt to rescue the body parts of a sheep from the mouth of a lion. While a leg or a part of an ear may be salvaged, death to the animal is certain.

The precise meaning of the last line of v 12 is not clear. The translation, **with only the head of a bed and a piece of fabric from a couch**, suggests that the people will escape with broken pieces of furniture. Samaria's destruction will be total; there will be nothing left that would be of any value. The alternate reading, "on the edge of their beds and in Damascus on their couches" (see NIV footnote), does not make much sense.

■ **13** Verses 13-15, addressed to an unnamed audience, begin with a call to **hear** (*šāmaʿ*) the pronouncement against God's people. Verse 13 functions rhetorically to introduce a legal hearing. Yahweh is about to bring charges against his covenant people. The unnamed audience is called to bear witness (**testify**) against Israel.

Amos identifies Israel as **the descendants of Jacob** in v 13; the reference to Israel as Jacob or as his descendants is a common practice among the prophets. The name is especially fitting here since v 14 mentions Bethel. The one who speaks is ***Lord, Yahweh God of hosts***. The title "Yahweh of hosts" (*yhwh ṣĕbāʾôt*) is very common throughout the OT. Amos is particularly fond of the phrase ***God of hosts*** (see also 4:13; 5:14-16, 27; 6:8, 14; 9:5). The phrase ***Yahweh of hosts/Yahweh God of hosts*** may be traced to Israel's holy war tradition that portrays Yahweh as the divine warrior who leads his hosts (stars, divine beings, and/or the armies of Israel) in his battle against the enemy. In Amos, the title coincides with the concept of the Day of Yahweh, the day of Yahweh's judgment of Israel and the nations.

■ **14-15** In 3:14-15, the prophet finally announces the divine judgment. Twice in v 14 he speaks of Yahweh's visitation. God will ***visit*** (*pāqad*; see v 2) Israel's ***transgressions*** (*pešaʿ*, **sins**; see the use of *pešaʿ* in 1:3, 6, 9, 11, 13; 2:1, 4, 6) upon Israel. Yahweh will also ***visit*** [*pāqad*, **destroy**] **the altars of Bethel**. The **horns** were four horn-shaped projections, one on each corner of the altar. They represented the efficacious power and protection that a worshipper could seek at an altar. The law seems to have allowed criminals to find safety by taking hold of them (see 1 Kgs 1:50; 2:28; see also Exod 21:13-14). Yahweh will **cut off** the horns and they will **fall to the ground**. There will be no protection for

Israel from Yahweh's judgment; even the places of their worship will have no power to save them.

The text concludes in Amos 3:15 with four distinct references to houses (*bayit*, **winter house**, **summer house**, **ivory** houses, great or many houses [**mansions**]). The various houses described by the prophet demonstrate the corruption that has swept across every facet of Israelite life: political (house of Jacob), religious-cultic (house of God/Bethel), socioeconomic arena (multiple luxurious houses of the elite).

Yahweh will fatally smite (**tear down**) the **winter house** that is inhabited at the time of the autumn harvest as well as the **summer house**, the dwelling for summertime. The elite of Israel constructed dwelling places for the extremes in climate. Both luxurious dwellings and their furnishings would have ivory inlaid into wood or stone (see 6:4). However, these luxurious homes will ***perish*** (**be destroyed**); the ***many houses*** (**mansions**) will come to an end (**be demolished**). These houses were also places of luxurious living as well as protection and safety for the wealthy people of Israel. They were built and they existed at the expense of the poor that the wealthy were to protect. Amos announces the destruction of all the places that the powerful people of Israel trusted in for their safety and protection.

FROM THE TEXT

This text reminds the readers that God is no respecter of persons or na- 3:9-15
tions when he carries out his judgment on those who are involved in promoting violence in the world. The community of faith is not a safe place for those who oppress and exploit others. It is ironic that in this text God calls the sinful and violent nations in the world to testify against his own people. The people of God are to be a witness of God's saving grace to the sinful world; when they fail to carry out their mission and become like the world, they would be no better than the rest of the world. The text is heard again in the words of the epistle writer Peter: "For it is time for judgment to begin with God's household" (1 Pet 4:17).

The repeated use of *bayit* ("house") in the text serves as an unmistakable literary device to draw the reading audience into the intricate web of their political, socioeconomic, and religious structures. From the source of political power (house of Jacob) to that of religious power (house of God or Beth-el) to that of economic power (winter and summer houses, ivory houses, many houses), Israel represents a dysfunctional and corrupt *house*. The text challenges its hearers to evaluate how such a web exists in their own world and identify for themselves their own dysfunctional and corrupt *houses*. The world outside is often critical of the church, the people of God, for their perceived hypocrisy and claim of self-righteousness. The church has been too quick to judge the world and too slow in acknowledging its own faults. The text calls for an end to all claims of moral superiority by members of the faith community and finger pointing at the dominant cultures. The imagined world of this text is a world of faithful living and covenant keeping. In this imagined world of the text, the people of God find their security neither in the political, social, or religious structures nor in the number of houses they own or the wealth they possess. The text reminds its readers that protection can come only from God, and it is offered to those who are committed to a covenant way of life.

The prophet understands the punishment upon Israel to be the visitation of God. The divine visitation reflects the central conviction behind the prophetic understanding of the Day of the Lord. There is no thought of capricious punishment or arbitrary reward in this text. Instead it reminds the readers that the seed planted produces specific fruit. The life lived by a community returns back upon that community.

E. Indictment against "Secondhand" Oppressors (4:1-3)

BEHIND THE TEXT

The oracle in 4:1-3, an independent unit, addresses the behavior of the wives of the elite and announces their concomitant doom. It follows the general pattern of prophetic oracles; it first provides the rationale for judgment in v 1 and then provides the divine response in vv 2-3. It continues the plural imperative ("hear this word") begun in 3:1 and repeated in 3:13. The oracle concludes with a typical conclusion of Amos: "declares the LORD" (see 2:16; 3:15). The judgment against the political, religious, and economic *houses* of Israel (3:9-15) is continued here; the specific target of judgment is the women of the *house* who carry out oppression indirectly by making demands on their husbands.

IN THE TEXT

■ **1** Verse 1 begins with a call to **hear** Yahweh's word addressed to the **cows of Bashan on Mount Samaria**. **Cows of Bashan** is a metaphorical designation of the women who live in the opulent houses in Samaria. Amos uses the label to depict the sleek, luxurious, even pampered character of these women. The region of Bashan, located in today's Golan Heights, has rich soil and abundant rainfall. Agricultural fertility abounds in the area. Consequently, the region is renowned for its cattle. The women are part of the political, economic, and social life of Samaria; thus, they belong to the elite class of people in the northern kingdom. The Hebrew text does say **you women** but simply addresses **the cows of Bashan . . . who oppress** and **crush**. Both verbs indicate brutal and inhumane treatment of the vulnerable members of the community by the violent and powerful people. The prophet identifies the oppressed and crushed persons as the ***weak*** (*dal*) and the **needy** (*ʾebyôn*) (see 2:6-7). Amos indicates that these women carried out their oppressive action by the demands they made to their husbands (*ʾădôn* literally means a "lord" or "master"): ***Bring and we will drink***. By making this demand, they become participants and coconspirators in the acts of extortion and oppression committed by their husbands/lords. These consumers are never satisfied with the abundance of resources they have; they want more even if that meant the oppression of the poor and the needy in the land.

■ **2-3** In vv 2-3, the prophet announces the divine response with a divine oath formula: ***Lord Yahweh*** **(Sovereign Lord) has sworn by his holiness**. Holiness is the essence of God, who God is. The holy God who is dependable and trustworthy pronounces a word that is also dependable (see Ps 89:35); God's holiness is the guarantee of its fulfillment.

Yahweh's word begins with the announcement of the ***days*** that are ***coming upon you***; the second person plural (**you**) refers to both the cows of Bashan and their husbands/lords. Days are the time of Yahweh's visitation upon his people.

The obscure nature of the words translated as **hooks** and **fishhooks** makes it difficult to determine the specific details of the events described in vv 2-3. The depiction of those under Yahweh's judgment being **taken away with hooks** fits very well with the notorious ancient Near Eastern practices of conquering armies putting hooks through the noses of their captives. This may be the likely meaning of the judgment word in v 2.

The location of **Harmon** (v 3) is uncertain. The text may have originally read Hermon, which is located within the Bashan region. In this case, the fertile heifers in the fields become dead bodies strung out on the mountains (for extensive discussion of possible renderings of the text, see Paul 1991, 130-36). The suffering that they have brought upon the needy and the weak is multiplied as it comes back upon them.

FROM THE TEXT

Contemporary readers of this text—who are for the most part consumers who make demands of the political, business, religious, and economic network to supply them with niceties that make their lives rich and well-maintained—hear in this text a word of judgment. Consumers/readers whose appetites are never quenched are participants, like the cows of Bashan, in the crimes of oppression and extortion.

The text makes no distinction between "firsthand" acts of violence and the "secondhand" demand for goods gained through violence. Therefore, it challenges the reading audience to ask penetrating questions that deal with their consumer demands, the oppressive and exploitive ways by which suppliers produce goods to satisfy such demands, and the political-religious-economic systems that seduce them into consumer-driven appetites. The text also compels its readers to imagine a world where life is lived in freedom from these appetites and desires, freedom possible through the work of God's grace in their lives.

F. Call to Worship (4:4-5)

BEHIND THE TEXT

The language of a traditional call to worship comprises these two short verses: come, bring, burn (e.g., see Pss 34:11; 46:8; 66:5; 95:1, 2, 6; 96:8; 100:2; 134:1). Through the call to worship, the priest invites the worshipping community to gather at the cultic site and to bring their offerings and sacrifices. Amos takes the priestly prerogative and extends this call.

The prophet's call to worship in Amos 4:4-5, however, is replete with irony and sarcasm (regarding the passage as "parody of priestly torah," see Wolff 1977, 211-12). Rather than inviting the community to worship at the cultic sites, Amos invites the people to rebel. Rather than expressing divine delight in the people's sacrifices, Amos ridicules the people's love for and personal delight in making sacrifice. These sacrifices bring joy to the people rather than to Yahweh.

This call to worship is the first of three in the book of Amos. The movement from one call to worship to the next demonstrates a progression in the book itself. Each call to worship builds upon the previous one. In vv 4-5, the prophet simply invites the people to come to the cultic sites and to bring their sacrifices. The second call to worship (5:4-5) calls upon the people not to go to the sites of worship but to seek Yahweh. The final call to worship (5:14-15) calls upon the people to seek good and not evil, to hate evil and love good. In so doing, they seek Yahweh.

IN THE TEXT

■ **4** Amos begins this call to worship with an imperative (*bô'* could mean **go** or ***come***). The verb suggests pilgrims' entrance into a holy site (see Wolff 1977, 218). In addition to **Bethel**, the primary Yahwistic cultic site of the northern kingdom, the prophet also names **Gilgal** (see Hos 4:15; 9:15; 12:11). Just after entering into the land, the people set up a twelve-stone memorial, underwent circumcision, and celebrated their first Passover in the land of promise at Gilgal (Josh 4—5). Two centuries later, Samuel anointed Saul as Israel's first king at Gilgal (1 Sam 11). Together Bethel and Gilgal signify two of the most significant locales in which Yahweh had acted in Israel's history. Consequently, they represent two of the most sacred sites at which the people gathered to worship Yahweh.

The statement, ***Come* to Bethel and *transgress*, to Gilgal and *multiply transgression*,** indicates Amos' evaluation of worship at Bethel and Gilgal. Rather than being a cult that encourages reconciliation with God and with neighbor, Israelite worship at Bethel and Gilgal promoted outright, purposeful rebellion/transgression (*peša'*). The second line of Amos 4:4 implies that worship sites have become places of many and great transgressions. Amos does not make clear why he regarded Israel's worship at Bethel and Gilgal as transgression. It is possible that he viewed worship at these places as nothing more than acts of transgression because of two reasons: (1) these places promoted illegitimate and idolatrous worship; (2) the worshipping community paid no attention to God's covenant requirements of justice and righteousness in community life.

Amos' call to worship at Bethel and Gilgal continues with a description of the various sacrifices and offerings given at the cult sites (v 4*b*). The prophet invites the people to bring their **sacrifices** and **tithes**. The generic term for sacrifice (*zebaḥ*) can refer to any offering of a slaughtered animal given for various reasons (i.e., thanksgiving, fulfillment of vow, atonement). The northern kingdom traced the practice of giving a tenth (i.e., **tithe**) to Jacob's divine encounter at Bethel (Gen 28:22).

Every three years literally reads ***every three days***. Deuteronomy 14:28 and 26:12 does make provision for a tithe every third year. The prophet's declaration of ***every three days*** could certainly be a parody on the every three years prescribed in Deuteronomy. On the other hand, the preposition *lĕ* before **morning** and ***days*** may function temporally, thus indicating the time at which offerings of sacrifices and tithes occurred in the northern kingdom: sacrifices every morning and tithes on the third day. In light of the broader context, the statements seem to convey the people's overzealousness in bringing their tithes and offerings. Nevertheless, according to Amos, their exuberant activity is outright rebellion.

■ **5** In Amos 4:5, the prophet calls upon the people to cause the sacrifices of leavened bread to go up in smoke (**burn**) as a **thank offering** (*tôdâ*). This offering ordinarily expressed gratitude and praise to God for answered prayers. Leavened bread could accompany it (see Lev 7:13). The **freewill offerings** (*nĕdābâ*) were voluntary gifts that express the worshipper's dedication to Yahweh. They could include whole burnt offerings or peace offerings (see Ezek 46:12). Both the thank offering and the freewill offering took place within the context of enthusiastic joy and celebration as Amos 5:21-23 depicts. The NIV interprets the mere proclamation and announcement of freewill offerings as expressions of pride (**brag** and **boast**). However, the prophet seems simply to call for the publicizing of the offerings so that the people can participate in them and thus join in the transgression that takes place at the worship sites.

Verse 5 ends with the prophet's assessment of the people that they **love to** be involved in the rituals of offerings and sacrifices. The verb "to love" (*'āhēb*) conveys not only affection for another but also commitment to another. How ironic that a people called to *love* Yahweh with all their heart, soul, and strength (Deut 6:5) *love* the system of offerings and sacrifices made to Yahweh. The worshippers have become absorbed in, affectionate toward, and committed to the act of worship rather than to the God whom they are called to worship. Displacing God, the people have substituted themselves along with their offerings and sacrifices as the focal point of their worship.

FROM THE TEXT

This brief text challenges the reading audience to ask in what ways the context for reconciliation with God through worship has become the context for rebellion against God. The text holds up a mirror of a generation that was exuberant with its sacrifices, offerings, and other acts of worship, but in its exuberance, it sinned all the more. Gazing into the mirror provided by a previous generation, a contemporary generation of readers sees itself honestly. It, too, begins to explore those acts of worship that have become the substitute for the life lived outside of public worship.

The text obliges the contemporary worshipping community to ask, "How does worship and sacrifice, even self-sacrifice, become more about pleasing the worshipper than pleasing God?" It confronts the reading community with the question, "What is it about public worship that we *love*? Why?" The words of the prophet challenge readers to contrast their own joy and delight in the acts of public worship with the divine reaction to exuberant worship practices. Later in the book, God speaks, "I hate, I despise your religious festivals; your assemblies are a stench to me" (5:21). The psalmist points us to worship that is pleasing to God, "You do not delight in sacrifice . . . The sacrifices of God are a broken spirit" (51:16, 17 footnote). Hosea puts it differently, "For I desire mercy, not sacrifice, and acknowledgment of God rather than burnt offerings" (6:6; see Matt 9:13).

G. A Rehearsal of Divine Attempts to Save (4:6-12)

BEHIND THE TEXT

The ideology of the ancient Near Eastern treaty curse or malediction lies behind the systematic review in Amos 4:6-11. The treaty curse warns the vassal of impending destruction by the suzerain if the vassal breaks the treaty (see Lev 26:14-39; Deut 28:15-46). Rather than prescribing the curses for the future, he articulates them as already having taken place. The text gives a catalog of Yahweh's judgment actions he carried out against Israel across their history. At the end of the report of each judgment event, the prophet makes the same declaration concerning Israel's response: "yet you have not returned to me." The case logically unfolds: five times, God acted and the people did not return (Amos 4:6-11); as a result ("therefore"), God will act (v 12). Hence, Israel should prepare for an encounter with its God.

IN THE TEXT

■ **6-11** In vv 6-11, the text outlines Yahweh's repeated attempts to bring his wayward people back to him through a series of plagues: famine, drought, horticultural disaster, fatal plagues, and military conquest. The first-person verb (**I gave**, **I . . . withheld**, **I sent**, **I struck**, etc.) appears as many as ten times in vv 6-11 to demonstrate Yahweh's repeated disciplinary actions. These first-person verbs of God's past activity conclude with the twice-repeated first-person verb of God's imminent activity in v 12 (**I will do**). Based on God's response to his people and their lack of response, God will soon act.

Through the metaphor of ***cleanness of teeth*** (**empty stomachs**), v 6 depicts widespread famine and consequential hunger. In vv 7-8 the text depicts vivid results of drought. The portrayal of rain on some locations without rain on other locations demonstrates the divine source of the disaster. With lack of rainfall early in the season (**harvest was still three months away**), crops were devastated entirely. Entire populations migrated to towns in search of water. Just as food was found nowhere (v 6), there was never enough water to satiate the people.

In v 9, the prophet depicts the utter destruction of fertile vineyards and trees brought about by horticultural diseases (regarding **blight and mildew**, see Paul 1991, 146) and locust infestations. The listing of one plague after another with the people's refusal to act sounds eerily reminiscent of Yahweh's actions against Egypt in Exod 7—10 and the Egyptian refusal to act. In Israel's memory, the series against Egypt ended with the death of each household's firstborn. In 4:10, Amos specifically cites the Egyptian plagues (see Exod 9:3-7, 15).

The final catastrophe in Amos 4:11 is compared to the destruction that happened to the people of **Sodom and Gomorrah** (Gen 19:24-25). By setting Israel alongside the nation of Egypt and the cities of Sodom and Gomorrah, the prophet makes clear that Yahweh is not a respecter of persons, cities, or nations. On the day of his visitation (the Day of Yahweh), God will hold all peoples, including the covenant community, responsible.

As noted above, the prophet employs a common statement five times in the series: **yet you have not returned to me**. This refrain affirms that the calamities experienced by Israel were purposeful and not punitive as ends in themselves. Through them, Yahweh desired his people to turn back (*šûb*; also ***repent***, **return**) to him. The preposition employed in the phrase **to me** indicates the divine desire that the people not simply turn *toward* or *in the direction of* Yahweh but to Yahweh as the terminal point. This repeated line reaches its logical climax in v 12; the people must finally make themselves ready to encounter their God. While they had anticipated such an encounter or visitation for the other nations, they had never imagined the same for themselves. Although they had not returned to him in the past, they have no option but to face him now. For Amos the divine patience has come to an end (see 7:1-6); indeed, the end is imminent (see Amos' emphasis upon *the end* in 7:7-9; 8:1-3).

■ **12** On the basis of repeated divine attempts to gain Israel's attention, the text announces God's response to his covenant people in v 12. Verse 12 employs the first-person verb **I will do** twice. Without describing the specific divine action (i.e., what God will do), the text states simply that Yahweh is preparing once again and once and for all to act in the life of his people Israel. The prophet specifically refers to the covenant community as **Israel** twice in v 12.

The particle *lākēn* (**therefore**) links the announcement of forthcoming divine activity to the preceding verses (e.g., see similar use of the particle in Isa 5:13-14, 24; 7:14; 10:16; Jer 6:15; 8:10). Based on what God has done in previous generations, he is about to act (**do**) once again. Likewise, based on God's intention to act (**do**) in the present generation, the people should make themselves ready; they should **prepare to meet** their **God**. The verb **prepare** conveys a sense of firmly establishing oneself or making oneself ready. While the verb **to meet** can convey the simple notion of encountering another, it quite often depicts a military encounter (see Judg 7:24, for example). The people who never returned to God have no option now but to encounter him and thus to be encountered by him.

The phrase **your God** reminds Israel that the God they are about to encounter is Yahweh the covenant God of Israel, as often found in the covenant formula, "I will be your God and you will be my people" (Jer 7:23; see Lev 26:12; Jer 11:4, etc.). However, this time the visitation of Israel's God will not be for the purpose of salvation but for the purpose of judgment. As Yahweh prepares to war against his own people, the prophet warns them to make battle preparations. Indeed, they will soon encounter their God as this long-expected day of divine visitation imminently looms on the horizon.

FROM THE TEXT

We hear today this rehearsal of the Lord's repeated attempts to bring his people back to himself, and its call to repentance in the backdrop of other prophetic calls to repentance. Jeremiah's repeated calls to turn back to the Lord (Jer 3:12, 14, 22; 4:1) remind the reader of the addictive behavior of God's people in their turning to other deities (Jer 2:9-28). Hosea's calls for Israel to return to its covenant God (Hos 12:6; 14:1-2) and the prayers of repentance he provides (Hos 6:1-3; 14:2-3) challenge the reading community not only to hear the call to repentance but to embody the prayer of repentance. Joel's call to repentance (Joel 2:12-14) reminds the reader that human repentance is grounded in the prevenient grace and sovereignty of God (see also Ezek 14:6; 18:30; Zech 1:3-4; Mal 3:7). This prophetic call does not stop with the OT prophets. The announcement of John the Baptist, the keynote message of Jesus, and the proclamation of the early apostles link the good news of Jesus Christ directly to the prophetic call to turn to God (Matt 3:2; 4:17; Mark 1:15; Acts 2:38).

Amos' rehearsal of divine activity leaves the reader asking, "Why?" "Why do God's people struggle in their covenant loyalty? In spite of seasons of want and seasons of plenty, why does the covenant community refuse to turn back to its covenant God?" The text moves the reader to a keen awareness that the covenant people not only *can* turn away from their God but have the propensity *to* turn away from their God. Nevertheless, this covenant God remains faithful in his continual and repeated calls for the people to turn to him in faithfulness and loyalty.

Amos also vividly announces God's intent to hold his people responsible for their failure to return to him. While the Lord is indeed gracious, merciful, slow to anger, and abounding in covenant faithfulness (see Exod 34:6), this divine grace is not cheap or frivolous. The people of God cannot afford to take it lightly or treat it with contempt. Divine mercy demands faithful responsibility. Divine love calls forth a community of love. Divine faithfulness calls for and expects the people's response of faithfulness. The God for whom Amos speaks refuses to stay silent and aloof from his people. He will come; he will act. According to Amos, "He will do." Therefore, the people who testify to the grace, mercy, and love of their covenant God must prepare to come face-to-face with their God. They must be ready to account for the divine grace, mercy, and love entrusted to them.

H. Doxology One (4:13)

BEHIND THE TEXT

This doxology is the first in the series of three doxologies that hold the book of Amos together as a literary and theological document (4:13; 5:8-9; 9:5-6). These hymns praise Yahweh as the one who holds life in his hands. In them, he creates life; he sustains life; he destroys life. These doxologies certainly find their home in the setting of Israel's corporate worship. Each doxology makes declaration of the divine name: ***the Lord, the God of hosts, is his***

name (see similar declaration in Exod 15:3 and Ps 68:4). Each also uses the participial form of the verb to depict the ongoing nature and character of the divine activity. With common content, verbal forms, and refrains, the three separate hymns may have originally comprised one hymn (→ Introduction: The Book of Amos as a Literary Work for more details).

IN THE TEXT

■ **13** Amos 4:13 brings the preceding verses to an appropriate conclusion. This verse utilizes the traditional Creator language from the Israelite cult to depict and name the God whom Israel will encounter. He is Yahweh who makes himself known through the lightning, the wind, and the darkness of the thunderstorm (see similar language in Pss 29:3-9; 46:6). The thunderstorm theophany is one of the most ancient and familiar depictions of deity in the ancient Near East.

The NIV fails to translate the important bridge linking the call to prepare to meet God in v 12 with the hymn itself. The phrase *kî hinnēh* ("for lo" [NRSV]) connects the depiction of Yahweh in v 13 directly to the God whom Israel will soon encounter. This divine appearance on the Day of Yahweh is certain; it looms on the immediate horizon.

The hymn itself employs five participial verbs: the one who **forms**, the one who **creates**, the one who makes known (**reveals**), the one who ***makes*** (**turns**),
4:13 and the one who **treads**. The verbs **forms** (*yāṣar* in Gen 2:7, etc.), **creates** (*bārā'* in Gen 1:1, etc.), ***makes*** (*'āśâ* in Gen 1:7, etc.) depict the creative activity of God. Like a potter, he crafts or **forms the mountains**. Yahweh also **creates the wind**. He not only forms the unmovable mountains that remain forever visible but also creates the constantly moving wind that is never visible. Yahweh also ***makes*** **dawn to darkness** and **treads** upon the high places of the earth. These verbal forms convey the destructive effect of Yahweh's appearance (see Isa 45:7; Mic 1:3). It is possible the first two lines celebrate the creative power of God and the last two lines convey the power of God to undo what he created. The middle line, **who reveals his thoughts to mankind**, is somewhat ambiguous. Does God make known his *own thoughts* to humans or does he make known *the thoughts of humans* to humans? The root of the word **thoughts** often denotes "negative thoughts" or complaints (e.g., see Job 7:11; Ps 64:1). If this term is referring to complaints, the line apparently depicts Yahweh's making his complaints or charges known to human beings (Gowan 1996, 382). If this is the case, then this line shows that God the Creator does not undo his creation without announcing his charges beforehand to humanity.

The series of statements culminates in the hymn's naming the one who creates, reveals, uncreates: **the LORD God Almighty**. The other two doxologies in Amos (5:8; 9:6) will also make specific declaration of the divine name.

FROM THE TEXT

When we read or even sing this verse today in isolation from the remainder of the book, we may be tempted to find here a song of joy and triumphalism. However, when we place it in the new context provided by Amos, the triumphal song and popular worship reflected by that song undergoes deconstruction. In its proper context, the song reveals the barren emptiness of popular worship of ancient Israel. The recontextualized hymn beckons the reading community to hear and to sing it not in joyous triumphalism but in covenant accountability. The text invites the reader to reimagine the anticipated arrival of God and the worship that celebrates this anticipated arrival. It reminds the reader that the God who creates, sustains, and destroys is also the God who will visit his people and hold them accountable for their covenant identity. The worshipping community now resings the familiar worship song to the God who is about to act, to the God whom they are preparing to meet (4:12).

I. A Song of Death (5:1-3)

BEHIND THE TEXT

The funeral dirge or "lament" (*qînâ*) that follows in 5:1-3 is set in the context of the preceding doxology. The destruction of Israel implied in 4:13 naturally leads to the lament over the dead in 5:1-3.

The lament typically took place during the period of mourning that followed the death of an individual in ancient Israel (see 2 Sam 1:17-27). For Amos, the victim of calamity is the "Israel" that is living in its final days. The dirge anticipates the total destruction of the nation; total destruction means no one will be left to perform the customary ritual of mourning for the dead. Amos, who spoke of the imminent destruction of Israel, now performs the funeral lament for the nation by assuming that the destruction has already taken place. The dirge characteristically follows an uneven meter of three beats in the first line and two beats in the second line. Amos 5:2 mourns the downfall of Israel; v 3 depicts the subsequent paucity of life.

IN THE TEXT

■ **1** In v 1, Amos addresses the ***house of Israel*** with an imperative, a command to **hear** (*šāmaʿ*) a specific **word** (*dābār*). Verse 1 identifies the word as a **lament** (*qînâ,* a funeral song) spoken by Amos. The verb **take up** (***raise***) is often found alongside *qînâ* (see Jer 7:29, for example). The first-person pronoun **I** does not have a specific referent. The pathos of the prophet would indicate that God's lament becomes the prophet's lament. Hence, the first-person pronoun may depict both divine and prophetic grief.

■ **2** In the dirge proper (v 2), Amos depicts Israel as a virgin (*bĕtûlâ*). This term may also be translated as "maiden" (NRSV) or ***young woman***. Amos' reference to Israel as *bĕtûlâ* suggests the nation as "still enjoying its vibrant political, economic, and military vitality and yet in the flower of youth" (Paul 1991, 160). As portrayed in the narrative of Jephthah's daughter (Judg 11:29-40), to die a virgin was among the greatest of calamities. In ancient Israel, the deceased individual continued to live through children. Therefore, for a woman to die a virgin meant that her life came to a complete and dreadful end. Amos depicts Israel's fall in a similar manner. There is no hope of life for Israel. The present generation is completely cut off, which means there will be no future generations.

The text articulates Israel's calamity as falling without any hope of rising. As humanity (*ʾādām*) dies and returns to the ground (*ʾădāmâ*) from which it came (Gen 3:19), the fallen corpse of Israel lies forsaken upon her **land** (*ʾădāmâ*). The land here may also refer to the land of promise that Israel received as an inheritance from God. The very soil that Yahweh had given her and from which she had come (i.e., **her own land**) has become the sight of her demise.

Israel's hopelessness is not merely in her falling; no one, including Yahweh, apparently, is present to **lift** or raise her up. She is **deserted** by all and remains in her fallen state without any hope of being able to rise again (***no more to rise***). Israel may have fallen in the past, but she was able to rise to her feet. However, this time, the dirge concludes and no one can raise her up.

■ **3** Verse 3 conveys another word from the **Sovereign Lord.** It is possible that v 3 is a separate oracle (see Gowan 1996, 386). This oracle depicts the scant remains of Israel's life after its demise. This verse portrays the imagery of a city that went out to battle and was reduced to a few survivors. Where a thousand went to battle, only a hundred remain. Where a hundred went out, only ten remain. Israel's destruction will not be total; some will survive (see 3:12); however, this small number of survivors does not imply a remnant upon which a future nation can build. Indeed, the prophet describes a situation in which "the death sentence has been pronounced over the state of Israel" (Wolff 1977, 237). While the NIV twice adds **strong**, the Hebrew text simply states the numbers one thousand and one hundred without the added adjective.

FROM THE TEXT

As the lament is an expression of grief, this text demonstrates the pathos of the prophet and the pathos of God for the people. This dirge certainly does not depict a prophet or a deity who celebrate the defeat of a people. They mourn its decimation. Heschel has aptly described the divine pathos as defining the prophets' consciousness of God. He observes that God

> does not simply command and expect obedience; He is also moved and affected by what happens in the world, and reacts accordingly. . . . God

> does not stand outside the range of human suffering and sorrow. He is personally involved in, even stirred by, the conduct and fate of man. (1962, 288-89)

The text makes clear that the prophet participates in and sympathizes with the grief-stricken heart of God. The text also engages the reader in the divine grief and the prophetic mourning over the incurable wound and untimely death of the covenant community. There is no celebration in this text over sinners "getting what they deserve." The text imagines the reading community (i.e., subsequent generations of God's people) participating in the divine pathos and prophetic empathy with lamentation and weeping. God's people weep with a weeping world, hurt with a hurting society, die with a dying community, and suffer with a broken church.

J. A Second Call to Worship (5:4-7)

BEHIND THE TEXT

This unit is another call to worship. However, in this instance, he reverses the call. Rather than seeking Bethel and Gilgal as before (4:4-5), the people are *not* to seek these sites. In contrast, they are to seek Yahweh himself. In light of the previous sarcastic call to worship, the prophet establishes *seeking* Yahweh as the antithesis to *seeking* the popular cult. The book of Amos will return again to similar language in 5:14-15 where the prophet will further explicate *seeking Yahweh* as *seeking good, hating evil,* and *loving good.*

IN THE TEXT

■ **4-5** Three times in vv 4-6, the prophet employs the verb **seek** (*dāraš*), a pursuit for inquiry and consultation. As applied to the cult, the verb denotes the worshippers' searching for a deity through acceptable ritual and prayer (see Deut 4:29, for example). Amos calls the people to *seek* Yahweh himself rather than to *seek* the worship site and its accompanying practices and rituals. Previously, the prophet depicted the people as loving to participate in such cultic practices as sacrifice and offerings (Amos 4:4-5).

Although the preceding dirge left no possibility for life, the prophet now appears to open the door for the people to live. However, the only hope for Israel is in its seeking Yahweh. The use of the double imperatives (**seek** and **live**) joined by the *vav* conjunction indicates that life is the purpose or the result of seeking Yahweh. The verse may be translated either ***Seek me so that you will live*** or ***Seek me, and you will live as a result***. In either case, the life of the people is interwoven with their dependency upon Yahweh. If they are to live, they must seek the divine source of their lives. Amos' call to seek Yahweh and live is rooted in Israel's understanding of Yahweh's blessing upon those who seek his face (see Pss 24:6; 27:8).

Through a chiasmic structure (Bethel-Gilgal-Beersheba-Gilgal-Bethel), the prophet contrasts seeking Yahweh with various worship sites. Seeking **Bethel** accomplishes the opposite goal of seeking Yahweh. Bethel cannot save; only Yahweh can. The people are not to **go** to Gilgal (4:4). Neither are the people to ***cross over*** to **Beersheba**. These verbs convey the idea of pilgrimage to these cultic sites. Both Bethel and Gilgal were sacred shrines in the northern kingdom. Beersheba, associated primarily with Abraham and Isaac, was the southernmost outpost of Judah. The familiar OT phrase "Dan to Beersheba" depicts the northern and southern extremes of united Israel (e.g., see Judg 20:1; 1 Sam 3:20; 2 Sam 3:10). Amos indicates here the practice of northern kingdom people crossing over the boundary of Israel into Judah in order to worship at Beersheba.

The remainder of Amos 5:5 returns to the two northern shrines and depicts the complete futility of anticipating life at either one. Gilgal and Bethel produce nothing but exile and futility. With a creative triple alliteration through the almost-gurgling sound of *gl* (repeated twice in the name Gilgal itself), Amos describes Gilgal as going into **exile** (*gilgāl gaʾlōh yigleh*). He proceeds to describe Bethel as changing its being into (or becoming) ***wickedness*** (*ʾāven*; see Hosea's naming of Bethel as Beth Aven in 4:15, etc.).

■ **6** Repeating the call to **seek . . . and live**, in v 6 the prophet speaks of Yahweh in the third person. The call of the prophet assumes that the people still have the possibility of survival. This assumption stands in stark contrast to many of Amos' declarations concerning an irreversibly impending doom. In the remainder of v 6, the text warns of Yahweh's consuming fire that will utterly devour both the people who seek the worship sites for life and the worship sites themselves. The designation **tribes of Joseph** more generally refers to the northern kingdom in which the Joseph tribes (Ephraim and Manasseh) occupied a prominent place. Verse 6 concludes with the words ***there will be no extinguishing for Bethel***. Bethel is destined for total destruction; there will be none left in the city to save the city from its total destruction.

■ **7** The grammatical construction of v 7 makes for an awkward statement in its present context. The NIV reading, **There are those who turn justice into bitterness and cast righteousness to the ground**, is an adequate reading of the text. The hymn in vv 8-9 seems to interrupt the logical flow of vv 7 and 10 (see Paul 1991, 167); v 10 resumes with the third-person plural verb (imperfect): ***they hate*** and ***they despise***. The third-person plural verbs in v 7 most likely refer back to the tribes of Joseph in v 6.

The word pair in v 7, *mišpāṭ* (**justice**) and *ṣĕdāqâ* (**righteousness**), occurs twice again in the book of Amos (5:24; 6:12; see *mišpāṭ* by itself in 5:15). For

Amos, this word pair functions to describe the measurement to which Yahweh calls his people in their dealings with one another. Mays has described this word pair as depicting the "quintessence" of Yahweh's will (1969, 92). Amos charges the worshipping community with the perversion of justice and righteousness. Turning justice into **bitterness** (***wormwood***) conveys the idea that the powerful people, by their perversion of justice, have made life bitter tasting for the powerless in the society (see 6:12). Native to the geography of Israel, wormwood has an extremely bitter taste. Life that was meant to be pleasant had become nothing but bitterness for the poor in the northern kingdom. Likewise, the wealthy have cast all sense of communal right-relatedness (*ṣĕdāqâ*) to the ground and thus destroyed the proper ordering of the covenant community. Following the doxology in 5:8-9, the text resumes the thought of v 7 and illustrates how the wealthy have perverted justice and righteousness.

Justice and Righteousness in the OT

The term most commonly translated in the OT as "justice" is *mišpāṭ*. This word derives from the verb *šāpaṭ*, which means "to judge" or "to govern." It expresses the litigation at the city gate and the subsequent judgments rendered (see Deut 25:1) as well as the acts of governance by public officials (see 1 Sam 8:11). As such, *mišpāṭ* embodies and protects the social order.

The term *ṣĕdāqâ*, most often translated as "righteousness," refers to the social order itself or the proper ordering of relationships within the society. Thus, it is a relational term. For the covenant people, this relationship was twofold: relationship with Yahweh and relationship with neighbor. Mays has observed that *ṣĕdāqâ* "is the quality of life displayed by those who live up to the norms inherent in a given relationship" (1969, 92-93). A society's *ṣĕdāqâ* determines its understanding of *mišpāṭ*. Therefore, *mišpāṭ* is not an abstract and absolute concept determined outside of a culture, society, or religion. It is the product of a society's sense of appropriate social ordering (i.e., *ṣĕdāqâ*). The concepts of justice and righteousness in ancient Israel were directly linked to the people's recognition of Yahweh as the God of justice and righteousness and of themselves as a nation that stood in a covenant relationship with their God and others in their community.

FROM THE TEXT

The text invites its contemporary readers to reflect on what it means to truly seek the Lord and popular practices of worship. To seek God means to live in faithful covenant relationship with him. There is intentionality and purpose in one's seeking of God. The God spoken of by Amos is the source of life. To seek God is thus to seek life. The text also cautions the readers that various forms of popular worship can become a substitute for true worship of God. The forms of worship addressed by Amos do not lead to life; they engender death.

The text also invites the readers to reflect on how justice becomes bitter wormwood in their communities. Do they participate in life-giving activities or life-taking activities? How do they help others enjoy the sweetness of justice? How are they involved in making life painful and troublesome for others? God's call to his people is to follow the path of justice and righteousness not only for those who belong to the community of faith but to all human beings. God called Abraham and his descendants "to keep the way of the LORD by doing what is right and just" (Gen 18:19). The call to the church is to be "peacemakers" in the world (Matt 5:9). That mission can become a reality only if the church would pursue the path of justice and righteousness to all humanity.

K. Doxology Two (5:8-9)

BEHIND THE TEXT

This doxology seems to interrupt the flow between Amos 5:7 and v 10. It is possible that the verb *hāpak* ("turn," "turn over") in both v 7 ("turn justice into bitterness") and v 8 ("turns midnight into dawn") functions as a catchword that links the two verses. The language of v 8 recalls the creative work of God in Gen 1; the language of Amos 5:9 recalls his judgment words pronounced against the nations and Israel in chs 1—2.

Though 5:8-9 interrupts the continuity between v 7 and v 10, most likely these verses are strategically placed by an editor as a theological and literary *interruption* to the misdeeds of the powerful elite in Israel. The portrait of Yahweh's life-giving and life-taking power in vv 8-9 contrast the catalog of the unjust practices in vv 7 and 10. The people who love to go to Bethel and Gilgal hear a doxology praising the sovereign power of Yahweh as they continue in their perversion of justice and righteousness. As in the previous doxology (4:13), this hymn also emphasizes God's power both to create and to uncreate. This hymn preserves continuity with the other two doxologies with the declaration that weaves the three doxologies together as a whole: "the LORD is his name."

IN THE TEXT

■ **8** Verse 8 utilizes three participles to describe the divine creative activity: Yahweh is the one who **made**, who **turns**, and who **calls**. The verb **made** is one of three primary verbs of God's creative activity in Gen 1—2. Genesis 1:16 reports that "God made two great lights" along with "the stars"; Amos observes that Yahweh **made** the seven-starred cluster **Pleiades** and the hunter-ironworker constellation **Orion** (see Job 9:9; 38:31). Regarding the association of one or both of these constellations with agricultural and navigational signs/seasons, see Robbins 2009, 547; Paul 1991, 168; Wolff 1977, 241.

The second divine activity is the turning of ***darkness*** (*ṣalmāvet* literally refers to the death-shadow or a deep shadow; see Job 3:5; Ps 23:4) into **dawn.** The NIV **midnight** does not convey the terrifying, death-evoking sense of this word. Ironically, the people *turn* that which is life-giving into bitterness and death (Amos 5:7); Yahweh *turns* that which is terrorizing and life-threatening into light (v 8). However, Yahweh also **darkens day into night**. In Gen 1:3-5, God made light and separated the light from the darkness. Amos depicts here God bringing the darkness of nighttime back into the day. God has power over light and darkness, day and night.

The third divine activity in Amos 5:8 is the calling for **the waters of the sea**. This divine summons of the waters echoes the language of Gen 1:9-10, which describes God's activity of gathering the waters into one place and naming it as sea. According to Amos, however, Yahweh calls (or gathers) the waters of the sea and he **pours them** (*šāpak*) upon the surface of the land. This may refer to Yahweh's giving of the rain through which he brings life and productivity to the land. However, the verb *šāpak* may also refer to the destructive nature of water through flood (see Amos 9:6). The concluding declaration of 5:8, ***his name is Yahweh***, links the doxology with both the preceding (4:13) and concluding (9:5-6) doxologies.

■ **9** The text moves from a life-giving portrayal of Yahweh in 5:8 to a life-threatening and even life-taking portrayal in v 9. Twice in v 9, the common word for devastating destruction or violent oppression appears (*šōd*, **destruction; brings . . . to ruin**). The phrase **with a blinding flash he destroys the stronghold** conveys the idea of destruction by fire; as in the judgment speeches against the nations in 1:4, 7, 10, 12, 14, and 2:2, 5, the focus here is on the destruction of the fortified cities.

FROM THE TEXT

As it stands apart from its present literary context, the second doxology depicts a triumphalist life-giving and life-taking God just as did the first doxology (4:13). Indeed, the Lord is the God who creates and uncreates. Amos' immediate audience and contemporary readers of Amos hear this doxology in light of their own perversion of justice (see 5:7, 10). The unique placement of vv 8-9 between v 7 and v 10 allows for the invasion of God who creates and destroys into the everyday practices of injustice. The doxology exposes the worship of God's people as empty and destructive when unaccompanied by justice and righteousness. The hymn deconstructs the bifurcation of worship and social behavior (i.e., relationship with God and relationship with people). This doxology in its contemporary hearing calls for the integration of the worship of God and faithfulness to one's neighbor. The hymn also reminds the readers that the God who gives life and who takes life demands justice from all human beings, particularly those who claim to worship him.

L. Social Justice and a Call to Proper Worship (5:10-15)

BEHIND THE TEXT

The accusations in 5:7 resume in vv 10-13. These verses list various ways in which injustice was carried out by the powerful in the society. Verdict statements are found in vv 11*b* and 13. The oracle in vv 14-15 likely represents a unit distinct from vv 10-13. However, in the present literary context, these two verses offer the alternative to the practice of injustice and destruction of vv 10-13. The language of the call to "seek good" in v 14 links vv 14-15 with the call to worship in 5:4-6 ("seek me . . . Seek the LORD"). Verse 15 conveys some hope, though not with absolute certainty.

IN THE TEXT

■ **10** Verses 10-12 give specific ways in which perversion of justice and destruction of righteousness took place in Israel. Verses 10 and 12 mention the city ***gate*** (*šaʿar*, **courts**; see also v 15) where judicial hearings took place in ancient Israel. Elders of clans administered justice at the city gate (see Deut 21:19; 22:15; 25:7). For Amos, the perversion of justice in the legal system is the context for all other acts of injustice in society. If one cannot receive a fair hearing, political, economic, and religious injustices will pervade the social fabric.

Amos 5:10 depicts those who pervert justice (see v 7) as those who **hate** and ***despise*** others who are committed to promoting truthfulness and justice in the society. The verbs **hate** and ***despise*** convey strong abhorrence, animosity, even hostility. This occurrence of the verb **hate** is the first of four occurrences in the book of Amos. It appears twice as a disposition of the people and twice as a disposition of God (see 5:15, 21; 6:8). The word pair **hate** and ***despise*** reappears in 5:21. However, the occurrence in 5:21 refers to Yahweh's hatred of worship festivals.

The objects of hatred are **the one who upholds justice in *the gate*** (*yākaḥ* means "judge," "decide," "convict," etc.) and **the one who tells the truth**. Both verbs are in the participial form, thus indicating ongoing, continuous activity of judging and speaking. Rather than the common word for truth (*ʾemet*), the prophet employs a word that specifically indicates entirety, completeness, or integrity (*tāmîm*). In other words, these persons are ones who tell the *whole* truth. Perverted justice despises both the judge and the honest witness.

■ **11-12** Verse 11 begins with two particles side by side: ***therefore*** (*lākēn*) and ***because*** (*yaʿan*) (***Therefore because you trample on the poor***). The NIV assigns the particle **therefore** to the subsequent line and omits the translation of *yaʿan*. The word *lākēn* often functions in prophetic texts to introduce a divine announcement based upon preceding grounds. In v 11, this first *lākēn* introduces the result of vv 7 and 10. The second particle, ***because***, does not indicate a *result* of what precedes, but rather it indicates a *cause*. Therefore, the lines that will follow describe the effect of a cause.

Those who hate justice and truth telling also ***trample on the poor*** (**levy a straw tax on the poor**). The verb translated ***trample*** occurs only here in the OT; it conveys the idea of oppressive and violent behavior. The second line identifies the forceful taking of grain as tax from the poor as the specific act of trampling (**impose a tax on their grain**). The text conveys the idea of the tax as a load or a burden on the poor. The precise nature of this tax is not clear in the text. It may have been unfair taxation of the poor or bribery fees paid by the poor in order to be heard at the city gate. Or, it may have been "legal" levies required of persons in a hearing, levies that would have depleted the poor of their own food supply.

In the second half of v 12, the prophet returns to language similar to v 11. Again the ***the gate*** (**courts**) is the location where perversion of justice is taking place. Three verb forms describe the oppressive actions of the powerful: ***harass*** (**oppress**); **take**; ***thrust aside*** (**deprive**). Verse 12*b* literally reads: ***harassing the righteous, taking a ransom, they thrust aside the needy at the gate***. The object of the oppressive action of the powerful is ***the righteous*** (*ṣaddîq*, **innocent**). This term likely refers to those who are in the right.

The list of violent acts in v 12 includes the taking of a ***ransom*** (*kōper*, **bribes**) by the officials at the gate, a payment given for the sparing of one's life. Though this could mean the payment of bribes, the word points more concretely to payments made as a "cover-up" (literal meaning of *kōper*) for the guilty. Officials at the city gate not only gain economic advantage through fining the poor but also exonerate the wealthy elite who can *pay their way* out of their guilt. The last line of v 12, ***they thrust aside the needy at the gate*** (**deprive the poor of justice in the courts**) indicates that the powerful in the community pushed their powerless dependents out of the way. The text does not specifically mention "justice" (*mišpāṭ*) here but simply speaks of a hostile pushing aside of needy people.

Verses 10-11*a* and 12*b* form an inclusio of evidence against the powerful; vv 11*b* and 12*a* interrupt the evidence with both a divine sentence (v 11*b*) and divine rationale for that sentence (v 12*a*). The divine sentence in v 11*b* is a classic announcement of reversal of fortunes (see Deut 28:30-32). In the end, the powerful will not find that which they sought. That which they built, they will not inhabit. That which they planted, they will not ingest. **Mansions** made of hewn or ***cut*** stones and lush **vineyards** demonstrate the luxuriant nature of houses and gardens. Cut stones required hard manual labor. Implied here is perhaps an additional charge of forced labor practiced by the wealthy.

In v 12*a*, Yahweh declares his keen awareness of the people's multiple (**how many**) ***transgressions*** (*peša*ʿ, **offenses**) and ***countless*** (**great**) **sins**. God himself is the witness to their rebellion; he knows it. The divine knowledge of the people's transgressions and sins leads to the divine verdict in v 11*b*.

■ **13** Verse 13 may be an isolated saying from the wisdom tradition (for various interpretations, see Paul 1991, 176). The reference to the **prudent** (*hammaśkîm*) expresses concern for wise behavior. This verse reflects wisdom's typical concern for the appropriate *time* to speak and the appropriate *time* to be silent (e.g., see Prov 11:12; 17:28; Eccl 3:7). It also refers twice to the context in which the people live (i.e., **the times**) as **evil**. In such a context, the wise person remains **quiet**.

One may interpret this saying in various ways. Certainly it is not a call to be silent over injustice. However, the saying may simply declare that nothing else can be done in light of the imminent divine judgment (see Wolff 1977, 250). Therefore, one can only remain silent and wait. On the other hand, one may interpret the saying to describe the wisdom of silence in order to halt further repercussions. Recognizing that complaints against injustice will only bring greater trouble (i.e., **evil**) upon themselves, the **prudent** will take the recourse of remaining **quiet** (see Mays 1969, 98). It is also possible that *hammaśkîm* (**prudent**) may refer to those who are "prosperous"; also, **quiet** may mean "death." This way of reading the text would lead to the translation, "Therefore, the prosperous will be silent (i.e., dead) in that time, because it is a time of destruction." If this is what is intended by the text, then Amos 5:13 declares that death and destruction await the prosperous ones who have planted luxurious gardens and who live in fine homes (see Gowan 1996, 390).

■ **14-15** The imperatives of vv 14-15 comprise a distinct unit. These verses flesh out the meaning of "seek the LORD" in 5:6. To seek Yahweh means to **seek good, not evil**. To seek Yahweh means to **Hate evil, love good; maintain justice in the *gate***.

These verses establish a poignant and radical alternative to the evil times of v 13. In this call, the prophet admonishes the people not to succumb to (i.e., not to seek) the evil that is prevalent in their time. Rather, they are to aggressively and passionately **seek good, hate evil, love good**, and actively **maintain justice**. Amos' call to **seek good** and **hate evil** conveys life-and-death options before his audience (**that you may live**). **Seek good** means "seek life." **Seek good** also means **love good** (see the parallel expressions in vv 14 and 15). **Love** expresses the idea of passion, loyalty, and commitment; in this context to that which is life-giving (**good**). In the same way **hate evil** means "hate death" (and by inference "choose life"). The prophet calls the community to have nothing to do with that which is destructively life-taking and life-threatening (i.e., **evil**). That which is life-giving is contrasted here with that which is life-taking (see Deut 30:15 for a similar call to choose life). The verbs **hate** and **love**, though they convey passionate emotions, also depict decisive actions related to one's choosing (e.g., Mic 3:2; 6:8) or one's rejecting (e.g., Mal 1:2-3). Mays has observed that "loving and hating mean bringing into force all the resources and powers of feeling, will, and thought in devotion to or rejection of a person or value" (1969, 100).

The third imperative in Amos 5:15 corrects any mistaken notion that the prophet's call to hate and to love is merely an intellectual commitment toward an idea or an ideal. The community ultimately must incarnate its hatred of evil and its love of good in the establishment of **justice**. The verb *yāṣag* calls for more than the simple act of maintaining justice; it calls for the proactive establishment so as to make justice "effective" (see Koehler and Baumgartner 1995, 427). This establishment of justice stands in sharp contrast with the behavior of vv 10-12. Hatred of evil stands in direct contrast to hatred of ones who administer justice and who speak with integrity at the city gate (v 10).

Amos announces in vv 14-15 that the worshipping community that seeks Yahweh through loving good and hating evil will indeed find that which they had been seeking through the cult: life (**you may live**), presence of Yahweh (**the Lord God Almighty will be with you**), and Yahweh's **mercy** (*ḥānan*). Life will be given to them. The divine presence that the worshipping community anticipates and celebrates will become a reality. They will experience Yahweh's mercy. Amos insists in vv 14-15 that the divine presence is first discovered in the orbit of social relationships rather than in the cult and its rituals of worship.

Intentionally the prophet precedes the announcement of divine mercy with an adverb (*ʾûlay*, **perhaps**) of hope-filled uncertainty. As the people well know, Yahweh will show his gracious favor (*ḥānan*) to whomever he shows his gracious favor (see Exod 33:19). Just as the community cannot manipulate this covenant deity through cultic ritual, they cannot control him through just and righteous behavior. They ultimately must embody their sacrifices and offerings in justice and righteousness.

The text identifies **the remnant of Joseph** as the recipient of the divine mercy. The reference to **remnant** indicates that the divine visitation will bring widespread destruction with few survivors (see Amos 3:12; 5:3; 9:9-10). While the reference holds out an element of hope by implying that some form of life will remain, the emphasis here is not so much upon the hope after judgment but upon the prevalence of destruction. As in 5:6 and 6:6, the prophet refers to the northern kingdom as **Joseph**.

FROM THE TEXT

In this text Amos vividly and imaginatively contrasts good and evil and integrates acts of justice and the act of worship. Acts of justice and the act of worship, according to Amos, cannot be bifurcated into separate realms. The text confronts the worshipping community that hates those who impartially dispense justice (5:10) with a call to hate their own evil disposition to promote injustice in the society (v 15). The text further equates *seeking* Yahweh in worship (v 6) with *seeking* good (v 14), and it announces that both will engender life. The text portrays the incarnation of seeking good (v 14) to be the passionate, active hatred of evil and the passionate, active love of good (v 15). In the end, this embrace of good and rejection of evil must be fleshed out in the daily, even mundane, practices of justice at the gate.

The "perhaps" of v 15 precludes all attempts by the people of the Lord to coerce divine grace. Mercy is mercy because the Lord himself freely bestows it upon his people. The "perhaps" of Amos recalls the tentative nature of Joel's promise following his prophetic call to return to the Lord: "Who knows? He may turn and relent and leave behind a blessing" (Joel 2:14). Nevertheless, the prophet remains insistent on one truth: justice must become an integral part of the worshipping community's life, or its worship is meaningless, empty, and even self-destructive.

The text of Amos clearly echoes similar words of Isaiah, who also challenged his audience who were preoccupied with rituals of worship without any regard for justice for the marginalized in the society: "Learn to do right; seek justice. Defend the oppressed. Take up the cause of the fatherless; plead the case of the widow" (Isa 1:17).

The text confronts its contemporary readers with several critical questions: What is the gate in our time? Where is justice expected but injustice carried out? How does the text relate to our judicial system and the modern-day courts? How does this text speak to governments and their political and economic policies, particularly to the tax systems that benefit the wealthy? How does it speak to justice in the workplace, in the church, in the community, and in the home?

The text is a powerful challenge to its readers to be involved in life-producing activities that benefit the whole community. Seeking good for self-serving purposes will eventually lead to the deprivation of life from others. The text also warns the readers that seeking good for self-serving purposes does not have any enduring quality; what is gained for self-gratification at the expense of others (mansions and vineyards in Amos 5:11) is destined for destruction.

M. An Unexpected Day of Mourning (5:16-20)

BEHIND THE TEXT

The unit in vv 16-20 is comprised of two distinct oracles (vv 16-17 and vv 18-20) as indicated by the messenger formula ("says the LORD") at the conclusion of v 17. However, both oracles indicate the reversal of fortunes expected on the Day of Yahweh. In contrast to the expectations of Israel's victory and subsequent exaltation over the nations, Amos depicts the day as one of great mourning and grief. Twice in v 16 and once at the beginning of v 18, the prophet employs the interjection of pain found in the lament (*hô/hôy*) in order to express this day's excessive despair.

The oracle in vv 16-17 depicts utter grief without describing precisely what has occurred to evoke the grief. The oracle in vv 18-20 reverses the anticipated light and salvation of the day and portrays it instead as one of darkness and destruction. With the pairing of these two oracles, the text places effect (vv 16-17) before cause (vv 18-20). The text climaxes in the second oracle by providing the source of the misery: the expected day of salvation had become a day of destruction.

The Day of Yahweh in Ancient Israel

The origins of the notion of the Day of Yahweh (*yôm yhwh*) are uncertain (regarding various suggestions, see Mays 1969, 103-4). Certainly, the concept appears to have been prevalent at the political and economic height of the northern kingdom in the first half of the eighth-century B.C. The earliest specific reference to the Day of Yahweh occurs in Amos 5:18-20, in which the prophet makes three references.

The concept of the Day of Yahweh likely emerged out of the understanding that the divine warrior, Yahweh, fought on behalf of his covenant people. Just as he had battled the armies of pharaoh at the Red Sea, so he would continue to battle Israel's enemies. The divine title "Yahweh God of hosts" ("the LORD God Almighty" [NIV]; see Amos 3:13; 4:13; 5:14, 15, 16, 27; 6:8, 14; also 9:5) expresses Yahweh as the God of the hosts of divine armies. Early on in Israel's history, these hosts might have referred to the astral hosts or to the hosts of divine beings who fought under Yahweh's command. Eventually these hosts would also have been used in reference to the armies of Israel itself.

The Israelites popularly understood this day as the time of Yahweh's destructive visitation against the surrounding nations (Amos 1—2). Typical of a national deity, Israel's God would judge and punish the nations on this day while he would bring deliverance and salvation to his covenant people (see Isa 13:6-9; 34:8-12; Jer 46:9-12; Ezek 30:1-9; Obad 15-18; Zeph 2:1-5). Obviously, the popular understanding was filled with nationalistic overtones.

Amos' unique prophetic task was to announce that this divine visitation would bring judgment not only upon surrounding nations but upon the covenant community as well. Prophets subsequent to Amos followed a similar line of reasoning (see esp. Zeph 1:14-18; also Isa 2:6—3:15; Ezek 7:19).

IN THE TEXT

■ **16-17** Although the unit in Amos 5:16-17 is distinct, the particle *lākēn* (**therefore**) directly links Yahweh's announcement that he will **pass through your midst** (v 17) with the injustices described in the preceding verses. This divine visitation will result in wailing and cries of anguish everywhere. The one who comes to visit Israel is the ***Lord, Yahweh God of hosts***, the sovereign God of the universe (v 16).

The remainder of the oracle in vv 16-17 depicts graphic illustrations of public mourning. These expressions of grief take place in town squares, streets, and outlying vineyards. The interjection of ***Woe*** or ***Alas*** (*hô*) appears twice in v 16. The phrase **cries of anguish in every public square** literally reads, ***In all the squares, they cry, "Woe! Woe!"*** This interjection expresses the agonizing pain of a mourner; it is also used to introduce judgments that evoke severe anguish (see 5:18; 6:1, 4). The prophet envisions the widespread expressions of grief in 5:16-17. Persons who regularly plow the ground will grieve (see 8:8; 9:5; see also Hos 4:3; Joel 1:10). Persons skilled in expressions of public mourning will cry out in bereavement.

This outburst of lamentation results from Yahweh's *passing through* the **midst** of his people. Israel's ancient traditions recalled Israel's God *passing over* the people of Israel when he *passed through* Egypt (Exod 12:12-13, 23). God saved Israel by passing over them when he passed through Egypt in judgment. Now, however, this same God will **pass through** his people; Israel will no longer experience salvation, but the judgment of destruction and death.

■ **18-20** The second oracle (Amos 5:18-20) depicts the radical reversal of the anticipated Day of Yahweh. With the interjection **woe**, Amos introduces death and destruction that awaits those **who long for the day of the Lord** (v 18). By means of a rhetorical question fraught with irony, the prophet asks: **Why do you long for the day of the Lord?** The answer is clear; no right-thinking person in this covenant community of injustice and oppression would desire Yahweh's visitation. Amos announces that this day will not be life-producing (**light**). It will be a death-producing day (**darkness**).

By means of two vivid images, the prophet demonstrates the reversal of expectations. The people anticipated a day of safety and rescue; in reality they will be faced with a day fraught with danger and defeat. Amos compares those who long for this day to a person who escaped the attack of **a lion** only to encounter **a bear**. They would be like a person who thought he was safe within the walls of **his house** but was bitten by a venomous **snake** (v 19). Amos warns those who think they are safe that what awaits them is a day of their destruction.

Amos' rhetorical question, **Will not the day of the Lord be darkness, not light—pitch-dark, without a ray of brightness?** (v 20), gives clarity to the images in v 19. **Darkness, pitch-dark**, and the absence of **a ray of brightness** indicate the total absence of life for the unjust on the Day of the Lord.

FROM THE TEXT

This text is an excellent example of how biblical writers with courage confronted their audience's settled, popular theological perspectives, which were built on certain assumptions they have maintained about God's covenantal obligations to them. Amos clearly reverses Israel's eschatological expectation and places the covenant people of God at the receiving end of God's judgment, which in their popular thinking was something that was reserved for their national enemies.

It is reasonable to assume that this message would have placed Amos at the top of the list of unpatriotic and anti-Israel preachers in the land—an enemy of the people and a friend of the enemies of Israel. Prophets who speak the truth with conviction seldom receive any respect or welcome among any nation that claims a "God on our side" theology and political ideology. Amos in many respects was a forerunner of many who followed him, including Jeremiah and Jesus, who courageously confronted popular theological ideas and self-serving political ideologies. Amos models for us what truly constitutes "prophetic preaching" in our day.

Often prevalent in the minds of God's people is the notion that divine retribution is for sinners and divine reward for believers. However, this text vividly calls the people of God to accountability for responsible grace. The text refuses to allow the people of God to anticipate a day of punishment for "outsiders" and a day of reward for "insiders." The text brings into sharp focus the manner in which the covenant God will hold his people accountable for covenant responsibilities. The text's focus is clearly upon the "insider's" accountability to God rather than the "outsider's" accountability.

These oracles challenge the reader to pay careful attention to the words of Jesus:

> Not everyone who says to me, "Lord, Lord," will enter the kingdom of heaven, but only the one who does the will of my Father who is in heaven. Many will say to me on that day, "Lord, Lord, did we not prophesy in your name and in your name drive out demons and in your name perform many miracles?" Then I will tell them plainly, "I never knew you. Away from me, you evildoers!" (Matt 7:21-23)

N. Reflecting on True Worship (5:21-27)

BEHIND THE TEXT

In this text Amos returns to the use of the verb *to hate* (see 5:10, 15), but here the verb conveys Yahweh's hatred of the popular practices of the Israelite cult. These practices include the three annual pilgrimage festivals, other sacred gatherings such as the new moon celebrations, the plethora of sacrifices, and festive music. As in 5:7, the prophet once again pairs the concepts of *mišpāṭ* and *ṣĕdāqâ* ("justice" and "righteousness"); however, in this passage these concepts serve as the contrasting alternative to the popular practices of the cult. The prophet's reference to the wilderness period assumes that the sacrificial system was not in place at that time. However, the wilderness traditions in the Torah depict the practice of sacrifice (see for example, Exod 24:5-8; Lev 1—7; Num 7:1-88, etc.).

IN THE TEXT

■ **21-23** The opening verb of Amos 5:21 is shocking as God himself appears to be the subject of the verb: **I hate**. The second verb **despise** in v 21 defines and clarifies the divine hatred as rejection or refusal of something. Yahweh's hatred of the people's festivals is not merely divine disdain but the complete divine separation from, rejection of, and refusal to participate in these cultic gatherings.

The reference to the **festivals** (*ḥag*) indicates the three annual pilgrimage feasts: Passover and Unleavened Bread, Weeks (Pentecost), and Tabernacles (Booths, Ingathering) (Exod 23:14-17; 34:18-26; Lev 23:1-44; Num 28—29; Deut 16:1-17). They recalled deliverance from Egypt and passage through the Red Sea (Passover and Unleavened Bread), the provision of manna and water in the wilderness (Tabernacles), and the covenant at Sinai (Weeks). With irony, Amos refers to festivals that celebrate the acts of God as ***your festivals***. That which was intended to celebrate Yahweh's mighty deeds had become the possession of the people.

The text also announces that the people's sacred **assemblies** are a **stench** (from *rîaḥ*, means "to smell an odor") to Yahweh. The text also depicts these holy gatherings as **your assemblies**. Like the festivals, the sacred assemblies in honor of God had become the people's property. Perhaps what is intended here is Yahweh's total rejection of sacrifices offered up during these festivals by those who oppress the poor; they do not yield "an aroma pleasing to the Lord" (see Lev 1:9).

Amos 5:22 addresses Yahweh's refusal to accept various sacrifices made by the worshipping community (**burnt *offering*** [*ʿōlâ*], the **grain *offering*** [*minḥah*], and the peace or choice **fellowship *offering*** [*šelem*]) (see Lev 1—3 for the nature and purpose of these offerings). Yahweh who hates and rejects the communal gatherings (Amos 5:21) will not favorably **accept** or even pay attention to (**regard**) the diverse sacrifices.

Amos proceeds in v 23 with further statements of Yahweh's refusal to participate in the worship of the people. Yahweh will cease to listen to the music of the worshipping community. Amos uses a unique prepositional phrase, *mēʿālay* (meaning "from upon me"), to indicate that Israel's noisy singing has become a burden to him. Yahweh states, ***Remove the roar of your songs from upon me***. Yahweh also announces that he will not **listen to** the melody played upon their ***stringed instruments*** (**harps**).

Verses 21-23 clearly show that Yahweh rejected Israel's worship because it had nothing to do with him but more to do with what the people enjoyed and what they did to please themselves. Worship belonged to the people (see the frequent use of **your** in these verses), and not to Yahweh.

■ **24** In v 24, the prophet announces in a brief declaration of six words what Yahweh desires from his people. Through the image of fresh-flowing water, Amos portrays the context within which the people's worship was to occur. The six words form a perfect chiasmic structure:

A Let flow
- B Like waters (comparison to liquid)
  - C Justice
  - C' Righteousness
- B' Like a torrent valley (comparison to liquid)

A' Ever-flowing

Literally the statement reads, ***Let justice flow like waters, righteousness like an ever-flowing stream***. At the center of the six-word statement are the two cornerstones for the life of God's people: *mišpāṭ* (**justice**) and *ṣĕdāqâ* (**righteousness**).

The prophet employs two liquid images to depict the manner in which justice and righteousness were to appear in the community. They were to be nonstagnant, life-giving, and life-sustaining forces. The first image is ***waters*** (**river**). The second image is a wadi of water (**stream**) that rushes through narrow channels in the desert or the torrent-valley that flows vibrantly in depths of the stream. Both images emphasize the free-flowing, nonstifled nature of water. Similarly, justice and righteousness were to roll along freely, abundantly, perennially in the communal life of Yahweh's covenant people.

■ **25-27** The remaining three verses of ch 5 pose some difficulty in their interpretation (see Mays 1969, 110-13). Clearly v 25 continues the notion of Yahweh's rejection of cultic ritual. Amos argues that as Yahweh did not require the people to bring sacrifices during the wilderness period (see 2:9), sacrifices are not essential to the covenant bond between Yahweh and his people (see Jer 7:21-22). In contrast to this statement, however, the extant wilderness traditions consistently depict the sacrificial system as present and practiced during this forty-year period. Interestingly, while Amos opposes the people's offering of sacrifice void of justice and righteousness, he does not make an argument or demonstrate support for the abandonment of the sacrificial system.

Modern translations show significant variances in the translation of v 26 (contrast NIV with NRSV). However translated, the verse obviously departs from Amos' dominant concern over issues of justice and righteousness. The verse actually addresses an issue over which Amos reveals very little concern, that is, idolatry and the worship of gods. The Hebrew text makes reference to *sikkût* and *kiyyûn*. The proper names Sakkuth and Kaiwan (see NRSV) appear in Babylonian sources in reference to the astral god Saturn. The Hebrew text depicts *sikkût* as "your king." This depiction may certainly be a reference to deity. It then depicts *kiyyûn* as both ***your images*** and ***your astral god(s) which you make for yourselves***. These two references could quite simply denote the people's astral worship and their subsequent lifting up of these astral deities in order to carry them into imminent exile (v 27; thus see NRSV). The verse would demonstrate the relationship between the people's worship of these astral gods and the exile they will experience.

In contrast to the NRSV, the NIV does not translate *sikkût* and *kiyyûn* as proper names for astral deities. Rather, it translates *sikkût* as **shrine** and *kiyyûn* as **pedestal**. The NIV then provides three genitive construct phrases: **shrine**
5:25-27 **of your king, pedestal of your idols** (literally "images"), and **star of your god**.
In the NIV, the lifting up is not the people's future action in relationship to an imminent exile. Rather, it is their past action (**you have lifted up**) that has resulted in the judgment of exile.

In either translation, rather than continuing the theme of justice and righteousness, the text provides rationale for exile. In one instance (NRSV), the emphasis is upon the worship of other deities. In the other instance (NIV), the emphasis is upon the exaltation of the king and the exaltation of other deities. The reference to **exile beyond Damascus** indicates a later perception of exile to Assyria as judgment especially for the worship of other deities (see 5:5; 6:7; 7:11, 17).

Mays has suggested that the reference to the worship of false deities and the Assyrian exile in 5:26-27 may be a later editorial comment "to explain the exile in terms of the Deuteronomic passion against foreign gods and to make the prediction of punishment precise" (Mays 1969, 113). However, Paul has made a convincing argument that vv 26-27 reflect a parody made by Amos himself (1991, 194-98). The prophet's consistent depiction of Yahweh as the ***God of hosts*** **(God Almighty)** certainly would have included the starry hosts. Paul interprets this passage as Amos' purposeful and satirical reference to the two astral deities. Ridiculing "the great cult processionals, when statues of gods were carried triumphantly on high by their worshippers," Amos "has another processional in mind—one of deportation" (1991, 197). As ***the* Lord . . . *God of hosts*** leads Israel into exile, "the Lord of all the *astral* hosts will deport them along with their *astral* deities" (Paul 1991, 198).

FROM THE TEXT

Amos addresses in 5:21-24 a community that has separated worship from life. The God worshipped by the community has nothing in common with the people who worship him. God delivers, provides, and remains faithful to his covenant; the community is violent, self-serving, and unfaithful to its covenant with God. God is just and righteous; the community commits injustice and unrighteousness. God gives life; the community takes away life from others. The contrast between the character of the worshipping community and that of God worshipped by the community could not be greater. Amos' challenge to his audience then and to his readers now is that they become like the God they claim to worship; be self-giving and life-giving in their private and public life. Amos challenges his readers to make worship a way of life. Amos' words here echo the words of Micah: "He has shown you, O mortal, what is good. And what does the Lord require of you? To act justly and to love mercy and to walk humbly with your God" (6:8; see also Pss 40:6; 51:16-17; Isa 1:11-12; Hos 6:6).

This text does not substitute acts of social justice for corporate worship or its rituals. Rather, Amos' call to let justice and righteousness flow like fresh water provides the context in which the worshippers enter into the various acts of worship. Apart from this context, the rituals of worship are meaningless. In 1 Cor 13, the Apostle Paul speaks of this context as self-giving love. While not calling for an end to acts of worship, prophecy, faith, and mercy, Paul declares such acts as nothing more than the cacophony of a clanging cymbal apart from self-giving love.

O. Indictment against Indulgence and Pride (6:1-14)

BEHIND THE TEXT

This chapter consists of various prophetic oracles ranging from the woe oracle in vv 1-7 to various announcements of judgment in vv 8-14. As a collection, these oracles construct an argument against the ruling elite of ancient Israel so that the divine hatred (v 8) of their arrogance is appropriate. Regarding the nature of the woe oracle, see 5:18. In the divine oath of 6:8, the prophet employs the ancient warrior formula familiar in Amos (***Yahweh God of hosts***; see 3:13; 4:13; 5:14, 15, 16, 27; 6:14). Oracles that announce Israel's complete destruction follow the divine oath statement in v 8. Twice in this chapter, the prophet makes specific reference to the conquest of various other sites (Kalneh, Hamath, and Gath in v 2; Lo Debar and Karnaim in v 13).

IN THE TEXT

■ 1-8 Amos introduces vv 1-8 as a woe (*hôy*) oracle (see 5:18). In vv 3-7, the woe of v 1 continues after the interruption of v 2 (see separate discussion of v 2 following v 7). Verses 3-6 depict the arrogant behavior of the elite; v 7 announces their demise. Verse 8 functions as a summative declaration of Yahweh's hatred for Israel's arrogant pride in their fortress-like capitals (see 6:1).

In v 1, the prophet addresses the woe against persons who are **complacent** and confidently **secure**. Both terms depict a sense of the arrogant ease and overconfidence of the people. This misplaced trust and false security embodies itself in their longing for the Day of Yahweh. The text locates these persons in the political capitals of the southern and northern kingdoms, Zion (i.e., Jerusalem) and Samaria respectively. The preposition **in** or **on** (*bĕ* in both instances) may simply indicate the persons' geographical location. However, based upon the prophet's indictments against misplaced confidence, the preposition may likewise indicate the object of the people's trust. The people do not merely reside in these cities. Their confidence is *in* Zion; their trust is *in* the mountain of Samaria.

The word *bāṭaḥ* (**feel secure**) is the common Hebrew verb for "trust." The

choice of the terms **Zion** (rather than simply Jerusalem) and **Mount Samaria** (rather than simply Samaria; see also 3:9; 4:1) imply their elevated place, both in height and power, and the security these cities claimed and offered to the people. In 6:8, Yahweh announces the divine abhorrence for Jacob's majestic exaltation or "pride" and hatred for its mighty strongholds or "fortresses."

In the second half of v 1, the prophet depicts these complacently secure persons as the designated leaders to whom the ***house*** **(people) of Israel** comes. The phrase **notable men** conveys the idea of those who have been distinguished from the rest of the population. They pride themselves as the leaders of the **foremost** or the first ***of the nations***. Obviously, the reference here is to the nation of Israel.

Through images of grandeur in v 1, the prophet vividly depicts an exalted nation with exalted leaders residing on exalted mountains. In vv 3-6, the prophet explicates the self-serving, overindulgent lifestyle of these leaders (see v 2). Amos sarcastically and rhetorically asks if these rulers are putting off the **day of disaster (*evil*)** as they **bring near** or establish a ***throne of violence*** **(reign of terror)** (v 3).

In vv 4-6, the prophet depicts the haughty yet nonchalant behavior of the elite. They are totally unconcerned about the day of divine visitation and Israel's impending destruction. They recline on luxurious beds, eat of the finest meats, engage in soothing music, indulge in gluttonous drinking, and rub fine oils on their bodies.

Amos sees in the hedonistic lifestyle of the ruling elite a clear lack of concern over Israel's ruin (v 6*b*). The participial verb forms in vv 4-6 depict the ongoing, persistent nature of the various activities of the wealthy people. The text also emphasizes their excessive nature.

The wealthy displayed their life of luxury and prestige by reclining on beds inlaid with **ivory** and stretching out on **couches** (v 4). Ivory beds were most likely imported into Israel in exchange for grain and oil, which the wealthy accumulated by their oppressive treatment of their tenant farmers. The wealthy also ate ***lambs from the flock*** (**choice lambs**) and ***calves from the midst of the stall*** (**fattened calves**). Verse 5 describes the idle, even careless way the wealthy played (**strum**) stringed instruments, such as **harps**. Amos compares the elites' skill of improvising on musical instruments to that of David (see 1 Chr 15:16; 23:5; 2 Chr 7:6; 29:25-27). Amos portrays here a world of disparity; the wealthy live a self-indulgent life while the poor in the community suffer under the oppressive actions of the wealthy.

Amos' depiction of the lavish lifestyle of the wealthy reaches its climax in 6:6. They extravagantly and wastefully consume Israel's essential products of wine and oil. They do not merely drink the wine; they drink it from large basins (**bowlful**) (see 2:8*b*). The text portrays the wealthy pouring out (i.e., anointing) on their head **finest lotions**. With oil running down their bodies and with stomachs overflowing with bowls of wine, the ruling elite had become gluttons of wasteful luxury and careless extravagance. In 6:6*b* Amos charges that the wealthy who are engaged in gluttonous practices are not the least bit affected by **the ruin of Joseph** (see 5:6, 15). The poor in the land are like broken and shattered pottery; however, the wealthy are not sickened or weakened (**grieve**) by the broken condition of the poor. They distance themselves from the poor and continue to relax, dine, play, and wastefully consume the hard-earned produce of the people.

Verse 7 of ch 6 makes clear that the life of luxury and extravagance of the wealthy and their uncaring attitude to the poor are the reasons for their impending exile. The elite will be **the first to go into exile**. They have sought to be first; they will indeed be first. True to the prophetic concept of the Day of Yahweh, the life that the ruling class has sought will return to them in its fullest sense. As a result, their revelry will end. The Hebrew text does not actually state that the **feasting and lounging will end**. It conveys the idea that the sprawling cry of revelry will go away as the wealthy go into exile.

Verse 2 interrupts the condemnation of the leaders (see v 1) and the subsequent depiction of their lavish, carefree lifestyle (vv 3-7) with a statement of shock and bewilderment. It interjects the flow with the observation that if other great city-states could not evade destruction, neither could Israel. If other nations could not survive divine scrutiny, how much more must Israel face the judgment of its covenant God? Kalneh and Hamath are city-states that the Assyrians incorporated into their empire in the second half of the eighth century B.C. Gath, one of the cities of the Philistine Pentapolis, was captured by King Hazael of Damascus in the late ninth century B.C. Gath does not reappear in the biblical text except here and Mic 1:10. As Amos scanned the historical horizon, he witnessed the fall of powerful city-states both in his time (Kalneh and Hamath) and in former generations (Gath). Pointing to their demise, the prophet deconstructs the fiction of national invincibility. The interjection into the text (vv 1-7) functions to inject a sense of reality into the ruling elite's complacent state of mind.

In v 8, Yahweh announces his utter abhorrence for the leader's arrogant complacency described in the preceding verses. Yahweh is now determined to hand over the city to the enemy along with all that is in it. The divine determination is resolute; ***the Lord Yahweh*** (**Sovereign Lord**) swears on his own divine character or even on his own "divine life" (*nepeš*; see also Jer 22:5). In Amos 4:2 (see also 8:7), a similar divine oath introduced divine judgment. The one who announces disdain and who is determined to destroy is once again Yahweh ***God of hosts*** (see 3:13; 4:13; 5:14, 15, 16; 5:27; 6:14).

Amos employs two terms to express Yahweh's revulsion to and hatred (**abhor**; **detest**). The first term, **abhor**, conveys his disdain toward **the pride of Jacob** (see also 8:7). Mays defines the **pride of Jacob** as "Israel's preening national self-confidence which had become the real centre and concern of the nation's upper classes" (1969, 118). The leaders' self-exaltation through status, power, and affluence had become an abominable thing to Israel's God.

Similarly, the protective, self-securing **fortresses** (see 3:10) filled with plunder and loot had become the object of Yahweh's hatred (see the use of the verb "hate" in various contexts in Amos [5:10, 15, 21]). Yahweh announces in 6:8 that he hates the city's self-securing citadels. Yahweh who hates the festivities of Israel (5:21) also hates the fortresses of Israel. Both were objects of the people's self-securing, misplaced trust. Amos understood both of these as examples of the pride of Israel.

In the concluding announcement of v 8, divine abhorrence becomes expressed action. Yahweh will **deliver up** (*sāgar*) the city along with all that fills it up. Yahweh will *sell* the city and everything in it just as a nation might *sell* its captives to another nation (see the same verb in 1:6, 9).

■ **9-10** In 6:9-10, the prophet reiterates the utter death and destruction about to occur. These verses reflect the scene of a national calamity, such as disease, pestilence, or war. Regardless of how many persons remain (**are left**) **in one house**, death will eventually come upon all inhabitants.

The meaning of v 10 remains obscure and ambiguous. Ancient Israel does not appear to have practiced cremation other than following a contagious plague. However, the scenario implies cremation as a rescuer removes corpses from a house in order to burn them. In the process, the rescuer asks either a fellow rescuer or a survivor whether other persons survived (see Paul 1991, 214-16, for various interpretations). The response to the question is first *ʾāpes*, a noun that means "nonexistence" or "cessation." In other words, that which has survived is nonsurvival; that which continues to exist is nonexistence. The respondent continues with *hās*, an interjection meaning **Hush!** or ***Silence!*** The explanation then follows: they **must not mention** [i.e., bring to remembrance] **the name of the Lord**. The very mention or remembrance of Yahweh's name would engender even more destruction. The name celebrated in the Israelite cult has become a harbinger of death rather than a herald of life.

■ **11** The terrorizing devastation of vv 9-10 multiplies in v 11. Yahweh stands behind all that has taken place. The text does not provide a direct object; Yahweh simply commands. As a result of the divine directives, houses, large and small, become obliterated into smallest particles (i.e., nonexistence).

■ **12-14** Verses 12-14 address the futility of the ruling elite to hope for salvation once Yahweh has declared otherwise. Although the rulers may point to past victories, their complete perversion of justice and righteousness makes any attempt to save themselves an utter absurdity. The unit opens with two rhetorical questions that demonstrate complete irrationality. The NIV interprets both questions around the absurdity of activities carried out on rocks. **Do horses run on rocky crags?** ("perpendicular cliffs"; Mays 1969, 121). For the second question, the Hebrew text literally reads, ***Does one plow with oxen?*** Obviously the question as stated makes complete sense. The NIV separates the plural ending (*îm*) on the phrase **with oxen** (*babbĕqārîm*), allowing the ending to stand alone as the word *yam* (sea); thus, the translation **plow the sea with oxen**.

Even more absurd, however, is the manner in which the elite have perverted or **turned** life-giving and healing **justice** (*mišpāṭ*) into an agent of death and destruction (*rōʾš*, a poisonous herb or venom). Similarly, they have distorted the sweet-tasting, life-preserving fruit that comes from ***right-relatedness*** (*ṣĕdāqâ*, **righteousness**) within the community into ***wormwood***, the most bitter and deadly of plants (see 5:7). What Amos sees all around him is death and destruction and bitter-tasting life experiences instead of life-producing activities of justice and righteousness.

In 6:13-14, Amos contrasts the self-confidence of the ruling elite with Yahweh's plans for them. Israel's rulers are confident in their **own strength**, and they continue to take pride in their victories over **Lo Debar** and **Karnaim**. Jeroboam II regained territory on the eastern side of the Jordan when Syria was weakened by the Assyrian invasion (see 2 Kgs 14:25). **Lo Debar** is likely a reference to the city of Debir (*dĕbir*) in northeastern Gilead (see Josh 13:26). Amos makes a pun on its name by calling it *lō' dābār* (meaning "not a thing" or "nothing"). Amos cynically quotes the leaders as saying, "Rejoicing over (the conquest of) nothing!" Similarly, **Karnaim**, located in the Syrian territory of Bashan, conveys prophetic sarcasm. The Hebrew word *qarnāyim* means "horns," a symbol for strength; Amos mocks at the ruling elite because they proudly say to themselves: "Did we not capture strength for ourselves by our own strength?" The complacent, arrogant leaders of Israel persist in boasting about their capacity to deliver. However, all that they have captured is their own strength. Ultimately all that they have conquered is *not-a-thing.*

Against the pride, self-confidence, and self-security of Israel's elite, ***Yahweh God of hosts*** announces that he is raising up (**will stir up**) **a nation** against the house of Israel (Amos 6:14). Although the text does not mention the specific **nation**, based on the historical context of later eighth century B.C., we may assume that the Assyrian Empire that had brought an end to Kalneh and Hamath (v 2) in 738 B.C. is intended here. This nation will **oppress** the house of Israel from **Lebo Hamath** at the northern limits of Jeroboam's territory (2 Kgs 14:25) to the wadi **Arabah** at the southern reaches of Jeroboam's territory (thus NIV adds **all the way**).

FROM THE TEXT

The various oracles of ch 6 speak into contexts of complacency and self-aggrandizement particularly among leaders in the household of God. Through the series of prophetic announcements, Amos reminds the reading audience of the seductive, addictive, and abusive nature of self-serving power and misused authority. The text brings the reader into a narrative world in which persons entrusted with authority have become preoccupied with luxury, opulence, and extravagance. In turn, they have become blind to their own perversions and deaf to the suffering cries of those under their care and supervision.

The oracles move the reading audience to examine and to reflect upon the self-deceiving and destructive nature of human pride. It invites the reader to engage further in canonical statements concerning the human pride that seeks to exalt oneself over others and over God himself (for example, Prov 11:2; Isa 2:11-17; Jer 49:16; Ezek 16:1 ff.; Hos 5:5; contrast John 13:1-16; Phil 2:1-11).

The text serves as a warning to subsequent generations concerning ecclesial complacency. It brings to mind the legend of the Roman emperor Nero's playing the stringed instrument while Rome was burning. How seductive is the power that convinces leaders to believe that all is well when in reality that which has been placed in their charge is decaying and coming to ruination.

The text vividly paints a portrait that points to the teaching of Jesus Christ that those who seek to be first will ultimately be last, and those who attempt to save their lives will ultimately lose their lives (Mark 8:34-38). It reminds the reading audience that this ultimate reality is inescapable; even the "first among nations" will not be exempt from this reversal of fortunes. The long list of great powers, leaders, and institutions that have faced the same fate serves as evidence.

Finally, the text encourages the reading audience to become keenly aware of how its own generation may take the life-giving intentions of God and pervert them for life-taking, self-serving purposes. How might justice and righteousness be perverted and misused to promote death instead of life? Images of wormwood and poison remind the readers of the destructive power of injustice and unrighteousness in the world in which they live. The text conversely invites the readers to imagine the alternative: their involvement in life-giving activities that would transform their world into a place of healing and peace to all humanity. The text also reminds the readers that for this to happen, they must be willing to be servants of all by rejecting the temptations of pride and arrogance—the desire to be "first among the rest."

IV. THE VISIONS OF AMOS AND THE CONFRONTATION WITH AMAZIAH: AMOS 7:1—8:3; 9:1-4

A. The Visions of Amos (7:1-9; 8:1-3; 9:1-4)

7:1-9; 8:1-3; 9:1-4

BEHIND THE TEXT

In the closing chapters of Amos, a series of five visions provides the framework for the text. In the first two visions of locusts and subterranean fire (7:1-6), the prophet cries out on behalf of the people, and Yahweh compassionately relents. In the third vision of the plumb line (7:7-9), the prophet recognizes that Israel is indeed askew from the will of its covenant God. As a result, the prophet can no longer protest. A narrative of the prophet's confrontation with the priest Amaziah at Bethel along with Amos' oracle of judgment (7:10-17) interrupt the series of visions. This interruption functions narratively to demonstrate that Amos, now fully aware that Israel is awry, faithfully proclaims the prophetic word at Bethel. In the fourth vision of the basket of ripe fruit (8:1-3), the prophet announces Israel's imminent end. Once again, as in 7:10-17, a break occurs in the flow of the visions as Amos confronts the injustices carried out by the ruling elite (8:4-6) and announces certain doom of the nation (8:7-14). The series of visions reach their climax in the fifth and final vision of an earthquake in the temple (9:1-4).

The breaks in the text (7:10-17; 8:4-6; 8:7-14) are significant statements of the prophet's confrontation at Bethel, his central indictment against Israel, and his announcement of imminent judgment. However, the discussion below will examine Amos' five visions together before considering the confrontation with Amaziah in 7:10-17 and the injustices and doom in 8:4-14.

The first four vision reports follow a common structure: (1) Introduction of the vision (i.e., the deity causes the prophet to see something); (2) Report of the vision; and (3) Dialogue between the prophet and God. In the first two visions of disastrous events, Amos initiates the conversation; in the third and fourth visions of commonplace objects, God initiates the conversation. In the final vision of the catastrophic quaking of the temple, no dialogue occurs.

In all five visions, the text employs the common verb for "see" (*rāʾâ*) rather than the more specific verb for "see" as in a vision (*ḥāzâ*). In the first four visions, the prophet employs the causative form of the verb (i.e., "Yahweh caused me to see"). In the final vision, the simple active form appears (i.e., "I saw"). The superscription refers to the content of the book as the "words" that Amos saw (*ḥāzâ*) as in a vision. Likewise, in 7:12 the priest Amaziah refers to Amos as a *visionary* (*ḥōzeh*, from *ḥāzâ*). The text, however, never refers to Amos as a *rōʾeh* ("seer," from *rāʾâ*).

7:1-9; 8:1-3; 9:1-4

According to the verb throughout the visions of Amos, the prophet simply *sees* the various sights (locusts, fire, plumb line, summer fruit, and shaking of the temple). However, he goes no further in describing them as extraordinary visions. Perhaps as the prophet Isaiah saw the common sights (e.g., cherubim, incense) of the temple "come to life" (Isa 6:1-8) and take on greater meaning, so, too, did Amos.

The Prophetic Vision

Throughout the OT, the vision is commonly associated with the office of the prophet (e.g., see 1 Kgs 22:17-19; Isa 6:1-8; Jer 1:11-13; Ezek 1:4—3:3; Joel 2:28; Zech 1:7—6:15). While in some instances, the prophetic vision reflects a mysterious, almost ecstatic experience (e.g., Ezekiel and Zechariah), in other instances common sites engender deeper, reflective thought by the prophet (e.g., Isaiah, Jeremiah, and Amos). These visions may occur during daytime or in night dreams. The common factor in all of them is that the prophet *sees* something that leads to a deeper meaning embodied in a message to the people. The prophetic vision is never an end in itself, but it consistently serves to prompt, inform, and move the prophet to speak a word to the community.

1. Vision of Locusts (7:1-3)

IN THE TEXT

■ **1-3** In the first, second, and fourth visions, the text describes God as the ***Lord*** [*ʾădōnāy*] ***Yahweh***. In the third and fifth visions, the word *ʾădōnāy* appears without specific reference to Yahweh. All five visions agree that the deity who is making preparations is the master or Lord of the people. The first vision (vv 1-3) depicts Yahweh's active engagement in **preparing swarms of locusts**; the verb used here (*yāṣar*) elsewhere describes the activity of a potter forming or molding a piece of pottery (see Gen 2:7, 19).

In the first vision, God is forming swarms of locusts to invade at the most formidable time, just as the later planting (*leqeš*) began to sprout after the first harvest. The loss of this crop would place the entire community at risk, as there would be nothing harvested for the dry season of summer. While the royal entourage would be well cared for from the first harvest, the common people of the land would suffer most. Ironically, the ones whom Amos has previously portrayed as living a life of opulence would continue to thrive while the ones depicted as dependent and weak would languish.

Such a divine visitation upon the people would lead to a total destruction of the people who are already helpless and weak because of the burdens imposed on them by the wealthy ruling class. Swarms of locusts have already ***finished eating the grass of the field*** (**stripped the land clean**) and are about to consume the latter growth (v 2). Seeing the desperate outcome of this destruction, Amos cries out to Yahweh to **forgive** (*sālaḥ*) his people. The prophet refers to Israel by the name **Jacob**, the ancestor of the nation with whom God entered into a covenant, when he was running away as a fugitive to escape the wrath of his brother (see Gen 28:13-15).

Amos' description of Israel as **small** evokes the weak and helpless condition of their ancestor when he was met by God at Bethel. Yahweh responds to the prophet's intercession for his forgiveness; Yahweh relents (*niḥam*) or changes the course of his action. The word *niḥam* indicates a change of mind out of sorrow, compassion, or pity. The weakness of Jacob to which the prophet refers likely engenders the compassionate relenting in the divine course of action. The request for forgiveness and the divine change of mind based upon compassion (*niḥam*) were not unfamiliar to Israel's understanding of Yahweh's character (see Exod 32:11—34:9; Num 14:13-25; see also discussion of Joel 2:12-14). Yahweh's statement, ***It will not be*** (**This will not happen**), confirms the divine change of mind.

2. Vision of Fire (7:4-6)

■ **4-6** The second vision in vv 4-6 follows a structure very similar to the first vision. In this report, the prophet employs the title ***Lord*** [*ʾădōnāy*] ***Yahweh*** three times. In this vision, Yahweh is **calling** (*qārāʾ*) for fire. As in "forming" in the first vision, this action depicts Yahweh's sovereignty over that with which he works. In the Hebrew text, Yahweh actually does not call for fire but rather for a trial or lawsuit (*rib*, alternative form of *rîb* as occurring elsewhere in the text) with **fire**. While the Hebrew text indicates that the trial will be carried out by means of fire, the NIV interprets the **judgment** itself to be in fire. The NRSV follows an alternative word division in the text here, which has resulted in the translation "for a shower of fire." In the various curses against the nations (1:4, 7, 10, 12, 14; 2:2), Amos depicted a divine fire consuming the secure fortress cities (see also 5:6 concerning "the tribes of Joseph"). In this vision, however, the text specifically describes the result of the fire; it consumed or **devoured** (*ʾākal*) both water and dry ground.

Rather than using generic terms for water (*mayim*) and land (*ʾereṣ*), the prophet employs much more concrete language. The fire consumes the subterranean waters of **the great deep** (*tĕhôm rabbâ*; e.g., see Gen 7:11; 8:2). It also devours the tracts of apportioned **land** (*ḥēleq*), that is, the land divided among tribes, clans, and families as their inheritance.

With both agricultural apportionments and the subterranean waters consumed by the fire, the situation of the people was hopeless. Drought or famine would bring the same devastation brought on by the locusts in the first vision. Once again, the plight of the ones for whom the prophet had been calling for justice was dismal. Amos cries out to Yahweh again. As in response to the first vision, the prophet cites the helplessness of **Jacob**. This time, however, rather than asking Yahweh to forgive, Amos simply asks the Lord Yahweh to **stop**, or more literally, to bring the vision to an end (*ḥādal*). As in Amos 7:3, Yahweh responds accordingly.

3. Vision of a Plumb Line (7:7-9)

■ **7-9** The third vision, in vv 7-9, departs from the customary language of the first two. The title Lord Yahweh is lacking in this vision. The text simply states **He showed me**. Amos sees this time ***the sovereign*** (*ʾădōnāy*) who has stationed himself (**standing**) beside a vertical (*ʾănāk*) **wall**. In his hand is an instrument (also *ʾănāk*; thus often interpreted as **plumb line**) for measuring the perpendicular accuracy (i.e., level nature) of the wall.

In contrast to the first two visions, in which the prophet initiates the dialogue, Yahweh proceeds to initiate the conversation in v 8. Yahweh addresses Amos by calling out his name and engages the prophet with the question,

What do you see? Not only is God *doing* something in these visions, but he invites Amos to become a participant by *seeing* what God is *doing.*

Amos answers with a single word: **a plumb line**. Yahweh responds to Amos and announces that he is in the process of **setting a plumb line** (*ʾănāk*) in the midst of Israel. Yahweh refers to Israel as **my people**, which indicates the covenant relationship between Yahweh and Israel. Since Yahweh engaged the prophet in the vision, perhaps the plumb line in the hand of God was actually the prophet himself. Yahweh's word that the prophet spoke examined the uprightness of the people. This task is precisely the concern of the book of Amos. Yahweh announces that he will not continue to ***pass over*** (*ʿābar*; **spare**) the people. Yahweh saved Israel from Egypt by *passing over* them when he *passed through* Egypt in judgment (Exod 12:12-13). In the past, Yahweh spared the nation from total destruction when they broke their covenant with him (see Exod 32—34; Num 14). Yahweh declares here that his relationship to Israel as its deliverer has come to an end. His patience with his people has reached its limit. The vision does not record Amos' appeal to Yahweh for mercy.

Amos 7:9 conveys Yahweh's judgment word against Israel. The cultic sites of Israel (**high places** and **sanctuaries**) will be utterly **destroyed** and **ruined**. Amos uses the name **Isaac**, Israel's ancestor, as the identity of the nation. **High places** refer to the fertility cultic sites of Canaan located on high hills or mountains. Jeroboam is said to have constructed temples to Yahweh on the high places of Dan and Bethel (see 1 Kgs 12:31-32; 2 Chr 11:15). The **sanctuaries** or holy places mentioned here perhaps were the shrines at Bethel in the south and Dan in the north.

Amos 7:9 ends with the judgment pronounced against the political house that ruled Israel. Yahweh the divine warrior will raise his **sword . . . against the house of Jeroboam**. Amos perhaps anticipates here the invasion of Israel and its destruction by Assyria. Yahweh's judgment will thus bring an end to both the religious and the political realms, which are ultimately responsible for the crookedness of the nation.

In the present arrangement of the book, the Amaziah-Amos confrontation narrative (7:10-17) interrupts the third and fourth visions. It is likely that the editors of the book inserted this text after the third vision because of the judgment words against Jeroboam in both texts.

4. Vision of a Basket of Summer Fruit (8:1-3)

■ **8:1-3** As previously noted, we will consider the fourth and fifth visions before returning to the confrontation narrative.

In the fourth vision, Yahweh shows Amos a basket of summer or ripe fruit (8:1-3). Just as God had asked the prophet what he saw in the third vision, God continues to guide the direction of the dialogue by asking the question again. Amos responds that he sees **a basket of ripe fruit** (*qayiṣ*). As *qayiṣ* can refer to the season of summer (see 3:15), the fruit seen by Amos is the fruit harvested toward the end of summer (Wolff [1977, 319] and Paul [1991, 253] suggest figs). Mays thinks that the basket of fruit may be an offering given at the annual harvest festival, in which worshippers anticipated blessing for the coming year (1969, 141). Gowan treats the basket of fruit as a vision (1996, 414).

The divine response to Amos provides interpretation to the vision. The NIV attempts to portray the wordplay of the text in the translation: **ripe fruit** and **time is ripe**. The text is not as concerned with the **ripe** nature of Israel (i.e., time for harvest) as it is with the paronomasia of *qayiṣ* (summer fruit) and *qēṣ* (***end***). These words both sound and look similar. Therefore Yahweh declares, ***The end has come to my people Israel***. As in the third vision (7:8), Yahweh employs the covenant language of **my people** in referring to **Israel**. As in the third vision, God announces, **I will spare them no longer**. The fourth vision concludes with a judgment word against **the temple**. In the third and fourth visions, the prophet thus focuses on the end of Israel's cultic life by citing three worship sites: high places, sanctuaries, and temple.

In that day in v 3 refers to the Day of Yahweh. With poignant irony, the prophet announces that the temple songs will become ***howlings*** (**turn to wailing**). Amos employs the verbal form *hêlîlû*, which vividly contrasts with the familiar praises of the temple, *halĕlu(yâ)*, that is, "praise the LORD." The prophet concludes with a declaration of the utter devastation: ***Many the carcass cast out in every location!*** The prophet does not merely speak of **bodies** strewn around, as described in the NIV. These bodies are corpses; they have been wastefully **flung** out; they appear in every place. In a sense of awestruck amazement, the prophet concludes with the interjection *hās*, ***Keep silent!*** This is clearly reminiscent of the same command in the scene of utter devastation in 6:10.

5. Vision of the Temple Destruction (9:1-4)

■ **9:1-4** In the final vision report (9:1-4), Amos depicts the temple destruction brought about by an earthquake. As in the third vision, Amos sees **the Lord** (*ʾădōnāy*) in this vision. In both instances, the Lord is positioned (**standing**) beside an object, a wall in 7:7 and an **altar** in 9:1. The setting for this vision is clearly a worship site, likely the temple at Bethel. However, in contrast to the four preceding vision reports, no dialogue between God and prophet occurs. No one interrupts; no one asks questions; no one gives responses. God gives a directive, and complete destruction ensues.

At the outset of the vision report, the Lord utters a command. The report does not specifically indicate the identity of the recipient of the command; it is unlikely that Amos is the recipient, since the prophet is not responsible for carrying out destruction but simply for announcing it. Perhaps the recipient is the divine army, that is, the *hosts* that carry out the directives of the divine warrior Yahweh (God of hosts). Perhaps the recipient is simply the land itself as it responds to the divine command by shaking and bringing down the temple.

The divine command is to **strike** the columns so that **the thresholds** supporting the temple **shake** and ultimately **bring . . . down** the temple. As a result, all who are inside perish. Ironically the site that the worshippers thought brought life becomes the site that brings death. As the divine fire devours the cult site (5:6), the temple is reduced to nothing (5:5). The remainder of the vision depicts the destruction of those who are left and those who may try to escape. Yahweh's sword will kill them. In times past, worshippers had celebrated the inescapability of the divine presence (see Ps 139:7-12). Now, however, that inescapability becomes the basis for destruction.

Throughout these verses (Amos 9:1-4), graphically violent language emerges in the text with Yahweh as the subject of destruction. He himself **will kill** (v 1), **take them** up from Sheol (v 2), **bring them down** from the sky (v 2), **hunt them down and seize them** from Mount Carmel (v 3), **command the serpent to bite them** as they hide in the sea (v 3), and **command the sword to slay** the captives (v 4). The text follows a chiasmic structure as the **sword** (*ḥereb*) envelops the destruction of any remnant, that is, ones whose lives are spared but captured (see the sword also 7:9, 11, 17). Between the two depic-
9:1-4 tions of the sword, a pattern of (*a*) depths and heights, (*b*) heights and depths appears. The prophet employs hyperbole to depict the extreme locations of escape. The chiasmus may be represented as follows:

A Sword against survivors
  B Lowest depths of Sheol (***grave***)
    C Highest heights of the sky (**heavens**)
    C' Highest peaks (***top***) of Mount Carmel
  B' Lowest depths (**bottom**) of the sea
A' Swords against surviving captives (exiles)

The inescapability of destruction is unquestionable. There is no escape for anyone, even to those who will go **into exile**. Yahweh declares that he will **command** the most destructive forces, **serpent** and **sword**, to do his bidding.

With irony, 9:3 portrays persons who attempt to **hide** from God. However, in the concluding statement of the vision report, Yahweh announces that he will ***fix*** his eyes upon them. Indeed, no one will be able to escape, for no one will be able to circumvent the eyes of Yahweh. Israel traditionally understood that the divine seeing of his people would bring deliverance and life (e.g., Ps 33:18); this time, however, it will bring only life-taking injury (*rāʿâ*, **harm** or ***evil***) rather than life-giving welfare (*tôbâ*, **good**).

FROM THE TEXT

Amos' series of vision reports vividly depicts the dual nature of the prophetic task. On the one hand, the prophet is to speak the word of the Lord faithfully to the covenant community. On the other hand, even as the prophet speaks the divine word, he remains in solidarity with God's people. The prophet is simultaneously the voice of God to the community and the intercessor on behalf of God's people.

The prophet's outcry in the first two vision reports reminds the reading community that the prophetic ministry never sets itself up in combative opposition to God's people. The prophet is no outsider to the community under divine scrutiny. The prophet is a member of and an engaged participant in the life of the covenant community. To preach judgment upon the people is ultimately to participate in the effects of that judgment.

Amos' outcry to God on behalf of the people recalls the prophetic intercession of the prophet par excellence, Moses, in Exod 32:11-14 and Num 14:13-20. The one who speaks for God to the people also speaks for the people to God. The prophet cries out to God on behalf of the people, "Forgive!" The authentic prophet envisions and longs for a divine change of mind concerning judgment against the people.

For subsequent generations who read the text, this prophetic task belongs not only to the clergy and ecclesial leadership on behalf of congregations but also to the church on behalf of the world and all creation. The prophetic church intercedes on behalf of the world; the prophetic church cries out, "Forgive!" It does not dream of divine judgment; it hopes for divine grace, mercy, and pardon.

The sequence of vision reports, however, also portrays the prophet's deep commitment to the God who has called and who has entrusted the divine message to the prophet. The prophetic voice must speak this message faithfully. Commitment to the community does not assuage commitment to the God who has called. In the end, the prophetic voice refuses to silence the divine word. The prophet speaks poignantly and clearly to the people of God, realizing that the word (*dābār*) spoken will become the very thing (*dābār*) that God has declared.

Therefore, even as the prophet intercedes for the people, the prophet receives and speaks the word given by God. Ultimately, the prophetic task is cooperation with the one who has called. The prophet recognizes his accountability and responsibility to the one who has called him, his master, his *ʾădōnāy*.

According to the third vision, a measuring line ultimately must be established in the midst of the community. It will ultimately demonstrate uprightness or the lack thereof. As apparent throughout the oracles of Amos, the prophet himself will ultimately function as the plumb line among God's people. Heirs of the prophetic task—including clergy, ecclesial leaders, and the prophetic church—continue to serve as a "plumb line" both for the covenant community and for the world. Placed in the midst of God's people and God's world, the prophetic voice functions to speak God's will to the people so that the people can be measured accordingly. While this prophetic task is persistent throughout the book of Amos, it is made concrete in the narrative of Amos' encounter with Amaziah (see discussion below).

The dialogue between the prophet and God in this text presents the reading audience with a challenging portrait of an authentically relational God. The text challenges the reader to encounter a deity who partners with his prophet and with his people. Unlike the Greek deities of Mount Olympus who remain aloof and stoic, impassable and detached, the God of Mount Sinai invites participation, cooperation, and reciprocity. The prophet is not a passive bystander; the deity is not a manipulative micromanager. The God of Amos is capable of changing his course of action based upon compassion and mercy toward his people. Likewise, the God of Amos works cooperatively with his prophet and not over and against his prophet. The relationship between God, prophet, and people is genuinely mutual and reciprocal.

B. Interlude: Amos-Amaziah Confrontation (7:10-17)

BEHIND THE TEXT

As noted in the discussion of Amos' five vision reports, the narrative of the prophetic confrontation in vv 10-17 interrupts the flow of the reports. The editors most likely inserted the account of the Amaziah-Amos confrontation here because it shares with the third vision the judgment words against the sanctuary at Bethel and the house of Jeroboam.

The genre of prophetic conflict is not unfamiliar to the OT. Prophets articulate this type of conflict (e.g., Hos 9:7; Mic 2:6), and narratives depict it vividly (e.g., Ahab and Elijah in 1 Kgs 18:17). The narratives of Jeremiah portray a prophet designed for conflict (Jer 1:4-10, 17-19; 18:18) with kings (Jer 36:1-26), priests (Jer 20:1-6), fellow prophets (Jer 28), and religious leadership in general (Jer 26:7-23).

Typically, the prophetic conflict narrative depicts the collision between the prophet and a recognized political or religious authority. This type of prophetic narrative characteristically includes an accusation against a prophet and the prophetic response. The accusation and response serve as the context for an oracle of judgment. The prophetic confrontation in 7:10-17 follows a simple structure:

1. Accusation against the prophet (vv 10-11)
2. Command for the prophet to return home (vv 12-13)

3. Prophetic response to accuser (vv 14-15)
4. Oracle of judgment (vv 16-17)

IN THE TEXT

■ **10-11** The priest Amaziah appears abruptly in the text. The name (meaning "Yahweh is mighty") also appears in the OT as the ninth ruler of Judah (see 2 Kgs 14; 2 Chr 25) and as a song leader among the Levites (1 Chr 6:16, 31-32, 45). However, only in this narrative does the name refer to a priest at an Israelite sanctuary.

Bethel functioned as the primary Yahwistic cultic site for the northern kingdom. Bethel is the primary site against which Amos pronounced earlier oracles (3:14; 4:4; 5:5-6). Amaziah's words in 7:13 indicate that Amos actually preached at the site of Bethel. He likely declared the oracle against the high places, sanctuaries, and house of Jeroboam (v 9) at this prestigious cult site.

In vv 10-11, Amaziah makes accusation against Amos to King Jeroboam. He describes the prophet as **raising a conspiracy** against the king. The verb *qāšar* ("conspire," "bind") denotes the action of joining a league with others. Amaziah's message to the king emerges directly out of the divine oracle attached to the third vision (v 9). In light of the frequent assassinations of kings in the northern kingdom's history, it is possible that Amaziah interpreted Amos' announcement of Yahweh's "sword . . . against the house of Jeroboam" as the prophet's instigation for another coup d'etat.

The priest sees the prophetic word at work **in the very heart of Israel**; he is well aware of the power and effectiveness of the prophetic word. He reports to the king that **the land cannot bear all his words**. The phrase translated **cannot bear** is actually the double appearance of the same verbal root *yākōl* ("to have power," "prevail," "endure"). The priest literally says that the land ***does not have power to have power*** to deal with the prophetic words spoken by Amos. It is unable to overcome the effectual, pervasive (**all**) words of the prophet.

Amaziah's quote of Amos in v 11 begins where v 9 ended. He focuses on Yahweh's sword "against the house of Jeroboam" (v 9) and interprets it as an announcement of the impending death of the king by **the sword**, perhaps the sword of the enemies of the king. The report augments v 9 with an additional reference to Israel's **exile . . . from their native land**. Although v 9 does not mention exile, previous oracles speak of the exile of Israel (5:5, 27; 6:7). The confrontation with Amaziah climaxes with an oracle of Amos in 7:17. In this oracle, the prophet quotes Amaziah word-for-word: **Israel will surely go into exile, away from their native land** (v 11). In both instances, the exile is announced as a certainty. Israel will be removed from their homeland, the ground (*ʾădāmâ*) that provided them with a home.

■ **12-13** Although vv 10-11 report Amaziah's words to King Jeroboam, the text does not record the king's response. Perhaps the king expected the priest to handle this matter and silence the prophet. In vv 12-13, Amaziah continues to speak; this time he speaks to the prophet himself and exercises his priestly authority, perhaps as the voice of the king. The text seems to portray Amaziah the priest as the religious "pawn" in the hands of the royal system.

Amaziah begins his speech with a direct address, **O *visionary*** (*ḥōzeh*, **seer**) and commands Amos, ***go*** (**get out**). The priest recognizes Amos as one who claims to receive visions from God (see 1:1, which introduces the content of the book as what Amos "saw" (*ḥāzâ*). In the early history of Israel, it was customary for people to give something as payment for the services of a seer or a visionary (see 1 Sam 9:1-10, which uses the synonym *rōʿeh*). Amaziah further commands Amos to go back to **Judah** and earn his living there by **prophesying** to the people of Judah (v 12). The command to flee (**go back**) contains an element of haste. For a southern prophet to speak such violent words in the north is nothing less than an attempt at insurrection. As a foreign rebel, Amos should hurry to make his escape. The command to ***eat bread there*** indicates Amaziah's assessment of Amos as a professional prophet who earned his living by his prophesying activity.

The priest's inferences in v 12 become clear in v 13. The prophet is not welcome at Bethel. In the Hebrew text, **Bethel** precedes the command not to **prophesy** (*nābāʾ*). Literally, the priest declares, ***(At) Bethel, you will no longer continue to prophesy***. As in v 12, Amaziah's concern is over the location where Amos is prophesying (i.e., Bethel and the northern kingdom).

The rationale behind Amaziah's command to Amos is filled with irony. Although the name of the site is *bêt ʾēl* ("house of God"), Amaziah declares it to be *bêt mamlākâ*, ***house of the kingdom***. The NIV translation **the temple of the kingdom** does not adequately convey the irony of the manner in which this *house* of God has been altered into a *house* in service to the kingdom. Not only does Amaziah describe Bethel as the ***house of the kingdom***, but he also observes that it is **the king's sanctuary** (*miqdaš melek*), the holy place of the king. Amos had previously announced that such holy places of Israel would be made a wasteland (see v 9). It is ironic that the holy place set aside for the worship of God had become a holy place set aside for the perpetuation of the king and his kingdom. Even more ironic is that a priest of Yahweh would have become the spokesperson of the king and of the dominant political-economic system rather than of the God whose Torah he was to teach.

■ **14-15** Amos' response to Amaziah in vv 14-17 occurs in two segments: (1) report of divine commission (vv 14-15), and (2) oracle of judgment (vv 16-17). At the outset of his response, Amos explicitly speaks of his own identity (v 14), using the first-person subject pronoun (**I**) three times. Twice he denies his identity as a **prophet** (*nābîʾ*) by saying that he is neither a prophet nor a son of a prophet. Mays has referred to the interpretation of the prophet's statement as "the most controverted problem in the Book of Amos" (1969, 137). Because there is no verb in the sentence, it is impossible to know if the statement speaks in the past (i.e., I was not a prophet, thus NIV) or in the present (i.e., I am not a prophet, thus NRSV, NASB). Regarding various interpretations, see Mays (1969, 137-38) and Paul (1991, 244-47). If translated in the past tense, Amos states that he was not a prophet prior to his call to go to Israel (v 15). If translated in the present tense, Amos rejects Amaziah's charge that he is a professional prophet. Amos understands his task in the context of Yahweh's command to him to prophesy (v 15; *nābāʾ*), though he was commanded by Amaziah not to prophesy (v 13; *nābāʾ*). Amos' claim that he is not a ***prophet's son*** indicates that he does not have membership in the prophetic guild. In Israel, younger prophets were often known as "sons of" a leading prophetic personality (e.g., see 1 Sam 10:9-14; 2 Kgs 2:5-15; 4:1, 38; 5:22; 6:1; 9:1). Whether one interprets the statement as past tense or present tense, the primary issue at stake in the text is the clash between the divine command to prophesy and the priestly command not to prophesy.

In v 14, Amos identifies himself as a ***herdsman*** (*bôqēr*, **shepherd**). The NIV interprets *bôqēr* (meaning "large cattle" or "herdsman of large cattle") as a transcriptional error of *nôqēd* (meaning "shepherd"). While the words do not sound alike, their similarity in appearance could easily result in a scribal error. Amos 1:1 indicates that Amos was among the *nōqdîm* ("shepherds"); in 7:15, Amos claims that Yahweh has taken him from following after the flock (*ṣôʾn*). As a herdsman, Amos certainly could have tended smaller flock, such as sheep and goats, as well as larger cattle.

The prophet also depicts himself as one who **took care of sycamore-fig trees**. These trees usually grow at higher altitudes than Amos' hometown of Tekoa. The verb **took care of** may indicate an act of horticultural husbandry in which one cuts or pinches figs in order to allow them to ripen at a quicker pace or to prevent insect infestation. However, the verb may also simply depict the gathering of figs or the sycamore leaves as fodder for animals (see Hayes 1988, 237-38).

Amos continues his speech and establishes himself as an authentic spokesperson for Yahweh in v 15. That Yahweh **took** [*lāqaḥ*] **me** indicates the divine initiative behind his prophetic activity. The verb *lāqaḥ* depicts the acquisition of a person or an object *for oneself*. In this case, Yahweh took Amos *away from* his ordinary task of ***following after*** **(tending) the flock** in order to make him his messenger to Israel.

The divine command to Amos in v 15 is in stark contrast to Amaziah's command in v 12 (see also v 16). Yahweh directs Amos to **go** (*lēk*) and to

prophesy (*nābāʾ*). Yahweh's directive to Amos is to prophesy to **my people Israel**. Amos' prophetic task functions within the context of the covenant between Yahweh and Israel. The prophet ultimately functions as the enforcer of the covenant.

■ **16-17** The judgment word in vv 16-17 is preceded by the introduction, ***Now, hear Yahweh's word***. The oracle of judgment begins with a direct quote of Amaziah's injunction against Amos' prophetic activity (v 16), which would then become the basis for the actual words of judgment in v 17. Yahweh commands Amos to prophesy to "my people Israel" (v 15); Amaziah commands Amos not to prophesy **against** [*ʿal*] **Israel** (v 16). The command to **stop preaching** (*nāṭap* literally means "to drip"; see also Mic 2:6, 11) stands in parallelism with the command **not** to **prophesy**. The phrase **descendants of Isaac** is in the same way parallel to **Israel** in v 16.

The priest's command in v 16 becomes the grounds (hence **therefore**) for divine judgment in v 17. Similar to other prophetic texts in which attempts are made to silence the prophet (e.g., Pashhur the priest Jer 20:1-6; Hananiah the prophet in Jer 28:15-16; see also Mic 2:6-7), divine judgment will come upon Amaziah for his attempt to hush the prophetic voice.

The comprehensive nature of divine action against the priest, his wife, his children, and his land reflects the corporate nature of judgment. However, in this passage the all-inclusive judgment also seems to indicate the complete end of Amaziah's priesthood. There is no hope of its return. The language of one's wife becoming a prostitute, one's children being violently killed, and one's land being parceled out to others reflects the language of the curse against covenant infidelity (see Lev 26:22; Deut 28:30-32, 41; Job 31:9-10; Jer 6:12; Mic 2:4-5). The image of the destructive sword was present in the oracle that sparked the prophetic controversy at the outset (see Amos 7:9, 11).

Amos announces that Amaziah, the priest whose task was to maintain the purity of the community, would himself die in an ***unclean land*** (v 17). The priest will be removed from Yahweh's holy land (i.e., Israel). Not only will the priest and his family be removed from the land of promise, but all of **Israel** will **go into exile**. Amos' concluding statement of v 17 regarding Israel's exile is word-for-word repetition of Amaziah's quote of Amos in v 11.

FROM THE TEXT

There is a subtle warning in the text that "the house of God" can become "the house of the kingdom" by attaching itself to political ideologies and by becoming the voice of politicians of any given nation. God's people hear in this text a call to resist the temptation to seek identity with the dominant empire in which they live and to subscribe to its political and economic ideologies.

The text clearly depicts exile of the people of God as the outcome when they become the voice of the kingdoms of this world.

Amos and Amaziah present two contrasting alternatives to ministry; one speaks for God and the other speaks for the kingdom. One follows the call of God and leaves his vocation, livelihood, homeland, and family to be faithful to God who called him; the other abandons his task to faithfully teach the *torah*/the Law and warn his people of the consequences of their covenant disobedience. One is not afraid to speak against an unjust king; the other is more concerned with defending the king. The text invites contemporary religious leaders and laity alike to ponder their loyalties and responsibilities as members of the kingdom of God. Who do they serve? For whom will they speak? Amos' stubborn refusal to bend to the popular wishes of the kingdom and the priest recall his conviction: "The lion has roared—who will not fear? The Sovereign Lord has spoken—who can but prophesy" (3:8)? When God speaks, the prophet, both ancient and contemporary, must also speak. The prophet must permit no priest, no king, or no fellow prophet to stand in the way of faithfulness to the divine word given by the Lord.

8:4-14

V. ORACLE AGAINST ISRAEL: AMOS 8:4-14; 9:5-10

A. Social Condemnation (8:4-14)

BEHIND THE TEXT

The collection of oracles in vv 4-14 interrupts the prophet's fourth and fifth visions (8:1-3; 9:1-4) in much the same way that the narrative of Amos' encounter with Amaziah (7:10-17) interrupted the third and fourth visions. In 8:4-6, Amos gives a list of the socioeconomic crimes of Israel's wealthy people. This is followed by a scenario of the impending judgment and its devastating consequences (vv 7-14). Amos' language describing Israel's socioeconomic crimes is reminiscent of previous oracles (2:6-8; 4:1; 5:10-12). Likewise, indirect references to the Day of Yahweh ("in that day," "the days are coming") reemerge in 8:9-14 (see 2:13-16; 3:14-15; 5:18-20).

IN THE TEXT

4-6 In 8:4-6, the prophet once again condemns the social and economic practices of Israel's leaders. The prophet summons the Israelites to **hear this**, but he does not specify the word that the people are summoned to hear in vv 4-6. What follows is a description of the social crimes committed by the addressees. The demonstrative pronoun **this** perhaps points forward to the judgment words in vv 7-14.

Amos depicts his addressees (the wealthy and powerful in the land) as those who **trample** [see 2:7] **the needy** [see 2:6] and bring an end to (**do away with**) **the poor of the land**. In 8:5-6 Amos quotes the words of the wealthy to describe the way they mistreat the weaker members of the society. By quoting the nobility, Amos establishes their guilt in vv 5-6. They are impatient with the length of time dedicated to celebrate **New Moon** and **Sabbath**; they hope these celebrations would end soon so they could return to their dishonest economic practices. In v 4, the prophet employs the causative form of the verb *šābat* (meaning "to cease") to show that the wealthy are involved in the cessation of the life of (**do away with**) the poor in the land. Instead of thinking of ways on the day of **Sabbath** (*šabbāt* means "rest," "cease") to bring an end to the impoverishment of the poor (to give rest to the poor), the wealthy are thinking of ways to bring an end to their life (see v 5). The festival of **New Moon** (*ḥōdeš*, literally *new*) occurred at the appearance of the lunar crescent (i.e., first day of the lunar month). Pairing the New Moon with Sabbath indicates that the New Moon apparently functioned also as a day of rest as did Sabbath.

Sabbath

The law of Sabbath (*šabbāt*) required all members of the community to experience a complete rest from productivity and labor (Lev 23:3). This rest included animals, servants, and aliens (Exod 23:12). Rooted in the divine rest at creation (Gen 2:2-3; Exod 20:8-11) and Israel's deliverance from Egypt (Deut 5:12-15), Sabbath functioned as the sign of covenant between Yahweh and Israel (Exod 31:12-17). Later in Israel's history, Sabbath expanded to include the fallow year in which land lay dormant (Exod 23:10-11; Lev 25:1-7), the remission of debt (Deut 15:1-18), and ultimately Jubilee (Lev 25:8-55).

Amos describes in 8:5 why the wealthy long for the celebration of New Moon and Sabbath to **be over**; they are eager to open their business to **sell grain** and **market wheat**. The verb *pātaḥ* means "to open" (perhaps to open the grain sacks for sale; **market**). Because the verb is concerned more with the sack's content than with the sack itself, Wolff suggests that the word means "to offer (for sale)" (1977, 327).

The text does not make clear where the nobility's saying ends. The verbs translated **skimping, boosting, cheating,** and **buying** are all infinitives in the Hebrew text, which contribute to the uncertainty regarding the length of the words of the nobility. The NIV reading suggests the nobility's desire to return to their business (v 5*a*) and the prophet's description of their business practices as dishonest (vv 5*b*-6). In contrast, the NRSV treats vv 5*b*-6 as the nobility's words—their articulation of the dishonest manner in which they will sell grain. Because the final line of v 6 includes a first-person plural verb (***we will sell***), the merchants' quote seems to be the full statement in vv 5-6.

Although the NIV takes creative liberty in v 5*b*, the phrases **skimping on the measure** and **boosting the price** adequately convey Amos' thought. The prophet depicts the nobility's engagement in fraudulent practices of containers, weights, and balances. Making reference to the basic units of weight (***shekel***) and measurement (***ephah***), the text portrays the greedy nobility as fraudulently reducing the container for measurement (i.e., ***making the ephah small***) and enlarging the heaviness of weights (i.e., ***making the shekel great***). "Packaging" the grain in smaller units than the legal ***ephah*** and making the valid weight of the ***shekel*** heavier, they defraud the people in two ways. While the NIV infers that the ***shekel*** is a coin (i.e., **boosting the price**), the reference is likely to an increase in the weight used in measurement. The merchant thus charges a stipulated price for a deceptively smaller amount. Ancient Israel's legal tradition banned such fraudulent practices (see Lev 19:35-36; Deut 25:13-16; see similar concerns in other eighth-century B.C. prophets, Hos 12:7 and Mic 6:9-11).

As if false weights and measurements were not enough, the merchants also rig the scales. Amos describes the merchants as ***bending*** or ***perverting*** **(cheating)** with **dishonest scales**. Wolff suggests that the reference is to merchants' bending "out of shape the crossbeam of the balances" (1977, 327). The wisdom tradition denounced such dishonest practices (see Prov 11:1; 16:11; 20:10, 23).

Ephah and Shekel

The ephah refers to dry measure while the shekel refers to the weight used in determining a purchase price. In ancient Israel, the ephah was the primary unit of dry (grain or corn) measurement. It consisted of ten omers (Exod 16:36). The homer was the largest dry measure and contained ten ephah (see Ezek 45:10). Equivalent to approximately forty liters, the ephah could also refer to the container itself. As the basic unit of weight and weighing approximately 11.33 grams, the shekel determined all smaller and larger weights. It became a coin only during the postexilic period.

Amos 8:6 depicts the manner in which the powerful elite engaged in economic exchange of **the poor** and **the needy** (see 2:6-7). Using language similar to that found in 2:6, the prophet depicts not the ***selling*** but the ***buying*** (*qānâ*) of the destitute. The term *qānâ* demonstrates that the wealthy nobility acquired the poor as personal property. Mays has attributed this practice particularly to an emerging urban culture in mid-eighth-century Israel (1969, 143).

In 8:6 and in 2:6 the preposition *bĕ* (***with***) indicates the means of transaction, that is, human beings exchanged for silver. Amos' indictment may have been directed against those who extend loans to **the poor**, which would eventually lead to the enslavement of the borrower. Gowan asserts the common practice in which wealthy landowners would "make it all the more certain that the poor would be unable to repay the loans and would have to become debt-slaves (cf. Exod 21:2; 22:24; Lev 25:39-42)" (1996, 416).

The phrase **the needy for a pair of sandals** is identical to 2:6. As noted in 2:6, the reference to a pair of sandals may indicate the exchange of land itself. It is fitting that Amos' opening indictment concerning economic injustices and closing indictment concerning economic injustices is framed with **buying** and **selling**. The full economic enterprise is corrupt and unjust. Both consumer and merchant are engaged in human trafficking; the destitute and dependent persons are mere commodities in the hands of the wealthy and the powerful. Amos makes clear the merchants' greed in the last line of 8:6; their strategy is to sell even the **sweepings** with the wheat in order to make a profit. Mays describes the sweepings as a "mixture of chaff and trash left after winnowing" (1969, 144). Smith suggests that the refuse of grain at the bottom of containers would further increase the product's weight (1989, 254). Such a practice would coincide with the fraudulent practices of heavy weights, smaller containers, and bent scales. That which the wealthy rulers anticipate to do when the festivals conclude becomes a reality as they sell the debris-filled wheat. The prophet Micah depicts a similar scenario in which the nighttime plans of the wealthy become reality at the outset of the next day (Mic 2:1). As Micah observes, the nobility is able to carry out the plans they devise because they have the power to do so.

■ **7** In Amos 8:7-14, the prophet declares diverse announcements of divine judgment. The oracles begin with such references as "in that day" (vv 9, 13) and "the days are coming" (v 11), implying the much-anticipated but highly misunderstood Day of Yahweh. Amos presents the Day of Yahweh as a certainty and the destruction of Israel as undeniable and unconditional. Hopelessness permeates the text as language of grief and lamentation prevails throughout. These verses graphically depict the thought behind Amos' lament over fallen Israel in 5:1-2.

Amos introduces the pronouncement of judgment by means of divine oath in 8:7 (see divine oaths also in 4:2; 6:8). Mays has described the oath as "a particularly intense form of the announcement of judgment" that expresses the absolute certainty of divine punishment (1969, 145). Amos says that Yahweh has **sworn by himself** that he will not **forget anything**. The text literally states that Yahweh will not forget ***all their deeds***. Israel had always hoped for Yahweh's memory of his people; it was horrifying for Israel to conceive of Yahweh's forgetting of his people (see Ps 10:11-12, for example). It is ironic that Amos speaks here of Yahweh's unending memory of Israel's infidelity; it will endure without end (**never forget**).

The prophet grounds the divine oath in **the Pride of Jacob**. The phrase here is somewhat enigmatic considering its occurrence in 6:8 (for diverse interpretations, see Gowan 1996, 417). The phrase occurs only twice outside of Amos. In Ps 47:4, Yahweh chooses the "pride of Jacob" as an inheritance. In Nah 2:2, Yahweh restores or returns the "pride ['splendor' (NIV)] of Jacob." In both texts, the phrase likely refers to the land.

In light of Yahweh's swearing "by his holiness" (4:2) and "by himself" (6:8), the phrase **Pride of Jacob** may function as a divine title (see 1 Sam 15:29; Mays 1969, 145; Smith 2005, 254-55). If so, then once again Yahweh's oath is based upon his own divine nature. The NIV's capitalization of the word suggests such an interpretation (contrast NRSV).

However, the phrase encounters a problem in light of its appearance in 6:8, where it clearly refers to Israel's haughty self-sufficiency embodied in its fortresses. Paul treats this as an example of prophetic irony in which Yahweh sarcastically swears "by the very attribute of the people that he has formerly condemned" (1991, 260; see also Wolff 1977, 328).

Interpretation of this phrase as prophetic irony, however, overlooks the serious nature of ancient Near Eastern oaths in which the power of the oath rests on the power of the name of the deity who is involved in the oath. The phrase is the basis for Yahweh's resolve that he will not forget. Thus it is more likely that here we have a divine epithet or a reference to Yahweh's heritage.

■ 8 A series of judgment oracles follows Yahweh's oath in 8:7 (v 8, vv 9-10, vv 11-12, vv 13-14). The first announcement of judgment (v 8) is cast in the form of a rhetorical question that affirms the desolation of the land and the grief of its inhabitants. The question actually opens by pointing the audience to the actual cause of the coming disaster: ***is it not on account of this*** (*haʿal zōt*). Although the demonstrative pronoun (**this**) has no specific referent, it likely refers to the economic injustices depicted in vv 5-7.

The reference to the land's ***shaking*** (**tremble**) may point to Amos' final vision of the earthquake (9:1-4; see also 1:1). Language of the earth's shaking frequently occurs alongside depictions of military battle, including the exodus event itself (e.g., see 1 Sam 14:15; Joel 2:10). As the land quakes, its inhabitants ***grieve*** (**mourn**; see similar response in Amos 9:5). For Amos, the grief is not limited to certain inhabitants; it is comprehensive.

The second half of 8:8 poetically compares the movement of the land at the time of its quaking to the rise and fall of the Nile at the time of the river's flooding. Mays observes that "the comparison of an earthquake's tremors with the seasonal rising and falling of the Nile is hardly apt and betrays an awareness only that the river did go up and down without any knowledge of how it occurred" (1969, 145; as to why such an odd image for an earthquake occurs, see Wolff 1977, 329). Paul, however, describes the depiction of the Nile as a "potently and picturesquely portrayed" image of "the rise and fall of the earth's surface during an earthquake" (1991, 260-61). The text employs three verbs to describe this movement. Literally the text reads: ***It rises like the Nile, all of it; it is tossed; it sinks like the Nile of Egypt***. The succinct depiction poignantly portrays the rapid movement not only of the Nile's flooding but also of the earth's quaking. Once again the text depicts the catastrophe as all-inclusive (**whole land**, literally, ***all of it***). Similar language of both all-inclusive mourning and of the rise and fall of the Nile reappears in the final hymn of the book (9:5).

■ **9-10** The second announcement of judgment (8:9-10) depicts the reversals that will occur at the time of divine visitation. The announcement begins with the familiar phrase ***and it will happen*** **in that day** (see Hos 1:5; 2:16, 21; Joel 3:18). Mays has observed that for Amos the phrase **in that day** "is more a matter of what than when" (1969, 146; see 2:16; 8:3, 13; 9:11).

The divine announcement that follows depicts the reversal of light into darkness (8:9) and joy into grief (v 10). This reversal comes as no surprise in Amos. The hymn fragments (5:8-9; 4:13) have affirmed that the God who creatively brings light into darkness has the destructive capacity to bring darkness into light. The community that has consistently reversed justice and righteousness (see 5:7, 10; 6:12) will now come face-to-face with its covenant God who can likewise reverse his life-giving creativity to life-taking destruction. This notion of Yahweh and the day of his visitation, however, provides a sharp contrast to the popular notion of the day as one of security for and exaltation of God's people. The divine subject of the destructive action is evident throughout vv 9-10 (see the first-person verbs, **I will make**, **I will turn**, **I will make**, **I will make** in vv 9-10).

Amos utilizes the causative forms of the verbs "to go" and "to become dark" to depict Yahweh as the instigator of the coming darkness. As eclipses "were considered portents of disaster throughout the entire ancient world" (Paul 1991, 262-63), the prophet certainly may have a solar eclipse in mind (see Isa 13:10; 50:3; Joel 2:10; 3:15 [3:3-4; 4:15 HB]). A partial solar eclipse appears to have occurred in 763 B.C. and a total eclipse in 784 B.C. (see Wolff 1977, 329; Paul 1991, 262-63). However, Amos conveys something far beyond an ordinary solar eclipse in his language of darkness (see Simundson 2005, 229). His depiction embodies his understanding of the Day of Yahweh as a moment of darkness rather than light (see 5:18; also Joel 2:10 in which darkness and quaking appear together). As the prophet describes darkness that invades light at the time in which only light is present (**broad daylight**), he overturns universal expectations of light. That which no one would anticipate will become the reality. Likewise, Yahweh will do the same on the day of his visitation as he overturns all popular expectations. Indeed, the anticipated day of brilliant light will be only a day of sheer darkness.

Amos 8:10 continues to describe the divine reversal or "overturning" of ordinary expectations. Speaking directly to the Israelite people (**your**), Yahweh declares that he will reverse their feasts so that they become occasions for **mourning**. While the reference to feasts (*ḥag*) can indicate any of the communal days of celebration, it particularly refers to Israel's three great pilgrimage festivals (see Exod 23:14-17; Lev 23:1-44; Deut 16:1-17). Jubilation typically characterized these festivals as the people recalled Yahweh's deliverance at the sea, provision in the wilderness, and covenant at Sinai. However, Yahweh would now reorder them. Rather than days of robust joy, they would become days of overwhelming grief. Days of festivities in which singing is heard would become days of **mourning and *lament*** (*qînâ*, **weeping**).

As the day of despair arrives, Yahweh himself will place customary signs of mourning upon the people. The text depicts Yahweh as raising **sackcloth** upon all their loins. While the loins refer to the body's mid-part, they metaphorically indicate the seat of strength. Hence an emblem of grief will clothe the very symbol of life and vigor. Likewise, Yahweh will bring baldness upon their heads (**shave your heads**).

The closing line of Amos 8:10 depicts the people's extreme grief. The text compares their mourning to grief over the death of one's **only son** (see Jer 6:26; Zech 12:10). Through posterity, life continued; however, with the death of posterity, life would end forever. The days that follow such a loss are replete with **bitter** anguish and mourning. Previously the prophet depicted the people as turning justice and righteousness into bitter-tasting wormwood (5:7; 6:12). Through the grief and calamity of death, the people will experience the bitter fruit of their own actions. The verb **I will make** links God directly to the bitterness that will be experienced by the people.

■ **11-12** The third announcement (vv 11-12) begins with the announcement that **the days are coming**. As in vv 9-10, Yahweh's direct intervention is very clear: **I will send a famine through the land** (*ʾereṣ*). Amos previously observed the people's failure to return to Yahweh at the time of divinely appointed famines and draughts (4:6-8). While earlier famines would have evoked lamentation (e.g., Joel 1:8-15; 2:12-17), the scarcity described by Amos in 8:11-12 is not **a famine of food** or **a thirst for water**. Rather it is scarcity of **hearing the words of the LORD**.

In ancient Israel, the divine word (*dābār*) was directly associated with the office of prophet (see Amos 1:1; Hos 1:1; Joel 1:1). It is certainly possible that Amos has in mind Yahweh's removal of his prophets from Israel (see Nogalski 2011, 346). In 2:12, Amos charges that the people of Israel had "commanded the prophets not to prophesy." In 7:10, Amaziah exclaimed that the land (*'ereṣ*) was not able to endure all of Amos' words. In 7:13 the priest finally commanded Amos not to prophesy at Bethel. Ironically, after a history of shutting down the divine word, the prophet declares in 8:11 that there will be now be **a famine of . . . the words** (*dābār*) in **the land** (*'ereṣ*). Mays comments that such a famine would ultimately indicate to the Israelites that "Yahweh had turned away from them and abandoned them to their troubles" (1969, 149; see Ps 74:9; Jer 37:17; Lam 2:9; Ezek 7:26). The very thing sought by the people (i.e., absence of the divine word) would return upon them. Simundson rightly observes that "they asked God to be silent and leave them alone. In a bizarre way, their prayer will soon be answered" (2005, 230). Interestingly the text does not depict a famine of a spoken word but rather **a famine of hearing the words of the LORD**. Outside of Amos, the expression "hearing the words of Yahweh" occurs only in Jeremiah (36:11; 37:2; 43:1; see Wolff 1977, 330). For Amos, even if the people did desire to hear the divine word (see 8:12), there is no divine word to hear.

The prophet depicts the people in v 12 as staggering as if they are drunk (see also 4:8; Isa 24:20) or blind (Lam 4:14-15). The phrase **sea to sea** may refer to the Dead Sea in the south and the Mediterranean in the west; Wolff interprets the phrase more broadly "to designate the uttermost boundaries of the earth, as in Ps 72:8 and Zech 9:10" (1977, 330-31). The text also depicts the people as roaming about **(wander) from north to east**. The odd combination of **north** and **east** may be linked to the reference to **sea to sea**, a sea in the south and another in the west. Thus, the prophet portrays the people as frantically wandering all around (north, south, east, and west) in order to seek the divine word. The people of God who refused to hear the divine word throughout their history, now anxiously seek a divine response to their cry. Amos has repeatedly called upon Israel to seek Yahweh and to seek that which is good (5:4-6, 14). While the language of seeking Yahweh is common in the OT, only in 8:12 does the text refer to seeking and finding Yahweh's word. Their frantic search ends up empty (regarding the divine silence, see 1 Sam 14:37; 28:6; Ps 74:9; Lam 2:9; Hos 5:6; Mic 3:5-7). Mays expresses the scenario in which the people of God find themselves:

> They ignore the word of the Lord in their prosperity and security, but when they suffer under the wrath of God they will learn anew that what they spurned was the only source of life and they will seek it with the desperation of men with empty stomachs and parched tongues. (1969, 149)

■ **13-14** The final announcement of judgment builds upon the famine in Amos 8:11-12. For a third time, the series refers to the day of divine visitation (**in that day**). The reference to **young women** (*bĕtûlōt*) and **young men** (*baḥûrîm*) conveys images of youthfulness and vitality. Amos announces that even the strongest, those who are in the prime of their life, would faint on the day of Yahweh's visitation. In the end, **they will fall, never to rise again** (v 14). Characteristic of the prophet, Amos once again depicts the Day of Yahweh as a reversal of expectations.

Yahweh makes an oath three times in the book of Amos (4:2; 6:8; 8:7). In each instance, he swears by himself. In v 14, the prophet depicts the fate of the Israelites who take oaths by the idols they worship. Wolff has observed that for one to take an oath in the name of a deity places "oneself under the power of a god affirmed to be one who lives" (1977, 331). The text is not clear by which deity's name these persons swear (see Gowan 1996, 419). Therefore, one cannot be certain whether these persons place themselves under the power of Yahweh or another deity. The reference to the locations (Dan and Beersheba) indicates the peoples' "defection from Yahweh," who has chosen for himself Jerusalem as the place of his sanctuary (Wolff 1977, 331).

Verse 14 begins with a general description of those under judgment as **those who swear by the *shame* of Samaria**. The precise meaning of this phrase remains uncertain (see Wolff 1977, 323, note *x*; Nogalski 2011, 347; Paul 1991, 268-70). On one hand, the feminine noun *ʾašmâ* may depict ***shame*** engendered by the people's offenses against Yahweh. Comparing Amos' use of the word to such texts as Hos 4:15 and 13:1, Wolff understands the term to be consistent "with the prophetic device of injecting a note of judgment into a fictitious quotation" (1977, 332). Therefore, the reference could function as a prophetic judgment against a cultic object in Samaria, such as the calf to which Hosea refers (Hos 8:6; see Gowan 1996, 419). Likewise, the reference may be to Samaria itself, as its strongholds have provided a sense of false security to the people. Amos' frequent references to Mount Samaria (3:9; 4:1; 6:1) especially convey the pride and self-assurance of the inhabitants of the city because of its fortresses.

On the other hand, in light of the references to oath making and to the gods of Dan and Beersheba, *ʾašmâ* may refer to the proper name of a goddess related to the ancient Semitic goddesses, such as Asherah or Astarte. As Assyria resettled foreign peoples in Samaria after 722 B.C., the people of Hamath introduced the worship of Ashima into Samaria (2 Kgs 17:30). If the text is making reference to this deity, however, the reference would likely be a later editorial addition. Mays has suggested that a later editor sought to make Amos' eighth-century message contemporary with "the situation in Samaria after its resettlement by Assyrian deportees who established their own cults there" (1969, 149). Noting that Amos does not emphasize the worship of other deities, Gowan suggests that the references to Samaria, Dan, and Beersheba are all attempts to provide "additional examples of apparent piety that he sees to be no better than hypocrisy" (1996, 419).

The oaths taken by the people—**as your god lives, Dan** and ***as the way of*** **Beersheba lives**—convey the loyalty of the people to the deity whom they invoke as a living deity. Such oaths are common to the OT (see Gen 42:16; Judg 8:19; Ruth 3:13; 1 Sam 14:39; etc.). **Dan** and **Beersheba** were the northern and southern boundaries of ancient Israel (Judg 20:1). Dan's **god** could be the calf-idol set up at Dan by Jeroboam I (1 Kgs 12:29) or a deity other than Yahweh (Smith 2005, 257). The phrase the ***way of*** **(god of) Beersheba**, may mean pilgrimages made to this traditional cultic site rather than a specific deity or idol (regarding interpretations of this phrase, see Paul [1991, 271-72] and Smith [2005, 258]). In 5:5, the prophet sets Beersheba alongside the cultic sites of Bethel and Gilgal. While Amos' message primarily concerns the northern kingdom, his reference to Beersheba indicates that he has the full perimeters of a united kingdom in mind.

Amos ends his judgment word with the announcement **they will fall,** 8:13-14
never to rise again (v 14). Regardless of the piety they express through their rituals and pilgrimages, the people of Israel are destined to die. They are faced with their inevitable doom for two reasons: (1) their crimes against others in their covenant community; (2) their loyalty to gods other than Yahweh, the covenant God of Israel. Amos' words here resonate with his earlier pronouncements: ***The end has come to my people Israel*** (8:2), and "Fallen is Virgin Israel, never to rise again" (5:2).

FROM THE TEXT

Amos' indictment against the dishonest economic practices of the ruling class vis-à-vis the poor of the land have significant implications for subsequent generations. In light of the prophetic concerns over fraudulent gain and dishonest practices, the text challenges the reader to examine critically and honestly its local community and to see where such practices occur. Not only does the text call upon the prophetic community to see such practices but also to name them. Mays has accurately described the individual, community, and/or institution that participates in such practices as ones who can "see only profit and are blind to the reality of the man whom they exploit. They love the Lord less, mammon more, and their fellows not at all" (1969, 145).

The text not only calls upon its readers to see and name practices of dishonest and fraudulent gain, but it also challenges its audience to become aware of and abstain from its own inadvertent participation in such practices. In certain instances, such participation may even be indirect. Birch associates Amos' eighth-century indictments with such contemporary practices as

> misleading bait-and-switch advertising, high-pressure sales tactics, misrepresentation of inferior goods, loans made at exorbitant rates, complex credit schemes for purchase of high-price goods, high prices for doing business in the inner city, redline real estate practices. (1997, 245)

The twenty-first-century context of the reading of Amos calls the reader to hear Amos in light of global realities as well. The text compels the reader to explore how such fraudulent and self-serving political and economic realities exist and thrive globally. It not only challenges the reader to avoid firsthand participation in such practices but also moves the reader to consider how he or she might unintentionally participate in practices that dehumanize human beings around the world. Concerning Amos' challenge to the contemporary global context, Nogalski has noted that

> as long as wealthy nations take advantage of poor nations, and the wealthy within nations continue to oppress the poor, the words of Amos need to be heard. As long as problems continue to be addressed by violence that one group, rich or poor, perpetrates upon another, the words of Amos need to be heard. (2011, 351)

Even as the text challenges the reading audience to consider self-serving, dehumanizing political and economic practices, it alerts the reader to the human propensity toward the bifurcation of "sacred" and "secular." It asks the reader to consider how one might simultaneously engage in the worship of a God who delivers and in practices that imprison other human beings. How is it possible for one be "at home" in religious institutions and practices that celebrate surrendering one's life for another while concurrently being "at home" in political-economic institutions and practices that applaud gain by dehumanizing life? The text moves the reading community to examine, confess, and turn from the lack of correspondence between the God it worships and the public life it lives. Mays' question concerning those who were "respectful of religion" in Amos' day just as easily addresses many popular practices of religion in the twenty-first century (1969, 144). He asks, "What matters this keeping of holy days, this proper piety in the sight of God and man, if all the while they are straining toward the 'unholy days' when their true dedication to greed fills the time?" (ibid.).

Amos' words, "they will fall, never to rise again," are reiterated by Jesus in his teaching, "Whoever wants to save their life will lose it" (Mark 8:35). Wolff has astutely commented that "those who would gain life for themselves by oppressing the weak, by practicing deceit in the economic realm, or through cultic-political attempts to establish security will in one way or another surely lose the same" (1977, 333). Moreover, the reading audience hears reverberations of Jesus' question, "What good will it be for someone to gain the whole world, yet forfeit their soul?" (Matt 16:26). Each generation of God's people must examine itself, asking what benefit there is in securing its survival yet losing its call and purpose in the world. What has it secured if it has lost its very identity?

The text further invites the reader to imagine forms that a famine of God's word might take in the present day. Does God *ever* stop speaking, or rather, do prophets become silent and communities become deaf? Indeed, the famine depicted by Amos is not the absence of sound; it is the absence of hearing. But then the reader must ask, Why would a prophet be silent? Does the silence emerge from fear? Intimidation? Ignorance? Cooperation with outside powers? The reader must also question, How does a community of God's people become deaf? Do they refuse to listen? Have they listened for so long that they are immune to the voice? Do other voices drown out the divine voice?

The image of a famine not of bread but of hearing the word of the Lord reminds the reading audience of the declaration first in Deuteronomy and later in Jesus' pronouncement to the devil. "Man does not live on bread alone but on every word that comes from the mouth of the LORD" (Deut 8:3; see Matt 4:4). In light of Amos' unique depiction of famine and in light of a Christian theology of preaching (e.g., see Rom 10:13-15; 1 Cor 1:18-25; 2 Tim 4:1-5), the reader might rightfully associate the hearing of the divine word with the centrality of faithful proclamation. Gowan poignantly asks,

> Does the church recognize that its health and vigor, its very life, depends on one thing only—not on efficiency of organization, not on breadth of programs, not on attractiveness of sanctuaries, services, and clergy—solely on the clear and faithful preaching of the Word of God as found in Scripture? (1996, 419)

B. The Final Doxology (9:5-6)

BEHIND THE TEXT

The hymn fragment in 9:5-6 continues the language and themes present in 4:13 and 5:8-9. While the first two doxological fragments depicted both the creative and destructive power of God, the concluding fragment portrays the effect of the divine touch as the land melts and the land's inhabitants grieve. The image of the land's rising and sinking like the Nile (see 8:8) vividly conveys the effect of an earthquake. Therefore, the fragment logically follows the final vision, which depicts the scene of an earthquake (9:1). Although the cult might celebrate Yahweh's constructive powers (see "builds" and "sets" in 9:6), these powers now serve in a destructive manner as Yahweh pours the stored waters upon the land. Overall, the fragment graphically portrays the effect of the God who fixes his eyes upon the people "for harm and not for good" (9:4).

As noted in 4:13 and 5:8-9, the declaration of the divine name functions as the literary link between the hymn fragments. With the divine name at the center of the Israelite cult, Israelites who gathered for worship at Bethel, Gilgal, Beersheba, and Dan likely knew the language of the complete hymn. However, the editor's interweaving of the familiar hymnic language into prophetic declarations on unjust socioeconomic practices and flawed worship practices recontextualizes both the hymn and the much-anticipated Day of Yahweh.

The text of the first hymn fragment (4:13) declares the divine name "LORD God Almighty." The second fragment (5:8-9) declares only the divine name "LORD." The epithet of the final fragment declares Yahweh as "the Lord, the LORD Almighty." The hymn concludes in a manner similar to 5:8-9 by declaring the divine name "LORD."

IN THE TEXT

■ **5** The hymn begins with the declaration of the divine name **the Lord, the LORD Almighty**. As in the earlier hymns, the text proceeds to describe Yahweh's activities. In v 5, Yahweh is the one who **touches the *land*** **(earth)**. While the verb *nāgaʿ* can mean the simple action of physical contact, it often indicates a form of harmful striking (e.g., see Gen 26:11; Josh 9:19; 2 Sam 14:10; Jer 12:14). In other instances, it even depicts divine chastisement (1 Sam 6:9; Job 1:11; 19:21).

The word *ʾereṣ* typically denotes land itself. Hence, the hymn does not portray a final destruction of the planet Earth. Rather, the hymn depicts a cataclysmic event that occurs upon the land. The depiction of the land's melting away indicates that Yahweh's touch indeed has destructive consequences for the land (for the same image of the land's melting because of Yahweh's voice, see Ps 46:6). With language similar to Amos 8:8, 9:5 indicates that the destructive event is an earthquake (see discussion in 8:8; Gowan [1996, 422] suggests volcanic activity). Although 9:5 depicts the land as melting, the reference in 8:8 to the land's trembling further indicates seismic activity. In response to the land's melting and trembling, the inhabitants mourn (see 8:8). See 8:8 for the explanation of **the whole land rises like the Nile, then sinks like the river of Egypt**.

■ **6** In contrast to the destructive nature of Yahweh's touch upon the land in 9:5, v 6 opens with a depiction of divine construction (compare constructive/creative language in 4:13 and 5:8). As in the previous hymn fragments, the text again employs a participial verb: ***he who builds***. The **lofty palace** ("upper chambers" [NRSV]) that Yahweh constructs in the sky is literally a means of ascent or a staircase. The NIV's translation of **palace** may portray more than the hymn intended; however, Mays (1969, 155) has described these chambers as "the heavenly residence" (see Ps 104:3, 13).

The hymn poetically depicts the sky as comprised of various floors so that Yahweh has extended the divine "staircase" into the far reaches of the sky. The poem conveys the manner in which God carries out his constructive activity in the furthest reaches of the sky, and it extends his divine productivity into the deepest recesses of the land. The text affirms that Yahweh has firmly established or fixed (**sets**) **its** [i.e., the sky's] **foundation on the earth**. The NIV **foundation** ("vaults" [NRSV]) appropriately conveys the sense of that which is firmly secured or bound. The word pair **heavens** and **earth** implies the totality of created space (Gen 1:1). As the hymn moves from the highest heights to the lowest depths, it is all-pervasive in its concern.

Yahweh, who firmly constructs the expanse of creation from heaven to earth, is ironically the very one who can call for destruction. For Amos, this Creator God whom the Israelites worship is similarly the life-taking God who will judge not only the nations but his own people as well. The notion of Yahweh's creative-destructive power is consistent with the previous hymn fragments.

Repeating precisely the destructive language of 5:8, the hymn shifts from images of cataclysmic earthquake to catastrophic flood in 9:6*b*. Yahweh the Creator is indeed Yahweh the destroyer (see 5:8). With irony the hymn depicts the one who is builder as the one who calls for destructive waters. The deity who has called a community into existence can, and in this case will, call for that community's annihilation.

FROM THE TEXT

The very nature of the genre of hymn compels the reader to move from reader-observer to reader-participant. The worshipping community who sings this hymn acknowledges that it worships the God who refuses to be trapped. He will not permit his covenant people to lock him into a position of "siding" with his people. He will make his people accountable for the manner in which they have embodied covenant fidelity.

As in the previous hymn fragments, 9:5-6 strikes the reader with irony in its portrayal of the Creator God as the destroyer God. Gowan goes as far as to say that "these verses are scarcely a doxology or a creation hymn, as they have often been called, for their contents speak of nothing but destruction" (1996, 422). The hymn ultimately undergirds the prophetic conviction that the community's life-giving deity is capable of becoming their life-taking deity. The hymn fragment encourages its reading community to consider the serious nature of being in covenant with this God who is both life-giving and life-taking. It entails both joyous privilege and frightful responsibility.

Amos' hymn reminds the reader of Isaiah's Song of the Vineyard (Isa 5:1-7). Although the vinedresser carefully tends to his vineyard, it only yields corrupt fruit. Therefore, the vinedresser destroys its hedge, tramples its wall, and makes it a wasteland. Likewise, Jesus' parable of the ill-prepared servant depicts the returning master who cuts the ill-prepared servant to pieces and assigns him "a place with the unbelievers" (Luke 12:46).

The hymn is a vivid portrayal of darkness replacing light and death overtaking life. The Creator has become the destroyer. The finality of the Day of the Lord is unquestionable (see also 5:2; 8:11-14). Nevertheless, the text is clear that the final statement of the hymn is not another depiction of death. The hymn concludes with the declaration ***Yahweh is his name***. The hymn leaves the reader to ponder and to imagine just what that line actually means. Will the deity named Yahweh who has consistently declared, ***I will be whoever I will be*** (Exod 3:14), continue to be *with* and *committed to* his people? Is it possible that the one who has consistently brought existence into nonexistence will again be faithful to his character even after the finality of exile and destruction? The community that sings this hymn not only ponders and imagines but ultimately hopes.

The eighth-century prophet seems all but certain that a hopeless future awaits the people. However, the reader of the text sings the hymn's dark ending in contexts beyond the eighth century. The reader sings the hymn in the pain of exile, in the persecution by powers and principalities, in the agony of a crucified Messiah, and in a church that seeks to find its place within the empire. Is it possible that the God who creates and destroys would once again create? The concluding verses in the canonical book of Amos, whether from Amos himself or from one of those subsequent generations, would answer in the affirmative. Certainly, the people who witnessed the finality of a sealed tomb would respond, "He is risen indeed!"

C. A Leveling of Identity (9:7-10)

BEHIND THE TEXT

By means of two rhetorical questions, the prophet engages in a disputation speech with his audience in vv 7-10. The core theological conviction that informs the prophet shapes his speech: while Yahweh is in a unique covenant relationship with Israel, he is sovereign over all nations (see this foundational claim of Israel in Exod 19:5-6; see Amos 1:3—2:5). At the outset of 9:7-10, Amos takes the conviction of Yahweh's sovereignty a step further. Though Yahweh holds all nations accountable, and though he has a special relationship with Israel, Israel is not the exclusive recipient of Yahweh's deliverance. According to Amos, Yahweh has acted in the history of other nations also to bring about their liberation.

Amos, after placing Israel on a common playing field with the nations, proceeds to argue that Yahweh will likewise hold all sinful nations accountable. This accountability pertains both to Israel and to her neighbors. While v 8 does not specify a particular kingdom as the sinful kingdom, the divine judgment of all sinners, both Israelite and non-Israelite, is obvious.

IN THE TEXT

■ **7** Yahweh's first rhetorical question is intended to debunk Israel's popular attitude of a superior standing with God because of his covenant relationship with them. The question literally asks: ***Are not like the Cushites, you to me, O Israelites?*** The phrase ***you to me*** (*ʾatem lî*) is central to the prophet's question. Yahweh conveys to the Israelites that the Cushites are like ***you*** (Israel) ***to me*** (Yahweh).

Nogalski has interpreted Amos' reference to the Cushites as evoking "a sense of an exotic, faraway people—a people who would seem as far removed from Israel culturally and historically as they are geographically" (2011, 354). Although Simundson interprets Amos' reference to be "particularly humiliating" and "a serious affront" to Israel's pride, there is no textual evidence that Israel looked upon the Cushites as inferior (2005, 234). The prophet does not state specifically how the Cushites are like the Israelites to Yahweh. However, Israel's location northeast of Egypt and Cush's location south of Egypt may imply that Yahweh had acted in both nations to establish them outside of Egypt.

Cushites in the OT

Genesis 10 depicts Cush as the oldest of Ham's sons and ancestor of North African tribes (see Jer 13:23). Moses' wife was also a Cushite. Cush appears in texts as representing the furthest extent of the world (Esth 1:1; Isa 18:1; Ezek 29:10). Cush had fluctuating relationships with Egypt, and the Cushites served in the Egyptian military (see 2 Chr 12:3). Because the Greek version translated *kûš* as *Aithiopia*, English versions often translate the word as Ethiopians rather than Cushites. However, Cush likely refers to a region just south of Egypt (roughly present-day Sudan). As Cush was a source for gold (Egyptian *nub*), Nubia became an appellation for Cush.

The second rhetorical question in Amos 9:7 takes the issue of Yahweh's involvement in other nations even further than the first. Verse 7 claims that Yahweh who had brought Israel **up from Egypt** was also at work in the deliverance of the **Philistines** and **Arameans**. This statement actually comes near to bringing into "question the belief in election that was appealed to in 3:2" (Gowan 1996, 423).

In contrast to the Cushites who lived far away from Israel, the Philistines and Arameans, the neighbors of Israel, were Israel's "two great arch-enemies" (Wolff 1977, 347). Amos had already placed these two nations side-by-side in his oracles against the nations (1:3-8). However, this time they represent objects of Yahweh's care. As Paul has observed, "This symmetry creates one grand inclusion for the entire book" (1991, 283). As evident in the NIV, the text does not actually employ a verb to describe what Yahweh did for the Philistines and Arameans. However, it clearly implies that he did for these nations exactly what he had done for the Israelites in "bringing them up."

The lineage in Gen 10:14 traces Caphtor to Egypt; however, Jer 47:4 depicts Caphtor as an island. It is likely that Caphtor is the present-day island of Crete (regarding suggestions concerning the location of Caphtor, see Paul [1991, 283, note 13]). Isaiah 15:1 refers to a Moabite city by the name of Kir. In his oracles against the nations, Amos notes that the Aramean people would go into exile to Kir (1:5). In contrast, 9:7 mentions Yahweh bringing them up **from Kir**.

Verse 7, when placed within the context of the oracles against the nations (1:3-8), reiterates Amos' conviction that Yahweh is no "respecter of persons." The prophet's intent is not as much to emphasize Yahweh's deliverance of Israel's enemies but more to demonstrate that Yahweh will judge and, if necessary, destroy the very nations that he once delivered. Divine deliverance does not preclude divine judgment. In the end, Israel is no exception.

■ **8** Verse 8 begins with the particle *hinnēh* (**surely**), which introduces the divine intention to act imminently. The specific identity of **the sinful kingdom** (lit. ***kingdom of sin***) is not clear. Based upon Amos' concern with violence and injustice both outside (1:3—2:5) and within Israel (2:6-8, etc.), Gowan appropriately concludes that the phrase refers to "any kingdom whose behavior leads Yahweh to intervene as an advocate of the oppressed" (1996, 424). By placing Israel alongside Philistia and Aram, Amos implies that "Yahweh's dealing with a political entity is not determined by their election but by the norm of *sin*" (Mays 1969, 159). The word **kingdom** (*mamlākâ*) may refer more broadly to the state itself (thus Paul 1991, 284) or more narrowly to the specific ruling dynasty or king (thus Wolff 1977, 348). Amos may have in mind the temple at Bethel, the temple of the kingdom, as a temple in a kingdom of sin (see 7:13). In this ***kingdom of sin***, the temple of the kingdom provided opportunity for rebellion against Yahweh (see Amos' call, "Go to Bethel and sin," in 4:4).

In the second part of 9:8, Amos describes the devastating annihilation that will come upon the sinful kingdom. The causative form of the verb *šāmad* here conveys the notion of extermination or obliteration. Destruction **from**

the face of the earth conveys the idea of complete separation of the sinful kingdom from the ground (*ʾădāmâ*), the productivity of which humans depend on for survival (see Gen 3:17-19; 4:14).

Though Amos insists on the destruction of God's people who have become sinners, the closing line of Amos 9:8 introduces a qualifying exception. The statement begins with the negative particle ***No*** (*ʾepes*, **Yet**; see 6:10) followed by the conjunction *kî*, which qualifies or delimits the preceding declaration. The construction does not express a contradiction to the preceding statement but a reservation (see Paul 1991, 284). With the negative particle, the construction indicates that the action will not be complete or total.

In light of Amos' frequent references to Israel's eponymous ancestor (3:13; 6:8; 7:2, 5; 8:7), the phrase ***house* of Jacob** in 9:8 refers to the northern kingdom; however, the likelihood that the phrase refers to the covenant people remains. Attributing the statement to the eighth-century prophet himself, Paul concludes that Amos understands that "the *nation* of Israel (as well as all other immoral nations) shall be destroyed, but the *people* of Israel shall not be totally eradicated" (1991, 285).

Interpreters are likely correct in concluding that this line and perhaps the remaining verses are later editorial additions (see Mays 1969, 160). Perhaps in the devastation of exile or in the uncertainty of the postexilic period, such affirmations of hope became essential to the people's future. Nevertheless, the closing line of v 8 and the subsequent verses of hope are consistent with the theology of both the Former and the Latter Prophets. Exile itself would not be the final divine response.

■ **9** Verses 9-10 depict Israel's imminent destruction; however, these verses also build upon the glimpse of hope in the final line of v 8. Through the image of the sieve, the text conveys a partial but incomplete annihilation of the Israelite population (see Paul 1991, 285). Likewise, these verses anticipate the restoration described in the concluding five verses of the book.

Verse 9 announces Yahweh's imminent activity of issuing a command. As the sovereign who functions as "commander," he will cause the nations, including Israel, to tremble. The verb *nûaʿ* (**shake**; see 4:8; 8:12) conveys an action of tossing or quivering. The image of a sieve illustrates the nature and purpose behind this divinely ordered shaking. This tool functioned to separate pebbles from grain (see Paul 1991, 286; Mays 1969, 161). Though 9:9 clearly depicts the judgment of "all the sinners among" Israel (v 10), the image of a sieve seems to convey the hope for a remnant. While the sieve holds back the pebbles, the fine grain survives (regarding whether the rarely occurring word *ṣĕrôr* refers to grain or to pebbles, see Gowan 1996, 424-25; Smith 2005, 272). Wolff refers to this divine sifting as simultaneously a "punitive intervention" and a "purifying judgment" (1977, 349; see also Simundson 2005, 234-35).

In contrast, however, Mays insists that Amos' message announces historical Israel's complete annihilation without a remnant (1969, 162). He argues that the image focuses entirely upon that which catches stones (i.e., sinners) and not at all upon that which separates the good grain.

■ **10** The opening statement of v 10 is unambiguous concerning the sword's victims. The sword of judgment will kill **all the sinners among my people**. This statement preserves the covenant commitment that Yahweh has made to his people. Though Yahweh will not bring an end to the covenant community as a whole (i.e., **my people**), he will hold individuals within the covenant community accountable for their sin. Both Jer 31:29-30 and Ezek 18:1-29 express a similar theological conviction.

At the conclusion of Amos 9:10 the prophet once again employs a direct quotation of the accused (see 4:1; 6:13; 8:4, 14). Their own words demonstrate their outright rebellious character; they are overly confident that **disaster (*evil*) will not overtake** them or **meet** them along their path. Either they trust in the fortresses in which they live for their security or in the efficaciousness of their rituals at their holy places for their deliverance. They reject the prophet's warning that the Day of the Lord will be a day of disaster for Israel (see 5:18-20). Amos warns that their death is certain and there is no escape from the Day of the Lord.

FROM THE TEXT

These brief verses invite the reader to consider two significant characteristics of covenant. On one hand, while the biblical concept of covenant calls the community to love the Lord alone (see Deut 6:4-5; Matt 22:35-38), it does not confine the Lord's love to the covenant community alone. The Lord is God of all peoples and of all creation. While the Lord has exclusive claims upon the covenant community, the covenant community does not exercise a monopoly over God. Therefore, the text challenges the reading audience to consider and confess God's activity in the lives of those outside the covenant community. In ways in which the covenant people may not even be aware, God is active in the most remote and faraway places. The Lord is at work in the most-feared enemies of God's people. Indeed, as Birch has rightly noted, "God is constantly active in all human history, actualizing possibilities for life and wholeness" (1997, 253).

The text urges the reading community to imagine and to enact its divine commission vis-à-vis the nations. If indeed God is already at work bringing deliverance in the most remote and threatening places, how might the covenant people join him in those places? As all of the earth belongs to God, how might this "treasured possession" become an incarnate "kingdom of priests and a holy nation" (Exod 19:5-6; see 1 Pet 2:9-10)? In what flesh-and-blood ways do the *blessed people* become a *people of blessing* to the nations of the world (Gen 12:2-3)? The prophet's pronouncement clearly relocates the reading community from a position of superiority *over* the world to participation in the life of God *in* the world.

The text challenges the reading community to consider a second factor in relationship to covenant. Challenging the cavalier—even rebellious—denial concerning accountability to God, the text insists upon the ultimate deathly ramifications for covenant-breaking. Divine judgment is not an option in the text. In a culture and era in which businesses break covenants, governments terminate promises, and family and friends sever relationships, the reader hears of a deity who takes covenant with utmost seriousness. The text reminds subsequent generations whose identity the sacred Scripture shapes: covenant-breaking bears dire consequences.

Without the slightest compromise to the preceding conviction, however, the final canonical text also insists upon divine persistence and faithfulness to his covenant. The Lord will not completely cut his people off, nor will he cease to be their God. In spite of the prophet's multiple announcements of divine judgment, the hope for a remnant remains.

VI. EDITORIAL CONCLUSION: HOPE BEYOND JUDGMENT: AMOS 9:11-15

9:11-15

BEHIND THE TEXT

The oracles of salvation in vv 11-15 naturally emerge from the divine announcement in v 8 that Yahweh "will not totally destroy the descendants of Jacob." While sinners die by the sword, vv 11-15 understand that Yahweh fully intends to "restore," "repair," and "rebuild" that which has collapsed in Israel (v 11). He will "plant" Israel in the very land he provided for them so that they will never again be uprooted (v 15).

Scholars are in general agreement that vv 11-15 are later editorial additions. During the catastrophe following the fall of Samaria in 722 B.C. and certainly following the destruction of Jerusalem in 587 B.C., questions concerning a future for God's people emerged. Amos' unqualified message of final destruction offered no hope to the generations after the destruction of the kingdoms. Prophets living through the exile, such as Jeremiah and Ezekiel, shifted their messages from judgment to salvation following Jerusalem's destruction (see also Isa 40—66). However, as Amos does not appear to have prophesied after 722 B.C. and as he lived two centuries prior to the fall of Jerusalem, it was the responsibility of those who preserved his work to contemporize his message for a new day.

In spite of popular support for viewing vv 11-15 as subsequent editorial additions, Paul provides significant refutation to the various linguistic and ideological arguments offered (1991, 288-90). He argues that "punishment for punishment's sake is not the prophetic ideal. The prophet's chastisement is meant to serve as a transitional stage to a period of future restoration, at least for the surviving remnant" (1991, 289). Likewise Birch, who has argued that vv 11-12 are "the addition of a Judean editor during or after the Babylonian exile," keeps open the possibility that vv 13-15 emerge from the eighth-century prophet himself (1997, 258).

One can subdivide the closing verses of the book of Amos into two sections. Each of the two sections begins with phrases that anticipate imminent divine activity in the prophetic books: "in that day" and "the days are coming."

The first section (vv 11-12) envisions the restoration of the Davidic kingdom, which will ultimately extend far beyond the reaches of Israel. The ancient tradition of Yahweh's covenant with the Davidic house (dynasty) clearly informs these verses (e.g., see 2 Sam 7:11*b*-16; Pss 2:6-9; 89:3-4, 19-37; 110:1-7; 132:10-12). The references to the fallen Davidic house and the remnant of Edom in Amos 9:11-12 indicate a setting after Jerusalem's fall in 587 B.C. for these verses.

The second section (vv 13-15) imaginatively portrays the fertility, life, and security that follow the restoration of David's kingdom depicted in vv 11-12. The books of Hosea and Joel both conclude with similar images (Hos 14:4-7; Joel 3:18). The covenant theology of retributive curse and blessing (see Lev 26; Deut 28) informs the language and thought of these verses; this theology viewed fertility as the direct consequence of divine blessing.

IN THE TEXT

■ **11** Verses 11-12 anticipate Yahweh's restoration of the Davidic kingdom at an indefinite time in the future (**in that day**). The contrasting verbs ***raise up*** (**restore**) and **fallen** indicate Israel's ultimate reversal of fortunes. The ***booth*** (*sûkkāh*, **shelter**) of David is reminiscent of the temporary dwellings of boughs constructed during the harvest festival of Tabernacles/Booths (see, for example, Lev 23:42-43). The term ***booth*** is seldom applied to the house of David in the OT (see "tent of David" in Isa 16:5 [NASB, NRSV]); the most common term for the ruling family is "house" ("house of David"; see 1 Kgs 12:26; 13:2; Isa 7:2). Amos' unique choice of this term may emphasize the temporary nature of the Davidic household. As a human institution it fell just as these temporary habitations would fall, yet the text asserts that Yahweh would raise it once again. Hence, Smith interprets the image as a reference to God's ultimate restoration of that which has fallen (2005, 280-81). However, the image may function primarily to evoke the sense of security provided by such booths. Thus, Mays concludes that the image recalls "the remembered security of national life under the umbrella of David's rule and announces that freedom from fear of foes will be established again by the revival of the Davidic kingdom" (1969, 164).

Through a series of first-person verbs (**restore, repair, rebuild**), Amos 9:11 describes the action of Yahweh himself in order to resurrect that which had fallen. Yahweh promises to repair the breaches in the city wall that the invading enemy had apparently brought about (see the city wall also in 4:3). The divine construction of David's booth will return to its former glory as in the ancient days (**as it used to be**).

■ **12** According to v 12, this divine restoration has an end in mind. Ultimately, Israel will possess that which remains of both Edom and all the nations. Interpreting the concluding verses as authentic to Amos, Paul suggests that v 12 is a reference to "future rulers of the Davidic dynasty" (1991, 291). He comments that as these rulers reassert the dynasty's "authority over all the nations that formerly were under its suzerainty," the extent of the empire would ultimately recur (ibid.). The verb *yāraš* (**possess** or ***inherit***) recalls Israel's foundational story of the divine gift of land to the Israelites (see verb in 2:10; see also Gen 15:7, 8; Num 13:30; Josh 24:8; Judg 2:6). Whatever Israel might inherit in the future would indeed be the gift of God once again.

The text envisions not only a remnant of the covenant community but also survivors from the various nations. While these verses do not portray Israel's dominion over the nations, they envision the reincorporation of the territory that once belonged to the Davidic kingdom. The specific reference to a **remnant of Edom** may indicate the situation after 587 B.C. (see Mays 1969, 164). However, Paul has suggested that this remnant refers to the port at Elath, which Israel regained after previously losing it during Ahaz's reign (2 Kgs 16:6) (1991, 291).

Noting the parallelism of Edom and the nations (see also Isa 34:1-8; 63:1-6; Obad 15-21), Smith has advocated for a literary rationale for the choice of Edom; he understands the term to function as a "representative of the human race" (i.e., *ʾādam*) (2005, 281). The Septuagint translates here *anthropos*, thus reading the Hebrew text as *ʾādam* instead of *ʾĕdôm* (Edom). In the canonical arrangement of the twelve, Amos' reference to **the remnant of Edom** sets up Obadiah's message, which will depict the Israelites' dispossession of and rule over Edom (Obad 17-21). However, Amos' depiction of a remnant contrasts with Obadiah's announcement of no survivors in Obad 18 (see Gowan's refutation that Edom receives any form of promise [1996, 427-28]).

While Amos specifically mentions Edom, his concern is much more comprehensive. Throughout the book, the prophet has consistently viewed Yahweh as God of all nations (see Amos 1:3—2:8; 6:2; 9:7). The envisioned future in which the people of God would inhabit the nations is consistent with this line of thought. Paul has suggested that the phrase **all the nations that bear my name** refers to nations David had conquered and thereby became Yahweh's possessions (1991, 292). Similarly, Mays comments that v 12 depicts Yahweh's reestablishment through the Davidic kingdom of "his claim to all the nations that once had belonged to him" (1969, 163-64). The qualifying phrase **that bear my name** implies Yahweh's possession of the nations and their subsequent loyalty to Yahweh; Smith concludes that Israel's possession of nations is not a statement of doom but a "promise of blessing" (2005, 282). Based on the broader context and convictions of the book of Amos, the presence of God's people in the nations is not to be viewed as a presence of prideful nationalism but a presence of justice and blessing.

Verse 12 ends with the announcement that Yahweh himself is the one who is in the process of carrying out this act of deliverance. The restoration of Israel, Edom, and the nations is not historical coincidence; it is the work of God.

■ **13** The concluding oracle of Amos (vv 13-15) projects beyond the restoration of the Davidic dynasty and depicts the life, fertility, and peace that will ensue. As noted previously, vv 13-15 are perhaps from an exilic or postexilic editor (see Mays 1969, 166). In its final canonical form, however, the book that began with curse against the various nations concludes with a reversal of curse by announcing blessing.

Verse 13 opens with the announcement that **the days are coming**. The text describes the one who has prepared the field (**plowman**) as drawing near to the one who harvests the field (**reaper**). Likewise, the one who treads upon the harvested grapes approaches the one who first threw out the seed (**planter**). The text portrays the readiness of a fertile and abundant harvest by merging the activities of sowing and reaping. The ordinary half year lapse between planting and harvesting grain and the one- to two-month lapse between sowing and treading grapes merge as one. Gowan has observed that the text portrays a harvest in which the barley "will be so large [that] the harvesters will still be at work in October/November, when plowing for the next planting would be done" (1996, 430). Likewise, the grapes will be "so plentiful that wine making will overlap planting time" (ibid.; regarding these metaphors, see also Mays [1969, 166-67] and Paul [1991, 292-93]). The language of mountains that drip and hills that flow with sweet wine recalls the concluding declarations of Joel (see 3:18 that adds flowing milk). The **new wine** envisioned by both Joel and Amos refers to the juice that emerges from the crushing of recently harvested grapes.

■ **14** The covenant language reappears as the images of restoration and fertility continue in v 14. Yahweh declares that he will **bring . . . back** his (**my**)

people from their captivity (lit. "turn or return captivity"). The text does not specify what Yahweh will return; the direct object here (*šĕbût*) derives from the verb *šābâ* ("to take captive"). A form of this word also appears in Amos 4:10 and 9:4. In both passages, it denotes that which has been captured. The NIV interprets the word in a broad sense to depict a return from exile itself. More narrowly, however, the return is of something specific, that is, captured people or captured goods (thus "fortunes" [NRSV]).

In either interpretation, Yahweh is actively engaged in bringing back that which the enemy had taken captive. Mays describes the phrase *šûb šĕbût* as a frequently occurring formula that depicts Yahweh's "shift from wrath to mercy" (1969, 167). As a consequence of the divine shift, the people's circumstances also change. More generally, Paul has interpreted the phrase to indicate "that Israel will be restored to its former state (of well-being)" (1991, 294).

The people themselves will **rebuild** (***build***) the cities that the invaders left desolate (**ruined**) (see v 11 where Yahweh promises to "rebuild"). The text clearly envisions a reversal of 5:11. The people will not merely plant vineyards and make gardens, but they will eat and drink from their produce, also a clear reversal of 5:11. The images of 9:14 convey not only reconstruction but also rebirth and life. In a manner similar to Amos, the prophet Jeremiah also depicts rebuilt and subsequently inhabited cities, sown vineyards and subsequent drinking of the vineyards' wine, and planted gardens and subsequent consumption of the gardens' produce (29:5, 28).

■ **15** The closing verse of Amos moves beyond the repair of a dynasty, the construction of cities, and planting of gardens. While v 14 depicts humans who plant vineyards and gardens, v 15 portrays God himself who will **plant** the people of God. Verse 15 literally reads: ***I will plant them upon their soil, and they will not be uprooted again from upon their soil.*** Although the Hebrew text simply employs the third-person plural pronoun (***them***) and does not specifically mention **Israel** as does the NIV, the context is clear that the identity of Yahweh's planting is "my people" (see v 14). Yahweh himself will plant his people upon the very soil (**land**, *ʾădāmâ*) from which Yahweh had destroyed the people (v 8). The text employs three words that each begin with similar pronunciation: *nāṭaʿ* ("plant"), *nātaš* ("pluck up"), *nātan* ("give"). Yahweh who will *plant* his people in their soil will never again allow them to be *plucked up* from the soil that he has *given* them (see similar language of planting, uprooting, and building in Jer 1:10; 24:6). Amos 9:15 ends with a note that the land is the possession of Israel; nonetheless it is Yahweh's gift to his people (**I have given them**).

The concluding formula affirms the covenantal relationship of Yahweh to Israel (**says the LORD your God**). These hope-filled promises no longer "speak about" the covenant community; they directly "speak to" the covenant community. In the same manner that the reference to "my people" in v 14 recalls the covenant identity of Israel, the final word of the text, **your God**, recalls the covenant identity of Yahweh. As the restoration of Yahweh's people is complete, covenant identity is restored: "I will be your God and you will be my people" (Jer 7:23; see Hos 2:23).

FROM THE TEXT

The closing five verses of Amos breathe life-filled hope into the despair and deathliness of divine judgment. The text focuses on the future of God's restorative activity and refuses to entrust to subsequent generations a formative text that merely rehearses the sins of former generations. In the end, the message of Amos is not merely one of God's former activity but of God's forthcoming activity. The repeated first-person verbs remind the reader that tomorrow's hope emerges from God himself.

As God's future breaks in upon God's people, the faithful community begins to participate in the divine restoration not only of their own community but of the world. As they lean into the future, they have a foretaste of divinely initiated life as God himself would imagine it. Nogalski insightfully observes:

> These verses do not say "I told you so," nor do they present a homily saying, "Amos was right." Rather, they address a people humbled by circumstance, searching for a reason to put the pieces back together. They convey the message, "the story is not over." These verses assume a relationship with a faithful God and offer hope that the future will be better, that God will not abandon the promises of the past. (2011, 360)

As noted above, scholars generally and perhaps correctly agree that these closing verses may be subsequent editorial additions. Such a proposal may challenge the reading community with questions concerning the nature of Scripture itself. How would such a phenomenon influence the understanding of biblical inspiration and authority? In light of such a phenomenon, how is one to understand the "authenticity" of these verses? Are they "less" credible than the rest of the book?

The authority of any text is ultimately embodied in the shaping of a community. The activity of the Holy Spirit in and through the life of the text (i.e., inspiration) continues to occur in the rereading of the text. The Spirit of God at work in the eighth-century prophet continued to be at work in those who maintained and preached the words of Amos. That same Spirit continued to respeak and to retradition the message of Amos to generations living in exile, seeking identity in the Second Temple community, facing religious persecution under the Greek and Roman empires, and daring to confess Jesus as Messiah. The message of Amos functions at the purest level of Scripture and carries the greatest authority as it spoke and respoke to subsequent generations. Wolff rightly observes that "the conclusion of the book witnesses to the assurance that the proclamation of Amos concerning the end of Israel was not God's last word. . . . Thus the old word was no longer to be transmitted without the new" (1977, 354).

This reality of the ongoing, living, formative authority and inspiration of the text becomes particularly evident in James' speech at the gathering of the church leaders in Jerusalem (Acts 15:16-17). In his speech, James depends upon Amos 9:11-12 to demonstrate that God had ordained Paul's mission to the Gentiles. The text in Acts reveals the author's dependence upon the Greek translation of Amos rather than the Hebrew text used by translations today. James declares: "That the remnant of *mankind* may *seek* the Lord, even all the Gentiles who bear my name, says the Lord, who does these things" (Acts 15:17, emphasis added; see Amos 9:12). Whether they emerge from the eighth century B.C. or from a subsequently inspired voice, and whether they derive from the Hebrew text or from the Greek translation, the passages in both Amos and Acts comprise sacred Scripture. Through these passages, the Spirit of God was at work in forming the subsequent Christian community. Indeed, they functioned authoritatively in shaping the people of God just as they continue to do.

In fear that the closing verses might nullify Amos' indictments concerning and judgments against violence and injustice, the reader might regret their inclusion. These verses of hope and restoration in no manner nullify the message of death and judgment. However, announcing judgment simply for the sake of invoking the fear of judgment is neither the task of the prophet nor the concern of the book of Amos. Prophets sought to shape the identity and ethic of a community, not simply to frighten a community. The canonical book seeks to declare boldly divine judgment against all acts of violence and injustice. Simultaneously it seeks to engender hope in the covenant God who will tenaciously remain committed to the covenant community, to the human race, and to all creation.

The language of raising up, repairing breaches, and building as in former days is not only a consistent and coherent prophetic theology but ultimately the language of new life and the hope of resurrection. Reading the text of Amos through Christian lenses, resurrection must be the final word. The God who stepped into the dark tomb and restored life is the same God who stepped into the abyss of Assyrian defeat and the despair of Babylonian exile and spoke hope and restoration. From a Christian perspective, the message of Amos is not complete without the concluding verses.

The reading audience may be tempted to hear the concluding verses of Amos as words of exclusive parochialism, haughty nationalism, or narrow ethnocentrism. Unfortunately, the reader that stops short with such a myopic reading of Amos has heard neither the full message of the prophet nor the message of those communities that follow in the tradition of the prophet. The Lord is God of all peoples—those who are well-known and those who are a mystery, those who are friends and those who are foes. As these verses depict the nations that *bear the name* of the Lord, the Christian reader anticipates a tomorrow in which the good news of God resounds in every people group. The reading community lives into a future in which the kingdom of God has embraced and been embraced by all peoples. It lives toward the vision in which "there is neither Jew nor Gentile, neither slave nor free, nor is there male and female" (Gal 3:28). Certainly, the vision of the revelator transforms all narrow and myopic readings of this text:

> There before me was a great multitude that no one could count, from every nation, tribe, people and language, standing before the throne and before the Lamb. . . . And they cried out in a loud voice, "Salvation belongs to our God, who sits on the throne, and to the Lamb." (Rev 7:9-10)

In his speech to the first-century Christian leaders, James clearly heard Amos through such lenses (see above). He perceived what Amos also knew: the Lord entered into a unique covenant with a community in order that this community might become the means of divine blessing to the world. The dreams and hopes of this community are not for its own salvation or exaltation but for the salvation and life of the world and all creation.

OBADIAH

INTRODUCTION

A. Obadiah the Prophet

The brief book of Obadiah, including the superscription, provides no information concerning the prophet's background, provenance, family, or historical setting. The name Obadiah ("servant of Yahweh") occurs numerous times in the OT along with its variant, Obed; therefore, the name appears to have been quite common. At a much later date, the Babylonian Talmud depicts Obadiah as one of King Ahab's servants who provided protection for Elijah (see 1 Kgs 18:3-16). However, the separation between the ninth century B.C. and the sixth-century B.C. situation reflected in the book of Obadiah makes the historical certainty of this tradition questionable.

The opening line following the superscription concisely informs the reader that the book contains Yahweh's sayings concerning the nation of Edom. Based on historical and geographical references in the book, the prophet was well aware of the Babylonian conquest of Jerusalem in 587 B.C. and of Edom's jubilant celebration of Jerusalem's fall. References within the text also indicate that the prophet was likely aware of Edom's downfall or imminent downfall (see discussion of historical context below).

B. The Historical Context and Audience of Obadiah

Although it is possible to understand the book of Obadiah as reflecting Edom's rebellion against Judah during the reign of Joram in the ninth century B.C. (2 Kgs 8:20-22), the book is much more likely a reflection of the situation following the fall of Jerusalem in 587 B.C. when Edom occupied the Negev (Wolff 1986, 18-19; for various scholarly suggestions concerning the historical context, see Raabe 1996, 47-56). Similar to curses against surrounding nations in various prophetic texts, Obadiah's depiction of Edom's imminent downfall reflects the popular anticipation of Yahweh's judgment upon Judah's enemies. It is certainly possible that Obadiah "saw" Edom's disastrous future on the horizon with either the military campaign of Nabonidus of Babylon in 552 B.C. or the Nabatean invasions of Edom in the second half of sixth century (Nogalski 2011, 385).

The history and tradition of Israel and Judah's relationship with Edom informs the historical depictions in the text. Edom was located just south of the Dead Sea in the Transjordan. Ancient Israelite tradition viewed Edom as Israel's "brother" as it traced the lineage of the nations back to Jacob/Israel and his firstborn twin brother Esau/Edom (see Gen 36; Deut 2; see filial language of the nations in Gen 25; 27; Num 20:14-21; Deut 2:4-8; Jer 49:7-11; Amos 1:11-12; Mal 1:2-4). The reddish color of soil in Edom engendered various etiologies related to Esau, including Gen 25:25, 30. Throughout the histories of the two nations, Israel and Edom shared a unique sociopolitical relationship of both camaraderie and hostility.

The Edomites appear to have settled in their land around 1300 B.C., perhaps just shortly before the Hebrews settled in Canaan. As anticipated in the etiology of the twins' struggle in their mother's womb (Gen 25:22-26), the nations were often hostile to each other. Various acts of animosity between the two nations occur throughout the biblical text (e.g., see Num 20:14-21; 1 Sam 14:47; 2 Sam 8:13-14). From Judah's perspective, this animosity reached its climax during the Babylonian assault on Jerusalem in 587 B.C. as Edom neglected its "covenant of brotherhood," encouraging and benefiting from Jerusalem's destruction (see Isa 21:11-17; Jer 49:7-22; Amos 1:11-12). Psalm 137 particularly recalls Edom's antagonistic attitude toward Jerusalem at the time of the city's fall (v 7). Although we cannot be certain, it is possible that Obadiah was present in Jerusalem or its vicinity to witness both Edom's passive-aggressive action vis-à-vis Jerusalem as well as to see the aftereffects of 587 B.C.

The historical context of Obadiah clearly establishes the nature of the prophet's audience: Edom and the remnant of Jerusalem. After the opening statement concerning Edom in v 1, vv 2-16 consistently and repeatedly employ the second-person pronoun (you) in direct address to Edom. The text does not specify, however, whether the prophet is speaking to the national identity of Edom, to the general populace of Edom, or to the Edomite leaders. As the text shifts to the depiction of Zion's restoration in v 17, the second-person pronoun drops out entirely. One might understand Edom as the audience that now "overhears" the statements concerning Yahweh's restoration of Jerusalem. While Edom is the primary focus of the book of Obadiah, undoubtedly the book also understands that the people of God in Jerusalem and beyond are a secondary audience that "overhears" Obadiah's message of divine vindication on behalf Judah.

C. The Book of Obadiah as a Literary Work

1. Genre

In its judgment upon Edom, the full text of Obadiah is similar in form and function to oracles against the nations found in other prophetic texts (Amos 1—2; Isa 13—23; Jer 46—51; Ezek 25—32). The genre of prophetic oracle of judgment and curse against the nations likely reflects a customary prophetic practice in ancient Israel carried out at cultic festivals in anticipation of Yahweh's triumph over Israel's enemies. Edom frequently appears in these curses (Amos 1:11-12; Isa 21:11-12; Jer 49:7-22; Ezek 25:12-14; Mal 1:2-5).

Raabe (1996, 7) has suggested that "the book of Obadiah moves gradually from pure poetry through v 15 to slightly more prosaic poetry in vv 16-18, followed by pure prose at the end." The purpose of this transition, however, is not clear. In contrast to Raabe's suggestion, the full book may be comprised of "six short poems in chiastic form."

2. The Development of the Text and the Relationship to Other Prophetic Texts

Two significant issues are important to our consideration of the development of the text of Obadiah. The first concerns the relationship of the book to other prophetic books with which Obadiah shares similarities in language and thought (for extensive analysis of similarities, see Allen 1976, 140-43). Obadiah 1-6 shares word-for-word similarities with Jer 49. In his extensive analysis of both texts, Renkema has suggested that Obadiah concluded that Jeremiah's earlier prophecy concerning Edom would be fulfilled imminently. Thus, according to Renkema, Obadiah understood himself as being "one with Jeremiah, the first to hear this divine message, in terms of prophetic succession" (2003, 117; see also Raabe 1996, 22-31). While it is certainly possible that Obadiah may have taken the oracle from Jeremiah or vice versa, it is also possible that both texts were dependent upon material in existence within prophetic and/or cultic settings (see Stuart 1987, 415-16). Likewise, it is possible that the similarity between the two texts is the result of subsequent editorial activity.

In addition to the direct correlation between the texts in Obadiah and Jeremiah, Obadiah shares similarities with other prophetic texts, including

Amos 9 and Malachi's depiction of divine retribution upon Edom in 1:2-5 (see Nogalski 2011, 371-72, 377-79). Because of the various similarities with other prophetic texts, Limburg has referred to Obadiah as "a skillful and imaginative interpreter of the older prophetic tradition" (1988, 128). While the book of Obadiah shares a significant amount of material with Joel (Obad 11 in Joel 3:3; Obad 15 in Joel 1:15; Obad 16 in Joel 3:17; Obad 18 in Joel 2:5; Obad 21 in Joel 2:32), the book of Joel characteristically employs texts from and allusions to various prophetic books (→ Introduction to Joel; see, however, Pagan's suggestion [1996, 436] that Obad 1-14 provides commentary on Joel 3:19 [4:19 HB] while Obad 15-21 provides commentary on Amos 9:12).

The second matter concerning the development of the Obadiah text regards its compositional history (concerning compositional levels, see a thorough analysis in Nogalski [2011, 368-76] and Raabe [1996, 14-18]). It is possible that an original text of Obadiah composed shortly after Jerusalem's fall in 587 B.C. consisted of vv 2-14, 15*b*. Subsequently the military campaigns of Nabonidus of Babylon in 552 B.C. or the Nabatean assault on Edom in the second half of the sixth century might have engendered the addition of vv 15*a*, 16-18 (or vv 15*a*, 16-21; regarding the unity of the book, see Achtemeier [1996a, 240-41] and Pagan [1996, 438-39]). However, one cannot confirm these two levels of the text with certainty.

3. Movement and Structure of the Book

The progression of thought in the book of Obadiah moves from judgment against Edom in vv 2-9 to a depiction of crimes committed by Edom in vv 10-14. The statement concerning the Day of the Lord in v 15 functions as a "hinge" as the book moves into a depiction of the results of the divine visitation upon both the nations and the people of God in vv 16-21. As these concluding verses extend beyond the historical realities of divine judgment upon Edom for its crimes against Jerusalem, they reflect a more general, even eschatological, depiction of divine judgment upon the nations of the world (see Pagan's suggestions [1996, 439] of a chiasm comprised of six poems in Obadiah). Based upon this general movement within the book of Obadiah, the commentary will follow the following structural outline:

I. Edom's Judgment and Destruction (vv 1-14)
 A. Announcement of Judgment (vv 1-4)
 B. Edom's Destruction (vv 5-9)
 C. Rationale for Judgment (vv 10-14)
II. Judah's Salvation (vv 15-21)
 A. The Day of the Lord (vv 15-16)
 B. Zion's Restoration (vv 17-18)
 C. Prose Conclusion (vv 19-21)

D. Theological Themes

1. The Day of the Lord and the Nature of Judgment

While the literary and theological "hinge" of the book in v 15 does not introduce a new theological concept, it certainly provides one of the clearest expressions of the Deuteronomic-prophetic notion of divine judgment. For the prophets, Yahweh's judgment is neither arbitrary nor capricious. As the prophets perceive judgment or retribution, the life that a community lives will ultimately come back upon that community (e.g., see Hos 8:7; 10:12-13; Amos 4:1-3; 5:11; 6:4-7). The seed that a community sows will produce a specific and concrete harvest. This theological conviction informs the Deuteronomic understanding of life and death (see Deut 30:15-20) and the prophetic perception of divine judgment (e.g., Hos 8:7; 10:12-13; Amos 4:1-3; 5:11; Mic 2:1-5; 3:5-7; 6:10-15). However, the conviction also clearly informs wisdom's understanding of the two paths and the final destination of each (Ps 1; Prov 4:10-19; 7—8). For wisdom particularly, this conviction is grounded in a theology of creation and order. Obadiah moves beyond the agricultural metaphor of planting and reaping to a succinct, almost proposition-like, statement in v 15: "As you have done, it will be done to you; your deeds will return upon your own head." Obadiah links this conviction directly to the divine visitation upon a nation or a group of people, that is, the Day of Yahweh. While other prophets speak of this day in relationship to Israel and the surrounding nations (e.g., Joel 1:15; 2:1; Amos 5:18, 20; Zeph 1:7, 14), Obadiah presents an unambiguous theological understanding of why specific forms of destruction will occur on that day; that is, because those forms reflect the "form of life" of the community that Yahweh visits. The day of divine visitation thus stands in direct correlation to the life lived by the community.

2. Yahweh as Lord of the Nations, Covenant Partner, and Vindicator

As all of the prophetic oracles against the nations demonstrate (e.g., Isa 13—27; Jer 46—51; Ezek 25—32; Amos 1—2), Obadiah's judgment against Edom clearly reveals the conviction that Yahweh is not merely the covenant God of Israel and Judah but is the Lord of all nations. The language in Obad 21 recalls the consistent theme of Yahweh's cosmic sovereignty found not only in prophetic oracles against the nations but also in the psalter's enthronement hymns (e.g., Pss 47; 93; 96-99).

While the text of Obadiah clearly recognizes the sovereignty of Yahweh over all nations, it also is committed to the understanding of a unique relationship that exists between Yahweh and Israel/Judah. Within the context of this unique relationship, Yahweh not only acted as the covenant community's deliverer and provider in the past but will continue to deliver his people from oppression and to provide protection for and vindication on behalf of his people. If one inaccurately understands Obadiah's words to be declarations of personal, hate-filled revenge, the text is capable of erroneously legitimating acts of hatred and violence. Just as the theological context of Yahweh as covenant vindicator is essential to an appropriate understanding of the imprecatory psalms that plea for divine vengeance (e.g., Pss 69; 109; 137; 139), so this context is essential to an appropriate theological reading of Obadiah. As Israel's covenant deity, Yahweh had committed himself to protect and defend his people from those who seek their destruction. Because Edom had acted violently and without compassion toward Yahweh's covenant people, Yahweh announces his determination to vindicate his people who are under his care and protection.

COMMENTARY

BEHIND THE TEXT

The genre of the book of Obadiah reveals the primary function of the text (→ Introduction). As an oracle of curse, it denounces Edom for its crimes against God's people and announces Yahweh's imminent judgment upon the Edomites. Israel's prophets spoke the divine word not only to Israel but to all nations. In contrast, Obadiah speaks out solely against Edom (see also Nahum's accusation against Assyria). However, even Obadiah generalizes the accusation in vv 15-16 and broadens it in vv 19-20.

Similar to the judgment oracle, the curse against nations is comprised of two primary elements: (1) the rationale for judgment (i.e., depiction of specific sins); (2) the judgment proper. The judgment against the nations theologically assumes both the sovereignty of Yahweh over all peoples and the unique nature of Israel as Yahweh's covenant people. Based upon the latter assumption, oracles against neighboring nations tend to climax with an announcement of Yahweh's ultimate salvation and elevation of his covenant people (Obad 15-21; Isa 24—27; Ezek 36—48).

Though Obadiah was most likely familiar with the Jacob-Esau narrative and the long history of animosity between the nations, Edom's response to Judah at the time of Babylon's invasion in 597 and 587 B.C. is foremost in the prophet's thinking. As the Babylonians invaded the city of Jerusalem, looted its valuables, exiled its citizens, and destroyed its temple, Edom stood by and refused to assist its "brother." Even more, Edom appears to have encouraged the Babylonian destruction of Jerusalem, perhaps even participating in it (see Ps 137; Isa 21:11-17; 34:5-6; Jer 49:7-22; Lam 4:21-22; Ezek 25:12; 35:3, 15; Joel 3:19 [4:19 HB]; Amos 1:11-12).

Edom likely survived the Babylonian onslaught for a few more decades, perhaps seeing its own demise under Nabonidus' campaigns in the second half of the sixth century B.C. (perhaps depicted in Obad 1, 7; see Bartlett 1992, 293). As late as Malachi in the mid-fifth century B.C., the people of God questioned Yahweh's relationship to the Edomites, and they consequently debated their own relationship to the inhabitants of Edom's former territory (Mal 1:3-4).

I. EDOM'S JUDGMENT AND DESTRUCTION: OBADIAH 1-14

A. Announcement of Judgment (vv 1-4)

IN THE TEXT

■ **1** Verse 1 begins a superscription that introduces the content of the book as **the vision** [*ḥăzôn*] **of Obadiah**. The word "vision" also occurs in the superscriptions of Isaiah and Nahum; in all these instances the word refers to the content of the prophetic books and not to the process by which these prophets have received their message from God. In contrast to many other prophetic books, the text provides no personal information concerning the prophet (e.g., his location, time period, name of father).

The prophetic proclamation begins with the typical messenger formula. The one who speaks the message is the Lord Yahweh or **the Sovereign LORD** (*ʾădōnāy yĕhwih*). The preposition *lĕ* could be understood either as "to" or "about"; thus, the message is ***to Edom*** or **about Edom**. The latter seems to be the case here.

The opening verses in Obadiah share numerous direct similarities with Jeremiah's oracle against Edom in 49:14-16. Obadiah 1*b* introduces the initial oracle (vv 1*b*-4) as **a message** that **we have heard**. The referent of the plural pronoun **we** is not clear (contrast singular pronoun "I" in Jer 49:14). Though the pronoun may refer to the people of Judah or to a prophetic group within Judah, it is also likely that the prophet may be conveying here what he heard as a participant in the divine council (e.g., 1 Kgs 22:19-23; Isa 6:8; see Nogalski 2011, 383; Renkema 2003, 117). Renkema interprets the plural to be the prophet's reference to himself and to Jeremiah, thereby "protecting himself against accusations of prophetic plagiarism" (2003, 117). The reference to **the nations** may even imply that the plural pronoun is simply a broad, perhaps universal, audience that is called to arms against Edom.

Yahweh's message comes through **an envoy**, perhaps the prophet, that **was sent** by Yahweh to call **the nations** for an "international" uprising or **battle** against the Edomites. The term *ṣîr* (**envoy**; also found in Jer 49:14) is uncommon in the OT (see the use of *mal'āk* [messenger] for prophets in Isa 42:19; 44:26; Hag 1:13; Mal 3:1).

■ **2-4** Obadiah 2-4 poetically depicts the collapse of once-mighty Edom as the nations heed the call in v 1*b*. In vv 2 and 4*b*, the oracle provides a frame or inclusio of Edom's assured fall. Within that frame, vv 3-4*a* employ numerous images of loftiness, self-security, and exaltation. These verses depict Edom as dwelling **in the clefts of the rocks** and **on the heights**, questioning who can bring them **down to the ground**, soaring **like the eagle**, and making their **nest among the stars**.

With the exception of the concluding words, v 2 replicates Jer 49:15 word-for-word. Obadiah 2 begins with a second-person address (**you**) that is continued through v 16. The goal of the battle against Edom is to make it **small among the nations** (v 2*a*). As a result, Edom will be regarded by the nations as an utterly **worthless** nation, a nation with no value in the eyes of its neighbors.

According to vv 3-4, the nation that boasted with pride that no one can bring it down finds an unexpected enemy who is able to bring down the nation that lived **in the clefts of the rocks** and **soar**ed **like the eagle**. The Edomites have settled and made their homes in **the clefts of the rocks** (*sela'*). The word *sela'* is the name of an Edomite stronghold (2 Kgs 14:7), so that the text could read ***the clefts of Sela***. The term is also a generic reference to the mountainous cliffs that provide secure dwelling for animals and humans alike. **Make your home on the heights** is parallel to **live in the clefts of the rocks**.

The prophet continues his emphasis upon the Edomites' pride and self-exaltation in v 4 by comparing them with eagles that **soar** far into the sky and build their **nest among the stars** (see variant in Jer 49:16). In comparing Edom to these mighty fowl, the author may have had several traits in mind: the height at which they fly, their large size, their feeding on prey, and perhaps their tendency to build nests in secluded locations (see Pagan 1996, 447). In this comparison with the eagle, **soar** is an appropriate translation of the verb *gābâ*, though literally the verb means "to be high" or "exalted."

In v 3, the prophet mentions Edom's **heart** (*lēb*) twice. Wolff describes Edom's heart as the nation's "self-awareness and the bearings from which it lives" (1986, 48) while Jenson describes it in terms of "the core of the personality that guides behavior" (2008, 13). Thus, within their own corporate "self-awareness," the Edomites engage in a dialogical soliloquy (**say to yourself**) as they question: **Who can bring me down to the ground?** The prophet portrays this corporate consciousness (i.e., *lēb*) as moved by arrogant **pride** (*zādôn*; see Jer 49:16; 50:31-32). The self-sufficient arrogance of Edom's communal *will* actively enticed or **deceived** Edom into a false sense of self-sufficiency. In spite of their illusionary self-perception, however, this self-exalted community will find itself brought down **to the ground**.

B. Edom's Destruction (vv 5-9)

■ **5-9** Verses 5-9 show similarities to Jer 49:7-11. Both texts portray the utter destruction and complete pillaging of Edom (Jer 49:9-10; Obad 5-6). Even Edom's traditional wisdom ceases to exist (Jer 49:7; Obad 8). However, the statements concerning the betrayal of **allies** and **friends** in v 7 are unique to Obadiah. Obadiah's emphasis upon the rejection by its allies prepares the way for the prophet's depiction of Edom's/Esau's betrayal of his brother Jacob in the subsequent section (vv 10-14).

Verses 5-9 vividly portray the fallout of the divine visitation upon Edom. In v 5, the prophet contrasts the activities of **thieves** and **grape pickers** with the fate of Edom. **Thieves** steal **only as much as they wanted**. They steal at nighttime when no one can see them. Still they exercise restraint. In the same way, grape pickers are known for leaving **a few grapes** for those who glean the vineyard after the harvest (see Lev 19:9-10; Deut 24:21). The prophet's lament over Edom, **Oh, what a disaster awaits you**, indicates that there will be no sparing of anything of Edom; its destruction will be total.

Obadiah 6 gives more details on Edom's destruction. Invaders of Edom will ransack and pillage the **hidden treasures** of Edom. For the first time in the book, the prophet refers to Edom by the name of its patrimonial ancestor **Esau** (see also vv 8, 9; Jer 49:8, 10). This reference anticipates the prophet's discourse on the breakdown of brotherhood in Obad 10-14.

Verse 7 announces that no will come to the aid of Edom when it is under attack. Neither **allies** (those with whom Edom had a covenant) nor **friends** (those with whom Edom had peaceful relation) nor **those who eat your bread** (those who depended on Edom for economic assistance) will provide aid. In fact, these once-trustworthy friends will become deceitful betrayers. They themselves will become pillaging enemies. Edom will experience from the nations what Judah had experienced from Edom.

The precise meaning of the phrase **force you to the border** is not clear. The text may indicate the expulsion of the Edomites from the boundary of their land. Jenson thinks the phrase refers to the Edomite refugees being sent back to the "borders of Edom" by Edom's former allies who refused to give them asylum (2008, 16; see also Renkema 2003, 141-44).

The concluding statement of v 7, **but you will not detect it**, suggests the total lack of wisdom on the part of the Edomites to perceive the actions of their former allies and friendly neighbors. The idea is reiterated in v 8, which deals with the disappearance of the wise people (*ḥăkāmîm*) from Edom.

Edom and Wisdom

Edom is believed to have been a center of ancient Near Eastern wisdom. Jeremiah speaks of Edom's wisdom (*ḥokmâ*), counsel (*ʿēṣâ*), and understanding (*bîn*) in 49:7. Each of these terms is at home within the Israelite wisdom tradition. The apocryphal wisdom book of Baruch reflects a similar tradition associating Edom (Teman, see v 9 below) with wisdom (Bar 3:22-23). Job's reference to "the east in the land of Uz" may set Job in Edom as well (Lam 4:21 depicts the daughter of Edom living "in the land of Uz"). Among Job's three companions who represent traditional wisdom thought, the most prominent, Eliphaz, is from Teman (Job 2:11; 4:1; 15:1, etc.).

Obadiah 8 begins with a veiled reference to the Day of Yahweh (**in that day**). Yahweh announces that he will cause **the wise men** [*ḥăkāmîm*] **of Edom** and the ***men*** **of understanding** [*tĕbûnâ*] **in the mountains of Esau** to ***perish*** (*ʾābad*, **destroy**). Jenson is likely correct in interpreting the **understanding** as a reference not merely to wisdom in general but to the "failure of political and diplomatic skills" (2008, 17).

Verse 9 describes the fate of warriors and those who lived in the safety of **Esau's mountains**. According to Obadiah, just as the **wise** will perish, so the **warriors** will be utterly dismayed (**terrified**). The text depicts the warriors as being from Teman. Obadiah may be employing **Teman** as a synonym for Edom (see Jer 49:7, 20), though elsewhere Teman appears as a city or a region within Edom (Amos 1:12). In Esau's genealogy (Gen 36:9-11), Teman is the son of Eliphaz and thus the grandson of Esau.

The statements concerning **Esau's mountains** in both Obad 8 and 9 refer to the mountainous terrain of the region. These mountains provided safety and a sense of security for the Edomites. Obadiah announces the enemy nations' slaughter of those who once thought of themselves as unassailable.

C. Rationale for Judgment (vv 10-14)

■ **10-14** The often-repeated phrase **you should not** in vv 12-14 depicts the primary theme of vv 10-14. The repetition is even more pronounced in the Hebrew text (the negative particle *ʾal* appears eight times in vv 12-14). In seven of these instances, he ends statements with the phrase **in the day of** (*bĕyôm*). In these statements, the prophet describes the day as **misfortune** (v

12*a*), **destruction** (v 12*b*), **trouble** (vv 12*c*, 14*b*), and **disaster** (v 13*a*, *b*, *c*). Through this series of indictments against Edom for its crimes against Judah, the prophet emphasizes Edom's broken oath of brotherhood.

Verse 10 indicates that shame and destruction will come upon Edom because of its violence against his brother Jacob. Edom **will be covered with shame** and it **will be destroyed forever**. The once lofty and arrogant nation will cover itself with shame and disgrace. **Destroyed forever** suggests the cessation of its very existence; the phrase may also mean Edom's exclusion from the neighboring nations. Edom's shame and isolation will be permanent or **forever** (*lĕ ʿôlām*).

In vv 11-15, the word **day** appears eleven times. While most of the references refer to the Edomites' specific actions at the time of Babylon's pillage of Jerusalem, the text reaches its climax with the divine activity on the **day of *Yahweh*** (v 15). In the MT the phrase **on the day** appears twice: the day when Edom stood afar or **aloof** from the people of God and the day when **strangers** [*zûr*] **carried off** Jerusalem's might (**wealth**). Up to this point in the text, Edom was the guilty bystander who watched the crime take place but did not directly participate in the crime. However, in the closing line of v 11, that scenario changes dramatically. The accusation, **you were like one of them**, identifies Edom as an active participant in the crime itself.

As noted above, the prophet proceeds to carry out a series of eight **you**
10-14 **should not . . .** statements in vv 12-14. The negative particle *ʾal* followed by the jussive verb creates a direct prohibition. Therefore, the repeated phrases are negative imperatives (thus, ***Do not*** . . .). These prohibitions outline a proper code of conduct for brothers; obviously, Edom violated all these prohibitions. Thus, the prohibitions serve here as indictment against Edom.

Obadiah's first negative command**, *do not* gloat over your brother in the day of his misfortune** indicates that Edom displayed prideful disdain and joy over the calamity that came upon Jerusalem. The reference to **your brother** assumes the Jacob-Esau narrative. The nations descended from these brothers were to embody the shared covenant of brotherhood.

Obadiah's second prohibition indicts Edom for rejoicing **over the people of Judah in the day of their destruction**. Similarly, the third prohibition implies that the Edomites opened ***their mouths wide* in the day of their trouble**. The image of opening one's mouth wide is a euphemism for the audacious display of pride and mocking triumph (Renkema 2003, 176). All three of the opening negative imperatives dictate against self-satisfaction and maltreatment of a brother through disdain, rejoicing, and prideful boasting.

In v 13*a*, the fourth command directs Edom not to **march through the gates of my people in the day of their disaster**. Here Obadiah indicts Edom for its direct involvement in the tragedy that came upon Judah. For the first time in Obadiah, the prophet draws upon the familiar covenant language **my people** (i.e., "I will be your God and you will be my people" [Jer 7:23]; → Hos 1:9; 2:1, 23). Edom has not simply mistreated another nation; Edom has transgressed the boundaries of the people who are in a unique covenant with Yahweh.

The fifth command (v 13*b*) conveys the same idea expressed in v 12*a*. Again, the indictment is against Edom's disdain and lack of compassion for Judah. In the sixth prohibition (v 13*c*), the prophet directs Edom not to **seize their wealth in the day of their disaster**. **Wealth** here perhaps includes both material resources as well as military strength. The prohibition implies Edom's participation in the crime of seizing Judah's wealth, committed by the invading forces (see v 11).

In the seventh command (v 14*a*), the prophet prohibits Edom from standing (*ʿāmad*) **at the crossroads** in order **to cut down their fugitives**. The prophet previously accused Edom of standing (*ʿāmad*) aloof during Judah's calamities (v 11); however, now he locates Edom within the distress itself. The Edomites are active participants in the crime. The **fugitives** are those who have tried to escape from destruction. Verse 14 ends with the fate of the survivors; Edom handed them over to the invaders.

II. JUDAH'S SALVATION: OBADIAH 15-21

A. The Day of the Lord (vv 15-16)

■ **15-16** The hinge of the book of Obadiah is vv 15-16. The Day of Yahweh is the focus of these verses. Obadiah begins with the announcement that this day is **near for all nations** (v 15*a*). In vv 15*b*-16, the prophet describes this day as a day of reaping that which a nation has sown. Thus, it was not an arbitrary day of divine punishment. It was the result of and directly related to the specific actions committed by a people. Simundson articulates this conviction in his observation that "though God rewards and punishes, Edom has already determined its own fate by its behavior. Actions have consequences" (2005, 248).

Verse 16 employs the familiar image of drinking from the cup of divine wrath. While the second-person singular pronoun ("you") in the opening verses of the book referred to Edom, the text is not precisely clear as to whom the second-person plural pronoun refers in v 16. Within the broader context of the book itself, it is likely that the speech is directed to Edom. Edom's drinking on Mount Zion in celebration of Judah's defeat will come back upon their own heads by the actions of other nations (see Craigie 1984, 206; Sweeney 2000, 294; Jenson 2008, 23-24). However, if Judah is intended by the second-person reference, as some commentators think, then the prophet may be saying that just as Judah has already drunk from the cup of Yahweh's wrath through the destruction of Jerusalem, Edom and the other nations will now drink from that same cup (see Limburg 1988, 133-34; Wolff 1986, 63-65; Barton 2001, 151-52; Nogalski 2011, 389; Renkema 2003, 190-98).

B. Zion's Restoration (vv 17-18)

■ **17-18** Verse 17 presents **Mount Zion** as the place of **deliverance** for the people of Judah who were mocked and attacked by Edom. Deliverance in **Mount Zion** provides a sharp contrast to the destruction of the "mountains of Esau" (vv 8-9). Mount Zion is the dwelling place of the holy God of Israel; though it was attacked and pillaged by the enemy, it will once again become **holy** (*qōdeš*, "set apart") to the people of Yahweh as the place of their deliverance.

In the remainder of vv 17-18, the prophet seems to be focusing on the restoration of the northern kingdom (***house of Jacob, house of Joseph***). Although Jacob functions as the eponymous ancestor of the northern kingdom, the term can refer to the united kingdom (see Jenson 2008, 24; Amos 3:13; 9:8; Mic 2:7; 3:9). However, it is possible that ***house of Jacob*** here is Judah and ***house of Joseph*** the northern Israel; if this is the case, Obad 18 conveys the hope for a reunited Israel (see Renkema 2003, 205). Joseph fathered the two powerful northern tribes of Ephraim and Manasseh; Ephraim gained preeminence among the northern tribes and became a representative of the northern kingdom (see Hosea, where "Ephraim" is a synonym for "Israel").

The last line of v 17, **Jacob will possess his inheritance**, literally reads in the Hebrew text as follows: ***the house of Jacob will possess the ones who possessed them*** (see NRSV). The verb *yāraš* ("take possession of" or "inherit") occurs twice in the verse. In the first instance, the house of Jacob *possesses*. In the second instance, the verb appears as a plural participle. It indicates that the house of Jacob is *possessed* by another, presumably Edom. Therefore, Edom not only loses what it has but loses back to Israel what it had previously taken from Israel.

The prophet makes a threefold reference to ***house of*** in v 18: houses of **Jacob**, **Joseph**, and **Esau**. Using images of burning (**fire** and **flame**), Obadiah depicts the manner in which Israel will turn back upon Edom. Within these images, the houses of Jacob and Joseph will burn and devour the house of Esau. As a result, Edom will become nothing more than **stubble**. In contrast to Jerusalem's "survivors" handed over by Edom (v 14), no Edomite will survive the ravaging fires of Jacob and Joseph. Using the causal particle *kî* (***for*** or ***because***), the prophet states the cause of Israel's rise and Edom's fall. Edom's destruction is not a matter of historical coincidence. Its demise is the result of Yahweh's spoken word (**The Lord has spoken**).

C. Prose Conclusion (vv 19-21)

■ **19-21** The unusual nature of vv 19-21 may indicate that the text originally occurred in prose rather than poetry (see Allen 1976, 168-72; Wolff 1986, 65-68). In vv 19-20, Obadiah expands the restoration to include both Israel and Judah. These verses begin and end with a reference to the southern territory of **the Negev**. The verb *yāraš* ("possess," "dispossess," or "inherit") appears three times in vv 19-20. The southern territory of Judah (**the Negev**) will dispossess (*yāraš*, **occupy**; see v 17) Mount Esau. Consistent with vv 8, 9, and 21, the NIV translates the plural **the mountains of Esau** although the Hebrew text uses the singular mountain. The southwestern territory of Judah, the Shephelah (**the foothills**) will dispossess the Philistines along the Mediterranean coast. This southern section of hills and valleys divided Judah's hill country from the Mediterranean coastal plains. Because of its strategic location, it served as a defensive zone from the Philistines on the coast. For both the Negev and the foothills, the NIV adds **people from**, a phrase lacking in the Hebrew text.

Again employing the verb *yāraš*, the text states that they will ***possess* the fields of Ephraim and *the field of* Samaria**. The subject of the verb ***possess*** is not stated; however, it is likely the reference is to the inhabitants of the Negev and the Shephelah. In other words, those who inhabit the south will move northward. Such a movement is evident in the text as **Benjamin** possesses the mountainous region in Transjordan known as **Gilead**. Although southern Gilead was apportioned to the northern tribes of Reuben and Gad, Israel did not maintain control over it. Rather, it corresponded to the kingdoms of Moab and Ammon. Although contested by both the Arameans and the Ammonites, northern Gilead remained a part of the tribe of Manasseh until the fall of the north.

In v 20, the text makes two distinct references to the **exiles**; those from **Israel** and those from **Jerusalem**. This term often functions to depict the collective nature or the community of persons in exile (e.g., see Isa 20:4; 45:13; Jer 24:5; 28:4; 29:22; 40:1). While several of the prophet's references in Obad 20 are not clear, the geographical relocation described in v 19 continues in v 20. The opening line of v 20 refers to ***this army*** (**this company**). The prophet is referring to a particular group among the Israelite exiles. He anticipates that this group of exiled people, when they return to **Canaan**, will possess the land as far **as Zarephath**. Best known from the Elijah narrative in 1 Kgs 17, Zarephath is located on the Phoenician coast between Tyre and Sidon.

Obadiah refers to a second group of exiles—those **from Jerusalem** who were in **Sepharad** (v 20). The text depicts their possession (*yāraš*) of the cities in **the Negev**. The exact location of Sepharad is also unknown (for various suggestions, see Wineland 2009, 169; Watts 1969, 64; Wolff 1986, 67-68; Jenson 2008, 26).

The book of Obadiah reaches a crescendo as v 21 announces that ***those who have been delivered*** or ***saved*** (reading the verb as passive instead of the active form of *yāša*ʿ in the MT; NIV **Deliverers**) will **go up *to* Mount Zion**. Whether the text denotes the deliverers or the delivered, it is clear that these persons will ultimately carry out the role of Israel's early judges and ***judge*** [*šāpaṭ*, judge; **govern] the mountains of Esau**. Ben Zvi has even suggested that Obadiah does "not express any desire for a return to the rule of Davidic dynasty, or to a period whose government may resemble that of the monarchic period. On the contrary, it suggests a world reminiscent of that of the Judges" (1996, 228).

The object of the judgments is clearly Mount Esau. With God's people residing on Mount Zion and with justice coming to those who perpetrated evil against God's people, the reign of Yahweh will be complete. Watts has noted, however, that these judges' "ultimate objective will be neither the destruction of Edom nor the rescue of Israel. Through their activity Jahweh will establish his reign and dominion in history" (1969, 65). The concluding announcement of the text makes this divine objective clear: ***the kingdom will be to/for Yahweh.***

FROM THE TEXT

Obadiah's emphasis on the downfall of the high and lofty and the exaltation of the humiliated is a central theme in the Bible (see an early expression of this theology in Hannah's song in 1 Sam 2:3*a*, 4*a*; also Isa 26:5; Jer 48:29, 39; Ezek 28:2, 8). Jesus' admonitions to his disciples to be the "last" and the "servant" of others (see Mark 9:35) offer the Christian alternative to the Edomite way of thinking and living life in the world. Paul's portrayal of Jesus' exaltation through self-emptying provides the ultimate contrast to human pride: "In your relationships with one another, have the same mindset as Christ Jesus: who, being in very nature God, did not consider equality with God something to be used to his own advantage, rather, he made himself nothing" (Phil 2:5-7*a*).

Obadiah also confronts his readers with a strong reminder that what they sow indeed will be what they reap. The seed one plants will indeed produce a crop consistent with that seed. Edom's judgment in Obadiah is not an arbitrary judgment but is clearly the outcome of the evil it committed against Israel. Nogalski has clearly articulated this understanding: "God has structured the world so that actions have consequences, and when human beings work at cross purposes to God's intentions, God will allow, or cause, those consequences to come to fruition" (2011, 354). The precise and definitive manner in which Obadiah presents this reality compels the reader to ask, "What will the seed planted produce in the end?"

Although the greatest portion of Obadiah addresses the realities of human pride and the consequences of one's actions, the text's concluding declaration shapes a third essential reality for the reading community. For Obadiah, the Lord is not the deity of a single people group. The Lord is God of all nations. Therefore, the ultimate concern of the text is not the establishment of a people group but rather the establishment of the reign of God. In the end, an authentic theology of hope emerges for the reading audience. Obadiah's final eschatological exclamation that the kingdom will belong to the Lord should remove parochial, nationalistic, and ethnocentric readings of the text. The declaration refocuses the reader to the essential message of the prophet: the Lord will ultimately establish *his* kingdom. The kingdom of God is not associated with the reign of a nation, an economic powerhouse, or a religious or ideological system. Read within the full context of the Christian canon, Obadiah's concluding declaration points toward a hope in which "the kingdom of the world has become the kingdom of our Lord and of his Messiah, and he will reign forever and ever" (Rev 11:15*b*). This hope leans into a coming kingdom comprised of "a great multitude that no one could count, from every nation, tribe, people and language" (Rev 7:9).

JONAH

INTRODUCTION

A. Jonah the Prophet

The book of Jonah is unique among the prophetic books in that it contains only one brief oracle: "Forty more days and Nineveh will be overthrown" (3:4). Otherwise the book is mostly in the form of a narrative interrupted by a hymn of thanksgiving (ch 2). Though the book is somewhat "biographical," it contains no actual biographical information, except the name of Jonah's father, Amittai, which is found nowhere else in the OT. The book also lacks superscription, which is usually found in other prophetic books; thus, it provides no historical data, geographical origin of the prophet, or names of the kings of Israel and Judah.

The prophet's name, Jonah (*yônâ*, meaning "dove"), may narratively coincide with other nonhuman characters in the book. In the narrative of Jonah, fish, wind, storm, vine, worm, and east wind all carry out the directives of God. In contrast, "the dove" runs away from the divine presence.

The name Jonah son of Amittai is also found in 2 Kgs 14:25. The tradition in 2 Kings identifies Jonah both as Yahweh's "servant" (*'ebed*) and as "the prophet [*nābî'*] from Gath Hepher." However, the book of Jonah does not identify Jonah as a prophet. The tradition in 2 Kings recalls Jonah's message concerning Jeroboam II's restoration of Israel's borders, which places Jonah in the eighth century B.C. Gath Hepher, which is not mentioned in the book of Jonah, is a town in the hill country of upper Galilee (see Josh 19:13).

B. The Historical Context and Audience of Jonah

The book of Jonah demonstrates the significance for understanding both the historical setting *within* the narrative's plot and the context *into which* the narrative speaks. The historical context within the narrative itself assumes the Assyrian power and the existence of Nineveh, the capital of Assyria. The narrative describes Nineveh as a large and domineering city (1:2; 3:2-3; 4:11). It remained the capital of the Assyrian Empire until its fall to the Babylonians and Medes in 612 B.C. The text in 2 Kings depicts Jonah's activity during the reign of Jeroboam II (786-746 B.C.), which places Jonah *prior* to both Tiglath-Pileser's (745-727 B.C.) expansion of the Assyrian Empire and the establishment of Nineveh as capital by Sennacherib (704-681 B.C.).

The Jonah narrative gives no indication of even a general time period in which the story occurs. It describes the ruler in Nineveh simply as "the king" and provides no name. In light of the detail often provided in biblical texts, such as prophetic superscriptions and the reference to Jonah in 2 Kgs 14:25, the narrative seems almost purposeful in its ambiguity regarding the king.

The book also lacks specific details of the context into which it speaks (for an overview of various dates see Limburg 1993, 28-31; Sasson 1990, 27-28). Scholarly date for the book ranges from the eighth century to the second century B.C. Both Fretheim (1977, 36) and Achtemeier (1996a, 258) suggest the first half of the fifth century B.C., the period in which Malachi was likely active. Trible summarizes quite well the context into which the narrative speaks:

> With no secure evidence to date Jonah, scholars have wandered throughout seven centuries to find it a home. . . . Although a majority of opinions clusters around the sixth, fifth, and fourth centuries, it but shows how indeterminate is the date. . . . Perhaps the best interpretive efforts allow Jonah to move among centuries. (1996, 466)

Within the narrative's own context, the brief message of Jonah (3:4) is addressed to an Assyrian audience. While the text does not mention who specifically heard Jonah's message, the word finally reaches the king of Nineveh. Because of the narrative nature of the book of Jonah, one might best understand the "audience" as the community for whom the narrative was written.

This audience may have been the Jewish community in the early fifth century B.C. However, as this conclusion is not conclusive and based upon the nature of narrative, one might best understand the "audience" of Jonah to be all reading communities subsequent to the writing of this short story.

C. The Book of Jonah as a Literary Work

As noted above, the narrative nature of the book is unique among the prophetic books. Although comprised of various episodes with their own subplots and resolutions, the narrative follows the single, overarching plot of the reluctant or even rebellious prophet. It moves swiftly from dilemma to resolution as God calls and Jonah flees, as God rescues and Jonah preaches, and as Nineveh repents and Jonah sulks. Although resolution occurs when Jonah finally goes to Nineveh, the conflict concerning the prophet himself remains without resolution. The narrative ends without an answer from Jonah to God's question, "Should I not have concern for the great city of Nineveh?" (4:11).

The book of Jonah is a literary masterpiece as it demonstrates eloquence in character depiction, plot development, strategic placement of prayers and direct discourse, repetition and hyperbole, wordplay and use of imagery (see Craig 1999; Trible 1994, 107-22). Repetitive hyperbole occurs through the use of the adjective "great" fourteen times in the narrative (Nineveh, wind, storm, Ninevites, fish). Repetition also occurs with the verbs "go down" (1:3, 5; 2:6) and "hurl" (1:4, 5, 12, 15).

The narrative is filled with irony. The narrative portrays characters that normally would not believe in God as actually believing: pagan sailors, Ninevite king, and Ninevite citizens (i.e., non-Israelites). Similarly, nonhuman characters function in the narrative as obedient and willing instruments of God: wind, storm, fish, worm, plant, hot east wind. Ironically, however, the human character that God has called is the single creature that is unwilling to respond obediently to the Lord. Jonah preaches "against" Nineveh, but Nineveh repents (Jonah's call was not to preach repentance). The king of Nineveh assumes the more traditional roles of prophet and priest and calls upon the Ninevites to repent and fast. When the Ninevites repent, God also repents and withholds his judgment.

In each of the four episodes, prayer plays a significant role and shows the contrast between characters. Jonah does not pray to his God when the sailors' lives are at risk (1:6), but the sailors do (1:14). However, he cries out to God when he finds himself in the belly of a large fish (2:2-9). In ch 3, the king urges his citizens to call upon God and hopes that he may show compassion (3:8-9). In the final prayer of the book, Jonah expresses his utter frustration with God for showing compassion to Nineveh (4:1-3).

Direct discourse is also prominent throughout the narrative. God, Jonah, the captain and the sailors of the ship, and the king of Nineveh all speak. Limburg has observed that "two-thirds of the sentences or verses in the narrative are in the form of direct discourse" (1993, 26). He states, "Direct discourse enlivens a story by making it possible for the reader or storyteller to take the role of the various characters in the story" (ibid.).

The words of Jonah particularly appear in strategic places throughout the book. The three liturgical statements of Jonah are crucial to the progression of the narrative: Jonah's confession of Yahweh as Maker of sea and dry ground (1:9), Jonah's song of thanksgiving (2:2-9 [2:3-10 HB]), and Jonah's creed-like statement concerning Yahweh's character (4:2). However, once again with irony, all of these liturgical statements are "out of place" in their specific contexts.

The only other statements made by Jonah in the book are his instructions to the sailors to throw him overboard (1:12), his brief prophetic oracle of judgment in Nineveh as he marches through the great city (3:4), and his angry outbursts in which he desires to die (4:3, 8, 9). In other words, he makes two statements that call for his death and one statement that announces the death of Nineveh! Although his brief oracle in Nineveh moves the king and the city to repent, no dialogue occurs between Jonah and the king. Similarly, no authentic dialogue takes place between Jonah and God throughout the narrative until the final chapter. However, even then the dialogue focuses upon Jonah's anger and his death wish.

The literary function of the Jonah narrative has been interpreted in a variety of ways, including didactic story, parable, prophetic legend, and novella (particularly regarding the didactic function, see Limburg 1993, 22-28; for extensive discussions of the genre classification of the book of Jonah, see Trible [1996, 467-74] and Simundson [2005, 256-58]). Eleven questions within the narrative (seven in ch 1; three in ch 4) likely demonstrate the didactic nature of the narrative. Regarding the didactic function of questions, Limburg has observed that "if a story is skillfully told, the storyteller can use questions to put each listener in the place of the one being questioned" (1993, 25).

English versification differs slightly from Hebrew versification; in the Hebrew text ch 2 begins with the account of God providing a fish to swallow Jonah (English 1:17) and ends in v 11 (English v 10).

The commentary will follow the general structure of the book as outlined below:

I. Episode 1: Escape and Rescue (1:1-16)
II. Episode 2: A Song of Gratitude (1:17—2:10 [2:1-11 HB])
III. Episode 3: A Reluctant Messenger, an Unexpected Response (3:1-10)
IV. Episode 4: An Angry Messenger, a Compassionate God (4:1-11)

D. Theological Themes

1. The Mission of God

The theological dilemma within the character of Jonah himself establishes the primary theological dilemma for the book: What is God's relationship to those persons and communities outside of the covenant community? Any community that understands itself to be in unique covenant with God must finally confront this question: Will the deity with whom a community shares covenant extend gracious fidelity beyond that community to all people groups? What if those people groups represent the very enemies who have attempted to destroy the covenant community?

The text does not provide final propositional answers to these significant theological questions; however, the narrative with its ironies and suspended conclusion invites the readers to reflect on this question. What does it mean for both the Assyrians and various nonhuman members of creation to demonstrate a greater readiness to participate in the divine mission than what has been demonstrated by the prophet himself? How does the community's parochialism and exclusivism as embodied by the prophet counteract and oppose the will of God vis-à-vis communities outside of the covenant?

If the literary work of Jonah does emerge in the fifth century B.C., it is certainly possible that it spoke into a context in which the covenant people were attempting to make sense of their God and of their own role in the world. The narrative may have spoken into a context in which it would have been easier for the community to define itself "against the world" (e.g., Ezra and Nehemiah's reactions toward foreign spouses and especially Moabite spouses; see Neh 13:23-31) rather than to define itself as citizens in the world.

2. Creation, the Sovereignty of God, and Universal Grace

Achtemeier has suggested that the primary purpose of Jonah is to reveal "the character of the creator and sovereign of the world" (1996a, 258). Throughout the narrative of Jonah, creation and members of creation—both non-Israelite and nonhuman—are active participants in the work of God: captain, sailors, king, cattle, wind, storm, fish, vine, worm, hot east wind. The book of Jonah's theological vision is clearly nonparochial and nonpartisan. Yahweh is Creator and sustainer of all life. The *missio Dei* (mission of God) is all-inclusive and has no boundaries. It is Israelite; it is Assyrian. It is human; it is nonhuman.

The narrative eloquently portrays divine sovereignty by means of depicting various obedient responses by God's creatures to their Creator's command (with the exception of the prophet). Even the Ninevite king recognizes the sovereignty of God in his declaration in 3:9, "Who knows? God may yet relent." He refuses to permit Nineveh's fasting and repentance to overpower this sovereign deity.

In a somewhat subtle manner, the text demonstrates the ultimate expression of God's sovereignty in its depiction of the divine change of plans regarding Nineveh. The book of Jonah is not unique among OT texts in depicting God's "relenting" or changing his mind. However, the instances in which God does change his mind throughout the OT are never arbitrary or haphazard. These occasions are consistently grounded in the grace, mercy, and forgiving nature of God. Jonah's creed-like confession of God's mercy in 4:2 frequently accompanies narratives in which God changes his mind or may change his mind (e.g., Exod 32—34; Num 14; Joel 2:12-14). Consistent with ancient Israel's confession of God's unique and holy character of love and compassion, the book of Jonah is comfortable with a divine change of plans toward salvation and away from destruction. This change in divine action ultimately functions as an expression of divine sovereignty and grace.

Ancient Israel ultimately had to take their creed-like confession concerning God's gracious and merciful character to its logical conclusion: How far does divine grace extend? What are the boundaries of grace? That logical conclusion to Israel's confession ultimately appears in the narrative of Jonah. In the end, the book of Jonah bursts through all boundaries and barriers that human beings have placed around divine grace. For the book of Jonah, divine grace is universal as it extends even to the fiercest enemies of God's people. Interpreting the book's satirical outlook upon "the whole prophetic enterprise," Brown has masterfully articulated the book's primary concern to be "the wideness of God's mercy and the narrowness of human judgment" (1996, 17).

3. The Open-endedness of the Narrative

God's question at the end of the narrative is one of the most theologically ironic statements in the book. Although the narrative portrays God as asking Jonah for his response, the question is addressed to the reader: "Should I not have concern for the great city?" Jonah does not respond. The silence of Jonah at the end of the narrative means that the reader now hears this question, which demands an answer. Will the reader join Jonah and remain silent? Or, will the reader through faithful response break the silence of Jonah and say yes to God's great question? Ironically, to say yes to God is to find oneself right back at Nineveh.

COMMENTARY

I. EPISODE 1: ESCAPE AND RESCUE: JONAH 1:1-16

BEHIND THE TEXT

The narrative of Jonah reflects the genre of the prophetic call in which Yahweh commissions a prophet, and the prophet willingly or in some instances reluctantly acquiesces to the divine call (e.g., Exod 3—4; Judg 6:11-27; 1 Sam 3:1-18; Isa 6:1-8; Jer 1:1-13). The narrative of Jonah gives extended attention to the prophet's resistance to the divine call. In contrast to the familiar prophetic hesitancy in other narratives, Jonah does not question. He simply flees in the opposite direction to which Yahweh has called him to go.

The size of Nineveh, Assyria's capital, at the height of its glory in the seventh century was about 1,850 square acres; it was surrounded by a double perimeter wall and had canals and parks. The narrative statement, "It took three days to go through it" (3:3), indicates the vast size of the city. The narrative assumes that the reader is familiar with Joppa's port location on the Mediterranean as well as Tarshish's western location (i.e., the opposite direction of Nineveh, the capital of Assyria).

The narrator also assumes the reader's awareness of the common ancient Near Eastern notion of *the sea* (*yām*) as a life-threatening, watery chaos. In both ancient Israel's creation narrative in Gen 1 and its redemption narrative and hymn in Exod 14—15, the covenant community testifies to Yahweh's power and authority over the sea. In the Jonah narrative, the numerous references to the sea (1:4, 5, 9, 11, 12, 13, 15) denote more specifically to the Mediterranean. The storm in the sea reflects the Deuteronomic-prophetic theme of retribution; the narrative seems to link the storm to Jonah's rebellion, and thus God's punishment for his disobedience.

The first chapter focuses upon the rapid actions of the prophet, Yahweh, and the sailors (see suggestion of chiasmic arrangement of ch 1 in Nogalski 2011, 412). The narrative gives little attention to the words of the prophet, except the statements he made to the sailors (see vv 9, 12).

IN THE TEXT

■ **1-3** In vv 1-3, Yahweh commissions Jonah. The book opens with the verb *vayĕhî* (from *hāyâ*, meaning "to be"), which functions narratively to introduce the story in a manner similar to the phrases "Once upon a time" or "It came to pass that" (Limburg 1993, 37; Jenson 2008, 42). Jonah is the only prophetic text to open in this way. The term *dābār* (**word**) functions similarly to the way it does in other prophetic texts (e.g., Hos 1:1).

The only other reference in the OT to **Jonah son of Amittai** is 2 Kgs 14:25. His father's name derives from the verb *ʾāman,* and it conveys the idea of belief or Yahweh's faithfulness.

Although the book of Jonah occurs within the collection of the Prophets in the Hebrew Bible (*nĕbîʾîm*), the narrative never refers to the character as a prophet (*nābîʾ*), nor does it refer to his activity as prophesying (*nābāʾ*). Rather, it depicts God's command to Jonah to ***call out*** (**preach**). With three imperatives, Yahweh commissions the prophet to ***arise***, to ***go***, and to ***call out***. The destination of the divine call is **Nineveh**, described by God as **the great city**. In the depiction of Nineveh, the narrator introduces for the first time the adjective *gādôl* (**great**) that will often reappear in the book.

Yahweh's commission does not specifically cite the evil deeds of the Ninevites; Yahweh states more generally that their ***evil*** has risen (**come up**) into his presence (**before me**). As the wickedness of Nineveh has captured the divine attention, Yahweh brings the matter to Jonah's attention. The narrative reports Jonah's response in a rapid succession of eight verbs (v 3). Although **Tarshish** appears only twice in v 3 in the NIV, it appears three times in the Hebrew text (NIV translates once **that port**).

The prophet's first action in v 3 was to rise (*qûm*), but instead of going to Nineveh he **ran away** (*bāraḥ*) from Yahweh's presence. The preposition ***before*** or ***in the presence of*** (*lipnāy*) occurs three times in relationship to God in vv 2-3. Nineveh's evil **has come up before** Yahweh (v 2); and Jonah **ran away from *the presence of Yahweh*** (v 3); Jonah boarded a ship and **sailed for Tarshish to flee from the *presence of Yahweh*** (v 3). The narrator also twice uses the verb *yārad* (**went down**; **went aboard**) to further emphasize Jonah's fleeing from Yahweh's presence. As the prophet moves in the opposite direction of Nineveh's evil, he simultaneously moves in the opposite direction of Yahweh himself. The narrative at this point does not say why Jonah ran away from the presence of God (see 4:2 for Jonah's explanation). Fretheim has observed that

> when Jonah resolves to flee from the presence of the Lord, he is not intending to cut himself off completely from God. . . . He seeks a place, not where he would be removed from God's rule, but where he would not have to continue to hear that word of God's commissioning him to go to Nineveh. (1977, 80-81)

Joppa and Tarshish

Strategically located thirty-five miles northwest of Jerusalem, the port city of Joppa served as a major economic and military crossroads between Egypt and Mesopotamia. Its Phoenician name literally means *beautiful*. With the city located on a one hundred foot cliff, it provided a safe harbor for ships sailing on the Mediterranean. According to 2 Chr 2:16, the lumber for Solomon's temple arrived into Joppa's port from Lebanon.

While the precise location of Tarshish is uncertain, both Jeremiah and Ezekiel describe the city as a producer of precious metal (Jer 10:9; Ezek 27:12; 38:13). Other texts associate Tarshish with islands or coastland (Ps 72:10; Isa 23:6; 66:19). Suggestions as to its location range from southwestern Spain to northern Africa (see Baker 1992, 331-33). A site along the Mediterranean coast is certainly probable.

■ **4-5** Verses 4-5 depict Yahweh's response to Jonah's decision to move in the opposite direction of his command to Jonah. Yahweh ***hurled out*** (causative form of *ṭûl*; **sent**) a **great wind** to **the sea**. The **great wind** produced a ***great* storm**. Just as Nineveh was great (*gādôl*), so, too, are the wind and the storm.

Verse 4 ends with the scene of the impact of the great storm on the ship. The phrase **threatened to break up** in Hebrew (*ḥiššĕbâ lĕhiššābēr*) "captures the sound of planks cracking when tortured by raging waters" (Sasson 1990, 96). The narrative moves to the next scene, which shows the fear and panic of **the sailors** (v 5) because of the storm that was threatening to break up the ship. Their crying out (*zāʿaq*), **each . . . to his own god**, is parallel to the crying out (*zāʿaq*) of the Assyrian king (see 3:7) who will command the Ninevites to call out to God for deliverance. Such a cry to Yahweh for deliverance was not unfamiliar to the Israelites in their seasons of distress (see Judg 3:9, 15; 6:6, 7; 10:10; 1 Sam 7:8-9; see Israel's general cry of distress in Exod 2:23).

The sailors' response to the storm also includes their hurling out (*ṭûl*; see Jonah 1:4) **the cargo into the sea to lighten the ship** (v 5). Fretheim suggests that while the sailors may have been attempting to lighten the ship by hurling its cargo overboard, the phrase may indicate "that the cargo is a sacrifice to the gods in order that the *sea* might be lightened" (1977, 82-83). Later, Jonah suggests to the sailors that they do the same to him "to make the sea calm down" (vv 11-12).

Verse 5 ends with the scene of Jonah's response to the storm that threatens the ship and the fear and panic of the sailors: he goes down **below the deck**, lays down, and falls into **a deep sleep**. The narrative again focuses on the descent of Jonah (*yārad*; twice in v 3) **below deck** (*yarkâ*, remote parts), indicating the deepest recesses of the ship. Verse 5 concludes with the portrait of Jonah in a **deep sleep**; the verb *rādam* used here indicates an intense, almost trance-like sleep (see Gen 2:21; see also Limburg 1993, 50). The Septuagint humorously depicts Jonah as lying down to sleep and snoring (regarding various interpretations of Jonah's deep sleep by Philo, Josephus, and the church fathers, see Sasson 1990, 101).

■ **6** The scene quickly moves to the captain's speech to Jonah (v 6). His question to Jonah, **How can you sleep?** indicates, on the one hand, the captain's concern over the imminent doom at sea; on the other hand, this question reveals Jonah's total lack of concern over the destruction that is about to happen to the ship and its sailors. His only concern at this point is his own comfort—his sleep—which takes him far away from the real-life issues and concerns of others. The captain, who is not even a worshipper of Yahweh, urges Jonah to call upon his god. Fretheim has commented that "the pagan has to remind Jonah of his religious responsibilities" (1977, 84)! The captain's command to Jonah parallels Yahweh's initial command to Jonah: ***rise*** (*qûm*; **Get up**). Likewise, his second command to Jonah is identical to the third divine imperative: **Call** out (*qārāʾ*). The captain acknowledges the possibility that Jonah's god may give attention to the sailors' distress and save them from their impending destruction. The captain's tentativeness concerning the divine deliverance foreshadows the cautious declaration of Nineveh's king in 3:9: "Who knows? God may yet relent" (see similar tentative statements in Exod 32:30; Joel 2:14; Amos 5:15; Zeph 2:3). In no less than the opening six verses of the narrative, twice Jonah receives a command to rise and to call out. In both instances, lives are at risk. In both instances, Jonah remains stubbornly resistant.

The narrative gives no indication that Jonah responded (i.e., rises and calls) either positively or negatively to the captain's request. The narrative's silence indicates Jonah's silence, which sharply contrasts the crying out of the sailors to their gods for help. The prophet continues to be the reluctant if not the recalcitrant prophet. Yet later in the narrative, this same prophet who appears not to care about his fellow sailors who are perishing (*'ābad*) becomes distressed over the destruction (*'ābad*) of a plant that provided him shade from the hot sun (4:6-10).

■ **7** In 1:7, the narrative moves from the captain's encounter with Jonah back to the sailors' desperate attempts for rescue. When both their crying out to their gods and their lightening the ship's load failed, they proceed to **cast lots** in order to discover **who is responsible for** the ***evil*** (*rā'â*; **calamity**) that has come upon them. Casting lots was a common practice in the ancient Near East to determine the divine will. Ancient Israelites employed this practice in order to determine such matters as kingship, guilt, appropriate sacrifice, land allotment, and settlement of disputes (e.g., Lev 16:7-10; Num 26:55; see Limburg 1993, 51-52).

■ **8** As the lot fell to Jonah, the sailors began their confrontation of Jonah with a general question about the source of **all this trouble**, followed by more specific questions directed to Jonah (v 8). The sailors wanted to know what kind of work he did, his point of origin, his homeland (**country**), and his nationality or ethnicity (**people**). They want to know about this person who shows no interest or concern about what is happening to them.

■ **9** Jonah does not respond to the sailors' questions concerning occupation, origin, or homeland; his reply focuses only on the people to whom he belongs: **I am a Hebrew** (*'ibrî*). The term "Hebrew" functions in the OT primarily as a reference to ethnicity or to the Israelite community at large. Jonah expands his ethnic identity with a confession that further reveals his religious identity. He confesses that he is a worshipper of ***Yahweh*, the God of heaven, who made the sea and the dry *ground*** (v 9). This confession indicates Jonah's faith in God as Creator. The sea and the dry ground are part of God's creative work (see Gen 1:10). In Jonah 2, he relates his faith in God as the one who delivers those who cry out to him for help. Jonah's response reveals the fundamental faith of Israel; Yahweh the God of Israel is the one who made the sea and the dry ground.

■ **10-12** The narrative reports the response of the sailors when Jonah revealed his ethnic and religious identity in v 10. They were in great fear (**this terrified them**). The conversation between the sailors and Jonah in vv 10-12 is rather unusual. Though the sailors are terrified because of the storm, they take logical steps toward resolving their crisis. The sailors' question, **What have you done?** and the parenthetical note about their knowledge of Jonah as a person who is **running away from** God indicate their awareness of Jonah's culpability in causing the storm that threatens to destroy them.

The sea is **getting rougher and rougher** (v 11), and they need to do something to make the storm go away. They know that the problem and the solution for their crisis is Jonah. He did something to bring the storm; now they need to **do** something to him to resolve the crisis. (**What should we do to you . . . ?**) It is ironic that the sailors ask for Jonah's suggestion as to what they should do to him; whatever they do to Jonah would be according to his decision and, thus they would be free from any guilt associated with their action.

In v 12, Jonah acknowledges his personal responsibility for the **great storm** that has come upon the sailors and suggests that they hurl or **throw** him **into the sea**. Fretheim sees here Jonah offering himself as both the sailors' sacrifice for deliverance and as a sacrifice to God, thereby satisfying divine justice (1977, 88; regarding Jonah's death wish, see Perry 2006, 6-7; regarding a "death wish" as an act of compassion, see Craig 1999, 145-46).

■ **13** Though the sailors would have been free from any culpability for their action, they refuse at first to sacrifice Jonah's life to escape the storm that threatens them (v 13). They instead try to do their best by risking their own lives **to row back to land** and thus avoid the need to sacrifice a human life. The narrator depicts them as digging into the water (**did their best to row**). In contrast to Jonah's lethargic, dispassionate response to both the storm and to Nineveh, the sailors will do all that is possible to preserve life. When the sailors recognized the difficulty of reaching the land, they ***cried out to Yahweh***. Their attention turned to Yahweh, the God whom Jonah worshipped. Though Jonah refused to call on Yahweh his God, the sailors did. Ironically, the rebellious prophet's mention of the name of Yahweh engendered faith in the pagan sailors.

■ **14** The sailors' prayer is not for deliverance from the storm, but rather they seek Yahweh's mercy and plead with him to spare them from any guilt for their forthcoming action toward Jonah (v 14). They plead with God not to let them **die for taking** Jonah's **life** (*nepeš*). They do not want to be held accountable for shedding innocent blood (**innocent man**). The final line of v 14 (**for you, Lord, have done as you pleased**) seems to convey the sailors' recognition that the storm was sent by God. Therefore, he must take responsibility for what they are about to do to Jonah.

■ **15** The sailors then did what Jonah asked them to do to calm the sea (v 15). They **threw him overboard** and the sea became **calm**, as Jonah had predicted (see v 12). The text places greater emphasis upon the cessation of the sea's angry rage (**the raging sea grew calm**).

■ **16** This part of the narrative ends with the report of the response of the sailors to what they have just witnessed (v 16). Instead of their great fear of the storm, they now have great fear of Yahweh; they worshipped Yahweh, Jonah's God, and **offered a sacrifice** and **made vows to him**. Both sacrifice and vow-making are familiar ancient Near Eastern responses of gratitude for divine activity.

FROM THE TEXT

One cannot read this portion of the narrative of Jonah without noticing its literary artistry and the use of literary devices. While a literary masterpiece, the narrative functions as much more. The very nature of this book and the techniques it employs attempt to beckon the reading audience to become participants in the story. By becoming engaged actors in the narrative, the reader will also encounter and be encountered by the image of the recalcitrant prophet, the obedient "foreigners," and the delivering, forgiving, nonpartisan deity, Yahweh.

In the opening chapter, the text challenges the reading audience to discover itself under the skin of obstinate Jonah. The narrative invites the reading community to see and name its own prophetic rebellion, its move in the opposite direction of the divine call.

The text also challenges the reading community to confess its own silence in the midst of death and destruction all around. It invites the reading community to hear the cries of the sailors who are perishing and to hear the entreaty of the captain, "Get up and call on your god!"

The opening episode of Jonah also confronts the reading community with the unnerving question: Is it even possible for "pagan sailors" to confess and call out to our delivering God in ways more honest than we? If "pagan sailors" cry out to God for deliverance, why would those who confess this God remain silent?

II. EPISODE 2: A SONG OF GRATITUDE: JONAH 1:17—2:10 (2:1-11 HB)

BEHIND THE TEXT

English translations present the rescue of Jonah in 1:17 as the conclusion to Yahweh's deliverance in ch 1 (2:1 in Hebrew). Not only does Yahweh rescue the sailors by bringing an end to the raging sea, but he rescues Jonah from the sea by providing a fish. Jonah is no longer on the raging sea running from God. He is now in the "vessel" of Yahweh's deliverance, a fish's belly.

Most of ch 2 is in the form of a thanksgiving psalm that celebrates divine deliverance. The typical form of the thanksgiving psalm combines elements of both lament and the hymn of praise. Language emerging from the lament frequently depicts the dire situation in which the psalmist once found himself. Such language commonly speaks of potential death in terms of disease, raging waters, the pit, and Sheol. Common language in the hymn of praise provides expressions of gratitude and worship to the God who creates and redeems. The general structure followed by the song of thanksgiving is: (1) depiction of the crisis; (2) reference to the worshipper's seeking of/cry to Yahweh; (3) Yahweh's subsequent deliverance; and, (4) expressions of gratitude and praise to Yahweh accompanied by the fulfillment of vows and sacrifices (for typical elements within the psalms of thanksgiving, see Pss 18, 28, 30, 116; regarding the relationship of the thanksgiving song to the hymn of praise and lament, see Anderson 2000, 97-119; Brueggemann 1984, 123-40).

IN THE TEXT

■ **17** In 1:17 the scene changes to the rescue of Jonah. God ***appointed a great*** **fish to swallow Jonah**. The intensive verb *mānâ* conveys the sovereign act of setting out or even *ordaining* the fish for a specific purpose. The verb appears again in 4:6, 7, and 8 to depict Yahweh's sovereign appointment of the vine, the worm, and the scorching wind for divine use. Although the fish provides safety for Jonah, the verb functions less to indicate provision and more to indicate divine appointment. With the recurring use of the verb, the narrator makes obvious that Yahweh's appointed agents, with the exception of Jonah, carry out their tasks promptly and appropriately.

The text employs the commonly used word *dāg* for fish. It provides no further description of the type or nature of the fish other than that it was ***great*** (*gādôl*; see 1:2). The common preposition *lĕ* attached to the infinitive construct **swallow** indicates that the fish was appointed to serve a divine purpose (see Williams 2007, 110).

Jonah remained in the *mēʿeh* (**belly**; more likely, intestines or bowels) of the fish for **three days and three nights**. The narrator will later describe the great size of Nineveh as taking three days to travel through the city (3:3). The reference to three days/third day does recur throughout OT. Hosea depicts a divine restoration of the people on the third day. As a result, Yahweh enables the people to live in the divine presence (Hos 6:2). In the Jonah narrative, the restoration that occurs after three days relocates Jonah from the sea (*yām*) to dry land (*yabbāšâ*). According to the Genesis creation narrative, God's formation and naming of both sea (*yām*) and dry land (*yabbāšâ*) occurred on the third day (Gen 1:9-10). Certainly in the narrative of Jonah, the prophet is a man of "the third day."

Three Days/Third Day in the OT

Other than the multiple references to seven days/seventh day, the reference to three days or the third day is the most frequently occurring reference to a specific number of days in OT. In the Genesis narratives, Abraham sees the place he is to offer Isaac "on the third day" (22:4), and Joseph instructs his brothers what to do in order to live "on the third day" (42:18). In the Sinai narrative, Yahweh descends to the mountain on "the third day" (Exod 19:11, 16). In the Deuteronomic narrative, Joshua announces that the people will cross the Jordan in "three days" (Josh 1:11). Likewise, in 2 Kgs 20:5 Yahweh promises healing to Hezekiah and instructs the king to go up to the temple "on the third day." In the narrative of Esther, the queen stands in the king's inner court dressed in royal garb in order to plea for the rescue of the Jews "on the third day" (5:1). In speaking of Yahweh's restoration of his people, the eighth-century B.C. prophet Hosea declares that "after two days he will revive us; on the third day he will restore us, that we may live in his presence" (6:2). While none of these texts provide precise significance of this number, they all share the notion of preservation of life, renewal of life, or a new beginning of life. Certainly for the early Christian community, Jesus' resurrection *on the third day* likewise points to the renewal of life for all creation.

■ **2:1-9** Following a brief introduction (v 1), the narrator records in vv 2-9 the prayer of Jonah while he was **inside the fish. Fish** is in the masculine gender in 1:17 and 2:10; it is in the feminine in 2:1. After noting various interpretations of the gender change, Sasson concludes that "a storyteller could simply use either gender for an animal—or both at once—when the sex of the animal was of no importance to the tale" (1990, 156). However, Trible argues that the feminine form "suggests female imagery: 'from the womb of the fish.' When Jonah prays to Yahweh from within the 'mother' fish, Jonah appropriately moves from death to life" (1996, 505).

Jonah's prayer begins with an acknowledgment that Yahweh **answered** him when he **called for help** and **listened** to his **cry from deep in the realm of the dead** (v 2). He cried (*qārāʾ*) to Yahweh in his **distress** though he refused to "preach" (*qārāʾ*) against Nineveh (1:2) and did not respond to the ship's captain's demand to "call on" (*qārāʾ*) his god (1:6).

Verse 2 of ch 2 affirms the character of Yahweh as one who responds to the cry of those who are in distress. This theme is consistent throughout the book. When one calls for mercy, whether that one be the sailors, the Ninevites, or the prophet himself, Yahweh responds with salvation.

The phrase ***from the belly of Sheol*** (**from deep in the realm of the dead**) parallels the **distress** depicted in the first half of v 2. **Sheol**, the realm of the dead, appears in Hebrew poetry as opening its mouth wide to devour the living to satisfy its insatiable hunger (see Prov 1:12; Isa 5:14; Hab 2:5). Jonah 2:2 portrays Jonah as having been **in the realm of the dead**; he has entered the world of death, and the prayer comes from the one who has been brought back to life.

Sheol: The Abode of the Dead

Although Sheol appears sixty-six times in the OT, the ancient Israelites never speculate on its nature in the OT text. As neither a reward for the righteous nor a punishment for the wicked, Sheol appears in OT texts as the underworld where all dead persons dwell (see Deut 32:22; 1 Sam 2:6; Job 7:9; Ps 88:1-12; Prov 15:24; 27:20; Isa 14:9). Most often, the word appears in poetic texts that depict potential death or life-threatening situations, such as disease, war, or other disasters. In the Septuagint, Sheol appears most frequently as Hades.

In Jonah 2:3 and 5, the text employs familiar language of life-threatening waters (see, for example, Pss 42:6-7; 69:1-2, etc.). These verses resemble a catalog of Hebrew terms for watery chaos: *mĕṣûlâ* (***the deep***), *yammîm* (**the** seas), *nāhār* (**the currents**), *mišbār* (**waves**), *gal* (**breakers**), *mayim* (**engulfing waters**), *tĕhôm* (**the deep**), *sûp* (**seaweed**; see *yam sûp,* "Sea of Reeds," in Exod 13:18). Within the context of the narrative, the images function as both common metaphors of destruction and vivid reminders of the threat of Jonah's literal drowning in the sea.

The poem, by the use of diverse verbs, brings the waters to life and gives them diabolical personhood. The verbs transform the turbulent water into a malevolent, life-threatening character. The various verbs (**swirled, swept over, threatened, surrounded**) suggest the action of hemming in or enclosing to the point of suffocation. Pressing in upon its victim, the water had an overpowering stranglehold upon Jonah. Cast out (lit. "sent out") into the deep waters, Jonah finds himself at the very center (**heart**) of the tempestuous sea. In the midst of the chaotic waters, the currents ***surrounded*** (*sābab*) him while the breakers and waves ***crossed over*** (*ʿābār*) him. In v 5, the waters ***encompassed*** (*ʾāpap*; **threatened**) his very life (*nepeš*; **me**). In Jonah 2:7, the text depicts this **life** (*nepeš*) as **ebbing away**. As the chaotic abyss (*tĕhôm*, ***the deep***; see Gen 1:2) surrounded the prophet, the binding, choking seaweed wrapped itself around Jonah's head.

Jonah 2:3 and 5 graphically depicts the final suffocating moments as the waters encircle their drowning victim. Verse 4 interrupts the death scene with the victim's statement of despair as well as hope. Jonah, on the one hand, recognizes that he has been **banished** (*gāraš*) from the presence of God (see Gen 3:23 and 4:14 for the use of the same verb); on the other hand, he is confident that he will **look again toward** the **holy temple** of God. The prophet who fled from the presence of Yahweh (Jonah 1:3, 10) now grieves his banishment from God's **sight**.

The second half of 2:4 opens with the adverb *ʾak* (**yet**), which introduces either a newly realized truth or a confident affirmation. In contrast to the grief of being driven from Yahweh's presence in v 4*a*, v 4*b* expresses the prophet's confident and persistent determination to **look . . . toward** Yahweh's **holy temple**. Even though Yahweh banished Jonah from his sight, he will continue to look toward Yahweh.

The transitional hinge of the poem occurs in v 6. In the first half of the verse, Jonah continues his descent. He had begun this downward spiral in his *going down* to Joppa, on *down* into the ship (1:3), and finally deeper *down* into the heart of the ship where he had fallen asleep (1:5). Sinking further into the depths of the sea (2:3-5), the prophet finally **sank down** (*yārad*) to the bottom of the sea (v 6). The image of the **roots of the mountains** depicts the ancient Near Eastern cosmological understanding of the mountain peaks that support the firmament and of the mountain's lowest extremities (i.e., **roots**), which plunge into the bottom of the sea (see Sir 16:19).

In running from the divine presence, Jonah has finally descended as far as the human being can go. **The earth beneath barred me in forever** sums up the plight of Jonah. The bar (*bĕrîaḥ*) to which the song refers often denotes wooden bars used in locking city gates. The reference to *hāʾāreṣ* (**the earth**) likely implies Sheol (see Eccl 3:21; Isa 26:19; Jer 17:13; Jenson, 2008, 66). The entangling power of death-ridden Sheol is capable of imprisoning the prophet **forever**. Jonah fled (*brḥ*) from the presence of Yahweh (Jonah 1:3, 10) only to discover that he was captured/barred (*brḥ*) by death. Once again, consistent with the Deuteronomic-prophetic conviction, the prophet has harvested what he has sown; he found that which he sought.

In the second half of v 6, the poem shifts suddenly and dramatically. The movement downward (*yārad*) becomes movement upward (*ʿālâ*, "go up"). Descent gives way to ascent. Addressing God directly (**you**) and identifying God specifically as ***Yahweh,*** **my God**, the prophet testifies that Yahweh **brought** (*ʿālâ*) his **life up from the pit**. Often translated as **the pit**, *šaḥat* appears frequently as a synonym for death or Sheol (2:2) in Hebrew poetry (see Job 33:22, 28, 30, etc.).

In Jonah 2:7, the text elaborates upon the situation in which Yahweh had brought up the victim's life from the pit. As his life (*nepeš*) was feebly fainting away, the prophet **remembered** Yahweh. His remembrance of Yahweh was accompanied by his prayer that went (*bôʾ*, "come," "go") to Yahweh, to his **holy temple**.

Verse 8 establishes a stark contrast between the one who remembers and prays to Yahweh (v 7) and the one who worships idols. Although the English translation of v 8 requires a number of words, the text itself is concise. The succinct statement declares in four expressions: ***Keepers [of] idols abandon loyalty.***

The first term is the participial verb *šāmar* (***keepers***, "watchers," etc.; **those who cling**), often used in the context of vigilant observance or obedience of covenant, commandments, and Sabbath (e.g., see Exod 31:13-14). The second expression is actually comprised of two words: the plural of *hebel* ("vapor," "air," "breath," "vanity," etc.) and *šāwʾ* ("emptiness," "nothingness," "worthlessness"). Taken together the two words mean ***vapors of nothingness*** or ***empty breaths***. Each of the two words can independently describe the emptiness of idol worship (e.g., *hebel* in Jer 10:15; 16:19; 51:18; *šāwʾ* in Jer 18:15). Although the expression in Jonah's song may indicate idol worship, it may broadly imply trust in any source other than Yahweh.

The other two words in Jonah 2:8 describe the action carried out by those who are ***keepers of nothingness***. These persons ***abandon*** (*ʿāzab*) their covenant faithfulness (*ḥesed*). Just as *šāmar* is a familiar Deuteronomic-prophetic expression for *keeping* covenant, *ʿāzab* is a common term for apostasy or abandoning Yahweh (Deut 28:20; 31:16). From the prophetic perspective, to place trust in idols is to forsake the covenant with Yahweh and thus to forfeit covenant loyalty to Yahweh (regarding *ḥesed* as covenant loyalty, see Hos 2:19, 21; 6:4, 6). They have not forfeited Yahweh's loyalty to them, but they have forsaken their own loyalty to Yahweh. The NIV **turn away from God's love for them** does not adequately express the text's conviction that misdirected trust is ultimately an abandonment of loyalty to God.

Jonah concludes his prayer with gratitude and testimony (2:9). Accompanied by a voice (*qôl*, ***song***) of thanksgiving, the rescued prophet promises to make **sacrifice** to Yahweh. The text's use of *šālam* (to be whole or complete) indicates that the prophet will bring his vow to a completion (**I will make good**). The prayer's reference to sacrifice and vows is not the first in the narrative (see 1:16). Whether carried out by "pagan sailors" or an "Israelite prophet," divine deliverance engenders worship, gratitude, and confession.

The song concludes with the grand declaration **Salvation *to Yahweh*!** Yahweh's action of deliverance (**salvation**) remains the consistent divine response to the cry for help. In response to the human outcry, Yahweh answers; in the distress-filled wail, Yahweh hears (see 2:2). The sailors witnessed this reality, and now Jonah sings of this reality. With this backdrop, the narrative anticipates that which will occur when the Ninevites, both human and animal, call out to God (3:8).

■ **10** The narrative resumes in v 10; Yahweh brings resolution to Jonah's plight. Yahweh spoke (**commanded**) to the fish; the fish **vomited Jonah onto dry land**. Trible observes that "at the boundaries of this episode . . . the unpalatable verbs 'swallow' and 'vomit' designate the opposite movements of descent and ascent" (1996, 507; see Jenson 2008, 68-69, regarding various interpretations of the fish's action). Reacting to Yahweh's direction, the fish becomes an instrument of divine deliverance (see wind in 1:4, bush in 4:6, worm in 4:7, east wind in 4:8). The prophet, after having been delivered from the destructive sea, is back on the **dry land**, the place of his life and vocation.

FROM THE TEXT

Removed from its narrative context, Jonah's song of gratitude could emerge out of multiple situations and emanate from the lips of any human being. It is certainly possible, even likely, that the song itself was familiar to many and may have existed long before the story of Jonah occurred. However, the reader of Jonah's song becomes keenly aware that songs are sung, prayers are prayed, and testimonies are given within contexts. Ultimately, poetry finds its home within narrative; song emerges from life. Likewise, testimonies and prayers continue to live as they find homes in multiple subsequent narratives.

Therefore, the believer continues to pray old prayers in new contexts and sing ancient songs in new settings.

Jonah's song of gratitude occurs within the narrative context of divine deliverance. The great fish becomes the means of God's deliverance from the sea in order that Jonah might ultimately find himself back on dry ground. Narrative of salvation brackets the song itself. The Lord's deliverance of Jonah *from* the sea precedes the song (1:17) while the Lord's deliverance of Jonah *to* dry ground follows the song (2:10). Through the images of life-threatening sea and life-preserving dry ground, the reader hears echoes of Israel's ancient confession of Yahweh as the deliverer of his people. While the contexts change, the salvific character of the Lord continues from one generation to the next. The reader finds hope for deliverance in Jonah's song; the song also reminds the reader that gratitude is the best way to respond to God's deliverance. In the Jonah story, deliverance comes from God even to those who attempt to escape God's presence.

For the early Christian community, the three days and nights spent by Jonah in the belly of the fish became a sign for the death and resurrection of Jesus Christ (see Matt 12:39-41; 16:4, 17; Luke 11:29-32). In light of the relationship between the common notion of *third day/three days* and the hope for divine rescue from a life-threatening situation, it is understandable how this tradition influenced the early followers of Jesus. For the early Christians the "sign of Jonah" testified to a central theological tenet of their faith. Just as God had delivered Jonah on the third day, so the Father raised the Son from the grave on the third day. In both instances, the third day pointed to hope that broke into despair, light that penetrated darkness, life that overcame death.

III. EPISODE 3: A RELUCTANT MESSENGER, AN UNEXPECTED RESPONSE: JONAH 3:1-10

BEHIND THE TEXT

The narrative continues in ch 3; Yahweh's word comes a second time to the previously recalcitrant prophet. The one who was returned to the dry ground from the depths of destruction receives another chance to respond to Yahweh's word. Though begrudgingly, the prophet will ultimately journey to Nineveh.

The narrative in ch 3 contains a systematic presentation of three actions and favorable responses to those actions. In each instance the response to an action prompts the next response. The central characters of the narrative are all involved: God, Jonah, and the Ninevites (embodied by the king). As Yahweh commissions Jonah, the prophet responds favorably. As Jonah proclaims a concise yet clear message in Nineveh, the Ninevite king and citizens respond favorably. As the Ninevites turn to Yahweh, Yahweh responds favorably to Nineveh. Unlike the narrative in ch 1 and ch 4, no dialogue occurs in ch 3. Though Jonah is a character in the narrative, the focus seems to be on the actions of the Ninevites and Yahweh's response to their actions.

The practices embodied by the Ninevite king and citizens in ch 3 are common in the communal fast, which occurs at times of national calamity, festivals of remembrance, or communal days of penitence (see Joel 1:13-14; 2:12-14). The language of the communal fast as well as the confession of Yahweh's character in Jonah 3—4 resembles the language of Joel 2:12-14.

IN THE TEXT

■ **1-2** Both in word selection and order, the statement in Jonah 3:1 is identical to 1:1 except that the phrase **a second time** replaces the phrase "son of Amittai." Likewise, the opening of 3:2 is identical to 1:2 (**Go to the great city of Nineveh and proclaim**); however, the prepositional phrase has changed from "against it" in 1:2 to the phrase **to it** in 3:2. In contrast to 1:2, in 3:2 Yahweh does not say why Jonah should preach to the city of Nineveh. He only tells him to proclaim **to it the message that I give you**. What Yahweh says, Jonah is to say.

■ **3** The first part of v 3 reports that Jonah ***rose*** [*qûm*] **and went to Nineveh** ***according to the word of Yahweh***. The text does not employ a verb that describes this action as obedience, though one may interpret Jonah's action, as the NIV does, as obedience to Yahweh's command.

In the second part of v 3, the narrator reports that **Nineveh was a very large city** (see 1:2; 3:2) and that **it took three days to go through it**. The phrase **very large city** (*ʿîr gĕdôlâ lēʾlōhîm*) conveys Nineveh's size and might. The report that **it took three days to go through it** further emphasizes the enormous size of the city (for various interpretations regarding three days, see Jenson 2008, 72). The reference to three days recalls Jonah's length of time in the fish (1:17). The reference to three days in 3:3 evokes suspense and anticipation that Nineveh may be the next recipient of divine deliverance.

■ **4** Verse 4 reports Jonah's action on his first day in the city. He travels through about one-third of the city (**a day's journey**) and announces Yahweh's message to the city. The prophetic message is very brief (only one line!), and it conveys no element of hope whatsoever. Jonah neither points to Nineveh's specific evils nor proclaims the typical prophetic message of repentance. He simply declares that in **forty more days . . . Nineveh will be overthrown** or ***overturned***. We may safely assume that the announcement of Nineveh's destruction was part of the message that Yahweh gave Jonah to proclaim, though we cannot be certain of the full extent of Yahweh's message to Jonah. One may entertain the likelihood of Jonah condensing the message from Yahweh to a one-line judgment speech. The narrator reports that Jonah announced this short message during his one-day journey through the city, which in turn means that two-thirds of the city's population may not have heard the message of judgment directly from the prophet.

Jonah's concise message has an ironic twist when we place it in the context of the entire narrative. The verb *hāpak* often means "to overthrow" or "to turn over"; the verb can also mean "to turn" or "to change." In the final chapter of the Jonah narrative, both Nineveh and Yahweh himself will undergo a complete change of heart (3:8-10). Jonah does not seem to realize that embedded in his judgment speech is the hope of salvation for a people who are willing to change their way of life.

■ 5 Verse 5 reports the response of the entire population of the city of Nineveh. We may assume that those who have heard the message of judgment Jonah preached spread it throughout the city since he himself went only a day's journey into the city. Verse 5 gives the key elements of a repentant response to a message of judgment. **The Ninevites believed God**. The narrator's use of the verb *ʾāman* to describe the Ninevites' belief in God provides an ironic pun on the name of Jonah's father, Amittai (means "belief"). Trible observes that "the 'calling' by the son of Belief elicits belief in God" (1996, 513).

The Ninevites' belief generates physical, corporate expression through the proclamation of a communal **fast**. The narrative demonstrates the all-inclusive nature of the fast, **from the greatest to the least** (the NIV adds **all of them**).

■ 6 In v 6, the ***word*** (*dābār*, "word" or "thing," **warning**) reaches **the king**. The text depicts the word as ***touching*** (*nāgaʿ*, **reached**) the king. He was deeply affected by what he heard. Throughout the episode, the narrator never makes mention of the king's specific identity; he is simply **the king of Nineveh**.

Verse 6 reports the response of the king to the word that reached him. He also followed the traditional rituals of mourning and repentance. He removed the symbols of his power by stepping down from the **throne** and taking off his **royal robes**. He put on **sackcloth** and **sat down in the dust** to display his sorrow and contrition. These rituals performed by the king indicate the depth and sincerity of the king's contrition and his utter dependence on God. Jenson has commented that "the movement from throne to ashes is a downward movement towards the grave but, unlike Jonah's downward movement in ch. 1, it is carried out voluntarily and from the best of motives" (2008, 76).

■ 7 The king, as a participant and leader in contrition and humiliation, proceeded to decree that all of the inhabitants of his kingdom, both human (*hāʾādām*, "the human") and nonhuman (*habbĕhēmâ*, "the beast"), should join him in doing the same. The royal decree emerged from both **the king and his nobles**. Although the emphasis upon the animals may reflect narrative humor, Jenson comments rightly that such an interpretation "may underestimate the close links between humans and animals that are found in traditional societies" (2008, 78). To underscore the comprehensive nature of the fast, the text makes clear that animals are to include both cattle (**herds**) and sheep (**flocks**).

The royal decree indicated what the people and animals were to abstain: **taste, eat, drink**. The word **anything** appears between the verbs **taste** and **eat**, and it could function as the object of either verb. Both the NIV and NRSV associate it with the verb **taste**; however, because the word ***water*** (omitted entirely in the NIV) appears before the verb **drink**, the word **anything** could easily be the object of the verb **eat**. The verse would thus read: ***No human or animal, cattle or flock, shall taste. They will not eat anything, and they will not drink water***. The second part of the decree, ***They will not eat anything, and they will not drink water***, seems to pertain more specifically to animals, since it employs the verb *rāʿâ* ("graze") rather than *ʾākal*, the more commonly used verb for human eating.

■ **8** The decree is continued in v 8. Both human and animal were to cover themselves (reflexive form of *kāsâ*; see v 6) with **sackcloth** just as the king had, and they were to **call urgently on God**. The crisis they were faced with required them to use their full strength (*ḥāzqâ*, **urgently**) when they made their appeal to God for help.

Verse 8 ends with the king's call to the city in crisis to **give up** [*šûb*, ***repent***] **their evil ways and their violence**. The community's call upon God is not expressed through mantic activity or raised volume but through authentic repentance. The NIV **give up** does not adequately convey the element of contrition involved in repentance. The city known for its violence and great wickedness heard from its king a demand to repent of their sinful way of life. The decree of the king echoes the words of the prophets of Israel.

■ **9** The king concluded his decree by declaring, **Who knows? God may *turn and change his mind***. The tentative nature of the king's statement recalls the sailors' statement in 1:6. Neither the sailors nor the king attempt to presume upon or manipulate God. Jenson rightly notes that rather than "skeptical resignation in the face of a situation that cannot be changed," the statement functions "to underline trust and total dependence, and to negate any notion of manipulation, guarantee or bargain" (2008, 79). The king's statement shares an uncanny resemblance to Joel's declaration, which also occurs within the context of a communal fast (Joel 2:14; see Nogalski 2011, 441). Both texts attempt to insure that the fast is not a manipulation of divine activity. Nevertheless, both texts assume that a change in divine action is possible. In Joel this change would be evident through a divine blessing. In Jonah this change would be evident through Yahweh's *turning* from his **fierce anger** against the Ninevites.

Verse 9 ends with the king's hope that God's favorable response to their repentance would spare them from destruction. This concern over someone or something dying or not dying occurs as a thread throughout the Jonah narrative (see 1:6, 14; see also 4:10). This reappearing thread functions to provide a stark contrast to Jonah's ambivalence toward Nineveh's potential death.

■ **10** Verse 10 reports God's favorable response to the Ninevites. Although the text by no means disparages the sackcloth, ashes, and abstinence from food and drink, it does not emphasize God's seeing these activities of the Ninevites. However, it does depict Yahweh's recognition that **they turned from their evil ways**.

In response to their turning (*šûb*; see 3:8), God compassionately changed his mind (*niḥam*; **relented**). While the verb *niḥam* conveys a sense of divine pity or ***compassion***, the remainder of v 10 clearly demonstrates that the verb indicates a change in divine intention (regarding the verb *niḥam* and the Israelite tradition of God's change of mind, see Joel 2:13-14; Hos 11:8-9; Amos 7:3, 6; Limburg 1993, 84-86). The text states that God changed his mind ***concerning the evil which he had spoken to do to them, and he did not do it***. As Nineveh turned (*šûb*) from its evil (*rāʿâ*), God changed the course of action (*niḥam*) concerning the forthcoming evil (*rāʿâ*) against Nineveh.

FROM THE TEXT

In the plot of the Jonah narrative, the opening line of ch 3 is literarily and theologically critical as the word of the Lord comes to Jonah a *second* time. Without this turn of events, Jonah remains the disobedient prophet and Nineveh's future remains hopeless. The essential theological vision of the Jonah narrative, however, is neither Jonah's recalcitrance nor Nineveh's sin. The narrative's focus is upon the God whose very nature allows him to change his plans of destruction. The Lord is indeed the God of the "second chance," whether that second chance is for the prophet himself or for Nineveh. The text's portrayal of a tenacious, determined deity calls upon subsequent generations of God's people to see and to confess where they have become disheartened or disillusioned and have consequently "given up" on their prophetic role in the world.

Though the Ninevites did not know Yahweh the God of Israel (notice the absence of the name Yahweh in the decree of the king), they call on God who sent his messenger to announce his judgment on the city of Nineveh. As limited and imperfect as Nineveh's theological understanding might be, Yahweh hears their cry. Throughout the Jonah narrative, the narrator seeks to demonstrate that Yahweh is *God* of all people groups regardless of national, cultural, or linguistic affiliation. Yahweh is *God* of all human beings, including those whose narratives vary from that of the covenant community. This God of the nations is *God* of even Israel's enemies. No group finds itself excluded from Yahweh's scope of authority, concern, and operation. The conviction underlying the narrative shares important dialogue with Amos' conviction that Yahweh was actively engaged in the deliverance of the enemies of Israel, the Philistines and the Arameans (Amos 9:7). Likewise, Paul's declaration in Athens (Acts 17) shares a significant conversation with the narrative's generic reference to God. Observing the altar inscribed *to the unknown god,* Paul announces, "So you are ignorant of the very thing you worship—and this is what I am going to proclaim to you" (Acts 17:23). He proceeds to give definition to this *unknown god* as the god who made every human nation from one human (Acts 17:26).

One of the most striking theological depictions in the Jonah narrative is one that has appeared rather consistently in *the twelve* (e.g., see Hos 11:8-9; Joel 2:12-14, 18-20; Amos 7:3, 6). In response to the repentance and petition of Nineveh, God changes the divine plans (i.e., changes his mind) concerning the destruction of Nineveh. The text challenges the reading audience to take seriously the role of human repentance as well as God's compassionate and gracious response to the human cry.

Texts such as this one in the OT do not challenge the notion of divine sovereignty itself as much as preconceptions of the *meaning* of divine sovereignty. The reader often comes to the biblical text with preconceived ideas of sovereignty and power. The God we encounter in the Jonah narrative is a God who is touched by the cry of his creation. He is a God who enters into relationship with his creation, which compels him to respond to creation with grace and compassion. Changing his mind is in the very nature and function of the sovereign God. Nogalski makes the following significant statement:

> Most instances where the Bible speaks of God changing God's mind involved human repentance or intercession. Theologically, this means we serve a dynamic God for whom the future is open. We do not serve a God who has preordained what will happen, but a God willing to wait for humans to change even though that waiting causes pain. . . . God changes God's mind *because* God responds to the responses human beings make, and the future unfolds accordingly. (2011, 349)

While the narrator is comfortable with a theological vision in which the God of compassion changes the divine mind, the narrator is equally careful to maintain the freedom of the Lord to act as he ultimately desires. Divine compassion does not result from human manipulation of divine power. The capacity of God to change his mind does not give to human beings the capacity to overpower God and thereby determine outcomes. God maintains control over his actions. The narrator clearly and poignantly emphasizes his commitment to divine transcendence and freedom through the king's declaration, "Who knows? God may yet relent and with compassion turn from his fierce anger so that we will not perish" (3:9; see also Joel 2:12-14).

IV. EPISODE 4: AN ANGRY MESSENGER, A COMPASSIONATE GOD: JONAH 4:1-11

BEHIND THE TEXT

The fourth and final episode functions as an epilogue to the narrative of Jonah. Though Jonah went reluctantly to Nineveh, his mission was "successful" in that the Ninevites responded favorably to his message (ch 3). However, in the final episode Jonah responds to the success of his mission with anger and expresses his own death wish three times (4:3, 8, 9). Within the broader context of the OT, the death wish is rare (see Nogalski 2011, 446). Even in the deepest despair and grief, the lament moves toward a cry for rescue rather than for death. While Job's death wish occurs within the context of his suffering and loss (3:1-19; 6:8-10), the death wishes of the prophets Elijah (1 Kgs 19:1-4) and Jeremiah (20:14-18) occur within the context of opposition and threat. In contrast to these rare death wishes, neither suffering nor loss, neither opposition nor threat, engender Jonah's death wish. Rather, prophetic "success" leads to his desire to die.

The concluding episode of ch 4 contains three subunits. In the first subunit (vv 1-4) Jonah cites Yahweh's compassionate nature (Exod 34:6-7) as the reason for his fleeing to Tarshish and expresses his death wish. Yahweh responds to Jonah with the question about the appropriateness of his anger.

In the second subunit (Jonah 4:5-9), three creatures serve at the divine disposal: a bush, a worm, and the wind. The Jonah narrative is already familiar with the divine deployment of creatures (e.g., wind and fish). This subunit also concludes with Jonah's death wish followed by the divine question concerning the appropriateness of the prophet's anger.

The final subunit (vv 10-11) takes the form of a divine monologue. In Yahweh's speech, Jonah's concern with the bush becomes a foil to God's concern with Nineveh. The final episode and the narrative as a whole end with Yahweh's rhetorical question, which seeks a response from Jonah, but he gives no reply. Inherent within the narrative's conclusion, the addressee of the question is not limited to Jonah. The reader of the text becomes an addressee as well so that the text leaves the audience to answer the divine question.

IN THE TEXT

■ **1-4** This subunit begins with a narrative introduction (v 1): ***it*** [i.e., this occurrence] ***was a great evil to Jonah and he was angry*** (**But to Jonah this seemed very wrong, and he became angry**). Nineveh turned from its *evil* ways and God changed his plans concerning the *evil* upon Nineveh (see 3:10), but Jonah saw these as *evil*. The narrator seems to suggest that Jonah took on Yahweh's anger, which he had turned away from the Ninevites. Jonah responded to his salvation with thanksgiving, but anger was his response to the salvation of the Ninevites.

Verses 2-3 are in the form of a prayer that Jonah prayed. The prayer begins with a question addressed to Yahweh: ***Is not this what I spoke when I was still in my land?*** Although the demonstrative pronoun (i.e., ***this***) has no direct referent, it likely indicates Yahweh's deliverance of Nineveh prompted by Yahweh's gracious character. Jonah then reveals the reason why he fled to Tarshish. The primary verb *qādam* ("go beforehand," "go in front of") followed by the infinitive form of *bāraḥ* ("to flee") indicates that Jonah carried out his action in advance or in anticipation of an action on the part of Yahweh. **That is what I tried to forestall by fleeing to Tarshish** is an adequate reading of the text. He was being proactive. He had hoped that his preemptive strike would spoil Yahweh's plans. Jonah then sums up his knowledge of Yahweh in the final segment of v 2. His words, **I knew**, reflect a confident "assertion of someone totally sure of himself" (Wolff 1986, 166). Fretheim has poignantly observed that Jonah fled "not because of *unbelief*, but because of a certain *belief* which he has" (1977, 78). As a member of the covenant community of Israel, Jonah fully knew the character of his God. What he knew about Yahweh was what Israel confessed about their God: ***Yahweh is* a gracious and compassionate God, slow to anger and abounding in love, a God who relents from sending calamity**. This ancient creedal statement has its origin in Yahweh's revelation of his character in the context of the golden calf incident in the wilderness (Exod 34:6-7; see also Num 14:18; Neh 9:17; Ps 103:8).

Israel's traditional faith, reiterated by Jonah in 4:2, emphasized Yahweh as a God who **relents** [*niḥām*] **from sending calamity** or evil on a sinful individual or people; this relenting on the part of Yahweh is grounded in Yahweh's grace, mercy, covenant faithfulness, and slowness to anger (→ Joel 2:13; Limburg 1993, 90-92).

Jonah's prayer ends with a death wish—**take away my life** [*nepeš*]**, for it is better for me to die than to live** (v 3). Previously when the prophet's *nepeš* was ebbing away, Yahweh had rescued him (2:7). Grateful praise was his response to God when God spared his life (2:9). His wish for death stems from his anger toward Yahweh, who rescued the Ninevites from their impending destruction. The life he once sought he is now willing to trade for death.

Verse 4 of ch 4 is Yahweh's response to Jonah, who viewed death as more appropriate (*ṭôb*) than life. God asked Jonah if his anger was appropriate (*ṭôb*). Yahweh's question (**Is it right** [*ṭôb*] **for you to be angry?**) is about the "rightness" or the appropriateness of Jonah's response.

■ **5-9** Jonah did not answer Yahweh's question; instead he responded with his 4:1-9
actions. He went out and sat down at a location **east of the city** and constructed a temporary **shelter** (*sûkkāh*) to provide shade and comfort to his life (v 5). The narrative does not deal with the significance of **east** [*qedem*] **of the city**. The location both establishes a context for the rising sun (i.e., from the east) and anticipates the **scorching east** [*qādîm*] **wind** that is soon to come upon Jonah (v 8). Jonah sat in the shade of the shelter **to see** [NIV adds **waited**] **what would happen to the city**. The narrator does not specify for what Jonah was looking. Wolff notes that "his very attitude is a defiant reply: we shall see whether my anger is justifiable or not! He shows his scorn of Yahweh by waiting for a change 'in the city' instead of examining himself" (1986, 169). It is possible that Jonah perhaps thought that the Ninevites would soon return to their wickedness, which would prompt Yahweh to suspend his mercy and carry out his judgment that he announced through Jonah. Jonah wants to see "what will happen *to* Nineveh, . . . what God intends concerning the city" (Perry 2006, 65).

In v 6, the narrator reports Yahweh's action to provide **shade** to Jonah and to **ease his discomfort. The Lord God *appointed*** a **plant** to **grow up over Jonah**. This is the only instance in the narrative where the narrator utilizes the divine name **the Lord God**. The verb ***appointed*** (*mānâ*) (see also 1:17;

4:7-8) indicates not only the will of the Creator at work but also the response of creation to the will of the Creator. The narrator refers to the plant as a *qîqāywōn*. This word occurs only in Jonah, so one cannot be certain as to its precise identity. However, the term may refer to a castor-oil tree or bottle-gourd with rapidly growing and rapidly withering vines. Although Jonah had already constructed a shelter, Yahweh now participates in the comfort-giving enterprise. The narrative literally describes the plant as being a means to ***deliver*** Jonah ***from evil*** (**ease his discomfort**). The narrator consistently points out Yahweh's propensity toward deliverance, whether the deliverance is of the sailors, Jonah, or Nineveh.

Verse 6 ends with a note about Jonah's ***great joy*** over the plant that gave him shelter. More than an inner emotional feeling of bliss (i.e., **very happy**), the verb conveys Jonah as actively engaging in jubilant celebration. Literally, the narrator describes the prophet as ***rejoicing a great joy***.

Verse 7 reports another divine action; God ***appointed*** [**provided**] **a worm** to act upon the plant. At the rise of dawn, the divinely appointed worm **chewed** (*nākâ*, "to strike") the plant. As a consequence of the worm's action, the plant **withered**. The report of the divine action is continued in v 8. As **the sun arose**, God ***appointed*** **a scorching east wind**. God again involves his creation to carry out his purpose. The narrative had already reported that God "sent a great wind on the sea" (1:4). Old Testament texts portray the seasonal winds emerging from the desert as divine instruments of both salvation (Exod 14:21) and judgment (Hos 13:15). Just as the worm *struck* (*nākâ*) the plant, the risen sun *struck* (*nākâ*, **blazed**) the head of Jonah. Jonah **grew faint** just as the plant withered.

Verse 8 ends with the report of Jonah's desire for death instead of life. Though the narrative does not make it clear, we may assume that it was the intensity of his physical distress that prompted the prophet to wish for death. Jonah repeats word-for-word what he already stated at the end of 4:3. He wants to live when God gives him life; he wants to die when God extends life to his enemies or withholds from him the comforts of life.

In v 9, Yahweh responds to Jonah's death wish word-for-word as he did in v 4: ***Is it appropriate for you to be angry?*** The phrase **about the plant** included in Yahweh's question reveals the motivation for Jonah's anger. Jonah responds in the affirmative, ***I am angry enough to die***. Jonah's anger concerning the plant leads to his resolute desire to die. It is ironic that the prophet who wanted to die because Nineveh lived now wants to die because a plant died. The narrative unambiguously depicts the prophet's misguided priorities, and Yahweh will all but say the same in the closing verse of the story.

■ **10-11** Yahweh's response to Jonah begins with his observation of Jonah's concern (*hûs* also conveys the idea of pity or compassion) for the plant. Jonah's pity toward the plant is likely in direct relationship to what the plant could do for Jonah. Viewing Jonah's pity as a "skillful use of irony," Wolff has observed that the meaning of Yahweh's statement is "the very opposite of what Yahweh says: Jonah is not really suffering with the withered plant at all; he is simply missing his own comfort" (1986, 173).

Yahweh also observes that Jonah **did not tend** or **make** the plant **grow** (*gādôl*; v 10). Yahweh describes the plant as coming into existence overnight and as perishing overnight. The concern over perishing (*ʾābad*) has already occurred twice in the narrative, first the sailors (1:6, 14) and later the king of Nineveh (3:9). Again it is ironic that Jonah demonstrates no concern over the perishing of either the sailors or Nineveh, yet he shows tremendous concern—to the point of death—over the perishing of the plant.

The narrative vividly contrasts Jonah's active pity with Yahweh's active pity in the concluding statement of the narrative (v 11). The negatively constructed statement in the Hebrew text can be translated as a rhetorical question by God to Jonah (thus, **Should I not have concern . . . ?**).

Verse 11 contrasts the pity of Jonah with the pity of Yahweh. Yahweh's reference to Nineveh as **the great city** at both the narrative's beginning (1:2) and end (4:11) functions as an inclusio for the book. Although the text depicts the greatness of many other objects (e.g., wind, storm, fish), the great city of Nineveh envelops the short story as the ultimate divine concern. While the narrator depicts the greatness of the city in 3:3 in relationship to its physical size, Yahweh describes its greatness in terms of the multitude of its residents, both human and animal.

Verse 11 of ch 4 shows the inclusive nature of Yahweh's compassion. His compassion reaches out to the city—its large human population and its many animals. The phrase **who cannot tell** [*yādaʿ*; ***know***] **their right hand from their left** indicates the almost childlike helplessness of Nineveh's inhabitants. Jenson interprets the reference as denoting a "relative lack of knowledge of God and his law" (2008, 93). Because of Nineveh's lack of knowledge, Jenson concludes that "they are thus worthy of compassion in comparison to Israel, which has all the benefits of the Torah (Deut 4:6)" (ibid.). God, who summons Jonah to "preach against" Nineveh at the beginning of the narrative (1:2), is portrayed at the end of the narrative as "a God subject to distress, disappointment, and suffering" (Craig 1999, 69).

The book ends with an open-ended question; it provides no narrative resolution. The narrative as it comes to us ends with the *great* silence of Jonah to Yahweh's *great* question. If Jonah responded, then it remains unknown to the reader.

FROM THE TEXT

At the end of the narrative, the readers of this little but profoundly significant narrative stand (or sit) with Jonah outside of *the city,* the object of God's compassion and mercy.

The angry response of Jonah compels the readers to reflect on their own anger toward God or toward the cities of their nation. Why do God's people get angry when things do not happen as they had planned it or when their comfort is threatened or when they see God's mercy at work in the lives of the so-called sinners in the world? After all, isn't God supposed to be in the business of destroying sinners and offering comfort and salvation to those who follow his precepts and commands? Why does he not protect the community of faith from the discomforts of life? The narrative also invites the readers to ponder how often do they grieve over their dying plants of shade and how seldom do they grieve over a dying Nineveh-like city in their world? How often do they seek the destruction of Nineveh rather than its repentance and deliverance? The narrative of Jonah challenges the readers to choose between the worldview of Jonah and the worldview of God. Jonah insists on judgment; God insists on salvation.

The narrative's description of Nineveh's lack of knowledge raises important questions for the reading audience. The text asserts a relationship between Nineveh's lack of knowledge and the divine pity upon the city. Jonah appears to hold Nineveh fully responsible for its actions; God's response suggests that Jonah does not perceive the situation correctly. As Wolff has observed, the "capacity for distinguishing and judging is not as fully developed among the Ninevites as Jonah would like to expect" (1986, 175). Therefore, that which "Jonah is inclined to despise is for Yahweh one more reason for compassion" (ibid.).

The reading community must at least consider the implications of the divine concern for those persons, societies, and cultures that have limited or no knowledge of God. What does the story suggest concerning the prevenient grace of God upon those who have limited or no knowledge of God? What does it say to God's people concerning their responsibility to those who have limited or no knowledge of God? What does the story say to God's people who are preoccupied with pronouncing judgment on the very same people that God seeks to save from death and destruction?

The narrative of Jonah also invites the readers to consider the breadth and depth of divine concern. The Lord's pity and care extends to both humans and animals. Though the concluding statement does not elevate nonhuman over human, it does depict God's care for the nonhuman alongside the human. Throughout the narrative of Jonah, God's creatures are vital to the divine endeavor. Wind, fish, worms, and plants are all integral to the mission and activity of God in the narrative of Jonah. Whether God employs light to divide darkness, firmament to divide water, land to contain seas and send forth plants, and luminaries to rule, the biblical narrative insists upon the participation of God's creatures in the creative and redemptive work of God. In the Jonah narrative, the prophet may be the only character that refuses to comprehend this reality and therefore the only character that refuses to positively participate in the divine story.

Finally, the open-ended rhetorical question that concludes the entire narrative of Jonah provides for the reading audience a poignant example of the Bible functioning as Scripture. The readers must decide an answer and therefore must finish the story. Refusing to provide a tidy, neat conclusion in which everyone "lives happily ever after," Scripture insists that the text must finally shape the identity and the ethic of the reading audience. Perhaps in the end, outside of God, the most significant character of the Jonah narrative is the subsequent generations of reading communities that must give an answer to the divine question. It is subsequent communities that must ultimately decide with which character it will identify. Will it stand with Jonah and pity that which protects it, so that its very reason for existence becomes its own survival? Or will it stand with God and pity the community that lacks knowledge—even when that community is its greatest enemy and threatens the very survival of God's people? The words of Jesus offer wisdom to the readers of Jonah as they ponder these questions: "Whoever wants to save their life will lose it, but whoever loses their life for me and for the gospel will save it" (Mark 8:35).

MICAH

INTRODUCTION

A. Micah the Prophet

Based upon the three kings noted in the editorial superscription to the book of Micah (Jotham, Ahaz, and Hezekiah), the prophet's activity occurred during the second half of the eighth century B.C., not before 742 B.C. and not after 686 B.C. While Simundson narrowed the window of Micah's activity to 730-701 B.C., Wolff has narrowed it even further to 733-722 B.C. (Simundson 2005, 293; Wolff 1990, 8). Mays has placed Micah within the extremely brief period of Sennacherib's siege of Jerusalem in 701 B.C. and the few months leading up to those events (1976, 16).

During the broader time span noted in the superscription, both the northern and southern kingdoms experienced a rapid decline starting with the aggressive policies of Tiglath-Pileser III (745-727 B.C.). Micah was fully aware of the advance of the Assyrian armies against the northern kingdom (1:2-7); he would have also known about the fall of Samaria in 722/721 B.C. The broader time span in the superscription includes Sennacherib's invasion of Judah (see 1:8-16) and his siege of Jerusalem in 701 B.C. (see historical context below). The prophetic activity of Micah therefore witnessed the great challenges, transformations, and defeats in the life of God's people.

While the superscription states that the book includes "the vision" that Micah "saw concerning Samaria and Jerusalem," most of Micah's oracles are addressed to Jerusalem and its vicinity. The superscription also describes Micah as being from Moresheth (→ Mic 1:1, 14). Because Moresheth was a village twenty-five miles southwest of Jerusalem and because of his affinity with the oppressed whom Micah depicts as "my people," Micah may have had a unique familiarity with the socioeconomic plight of Judah's agrarian farmers. However, one cannot be certain precisely what his relationship with them might have been. While the text does not directly address the significance of Micah's name, the name Micah (shortened form of Micaiah, "Who is like Yahweh?") literarily foreshadows the concluding question of the book itself (7:18): "Who is a God like you?"

While the book does not recount a specific prophetic "call experience" in the life of Micah, the prophet's depiction of himself in 3:8 provides significant insight into his perception of himself as a prophet. It is possible that Micah faced opposition to his prophetic activity and was told by other prophets not to "prophesy" (2:6; see Amos 7:10-17).

The prophet Micah reappears in the book of Jeremiah (ch 26). During Jeremiah's trial by the priests and the prophets, some of the elders reminded the people that Micah also prophesied about the destruction of Zion (see Mic 3:12) and that King Hezekiah did not put the prophet to death but instead sought the Lord's favor (Jer 26:17-19).

B. The Historical Context and Audience of Micah

As in many of the prophetic books, the editorial superscription supplies a historical context for the ministry of Micah. Verse 1 places the ministry of Micah during the reign of the southern kingdom kings Jotham (co-regent with his father Uzziah 750-742 B.C.; 742-735 B.C.), Ahaz (735-715 B.C.), and Hezekiah (715-686 B.C.). The superscription describes the book as the vision that Micah saw concerning both Samaria and Jerusalem. While most of the oracles in Micah are directed toward the southern kingdom of Judah, the first chapter does address the situation in the northern kingdom by making special reference to Samaria.

A brief overview of the period to which the superscription refers indicates the volatility of this era. Early in Ahaz's reign over the southern kingdom, the Syro-Israelite alliance against Judah occurred (ca. 735 B.C.). Later in Ahaz's reign, the northern kingdom of Israel with its capital in Samaria fell to the Assyrians (722/721 B.C.). At the end of the eighth century B.C., Sennacherib led a military campaign westward. After gaining a significant victory over the Egyptians at Ekron in Philistia, Sennacherib made his way into and through the southern kingdom of Judah. This Assyrian advance is reflected both in Mic 1:10-16 and Isa 10:28-31 (regarding the Assyrian advance and siege, see 2 Kgs 18:13—19:37; Isa 36—37; Anderson 1986, 347-48). Sennacherib gives the following report of his conquest of numerous villages and cities in Judah and finally his siege of Jerusalem in a clay prism:

> As to Hezekiah, the Jew, he did not submit to my yoke, I laid siege to 46 of his strong cities, walled forts and to the countless small villages in their vicinity, and conquered (them) by means of well-stamped (earth-) ramps, and battering-rams. . . . I drove out (of them) 200,150 people, young and old, male and female, horses, mules, donkeys, camels, big and small cattle beyond counting, and considered (them) booty. Himself I made a prisoner in Jerusalem, his royal residence, like a bird in a cage. I surrounded him with earthwork in order to molest those who were leaving his city's gates. (Pritchard 1969, 288)

While ch 1 mentions Samaria, the book focuses upon the city of Jerusalem and persons within Jerusalem who have the power to exercise authority in political, economic, judicial, and religious affairs (i.e., chiefs, rulers, prophets, and priests). Micah especially expresses a concern over the manner in which the powerful elite have used their legitimate offices for self-serving reasons at the expense of persons they are to protect. He emphasizes the manner in which they take, even hoard, land and houses (2:2, 8-9). While the means they employed may have been technically legitimate, Micah demonstrates a concern over the never-ending greed of those who exercise authority in the community (3:1-3, 5, 11).

Micah especially speaks on behalf of persons who experience oppression by the actions of the city's powerful elite. Perhaps his use of the phrase "my people" indicates a unique affinity that the prophet shares with these oppressed, powerless communities and individuals within Judah (see 2:8-9; 3:1-3). The audience addressed by Micah especially includes those persons in positions of power and authority who misuse their positions for self-serving and profiteering purposes. The superscription's specific reference to the capital cities along with Micah's early reference to Samaria and Jerusalem as "Jacob's transgression" and "Judah's high place" respectively foreshadows his concern with structures of power. The early depiction of Samaria's fall in 1:6-7 and the focus upon Jerusalem's fate, whether its destruction or restoration, throughout the remainder of the book affirms Micah's focus upon the political and socioeconomic centers of Israelite society.

C. The Book of Micah as a Literary Work

1. Literary Features and Genres

The book of Micah is predominantly comprised of judgment and salvation oracles. Following the typical structure, the judgment oracles first depict the sins of the people and proceed to announce the nature of divine judgment upon the people.

The oracles of Micah employ a variety of literary features and genres, including wordplays, metaphors, lamentation, and lawsuit. While some of the meanings have been lost over time, artistic devices and plays on words convey the onslaught of the Assyrian army against cities in Judah in 1:10-16. Similar to other prophets such as Hosea and Jeremiah, Micah employs various metaphorical images such as wild, howling animals (1:8), bald vultures (1:16), sheep gathered in a pasture (2:12-13), and the writhing pains of a woman in labor (4:9-10).

A unique feature in the book of Micah is the call to lamentation in 1:8-9 followed by a lament proper at the conclusion of the book in ch 7. By beginning with a call to lamentation and concluding with a lamentation, the text provides the community with actual words by which they might join their city in crying out to God. As the oracles of judgment and salvation are subsequent to the call to lamentation, they function structurally to engender the lamentation that concludes with expressions of trust and hope in God. The lament seems to emerge from the "mouth" of the city of Jerusalem. In ch 6 (see also 1:2-7), Micah employs the genre of prophetic lawsuit (*rîb*) in order to present the divine accusation and judgment against Jerusalem.

2. Historical Development of the Text

The canonical book of Micah reveals at least two levels of historical development. On the one hand, many of the oracles speak directly into the milieu of the second half of the eighth century B.C., that is, the period in which Micah was active. However, other texts seem to speak into the situation of the southern kingdom once the Babylonian Empire had replaced the Assyrian Empire (4:10) and once Jerusalem had fallen to Babylon in 587 B.C. (7:8-20). The messages of hope and restoration in chs 4—5 and ch 7 assume that Judah and its capital of Jerusalem have undergone catastrophic defeat and destruction.

Since the time of Stade's work in 1881, much of the history of modern critical scholarship has interpreted chs 1—3 and perhaps parts of Mic 6 and 7:1-7 as reflecting the words of the eighth-century prophet, and much of chs 4—7 as the work of later editors of the book (see esp. Mays 1976, 12-15, 21-33; Wolff 1990, 2-3; Andersen and Freedman 2000, 17-24; Allen 1976, 241-51; McKane 1998, 1-8). While Hillers agrees "that the present text shows signs of editing or alteration with the needs of a later, exilic community in mind," he ultimately concludes that "redaction-criticism of Micah fails to carry a satisfying degree of conviction" (1984, 3-4). Though biblical scholars have suggested diverse reconstructions of the historical development of the text, there is no consensus. Achtemeier's conclusion is insightful and helpful for interpreting the canonical text:

> Certainly there is no doubt that the prophet's own oracles have been revised or supplemented with later material over a number of years. . . . But to divide Micah into atomistic oracular units, to judge them genuine or nongenuine, and to separate them on the basis of the supposed historical background of each unit is to miss the overriding, unified message of the book. (1996a, 288)

3. Micah and Intertextuality within the Prophets

As Micah and Isaiah were later-eighth-century B.C. contemporaries in Judah, one might expect shared features, including references to a messianic figure, a remnant, and an anticipated future "day." Micah 4:1-4 and Isa 2:1-4 share the anticipation of Yahweh's imminent peace-filled reign (→ Mic 4:1-4). Achtemeier represents the opinion that material from Isaiah was "taken up and incorporated in the Micah corpus" (1996a, 290). However, it is difficult to be certain whether one prophet employed material from the other or whether they both relied upon a common tradition. It is certainly possible that a subsequent editor had a hand in both books. Regardless of the conclusions that one might make concerning the common features, from a canonical perspective, one should read and hear each text in light of the other.

The reference to Micah by Jerusalem's elders in Jer 26:18-19 (see Mic 3:12) demonstrates that the Micah text continued to speak into and inform subsequent situations and texts (regarding the general relationship between the Jeremiah text and Micah's overall ministry, see Hillers [1984, 8-9]; regarding various themes, vocabulary, and idioms of Micah that reappear in Jeremiah, see Andersen and Freedman 2000, 27).

4. Flow and Structure of the Book of Micah

The literary flow of the book of Micah moves back and forth between judgment and salvation three times. Subsequent to the brief judgment upon Samaria and the poetic depiction of the Assyrian onslaught in ch 1, chs 2—3 present various oracles of judgment against Jerusalem. A brief interlude of hope (2:12-13) is found between the oracles of judgment in 2:1-11 and ch 3. Chapters 4—5 shift dramatically toward a depiction of hope and restoration. Chapter 6 returns to a message of judgment with a court trial (lawsuit) as its setting. Chapter 7 introduces a formal lament spoken by the devastated city of Jerusalem. Finally, the text concludes with a promise of salvation (7:8-20). Typical of the lament structure, the declaration of patient trust in the Lord in v 7 functions as the "hinge" between the outcry of grief in vv 1-6 and the anticipated restoration in vv 8-20 (regarding four possible structures in Micah, see Simundson 2005, 291-92; regarding a single division between 1:2—5:15 addressed to all nations and 6:1—7:20 addressed to Israel, see Mays 1976, 3-12; see also Achtemeier 1996a, 288).

This alternating pattern of judgment (1:2—2:11; 3:1-12; 6:1—7:7) and salvation (2:12-13; 4:1—5:15; 7:8-20) within the flow of the book provides a structural framework by which one might examine the book of Micah. A plural imperative to "hear" (*šimʿû*; see 1:2; 3:1; 6:1) begins each section of judgment. These imperative calls indicate a primary structural division of the text as they separate the book into three judgment-salvation units (see Limburg 1988, 159-61). Reference to the nations in 1:2 and 7:16 also provides a framework for the book.

Based upon the three series of alternating judgment and hope within the book of Micah, the commentary will follow the structural outline below. The English versification slightly differs from the Hebrew versification in chs 4 and 5 (Hebrew 4:14 is 5:1 in English translations) (→ Mic 4—5). The Hebrew and English return to the same versification in ch 6.

I. Superscription (1:1)
II. Judgment and Hope: Series 1 (1:2—2:13)
    A. Oracles of Judgment (1:2—2:11)
        1. Against the Centers of Power (1:2-16)
        2. Against Self-serving Socioeconomic Practices (2:1-11)
    B. A Glimmer of Hope (2:12-13)
III. Judgment and Hope: Series 2 (3:1—5:15)
    A. Condemnations of Judah's Leadership (3:1-12)
    B. Oracles of Hope (4:1—5:15)
        1. A Vision of Restoration (4:1-13 [4:1-14 HB])
            a. Nations' Pilgrimage to Zion (4:1-5)
            b. Yahweh Will Gather the Exiled People (4:6-8)
            c. Judah's Exile to, and Rescue from, Babylon (4:9-10)
            d. Victory over the Enemy Nations (4:11-13)
        2. A Ruler from Bethlehem (5:1-6 [4:14—5:5 HB])
        3. The Emerging Kingdom (5:7-15 [5:6-14 HB])
            a. Judah's Triumph over Enemy Nations (5:7-9)
            b. Yahweh's Judgment of Idolatrous Nations (5:10-15)
IV. Judgment and Hope: Series 3 (6:1—7:20)
    A. The Divine Lawsuit (6:1-16)
    B. Lamentation with Hope (7:1-20)
        1. Jerusalem's Lament (7:1-7)
        2. Anticipation of Deliverance (7:8-10)
        3. Restoration and Rebuilding of Jerusalem (7:11-17)
        4. Who Is like Yahweh? (7:18-20)

D. Theological Themes

1. Divine Judgment and Divine Promise

The book of Micah provides a unique prophetic perspective concerning Jerusalem, which is shaped by and large by the theology of the Davidic covenant and a theology of Zion. On the one hand, Micah is adamant concerning divine judgment upon the city's leaders and the imminent catastrophic destruction of the city. On the other hand, the book anticipates the devastated city's restoration and its exaltation among the nations in days to come. While the book holds firmly to the prophetic conviction that Yahweh requires covenant fidelity and will hold Judah accountable, it is simultaneously resolute in the royal-priestly conviction that Yahweh has committed himself to the Davidic family and to his dwelling place in Zion. In its present form, the book of Micah allows for judgment and salvation, destruction and restoration, death and resurrection, to stand side by side without diminishing the significance of the other.

Micah's view of judgment is consistent with the Deuteronomic-prophetic conviction of "sowing and reaping" (see Hos 8:7; 10:12-13; Obad 15-16). The judgment of Yahweh is neither arbitrary nor capricious. Rather, it is in accord with and directly related to the specific crimes of the people (Mic 2:1-4; 3:1-4, 5-7, 9-12; see also the theological vision of Obadiah). Micah's view of restoration is also consistent with the prophetic understanding of Yahweh's commitment to be faithful to his covenant and his ultimate plans and purposes for the covenant nation.

2. Socioeconomic Condemnations and True Worship

Similar to Amos' depictions of Israel's socioeconomic crimes against one's neighbor and the extravagant worship of Yahweh, Micah vividly portrays the stark contrast between worship and daily life. He depicts the socioeconomic and judicial atrocities carried out by royal functionaries, landholders, and religious and judicial authorities as they engage in selfish acts of hoarding. What they desire, they are able to gain because of their positions of power and authority within the community (2:1). Motivated by gain (3:11), these powerful elite distort the very system intended to protect the populace in order to accumulate more. As a result, they leave the people in their care without both a dwelling place and land (2:2, 9). They act in the same manner as cannibals as they crush and devour the persons under their authority (3:1-3). In light of these atrocities, Micah is insistent that Yahweh does not seek the worship of these leaders through extravagant offerings and sacrifices. Rather, the worship that he seeks from their hands and from their hearts is expressed through actions of justice (*do* justice), faithfulness (*love* faithfulness), and humility (*walk* humbly; 6:1-8).

3. Authentic Prophetic Ministry

Likely resulting from opposition from religious and political leaders much like the opposition experienced by both Amos (7:10-17) and Jeremiah (20:1-6; 28:1-17; 36:1-26), Micah is sensitive to the nature of the authentic prophet. He contrasts his own ministry to the prophets who deliver a message according to the whims of the people (Mic 2:6, 11; 3:5). In similar manner, he views his own prophetic ministry as a foil to the priests and prophets who conduct their tasks solely for the rewards they receive (3:11). Micah considers the Spirit of the Lord, justice, power, and might as the marks of the true prophet. He is convinced that the prophet is never simply to speak the words that the people desire to hear. The true prophet is to announce to the people their transgressions and sins (3:8). This exemplary faithfulness to the prophetic task made Micah a reference point and a prophetic voice that was heard in the next century (Jer 26:18).

4. The Answer of Divine Grace and Forgiveness

The repeated movement of the text from judgment to salvation presents a final answer to a consistently rebellious people. Micah recognizes that Yahweh has committed himself to his people through covenant while he simultaneously recognizes that the community has habitually rebelled and must undergo divine judgment. In light of this complicated reality, Micah's final resolution is found solely in the gracious and forgiving nature of God. Indeed for Micah, the merciful nature of Yahweh sets him apart from all other deities and from all other powers. That which makes this God distinct, separate, or holy is his compassionate, faithful, and forgiving character. How else might the prophet announce the absolute uniqueness, the incomparable otherness, the utter holiness of the Lord God than to cry out, "Who is a God like you?" (7:18). However, from the beginning of the book, the prophet's name itself may have given a clue to the book's final answer: Micah—who is like Yahweh?

COMMENTARY

I. SUPERSCRIPTION: MICAH 1:1

■ **1** Characteristic of the prophetic books, the book of Micah opens with an editorial introduction (e.g., see Hos 1:1; Joel 1:1). The introduction affirms the divine source of the subsequent oracles and additionally provides information on the prophet's provenance, the historical context, and the primary recipients. The opening line is similar to Hosea and Joel (**the word of the Lord that came**; see Hos 1:1). Similar to Hosea and Joel but in contrast to Amos, the editor portrays the complete text as the word **that came to Micah**. The introduction acknowledges that the prophetic word did not originate with the prophet but with Yahweh himself. Addressing the theology of the prophetic word, Mays observes that the prophetic word "transcends the existence and experience of its spokesman, and has an independent self-contained reality and a power to actualize itself" (1976, 37).

In contrast to Hosea and Joel, Micah's introduction provides the prophet's hometown rather than his father's name. Employing the gentilic-adjectival form of the city, the text refers to Micah as the Moreshite (i.e., **of Moresheth**). In Jer 26:18 the prophet is referred to as "Micah of Moresheth." The name Moresheth means "possession." The name as it appears in 1:14 ("Moresheth Gath") implies an outlying village in the broader perimeters of Gath. Located in the eighty-kilometer long fertile region dividing the hill country from the coastal plain (i.e., the Shephelah), the city was likely one of many defensive cities in this strategic region. Moresheth was approximately six miles southeast of Gath itself, six miles northeast of Lachish, and twenty-four miles southwest of Jerusalem. See Historical Context in the Introduction for the names of the kings mentioned in v 1 and the setting of Micah's ministry.

In contrast to Hosea and Joel, the introduction to Micah implies that the prophet received the content of the book in a vision (**the word of the LORD that . . . he saw** [*ḥāzâ*]). Both Amos 1:1 and Obad 1 employ a similar form of the word. Micah's message specifically concerns the capitals of the northern and southern kingdoms, Samaria and Jerusalem respectively. In the opening oracle of the book, Micah specifically mentions the culpability of these cities (1:5). Two decades separated the fall of Samaria to Assyria in 722/721 B.C. and Sennacherib's advances toward Jerusalem in 701 B.C. An even greater period of time separated both of these events from Jerusalem's fall to the Babylonians in the early sixth century B.C. In light of this lengthy span of time, Mays has noted that the later Micah tradition understood the divine judgment upon Israel in 722/721 B.C. and upon Judah in 587 B.C. as "one unified action of God" (1976, 37, 39). Although the introduction of Isaiah refers to Judah and Jerusalem, no other prophetic introduction refers specifically to the capital cities of both the northern and the southern kingdoms. Micah's introduction is unique in its insistence that the prophetic message specifically addresses the central power structures of both cities.

II. JUDGMENT AND HOPE: SERIES 1: MICAH 1:2—2:13

A. Oracles of Judgment (1:2—2:11)

1. Against the Centers of Power (1:2-16)

BEHIND THE TEXT

The opening oracle of Micah is comprised of two primary units: theophany (vv 2-7) and lamentation (vv 8-16). The depiction of a theophany or divine appearance employs the two traditional elements of theophany: (*a*) announcement of divine appearance from the divine abode, and (*b*) effects of the divine appearance (regarding the theophany in biblical texts, see Wolff 1990, 46-47; Mays 1976, 42-43; Hiebert 1992, 508-10). Incorporating familiar language of the divine theophany (e.g., see Amos 1:2; Nah 1:2-5; Hab 3:2-15), the unit in Mic 1:2-7 depicts Yahweh's emergence from the temple in order to pronounce judgment against the northern kingdom of Israel. The judgment particularly emphasizes the political capital of the northern kingdom, Samaria, established by Omri in the ninth century (882-871 B.C., see 1 Kgs 16:21-29; see reference to "the statutes of Omri" in Mic 6:16). This judgment against the north is unique in the book of Micah, as most of the book addresses Judah. The concluding comment in 1:5 concerning Judah and Jerusalem demonstrates that Israel's demise provides a clear warning to Judah.

The second unit (vv 8-16) functions as a lament regarding the impending destruction of Judah and Jerusalem (regarding the text as a summons to lamentation, see Wolff 1990, 48-49). The lament commences in v 8 with Micah's own mourning and concludes in v 16 with a general call to participate in familiar practices of corporate lament (regarding corporate lament and fasts, see Joel 1:13-16; Jonah 3:6-9). In the present canonical structure of the book of Micah, lament both opens and concludes the text (see ch 7; see also lament in 2:4). However, in the concluding lament, the community waits in hope for divine deliverance.

Verses 8-16 may historically recall the advance of Sargon's Assyrian armies against Philistia (720 and 714-11 B.C.). However, they more likely reflect the devastating effects of Sennacherib's (704-681 B.C.) invasion in 701 B.C. during the reign of Hezekiah (see 2 Kgs 18:13—19:37; Isa 36:1—37:38; 2 Chr 32:1-23; Mays 1976, 52-54; Hillers 1984, 23, 30) (→ B. The Historical Context and Audience of Micah in the Introduction).

Wolff argues that Mic 1:8-16 anticipates imminent destruction of individual Judean towns rather than events that have already occurred; the lament thus reflects the decade between 733 and 723 B.C. (1990, 49-50, 53-54). In contrast to the traditional interpretation of 701 B.C., Shaw argues against 701 B.C. and for an earlier date during a period of what Shaw calls a "deep discontent over the policies of Jeroboam II" (1993, 56-67). Ben Zvi concludes, by noting the text's obvious avoidance of specific historical references, that the text actually "allows the intended audience of the written text of 1:2-16 to develop multiple readings and understandings of the text" (2000, 37).

Various cities named in these verses appear to be located in the western Judaean area of the Shephelah. As the Shephelah divided the Judean hill country in the east from the coastal plains in the west, it was comprised of fertile valleys dotted with hills (for general location of various towns, see Hillers' attempt to plot the cities on a map, 1984, 29). Several of the cities appear to have shared a direct relationship with Jerusalem. At Tell Ej-Judeideh (likely Moresheth) and Lachish, jar handles with the stamp *lmlk* ("to/for the king") have been found. David's provincial palace was located at Lachish, while Lachish along with Adullam, Gath, and Mareshah underwent fortification by Rehoboam (see 2 Chr 11:7-9). As the lament specifically cites these towns of the Shephelah, it suggests that as Yahweh's judgment reaches Jerusalem (Mic 1:12), the fertile, fortified cities of the Shephelah have already known firsthand the fate that still awaited Jerusalem. While the precise locations of some towns in ch 1 are well known, it is possible that the writer actually created other names in the text in order to provide wordplays (→ Mic 1:8-16, chart listing wordplays; see also Allen 1976, 278).

IN THE TEXT

■**2-7** Although the last line of 1:5 refers to Jerusalem, the oracle in vv 2-7 focuses upon the imminent divine judgment upon the northern kingdom alone (regarding these verses as a "transformation" of the ancient concept of a divine council and "patron deities," see Hillers 1984, 19). While the prophet directs most of his message to the southern kingdom, he understands the divine judgment upon the northern kingdom to point toward the forthcoming judgment upon Judah. The oracle in vv 2-7 reveals precedent for divine judgment upon Yahweh's covenant people, and it establishes the validity of Micah's message to Judah. As the prophetic word concerning the northern kingdom came to pass, the text assumes that the message concerning the southern kingdom will also come to pass. The passing reference to Jerusalem in v 5 makes this reality clear.

In vv 2-4, the text depicts the divine judgment in terms of a theophany (i.e., appearance of a deity). Within the context of a judicial hearing in which the indictment is about to take place, the imperative calls to **hear** (*šāmāʿ*) and to ***give attention*** (*qāšab*, **listen**) commonly occur together in prophetic accusations (e.g., Isa 28:23; 34:1; Hos 5:1). The language and metaphors of the courtroom will once again appear in Mic 6:1-8.

The reference to **peoples** and **earth** in v 2 may indicate that the addressee of the prophetic accusation is global, perhaps even cosmic (Hillers 1984, 19; Simundson 1996, 543). Assuming that the divine judgment on one nation (Israel and/or Judah) is within the broader context of Yahweh's "zeal to establish justice" universally, Hillers suggests that "the fate of God's own people is not the result of caprice, but the carrying out of a broader order" (1984, 19). Similarly, Mays has interpreted all of chs 1—5 to be Yahweh's "witness against the peoples of the earth" rather than simply a judgment against the covenant community alone (1976, 40). However, as *ʿam* (**peoples**) often refers to the inhabitants of specific localities or to a people group, the addressees may certainly be the people of Israel specifically. The word *ʾereṣ* (**earth**) most often refers to the land and certainly not the planet Earth; the addressee is most likely the land of Israel itself rather than the "globe." In light of the specific references to Israel and Judah in ch 1, the indictment is first and foremost **against** Yahweh's covenant people. By means of the phrases **all of you** and **all who live in it**, the text places emphasis upon the all-inclusive nature of the addressees.

The one who brings the charge against the people is the **Sovereign Lord** (*ʾădōnāy yĕhwih*). Amos often employs this phrase in reference to Yahweh (e.g., see Amos 1:8; 3:7). As will become evident in the text, Yahweh will function as judge, prosecuting attorney, and **witness** (*ʿēd*, regarding God as witness, see Gen 31:50; 1 Sam 12:5; Job 16:19; Jer 42:5; Mal 3:5) vis-à-vis his covenant people. Micah 1:2 makes clear that **the Lord** (*ʾădōnāy*) who dwells in **his holy**

temple in Jerusalem is the one who comes to witness against his people (see Jer 25:30-31; Joel 3:16; Amos 1:2).

Micah 1:3-4 gives the report of the coming of **the Lord . . . from his dwelling place** (theophany). The particle **look** (*hinnēh*) indicates that the theophany is already taking place. Yahweh has already come out of his temple and has begun his journey. As he **comes down** he **treads** [*dārak*] **on the heights** [*bāmâ*] **of the earth** (v 3; see Amos 4:13). Although the verb *dārak* can indicate simple, nondestructive action of marching forward, the theophanic nature of the hymn likely depicts Yahweh as leveling or pressing down upon the high places (e.g., see *dārak* in relationship to pressing grapes and olives in Isa 16:10; Jer 25:30; Amos 9:13; Mic 6:15). The term *bāmâ* (**heights** or ***high places***) can refer to the hills upon which fertility rites occurred (see 1:5 regarding Jerusalem as the *bāmâ* of Judah). However, the divine marching upon elevated places so that they become flat is a familiar motif in Israel's theophanic hymns (e.g., see Judg 5:4-5; Isa 40:3-5; Amos 4:13; Hab 3:6). Micah 1:4 describes the powerful effect of Yahweh's coming down from his temple; again, v 4 reflects the language of Israel's traditional theophanic accounts, which includes the melting of mountains (see melting mountains, rocks, or land in Ps 97:5; Amos 9:5; Nah 1:5). Images of melting mountains and bursting valleys reflect the cosmic convulsions brought about by seismic activity. Images of melting hot wax and water flowing down steep slopes reflect the flow of volcanic lava (see the quaking and fire of Sinai in Exod 19:18; see also quaking and downpour in Judg 5:4-5). The vivid portrayal of destructive eruptions foreshadows the massive destruction precipitated by the Assyrian onslaught in Mic 1:10-15.

The text proceeds to announce the reason behind Yahweh's prosecution of and testimony against Israel in v 5. While the demonstrative pronoun **this** does not have a specific referent, the phrase **all this** (*kol zōʾt*) likely refers back to the divinely produced cosmic convulsions. It simultaneously points forward to the destruction depicted in vv 10-15. Verse 5 describes the cause of the divinely led destruction: Israel's **transgression** (*pešeʿ*) and **sins** (*ḥaṭṭāʾt*). The phrase **Jacob's transgression** occurs twice in v 5, once in the causal statement at the opening of the verse and again in the rhetorical question in the second half of the verse. Although *pešeʿ* can specifically indicate willful acts of rebellion and *ḥaṭṭāʾt* can specifically denote both purposeful and inadvertent sin (i.e., missing the mark), the two terms likely occur in parallelism with each other in this instance. Though Wolff distinguishes between *pešeʿ* as "intentional criminal rebellion against the law" and *ḥaṭṭāʾt* as "objective error of one who loses the way and is confused," he concludes that in v 5 both words "equally characterize the guilt of the transgression" (1990, 56). The word pair reappears in 3:8. Similarly, the two primary names for the northern kingdom's eponymous ancestor, **Jacob** and **Israel**, occur in synonymous parallelism (see, for example, Hos 1:4; Amos 3:13; Obad 10). Both of these names more narrowly refer to the northern political entity. Mays suggests that a narrow reference occurs only in Mic 1:5. He also notes that otherwise the reference takes on more of "a religious than a political identification" and thus can denote Jerusalem and Judah as well (1976, 44).

Verse 5 proceeds to inquire concerning the identity of Jacob's transgression. A rhetorical question provides the response: **Is it not Samaria?** Amos and Hosea, the eighth-century B.C. prophets who preached specifically to the northern kingdom, brought indictments against its capital (see Hos 7:1; 8:5, 6; 10:5; 13:16; Amos 3:9, 12; 4:1; 6:1; 8:14). Hosea condemned the calf of Samaria while Amos condemned the false security engendered by Mount Samaria. In contrast to both Amos and Hosea, Micah simply refers to the capital city itself as the transgression of the northern kingdom. He specifies no further as to the sin committed by the people of Samaria. For Micah, the capital city in and of itself *is* the sin.

Micah 1:5 ends with question and answer concerning Judah. In the question, Micah names the sin of Judah (**What is Judah's high *places*?**). The answer, **Is it not Jerusalem?**, seems to suggest a single "high place," the mount of Jerusalem (see Hillers 1984, 20). However, the plural form in the Hebrew text indicates that the indictment is against all the illegitimate sites of worship in and around Jerusalem. High places were mountains or hills where people set up altars to carry out the fertility cult because of their proximity to heaven. Deuteronomistic texts repeatedly refer to the multiple cult sites constructed and visited by Solomon and left standing during subsequent kings' reigns (e.g., regarding Solomon, see 1 Kgs 3:3-4; 11:7; 15:14; 22:43; 2 Kgs 12:3; 14:4; 15:4, 35; regarding Jeroboam, see 1 Kgs 12:31-32; 13:33-34; regarding Rehoboam, see 1 Kgs 14:23). If the plural indicates these multiple sites, then the text envisions Jerusalem to be just as atrocious as the various high places elsewhere in the land. Just as the city of Samaria itself is the transgression of the north, the holy mount of Jerusalem is one and the same with the ***high places***. According to Micah, the rebellion for which Yahweh will judge both kingdoms takes place in their political, economic, religious centers. Micah's indictment thus strikes at the very heart of the kingdoms.

The prophet resumes judgment against the northern kingdom in Mic 1:6-7. At the time of Micah's ministry, the Assyrian assault demonstrated Yahweh's judgment upon the north. As noted above, most of the book of Micah is concerned with the southern kingdom. However, the fall of the north depicted in ch 1 provides a basis for the forthcoming judgment upon the south. According to vv 6-7, the result of Yahweh's visitation upon **Samaria** will be the city's utter devastation. The political-economic center that once stood tall and proud will become a **heap of rubble *in the field*** (see the same image in regard to Jerusalem in 3:12; see also Ps 79:1; Jer 26:18). Although the NIV omits the phrase ***in the field***, the fuller image of **a heap of rubble *in the field*** intensifies the portrait of Samaria's total destruction. The once-mighty political-economic center of the kingdom will become a mount of rubble rising from a wide-open countryside. Farmers will level this piled up ruin of the capital city and make it a place for **planting vineyards**. The text's depiction of Samaria's utter destruction continues in Mic 1:6 with images of the collapse of above-ground structures and the uprooting of underground foundations. Yahweh declares that he will hurl **into the valley** the very **stones** that once held the city's magnificent structures together. The reference to stones and foundations in v 6 echoes Amos' concern over false security and Hosea's concern over false worship. Yahweh will also uproot the **foundations** that once lay deep beneath the ground's surface so that they become exposed (**lay bare**). The depiction of demolished structures and exposed foundations evokes images of large trees uprooted by earthquake and storm.

Verse 7 focuses upon the destruction of the city's illicit cultic practices. The imminent and utter destruction in v 7 is clear: ***crushed by beating*** (**broken to pieces**), **burned with fire**, ***left in desolation*** (**destroy**). The threefold repetition of the particle *kāl* (**all**) emphasizes the all-pervasive nature of the destruction.

The first and third lines of v 7 employ two of the most frequently occurring words in the OT for idols. The verbal root of *pesel* (**idols**) depicts the action of hewing from stone (see, for example, Exod 20:4; Deut 4:16). The verbal root of *ʿāṣāb* (**images**) conveys the action of shaping or fashioning (see Isa 10:11; Jer 50:2; Hos 4:17). While slightly different nuances are present, the two words function similarly in their depiction of humanly crafted images employed in cultic settings.

In the second line of v 7, a single word appears three times: *ʾetnâ*. The NIV translates the term once as **temple gifts** and twice as **wages of prostitutes**. Derived from the verb *tānâ* or *tānan* ("to hire," see Hos 8:9, 10), the nominal form of the word refers to the payment made for a prostitute's services (see Deut 23:18; Hos 2:12 [2:14 HB]; 9:1). In Hosea's depiction of Israel's prostitution, this term functions figuratively to portray the people's idolatrous practices (9:1). Micah may also employ this image to depict Israel's idolatrous practices. However, Wolff interprets the indictment to be more of a political and economic nature and less of a cultic matter. He suggests that Micah understood "that Samaria gave commercial goods and tribute to the great power Assyria, and therefore 'gathered' 'whore's wages,' which made possible the splendid buildings for the royal residence" (1990, 58). The eighth-century B.C. prophets understood covenant infidelity vis-à-vis Yahweh in terms of both the worship of other deities and political-economic engagement with other nations (i.e., alliances and treaties). Fire will utterly consume these "payments" or offerings (**temple gifts**) that the leaders had presented whether the recipients of these offerings/payments were delicately hewn, finely formed images or the Assyrian Empire itself.

The second half of Mic 1:7 depicts both the manner in which the people received these wages and the manner in which they will spend them. Just as the Israelites have gathered them as payment for prostitution (see similar image in Hos 2:12 [2:14 HB]; 9:1), they will spend them as payment for prostitution. Hillers has observed that "as the precious things were gained, so they will be lost, the end will be like the beginning" (1984, 21; see also Simundson 1996, 544). Such an understanding of the correlation between crime and judgment is consistent with the prophetic concept of reaping and sowing (see Hos 8:7; 10:12-13; Obad 15).

■ **8-16** Micah 1:8-16 shifts focus on to the Assyrian assault upon the outlying towns of Judah. As noted previously, this devastation particularly was familiar to the people at the time of Sennacherib's advance toward Jerusalem in 701 B.C. Capitalizing upon the Assyrian onslaught, Micah is able to turn "political and military strategems into theological drama" (Mays 1976, 42). Various towns in vv 8-16 were located within the sphere of the Assyrian advance. Once defeating the towns and villages of Judah, the army ultimately made its way to Jerusalem's doorstep.

The text begins with a declaration of lament over Judah's destruction (vv 8-9). It concludes with the prophetic call for communal lament (v 16). Between these announcements of lament occurs the actual lamentation over the devastation taking place in the villages and towns that lay outside of Jerusalem. The lamentation opens with familiar words from David's lament over the deaths of Saul and Jonathan in 2 Sam 1:20, **Tell it not in Gath** (Mic 1:10; regarding the relationship between the two texts, see Simundson 1996, 547). In spite of textual corruptions and obscure terms, the meaning of the passage is clear. As the Assyrian army proceeds to make its way to Jerusalem, it leaves only devastation and destruction in its wake.

Micah 1:8 declares the prophet's own intent to lament; v 9 provides the rationale behind the lament, which will occur in vv 10-15. Micah announces that he himself will **wail** in deep lamentation (v 8). The first verb employed in the text, *sāpad* (**weep**), most often occurs in the context of mourning for the dead (e.g., Gen 23:2; 1 Sam 25:1; 28:3; 1 Kgs 14:13; 18; Jer 16:6; 22:18; Amos 5:16). Parallel to *sāpad* is *yālal* (**wail**), a verb that depicts loud and distress-filled howling (see this verb alongside *sāpad* in Jer 4:8; Joel 1:13).

The prophet also announces his intent to ***walk around*** **barefoot and naked**. Isaiah does a similar action in Isa 20:2-4 to depict utter shame brought about by defeat (see also Job 12:19; Ezek 24:17-23; Amos 2:16). Wolff has suggested that Micah's reference to **barefoot and naked** symbolizes imminent captivity rather than grief and sorrow (1990, 58). Verse 8 ends with the announcement of the prophet that he would **howl like a jackal and moan like an *ostrich*** (**owl**). The sound of his outcry will be like the agonizing screech or howl of animals in desolate, desert-like places: jackals (see Job 30:29; Isa 13:22; Lam 4:3) and ostriches. In OT texts, these animals commonly appear together in barren and isolated settings (see Job 30:29; Isa 13:21-22; 34:13; 43:20; Lam 4:3; regarding ostriches alone, see Jer 50:39 [NASB, NLT, NRSV]).

In Mic 1:9, the poetic meter of the text shifts to the *qinah* with its characteristic 3+2 pattern. The *qinah* is the meter in which the lament commonly occurs (→ Amos 5:2). This meter continues throughout the remainder of the lament. The prophet proceeds in Mic 1:9 to announce the reason behind his grief: Samaria's **incurable *wounds*** of destruction have **spread to Judah**. The Assyrian armies that had made destructive blows against Judah's neighbors, Israel and Syria, two decades earlier had finally made their way into Judah. The prophet expresses his grave concern over the rapidly approaching events by means of the threefold repetition of the preposition *ʿad* (up to, as far as): ***as far as* Judah, *as far as the gate* of my people, *as far as* Jerusalem**. In moving from Judah to the city gates to Jerusalem itself, the text depicts the spatial movement of the powerful Assyrian army as it quickly advances. The text further portrays the spatial movement toward Jerusalem through two verbal statements: they have ***come*** (*bôʾ*, **spread**) and they have ***touched*** (*nāgaʿ*; **reached**). The striking blows of Sennacherib's troops are no longer echoes of military activity heard from a distance. The devastation has finally come upon Judah and will soon arrive at Jerusalem.

Micah's use of the phrase **my people** in v 9 is the first of several occurrences in the book (2:4, 8, 9; 3:2, 3, 5; 6:3, 5, 16). As a covenant phrase, it would refer to all of the citizens of Judah. The first-person possessive pronoun would thus be from the perspective of Yahweh, so that the phrase **my people** would refer to Yahweh's covenant community (see Shaw 1993, 114-15). However, in the book of Micah, the first-person possessive pronoun in the phrase "my people" often appears to refer to the prophet himself rather than to Yahweh. In these instances, the phrase may suggest a unique relationship shared between Micah and the people for whom he is speaking. Understanding the phrase "my people" to refer to those impoverished persons who are oppressed by the community's elite, Mays and Wolff view Micah as particularly identifying with and representing the concerns of these persons so that they are indeed Micah's people (see Mays 1976, 55-56; Wolff 1990, 59, 82). However, in light of the close identification of the prophetic "self" with Yahweh himself (see Abraham Heschel's concept of *pathos* [1962, 285-98]), one must be cautious in making too much of a distinction between Yahweh and the prophet in relationship to the first-person pronoun (see Waltke 2007, 69). As this phrase in Micah can also include oppressors (2:8) and the guilty (2:4; 6:3), Waltke suggests one must avoid a monolithic definition of the phrase and must therefore interpret the phrase within its context for each occurrence (2007, 69).

The lament proper occurs in vv 10-15. Throughout the lament, the text engages in various wordplays on cities' names in order to depict the devastation that has either already occurred (for detailed analysis of cities, see Mays 1976, 52-54) or is about to occur (Wolff 1981, 40). Ben Zvi interprets the nature of the wordplays to be artistic devices that function as a taunt. He has noted that as the prophet mocks each city by relating its name to its fate, in a tauntingly ironic manner "what will happen to a town is what was supposed to happen to it from the very beginning" (Ben Zvi 2000, 36).

Because of unique attempts to coordinate town names with other words for the sake of wordplay, this unit presents significant challenges for precise translation. Textual corruptions also have compounded the difficulty of interpreting the text. Interpreters have suggested diverse interpretations of both literary devices in the text and possible textual corruptions that have occurred (e.g., see Waltke 2007, 62-64; Hillers 1984, 24-28; Mays 1976, 48-49, 51-52, 56-60; McComiskey 1993, 626-32; concerning the nature and function of wordplay, see McKane 1998, 54-58).

The geographical layout of Judah certainly allowed for Jerusalem and its immediate environs to become more vulnerable to Assyrian attack as defensive fortifications throughout Judah fell to the invaders. From the cities in the text that are familiar, McComiskey has suggested that the prophet himself was obviously familiar with these cities as they "comprise a circle of nine miles in radius around Micah's hometown of Moresheth-gath and are visible from there" (1993, 626; see also Waltke 2007, 89-90). While many of the towns are likely located along the route of the Assyrian army's advance toward Jerusalem (see Mays 1976, 52-54), it is possible that Micah chose some names simply for the sake of wordplay (see discussion above; Allen 1976, 278). Regarding the artistic nature of these verses, Mays has observed that Micah's lament "is a magnificent witness to Micah's literary ability, to the historical situation in which he spoke, and the profound emotion of his participation in the suffering of his people" (1976, 51). However, observing the "clear, unambiguous, and penetrating" language of the text for easy memory, Wolff concludes that the "the wordplays have no intrinsic significance" and that one should not "expect to find a great deal of theology in them" (1981, 41).

The chart below provides a summary of the town locations and/or significance in Israel's history, the likely wordplay employed by Micah, and the translation of the wordplay in the NIV.

Name of Town	Location/Significance of Town	Wordplay	NIV Wordplay or Association
Gath (gat)	A city of the Philistine Pentapolis (see I Sam 7:14) and associated with "giants" in ancient Israel's tradition (Josh 13:3; I Sam 17). Significant role in David's early reign (I Sam 21, 27). In lament over the deaths of Saul and Jonathan, David exclaims, "Tell it not in Gath" (2 Sam 1:20; see also reference to Gath in Amos 6:2).	*Gat* correlates with the verb *nāgad* ("to make known"; "to tell").	**Tell** (1:10).
Acco (corrupt text; MT reads *bākô*)	Coastal city north of Mount Carmel. Significant for trade throughout the Valley of Jezreel, and remained a Phoenician port. See reference in Judg 1:31.	*Bākô* correlates with the verb *bākâ* ("weep").	**Weep** (v 10).
Beth Ophrah (*bêt lĕ ʿaprâ*)	Benjamite city northeast of Bethel. See reference in Josh 18:23; I Sam 13:17. As home of Gideon (Judg 6—9), related to the tribe of Manasseh.	*Bêt lĕ ʿaprâ* means "house of dust"; form of *ʿaprâ* ("dust") appears once in the lament as a part of the name of the city and once as **dust.**	**Roll in the dust** (v 10).
Shaphir (*šāpîr*)	Various possible locations; however, location is uncertain. Only mention in the OT.	*Šāpar* ("to be beautiful," "fair," or "pleasant") provides contrast to the nakedness and shame.	**Naked and in shame** (v 11).
Zaanan (*ṣaʾănān*)	Perhaps Zenan in the Judean valley (Josh 15:37); however, uncertain. Only mention in the OT.	The word *ṣaʾănān* sounds similar to verb *yāṣāʾ* ("to go out"; "come out").	**Come out** (v 11).

Beth Ezel (*bêt hāʾēṣel*)	Identity and location are not certain. Only occurrence in the OT.	*Bêt hāʾēṣel* means "house of withholding."	**It no longer protects you** (meaning "it withholds its protection") (v 11).
Maroth (*mārôt*)	Unlikely to be Maarath in hill territory (Josh 15:59); therefore, location is not certain. Only occurrence in the OT.	*Mārôt* correlates with the adjective *mōrâ* ("bitter").	**Writhe in pain, waiting for relief** (v 12).
Lachish (*lākîš*)	Associated with royal stables, massive fortifications, and a large state center. Excavation of Level III shows destruction in 701 B.C. Sennacherib appears to have taken Lachish early and established a base there (see 2 Kgs 18:14, 17; Isa 36:2; 37:8). Sennacherib's Nineveh palace contains detailed reliefs depicting the defeat of Lachish.	*Lākîš* correlates with the noun *lārekeš* ("steeds").	**Harness fast horses to the chariot** (v 13).
Moresheth Gath (*môrešet gat*)	Likely related to the hometown of Micah, see 1:1.	*Môrešet* derives from the verb *yāraš* ("to possess" or "inherit"), thus "possession" (perhaps "possession of Gath").	**Parting gifts** (v 14). Correlation with *šillûḥîm* (**parting gifts**) conveys irony of the loss of possession. Regarding *šillûḥîm* as a bridal dowry, see Roncace 2009, 140; Luker 1992, 904-5; Waltke 2007, 82).

Akzib (*ʾakzîb*)	Tel located north of Acco on the Mediterranean coast. Conquered by Sennacherib in 701 B.C. (Josh 19:29; Judg 1:31). Other references include Gen 38:1-5 and Josh 15:44.	The term *ʾakzāb* also refers to a *deceptive body of water.*	**Will prove deceptive** (v 14).
Mareshah (*mārēšâ*)	Located twenty-four miles to southwest of Jerusalem and twenty-one miles east of Ashkelon, the city became a fortification during the reign of Rehoboam (2 Chr 11:7-9). See reference also in Josh 15:44.	Like the word *Moresheth,* the name *mārēšâ* also derives from verb *yāraš* ("to possess," "dispossess"). Thus, a "dispossessor" or conqueror inhabits the possession or inheritance.	**I will bring a conqueror** (v 15).
Adullam (*ʿădullām*)	See early references in Josh 12:15; 15:35. Location of caves in which David hid from Saul; later developed into fortification (see 1 Sam 22:1-4; 2 Sam 5:17; 23:13-17). As a protected route between the coastal plain and Judah, refortified by Rehoboam prior to Shishak's invasion (2 Chr 11:7).	The word *ʿădullām* may be associated with the verbal form *ʿādal* ("to turn aside"), and thus functions appropriately as a name for a refuge or retreat. Although no wordplay is apparent, the city name *ʿădullām* is preceded by the preposition *ʿad* ("as far as") in order to create a repeated effect, that is, *ʿad ʿădullām.*	**The nobles of Israel will flee to Adullam** (v 15).

The text concludes in v 16 with a call for the community to participate in the prophet's grief. Verse 16 begins with two feminine imperatives: ***make bald*** and ***sheer***. The NIV combines these into one imperative (**shave**) and adds the phrase **your head in mourning**. The double imperatives in the Hebrew text emphasize the intensity of the demonstration of grief. The imperatives are followed by an announcement of the cause of grief: ***because of* the children in whom you delight** (***your dainty children***; "your pampered children" [NRSV]). The text implies the exile of the population of Judah (Simundson views children as a reference to the towns of Judah [1998, 547]).

The second part of v 16 introduces another imperative that reiterates the previous call to show grief: ***enlarge your baldness as the eagle***. The reason for showing grief is made more specific at the conclusion of v 16: ***for they are removed from you***. The verb *gālâ* ("to remove") indicates exile or captivity. The exile of the population, or more specifically the separation of the people from the land, is the reason why the prophet calls his audience to show grief in all of its intensity. The prophet's use of the feminine verbal forms and reference to children are intended to evoke the image of mothers weeping over the loss of their young children.

FROM THE TEXT

The covenant conviction that the Lord will hold his people accountable for their infidelity informs the opening chapter of Micah. The reader of the text clearly perceives that this covenant deity will not sit aloof from his people's transgressions. He will ultimately require an answer from them. This same conviction shapes Amos' understanding of the Day of the Lord: "You only have I chosen of all the families of the earth; therefore I will punish you for all your sins" (Amos 3:2). Divine judgment is not merely to the nations outside of the covenant community. It particularly pertains to the covenant community itself as the Lord will hold this unique people accountable for their covenant responsibilities of fidelity to God and to neighbor. The same underlying conviction informs Jesus' parables concerning the tenants and the talents (Matt 21:33-44; 25:14-30). The text invites the church, the covenant community of Jesus Christ, to hear and respond to its call through honest examination and confession of its life in the world. In what ways is it living out the covenant responsibilities given to it by its Lord?

The text's specific reference to the political-economic centers of Samaria and Jerusalem invites the reader to ponder further the interrelationship between covenant identity and political-economic practices. As the remainder of the book of Micah will clearly demonstrate, the kingdom of God is not separate from structures of power and the use or misuse of political and economic resources (e.g., see 2:1-2; 3:1-3, 5, 9-11; 6:10-12, 16). The text challenges the reading community to examine honestly its use of resources of power, economy, and ideology in relationship to human beings. How does the church use its own resources selflessly for the sake of providing life to human beings rather than selfishly for preserving its own institutional life? In hearing the concerns of Micah over the centers of power, the reader hears the voice of Jesus as he instructs his disciples in Mark 10:42-44:

> You know that those who are regarded as rulers of the Gentiles lord it over them, and their high officials exercise authority over them. Not so with you. Instead, whoever wants to become great among you must be your servant, and whoever wants to be first must be slave of all.

The poetic nature of Mic 1, particularly the creative wordplays of vv 8-15, reminds the reader that art has historically been intertwined with communication of the divine message throughout the history of the people of God. In this instance, the art is first through oral communication and subsequently preserved in written literature. In subsequent generations such artistic expression of the divine word may occur through the visual arts of painting and sculpture, through music, or through architecture. The message to God's people is certainly not limited to a simple logical, propositional presentation. It is oftentimes communicated most appropriately through inspired artistic, creative, and imaginative expressions.

2. Against Self-Serving Socioeconomic Practices (2:1-11)

BEHIND THE TEXT

In ch 2 Micah focuses on specific socioeconomic practices of the politically and economically powerful members of the community in the eighth century B.C. By the middle of the eighth century B.C., the political situation had created an economic reality in which a small group of powerful elites controlled the community's judicial and economic affairs. The political elite who exercised power in outlying cities and villages controlled the land and its agricultural produce. They continued to enlarge their landholdings by the use of power and by exploiting the common practice of debt servitude, which ultimately gave them power to take over the family inheritance of the majority of the population, primarily comprised of agrarian farmers (regarding the process of land accumulation by the powerful and the context that gave rise to this process in the eighth century B.C., see Chaney 1982, 3-13; 1989, 15-30; 1991, 127-39; Green 1997, 365-97; Premnath 1988, 49-60; 2003, 43-98).

IN THE TEXT

■ **1-5** Formally, the unit in vv 1-5 functions as a woe oracle. Though a common interjection of pain often found in laments over the dead, **woe** (*hôy*) frequently introduces divine judgment (e.g., Isa 5:8; Amos 5:18; 6:1; regarding its setting in life, see Mays 1976, 62). Two participles, **those who plan iniquity** (*ʾāven*) and **those who plot evil** (*rāʿ*), serve to identify the recipients of the divine judgment (Mic 2:1). The verb *ḥāšab* ("devise," "scheme") portrays the addressees as first making plans to bring about trouble and then as proceeding to implement those plans (i.e., troublemakers in a literal sense). The parallel statement depicts these troublemakers as plotting (*pāʿal*) **evil**. **Plan** and **plot** and **iniquity** and **evil** are used here as synonymous terms.

Iniquity and evil are actions that violate the standards of behavior stipulated in the Sinai laws for the covenant community. They are destructive and damaging and result in trouble and injury within the community. According to Micah, these persons scheme while still lying upon their beds. Then as soon as the light of day appears, they act on their well-developed plans (**they carry it out**). Micah presents these persons as those who are fully capable of carrying out their plans (**it is in their power to do it**). They are the political and economical elite who take full advantage of the social structure and the power they have at their disposal. Wolff has observed that "their power is the basis . . . for the laying of their plans; it also provides the possibility for the execution of these plans" (1990, 77). In subsequent texts, Micah more specifically identifies the social roles of these powerful individuals to be heads and chiefs, prophets and priests (see 3:1, 5, 9, 11).

The first half of v 2 depicts the actions of the oppressive and powerful elite in the community. These include coveting **fields** and **houses** (see the commandment in Exod 20:17; Deut 5:21) that belong to others and taking them by force (**seize, take**) from the landholders. The verb **seize** (*gāzal*) suggests violent confiscation—even robbery—of that which belongs to another (see Gen 21:25; 31:31; Judg 21:23; Job 20:19; 24:9). The same verb reappears in Mic 3:2 to depict cruel treatment of the poor by the powerful ("tear"). Micah uses the verb *nāśāʾ* (**take**; lit. "lifting up" or "carrying away") instead of the more common Hebrew verb *lāqâ* (meaning "to take") to depict the forceful taking of the houses of the poor by the wealthy. Likely through legitimate means such as the recuperation of unpaid debts, imposition of fines, high interest, or collateral, the self-serving elite confiscate the fields and houses that they desire and make them their own possessions (see similar indictment in Isa 5:8).

Oppression within Ancient Agrarian Political-Economic Structures

The nature of the ancient agrarian political-economic structure allowed for and even encouraged oppressive practices. Through a series of relationships of reciprocity, landholders ("clients") were dependent upon state functionaries ("patrons") at the state, regional, and local levels. In theory, plots of land were inheritable property that ultimately belonged to Yahweh. However, in practice the king ruled over "Yahweh's land" and in turn appointed political-economic functionaries at various levels to supervise the land and to oversee the state's taxation system. As a result of consecutive agricultural calamities such as drought, famine, and locust plague, a landholder was unable to pay taxes and other fees and fines. As a result of his inability to pay, he resorted to debt servitude of both family members and himself. Ultimately, the inheritable land itself was lost to the family. Selfishly employed by the powerful, the political-economic structure—even under the guise of Yahweh's "promised land"—enabled the political elite to use their positions of power over vulnerable farmers in order to increase their own landholdings.

The second half of Mic 2:2 depicts the oppressive nature of the self-serving activities of the elite. Mays has observed that contexts in which the verb *ʿāšaq* (**defraud**, "extort," "oppress") frequently occur indicate the activity of "taking something away from another through an advantage of position or power" (1976, 63). The object of the verb is the politically and economically vulnerable members of the society (see also Deut 24:14; Prov 14:31; 22:16; Jer 7:6; Ezek 22:29; Amos 4:1; Zech 7:10). Micah describes the object of oppression in 2:2 as *geber* (***man***; **people**) and ***his*** (**their**) ***home***(s), and *ʾîš* (***fellowman***; **them**), and ***his*** (**their**) **inheritance**. Wolff interprets the term *geber* as one who is "capable of military service" or a "citizen who possesses full legal rights and obligations." Therefore, he argues that Micah is emphasizing the oppression of persons who possess "landed property as 'hereditary possession'" (1990, 78). The political and economical elite in the community have the power to act in self-serving ways, including the oppression of individuals who have strength to provide, to protect their household, and to pass inheritable property to their descendants. ***Home*** (*bayit*) probably refers to one's household and not to a physical structure. ***His*** **inheritance** likely refers to a deceased individual and his inheritance, particularly his land, left to his wife and children (see sidebar, "Land as Inheritance," below). As those in power employed ways to strip an owner of his land, they oppressed not only the landholder but also his entire family, his household and his heirs.

Land as Inheritance

The biblical tradition depicts Yahweh as primary landowner and the people as tenants. Apportioning Yahweh's land among the twelve tribes, the Israelites proceeded to subdivide the land among the tribes' various clans, extended families, and households (see Josh 13—19). While the oldest son received a double portion of the inheritance upon the death of his father, all other sons received equal shares. If a deceased man had no sons, his brothers, uncles, or other next of kin received the property. As a result, the man's inheritance—particularly the family land—remained within the extended family (see exception in Num 27; 36:6). The narrative of Naboth's vineyard (1 Kgs 21) demonstrates the concern to maintain land within the family unit. While likely never fully enforced, the laws of the Jubilee Year (Lev 25) attempted to preserve the inheritable land within the family unit.

The opening particle in Mic 2:3 (*lākēn*, **therefore**) indicates that vv 1-2 function as the basis for the divine response in vv 3-5. Now it is Yahweh's turn to plan (*ḥāšab*; see 2:1) evil. He is **planning disaster** or ***evil*** [*rāʿâ*] **against this people** (i.e., those who "plot evil on their beds" [2:1]). The powerful will be unable to reverse or to withdraw from the divine plans (**from which you cannot save yourselves**; lit. "from which you cannot remove your necks"). The language of removal implies a tight noose or burdensome yoke from which the powerful cannot escape. The once haughty leaders will suffer disgrace and humiliation when Yahweh brings evil against those who plot evil; they **will no longer walk proudly** (v 3; *rômâ*, sense of being "lifted up" or "exalted"; see Prov 21:4; Isa 2:11, 17; 10:12; Jer 48:29) because they will be faced with **a time of calamity** or ***evil*** (*rāʿâ*).

Micah 2:4-5 depicts how the powerful elite who once dispossessed others' land will now be dispossessed of their land. The subject of the verbs **ridicule** and **taunt** in v 4 is in the third-person singular; the NIV and other translations translate the subject in the plural form (**people, they**). **In that day** is the day when Yahweh humiliates the proud in Judah with his evil directed against them. Those who witness the humiliation of the oppressors in Judah will **ridicule** and **taunt you with** a **mournful song** (lit. "he shall take up a proverb against you, and lament with wailing"; the prophet poetically employs a threefold repetition of words comprised of the letters *n* and *h*: *nāhâ nĕhî nihyâ*). Micah's reference to taunt songs and songs of mourning recall his outcry in 1:8 and anticipate the lament in ch 7.

It is not clear who taunts and takes up the lament; translations, including the NIV, assume the enemies of Judah or those who witness Yahweh's judgment of the proud oppressors. If the third-person singular is kept following the Hebrew text, the prophet himself could be the one who taunts the proud, who soon will be humiliated. If so, the prophet composes this taunt song, which would be heard in the land as the lament of the proud oppressors who are faced with the impending judgment of God (dispossession of the land and exile). The taunt/lament implies that Yahweh will take the land/wealth from the proud oppressors and give them to their enemies: **We are utterly ruined; my people's possession is divided up. He takes it from me! He assigns our fields to traitors** (v 4).

The taunt/lament begins with the expression, **We are utterly ruined** (v 4). The reality of Yahweh's judgment will result in the total destruction of the wealthy. The second line, **my people's possession is divided up**, indicates the reversal of the covenant blessings. **My people**, the special possession of God through the Sinai covenant, received the gift of the land as the fulfillment of God's promise to the patriarchs. They took possession of the land and divided it among the tribes and the clans. The taunt reveals the irony of the division of the land again, this time because of the iniquity and evil of the elite in the land. **He takes it from me** most likely conveys the idea of Yahweh taking his land back from the oppressive landowners. The concluding line of v 4 shows Yahweh's plan after taking back his land; he will reapportion the fields to the **traitors** (*šôbēb* means "those who turn back or rebel"; thus, **traitors**). This reference is likely to those who will eventually capture Judah (i.e., ones who overturn the nation). Throughout this taunt, the prophet attacks the false claims of the powerful elite concerning the land; they have assumed that they owned the land and that it will never be taken away from them or be handed over to anyone.

The prophet makes clear in v 5 that his central concern is the land that the elite have oppressively taken from vulnerable landholders. As Yahweh removes the land from the powerful, he will not provide a means for the land to return to them. The oppressive ruling elite will have no one to ***establish the boundaries of*** **(divide) the land by lot** as had occurred in the original distribution of the land. Israel's narratives concerning the original distribution of the land to tribes and clans indicate the division of the land by lots (*gôrāl*) (see Num 26:55, 56; 33:54; Josh 18:6-11). The apportionment of land took place in public settings, or **the assembly of the Lord** (regarding such public gatherings, see Num 16:3; Deut 23:2-4; Josh 8:35). **You will have no one in the assembly of the Lord** anticipates the exile of Yahweh's covenant people from the land, which would leave the land in the hands of the invading forces.

■ **6-11** Just as Mic 2:1-5 contrasts the devising by the elite and the devising by Yahweh, vv 6-11 contrast that which the people desire to hear preached and that which Micah preaches (regarding the text's corrupt nature and various attempts of textual reconstruction, see Mays 1976, 68-73; Hillers 1984, 34-36). The following is a literal translation of v 6: "'You [plural] shall not proclaim,' they proclaim, 'They shall not proclaim these (things); disgrace shall not be turned back (on us).'"

The oracle opens in v 6 with the voice of someone saying to Micah not to ***preach*** (*nāṭap*; meaning "drop," "drip," "prophesy," "preach"). Most translations, except the NIV, recognize ***they*** in v 6 as the people (**their prophets say**). Within the broader context of the book of Micah, the persons who address Micah may be the prophets who lead the people astray by their proclamation of "'peace' if they have something to eat" (3:5). It is also possible that the directive may be coming from the powerful elite whom Micah condemns in the preceding verses as well as in 2:8-10. The peculiar word *nāṭap* occurs three times in v 6. Though **prophesy** is a possible rendering of this word, it often denotes the dripping of a liquid (see Josh 4:18; Judg 5:4; Ps 68:8; Joel 3:18; Amos 9:13). Outside of Micah, the term occurs for prophetic preaching in only two other instances (Ezek 21:2; Amos 7:16). Amos' use of the term in his response to Amaziah (Amos 7:16) is similar to Micah's statement. In both Micah and Amos, the term appears on the lips of one who instructs the prophet not to proclaim his message. Both Amos and Micah seem to interpret the term to be a pejorative. Wolff has suggested the colloquial translation *slobbering* or *babbling* (1990, 81). Its occurrence again at the end of this unit in Mic 2:11 clearly shows the contrast between the genuine prophecy of Micah and the "dripping" that comes from those who prophesy for "wine and beer" (v 11). Micah's opponents want him to stop preaching **about these (things)**; obviously Micah's message of disaster and judgment is what they would rather not hear. The concluding comment in v 6 conveys a type of security that is similar to 3:11. Micah's opponents seem to be secure about their future. They confidently declare that the humiliating acts announced by Micah will not overtake them. The plural form of *kělimmâ* (**disgrace**, "reproach," "insult") may refer back to the various acts of judgment previously announced by Micah. The passive form of the verb *sûg* (**overtake**; lit. "to turn back") with the negative particle (**not**) conveys the audience's confidence that Yahweh would never turn back such humiliating actions upon his own people as Micah has announced.

In v 7, Micah quotes two questions that the people have raised. He couches these questions within his own question, ***Should it be said, O house of Jacob?*** Although the NIV translates the first rhetorical question raised by the audience as two questions (**Does the Lord become impatient? Does he do such things?**), it likely consists of two statements linked by the particle *ʾim* (or, "if") so that the second statement provides an alternative to the first (see Williams 2007, 160). The text reads literally as follows: ***Is the spirit*** [*rûaḥ*, ***breath***] ***of Yahweh short or are these things (even) his doing?*** If the particle *ʾim* is functioning in a concessive manner, the second statement would read "*even if* these things are his doing?" The noun *rûaḥ* (***Spirit***) alongside the verb *qāṣēr* ("to be short") conveys the notion of impatience or discouragement (see, for example, Num 21:4; Job 21:4; Zech 11:8). The traditional notion is that Yahweh's spirit is "long" (*ʾārēk*, i.e., "slow") to anger (for example, Exod 34:6; see *ʾārēk rûaḥ*, "long of spirit," in Eccl 7:8 to indicate patience). The question raises a challenge to Micah's judgment words because they contradict Israel's traditional confession of faith that Yahweh is slow to anger. The answer to the second part, ***are these things his doing?*** is also clear as far as the audience is concerned. It is not in the nature of Yahweh to do such evil against his people.

The second half of Mic 2:7 also functions as a rhetorical question, taken from other settings in which Yahweh or the prophet himself has spoken about Yahweh's promise to **do good to the one whose ways are upright**. The question affirms that Yahweh does not withhold any good (*ṭôb*) thing from those who walk blamelessly (Ps 84:11). Again, Micah's audience raises doubt over Micah's words concerning the impending divine *rāʿâ* (see Mic 2:3; opposite of *ṭôb*). Other prophetic voices in the community were certainly not declaring such a message of devastation (2:11; 3:5). In contrast to Micah, these other messengers declared that no *rāʿâ* would come upon Judah (3:11).

Micah does not attempt to refute these questions directly. However, in 2:8-9 Micah does provide an indirect yet concrete refutation to the second question. The second question assumes that the community is walking in an upright manner. The prophet cites recent evidence (**lately**) as he indicts the covenant community (**my people**) who **have risen up like an enemy** (v 8). The phrase **lately my people** (*ʾetmûl ʿammî*), could be a corruption of the text that read "you against my people" (*ʾatem lĕʿammî*), meaning the leaders are rising up against **my people** (see NRSV). This reading is consistent with Micah's tendency to use the phrase **my people** for the victims of oppression (see subsequent verse). However, no extant textual evidence supports such a textual corruption.

In the remainder of v 8, the prophet provides further details of the manner in which the accused have risen up like an enemy. Like predators, they **strip** (*pāšaṭ*) the innocent of their ***garment*** (lit. "glory" or "magnificence"; thus, **rich robe**; see Gen 37:23). Much of the text in Mic 2:8 is rather dubious, perhaps as a result of textual damage. Although Mays suggests that "the sense must be guessed" at certain points, he concludes that "enough is clear to make out a recitation of precisely those actions which would be expected from conquering invaders" (1976, 71). The remainder of the verse depicts victims who trustingly (**without a care**) return from battle (see NRSV, "with no thought of war"). The text conveys an image in which violent victimization is unexpected.

The prophet continues to depict the accused as enemies against Yahweh's people in v 9. These powerful perpetrators of evil remove divine blessing from the most vulnerable of the covenant community (**my people**). They **drive** [*gāraš*] **the women** from their houses, and they take Yahweh's **blessing** (*hādār*, "splendor," "glory") from the children. The text implies the glory that Yahweh bestows to children, which is their inheritance that guarantees a future for them. Depriving the children of their inheritance means depriving them of a hope-filled future. As Mays has observed, the elite's maddening rush to acquire property has left the children "in poverty," and for them "there is no future but slavery and servitude" (1976, 71).

The prophet issues an imperative, a command to those who are the powerful oppressors in the community (v 10). The double imperative to **get up** and to **go away** conveys a sense of immediacy. Although the powerful might have acquired the property of the weak, they will not settle down on their acquisitions. Micah's observation that this place is not one of ***rest*** (*mĕnûḥah*, **resting place**) recalls Israel's cherished tradition of "final rest" in the divine gift of the land (see Deut 12:9; 1 Kgs 8:56). Hillers defines this tradition of *rest* as "a theologically important term for undisturbed enjoyment of God's gift of the land" (1984, 37). Yet now Micah depicts this "holy land" as having become ***unclean*** due to the corrupt practices of the rulers (see Ezek 36:16-36 for correlation between people's abhorrent practices and the land's uncleanness). Because the language of uncleanness is often associated with the idolatrous practices that led to Babylonian exile (see Ezek 36), this reference may reflect a subsequent exilic interpretation of Micah's message (see Mays 1976, 71-72).

In Mic 2:11 the prophet returns to the theme of proclamation (*nāṭap*) introduced in v 6. Micah portrays a scenario in which an individual filled with ***emptiness*** (*rûaḥ*; lit. "air" or "wind") walks around and ***lies*** [*kāzab*] ***falsehood*** (*šeqer*). He ***preaches*** or, literally, ***drips*** (*nāṭap*; see v 6) to the people (***to you***) about wine and intoxicating drink. The similarity in sound between "falsehood" (*šeqer*) and "intoxicating drink" (*šeqār*) intensifies the scenario in which the preacher speaks nothing but deceptive, drunken delusion. In a concise, four-word conclusion, Micah announces that this "make-believe preacher" is ***a preacher*** [*nāṭap*; lit. "one who drips"] **for this people**!

FROM THE TEXT

The oracles in vv 1-5 and vv 8-9 challenge the reader to consider and to confess the political-economic structures that permit and even encourage diverse ways of "land-grabbing" in any given historical, social, and religious context. The text also invites its readers to reflect on ways to overcome their covetous desires. What are our own covetous desires, and why do such desires continue to exist among a covenant people who claim undivided trust in our God? What is the socioeconomic, political, and religious identity of powerless persons who so easily become "objects" of our own self-serving and covetous desires? In the twenty-first century, as the people of God find themselves located not only in local and national contexts but within a global community, how do "land-grabbing" mind-sets and practices oppress the weak, the vulnerable, and the poor across the world?

The messages of judgment and impending doom in ch 2 make clear the Deuteronomic-prophetic conviction of retribution through the reversal of fortunes of those who are engaged in oppressive activities. The seed sown by an individual, a community, an institution, or a society will undoubtedly produce very specific fruit. What the powerful of a society *take*, they will ultimately *lose* (see vv 3-5, 9-10). This prophetic conviction that underlies vv 3-5 echoes the teaching of Prov 22:16: "One who oppresses the poor to increase his wealth and one who gives gifts to the rich—both come to poverty." Jesus reminded his followers that "whoever wants to save their life will lose it" (Mark 8:35). Jesus also asked: "What good is it for someone to gain the whole world, yet forfeit their soul?" (Mark 8:36). The ironic shift from "land-grabbing" (Mic 2:1-2) to land loss (vv 3-5), from oppression of the poor to impoverishment, and from gaining the world to losing everything moves the reading community to examine the trajectory of its present commitments. It compels the reading audience to see the seed it plants and to imagine the harvest that it and its posterity will reap.

The oracle in vv 6-11 echoes the prophetic dilemma faced by prophets such as Amos in his encounter with Amaziah (Amos 7:10-13) and Jeremiah in his encounter with Hananiah (Jer 28). The text reminds the reader that the authentic prophet must regularly determine whether he or she will succumb to the majority voice, bow to the wishes of the people, and conform to twisted, self-serving theological arguments. As the clergyperson and the church encounter daily poll numbers, popular opinions, and competition, ministry can all too easily evolve into a consumer-oriented enterprise. Within such a context, the good news of the gospel (i.e., evangelism) can unwittingly be reduced to attractiveness and appeal while the presentation of the gospel becomes diluted to advertising and sales. The world becomes a market; the congregant becomes a consumer; the church becomes a department store; and the gospel becomes a product. Micah reminds the reading audience that such societal, cultural, institutional, and even religious pressure to succumb to a domesticated message will always be present. Likewise, the text reminds the reader that the prophetic community understands itself and its message as alternative to rampant religious consumerism.

Through the questions raised by Micah's peers in Mic 2:7, the reader of the text observes the tendency for God's people to employ biblical and theological interpretations for self-serving and self-securing ends. As a result, God's people hear that which they desire to hear, remaining deaf to the prophetic message. The questions raised by the audience emerge from a nearsighted interpretation of a familiar and well-grounded confession concerning Yahweh's fidelity. This popular interpretation of divine grace has cheapened grace by emptying it of any form of responsibility.

Coining the term "cheap grace," Dietrich Bonhoeffer describes this "deadly enemy of our church" as

> the grace which amounts to the justification of sin without the justification of the repentant sinner who departs from sin and from whom sin departs. Cheap grace is not the kind of forgiveness of sin which frees us from the toils of sin. Cheap grace is the grace we bestow on ourselves." (1959, 43-44)

This understanding of divine mercy simply substantiates the audience's own self-assurance and false security. Just as Amos' ministry sought to overcome the self-serving popular theology of the Day of the Lord, Micah's ministry sought to overcome a self-serving popular theology that misconstrued divine fidelity and grace.

B. A Glimmer of Hope (2:12-13)

BEHIND THE TEXT

In contrast to the preceding oracles that describe Yahweh's removal of the powerful elite from their land (2:3-5, 10), vv 12-13 depict Yahweh's leading his people back to their homeland. Scholars generally regard these verses as a subsequent editorial interruption within the oracles of judgment in chs 1—3 (for various interpretations, see Hillers 1984, 38-40; Mays 1976, 73-76). However, since the text specifically addresses Jacob and Israel (i.e., the northern kingdom), it is possible that the text does not merely address a sixth-century B.C. exiled Judean community. The text does appear to speak to the northern nation that underwent the catastrophes depicted in the preceding oracles (especially 1:5-7) in the eighth century B.C.

In contrast to the oracles of judgment that precede and follow this oracle, the unit in 2:12-13 is an oracle of salvation (regarding the division of the book of Micah into three sections [chs 1—2; 3—5; 6—7], each beginning with the command to *hear* and moving from judgment to salvation, see Allen 1976, 257-58; Limburg 1988, 159). This oracle shares similar images with 4:6-7, which also depicts Yahweh's guiding the returnees back to the homeland. Micah's depiction of a king who leads his people to victory shares many similarities with texts in Isa 40—55 (see esp. Isa 40:11; 41:15 ff.; 43:5-6; 49:8-12).

IN THE TEXT

■ **12-13** The numerous first-person verbs in Mic 2:12 depict the manner in which Yahweh himself will restore those who have experienced dispersion from their land. In the opening line, the text employs two primary verbs to describe Yahweh's action: **gather** (*ʾāsap*) and **bring together** (*qābaṣ*). In both instances, the infinitive absolute verbal form alongside the finite form of the same verb provides emphasis to the action (i.e., **I will surely gather**; **I will surely bring together**). The adverb *yaḥad* (**together**) emphasizes the communal nature of the gathering of the exiled. The object of Yahweh's gathering is Jacob/the remnant of Israel. **Remnant of Israel** includes the survivors of the destruction of the northern kingdom in 722/721 B.C. as well as those who would survive the impending judgment of Yahweh.

The remainder of v 12 reflects the communal nature of the gathering of the exiled. The text is not concerned primarily with Yahweh's bringing individuals back to the homeland; he will **bring** the community **together like sheep in a pen**. The images of sheep within an enclosure (**pen**) and of a ***flock in the midst of a pasture*** portray a unified gathering of the remnant. The final phrase, ***they will make loud noise like people,*** indicates that sounds of the people will be heard again in the land.

The unit ends with the description of the coming up (ascending) of **the One who breaks open the way . . . before them** (the exiled people) (v 13). The text identifies Yahweh, their King, as the one who will lead the returning exiles in the last line of this verse. Whereas Israel's unfaithful and self-serving shepherd-leaders (2:1-2, 8-9; 3:1-3, 9-11; see also Ezek 34:1-6) caused the scattering and destruction of Yahweh's flock. The text anticipates the reversal of the misfortunes of the community. Under the leadership of Yahweh, his flock will **break through** and **go out** of the land of their exile. The people will be guided on their way by ***Yahweh*, their King**, who would **pass through before them . . . at their head**. Yahweh, who will come to deliver his people, will not abandon them after their rescue; he will guide them to their homeland by marching before them as their leader.

FROM THE TEXT

In this brief interlude, captivating images of salvation appear. The text calls upon the audience to imagine and thus to hope for a salvation not merely of individuals but of the people of God as a corporate entity. There is hope for the covenant community as the Lord is determined to deliver his people just as he had delivered them from Egyptian captivity. This God who once committed himself to a peculiar people and who had consistently acted to deliver his people will remain faithful to his covenant as he delivers and restores them.

The images of the text vividly engender a clear recognition that salvation is the act of God alone. The Lord himself leads his people; his people subsequently follow. The Lord himself prepares the way; his people subsequently traverse on the way. Salvation occurs by divine grace and by divine grace alone in the life of God's people. However, in a synergistic fashion, God's people join their leader who initiates and enacts their salvation.

For the reader of the biblical canon, the image of the divine Shepherd-King especially evokes Ezekiel's extensive and vivid image of the Lord as Shepherd-King of his people (ch 34). At the same time, the image of the divine Shepherd-King stands in stark contrast to Ezekiel's depiction of Israel's and Judah's shepherd-kings who parasitically survived on the life of the people they led. Ezekiel's depiction of self-serving leaders recalls Micah's images of cannibalistic leaders in 3:1-3, 9, 11.

The good news of the divine King who selflessly leads and serves his flock in this text is heard again in Paul's letter to the Philippians where the apostle portrays the one who "did not consider equality with God" as something to be grasped but took the form of "a servant" (Phil 2:6-7). The kingdom this divine King fashions is a kingdom that promotes a self-giving way of life, a kingdom where there is no place for selfish ambition, a community that looks "to the interests of the others" (Phil 2:2-4).

III. JUDGMENT AND HOPE: SERIES 2: MICAH 3:1—5:15

A. Condemnations of Judah's Leadership (3:1-12)

BEHIND THE TEXT

Micah 3 is made up of three distinct oracles (vv 1-4, 5-8, 9-12); each oracle addresses the community's corrupt leaders. In vv 1-4 and vv 9-11, Micah confronts the nation's authorities generally. In vv 5-7, 11 Micah specifically addresses the prophets (includes priests in v 11). Verse 8 concludes with a reference to his own prophetic identity. The charges in ch 3 culminate in v 12 by Micah's placing complete responsibility for the nation's collapse upon its rulers.

As observed in ch 2, the political and economic situation of the mid-eighth century B.C. created "the perfect storm" for leaders at every level (local, regional, state) to abuse authority for personal gain. The leadership at this time included both the king in Jerusalem and his royal functionaries in outlying cities and villages, as well as the religious leaders and functionaries, including temple priests and prophets.

IN THE TEXT

■ **1-4** The first unit begins with the prophet speaking in the first person (**I said**). Micah calls upon the **leaders** [*rōʾš*] **of Jacob** and **rulers** [*qāṣîn*] **of Israel** to listen to his words, which are words of accusation and indictment. The addressees are all who are in leadership positions, those who have military, civil, and judicial authority over the nation, referred to here as **Jacob/Israel**. Micah is addressing the leaders of both the northern and southern kingdoms. Micah's accusation directed at the leaders begins with a rhetorical question, **Should you not *know* justice . . . ?** The prophet claims that those who are in leadership positions ought to have an intimate awareness (***know***, *yādāʿ*, see Hos 2:8, 20; 5:4; 6:3) of **justice** (*mišpāṭ*; see Amos 5:7, 15, 24); they should know how to render appropriate decisions (i.e., justice) based upon the socioeconomic convictions of the Yahwistic faith. In v 9, the prophet declares that these rulers detest the very *mišpāṭ* that they should know. The prophet goes on to describe the actions of the leaders that are clearly perversions of justice. They **hate** that which is **good** and **love** that which is **evil** (v 2; see similar language of love/hate and good/evil in Amos 5:15; Isa 1:1-17).

Micah 3:2-3 uses verbs that convey the image of cannibalism to depict the brutality of leaders and their violence over whom they rule. They **tear the skin**, **eat . . . flesh**, **strip off . . . skin**, **break . . . bones**, and **chop . . . like meat** (see Ezekiel's image of self-serving shepherds who feed only themselves while their people/sheep have become prey to the enemy in Ezek 34:2-10). In five of the six instances in which these terms occur, the prophet employs the third-person plural pronoun (**their**) in order to connect the skin, the flesh, and the bones directly to the victims. Once again the text employs the relational phrase **my people** in depicting the victims of the rulers' violent activities (Mic 3:2; see phrase in 1:9; 2:8-9).

In 3:4, the prophet announces the verdict upon the rulers for their horrific behavior. **Then** and **at that time** indicate the time of judgment. When the judgment of Yahweh comes upon them, the oppressive rulers of Israel will **cry** [*zāʿaq*] **out** to Yahweh, but **he will not answer them**. Israel's communal memory celebrated Yahweh's hearing the cry (*zāʿaq*) of their ancestors enslaved in Egypt and his faithful response to deliver (Exod 2:23; 3:7, 9). Likewise, during the period of Israel's judges, the Israelites cried out (*zāʿaq*) under oppression by surrounding nations, and Yahweh heard their cries and responded with deliverance (Judg 3:9, 15; 4:3; 6:6-7; see also 10:10-15). Micah announces the reversal of these sacred traditions; those who disregard their duty to do justice cannot expect to hear Yahweh's answer to their cry for help. **He will hide his face from them** reiterates the idea of Yahweh's rejection of the leaders and their cry. **Hide his face** indicates Yahweh's total disapproval of, and withdrawal from, those who violated the norms of the covenant way of life. He will not be present in their life.

■ **5-8** The oracle in vv 5-8 addresses Israel's prophets. The charge against the prophets is given in v 5; the text proceeds with the divine judgment in vv 6-7. In v 8, Micah contrasts himself and his ministry with that of the unfaithful prophets.

The charge against the prophets is that they **lead** Yahweh's people (**my people**) **astray** (v 5). The causative form of the verb *tā'â* (**lead . . . astray**) conveys the action of causing another to wander about or to err. Amos 2:4 attributes this same action of leading astray to the false gods while Hos 4:12 attributes this action to a "spirit of prostitution." Isaiah more generally indicts Israel's leaders of having led the people in the wrong direction (Isa 3:12; 9:16). Similar to Micah, the prophet Jeremiah places direct blame upon the prophets for having led the people astray (Jer 23:13, 32).

Micah does not state specifically how the prophets have misguided the people. Micah's indictment may be against prophets who speak ***well-being*** (*šālôm*, **peace**) to persons who are able to pay (i.e., bribe), while speaking disaster to persons who cannot pay (see Wolff 1990, 102). In such a situation, the prophetic message becomes a commodity for exchange. Micah's later indictment of the prophetic task as a profiteering enterprise (Mic 3:11) certainly agrees with this depiction. These self-serving prophets clearly fashion their messages in such a way that the message benefits the prophet in the end.

However, Micah's indictment in v 5 may not merely be against "prophecy for profit." The phrase translated by the NIV as **if they have something to eat** literally reads, "those who bite with their teeth." While this phrase certainly can indicate the activity of the prophets chewing food (and speaking peace to those who feed them), it is an awkward expression. The phrase "those who bite with their teeth" can indeed mean oppressive activity. The verb translated ***bite*** (*nāšak*) most often depicts the action of a snake's biting (Num 21:8-9; Prov 23:32; Amos 5:19; 9:3). Thus, it is possible that Micah describes prophets who speak shalom to individuals who engage in oppressive activities. In contrast, however, these prophets do violence (**prepare to wage war**) against those who do not put something into the prophets' mouths (i.e., **feed them**). Wolff has noted that in this reference, "Micah thinks not only of poor people who can pay nothing, but also of honest and thoughtful persons who refuse to meet such expectations" (1990, 103). The last line, they **prepare to wage war** [lit. "sanctify a war"] **against anyone who refuses to feed them**, conveys the idea of the prophets carrying out a holy war against those who refuse to bribe them. They are determined to destroy those who are committed to preserving justice and righteousness in the land.

The divine judgment upon the prophets in vv 6-7 is replete with images of darkness (**night, darkness, sun will set, the day will go dark**) as Micah depicts utter divine silence vis-à-vis the accused prophets. Every form of receiving a divine word will become empty and silent. In v 6, Micah portrays the absence of both **visions** (*ḥāzôn*; see 1 Sam 3:1) and **divination** (*qesem*; see Num 22:7; Isa 2:6; Ezek 21:29). In Mic 3:7, he depicts the subsequent shame of ***visionaries*** (*ḥōzeh*, **seers**) and the disgrace of **diviners** (*qōsēm*). Noting that both **seers** and **diviners** "are represented as legitimate means of prophetic knowledge," Wolff concludes that "Micah is not at all concerned about the methods they use to attain knowledge of God. But he has sharply focused on the misuse of the authority of their office" (1990, 103).

Micah announces that Yahweh's judgment of giving **no answer** to these self-aggrandizing prophets' methods of inquiring a word from him will result in their shame, disgrace, and humiliation (v 7). They will display their shame and disgrace by covering **their faces** (regarding this gesture in relationship to the leper, see Lev 13:45).

Within the context of the profiteering prophets and their forthcoming silence, Micah provides a contrast as he describes his own prophetic ministry in Mic 3:8. Although Micah does not specifically refer to his "call" to the prophetic task (e.g., Isa 6:1-8; Jer 1:4-10; Ezek 1—3), he poignantly describes that which enables him to carry out his prophetic task. Using the strong adversative adverb *ʾûlām* (**but as for me**) and the first-person pronoun (i.e., ***I myself***), Micah depicts himself in direct antithesis to the accused prophets.

That which fills (*mālēʾ*) Micah stands in sharp contrast to the *empty* darkness of his fellow prophets. Compared to the emptiness that fills the corrupt prophets, Micah describes himself as a prophet who is **filled with power** (*kōaḥ*), the efficiency to carry out specific tasks. Mays interprets power as the capacity "to persevere in the face of opposition and discouragement" (1976, 85). Micah identifies power as Yahweh's **Spirit** (*rûaḥ*, also "breath," "wind"). The narratives of Judges and 1 Samuel report God empowering Israel's leaders with his Spirit and equipping them to carry out special tasks (see, for example, Judg 3:10; 1 Sam 10:6, 10; see the prophets and the role of the Spirit in Isa 61:1; Ezek 2:2; 3:12, 14, 24; 8:3; 11:1, 5; 37:1; Joel 2:28-29).

Micah also identifies himself as a prophet filled with **justice** (*mišpāṭ*) and **might** (*gĕbûrâ*). In direct juxtaposition to the self-serving, twisted practices of the prophets and other leaders, Micah perceives himself as having the capacity to make right and equitable decisions and to carry those decisions to their completion (see discussion of *mišpāṭ* in Amos 5:7, 15, 24). Micah's self-depiction as filled with **might** or the strength of a warrior conveys courage and the capacity to prevail over an enemy.

Micah's understanding of himself recalls Isaiah's depiction of the ideal King (Isa 11:1-5). Like Micah, Isaiah emphasizes the essential role of the divine spirit (Isa 11:2), warrior-like might (Isa 11:2), and the capacity to make upright and equitable decisions (Isa 11:3-5). Rather than intending to portray himself as a messianic figure, however, Micah employs these descriptions to establish himself as a prophet who is prepared to carry out the divine mission given to him.

In the concluding line of Mic 3:8, the prophet specifically states his mission. The verb *nāgad* (**declare**) indicates a task that is not merely uttering words or delivering speeches, but making something known or evident. The prophet understands himself to be equipped for the single purpose of making obvious to the covenant community, **Jacob** and **Israel**, its sin and transgression (regarding the names **Jacob** and **Israel** as an "all-Israel" identity, see Mays 1976, 45, 88).

■ **9-12** Micah returns in vv 9-12 to the same addressees as in 3:1. In v 1, the prophet portrayed the ruling elite as those who have the responsibility to know "justice" (*mišpāṭ*); in v 9, he describes them as abhorring **justice** (*mišpāṭ*), the very thing for which they were responsible. The verb *tāʿab* (**despise**) conveys a sense of having an aversion to something or even viewing it as an abomination. Wolff has noted that "just as others are repelled by filth and refuse," Judah's leaders "find the practice of justice highly disagreeable" (1990, 106). Moreover, they **distort** (*ʿāqaš* means "the perversion of that which is just or upright"; see Job 33:27; Prov 8:8-9; 10:9; 28:18) that which is **right** (*yāšar* refers to that which is straight, level, upright, etc.; see 1 Sam 29:6; Job 1:1; compare Mic 7:2).

In 3:10, Micah declares that the corrupt leaders of Israel have built their religious and political capital (**Zion/Jerusalem**) by means of **bloodshed** and **wickedness**. Wolff finds here a critique of Hezekiah's extensive building endeavors in Jerusalem, which would have involved a large number of workers from throughout Judah (see Wolff 1990, 106). The accusation perhaps is also against powerful elite who have built the city through violent seizure of property and houses, slave labor, and exorbitant taxation (see Simundson 1996, 560; Mays 1976, 88). However, building the city does not exclusively mean its actual physical construction. Micah may also be dealing with the prevalence of injustice and violent deeds with which the leaders govern the city. The city is no longer the symbol of justice and righteousness; the covenantal framework and foundation for its existence has collapsed, and it has become a city of bloodshed and violence (see Isa 1:21-23; 5:7).

Micah goes on to describe the civil and religious leaders of Judah and Jerusalem as those who carry out their tasks solely for gain (Mic 3:11). The **leaders** (*rōʾš*) of the community **judge** or dispense justice (*mišpāṭ*) **for a bribe** (regarding bribes, see Exod 23:8; Deut 10:17; 16:19; 1 Sam 8:3; Isa 1:23). The

priests who are entrusted with the responsibility to **teach** hire themselves out **for a price** instead of faithfully teaching the people the covenantal requirements of Yahweh. The **prophets**, instead of speaking faithfully on behalf of Yahweh, **tell fortunes** or practice divination **for money**.

Mays has observed that it was likely "not 'the fee' for service or profit from work that Micah sees as hideous, but the fact that gain had become the overriding basis of the practices of leader, priest, and prophet alike" (1976, 89-90). Yet these selfish and profit-seeking leaders are unconcerned, perhaps even oblivious to the fact, that Yahweh will hold them responsible. They continue to rely on Yahweh for **support** of their activities (v 11). They are confident that Yahweh is in their midst (**among us**) and therefore **no disaster** would come upon them. These leaders seem to be well acquainted with the cultic affirmation of Yahweh's presence in Zion (see Pss 9:11; 74:2; 76:2; 84:7; 132:13). The temple, Yahweh's dwelling place, in Jerusalem led to the development of an ideology of the protection and indestructibility of the city and the safety of those who resided in the city. This misdirected confidence in the temple and the city continued to have an impact on the nation until the city and the temple were destroyed by the Babylonians (see Jeremiah's indictment against the false sense of security in the temple in Jer 7:1-15).

In the closing verse of ch 3, Micah presents the ultimate irony concerning Judah: the ones responsible for building Jerusalem-Zion are equally responsible for its downfall. The adverbial construction *lākēn* (**therefore**) directly links the verdict and punishment in v 12 to the preceding accusations. With the threefold emphasis upon **Zion**, **Jerusalem**, and **the temple hill** (lit. "the mountain of the house"), the prophet makes clear that even Yahweh's sanctuary is not exempt from the impending disaster (see similar thought in Jer 7:12-15; 26:4-6).

As a result of the brutal activities in Jerusalem, the city built with violence and bloodshed will become a leveled wasteland. The images of a **plowed . . . field**, a **heap of rubble**, and an ***overgrown mound*** recall the former height and majesty of the city, particularly the elevated mound upon which the temple stood. Similar images appeared in 1:6 to convey the devastated and leveled plight of Samaria as well. Certainly the earlier destruction of Samaria provided the necessary evidence to Judah and Jerusalem that the covenant community was not immune to divine judgment and destruction.

Not surprisingly Micah's words become a touchstone in the next century as the religious leaders attempted to end Jeremiah's life on account of his temple sermon. Referring to the words of Micah in 3:12, the elders at the time of Jeremiah provided historical precedent for the religious leaders to spare Jeremiah's life as he was simply preaching a message similar to Micah's (Jer 26:16-19). Micah's explicit depiction of Jerusalem's downfall and of the temple's destruction in ch 3 establishes the context for the sudden shift of hope and restoration in chs 4—5.

FROM THE TEXT

This text particularly challenges the reading audience to consider the nature of leadership in all arenas of life—political, economic, and religious. The text moves the reader to examine honestly the manner in which leaders use their power and exercise their authority. It invites individuals and institutions that exert authority over the community of faith to examine their own fidelity to their divine calling and to their proclamation of the God-given message. It especially confronts the reader with images of persons and communities entrusted to their ministry, care, and protection. In the reading of this text, various questions arise: How might religious, political, and judicial leaders practice cannibalism of the very ones they are to protect? How might leadership roles become "life-taking" rather than "life-giving"? How might those under the care of authoritative figures become the fodder for survival of the power base? How do divinely given tasks become diluted to routine jobs, means of survival, or avenues for revenue? The text's graphic contrast between the prophets of Micah's day and the prophet who is equipped by God to carry out the prophetic task challenges the reader to examine the source and center of ministry. From where does power and might to practice ministry come; is strength discovered in the applause of others or in the call of God?

Boldly confronting self-confidence and false security grounded in a well-established popular Zion theology, the daring language in Mic 3:12 challenges subsequent generations to examine their own bases of false security. It moves the reader to confess the seductive self-confidence engendered by well-established theological traditions that unwittingly limit and confine the Lord. Overconfidence and delusional security in the Zion tradition moves the reader to listen again to both the temple sermon of Jeremiah (7:1-15; also ch 26) and the temple sermon of Jesus (Mark 11:15-17).

The subsequent use of Micah's message in Jeremiah's day (Jer 26:18) reminds the reader that the boldness to see and to name self-serving theologies will almost always raise suspicion and opposition. Preservers and perpetuators of such theologies will employ diverse means to still the voice of the prophetic message (Jer 26:7-16; Mark 11:18). The faithfulness of the prophet Micah in the eighth century B.C. had a direct effect in a later century. An intertextual reading of Scripture (i.e., Micah, Jeremiah 7, 26; Mark 11:15-17) challenges the reader to consider the significance of a message for future generations. The reader of the text must ask, "How will faithfulness of one generation provide encourage, hope, and even salvation to subsequent generations?" The reader of the text must likewise ask, "How would the lack of faithfulness on Micah's part have left subsequent generations empty and without recourse?"

B. Oracles of Hope (4:1—5:15)

BEHIND THE TEXT

In chs 4—5, brief depictions of the people's contemporary situation in 4:9, 11, and 5:1 likely reflect the advance of the Assyrian army and Sennacherib's siege of Jerusalem in 701 B.C. (see 1:8-16; Allen 1976, 341). At the same time, the specific reference to Babylon in 4:10 and the general tenor of anticipated exile likely reflects subsequent editorial activity at the time of Babylonian exile or shortly after (Mays 1976, 95-104; for a lesser-held perspective that the prophet envisions exile far in advance, see Kaiser, 1992, 61-63).

In contrast to the imminent divine judgment in chs 1—3 and ch 6, the tone of chs 4—5 abruptly shifts toward hope. The ruined city becomes the restored city (4:1-5). The people in exile become a people who return (4:6-13). A humble king and community replace the self-serving, abusive ruling class (5:1-6). The "Jacob community" that had disintegrated becomes a restored and enlivened community that trusts its covenant God alone (5:7-15). While one might examine each of these units and the oracles within them separately, taken together they provide a vibrant portrayal of Yahweh's restoration and the complete reversal of fortunes for the covenant community. The text presents a complete and radical transformation of temple, land, rulers, and community.

The ancient Zion tradition especially informs the depiction of the city of Jerusalem and its temple mount in these chapters. This ideology has its roots in Yahweh's covenant with David (see 2 Sam 7:12-16) and his choice of Zion/Jerusalem as his dwelling place. The tradition upheld the view that Yahweh ruled his people and the world from the city of Jerusalem through the Davidic rulers (see Pss 2:6-7; 72:2-4, 12-14; 89:3-4, 19-37; 132:11-12). The royal palace was situated in proximity to the divine palace to demonstrate the intrinsic relationship among Yahweh, Zion, and the Davidic family. In the Zion tradition, the cosmic reign of Yahweh, the divine covenant with the Davidic dynasty, and Jerusalem and its temple as Yahweh's earthly abode were thus inexorably bound up with each other.

Although the Zion tradition emerged as a justification for the Davidic dynasty in Jerusalem, it functioned in the exilic and postexilic periods to provide hope for return and restoration. This tradition became a significant basis for an emerging Jewish eschatology and messianism in the postexilic period.

Chapters 4 and 5 exemplify the ancient Israelite practice of retraditioning sacred traditions in light of changed circumstances (regarding the process of retraditioning within the prophetic tradition, see Zimmerli 1990, 69-100;

Steck 1990, 183-214; Ackroyd 1990, 215-34). In the preexilic period, the Davidic covenant had legitimated the Davidic dynasty's authority and the Zion tradition had legitimated Jerusalem's preeminence. In the exilic and postexilic periods, both the dynasty and Zion became the basis of hope for restoration in the absence of king and temple. Ancient Israel's core conviction that the future remained wide open to God's creative and redemptive activity vividly informs all of chs 4—5 (regarding Israel's core traditions, including a future of hope, see Harrelson 1990, 11-30).

The opening verses of this unit (4:1-3) share an obvious similarity with Isa 2:2-4. In almost every instance, Mic 4:1-3 is identical in both thought and vocabulary to Isa 2:2-4. Just as the poetic depiction of the temple's elevation in ch 4 follows Micah's statements of its leveling in ch 3, so, too, the Isaiah text follows divine judgment upon Jerusalem. While it is not possible to determine precisely if one text borrowed from the other, it is conceivable that both texts employed lyrics from a familiar Zion hymn (see Hillers 1984, 51-53; Mays 1976, 95; Simundson 1996, 564).

Chapters 4 and 5 are made up of the following oracles of restoration: nations' pilgrimage to Zion (4:1-5); Yahweh will gather the exiled people (4:6-8); Yahweh will rescue his people from Babylon (4:9-10); victory over the enemy nations (4:11-13); a ruler from Bethlehem (5:1-6); Judah's triumph over enemy nations (5:7-9); Yahweh's judgment of idolatrous nations (5:10-15).

IN THE TEXT

I. A Vision of Restoration (4:1-13 [4:1-14 HB])

a. Nations' Pilgrimage to Zion (4:1-5)

■ **1-5** In vv 1-5, the prophet describes how Yahweh will once again elevate the leveled hill of Zion above all other mountains as the destination of the pilgrimage of all nations. The opening phrase, **in the last days** in v 1, clearly anticipates a future day of restoration. This phrase also indicates a conclusion to the history with which the writer is particularly concerned. The historical era for which Micah is concerned is the period of Jerusalem's fall. Therefore, the prophet depicts the *end* of this period of divine judgment and destruction (v 4). When this historical epoch reaches its finale, Yahweh will restore Jerusalem and revive his people.

The opening verse portrays the restoration of both the destroyed temple and the hill upon which the temple stood. The **mountain of the *house of Yahweh*** or the temple mount will become firmly **established** as first among the mountains and ***elevated above all the hills***. The height of the temple mount and its elevation imply the greatness of Yahweh who has chosen it as the location of his house/the temple. The parallel lines in v 2, **let us go up to**

the mountain of the LORD, to the temple of the God of Jacob, further indicate that the focus here is not on the mountain but rather on the temple located on the mountain.

Micah envisions a day when various people groups (plural *ʿammîm*) **will stream** or flow like a river, to the mountain of the Lord's house (v 1), in order to receive his instruction. The pilgrims to the temple will be eager to learn from Yahweh: **he will teach us his ways** (*derek* here means a path of life or moral character and action; see Deut 9:12, 16; Prov 2:8; 3:6, 23), which would enable them to **walk in his paths**, the way of life he sets before them. Micah also anticipates **the law** (*tôrâ*) going out **from Zion**; the parallel expression, **the word** [*dābār*] **of the LORD from Jerusalem**, repeats the same idea. In a technical sense *tôrâ* refers to priestly instruction and *dābār* refers to prophetic proclamation. Micah here anticipates Yahweh himself being directly involved in giving his instructions/word to the nations in the eschatological era of restoration without the mediating agencies of priests and prophets who have perverted their offices for self-serving purposes (see 3:11).

In 4:3, Micah also anticipates Yahweh taking upon himself the task of judging **between many peoples**; the second line, (he) **will settle disputes for strong nations far and wide,** reiterates the role of Yahweh as the universal judge and arbitrator. In the days of restoration, all peoples—not just Israel, but all the nations in the world—will enjoy impartial judgments, which Jerusalem's rulers have failed to provide to Yahweh's people.

In v 3*b*, the text anticipates new realities that will come into existence in the world as a result of Yahweh's direct involvement in the affairs of the world through his instructions and impartial judgments. The nations and people who followed a path of war and destruction of each other will pursue peace by converting their weapons of war (**swords**, **spears**) to tools of agriculture (**plowshares, pruning hooks**). That which has notoriously functioned to promote death will promote life. One **nation** will not initiate war (**take up sword**) against another nation. As a matter of fact, there will even be an end to the teaching and training of war tactics and technology because of an entirely different "curriculum"—Yahweh's *tôrâ*—that will emerge from the restored Zion. What the prophet anticipates here is a peaceable kingdom of God initiated through Yahweh's instructions that would motivate the nations in the world to pursue the path of peace through unilateral disarmament.

Verse 4 vividly depicts the absence of war through the image of individuals ***sitting*** [*yāšab*] **under their own vine** and **fig tree. No one will make them afraid** conveys the idea of everyone pursuing the path of peace and harmony in relationships. In light of the prophetic indictments in 2:1-2, 9, the image perhaps extends beyond the absence of war. It portrays a family's inheritable land that will now stay within the family line. No longer will men, women, and children live in fear that their very survival and inheritance is at stake. No longer will the elite hoard property (2:2) or drive the women from their homes and children from their inheritance (2:9).

The reality of this peaceable kingdom is certain because he who wills it and intends to establish it is **the LORD Almighty** or ***Yahweh of hosts***. He has the power and commitment to fulfill what he **has spoken**. Micah is confident in the restoration of Israel and the nations' acknowledgment of Yahweh as the source of peace in the world. Judah's covenant deity who has fought his people's battles has declared restoration, and he himself will complete it.

Micah concludes the eschatological vision of restoration with the testimonial response of the community (v 5). The covenant people of God acknowledge that nations in the world **walk** or conduct their life **in the name of their gods**. However, Yahweh's people confess, **we will walk in the name of *Yahweh* our God for ever and ever**. It is possible that Micah imagines here the commitment of the covenant people to walk in the name of the Lord as the motivation for the nations to abandon their walk in the name of their gods and pursue the path that leads to Zion, "the mountain of the LORD" so that he may "teach" them to "walk in his paths" (v 2).

b. Yahweh Will Gather the Exiled People (4:6-8)

■ **6-8** The focus of vv 6-8, 9-10, and 11-13 is on the scattered covenant community. Verses 6-8 deal with the theme of Yahweh's assembling of the scattered exiles for an imminent return to Zion and the establishment of his kingship over them.

The opening phrase, **in that day** (v 6), connects vv 6-8 to the preceding eschatological oracle (vv 1-5). **The exiles** are portrayed in v 6 as **the lame**, a flock that limps (*ṣōlēʿâ*; see also v 7). Using synonymous expressions, **gather/ assemble**, Yahweh expresses his commitment to restore **the exiles** (lit. "those who were driven out or banished") on whom Yahweh has ***brought evil*** (**brought to grief**) by his judgment.

Verse 7 portrays a complete reversal of fortunes. The hopeless ones will become a restored nation. Yahweh will make the weak, limping flock to be that which remains (**remnant**) and make it **a strong nation**. For Micah, the remnant has indeed become what Mays describes as "the name for the eschatological goal of YHWH's way with Israel" (1976, 101). Yet this remnant, this "eschatological goal," is a helpless, lame flock. In the end, the weak will become strong and the lame will become the object of Yahweh's special care (see Jer 31:8-11).

Micah 4:7 ends with the announcement that Yahweh himself will be ***king*** over his gathered remnant in **Mount Zion**, the place of his eternal dwelling. Yahweh will rule over his flock from Zion **from that day and forever**. The day of restoration will initiate a new day of Yahweh's kingship over his people, which will continue uninterrupted forever.

In v 8, Yahweh speaks directly to Jerusalem personified as a woman (**Daughter Zion**; the imagery continues in vv 9-10; regarding the feminization of cities, see Weems 1995, 44-45). Verse 8 refers twice to the majestic city as **Daughter**. The city is described in this verse as a **watchtower** and a **stronghold**, a place of protection and safety for Yahweh's flock (regarding *migdal ʿēder*, **watchtower**, as the proper name of a location, see Gen 35:21; Mays 1976, 103; Achtemeier 1996a, 332). As towers rose above the fields in which sheep grazed, so the holy hill of Zion stood elevated in the midst of Jerusalem. The reference to **stronghold** (*ʿōpel*) indicates an elevated, fortified location within the city. Perhaps it refers to the old Jebusite City of David (see Simundson 1996, 567; Mays 1976, 103). The second part of v 8 announces the restoration of Zion's **former dominion**, the glorious place it once held as the place from where Yahweh ruled over the world. **Kingship will come to Daughter Jerusalem** reaffirms the reign of Yahweh from Zion/Jerusalem. Restoration thus includes the restoration not only of the exiled people but also of Yahweh's kingship over the world. When Yahweh reestablishes his reign over the world from Zion, the city will regain its former glory and preeminent place in the world.

c. Judah's Exile to, and Rescue from, Babylon (4:9-10)

■**9-10** The portrayal of Zion's future glory in v 8 stands in stark contrast to
4:6-10 the present reality of Zion depicted in vv 9-10. The present condition of Zion is continued in vv 11-13 and 5:1-6. Each of these units begin with the temporal adverb *ʿatâ* (***now***; see vv 9, 11; 5:1 [4:14 HB]. The ***now*** of these verses stands in juxtaposition to the "last days" and "that day" of vv 1 and 6. While the unit begins with images of a woman's labor pains (4:9-10), it concludes with a depiction of one who has been in labor finally giving birth (5:2-3 [5:1-2 HB]).

Two rhetorical questions follow the adverb ***now*** in v 9 (**Why do you . . . cry aloud—have you no king? Has your *counselor* perished, that pain seizes you like that of a woman in labor?**). Both the verbal and nominal forms of *rûaʿ* (**cry**) appear in the question. This word often refers to a communal war cry (Josh 6:10, 16, 20) or to the corporate outcry in worship (Pss 47:1; 66:1; 81:1). In this instance, the reference is to the cry of pain heard from **a woman in labor**. The addressee (**you**) is identified as **Daughter Zion** in v 10.

The reason for the cry of Jerusalem is clear; she has no king; he is gone from her midst. Her counselor has perished. It is possible that counselor here is a synonym for king since the function of a king included giving wise counsel to his people (regarding the identity and nature of this absent king, see Ben Zvi 2000, 115-16). The absence of a king causes agony and anxiety for the city, and it cries out in intense pain. In the end, the crying Jerusalem will produce a king who will bring hope and peace to the distraught community (5:2 [5:1 HB]).

In 4:10, the prophet issues an imperative to the distraught city already in intense pain **like that of a woman in labor** (v 9): **writhe in agony** [lit. "be in travail and burst forth"] **. . . like a woman in labor.** This imperative evokes the image of a mother's thrusting or bringing forth an infant from her womb as she gives birth (see Job 38:8; Ps 22:10).

The reason for the command to **writhe in agony** is stated in the next two lines; Zion must **leave** and **camp in the open field** for she will soon **go to Babylon** (v 10). Yahweh who announces the exile of his people also promises to rescue them from Babylon. It will be an intensely painful experience for the people of Judah to leave their land and their beloved city to begin life in the land of Babylon. However, she who is in labor pain will soon experience joy in that she will be **rescued** from Babylon. Yahweh will **redeem** her **out of the hand** of her **enemies** (v 10). The city in labor is thus also a sign of hope for the nation. The pain of exile anticipates the joy of restoration. What the community and the nations perceived as defeat and death will eventually give way to victory and life. Assyria was the aggressive power at the time of Micah, and Babylon emerged as a dominant power only in the second half of the seventh century B.C. Most scholars either place the text in the early part of the sixth century or find here a later editorial reworking of Micah's words.

By placing the text just before the fall of Jerusalem in 587 B.C. Mays has suggested that the metaphors in vv 9-10 should be "understood in a fuller sense as the birth pangs of a new era and the imperatives interpreted as a summons to a future of hope." He has also noted that in v 10 "the exile becomes a bridge from the loss of the city to the place of deliverance" (1976, 105).

d. Victory over the Enemy Nations (4:11-13)

■ **11-13** Similar to the preceding verses, vv 11-13 also contrast the present **now** with the anticipated salvation of the people. These verses also vividly contrast the plans of the nations with Yahweh's final intentions. This contrast revolves around the actions of the **nations** that are **gathered** [*ʾāsap*] **against** Zion (v 11) and Yahweh's gathering (*qābaṣ*) of nations **like sheaves to the threshing floor** (v 12). The NIV indicates the verbs' synonymous nature by translating both as ***gather***. The plan of the nations that have **gathered against** Zion is to defile the city for the satisfaction of seeing it in a dishonored and desecrated state. **Let our eyes gloat over Zion** literally is "let our eyes look upon Zion."

In contrast to the nations' plans, v 12 portrays Yahweh as having a very different intention. The opening line of v 12 makes obvious that the nations' thoughts do not coincide with Yahweh's thoughts. The scheming nations have absolutely no perception of the divine plans. As they are gathered against Zion, they have unwittingly participated in Yahweh's intentions to *gather* them. The text compares Yahweh's action to that of a reaper who assembles stalks on a threshing floor in order to separate the grain (see similar images in Isa 41:15 and Amos 1:3).

Just as the narrative of Israel's redemption from Egypt was less a contest between the Hebrews and Pharaoh and more a contest between Yahweh and Pharaoh, the present situation is a match between Yahweh and the nations. Nevertheless, just as Moses and the Hebrew escapees cooperated with and participated in the divine redemptive activity, the exiled people will take part in the divine redemption. They will not sit by in an idle or passive manner. In v 13 Yahweh calls upon **Daughter Zion** to **rise and thresh** the nations that he has gathered on the threshing floor and **break** them **to pieces**. The text anticipates not simply the defeat of the nations but their total destruction. Yahweh promises to **give** Zion **horns of iron** and **hooves of bronze** in order to accomplish the destruction of the nations. Iron and bronze are the strongest metals of warfare and agriculture. The image of the horn frequently depicts strength (Deut 33:17; 1 Sam 2:1; 2 Sam 22:3), even oppressive strength (Deut 33:17; Ezek 34:21; Zech 1:18-21 [2:1-4 HB]). The image of the iron horn intensifies the nature of that strength (1 Kgs 22:11; Pss 75:10; 89:17, 24). The text portrays Zion as having hooves that thresh out grain as they trample upon the stalks.

Vocabulary of holy war informs the second half of Mic 4:13 (see also holy war language in 3:5). Although Jerusalem will trample the nations with iron horn and bronze hooves, the city will not do so "for its own gain or glory. . . . Nothing that it gains from their defeat will belong to it" (Achtemeier 1996a, 336). Yahweh instructs Judah to impose the sacrificial ban (*ḥērem*, **devote**) on the **ill-gotten gains** (*beṣaʿ*; see Exod 18:21; Judg 5:19; 1 Sam 8:3; Isa 33:15; Jer 22:17) of the nations, the violently and improperly gained profit of the nations at the expense of Judah. The stipulation of the sacrificial ban demands that warriors engaged in holy war are to retain no spoils for themselves (see Josh 6:17-18; 7:1, 11, 15). Since the warrior-deity Yahweh ultimately carries out the battle, all war spoils belong to Yahweh alone. Therefore, they must become sacrifice to Yahweh. The text clearly affirms that this warrior-deity alone is the **Lord of all the earth** (*ʾădôn kol hāʾāreṣ*).

2. A Ruler from Bethlehem (5:1-6 [4:14—5:5 HB])

■ **1-6** As in the two preceding units (4:9-10; 4:11-13), 5:1-6 (4:14—5:5 HB) once again contrasts the **now** of the present situation with the salvation to come (5:1 [4:14 HB]). In these verses, the divinely led salvation emerges from the birth of a ruler. English translations begin a new chapter (ch 5) with this unit; in the Hebrew text, ch 4 ends with v 14, which is 5:1 in the English translations.

The opening imperative in v 1 (**marshal your troops**) is addressed to ***daughter troop*** (*bat gĕdûd*, **city of troops**). It is not clear if this imperative is a call to arms or a call to lament or wail. The verb *gādad* conveys the ideas of both *cutting*, a common practice during wailing and grieving, and *gathering as* *a marauding band*. The text appears to direct the raiders to *gather themselves* in troops. The addressee is not specifically mentioned as "Daughter Zion," but it is likely that the city, and not a division of the army, is intended here.

Whether the text intends a call to arms or a call to lament, it depicts Zion as under **siege** (*māṣôr*). Looking back to Micah's eighth-century B.C. context, the siege would likely refer to Sennacherib's siege of Jerusalem at the time of Hezekiah (see 2 Kgs 18—19; Isa 36—37). However, as the word *māṣôr* frequently appears in texts depicting Nebuchadnezzar's sieges of Jerusalem over a century later, it likely refers to the Babylonian siege of Jerusalem in the early sixth century B.C. (see 2 Kgs 24:10; 25:1-3; Jer 52:5; Ezek 4:3, 7; 5:2).

During sieges by foreign powers, Jerusalem would have undergone tremendous suffering accompanied by corporate shame. **They will strike Israel's ruler on the cheek with a rod** (Mic 5:1) indicates the utter humiliation of the Israelite king by the invading nation. The last king of Judah, Zedekiah, experienced shameful degradation and horrific torture when he was captured and brought to stand before King Nebuchadnezzar (see 2 Kgs 25:1-7). The text refers to Jerusalem's **ruler** as a *šōpēṭ* (judge). While this term commonly refers to the charismatic military leaders of the premonarchic period (Judg 2:16-19), the term often refers to rulers in a more general sense (1 Kgs 3:9; 2 Kgs 15:5; Isa 16:5; Amos 2:3). Mays suggests that the use of the term *šōpēṭ* in this passage provides a "scornful contrast" between Zion's humiliated king and "the old judges of Israel . . . (who) rose to the occasion when Israel was threatened" (1976, 114-15).

The derisive depiction of Jerusalem's humiliated king stands in contradistinction to the ruler depicted in Mic 5:2-6 [5:1-5 HB]. Just as the grave situation described in 4:9-10*a*, 11-12 stands in juxtaposition to the deliverance described in 4:10*b*, 13, the besieged city and the humiliated ruler in 5:1 stand in direct contrast to the glorious future imagined in the subsequent verses.

The threefold use of the temporal adverb *ʿatâ* (**now**) in 4:9, 11, and 5:1 transitions to a similar-sounding word *ʾatâ* (**you**) in the direct address in 5:2: **You, Bethlehem Ephrathah**. The conjunction **but** (*vĕ*) before *ʾatâ* (**you**) introduces the reversal of Zion's misfortunes. What follows in vv 2-5 is a depiction of the humble origins of Jerusalem's future ruler, along with the nature of his reign.

Rather than addressing a future king or a future kingdom, the prophet addresses a relatively insignificant (*ṣāʿîr*, **small**; see 1 Sam 9:21) clan in Judah. The text's reference to **Bethlehem** directly associates this anticipated ruler with King David's birthplace. Obviously, the long-held association between a coming ruler and the Davidic covenant had endured even through seasons of despair and disillusionment. The anticipated ruler's humble nature yet ultimate glory stands in direct contrast to the present ruler's humiliation in 5:1.

Israel's tradition remembered **Ephrathah** as the site of the matriarch Rachel's death (Gen 35:16, 19). The Davidic tradition remembered David's father, Jesse, also to be an Ephrathite from Bethlehem (1 Sam 16:18; 17:12, 58). In Ruth, a postexilic work concerning the ancestry of King David, the name Ephrathah occurs alongside Bethlehem (4:11; see also 1 Chr 2:24 and Ps 132:6). In placing Ephrathah and Bethlehem side by side, the text of Micah likely understands Ephrathah to be a clan that was scattered throughout Judah (for other suggestions of the relationship between the names, see Mays 1976, 115). As a clan, Ephrathah would likely have extended beyond the village of Bethlehem. However, the text depicts the part of the clan that had settled in Bethlehem. Although Bethlehem and Ephrathah were originally two distinct entities (village and clan respectively), their common association with the Davidic family led to their fusion as found in Mic 5:2.

The Tradition of Bethlehem

Bethlehem (*bêt leḥem*, meaning "house of bread") is located approximately six miles south of Jerusalem. Although it retained its identity as a small, rural village, it rose to prominence and maintained distinction in the biblical tradition as the birth city of King David. Likely written after the return from exile, the narrative of Ruth situates David's ancestors in the village of Bethlehem (1:1, 2, 19; 4:11). As David's hometown, Bethlehem was the site of his anointing as king over a united Israel (1 Sam 16). He continued to live in the village until he established his capital in Jerusalem (see 1 Sam 17:12; 20:6, 28). Any reference to a future ruler's coming from Bethlehem would undoubtedly have fueled messianic hopes in subsequent generations. This hope particularly became evident in the early Christian community as apparent in Matt 2:11 and Luke 2:4-7.

With its center in Jerusalem, the Davidic tradition clearly informs the messianic hope in Mic 5:2-5*a* (→ sidebar "The Davidic Tradition and Messianic Expectations," below). The phrase **out of you will come for me one who will be ruler over Israel** clearly indicates two things: (1) out of Bethlehem will come a ruler; (2) this ruler will belong to Yahweh, and not to himself or the city or its clan. He will reign on Yahweh's behalf and according to Yahweh's agenda. This ruler's reign will not be over the southern kingdom or the tribe of Judah or the city-state of Jerusalem alone. His reign will extend over all **Israel**, the territory that David once had ruled.

The concluding statement of v 2 establishes the coming ruler's direct continuity with the ancient Davidic line. This ruler is no new upstart. His **origins** are from ***a time long ago*** **(from of old)** and he proceeds **from ancient times** (*ʿôlām*). The reference is obviously not to the chronological age of the ruler but to the antiquity of the dynastic lineage to which he belongs, that is, the Davidic family (Hillers 1984, 66, suggests that the text may imagine a return of David himself).

The Davidic Tradition and Messianic Expectations

According to the Deuteronomic narrative concerning the establishment of the Davidic dynasty (2 Sam 7:4-17), David desired to build Yahweh a temple (*bay-it*, "house"). Responding on behalf of Yahweh, the prophet Nathan announced that David would not build Yahweh a house but rather that Yahweh would build David a house (2 Sam 7:11; *bayit*, i.e., "dynasty"). Nathan further declared that Yahweh himself would raise up David's descendants to succeed him, that Yahweh would be father to the Davidic descendants, and that they would be his sons (2 Sam 7:12*b*, 14*a*). The covenant between Yahweh and David engendered subsequent confidence that Davidic successors would remain on the throne for perpetuity (see Pss 2; 89; 110; 132). As Davidic descendants were anointed (thus the title "anointed one," *māšîaḥ*, or "messiah") to the office of king, they functioned under the title *son of God* (see 2 Sam 7:14; Ps 2:7).

As the office of kingship degenerated and as a Davidic king did not rule from the time of exile on, the divine covenant with David fueled the anticipation of a future Davidic Anointed One or *Messiah* (see Isa 9:6-7; 55:3-4; Jer 30:9; 33:14-26; Ezek 34:23-24; 37:24-25). This messianic anticipation provided the context for the early followers of Jesus to confess that he was the Anointed One who would ultimately establish the kingdom of God.

The text pauses in Mic 5:3 to reflect upon unfulfilled hope in the present circumstances of defeat and exile. Verse 3 reiterates the condition described in 4:9-10; the present time is indeed the period of labor pain for the people of God. Labor must occur first; however, birth would most certainly follow. The repeated use of **now** in the preceding verses reaches a climax in 5:3 in its reference to a designated **time** (*ʿet*). Only when the "now of labor" is complete and the "time of birth" has arrived will the present struggle give birth to the anticipated Davidic ruler.

The first part of v 3 is rather vague; it reads: ***he will give them until a time*** (**Israel will be abandoned**). The Hebrew text neither refers to abandonment nor mentions Israel. The reference to **time** is likely the time when the one who is in labor has actually birthed a child. Thus, the text clearly emphasizes the "waiting period" prior to birth, that is, the labor period. While the text certainly may be describing a mother who will give birth to a new king (see Isa 7:14; 9:6), it likewise employs the image of a woman as a depiction of the travail of 701 B.C. or of exile (see Achtemeier 1996a, 340; Simundson 1996, 571). For the writer of the text, the birthing process with its labor pains is not yet complete. However, when it is complete, the community that remains (*yeter*, **the rest**, i.e., "the remnant") out of the dispersed community will **return** to Jerusalem. Familial language (**brothers** and **Israelites**) expresses the communal and all-inclusive nature of the return of the "Israelite family."

In Mic 5:4, 5*a* (vv 3, 4*a* HB), the prophet depicts the anticipated ruler's reign both in terms of the ruler's subservience to Yahweh and in terms of the ruler's service to the community as the one who will be the source of **peace** (*šālôm*) for Israel. This ruler will function as servant both to his God and to his people, as the **shepherd** of **his flock**. The image of the shepherd is common in ancient Israel's depictions of royal rule, whether the ruler be divine or human (see 2 Sam 5:2; 7:7; Ps 23; Isa 40:10-11; 44:28; Jer 23:1-6; Ezek 34; 37:24; Zech 11:4-17). The text depicts an ideal ruler who will protect and nourish the citizens of his kingdom in the same manner that a shepherd protects and nourishes his flock.

The twice-occurring instrumental use of the preposition *bĕ* (**in** or "by means of") in Mic 5:4 indicates the means by which the ruler will oversee his people/flock. Yahweh's **strength** and **majesty** will direct the actions of the earthly shepherd. References to Yahweh's **strength** frequently occur in hymns extoling God for his extraordinary potency to act (see Exod 15:2; Pss 29:1; 59:17; 62:11; 63:2; 68:35; Hab 3:4). References to Yahweh's **majesty** indicate the exalted nature of Israel's divine King over all other divine and human rulers (see Exod 15:7; Job 37:4; Isa 2:10; 24:14). The sovereignty and lordship of Yahweh over Jerusalem's ruler will be the very means by which this ruler exercises his authoritative task. Moreover, he will shepherd his flock ***in the name of Yahweh his God*** in covenantal fidelity to Yahweh. Mays aptly observes that this ruler's "reign will be an expression, not a replacement of YHWH's kingship" (1976, 117). The Deuteronomic "Law of the King" (Deut 17:14-20) expresses a similar commitment to the king's subservience to Yahweh's sovereignty (see also Isa 9:6-7; 11:1-5). For this Davidic shepherd, Yahweh will be the ultimate and final shepherd through whom and by whom the ruler would be able to perform his royal tasks.

The final part of Mic 5:4 anticipates the secure and peaceful life of the people in the land and the **greatness** of the ruler reaching **to the ends of the earth** (lit. "they will inhabit and then he will become great until the ends of the earth"). Although the condition of the life of the people is not made clear in the text, it clearly assumes a period of peace and security for the people (hence, **securely** in the NIV). Both Isaiah (9:6; 11:6-9) and Ezekiel (34:25) imagine a similar peaceable kingdom under the reign of an anticipated Davidic ruler.

An inclusio provides the context for Mic 5:5-6: **when the Assyrians invade our land and march through our fortresses** (v 5); **when they** [the Assyrians] **invade our land and march across our borders** (v 6). The Assyrian domination of the ancient Near East in the eighth century B.C. is thus the historical context of these verses. The text begins with the announcement that ***this one*** (meaning, the ruler from Bethlehem Ephrathah) will be the source of **peace** (*šālôm*) for his people during the Assyrian invasion. Verse 6 ends with the anticipation that **he will deliver** Israel **from the Assyrians** who invade and march through the land. The nation will also **raise** up **seven shepherds** (or, ***rulers***) and **eight commanders** (or, ***leaders of men***) against the Assyrians **who will rule the land of Assyria with the sword** and **the land of Nimrod with drawn sword** (or, ***in its gates***) (vv 5-6). Numbers **seven** and **eight** convey the idea of a fully equipped and well organized cadre of leaders who will rise up to defend the nation and overtake the invading nation. While Nimrod is synonymous with Assyria in v 6, the legend of Nimrod evokes images of predatory warriors and hunters. With great irony, the text portrays the defeat of the mighty Assyrians and their domination by leaders who are raised up by the weak and powerless nation of Judah.

Even after the demise of the Assyrian Empire in the seventh century B.C., the myth of Assyria continued to function almost in the form of a code word for other empires that made incursions from the north (see Mays 1976, 120; Wolff 1990, 147; see the same use of Babylon in Rev 14:8; 17:5; 18:2, 10, 21). The Micah text thus continued to convey divine deliverance of the covenant people during the Babylonian period as well as in subsequent eras. Understanding the reference to Assyria in this pan-historical way, Achtemeier comments that Assyria here is to "any nation that would threaten Israel in the future" (1996a, 342).

The Legend of Nimrod

The genealogy of Gen 10 pauses to describe Nimrod as the first mighty warrior on earth and as a mighty hunter before Yahweh (see also 1 Chr 1:10). The great-grandson of Noah, the grandson of Ham, and the son of Cush (Sudan), Nimrod is associated both with Shinar (Babel and Akkad) and Assyria. The genealogy credits him with having built Nineveh. As Nimrod is a legendary figure associated with the origins of Assyria, identification of a historical personality is difficult if not impossible. Outside of the genealogical texts in Genesis and 1 Chronicles, the only other biblical reference to Nimrod occurs in Micah.

3. The Emerging Kingdom (5:7-15 [5:6-14 HB])

a. Judah's Triumph over Enemy Nations (5:7-9)

■ **7-9** The dominating presence of **the remnant of Jacob** in the world and their **triumph** over their **enemies** is the focus of vv 7-9. Verses 7 and 8 begin with the announcement that **the remnant of Jacob** will be **in the midst of many peoples** and **nations**. While only a trace (*šĕʾār*, **remnant**) of Jacob will remain, it will survive and will ultimately flourish. The reference is most likely to those who would survive the Assyrian and Babylonian invasion of the kingdoms of Israel and Judah in the eighth, seventh, and sixth centuries. Within the context of Jerusalem's exile in the early sixth century B.C., the reference to a remnant is as much—perhaps even more—a word of hope as it is a word of threat (see Simundson 1996, 574). In the end, Yahweh will not bring complete annihilation to his covenant people. This small group of people will live in their land surrounded by many and diverse people groups.

Verse 7 compares the remnant to **dew from the LORD**, like **showers on the grass**, whereas v 8 compares them to a **lion/young lion** that destroys **flocks of sheep**. These contrasting images—**dew/showers** and **lion/young lion**—convey the idea of the life-giving and life-taking presence of the remnant among the nations. The concluding lines of v 7 indicate that just as dew/showers do not depend on human effort, but come as Yahweh's gift, "the future existence of a 'remnant of Jacob' in the historical realm is also a wonder that can only be understood as coming 'from Yahweh'" (Wolff 1990, 156). Achtemeier has suggested that the image of the dew points particularly to a "mysterious, nonhuman origin" (1996a, 344). The remnant's presence among the nations will be divine blessing and gift first to the remnant itself but ultimately as a divine gift to the world.

The image of a ferocious, destructive lion that devours its prey provides sharp contrast to the image of dew. This image conveys the manner in which the residue of God's people will finally bring down—even destroy—the surrounding nations. The image of both the life-giving and the life-taking presence of God's people among the nations is consistent with God's word to Abram in Gen 12:3. While Abram's descendants would bring God's blessing to the nations that blessed them, they would likewise bring God's curse to the nations that cursed them.

In Mic 5:9, the text anticipates the power (**hand**) of the remnant being **lifted up in triumph over** their **enemies**. Ultimately, these **foes**, along with their military, political, and religious sources of strength, **will be destroyed**. It is possible to link the last line of v 7 to v 9. Both the life-giving and life-taking presence of Israel among the nations is the work of Yahweh. The remnant of Jacob must not wait for human help but rather must trust in the power and presence of Yahweh who delivers them from the power of their enemies. The victory of Jacob's remnant is the inexplicable act of Yahweh (see Wolff 1990, 157).

b. Yahweh's Judgment of Idolatrous Nations (5:10-15)

■ **10-15** In vv 10-15 Micah provides a catalog-like list of various objects of misplaced trust. The addressee of these verses is not clear in the text. The oracle may be addressing the nations that Yahweh and his shepherd will cut off (see vv 5-9). Achtemeier has interpreted the oracle as addressing primarily or solely the nations who "must also be purged of their idolatry and false trusts before they can become people of the Lord" (1996a, 346-47). However, the addressees likely include the covenant community, the remnant of Jacob, as well. The prophets often show that the people of Yahweh, like the nations around them, trusted in **horses** and **chariots** (see Isa 2:7; 30:15-17; 31:1-3; Hos 10:13) as well as **cities** and **strongholds** for their security. These objects of false security also included **witchcraft**, **idols**, **sacred stones**, and **Asherah poles**.

In these closing verses, the second-person singular pronoun and suffix (**you** and **your**) occurs over a dozen times, which indicates that the people possessed these objects and carried out these practices. In direct contrast, the first-person verb appears nine times in reference to Yahweh. Yahweh (**I**) himself will destroy all that have become objects and practices of the people's (**your**) trust. The verb **destroy** (*kārat*) appears four times in vv 10-13. Just as instruments of war, strongholds, and religious practices would not deliver those that trust in them, these human constructions would not provide deliverance to Jerusalem. Yahweh alone will be the source of his people's salvation and of their enemies' judgment. Yahweh alone would be able to do in and through his people what their objects of false security could not do for them.

The final verse of this unit (v 15) identifies the recipients of divine judgment: **the nations that have not obeyed** (NIV adds **me**). Just as the preceding verses could apply both to the nations and to the covenant community, this reference could refer to both. However, the specific reference to **vengeance** and the preceding references to divine deliverance from the enemies in vv 6-9 imply that Yahweh will act as the defender of his covenant people (→ sidebar, "Vengeance in the OT," below). In the end, he will carry out the same judgment upon the nations that he has executed on unfaithful Israel and Judah.

Vengeance in the OT

The concept of vengeance or revenge in the OT easily contributes to misunderstandings if removed from the context of covenant. The verb *nāqam* literally conveys the notion of vindication. The covenant between Yahweh and Israel provides the context for Yahweh's vindication on behalf of his people. Because the people cannot defend themselves from oppression or speak on their own behalf in the community of nations, Yahweh acts as their *gōʾēl* (see 4:10). He acts for the sake of his covenant people much as the redeemer-kinsman (*gōʾēl*) acted for the sake of the poor, the widow, and the fatherless child (e.g., see Lev 25:25; Ruth 2:20; 3:9, 12; 4:1, 3). Therefore the cry for Yahweh to "take vengeance" on an oppressor is a plea for Yahweh to remain faithful to the commitment that he has made through the covenant. Its intention is certainly not simply to request that Yahweh inflict pain or destruction in order to "get back" at an individual or group.

FROM THE TEXT

As chs 4 and 5 engage the imagination of subsequent generations of readers, they evoke hope-filled visions of the Lord's reign as the kingdom of God extends to all people groups, nations, languages, and cultures. Christian communities over the past two millennia have celebrated and affirmed Micah's hope-filled imagination as they participate in the life and covenant of God through Jesus Christ.

The underlying conviction concerning a remnant of God's people (4:6-7; 5:7-8) speaks hope and promise to all subsequent generations who have lost hope that there even is a future. In the bleakest of local circumstances and global crises, even when engendered directly from a community's rebellion, the Lord refuses to give up on his people. The most atrocious transgressions and sins of God's people will not bring the utter annihilation of the community with whom he has made covenant. When the Lord has made a covenant, he is faithful and true to the divine commitment.

As Ezekiel reminds the exilic generation in the next century, the self-serving, idolatrous confidence in the temple and Zion may result in the departure of the Lord's glory from his temple (Ezek 8:7-18; 10:18-19). However, the glory will indeed return (Ezek 43:1-5). The departure only provides the opportunity for the Lord himself to prepare his people (e.g., see Ezek 36—37) and to rebuild his temple (Ezek 40—42) so that his people and temple may provide life to the deadliest places on the face of the earth (Ezek 47:1-12). *Ichabod* ("the glory is no more") may be for a season (see 1 Sam 4:21), but the divine glory will ultimately make its way back home to the Lord's covenant people (1 Sam 6:1-16). The hope of the people of the Lord in all generations is grounded in the covenant-keeping nature of God himself.

The sharp juxtaposition of "now" in 4:9—5:1 to "in the last days" and "in that day" turns the readers' attention to the same juxtaposition of present realities and future hope. It invites the reader into a world of "the now and the not yet" as it functions to encourage the people of God in subsequent generations to remain steadfast and faithful. Suffering and loss may be a present reality; however, deliverance and salvation will triumph in the end.

Even as the anticipated salvation bursts forth into the present, however, the text calls the reading community to the honest awareness that the culmination of the kingdom is yet to be fully realized. In the midst of the present realities of suffering, persecution, and loss, the people of God continue to anticipate God's victory with the hope-filled prayer: "Your kingdom come; your will be done, on earth as it is in heaven" (Matt 6:10).

The literary-theological thread of a woman in labor provides a poignant metaphor of the profound paradox of exile and suffering for communities whose histories are deeply acquainted with exile, persecution, and holocaust. The experience crosses all boundaries within the human race: suffering in labor ultimately brings forth life. The shrill scream of pain begets the cry of a new creation. In the writhing agony of labor, new life awaits. For our ancestors, the hopelessness of exile anticipated return and restoration. The apparent defeat on a criminal's cross waited for resurrection. Present persecution called for hope in spite of the circumstances. Indeed, to labor in pain is to give birth to new life. To be poor is to inherit the kingdom of God; to hunger is to be satisfied; to weep is to laugh; to be hated and rejected is to be blessed (see Luke 6:20-22). The early Christian community would ultimately testify, "To die is to live" (see Mark 8:34-35; Rom 6:1-10; Phil 1:12-23). Human foolishness and weakness has indeed become the wisdom and power of God (1 Cor 1:18-25).

Although these chapters provide readers with hope-filled imagination, they simultaneously warn against parochialism, nationalism, and ethnocentrism that erroneously equates any one nation, ethnicity, or culture with the people of God. These verses shatter the constraining, limiting bounds created by human institutions and traditions, such as gender, ethnicity, and political-economic status. They anticipate Paul's pivotal declaration that in Christ "there is neither Jew nor Gentile, neither slave nor free, nor is there male and female" (Gal 3:28).

Read through the lenses of the instruction of the gospel of Christ to love and to bless one's enemies (Matt 5:43-44; Luke 6:27-28, 35; Rom 12:9-20), the text's graphic images of the wielding sword in Mic 5:6 call the reader to cautious vigilance. The reading community must remain alert to both external expressions and internal desires of violence and retribution on the part of God's people in any given generation. The Lord has never called upon his people to function as his curse upon the world but rather to serve as his means of grace for blessing to the world. The people of God must remain diligent in their refusal to function as prosecutor, judge, or executioner no matter what the perceived enemy has said or done. Indeed, texts such as Mic 5:6, 8-9 compel the reader to hear Paul's admonition to the church at Rome:

> Do not repay anyone evil for evil. . . . Do not take revenge, my dear friends, but leave room for God's wrath, for it is written: "It is mine to avenge; I will repay," says the Lord. On the contrary: "If your enemy is hungry, feed him; if he is thirsty, give him something to drink. . . ." Do not be overcome by evil, but overcome evil with good. (Rom 12:17, 19-21)

In like manner, the faithful reading community must maintain caution so as not to anticipate its own hand being raised above its "enemies" (Mic 5:9). For the text to stir such subconscious or emotional anticipation of the destruction of "enemies" all too easily promotes an erroneous biblical basis for violence or repressed violence. Rather than intending to encourage such anticipation, the text seeks to leave all judgment against "the enemy" to God.

Texts such as these oblige the contemporary community to hear and to receive them in the fuller canonical context of divine love and mercy to one's foes. Participation in the cross of Christ stands in sharpest contrast to exaltation above one's enemies. The heart of the God incarnate in Jesus Christ calls for an emptying of all forms of self-exaltation on the part of the covenant community. It calls for giving one's life on behalf of both friend and foe.

The concluding catalog-like depiction of objects in which both the nations and the people of God have placed trust (5:10-15) invites the reader of the text to imagine and to reflect upon objects of trust in the reader's own context. The futility of trust in military, political, economic, and religious systems transcends historical eras. Throughout the generations, the people of God unfortunately have continued to place their trust in such systems. The text invites the faithful reading community, the church, to consider its own horses and chariots, cities and strongholds, images, stones, and Asherah poles. It encourages the reader not only to name humanly devised systems in one's contemporary setting but also to acknowledge the impotence of these systems to provide life, salvation, and hope. It calls upon the people of God to confess that the Lord alone is deliverer and provider.

A final word must be said concerning the influence of Micah upon the Christian understanding of Jesus as Messiah. This text's unique association of the anticipated king with a small clan from the village of Bethlehem is consistent with the OT's proclivity to associate God-called leaders with human weakness. David himself was among the weaker candidates for leadership (1 Sam 16:1-14), but he was not alone (e.g., see Exod 4:10-16; Judg 3:15; 6:15; 1 Sam 9:21; Jer 1:4-10). The words of the Apostle Paul to the church at Corinth encapsulate this biblical conviction:

> But God chose the foolish things of the world to shame the wise; God chose the weak things of the world to shame the strong. God chose the lowly things of this world and the despised things—and the things that are not—to nullify the things that are, so that no one may boast before him. (1 Cor 1:27-29)

Undoubtedly this passage's anticipation of a humble ruler from Bethlehem provided and continues to provide the Christian community with lenses by which it understands the person and reign of Jesus Christ. Micah 5:2 establishes the context of a Davidic ruler who shepherds his kingdom through the majestic strength of Yahweh and who provides security to his people (Matt 5:6). He does not merely provide peace; he himself *is* the peace of his people. However, as anticipated by Micah, this peace is not merely an inner tranquillity within the individual. This Anointed One who humbly shepherds his flock brings peace and reconciliation to a broken and fragmented community and ultimately to a broken and fragmented world. The Christian reader of Micah cannot help but overhear the declaration to the church at Ephesus concerning Jesus Christ (Eph 2:14, 17): "For he himself is our peace, who has made the two groups one and has destroyed the barrier, the dividing wall of hostility . . .

He came and preached peace to you who were far away and peace to those who were near." Indeed, the Christian community has historically confessed Jesus Christ in terms of the idealized ruler in Micah. He not only humbled himself to the will of his Father (Luke 22:42; 1 Cor 15:20-28; Phil 2:5-11) but also is the "good shepherd" who knows his sheep by name and leads them (John 10:1-18).

IV. JUDGMENT AND HOPE: SERIES 3: MICAH 6:1—7:20

A. The Divine Lawsuit (6:1-16)

BEHIND THE TEXT

The chapter is well-known for its full development of the lawsuit or legal dispute genre in the prophetic literature. The genre of this oracle conveys the essential meaning of the text. This chapter presents Yahweh's legal case (*rîb*) against the covenant community (regarding the didactic nature of Mic 6:1-8, see Ben Zvi 2000, 149-51).

With the surrounding mountains as witnesses and jury and with Yahweh as prosecutor and witness, Yahweh the plaintiff presents his case (*rîb*) against the covenant community (vv 1-2). In vv 9-16, Yahweh also pronounces his verdict as the divine judge. Yahweh outlines in vv 3-5 the actions he performed to save them throughout their history. The covenant people (defendants) respond in vv 6-7 and sarcastically ask if there are other sacrificial requirements (and list a few examples) they need to fulfill in order to satisfy their offended covenant deity. The divine response (v 8) to their question is not a new response. It is a response that the people have known from the beginning.

While one might consider the oracle in vv 9-16 separately, these verses function as the divine verdict in the text's present canonical arrangement. Yahweh provides specific evidence of Judah's infidelity (vv 9-12) and proceeds to announce his judgment upon them (vv 13-16).

The text assumes the audience's familiarity with both the lawsuit genre and various ancient traditions, narratives, and historical eras. These traditions and narratives include prominent characters such as Moses, Aaron, and Miriam, and the narrative of Balak and Balaam. The text also assumes the audience's familiarity with sites related to the crossing of the Jordan River as well as the political-economic policies of Kings Omri and Ahab (see vv 4-5, 16). Likewise, vv 6-7 presume the audience's acquaintance with various elements of the sacrificial system. The Deuteronomic-prophetic conviction of sowing and reaping underlies the judgment words in vv 14-15.

IN THE TEXT

■ 1 While English translations interpret the term *rîb* in various ways (e.g., **case** in v 1; "accusation" and "case" in v 2; "charge" in Hos 4:1; "judge" in Isa 3:13), the notion of a lawsuit or a legal hearing undergirds the essential meaning of the term. Similar to the lawsuit in Hos 4:1, the text in Mic 6 opens with a plural imperative call for the audience to **listen** (*šāma*ʿ, translated as "hear" in Hos 4:1). The text is not precise in regard to the identity of the addressees. On one hand, they may be the broader audience of the people of God; on the other hand, they may be the mountains and the hills depicted in v 2 (regarding the diverse voices and addressees in Micah's lawsuit, see Ben Zvi 2000, 142-49).

In contrast to the plural form of the first imperative, the command to **stand up** and to state the **case** is singular. Likewise ***your voice*** (**what you have to say**) is also singular. These singular forms certainly may function as a collective singular in reference to Judah as an entity. However, as the only character in ch 6 bringing a lawsuit is Yahweh, v 1 likely introduces Yahweh, the plaintiff, as he takes his stand to present his case. If this interpretation is correct, then the first verse calls upon Yahweh to rise, state his case, and let the hills hear his voice rather than calling upon the people to bring their own lawsuit to court.

■ 2 The opening plural imperative *šāma*ʿ reappears at the beginning of v 2 (**hear**). In v 2, the addressees are clearly the mountains and hills along with the earth's foundations. Ancient Near Eastern cosmology understood the mountains to reach high toward the heavens thereby holding up the firmament itself. In the same manner that a building's foundations provide firm support to that building, the **foundations of the earth** extended far into the depths of the earth, thereby providing support and security to the earth itself (see similar images in Job 38:4; Pss 24:1-2; 89:11; 102:25; Isa 48:13). Therefore, the prophet calls to that which provides security both to the heavens and the earth, that is, the "highest heights" and the "deepest depths," to hear Yahweh's lawsuit against his people. The last line, he is **lodging a charge** (*yākaḥ*) also conveys the idea of a lawsuit (*rîb*).

As lawsuits operate within a specific relational context, the context for Yahweh's lawsuit against his people is the covenant long ago established between Yahweh and Israel. The reference to **his people** (*ʿammô*) recalls the covenant formula "I will be your God and you will be my people" (*ʿammî*, Jer 7:23; → Hos 1:9; 2:1, 23).

■ **3** In Mic 6:3-5, Yahweh the plaintiff (also the prosecutor), instead of presenting evidence to show the defendants' infidelity to the covenant, provides evidence of his own fidelity to his covenant.

Verse 3 opens with Yahweh addressing the accused as **my people** (*ʿammî*; see above and v 5). Yahweh begins his speech to his people with his questions that elicit a response from the covenant community: **What have I done to you? How have I burdened** [*lāʾâ*] **you?** The nominal form of the verb (**burdened**) occurs in other OT texts that depict Israel's weariness during their oppression in Egypt (Num 20:14) and their restlessness in the wilderness (Exod 18:8). Yahweh wants to know if he had acted in oppressive ways at any time in the past in his relationship with his people. Yahweh demands a response from his covenant partner (**Answer me**); however, the people are silent. They are unable to offer any evidence of divine maltreatment or infidelity.

■ **4** As the defendants remain speechless, Yahweh declares that his actions were not burdensome, but rather gracious and compassionate and salvific. Yahweh **brought** them up (*ʿālâ* sounds similar to *lāʾâ* [meaning "burdened"] in v 3) **out of Egypt**. Rather than weighing his people down, Yahweh has **redeemed** them from **the land of slavery**, where they were burdened by the Egyptians through hard labor and oppressive treatment. Yahweh not only redeemed Israel but also provided them with capable leaders. Though in the NIV Aaron and Miriam appear to have a secondary role to Moses (i.e., **also Aaron and Miriam**), the Hebrew text lists **Moses**, **Aaron**, and **Miriam** equally alongside each other as those whom Yahweh sent **to lead** Israel out of Egypt (see NRSV). While Moses appears first in the list, all three appear in Micah's list as equally significant leaders in the life of God's people. Certainly, ancient Israel's tradition remembered Moses as the leader par excellence, the nation's lawgiver, and the prophet without parallel (Deut 34:10-12). However, it also remembered the diverse roles played by Moses' brother and priestly leader Aaron during both the escape from Egypt and the wilderness sojourn (see Exod 3:10-16; 6:28—7:13; 16:1-34; 17:8-13, etc.). Israelite tradition remembered the significant role of Moses' sister Miriam especially in the community's worship that occurred just after the deliverance at the sea (see Exod

15:20-21; however, see also the tradition of Aaron's and Miriam's rebellion against Moses in Num 12).

■ **5** In v 5 Yahweh calls his people to **remember . . . that** they **(you) may know** his saving activities. Two incidents of historical significance are mentioned in v 5 that should evoke in Israel's remembrance Yahweh's fidelity to his covenant. The reference to **Balak** and **Balaam** recalls the incident in which Moab's king, Balak, entreated the diviner Balaam to curse the Israelites who were traveling through Moab on their way to Canaan (Num 22—24). Yahweh instructed Balaam not to curse the Israelites because they were a blessed people (Num 22:12). Throughout the remainder of the narrative, Balaam repeatedly insists to Balak that he cannot curse those whom Yahweh has blessed. The best that he could do was to pronounce blessing upon them since they were already a divinely blessed people.

Numbers 25 preserves the narrative of the Israelites at **Shittim** where they engaged in cultic prostitution with the Moabite women and made sacrifices to Baal Peor, the Moabite deity. Yahweh's speech, however, makes no reference to this rebellion of Israel, but mentions Shittim as a place significant to his saving acts on behalf of Israel. Shittim was Israel's final encampment east of the river Jordan; it was from here that Joshua sent out two spies to Jericho (Josh 2:1) and led the march across the river Jordan (Josh 3:1). **Gilgal** was Israel's first encampment in Canaan (Josh 4:19-24). Therefore, the phrase **from Shittim to Gilgal** (the NIV adds **your journey**) certainly would recall Yahweh's faithfulness to his people as they crossed the Jordan into the land of promise (see Joshua's words in Josh 4:21-24).

Ironically, however, just as Shittim was a site of rebellion, so, too, was Gilgal. At Gilgal, the Israelites made Saul their king (1 Sam 11:14-15). In the eighth century B.C., both Hosea and Amos portrayed Gilgal negatively (Hos 4:15; 9:15; 12:11; Amos 4:4; 5:5). While the phrase **from Shittim to Gilgal** no doubt testifies to Yahweh's faithfulness, it simultaneously evokes memories of rebellion and unfaithfulness.

The call to **remember** in v 5 reiterates a familiar Deuteronomic-prophetic concern (see Deut 5:15; 7:18; 8:18; 15:15; 16:12; 24:18, 22; 32:7; regarding not remembering or forgetting, see Deut 4:9; 6:12; 8:11, 19; 32:18; Hos 2:13; 13:6). Simundson has observed that this call to remembrance particularly means that the people are "to identify fully with the ancient stories, to know that they are not remote tales from long ago but are living examples of the ongoing presence and power of God in every age" (1996, 579). Mays has gone even further in describing the past events in Israel's life as more than "examples" for subsequent eras. He has observed that remembrance in this context means "to recall the past and confront it as present reality, to live and think by events whose force continues from the past into the present" (1976, 135).

The purpose of Yahweh's call to **remember** is to elicit the response of the people: ***in order to* know the righteous acts of the Lord** (v 5). The verb **know** (*yāda'*) means to enter into a personal covenantal relationship and experience with another party. The text suggests that the memory of Yahweh's saving acts by the people is critical to their covenantal knowledge of Yahweh and his righteous acts on their behalf. The prophet Hosea associated the lack of knowledge with Israel's ultimate destruction (Hos 2:8; 4:1, 6; 5:4; 6:3; 11:3).

Within the context of the covenant relationship between Yahweh and his people, the notion of righteousness (*ṣĕdāqâ*) signifies "right-relatedness." Yahweh's actions demonstrate that he has acted appropriately or "rightly" within the covenant relationship; it is thus apparent that he has remained rightly related to them. This divine "right-relatedness" (i.e., righteousness) stands in stark contrast to the community's actions both toward Yahweh and toward their neighbors (see Mic 6:9-12). Within the context of the covenant that they share with Yahweh and with each other, they are clearly "not rightly related" (i.e., unrighteous).

■ **6-7** Verses 6-7 function as the response of the defendants within the legal context of ch 6. These verses may be understood as the defendants' inquiry seeking Yahweh's instruction on how they may properly approach him in the setting of worship. However, the progression of the questions from a routine inquiry to sarcastic and hyperbolic questions implies a defiant attitude of the worshipping community that is under indictment for its covenant-breaking.

The opening lines of v 6 express the primary issue at hand. The worshipping community, the defendants in Yahweh's lawsuit, responds to Yahweh's case with a question concerning the offering (**with what**) they should bring with them that would please Yahweh when they come and bow down before him in worship. It is unlikely that the people express here their ignorance of the laws that regulated the act of worship; it is also unlikely that the questions come from a repentant community that seeks restoration of relationship with its covenant partner, and desires to know possible ways to properly worship Yahweh. Rather, the tone of the questions and the questions themselves suggests their utter disbelief in Yahweh's case against them. They seem to counter the charge against them by portraying Yahweh as a deity who expects more than what he stipulated in the laws of sacrifices and offerings he gave to Israel through Moses. Their questions also imply that they have fulfilled their obligations according to the cultic laws established by Yahweh. Therefore, they want to know what else they need to do to satisfy the divine requirements of worship.

The people speculate and give a list of several types of offerings in the remainder of vv 6-7 that they assume would perhaps please Yahweh and prompt him to withdraw his case against them. The first two suggestions, whole **burnt offerings** and **calves a year old**, are more costly than other common sacrifices.

In contrast to other animal sacrifices, the whole burnt offering reserved nothing of the animal for the worshipper or priest to consume. The entire animal was slaughtered and burned. The year-old calf depicts livestock at its prime. As the inquiry in v 7 proceeds with various suggestions, the possibilities become hyperbolic and extravagant, if not absurd. The suggestions of **thousands of rams** or **ten thousand rivers of oil** extend beyond that which is reasonably possible for any worshipper. In the suggestions of these extravagant possibilities, the focus shifts specifically to that which will please Yahweh and that which he will accept with favor. The second half of v 7 moves even beyond hyperbole and sarcasm. In utter disbelief, the defendants ask if Yahweh would be pleased with the offering of their **firstborn** for their sins. The worshipping community is well aware of Yahweh's hatred against this detestable practice (Lev 18:21: 20:2-5; Deut 18:10; Jer 7:30-31). The concluding statements of Mic 6:7 thus demonstrate that the inquiry in these verses do not concern routine acts of worship. Ultimately, all of these questions serve to characterize the plaintiff as an unreasonable and overbearing deity who simply cannot be pleased in ordinary ways of worship.

■ **8** Yahweh's case against Israel and Israel's response to Yahweh are followed by the statement in v 8, which most likely comes from the prophet who now functions as a witness for Yahweh in the setting of this legal dispute. This verse, well-known in both Judaism and Christianity, and even in secular settings, has the tone of a priestly instruction. However, in content and theology, this instruction is consistent with the teachings of Israel's prophets, and, in fact, it conveys the essence of prophetic teachings (see similar prophetic convictions in 1 Sam 15:22-23; Ps 51:16-17; Isa 1:12-17; Hos 6:6; Amos 5:21-24). Simundson, who finds a similarity between Micah's response here and Yahweh's speech in Job, has observed that "the answer changes the question" (1996, 580). No longer is the concern one of cult and sacrifice, but rather the concern is daily lifestyle and fidelity.

Micah 6:8 begins with a claim about what Yahweh has already revealed (**he has shown you**) as that which is **good** and that which he **requires**. There is no new revelation here, but a reiteration of what has already been revealed by Yahweh. The addressee in v 8 is identified by the more general term ***human*** (*ʾādām*, **mortal**). Mays, who places this verse in the ancient Israelite context, concludes that this address "is not intended to identify the questioner with humanity in general or to address him in some other identity than that given by his relation as an Israelite to Yahweh his God" (1976, 141). However, associating Micah's use of both *ʾādām* and *ṭôb* (**good**; see below) with creation itself as depicted in Gen 1, Achtemeier comments that the addressee is "creature before creator and subject totally to the creator's definitions of good" (1996a, 356). She concludes that "God has created human life on this earth, and as its creator, God alone can say what and how it should be lived" (ibid.). What Yahweh has already revealed is **good** (*ṭôb*) or appropriate and fulfills what he requires from *ʾādām*. The participle form of the verb *dāraš* ("to seek" or "demand," **require**) conveys an ongoing, uninterrupted nature of the divine demand.

The NIV does not translate the particle *kî ʾim* at the beginning of the last line of v 8. This particle may affirm the absolute certainty of that which follows. Alternatively, the particle may function to provide contrast or limitation to the preceding clause (thus "but" [NRSV] or "except"). Three infinitive verbs follow the particle in order to express that which Yahweh is seeking: ***to do, to love, to walk***.

The first verb ***to do*** does not mean *how* one is to act (as in **act justly**), but rather it calls for a specific deed; Yahweh has shown the worshipping community that it is appropriate or fitting ***to do justice*** (*mišpāṭ*) (see Amos' concern for *mišpāṭ*, the rendering of right judgments and appropriate decisions within the context of covenant in Amos 5:7, 15, 24; 6:12; see also Mic 3:1, 9).

The divine demand **to love** conveys much more than an emotive or sentimental affection. The verb *ʾāhab* denotes a sense of commitment or allegiance, in this context to *ḥesed* (***covenant loyalty*** or "fidelity"), which is embodied by the worshipping community in loyal and faithful actions both in its relationship to Yahweh and to other human beings (see Hosea's concern over Israel's lack of *ḥesed* in its covenant relationship with Yahweh in Hos 4:1; 6:4, 6).

6:8 The final verb (*hālak*, **to walk**) conveys the manner in which one conducts one's life; Yahweh has already shown the worshipping community that it is fitting and appropriate **to walk humbly with** their (**your**) **God**. This divine requirement addresses the day-to-day behavior of the community (see this verb also in Mic 2:3; 4:2, 5). In Prov 11:2, the only other instance in which the verb *ṣānaʿ* ("humbly") occurs in the OT, it stands in direct contrast to human pride. Limburg translates the verb as "circumspectly" or "carefully" and interprets it as "the theological dimension of the sort of life God wants" (1988, 192). Mays has noted that *ṣānaʿ* conveys "a way of life that is humble, not so much by self-effacement, as by considered attention to another. The humility lies in not going one's own way presumptuously, but in attending the will and way of God" (1976, 142; see also Achtemeier 1996a, 353). According to the wise saying in Prov 11:2, this humble or circumspect lifestyle goes hand-in-hand with wisdom.

Rather than an isolated, privatized lifestyle, the conduct of this *walk* is to be embodied in a life lived in direct relationship with God. Within the context of Yahweh's covenant with Israel, the phrase **your God** functions as a fitting counterpart to the earlier divine address, "my people" in Mic 6:3, 5. Throughout the divine lawsuit in vv 1-8, the covenant that exists between Yahweh and his people clearly functions as the context.

9-12 In vv 9-12 Yahweh elaborates his charges by listing specific acts of infidelity carried out by Judah. Yahweh begins his speech by raising his voice and calling the city, most likely Jerusalem (***The voice of Yahweh calls*** **to the city** [v 9]). A wisdom reflection interrupts Yahweh's announcement in v 9. Micah affirms that reverence (*yārāʾ*, **fear**, "awe") toward the divine name is well-advised (*tûšiyyâ*, **wisdom**). The precise meaning of the final line of v 9 is not clear. Translating *maṭṭeh* as **rod**, the NIV interprets the divine call to be obedient reception (*šāmāʿ*, **heed**, "obey," "hear"; see v 1) of both the rod of judgment and Yahweh who has appointed the rod of judgment (the NIV adds the phrase **the One**).

By means of rhetorical questions, Yahweh reminds the city's dishonest, violent, self-serving leaders of his awareness of their deeds (***Will I forget?*** [v 10]) and of his determination to prosecute (***Will I acquit?*** [v 11]). Clearly implied in these rhetorical questions is the understanding that the divine judge must proceed to execute judgment against his rebellious people.

In vv 10-12, Yahweh describes in detail the specific socioeconomic crimes of the covenant people that he will not forget or acquit. The list begins with the description of ***the house of the wicked*** (*rāšāʿ*) as ***storehouses of wickedness*** (*rešaʿ*). The text clearly indicates that the house has taken on the character of that which fills it up. Violent and criminal activities lie behind the treasures that fill the storerooms. The reference here may likely include the storerooms of the temple itself.

In the same way, Yahweh will not forget the condemned or **accursed** practice of making **ephah**, the dry measure, **short** and thus shortchanging the poor by greedy merchants (see similar indictment in Amos 8:5). In Mic 6:11, Yahweh states that he will not acquit those who do business with **dishonest scales** and **a bag of false weights** (see Amos 8:5; Hos 12:7). Israel's legal and wisdom traditions also condemned the use of deceptive weights, measurements, and scales (see Lev 19:36; Deut 25:13-14; Prov 11:1; 20:10, 23).

In Mic 6:12, Micah describes the wealthy beneficiaries of these fraudulent practices as filled with ***violence*** (*hāmās*; see Amos 3:10). Violence is the means by which the rich have gained their wealth. The second part of Mic 6:12 describes the total lack of honesty, integrity, and truthfulness in the society. The people are **liars**, and they do not speak the truth; what comes out of their mouth is ***deceitfulness***. Micah employs a noun (*rĕmiyyâ*, ***deceitfulness***) from the same root as the word that describes the weights in v 11 (*mirmâ*, **false**). Thus, tongues of the powerful elite have the same dishonest character as the weights they use. Verses 10-12 depict a wealthy ruling class whose actions are violent and unjust and whose character, both inside and out, is fraudulent and dishonest.

■ **13-16** The concluding four verses of ch 6 provide specific details of the divine judgment upon Jerusalem and its leaders. The opening phrase (**therefore** [v 13]) makes evident that the devastation that Yahweh is about to bring is quite clearly the result of the people's sins described in the preceding verses. Yahweh himself is preparing to ***attack*** (*nākâ*, **destroy**; see Hos 9:16; Amos 3:15; 4:9; 6:11). Micah 6:13 also links the destruction of the people by Yahweh to the **sins** (*ḥaṭṭā'ṯ*) of the people. A community that remains defiant before Yahweh who has brought his case against it cannot expect to receive anything from him but devastating judgment.

In vv 14-15 Yahweh announces that his judgment will result in the total futility of all the work they do to accumulate wealth and find satisfaction to their lives. Because of the difficulty of the text, both Mays and Allen understand the references to empty stomachs and the inability to save that which is stored up to the inability to produce children (Mays 1976, 143, note e; Allen 1976, 380). Mays suggests the translation, "Semen into your womb you will take, and not bring forth" (1976, 380; however, see Hillers 1984, 81, note n, for a sound argument against this interpretation). The underlying message of v 14 is clear: Yahweh's judgment will ruin the efforts of the wicked to stay wealthy and happy through their criminal activities.

Verse 15 reiterates the theme of v 14 by relating Yahweh's judgment to the agricultural activities of the wicked. Though they **will plant**, they will **not harvest**; though they **will press olives**, they will **not use the oil**; though they **will crush grapes**, they will **not drink the wine**. The clear message here is that they will not be left alive to enjoy the fruit of their labor.

Another reference to the sins of the people in the first half of v 16 interrupts the depiction of the imminent judgment. Yahweh adds to the list of crimes of those under his judgment, their carrying out of **the statutes of Omri and all the practices of Ahab's house**. Although Omri and Ahab were ninth-century B.C. kings in the northern kingdom, they must have become familiar to the southern kingdom as well. Their unjust socioeconomic practices stood in direct contrast and opposition to the socioeconomic practices of Yahwism. During the Omri dynasty, Israel's political and economic elite prospered significantly at the expense of the masses. Bernhard Anderson has described the socioeconomic situation under Omri as "something like an economic boom . . . with an inevitable widening of the gulf between the 'haves' and the 'have-nots'" (1986, 265). Rather than walking (*hālak*; see v 8) circumspectly with their God, Yahweh, the Jerusalem elite have ***walked*** (*hālak*, **observed**) according to non-Yahwistic ***principles*** (*mô'ēṣâ*, **statutes**) initiated by the Omri dynasty. As a result, Yahweh himself will hand the leaders and their rule over to utter ***devastation*** (see *šāmam* in v 13). As the city's inhabitants become the object of mockery, Yahweh will hand them over to ***derisive hissing*** (*šĕrēqâ*; see Jer 19:8; 25:9, 18; 29:18; 51:37).

The precise meaning of the concluding line of Mic 6:16 is somewhat difficult to interpret. According to the Hebrew text (see NRSV), the line states, ***You will carry the taunt of my people***. The Septuagint reads, "They will carry the taunt of peoples (i.e., nations)." The NIV, **You will bear the scorn of the nations,** conveys a similar interpretation. However, the phrase ***my people*** might be a reference more generally to the covenant community (see NRSV) or more narrowly to the oppressed community for whom Micah speaks. The addressees (**you**) in these verses are Jerusalem and its powerful elite; the text reminds the guilty leadership of Jerusalem that they will carry the scorn that has come upon Yahweh's (***my***) people.

These concluding verses in ch 6 clearly reflect the prophetic-Deuteronomic conviction of sowing and reaping. The powerful elite who have worked so diligently will ultimately achieve nothingness (regarding these verses as "futility curses," see Mays 1976, 147-48; Simundson 1996, 582). Instead of receiving praise, they will become objects of derision. Those who have given every effort to save their lives in the end will lose their lives.

FROM THE TEXT

The lawsuit between the Lord and his people poignantly reminds the reader of the covenantal relationship established by God with his people. Neither salvation nor judgment is arbitrary. Both occur within the context of the covenant relationship between the Lord and his people. The lawsuit genre establishes the Lord's legitimate, even legal, grounds for his accusation against his people. He is no petty deity. Within the context of covenant, he has expectations of his people, and he holds his covenant partner accountable.

The evidence of the Lord's faithful actions toward his people in vv 3-5 reaffirms the essential character of this covenant God as grace and mercy. Rather than exposing his divine character through disconnected propositions and abstract ideas, the Lord has revealed his nature through the concrete, historical acts of deliverance and provision. This God is not simply the highest ideal that the human mind can conceive. This God has acted in definitive ways to save his people from oppression and to provide for them in times of need.

The questions in vv 6-7 and the priestly prophetic *torah* in v 8 shape a clear and precise prophetic worldview for the reader of the text. Though the questions come from a community under indictment, these verses do not delegitimize rituals and sacrifices, but place them in their appropriate context (see 1 Sam 15:22-23; Ps 51:16-17; Isa 1:12-17; Hos 6:6; Amos 5:21-24; Matt 9:9-13; 12:1-8). In response to the all-consuming question pondered by human beings across time and space—"What does God desire?"—the text clearly articulates the divine desire for a lifestyle of justice and righteousness. The reader becomes keenly aware that Yahweh intends this lifestyle not only for the covenant community but also for the entire human race (*ʾādām*). This lifestyle is that which is appropriate, that which the Creator has deemed as good (*ṭôb*). Anything short of justice, fidelity, and a humble walk with God fails to fulfill the divine intention for the human race.

Canonically, the instruction of Mic 6:8 is in direct dialogue with Micah's fellow eighth-century B.C. prophets. It echoes Amos' concerns for justice (see Amos 5:7, 15, 24; 6:12), resonates with Hosea's emphasis upon covenant faithfulness (see Hos 4:1; 6:4, 6), and confirms Isaiah's admonitions to conduct one's life in a trusting walk with God (see Isa 7:4, 9*b*; 8:12-13; 30:15; 37:6).

Micah's instruction for proper worship encapsulates the essential message of all of the eighth-century B.C. prophets. Furthermore, this text boldly reminds its hearers that justice, fidelity, and a trusting walk with God are not mere theories to ponder, ideals to question, and thoughts to debate. Ultimately, justice, fidelity, and trust are actions to carry out. The faithful disciple is to *do*, to *love*, and to *walk*. Having become a hallmark of the Christian church and social justice movements, Mic 6:8 particularly challenges these communities to move beyond debate and theory and to move forward into action. The walk that recognizes the Lord as God is not merely expressed through internal confessions or oral testimonies. It has hands and feet. Indeed, Micah's prophetic instruction calls upon the people of God to see *word* become *flesh*.

Verses 6-8 also encourage the readers to recognize God's lordship over the totality of life. Though there is an explicit criticism of cultic sacrifice that separates itself from justice and fidelity in vv 6-8, these verses function to remind the reader of the ongoing necessity of sacrifice in its most basic sense. Mays has articulated the irony of the response in light of the worshipper's inquiry concerning sacrifice:

> So at a profound level the answer does call for sacrifice, but a kind quite different from that proposed by the question. It is not sacrifice of something outside a person which can be objectified as a means to deal with God. It is rather a yielding of life itself to God and his way, "repentance" of the most radical sort. What YHWH requires is not the life of some thing, but the living of the man who stands before him. (1976, 142)

Similarly Brown has observed:

> In the end, God's answer in verse 8 calls for a sacrifice to end all sacrifices, namely the sacrifice of the self in humble obedience to God. What we bring, apart from a listening and obedient heart, is unnecessary baggage, useless props that can only burden and divert us from faithful obedience, at best, and, at worst, encourage us in blissfully assuming that

everything is hunky-dory between God and us. Such presumption is deceptive, the prophet warns. (1996, 59)

The text particularly challenges and even warns its readers against the false assumption that God desires the sacrifice of "more things." In an era in which "more is better," the people of God might all-too-easily view "great sacrifices" as the evidence for commitment to God. Ultimately, God desires the undivided, consecrated life of the human being. This consecrated life will ultimately carry out justice, embrace fidelity, and trustingly journey with God.

In vv 9-12, the reader encounters concrete depictions of daily activities that impede the people of God from doing justice, loving faithfulness, and humbly walking with God. Through the depiction of activities such as self-serving business transactions, violence, and deception, these verses move the reading audience to see and to confess its own selfish desires, violent acts, and false dealings. These verses also warn the readers that injustice and greed cannot bring fulfillment to one's life. Micah anticipated empty stomachs or barns as the destiny of the unjust people he addressed in his day. Jesus offers the alternative to his disciples: "Blessed are those who hunger and thirst for righteousness, for they will be filled" (Matt 5:6).

B. Lamentation with Hope (7:1-20)

BEHIND THE TEXT

While several distinct oracles comprise ch 7, these oracles operate collectively as a single lament, with each oracle displaying a significant component of the typical structure of a lament. The general structural movement of the lament genre begins with an address to God with opening petition and moves to the lament proper with an outcry of despair. Oftentimes, the lament proceeds to confess trust in Yahweh followed by the petition for divine assistance. In anticipation of divine aid, the lament may conclude with either praise to Yahweh or a vow to praise Yahweh (regarding the structure and setting of the lament genre along with the role of the "enemy" in laments, see Westermann 1981, 165-213). The lament with its concluding declaration of trust in Yahweh serves as an appropriate literary conclusion to the book of Micah. Structurally, the lament of ch 7 carries out the opening call to lamentation in 1:8-16 that continues in 2:4.

In the opening cry of despair (7:1-6), the worshipper cries out concerning the distress. The focus of the despair is upon the sense of isolation and the incapacity to place trust in both family and neighbor. The lament's hinge that moves the text from despair to hope occurs in v 7, a confession of trust in Yahweh. The one in anguish declares the intent to wait patiently upon Yahweh's action.

In anticipation of divine activity, vv 8-10 specifically address the enemy who has brought the despair upon Jerusalem and who continues to gloat over the apparent defeat of the city. The lament genre frequently gives significant attention to both the destructive activity of the enemy and the ultimate defeat of the enemy (e.g., see Pss 13; 18; 57; 59; 69; 74; 143). Micah 7:8-10 affirm that the enemy will experience a similar defeat as Yahweh delivers the city in the end.

In vv 11-17, the lament shifts from the defeat of the enemy to the restoration of Jerusalem. Finally as one might expect, the lament concludes in vv 18-20 with an affirmation of the divine character. This closing affirmation functions as an appropriate conclusion both to the lament and to the book of Micah as a whole. It provides the context within which the lament and overall message of Micah occurs: Yahweh's consistent fidelity to his people embodied in his forgiveness of his people's transgressions.

The speaker of the lament may be either the prophet or an anonymous leader of the people (Simundson 1996, 584-85; Hillers 1984, 85). However, in light of the preceding outcry to the city of Jerusalem (6:9-16), the one crying is likely the city of Jerusalem itself (Mays 1976, 150-51, 158; Achtemeier 1996a, 358; regarding diverse voices, such as Jerusalem, the prophet, Yahweh, and the people, see Ben Zvi 2000, 167-68; Hillers 1984, 90). As early as 1:5, the text points to Jerusalem as the transgression ("high place") of Judah (see also 1:9, 12-13; 3:10, 12). Throughout chs 4—5, the prophet directly addresses both the present agony and the future restoration of Jerusalem/Zion (4:1-2; 4:8—5:1). In light of the devastation depicted throughout the preceding six chapters, the city responds to the verdict and judgment in 6:7 with an agonizing cry of lamentation.

IN THE TEXT

I. Jerusalem's Lament (7:1-7)

■ 1 Verse 1 opens with a phrase that conveys the idea that what follows is a lamentation: *ʾallay lî* (***Alas to me!*** Or ***Woe is me!*** See also Job 10:15; **What misery is mine!**). The first verse metaphorically depicts the agony detailed more fully in Mic 7:2-6. The city has become like those who glean the vineyard to gather the **summer fruit** after the harvest. **Cluster of grapes** or **early figs** are rarely left behind in the vineyards by farmers but are carefully harvested because of their high value. Those who glean the vineyards would not find them after the harvest; the empty vineyard cannot satisfy the hunger and craving of those who glean it for fruit.

■ 2 Verse 2 reveals the meaning of the metaphor utilized in v 1. The city remains like a harvested vineyard. Those who are **faithful** to the covenant (*ḥāsîd* from *ḥesed*) **have been swept** [or ***perished***; *ʾābad*] **from the land**. It remains empty without any **upright person** in it. Instead, what one finds in the city are those who look for an opportunity to **shed blood** and **hunt each other** [***his own brother***] **with nets**. With hostile intentions, every individual (***all of them***) lies in wait to shed blood. The image of hunting down one's closest kin with a net poignantly portrays the excessively violent nature of the community. Even closest relatives and friends have become hunted prey to each other. Using images of violence and hunting, v 2 thus portrays the city as a violent and deceptive place.

■**3** Verse 3 begins with the observation that those who remain in the city have become good (*ṭôb*, **skilled in**) at **doing evil** with **both hands**. Those who have been shown the ways of doing "good" (6:8) have become "good" at **evil**. The phrase **both hands** refers to total corruption; every activity of those who are left in the city reflects their skill in doing evil. The corruption of the city is seen in the way the ***official*** (*śar*, **ruler**) and the **judge** (*šōpēṭ*) and **the powerful** in the city carry out their responsibilities. ***The official*** and ***the judge*** ask for (or, **demands**) ***a bribe*** (*šillûm*). The civil and judicial leaders carry out their responsibilities solely for profit. Likewise, **the powerful** (*gādôl*) make known theirs **desires** or appetites (*nepeš*). They then proceed to ***weave it*** together. The NIV interprets the verb *ʿābat* (***weave***) as conspiracy of the leaders as a group to carry out what they desire and declare.

■**4** Verse 4 begins with a mocking description of the moral and ethical makeup of the leaders and their capacity to produce anything good for the well-being of others. **The best of them is like a brier. The most upright** among them is no better than an obstructing **thorn hedge**. The images of **brier** and **thorn hedge** show that these leaders use their power and position to inflict pain and agony to those whom they are called to serve with moral and ethical integrity. They bring destruction and death to the ones under their leadership and protection.

The second half of v 4 issues a warning to the city. Verse 4*b* literally reads: ***the day of your watchmen,*** (the day of) ***your visitation, has come; now will be their confusion***. The reference to **the day** often denotes the time of divine judgment against the nations as well as the covenant people (see 2:4; 3:6; 4:1, 6; 5:10).

Though **watchmen** is a term used by Israel's prophets to describe their office (Isa 56:10; Jer 6:17; Ezek 3:17; Hos 9:8), it generally denotes the lookouts who kept watch for invading enemies (1 Sam 14:16; 2 Sam 13:34; Isa 52:8; Ezek 33:2-6). Undoubtedly, frequent warnings went out from the city towers as the Assyrian armies in the eighth century and Babylonian armies in the sixth century advanced toward Jerusalem (see Mic 1).

Although the Hebrew text lacks reference to God as the subject in 7:4*b*, it is clear that Micah presents the sound of the alarm by the watchmen not only as a warning of the enemy's approach toward Jerusalem but also as God's visitation (*pāqād*; → Hos 1:4; 2:13 [2:15 HB]; Amos 3:2) of the wicked leaders of Jerusalem. God's visitation here is clearly for the purpose of carrying out the punishment of the wicked in the city, which he will accomplish through the enemy's onslaught.

■ **5** Verse 5 indicates that no one in the city is worthy of **trust**. One can place **confidence** in neither companions nor closest friends. The entire fabric of appropriate relationship has deteriorated to hostility. One must **guard** (*šāmar*) what comes out of one's mouth when speaking even with his wife with whom he maintains an intimate relationship of sharing the same bed.

■ **6** Verse 6 continues the description of the breakdown of relationships in the city, which has infiltrated into the family structure. Family relationships—**father-son**, **mother-daughter**, **daughter-in-law–mother-in-law**—have broken down; within these relationships there is dishonor, hostility, and hatred. Verse 6 concludes with the observation that one's **enemies are the members of his own household**. Commenting on v 6, Brown has poignantly observed that "the cloistered walls of hearth and home offer no safe haven in a society bent on self-destruction" (1996, 63). The very thread of covenant fidelity that holds this community together has disappeared, as all social relationships have disintegrated. (See Micah's depiction of the breakdown of intimate human relationships applied to Jesus' announcement in Luke 12:53.) Within the broader canonical context of the Book of the Twelve, however, Malachi's declaration concerning the Day of Yahweh reverses the societal breakdown depicted in these verses. He anticipates that before the "great and dreadful day of the LORD comes," the prophet Elijah "will turn the hearts of the parents to their children, and the hearts of the children to their parents" (Mal 4:5-6; see also Luke 1:17).

■ **7** Verse 7 abruptly shifts to a declaration of trust in Yahweh. The contrast between the lack of trust in the preceding verses and trust in v 7 is dramatic. This declaration functions as the hinge between distress in vv 1-6 and hope in the remainder of ch 7 (regarding v 7 as the bridge from despair to hope, see Mays 1976, 156; Hillers 1984, 85). The distressed and devastated city now eagerly, yet patiently, waits for Yahweh to act. Employing the first-person subject pronoun, the one lamenting announces, ***I, I myself will watch for Yahweh***. In the same way that the sentinels had watched (*ṣāpah*) for the approaching enemy in v 4, the city will now **watch** [*ṣāpah*] ***for Yahweh*** (NIV adds **in hope**). In ancient Israel's theological memory, Yahweh had repeatedly delivered his covenant people. Therefore, the city declares its intention to **wait for God my Savior** to act according to his nature as the Savior of his people. In the past history of Israel, God had always heard and responded to the cry of his people in their distress (e.g., Exod 3:7; Num 20:16; see also Gen 16:11; 21:17). The lamenting city affirms this faith when it declares its hope: **my God will hear me**.

2. Anticipation of Deliverance (7:8-10)

■ **8** The city that ends its lament with hope and trust in Yahweh in v 7, now speaks to the enemy and confidently expresses its faith that Yahweh will come to its rescue. In v 8, Jerusalem warns its **enemy** not to take joy (**gloat over**) in its present misfortune (regarding Edom as the specific enemy in Mic 7, see Mays 1976, 159; Obad 10-15). With two stark contrasts, v 8 anticipates a reversal of the situation: **fallen/rise** and **darkness/light**. The city confidently states that though it has **fallen**, it will indeed **rise** again. Though the city sits in **darkness**, Yahweh will be its **light** (see Ps 27:1; Isa 10:17; 60:19-20; compare Mic 7:9). What gives certainty to the city about the reversal of its misfortune is perhaps the memory of Yahweh's faithfulness to the city in the past and his continued commitment to be with his people, and the city he has chosen to be his dwelling place.

■ **9** In the first half of v 9, the city acknowledges that it is bearing Yahweh's **wrath** because of its sin against him. The term *zaʿap* (**wrath**) conveys the idea of angry rage resulting in destruction and violence (see Isa 30:30). In the second half of the verse, the city abruptly shifts from an admission of guilt to an anticipation of Yahweh's judicial intervention on his people's behalf. The city will not be under Yahweh's wrath forever; he will appear again in the setting of a court, this time to plead its **case** and ***do justice*** (*mišpāṭ*) for his people (compare with ch 6, where Yahweh is the prosecuting attorney and the judge who pronounces the verdict). The very *mišpāṭ* that is lacking in the city and that Yahweh seeks from his people is the justice that he will now provide on behalf of his people (see 3:1, 9; 6:8). Yahweh will thus **bring** the city **out** of its darkness **into the light**. The metaphor of darkness and light clearly implies Yahweh's work of salvation (→ v 8 above). The city will once again **see** Yahweh's **righteousness** (*ṣĕdāqâ*; see 6:5) in action. The covenant deity who has been faithful in his righteous acts in the past will remain faithful in his righteous acts in the future. Yahweh's justice (*mišpāṭ*) on behalf of his people is evidence of his right relationship with them (*mišpāṭ* and *ṣĕdāqāh* frequently appear together; see Isa 1:21, 27; 5:7, 16; 9:7; Hos 2:19; Amos 5:7, 24; 6:12).

Through the contrasting legal role of Yahweh in Mic 6 and 7, Micah demonstrates that the prophetic message is never monolithic. The God who has brought accusation and condemnation upon his people in the courtroom now comes to the defense and rescue of his people in the courtroom. The prophetic messenger of judgment in one context becomes the prophetic messenger of salvation in another context. Brueggemann has classically described this dual role of the prophet in terms of *criticizing* and *energizing* (2001, 39-79). Prophetic words of judgment seldom end in doom and gloom but are always followed by the prophet's energizing words that point to a future filled with hope.

■ **10** In v 10, the city speaks about the **shame** and the **downfall** of the **enemy** who mocked it when it sat in darkness. The enemies who have rejoiced over the apparent defeat of Yahweh's people have asked the question, **Where is *Yahweh* your God?** The enemies have concluded that Yahweh had abandoned his people with whom he had made a covenant. The city claims that these enemies of Yahweh and his people will **see** his justice and righteousness at work on behalf of his people. As a result, humiliation will spread over them just as a garment covers (*kāsâ* means "clothe," "spread over") one's body. Verse 10 ends with a note on what Yahweh's people will witness; now it will be their turn to witness what will happen to their enemies. They will see the humiliation of their enemies. Both the NIV and the NRSV supply the direct object **her downfall**; however, the Hebrew text simply states that the eyes of the lamenter will see ***her*** or ***it*** (feminine). The Hebrew words for **enemy** and **shame** are grammatically feminine; therefore, the reference is likely to either the enemy itself or the shame that has overwhelmed the enemy. The vivid image of mud trampled upon in the streets indicates that the eyes of the one lamenting will indeed witness the enemy's destruction, defeat, and humiliation (v 10).

3. Restoration and Rebuilding of Jerusalem (7:11-17)

■ **11-12** The reconstruction of devastated Jerusalem in vv 11-17 provides a striking contrast to the enemy's defeat and shame in v 10. The city that laments in the preceding verses now expresses hope in ultimate divine restoration. The opening lines of these verses refer three times to **the day** or **that day** (see *yôm* as either judgment or salvation in 2:4; 3:6; 4:6; 5:10; 7:4). The city's restoration will include both a rebuilding of its walls and a widening of its borders (v 11). These two actions placed side by side in the text create once again a remarkable image of compatible contrasts. Simultaneously, the construction of walls creates limits around the city while the widening of borders extends the reaches of the city. Mays has suggested that the phrase concerning the extension of boundaries may indicate that "Jerusalem will live in a world without limits which separate her life from the nations, and so prepare for the movement of people freely from all the world to her" (1976, 161-62). Achtemeier has described this image of expanded borders in metaphorical terms as Israel's experience of "'the wideness of God's mercy,' the freeing, liberating expanse of its future salvation" (1996a, 363).

Not only will the divine restoration include the refortification and expansion of the city, but the city will ultimately become the destination of persons from Assyria and Egypt (v 12). How ironic that the city that once symbolized shame and mockery to the nations now becomes a final destination! The verb **will come** actually lacks a specific subject in the Hebrew text. While the subject of this activity may be the citizens of the world powers that will make Jerusalem their destination (see Mic 4:1-2; Isa 2:2-3; 60:3), the statement likely emphasizes the return of Jerusalem's dispersed citizens (see Mic 2:12; Isa 11:11-16; 27:12; Zech 10:8-12; Simundson 1996, 588). In both of these interpretations, however, the text is clear that the city will not only undergo refortification and expansion but will once again be inhabited.

As the Euphrates is one of two primary rivers running through Mesopotamia, the phrase **from Egypt to the Euphrates** (***the River*** in the Hebrew text; see Num 22:5; Josh 24:3, 14) functions synonymously with the preceding reference to **Assyria** and **Egypt**. In ancient Israelite tradition, the **Euphrates** and **Egypt** represent the boundaries of Solomon's empire (see 1 Kgs 4:21; Ps 72:8; Zech 9:10). The phrases **sea to sea** and **mountain to mountain** depict the all-encompassing nature of the return of Jerusalem's scattered inhabitants.

■ **13** As is common to the lament genre, this lament once again shifts abruptly in Mic 7:13 from the hope of a renewed Jerusalem in vv 11-12 to the utter devastation (*šāmam*; see 6:16) of the ***land*** (**earth**). The emphasis upon the inhabitants of the land and the land's devastation is ironically similar to the depiction of divine judgment upon Jerusalem at the conclusion of ch 6. Mays notes that this similarity may express "the concept of the eschatological reversal—the city/land that was an island of humiliation in the midst of powerful nations will become an island of salvation in the midst of a world under judgment" (1976, 162). The concise declaration at the conclusion of 7:13 poignantly expresses the consistent Deuteronomic-prophetic conviction of sowing and reaping (e.g., → Mic 6:14-15; Hos 8:7; 10:12-13; Obad 15). The devastation that occurs upon the land in Mic 7:13 is not an arbitrary divine judgment. It is most certainly the ***fruit*** (*pĕrî*, **result**) of the people's **deeds**. The inhabitants of the land will indeed reap the harvest of the seed they have sown. MICAH

■ **14** The restored city and its inhabitants now turn to Yahweh who established justice for them (v 9) and appeals to him to **shepherd** them with his **staff** (v 14). The reference to **your people** again assumes the context of the covenant between Yahweh and his people (see 6:3, 5; 7:7, 10). **The flock of your inheritance** also implies the covenant relationship often portrayed in the OT through the shepherd-sheep metaphor. The similarity between the language of 5:4-6 and 7:14 suggests that Yahweh's rule over his people is directly associated with the faithful rule of Yahweh's Anointed One. A similar direct correlation between divine rule and messianic rule occurs in Ezek 34:11-31. 7:11-15

The restored people also anticipate that as Yahweh shepherds his flock, they will live **in a forest** and in **fertile pasturelands** (*karmel*, garden land) and that they will feed in the productive regions of **Bashan** (Jer 50:19; Amos 4:1) and **Gilead** (see Gen 37:25; Num 32:1; Jer 8:22; 46:11; 50:19) as in the former days, perhaps when they first came into the land. Micah 7:14 conveys hope in the well-being and fertility that will emerge in the future, in the day when Yahweh would restore his people. The hope being expressed here is that the land that now lies in devastation and ruin also will be restored to be the most suitable place for the settlement of the restored people.

■ **15** In response to the people's appeal, Yahweh declares in v 15 that he would **show** his people **many wonders**, or his marvelous deeds. The hope of the lamenting community will be fulfilled; Yahweh will once again provide his people with life-giving deliverance and nourishment as he did when they came out of Egypt. The future restoration, in a very real sense, would be a second exodus experience for the people who now live in exile and humiliation.

■ **16-17** Verses 16-17 return to the theme of the nations' shame (*bôš*) when they see Yahweh's marvelous deeds on behalf of his people. **All their power** will be gone at the sight of Yahweh's demonstration of his power (v 16). As expressions of utter humiliation, the previously gloating nations will refrain from both speaking and hearing. The text vividly depicts the nations' utter disgrace by employing the metaphor of a serpent that does no more than crawl on the ground and **lick dust** (v 17). In the end, the nations will recognize the futility of their own strength as they **come trembling out of their dens**. This depiction is consistent with a central OT conviction and particularly with a conviction of the prophetic faith: the mighty will fall; the proud will be humbled; the strong will become weak (see 1 Sam 2:3-8; Isa 14:4-21; Ezek 28:1-19; Amos 6:4-7; Obad 1-4). Just as fallen Jerusalem will rise again (Mic 7:8), the self-exalted nations will tumble to the ground in the end.

The closing line of v 17 expresses one of the great ironies of divine judgment. The nations that have caused Israel to tremble will finally stand in awe (*pāḥad*; → Hos 3:5) of Yahweh and will revere (*yārēʾ*, **fear**) him. While the NIV is not necessarily incorrect in translating *yārēʾ* as **be afraid of**, the word *yārēʾ* often indicates the sense of awe or veneration rather than terror. Verse 17 ends with the anticipation that the nations would **turn in fear to *Yahweh* our God**, to acknowledge his sovereign lordship over all nations.

4. Who Is like Yahweh? (7:18-20)

■ **18-20** The concluding three verses of ch 7 function as a hymn celebrating Yahweh's faithful nature. This hymn functions both as an appropriate conclusion to the lament of ch 7 and as an appropriate conclusion for the book of Micah itself. Consistent with the structure of lament that frequently concludes with praise or an expression of trust in Yahweh, the cry of despair ultimately gives way to the cry of hymnic praise (regarding praise in the genre of lament, see Westermann 1981, 81). Though the book of Micah opened with a depiction of Yahweh's coming to his people in wrath, it concludes with a praise-filled declaration of his forgiveness of and grace toward his people. The concluding verses of the book describe precisely the reason for the community's hope for salvation, forgiveness, and restoration: the faithful character of Yahweh himself.

The hymnic declaration begins with the rhetorical question, **Who is a God like you . . . ?** (see similar rhetorical questions in Exod 15:11; Pss 71:18-19; 77:13). Just as the name of the prophet himself means "Who is like Yahweh?" the question in Mic 7:18 is particularly fitting as a conclusion to the prophetic oracles.

The remainder of this hymn brilliantly depicts Yahweh's incomparable nature in terms of divine forgiveness, compassion, and faithfulness. In these verses, that which makes Yahweh distinct (i.e., holy) is not his creative capacity, his terrorizing actions against enemies, or his demand for judgment. For these verses, that which sets this God apart, making him a holy God from all other gods and powers, is not even the reality that no other gods or powers exist. That which distinguishes Yahweh from all other realities is his forgiving, gracious, and faithful character.

Although these verses do not directly quote from the traditional confession of Yahweh's character, the convictions and language are the same (→ Joel 2:13; Jonah 4:2; see also Exod 34:6-7; Num 14:18; Neh 9:17, 31; Ps 103:8). In describing its relationship to Exod 34:6-7, Brown views this text as "the prophet's recasting of God's sublime confession given to Moses" (1996, 65; see also discussion of the relationship to Exod 34:6-7 in Mays 1976, 167; Allen 1976, 403; Limburg 1988, 196).

Micah 7:18-19 begins and ends with references to ***iniquity*** (*ʿāwōn*, **sin**, v 18), **transgression** (*pešaʿ*, v 18; **sins**, v 19), and ***sin*** (*ḥaṭṭāʾt*, **iniquities**, v 19; see all of these terms in Exod 34:7). While *ʿāwōn* often indicates the guilt or consequence of sin (thus ***iniquity***), *pešaʿ* indicates purposefully rebellious acts and *ḥaṭṭāʾt* indicates the broader sense of *missing the mark*. Although the terms may have the poetic function of synonymous parallelism in these verses, Achtemeier rightly suggests that the hymn's use of all three terms may be an attempt to "deal with every form of sinfulness" in the life of God's people (1996a, 367).

Just as in the traditional confession of Exod 34:7, Yahweh ***forgives*** (*nāśāʾ*, "takes away," "carries," **pardons**) iniquity. He ***passes over*** (*ʿābar*, **forgives**) **transgression**. The participle form of both *nāśāʾ* and *ʿābar* indicates that the divine action of *taking away* iniquity and *passing over* transgression is the ongoing nature and activity of Yahweh. It is an act of covenantal faithfulness on the part of Yahweh to forgive and restore that which remains (**the remnant**) **of his inheritance** (see Israel as Yahweh's special possession in the world in Exod 19:5). If this covenant deity did not consistently take away and pass over the sins of his people, the community would remain hopeless. These actions depict Yahweh's consistent character and repeated acts of forgiving sin. It is also in the covenantal nature of Yahweh to **not stay angry forever** (see Yahweh's slowness to anger in Exod 34), but to **show mercy** (*ḥesed*, ***covenant faithfulness***; see Mic 6:8; Hos 2:19; 4:1; 6:6). Mays describes the *ḥesed* of Yahweh as "the gracious conduct which makes the most and best of a relationship, the deed which brings a relationship to its fulfillment, even when the partner is weak or fallible" (1976, 168).

Micah 7:19 continues the covenant character of Yahweh. The lamenting community is confident that Yahweh will once again show **compassion** (*rāḥam*; see Hos 1:6; 2:19, 23; Joel 2:13; Jonah 4:2) toward his people (**us**). The second half of Mic 7:19 describes how Yahweh will show his forgiveness; he will **tread** (*kābaš* means "to subdue"; see Gen 1:28; 2 Chr 28:10; Jer 34:11, 16) their **sins underfoot and hurl** their **iniquities into the depths of the sea**.

The specific language of passing over, treading underfoot, and throwing into the depths of the sea may be an allusion to Yahweh's deliverance of Israel at the Sea (see similar language in the Song of Moses in Exod 15). Noting the similarity between the language of Yahweh's forgiving nature and his deliverance at the Sea, Mays has observed that "the hymn regards even forgiveness as the work of majestic powers, a 'miracle' of the might of God" (1976, 168). Even more, however, the similarity to the deliverance at the Sea reminds Israel that just as Yahweh had saved his people in the past, he indeed would save them in the future. However, the good news for the covenant people this time is that their God would not only deliver them from their enemies but also free them from their rebellion, their sin, and their iniquity.

This testimony to Yahweh's forgiveness and compassion in Mic 7:18-19 finds its mooring in the covenantal promises of God to Jacob and Abraham,
7:18-20 the ancestors of Israel. The community confesses its faith: **you will be faithful** [*'ĕmet*] **to Jacob, and show love** [*ḥesed*] **to Abraham** (v 20). Although the text may intend two distinct thoughts in these expressions, they likely convey the single notion of "gracious faithfulness" (Mays 1976, 168). While **Jacob** served as the patronymic ancestor of the northern kingdom of Israel, **Abraham** functioned as the primary patronymic ancestor of Judah. With references to both Jacob and Abraham, the text makes clear that Yahweh's fidelity and forgiveness extends to all members of the covenant community, both north and south. He will be faithful to the oath that he had made to both Abraham and Jacob (Gen 15:1-21; 17:1-27; 28:10-22; regarding the divine oath, see Gen 22:16; 26:3; 50:24; Exod 13:5, 11; Num 11:12; 14:16; Ps 105:8-11). The land is consistently at the core of ancient Israel's tradition of the divine promise to the patriarchs.

In contrast to the pattern of infidelity by his covenant partners, Israel and Judah, Yahweh remains faithful and reliable in his covenant commitments. This divine fidelity engenders Yahweh's forgiveness of and compassion toward his people. Not only does the conviction of Yahweh's covenant faithfulness shape Micah's message of hope, but it also informs the hope of divine forgiveness and restoration in Hosea's message to Israel, Joel's message to Jerusalem, and Jonah's message to Assyria.

A concluding comment on these closing verses is necessary. Although the NIV alters the text to read that Yahweh will **hurl all our iniquities** into the depths of the sea, the Hebrew text reads, ***You will hurl all their iniquities***. Based upon the reading of the Hebrew text, Achtemeier has suggested that "Micah looks forward to the time when Yahweh will reign as Lord over all the earth . . . , and that reign will be made possible by Yahweh's universal forgiveness of the nations as well as of Israel" (1996a, 368). If her interpretation is correct, then both Jonah and Micah conclude with a note on Yahweh's concern for all nations. Yahweh, who shows concern for the Assyrians in Jonah, shows his compassion for all nations in Micah. Both prophets thus portray God as a God of all nations, and both offer hope to all who trust in him for their salvation.

FROM THE TEXT

The concluding lament of ch 7 provides the reader with an appropriate and beautifully constructed response to the message of the book of Micah. Consistent with the function of the lament genre, this text provides its hearers with language to express despair to God over present crises, hope-filled anticipation that God will act, and imagination of what may become of the future. The opening six verses particularly allow subsequent generations to utter particularly that which humans are hesitant to articulate: their own isolation and inherent mistrust of others.

For the Christian reading community, the text's hinge in v 7 recalls not only the hope of deliverance embodied in the return and restoration following the exile, but even more, recalls deliverance and hope embodied in resurrection following crucifixion. This verse expresses the sincere Christian prayer of trust in God between Good Friday and Easter Sunday. Where death appears to have been victorious and where the stone has sealed off all hope for the future, life will indeed emerge. Familiar with the reality of Holy Saturday, the Christian community often seems to reside somewhere between crucifixion and resurrection as it finds itself existing in the period of *the meantime*. The turning point of the text declares boldly that in the seasons of *the meantime*, in the Holy Saturdays of the Christian journey, "I will wait for God my Savior."

While most of the book of Micah consists of oracles of judgment (1:1—2:11; 3:1-12; 6:1-16) and salvation (2:12-13; 4—5), the incorporation of lament poignantly reminds the reader of the intimate, almost pastoral, relationship that the prophet shares with his people. Brown perceptively comments that "Micah is no doomsday prophet, isolated from the people whom he serves. Rather, he lives in solidarity with his people. He laments when they suffer (1:8) and rejoices in their restoration" (1996, 65). Simultaneous with the authentic relationship that the prophet shares with his people, he shares a profound relationship with the God who called him. Heschel has classically articulated this oneness that the prophet shares with God as "a fellowship with the feelings of God, a sympathy with the divine pathos, a communion with the divine consciousness. . . . He lives not only his personal life, but also the life of God. The prophet hears God's voice and feels His heart" (1962, 31). In the lament that concludes the book of Micah, the reader hears the agonizing cry of a triad of voices: people/Jerusalem, prophet, and God himself.

The incorporation of lament into this book of judgment and salvation oracles reminds the reading community of the significant role of lament in the life of the people of God. Rather than an expression of infidelity toward God, grief and lamentation are honest cries to God. Lament refuses to conceal; therefore, it must confess. It sees the present situation as it is and names it. Yet in all of its honesty, lament hopes beyond hope that God will creatively and redemptively work once again. Addressing the grief that one encounters in lament, Brueggemann has rightly observed that "grief is offered against establishment *denial* and *cover-up*" so that ultimately "newness comes out of grief articulated and embraced" (1986, 131; in regard to the prophetic grief of Jeremiah, see Brueggemann 1986, 10-47). As the people of God learn to wait between crucifixion and resurrection, their waiting will undoubtedly evoke lament as they cry out in honesty and faith to their covenant God.

As is the case in all of the biblical laments that speak of enemies, the reader must remain alert to the manner in which he or she receives the text. The enemies are not simply individuals who have offended. They are the powers and the principalities, the empires and the unjust forces of this world, the political and economic and religious systems that fight against the kingdom of God. However, the function of "enemies" in the lament is never to evoke hatred and bitterness in the reader's mind but to affirm that the establishment of God's sovereign reign will ultimately bring an end to all that is in opposition to the will of God.

References to "enemies" in the lament primarily carry two functions. On the one hand, they leave the establishment of the kingdom of God to the Lord himself and not to the devices of his people. On the other hand, they evoke hope in the reader's mind as they affirm that in the end the divine kingdom will come as his will is "done, on earth as it is in heaven" (Matt 6:10).

Read within the canonical context of the entire book of Micah, the recurrence of the divine court scene in the lament is particularly illuminating. As noted previously, Mic 6 depicts Yahweh as accuser, witness, and judge. Providing evidence against his people, the Lord pronounces sure and imminent judgment upon them. Yet before the book of Micah ends, Yahweh once again appears in court with his people. However, he appears this time neither to accuse nor to judge his people but to deliver them and to forgive them. The reemergence of the lawsuit brilliantly demonstrates that the God who takes his people to court is no deity of arbitrary accusation and judgment. He is a covenant deity. In both instances, the courtroom scene occurs within the context of the established covenant between the Lord and his people. All judgment in ch 6 occurs within the context of covenant; likewise, all salvation in ch 7 occurs within the context of covenant. Neither court scene is the result of divine random acts of judgment or divine "random acts of kindness." As the Lord is a covenant-making and a covenant-keeping God, covenant brings judgment and despair (see Amos 3:2) as well as restoration and hope.

As subsequent generations hear the words of the book of Micah, the concluding confession in 7:18-20 functions as a crescendo in its affirmation of the essential character of this covenant-making and covenant-keeping God. In response to the rhetorical question *Who is a God like you?* the text articulates the incomparable nature, that is, the holy nature, of the Lord God. That which sets this deity apart from all other deities, from political and economic powers, and from humanity itself is his gracious, faithful, and forgiving character. This creed-like confession has informed and shaped the faith, the character, and the life of the people of God throughout all ages. While this confession provided hope of divine forgiveness to a rebellious generation in the wilderness (Exod 34:6-7; Num 14:18), it provided the same hope to Israel's most despised enemy (Jonah 4:2).

This confession not only functions as an interwoven thread throughout the Torah and the Prophets but also foreshadows the character of the God who is incarnate in Jesus Christ. The Christian community confesses this God-in-flesh as the embodiment of the divine character and therefore as the "fleshing out" of all that is forgiving, merciful, compassionate, and faithful.

For the reader who believes that God is restoring humanity to the divine image as he transforms humanity into the likeness of Christ Jesus (2 Cor 3:18), Mic 7:18-20 functions in a secondary way. The God whose character is forgiving, merciful, compassionate, and faithful and who has revealed himself in Jesus Christ in the same manner subsequently calls his people to that same character. As God is by nature, he calls his people to be by grace (Athanasius of Alexandria). As God is distinct, as God is holy, he calls his people to be distinct. He calls his people to be holy. What does this distinctiveness, this holiness, look like? It looks like the character of God as revealed in Christ Jesus. It pardons and forgives; it is slow to anger and delights to show mercy; it has compassion even toward disloyal covenant breakers and the most horrific enemies.

In the face of violence, greed, and hatred within the human community across time and space, subsequent reading communities may question the reality of the hope expressed in this lament. In the midst of what all too often has appeared to be the reign of evil powers and principalities, readers of this text may even doubt the gracious and forgiving nature of the Lord himself. However, the text's conviction of the Lord's cosmic and universal sovereignty (7:17) undergirds the hope for the ultimate realization of both his character and his kingdom. He is no parochial, national, ethnic God; he is God of the universe.

The declaration of the Lord's cosmic reign moves the Christian reader of the text to anticipate the culmination of the kingdom of God as celebrated by the Apostle Paul in Phil 2:10-11: "At the name of Jesus every knee should bow, in heaven and on earth and under the earth, and every tongue acknowledge that Jesus Christ is Lord, to the glory of God the Father." Various empires throughout the ages may deceptively convince the citizens of the world to declare that the empire and its emperor are sovereign. Citizens may live under the delusion that political, economic, and ideological systems of the empire bring life, prosperity, peace, and hope. The powers may even coerce a confession that "Caesar is lord." However, this text affirms the futility of all empires and the fallibility of all "caesars." It is keenly aware that in time, the falsehoods and delusions shaped by the powers will become apparent. Read through the Christian confession that Jesus is Lord, this text anticipates that all creation will recognize and confess the sovereignty of the Lord God as revealed through the crucified and resurrected Messiah, the lowly shepherd born in Bethlehem, Jesus Christ. For the Christian community, the cosmic affirmations of Mic 7 anticipate the reign of God through his Messiah over saints "from every tribe and language and people and nation" (Rev 5:9). This text joins the Christian community in its bold and unreserved confession that this God is indeed "the blessed and only Ruler, the King of kings and Lord of lords" (1 Tim 6:15).